Movement Skill Development

MOVEMENT
SKILL
DEVELOPMENT

Jack Keogh • David Sugden

University of California, Los Angeles   University of Leeds

Macmillan Publishing Company
New York
Collier Macmillan Publishers
London

Copyright © 1985, Macmillan Publishing Company,
a division of Macmillan, Inc.

Printed in the United States of America.

Macmillan Publishing Company
866 Third Avenue, New York, New York 10022

Collier Macmillan Canada, Inc.

Library of Congress Cataloging in Publication Data

Keogh, Jack.
    Movement skill development.

    Bibliography: p.
    Includes index.
    1. Motor ability in children.   2. Child development.
I. Sugden, David (David A.)   II. Title.
BF723.M6K4   1984   155.4′12   84-10093
ISBN 0-02-362600-3

Printing: 1   2   3   4   5   6   7   8
Year: 5   6   7   8   9   0   1   2   3

ISBN 0-02-362600-3

Much of what is known about movement skill development derives from the work done by psychologists and medical personnel between 1920 and 1940. These researchers were concerned almost exclusively with describing movement changes as indications of general developmental progress. Movement change is readily observed during the early years of life and can be taken to represent the general developmental state of the neurological system and some aspects of perceptual–cognitive and personal–social functioning. Interest in movement skill development revived in the 1960s because of the concern for children with learning problems. Again, movement was viewed in terms of perceptual–cognitive development and little effort was made to describe and understand movement skill development. The few studies that focused directly on movement skill development failed to provide clear research directions.

A volume edited by Connolly in 1970 marked the beginning of what has become a more direct study of movement skill development, with more focused lines of research. The different authors in this volume pointed the way towards the study of the processes and mechanisms underlying movement skill development and towards finding better ways to describe movement changes. A considerable amount of work has been done since 1970 to expand our knowledge and our ideas about movement skill development. Our general goals in this book are to provide a comprehensive review of past work and a discussion of current thinking about movement skill development.

The study of movement skill development or any area of human behavior should have two major avenues of work. Bryant (1981) states it this way:

> There are two basic questions in developmental psychology. They are often confused with each other but really are quite separate. The first concerns what children are like at particular ages. How does a child of three, say, behave and what underlies his behaviour? What will be the difference between the things he does and the things he understands now and in a year's time? Two years time? The first question then asks what children are like and in what ways they change as they grow older. The second question is the casual one. Given that children do change as they grow up what exactly makes these changes happen? [p. 204]

The first avenue of work is to describe movement skill development so that we learn about the nature of the phenomena we seek to understand. The second is to examine the observed changes in ways that provide some understanding of how they occur. Careful and clever descriptions should lead to the identification of characteristics and qualities of change, and this in turn should lead to the propositions about the nature of change in movement skill development. These propositions provide the issues and questions which form the basis for discovering important determinants and influences. The two major avenues of research work identified as description and explanation are often viewed quite separately. We view them as transactional: explanations should proceed from the concerns identified in descriptions and they should lead to different levels and types of descriptions.

Thus, the two general approaches of this book, description and explanation, are in some ways tied to each other. Part I is descriptive and provides some sense of the nature of change in movement skill development. Part II is a discussion of the possible influences on movement skill development. It is largely speculative because clear lines of research are not well established and is intended to be provocative rather than definitive.

Chapter 1 is a general introduction to the book and provides our perspective on movement skill development. Part I, a descriptive review, focuses on the progressive resolution of movement problems. The two general movement problems are establishing control of one's own body and adjusting to a changing environment (e.g., when a baby gains control of upright posture and walks, when a child can walk on a crowded sidewalk where other people are moving). Within the context of these two general movement problems are other movement problems to be resolved (e.g., making more continuous and simultaneous movements in contrast to making a series of discrete and separate movements). Descriptions of change are presented in relation to chronological age, but our focus is upon the nature of change rather than the age at which it occurs.

Part II is structured in relation to systems or functions which contribute most directly to the production of movement. We view these systems or functions as resources, the development of which ultimately determines movement skill development. Chapters are organized around a general division by types of resources. The neuromotor system is the basic resource; other biological functions and processing systems which directly influence the neuromotor system are also important resources. Each resource is viewed in terms of development within the resource and in terms of the development of movement control

We believe that the lack of a general perspective limits the study of movement skill development to unrelated descriptions and trivial explanations. Thus, we made an effort to create and use a general framework, and this necessarily has limitations and contradictions. One difficulty pointed out to us is that a reader must be conscious of our framework and cannot treat each chapter as an isolated topic. We take this as a compliment because we intend that the book as a whole should provide a useful perspective, along with a considerable amount of new information, and should provide some challenging directions.

Our knowledge bases and points of view have been developed in many subtle and complex ways by colleagues and students who asked questions, offered new and contradictory information, proposed alternative explanations, and demanded clearer statements. We wish to acknowledge the contributions of Ruth Abernathy, James Oliver, Larry Rarick, Margaret Faust, William Faust, Kevin Connolly, Sheila Henderson and, most importantly, our wives, Barbara Keogh and Lorrie Sugden. The insightful and detailed review of the complete manuscript by Jane Clark was most helpful and led to major rewriting throughout the manuscript. We also appreciate the assistance of Rosie Connell, Mary Carter, Frank Powell, and Al Salmoni in reviewing one or more chapters. We were supported throughout our work by the cheerful and efficient manner in which Fran Wilson, along with several people at the Central Word Processing Center at UCLA, typed the many drafts of the manuscript.

J.K
D.S

vii

Movement Skill Development

1 | *An Introduction to Movement Development*

The moment development of babies and young children has a particular charm for most adults. We are delighted by the seemingly random arm and leg movements of babies and their efforts to accomplish the most basic achievements, such as grasping an object and holding their head upright. We are amused and impressed as we watch the clumsy but eventually effective movements of young children in mastering a wide range of skills, from putting on a jacket and pedaling a tricycle to washing their hands and throwing a ball. The purpose of this book is to look more carefully at the movement changes of babies and young children. We shall begin by discussing development and movement separately before we bring them together to form a framework for examining movement development.

Development

Development is the general process of change that refers to change in a particular type of human ability, such as reasoning and communication, or to a broader change across many types of human abilities. Change is so apparent and dramatic in children and youth that we tend to think of development as change that leads to full development or maturity as an adult. For example, we say that a mature person is fully developed. Yet now the concept of development is being broadened to recognize change as a lifelong process (Goulet and Baltes 1970). Maturity may be an appropriate term to describe some physical and biological changes, such as height and neural conduction rate, in which a point of maximum size and output are achieved by adulthood, but more general abilities are better described as having the potential to continue to develop throughout life.

Development is a difficult idea to comprehend because changes in human abilities are so vast and complex. The beginning of development is at conception, and our first view of newborns is at birth when they are small, not mobile, and without verbal communication. In 20 years, we see many changes, leading to larger, mobile, and skillful persons who can reason about and communicate abstract notions and who have a personal sense of self and are part of a social system. Examples will help us appreciate the nature of these changes before we examine them more formally and formulate a general definition of development. Our examples were selected to highlight the changes in human abilities that attract our attention. Some of them are quite visible, but others are inferred from the more visible ones.

Descriptions of Change

Physical growth changes are easily recognized, beginning with the observation that children get larger. Humans have a microscopic size at conception and grow to a length of about 20 inches at birth (after only 9 months of life) and a height of 60 inches or more at 20 years after birth. The proportions of babies change so that their heads, which are one-fourth of their body length at birth, become approximately one-tenth at age 20. We become relatively longer legged just before pubertal growth, when we are described as "leggy." Changes in body proportions during puberty distinguish male and female physiques, including changes in secondary sex characteristics. Internal systemic changes during puberty provide the capability for reproduction. Also, changes in body-tissue composition and physiological functioning give males relatively more muscle than females have and a greater capacity for taking in and transporting oxygen to fuel the muscular system.

Our control of movement changes so that we become more accurate as well as faster. We can control force better to make stronger as well as slower and softer movements. Movements become more coordinated with fewer extraneous movements and appear to be smooth, effortless, and unhurried. A richer repertoire of movements is established to produce variable and elegant solutions to movement problems. Multiple demands can be handled in a shorter time, including the ability to relate our movements to the movements of others. We can plan ahead by knowing what others are likely to do. Movement becomes more than just the skill to perform when personal-social requirements become an important part of movement situations.

Babies' communication is limited to nonverbal exchanges which often are quite effective, although not a satisfactory substitute for language. Babies' sounds later become speech in the form of words spoken in a particular language and accent, initially to represent objects and later to represent abstractions. Language follows when speech is organized to convey more complex meanings, but it is not yet communication with others until individuals exchange or interact. Young children with a basic language thus may carry on a collective monologue without communicating with others.

The ability to reason underlies the development of other abilities and is inferred from a wide range of behaviors. We depend first on more concrete items and thus need to have those things in hand or in view. Later we can keep objects in mind when they are not in sight. Even more dramatic is the ability to attach meaning to objects and then to symbols in the form of numbers and words. We become able to use words to represent ideas and to organize words to convey even larger concepts which we analyze, synthesize, and reorder with words. The ability to read is an important development in which words represent ideas, abstractions, and expressions of feeling to impart facts, opinions, and ideas. Similarities are perceived in what we see and hear, as in recognizing the same word when seen in lower-case and upper-case letters and written differently. We also can speak or write with different combinations of words to convey the same meaning. We can take different perspectives other than just what we ourselves see and understand. We can transform input to become or represent something else, and we can go beyond the information given to create more. Causality comes to be recognized as something that leads to something else; ambiguities are recognized and sometimes tolerated.

Human relationships develop as an interplay of self and others which requires communication and reasoning abilities. We become less egocentric and better able to take the position of others to understand their needs and feelings. We become able to internalize our relationships with the world to establish autonomy, independence, and control. That is, we initially perceive situations as controlled by others before we, to some extent and varying by situation, come to recognize that we can control or affect them ourselves. We become able to set our own goals and to evaluate and reward ourselves, while also becoming aware of the social evaluation of others. Social relationships change so that we relate to different groups, ranging from family to peers to a larger community, and we become part of a society that extends beyond our immediate social involvements.

Periods of Change

A listing of changes illustrates the enormity and complexity of human development, as well as the realization that individuals develop throughout all of their lives. We now need to reduce these changes into a better definition of development. We shall begin by looking at how periods of change have been described. These descriptions are based on individuals' new capabilities to do something that they were not able to do earlier. If we think of what we do as requiring some type of internal organization in relation to our surrounding environments, then major periods of change are those times when we reorganize how we do what we do and also do new things. In this view, the individual really does change into a different human being, and we recognize the change as another period of development.

Piaget (1964) describes four periods in intellectual development in which individuals differ in their intellectual functioning, or in their ways of knowing and reasoning (Ginsburg and Opper 1969). He begins with a sensorimotor, or preverbal, period in which practical information such as object permanence, temporal succession, and sensorimotor causality becomes the basis for later representational thought. The second period of preoperational representation requires that earlier information be reconstructed to establish the beginnings of language and symbolic function which are thought in a representational form. Piaget calls the third period concrete operations, in which children can operate on objects to formulate abstractions in the form of classes, relations, and numbers. The fourth period is the level of formal operations which is reasoning about hypotheses and not just objects. Piaget traces the development of reasoning as proceeding from direct knowing to abstract manipulations. He believes that an individual's intellectual functioning is sufficiently different in each period to be recognized as developmentally different, and his formulations provide a theoretical structure for studying intellectual development that has stimulated a vast amount of related research.

Erickson (1950) describes ego development as having eight stages which progress from the development of trust during infancy to ego integrity at maturity. Each of the eight stages is a conflict whose resolution leads to a positive or negative ego quality (for example, trust versus mistrust). Erickson sees the conflicts and related ego qualities as occurring progressively, with a time period for each, and he relates each stage of ego development to its social context and social expectations. For example, conflict during pubescence and adolescence leads to either identity (positive) or role diffusion (negative). This is followed by a conflict that leads to either intimacy (positive) or isolation (negative) in both a personal and a sexual sense.

Piaget's and Erickson's ideas show us ways to think about periods of change. Two more examples will help clarify the idea of two periods of change occurring simultaneously and thus influencing each other. Pubescence and adolescence are commonly recognized as major periods of change. Pubescence is a time of biological change when an individual becomes capable of reproduction and body form and composition are greatly altered. Adolescence is a time of social change when an individual becomes more personally and socially independent and more

3

involved in a peer rather than a family social setting. These two periods not only interact to influence each other but also change each other. Changes in secondary sex characteristics, which vary in age of onset and extent of change, often imply greater personal-social development and so change others' expectations and behaviors when interacting socially with these more mature looking adolescents. The reverse may be true when the social importance of pubertal body changes leads to an increase or decrease in amount of physical activity, which also can change body appearance.

Our descriptions of change and examples of periods of change should impress us with the scope of human development and should indicate how we can characterize its various aspects. We now shall consider some ways to think about development as a concept.

Characteristics of Change

Two points should be remembered when thinking about development. First, there are *different kinds of change*. From the many examples in our introductory comments and of major periods of change, it should be apparent that development is change in kind more than change in quantity. Second, not only does an individual change to become someone quite different, but surrounding environments also change in a *transaction* between individual and environments. Environments often are perceived differently as an individual develops, thus becoming different environments for the same person. The reverse also must be considered, that a different person now is in these environments.

The first point about kinds of change is illustrated by Flavell's (1972) description of five types of change processes in cognitive development. Keogh and Kopp (1978, p. 538) use these five processes to suggest how we can conceptualize "changes in terms of explanations of abilities, organization and reorganization of abilities, and consolidation of skills." We shall follow their description of Flavell's change processes to illustrate change in different developmental dimensions within one period and across periods. As used by Flavell, X_1 and X_2 represent a behavior, skill, ability, structure, concept, operation, bit of knowledge, or any other type of behavior unity.

Addition is a type of change in which behavior X_1 starts at one time, and behavior X_2 is added later. The two coexist as a permanent part of a child's repertoire, thus providing diversity in behavior and alternative modes of response.

Substitution is the gradual replacement of X_1 by X_2 so that both behaviors coexist for a period of time to alternate, complement, or compete with each other. X_2 eventually replaces X_1.

Modification is the refinement of X_1 to become X_2. Flavell proposes that modification occurs by means of differentiation, generalization, or stabilization to produce a change in adaptive quality rather than a change in kind.

Inclusion is the use of X_1 as a component of X_2 to form higher orders of behavior. X_1 maintains its own integrity and can be used as a component in a variety of higher-order behaviors.

Mediation is the use of X_1 as a bridge to influence the formation of X_2 without becoming a part of it. Presumably X_1 can mediate with other behaviors, a role that changes with time.

These different types of change are best illustrated in observations of early development. Babies and young children *add* many permanent behaviors to their repertoire without displacing existing behaviors, as seen with spoken language added to gestures and a thumb-finger opposition added to the use of all fingers as two different ways to grasp an object. *Substitution* can be found in the gradual replacement of babbling sounds by words and crawling by upright locomotion. *Modification* occurs in the perceptual change from grossly differentiating patterned and nonpatterned stimuli to discriminating patterns and in the movement change of modifying walking to adjust to different kinds of surfaces such as grass, sand, mud, and shallow water. *Inclusion* occurs when children incorporate thumb-finger opposition into other movements, such as holding a pencil or flipping a switch. *Mediation* is more difficult to explain but can be seen when children handle objects in order to learn more about their environment. As change becomes more complex, it is more difficult to characterize the type of change, as it probably is a mixture. However, the kinds of change that Flavell suggests do provide useful guidelines for thinking about development as a process of change.

The second point is that change is transactional, meaning that individuals and environments change in relation to one another. This follows from the notion that development is adaptive change, that change occurs in relation to biological, physical, and social environments to enable individuals and environments to become compatible. The interplay of individuals and environments is well accepted, but there are differing views about the nature of the interplay. One view is that there is a one-to-one, unidirectional correspondence, so that a specified amount of change in an environment will produce a corresponding amount of change in an individual. But most people consider the interplay to be more of an *interaction*, in which different levels of individual conditions and environmental conditions lead to different amounts of change. A more complicated view is that these interplays are *transactional* (Sameroff and Chandler 1975), that both individual and environment can change each other, thus leading to a different set of relationships rather than to an interactive set of relationships that are fixed by levels. The transactional notion recognizes that change can occur in both individuals and environments to produce different individuals and different environments over time.

Consider the interplay of babies and mothers when babies are developing feeding skills. We expect that the mothers' tone of voice and other communicative behaviors will influence when and how their babies will use a spoon and hold a cup. It is reasonable that the influence will be interactive, in that a soft and accepting tone of voice will have a positive effect on some babies but not others and that the opposite will be true for a loud and aggressive tone of voice. A transactional view would take into account, for example, that soft-speaking and accepting mothers become louder and more aggressive in their speech when their babies bang their spoons and turn their cups upside down.

Both the person and the environmental conditions can change and must do so in many ways. A transactional view makes things more complicated, but the very nature of development is change, which often means a change in both individual and environment. Although it is difficult to conceptualize change in a physical environment, think of the changes and variations in our perceptions of the physical world when snow is perceived as cold, beautiful, fun, or hard work. The mover–environment interplay as a transactional relationship is basic to our view of development in this book.

Definition

Development is adaptive change toward competence. Adaptive change is intended to draw our attention to the transactional relationship of individuals and environments. Our earlier comments on kinds of change should be kept in mind when thinking of change as occurring in many different ways. *Toward competence* directs us to think of a person in the process of becoming something, rather than what that person is at the moment. Competence conveys the meaning of a larger concern for being effective in our environment, rather than focussing on the achievement of specific skills (Connolly and Bruner 1974).

We should view development as a lifelong process, and we also should recognize that it is increasingly difficult to observe and understand as it continues within an individual. Early and more basic adaptations are observed in most people as similar changes in behavior. But adaptation becomes more variable and individual, and so later development is characterized by a wide range of kind and quality of behaviors.

A distinction needs to be made between development and learning. Piaget (1964) views learning as a function of development rather than development being the overall summation of a series of learnings. Learning in his view is shaped by the learner's developmental state. An individual in one period of change may learn quite differently, as well as learn something quite different, when compared with an individual in another period of change. Piaget sees development as a spontaneous process encompassing all structures, whereas learning is provoked by situations and is limited to a single problem or a single structure. Development, therefore, is not the end result of a series of discrete learning experiences but rather is the larger process of change. Each element of learning occurs as a function of the developmental state.

The distinction between development and learning can be illustrated in the analysis of children achieving a cognitive conservation of amount of substance, as well as weight and volume. The Piagetian task used to study these achievements involves a piece of clay that can be altered in shape. Children eventually recognize that each new shape will have the same weight and volume as the previous shape. But they can conserve or recognize the constancy of the amount of substance before they can recognize the constancy of weight and volume in the different shapes. Children will say that there is the same amount of clay in the new shape but will see its weight and volume as changed. This is an interesting observation, because they can be shown, and presumably can be taught, that the weight and volume remain the same, though not that the amount of substance remains the same; yet the conservation of amount of substance precedes the conservation of weight and volume. Piaget argues that this observation strongly favors a developmental rather than a learning explanation, and therefore, learning must be viewed as a subset of development and not the other way around.

In summary, we conceptualize development generally as a process of change and specifically as adaptive change toward competence. Individuals and environments are seen in a transactional relationship, in which each partner changes in relation to the other. Learning is part of experience and, as such, is a funtion of development. Development becomes more difficult to observe and study as individuals grow older, because a more complex organization of relationships is a natural consequence of developmental change. Different aspects of these relationships, too, may be more important at different times, which further complicates our conceptual sense of development.

Movement

Now that we have a general sense of development, we need to consider what movement is so that we can look at it in the context of development. Movement is such a common and ongoing part of our daily lives that we would chronicling all of our day if we tried to list our movements for a single day. We would need to begin with the movements of our fingers and related arm-hand body parts in order to describe using a pen to write this list. Our list would then include movements to dress and feed ourselves, change locations, and participate in work and play activities. Specific tasks might include buttoning a shirt, tying shoelaces, shaving or applying makeup, buttering toast, using a spoon to eat soup, walking on a crowded sidewalk, riding a bicycle, driving a car, using a typewriter, lifting a box, turning a page, playing a piano, throwing a ball, and dealing cards.

This brief listing of movements leads to the recognition of several considerations in defining what movement is. One important point is that movement often is described in functional terms, as we did in listing movements such as buttoning and throwing. This is quite different from describing the body movements that were made to achieve the functional outcomes of having the shirt held closed by the button and a ball propelled through the air. Movement can be described and analyzed strictly as *body movements* or *intended functions*. Both levels of description are useful, though we shall focus mainly on the broader and functional aspects of movement in considering movement development, while including many descriptions and analyses of changes in body movements.

Another consideration is that body movements must be adjusted to the existing circumstances, as when using a more delicate control of force to shave, in contrast with using maximal force to throw a ball, or walking carefully on an icy sidewalk, in contrast with running full speed in a footrace. The control of movement becomes more complicated when objects and other people are in the environment and are moving. Delicate and forceful movements must be adjusted in relation to the temporal constraints imposed by needing to move just before, just after, or in time with objects and other people.

Movement in a strict sense is the displacement of body parts and is properly called body movement. But we shall use a broader perspective that places the mover in the environmental context in which the body movements take place. This means that we shall be concerned with the movement's intent and function and its interplay with the environment in what is called *action*, in contrast with a more limited view of movement as an isolated *act*. We believe this more comprehensive perspective is necessary when trying to capture a larger view of movement development.

Production of Movement

An individual's movements are produced either directly or indirectly by muscle contractions. Movement is produced directly when muscles attached to bones are contracted in such a way that the bones are moved. We see this when the arm is flexed to move the hand to the head, whether to use the hand to salute or reach for a hat. Movement is produced indirectly when one part of the body moves because of contractions in other body locations. For example, the head moves forward during walking because leg movements are displacing the body in a forward direction. It soon becomes clear that analyses of movements in terms of muscle contractions become complicated and elusive if we try to explain movement by a complete account of all muscle activity. Some muscles must move key body parts, whereas other muscles must contract to limit movement in other body parts or to hold them in a desired position. Walking exemplifies the variety of outcomes produced by muscle contractions, in that legs are moved to provide the basic forward movement of the body and arm movements contribute to the forward movement but are more useful in counteracting forces produced by movement in the opposite leg. Additionally, the head is held in an upright position by other muscle contractions.

The neuromuscular system is responsible for contracting muscles and, therefore, for producing movement in the strict and limited sense of displacing body parts. Thus we shall call the neuromuscular system the *neuromotor system* when we speak of motor control. *Motor* will refer to the internal motor system, and *movement* will be the observable result we have defined as the displacement of a body part. This distinction is seen in our using the word *movement* in the title of our book to emphasize that we are concerned more with movement as an observable behavior than with internal motor functions.

Figure 1-1 diagrams the production of movement. The neuromotor system is in the center to show its central role in producing muscular contractions, which are observed as movements. The resultant movements often lead to related outcomes or consequences which are included in our description and analysis of movement. Movement is the primary outcome when individuals are dancing, swimming, or otherwise using movement as the end product or intended achievement. However, many movements are used to produce an effect or outcome beyond the movements. Examples are throwing to move a ball to another location and moving a pen to create words on a page. Movements and movement-produced outcomes often are difficult to separate for purposes of description and analysis. Our examples of dancing and swimming can also produce related outcomes, such as creating appreciation and excitement in others who watch the movements, particularly if the movers are seeking to produce such reactions. All of this merely

FIGURE 1-1

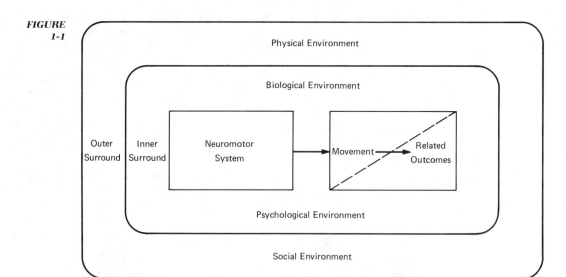

A general representation of the production of movement.

reaffirms the need to think of movement as more than the displacement of body parts.

We now shall go beyond the immediate production of movement by the neuromotor system to look at the many environments surrounding the neuromotor system and movement. We should explain our use of the word *environment*. The conventional use of the word *environment* is to identify the context in which an event takes place, which usually includes the assumption that these surrounding conditions have some influence on the event. We accept this usage, but we see a variety of environments rather than only one large one. We shall use *surround* to indicate the broader sense of an environment and divide it into *internal surround* and *external surround*, as shown in Figure 1-1.

Our next step in describing the production of movement is to look at the neuromotor system and movement in relation to the internal surround. All of a human's internal functions take place in both a biological environment and a psychological environment. An individual's many physiological systems can be regarded as part of this personal biological environment, which also affects the neuromotor system. This biological environment also includes bone structure and nonmuscle tissue, such as fat, tendons, and ligaments. The neuromotor system functions within the constraints of the biological conditions existing when the neuromotor system produces a movement. Examples are the size and weight of the skeletal structure to be moved and the current capability of the cardiopulmonary system to care for some of the muscle energy demands. The neuromotor system cannot function without some of the biological support systems and must function in relation to current biological conditions. The biological environment changes with maturity to become quite a different environment, as indeed the neuromotor system changes with maturity to become quite a different system. The state of the biological environment will vary somewhat in a short period of time and perhaps quite markedly and more permanently over a long period of time. The relation of the neuromotor system to the biological environment also will change in a transactional way. Movement leads to some immediate changes in some aspects of the biological environment, such as a lessened capability for supporting the neuromotor system, which then restricts the neuromotor system in subsequent movement production.

The psychological environment includes perceptual, cognitive, and emotional functions, which are biological systems conceived in psychological terms. Individual's perceptual-cognitive capabilities are necessary to process the information needed by the neuromotor system to produce movement. Each person's emotional state obviously will affect the functioning of his or her perceptual-cognitive mechanisms. Additionally, movement will influence the psychological environment in a transactional way that will lead to differences in it when preparing and producing the next movement. An example is that success and failure can change our perceptions of subsequent events and can lead to a greater or lesser involvement in some movements, as well as influence movement performance.

The outer surround is viewed as having a physical environment and a social environment. The outer surround is the more traditional sense of the environment within which movers move. The physical environment includes inanimate objects and structures that are part of our immediate outer surround, as well as the natural laws governing the physical environment. Movements must be planned and executed in relation to the location and condition of objects and surfaces and our knowledge of our physical world. We move differently when picking up small and large objects and when swimming above and below the water. Our social environment is perhaps the most complex and mobile aspect of our total surround, as we have many expectations and rules to learn and use. Our social involvements are complicated further because each participant may view a situation quite differently. Movements are an integral part of our social functioning, as exemplified by our walking style, the way we use our knife and fork, and the use of specific sport skills to participate with others.

Descriptions of Movement

Movement can be described in many different ways, depending on what one chooses to call a unit of movement and how the description will be used. Anatomical descriptors of flexion, extension, and the like provide information about the movements of body parts. Measurements of space, time, and force characteristics can be used to formulate more precise quantitative information about the movements of body parts. These measurements are useful in recording movement details, but we also need ways to categorize their overall patterns. We do this by including a functional sense of movement in such terms as walking, throwing, and swimming.

One problem in describing movements is to determine what we should use as a unit of movement. The difficulty is that every movement is really a combination and coordination of many smaller units. For example, walking and writing are commonly identified as movements, but each is really a composite of many separate movements. We see this when watching babies walking as they move one foot forward, followed by a pause and the movement of the other foot forward. Also, a pencil can be held in various ways to make single lines in different directions, as well as writing single letters and complete words continuously. The point is that each movement is a combination of other movements and also may be used as a part of another movement. This means that they can be labeled in various ways depending on what one chooses to view as a movement for purposes of description and analysis.

One developmental concern is describing and analyzing movement changes, particularly those that lead to organizing different movements and to moving in a *continuous* rather than a *discrete* manner. An important developmental change is the extent to which new movements are a sequence of discrete movements, such as early walking efforts, rather than the more continuous alternation of leg movements in a later walking movement. The same pattern of change from discrete to continuous is observed in using a pencil, as when children initially make a number of discrete or single lines before they move the pencil more continuously. Although many body movements do need to be made continuously, others should be made discretely. For example, a nail may be pounded with one discrete stroke at a time or with a continuous set of strokes. Pedaling a bicycle is usually more effective when maintaining a continuous alternation of leg movements.

Mover-Environment Relationships

We now shall categorize movement according to mover-environment relationships, using a framework proposed by Gentile and her colleagues (Gentile et al. 1975) and elaborated by Spaeth-Arnold (1981).

The Gentile framework helps us recognize the task requirements involved in making different types of movements in relation to different environmental conditions. It use two dimensions of movement and environment, which are then broken down into subunits. Movements are divided into *body stability* and *body transport* that, respectively, maintain and change body position. In addition, some movement tasks involve *limb manipulation*. The four limbs obviously are needed to maintain and change body position, but they also may be used separately or cooperatively for other purposes. For example, kicking or throwing a ball requires using a limb to impart force; turning a knob is accomplished by movements of the thumb and fingers, which are part of an arm movement. Limb manipulation also is required to clap our hands or stamp our feet, and it is used in the Gentile framework to describe the use of limbs to achieve outcomes other than body stability and body transport.

The two movement categories of body stability and body transport become four categories when recognizing that limb movements may or may not be involved. Examples for each of the four categories are listed in Figure 1-2. A baby standing on a chair is maintaining a body position without limb manipulation; reaching for a stationary object, such as a cookie held by a parent, adds a limb manipulation to move the arm to the appropriate spatial location and to use the thumb and fingers to grasp the cookie. A similar sequence becomes body transport when a baby walks across the floor without limb manipulation and then reaches for a cookie while walking. Eating the cookie while walking also is an example of limb manipulation during body transport.

Movements often are difficult to categorize because of the recurring problem of determining units and subunits. A baby may walk across a room, stop and reach for a cookie, and then continue walking while eating the cookie. The whole movement episode can be divided into several units, as we did in Figure 1-2, or into subunits, as when separating the leg movements of walking from the arm movement to reach for the cookie.

Recall that the movement classification in Figure 1-2 includes limb manipulation, as a distinction within both body stability and body transport. Limb manipulation

FIGURE 1-2

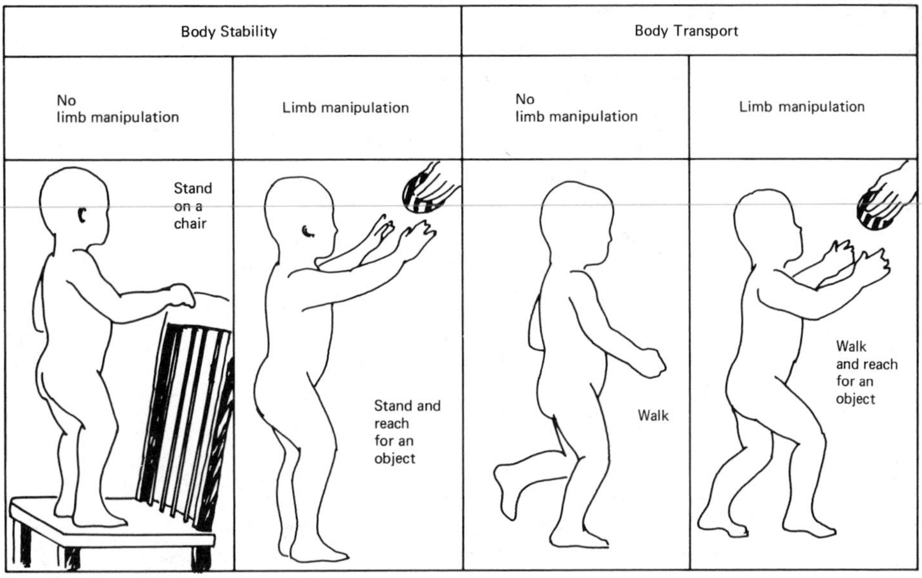

Analysis of the nature of body movements as proposed by Gentile. (Modified with permission from Spaeth–Arnold, 1981.)

often is the primary movement in the movement goal to be achieved, but the body also must be controlled in order to support the limb movements. Limb manipulation in combination with body transport really is the simultaneous performance of two tasks, such as walking and reaching, which early in life are difficult to do separately, much less together. Spaeth-Arnold (1981) adds that humans' upright posture increases their opportunity to use their arms for manipulative purposes. Thus, limb manipulation is a particularly important consideration in classifying humans' movements.

The second dimension of environment is a continuum to indicate the extent to which the environment is *stable* or *changing*. A stable environment provides a more predictable set of relationships. As noted by Spaeth-Arnold, the mover needs only to match the movements' spatial and directional characteristics with the environment's spatial characteristics. The mover determines the movement's temporal characteristics, without any constraints imposed by the environmental conditions as to when to start and finish the movements. The movement examples in Figure 1-2 are in a stable environment, in that the people and objects in the environment are stationary. The baby in our examples must move in relation to the environment's spatial requirements of reaching to the place where the cookie is being held, as well as walking toward the location of the cookie while avoiding chairs or other obstacles. But the baby decides when to start and stop the movements. Movement tasks of this nature have been described as *closed*, so as to indicate that the environmental conditions are fixed and not likely to change (Fitts 1962, Poulton 1957). Another way to describe a stable or closed environment is that it contains no other movement, which means that the movers do not need to adjust their movements to the environment's changing characteristics.

A changing environment is more unpredictable, and the mover must cope with both the spatial and the temporal constraints that it imposes. Examples are provided in the lower half of Figure 1-3. When a baby stands on a soft mattress, the weight of the body pushes down the mattress surface to create a changing surface. If the baby reaches for a moving balloon, movements must be adjusted spatially and temporally to the changing support surface and the changing position of the balloon. The situation becomes further complicated when the baby is walking, because this adds the continually changing location of the body to the problem of relating to location changes in the environment. Walking with a friend means an adjustment to maintain a position neither too far ahead nor too far behind; walking a dog on a leash adds the control of an arm to hold the leash in relation to the movements of the dog.

Movement tasks in a changing environment also can be described as *open*, thus indicating that the mover must control body movements in relation to both spatial and temporal requirements in the environment (Fitts 1962, Poulton 1957). Singer and Gerson (1981) make the additional distinction that some movement tasks (closed) are *self-paced* and others (open) are *externally paced*. The classification of movements as open and closed should be viewed as a continuum, because movement tasks often have both open and closed characteristics. Fitts recognized the continuous nature of the open-closed distinction by identifying an intermediate level. Using the arrangement in Figure 1-3, movement tasks will be more closed for body stability movements in a stable environment and will be more open for body transport movements in a changing environment. Movement tasks will be a mixture of open and closed for body stability movements in a changing environment and for body transport movements in a stable environment. That

**FIGURE
1-3**

	Movement		
	Body Stability	**Body Transport**	
Stable	Stand on a chair —and— Reach for an object (LM)	Walk —and— Reach for an object (LM)	S
Changing	Stand on a soft mattress —and— Reach for a moving balloon (LM)	Walk with a friend —and— Have a dog on a leash (LM)	S/T

Environmental Conditions

Spatial (S) — Temporal (T) Requirements

LM = limb manipulation

A classification of movement tasks as proposed by Gentile. (Modified with permission from Spaeth–Arnold, 1981.)

is, movement tasks will be open if either the mover or the environment is changing and will be even more open if both are changing.

Looking now at Gentile's classification of movement tasks in Figure 1-3, we can think of four general classifications for body movement and environment and the extent to which each is stable or changing. Although limb manipulations add another division to each of the four general classifications, they do not change their general meanings. The important distinction is to recognize the extent to which movers must cope with both *spatial* and *temporal requirements*. Spatial requirements are present in all movements, even if only to maintain a spatial location, and they can increase when more accuracy is required. And temporal accuracy is always a part of movements in terms of the proper timing or phasing of movements of body parts. Our main concern, however, is with temporal requirements in relation to the external environment, those that involve timing of movements so as to avoid a stationary object or to coincide with a moving object.

Movement Development

Development and movement, which have been described separately, now will be joined to present our perspective on movement development. As a starting point, we shall consider movement development as *development of movement control*. This emphasizes gaining control of body movements, rather than perfecting control, and includes control in relation to environmental conditions and outcomes to be achieved (Keogh 1971b). In the early years the developing mover must achieve body stability, body transport, and limb manipulation in order to move in a variety of changing environments and to create a wide range of movement-related outcomes. As we shall focus on these early refinements of movement control and mover-environment interplay in this book, we shall consider only briefly the refinements of movement control to produce maximal performance and shall concentrate instead on the development of movement control until an adequate level has been established, in both stable and changing environments. Thus our primary concern is how control is established, not how control is perfected.

Movement is produced by the mover, which means that we must decide how the mover produces movement and what influences the mover's movement production. Our representation of movement production presented in the previous section will be used in a framework in which we can describe and analyze the development of movement control. Our framework will place the production of movement in the context of a movement situation in order to identify the *movement problems to be resolved.*

Movement Situation

A mover functions in a *movement situation* composed of the mover and the various environments identified earlier as part of the inner and outer surrounds. A mover produces movement to resolve the *movement problems* created by an interplay of mover and environments. An individual wanting to eat food that is on a table in the next room presents a series of movement problems. The individual must get from here to there, get in position, reach for the food, and put the food into his or her mouth. An adult might walk to the other room, sit down, reach for a bowl of food, use a spoon to put the food onto a plate, and use a fork to move the food from the plate to his or her mouth. A child might crawl to the other room, be lifted onto a chair, be handed food to be held, and use a hand to place the food into his or her mouth. Both the adult and the child might create the movement problems in relation to an inner surround condition of being hungry, which may be both biological and psychological. A spouse or parent might help create the movement problems by calling the adult or child to dinner. Such movement problems generally are not recognized and solved consciously, although individuals can sometimes be aware of movement problems and their attempted solutions.

A mover has two roles in a movement situation. First, a mover helps create movement situations and movement problems in an interplay with different environments, as in the food-movement examples. Second, the mover organizes a movement plan and attempts to produce movements toward its outcome. Movement is what we observe, but we must recognize the interplays and decisions that precede and direct it. Again, the preparation and production of movement generally occur unconsciously, but we need to consider what is happening and how it might be happening.

A movement situation is the context in which movement takes place, as diagrammed in Figure 1-4. The interplay of *mover* and *environment(s)* creates a movement problem and a related *movement task. Environmental conditions* and *task requirements* are balanced against the *mover's resources* to establish *a level of individual demand* for a movement situation. All parts of the movement situation change in relation to one another, making movement development into a series

*FIGURE
1-4*

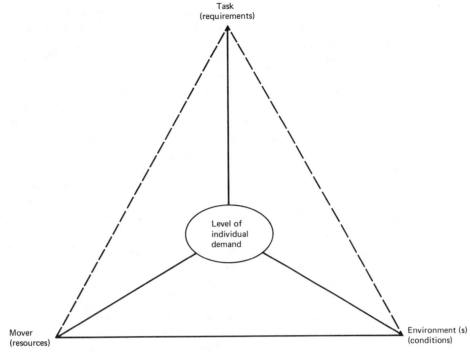

A general representation of a movement situation.

of transactional changes among mover, environment(s), and task across similar movement situations.

Movement Development Perspective

A basic point that we have stated in many ways is that the interplay of mover and environment(s) creates a movement problem. A movement task is created when a mover chooses an approach or a solution to the movement problem or a solution is imposed on the mover. Two children roll a ball to each other, and so we call the movement task "rolling a ball." The movement task can be imposed by having an adult hand the ball to one of the children and telling them to roll it back and forth. A movement task does not exist until the conditions are right for the mover and the environment to create it. The reason for belaboring this obvious, but often not recognized, point is that a movement task is not fixed and permanent. Changes in mover perceptions can lead to a change in the movement task, as when one child decides to throw rather than roll the ball. Changes in the environment also can change the movement task into finding a way to get the ball to a partner without rolling it through the puddle of water between them.

Dotted lines are used in Figure 1-4 to indicate the dependence of the movement task on the interplay of mover and environment(s). Some of these movement tasks are created often enough to be classified (see Gentile's classifications in Figure 1-3). In any case, the mover and environment(s) actually are the reality of a movement situation, whereas the movement task is a conceptual convenience to help us specify and analyze the requirements of a particular movement situation.

Movers must move according to specific environmental conditions and task requirements. Environmental conditions are the current state of affairs in all pertinent aspects of the internal and external surrounds. Task requirements usually reflect the spatial, temporal, and force requirements. Rolling a ball must take into account the weight and material of the ball, the position of the body at the start of the roll, the presence or absence of others and who they are, the appropriate force to roll the ball far enough and softly enough, the force directed to produce an appropriate direction and path, and perhaps a release at an appropriate time to intercept another moving object.

Analyses of movement situations generally are based on environmental conditions and task requirements, with little concern for their impact on the mover. But the idea of closed and open movement situations does include the mover, by recognizing that he or she will encounter different levels of demand. This means that a more open movement situation will place a higher load on the mover and thus will be more demanding, because the environmental conditions and task requirements have changed. The use of *demand* here should be expanded to include the level of demand in relation to the mover's resources, thus enabling us to think of demand as individual differences and developmental change.

An individual's level of demand in a movement situation is a function of movement conditions and task requirements balanced against mover resources, as represented in Figure 1-5. A movement situation is demanding for an individual to the extent that many of a mover's resources are needed to cope with environmental conditions and task requirements. If the movement task is putting on and buttoning a shirt, the level of demand will be low for a normal adult or an older child, because they have sufficient resources to complete the task while doing something else. But the level of demand for a young child probably will be quite high, to the point that the conditions and requirements may exceed his or her resources.

If conditions and requirements are held constant, the level of individual demand will change according to the mover's resources. Some individuals may have better neuromotor control and better physiological and psychological resources for dealing with certain environmental conditions and task requirements, and so there will be individual differences in level of demand. Kay (1970) describes this as the *evergreen principle*, in which the less efficient the mover is, the harder the task will be. Indeed, less able movers contribute to their own high level of demand because they also must cope with their movement errors. This reasoning can be extended to define *movement development as the development of the mover's resources*. If movers have more personal resources, they can function better in a movement situation. Changes in mover resources, therefore, become the key to understanding changes in movement development.

The level of individual demand is transactional, because the interplay of conditions and resources establishes task requirements, followed by the use of these

FIGURE 1-5

$$\frac{\text{Conditions \& Requirements}}{\text{Resources}} = \begin{array}{l}\text{Level of}\\\text{Individual}\\\text{DEMAND}\end{array}$$

A general representation of level of individual demand as a function of environmental conditions, task requirements, and mover resources.

16

resources in relation to conditions and requirements. The representation in Figure 1-5 is not a formula by which the precise values for each component can be used to calculate a level of demand; rather, it suggests what is involved when an individual produces a movement. Matters become more complicated when we include the mover, particularly mover resources, instead of concentrating only on environmental conditions and task requirements. But movers and their personal resources are movement development and cannot be ignored.

Chapter Summary

The framework in Figure 1-4 is intended to take us beyond the classification of movement to a perspective for thinking about movement development. The Gentile classification of movement tasks relates the mover and the environment, and we expanded it to include the transactional nature of the many interplays and to stress the importance of the mover's resources and the individual level of demand when thinking beyond a single movement situation to study movement development. We noted that development is more than quantitative changes and can be described and analyzed as movement problems to be resolved. This requires understanding the changes in the mover's resources and the transactional nature of changes in mover-environment(s) relationships.

PART ONE

DESCRIPTIONS OF CHANGE

This book is divided into two parts. The first describes changes in movement development and the second examines possible influences on these changes. If we can formulate some ideas about the nature of the changes we observe, we have a starting point for studying its determinants. Movement development is difficult to characterize, however, because there are so many movement skills and individuals vary considerably in their movement experiences. Also, the descriptions of change must be organized in relation to different movement perspectives.

Our basic movement perspective, as presented in Chapter 1, focuses on the development of movement control. This means that we are more interested in changes related to establishing control of body movements than changes related to perfecting control of body movements. Although the distinction becomes blurred in many movement skills, we can separate establishment of control and perfection of control as two major perspectives in describing change. Establishing control involves the initial mastery of a movement skill, as well as achieving its basic refinements, modifications, and variations. Perfecting this control leads to higher levels of performance and functioning in complex movement situations. Establishing control is a general movement problem to be resolved in the early years; perfecting control is the effort in the later years to achieve maximal performance. Standing upright and walking are establishing control of a movement skill; running fast is perfecting control of a movement skill.

Three changes characterize movement development in the earlier years and are used to organize our description of development of movement control. First, basic movement control must be achieved to enable babies and young children to control their own body and limb movements. Second, this basic control of self-movements must be refined, modified, and varied to become new movement patterns, particularly as fundamental play-game skills of running, jumping, and the like and as functional hand skills for daily living tasks. Third, movements must be adjusted spatially and temporally when moving in more open movement situations. Additionally, we include a brief review of changes in maximal performance efforts.

Before we begin our descriptions of change, we need to discuss age which is an ever-present and a confusing term in studying development. Age, as chronological age, is the time line along which change is traced to the point that age often is mistakenly viewed as an agent of change. Age periods are used to designate spans of time which also take on the aura of an agent of change. We shall identify some of our uses of age as time, with a caution about perceiving age as an agent of change.

A simple age line is presented in Figure I-1 to indicate several considerations in measuring the age of an individual. Life begins at conception (C). The

FIGURE
I-1

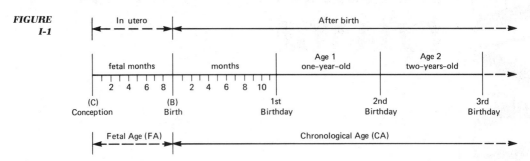

Age line to illustrate different designations of age.

approximately 9 months (40 weeks) in utero are identified as fetal months.
Chronological age (CA) is calculated from the time of birth, which means that the
approximately 9 months in utero are not included in CA, an important omission in
the early years, because 9 months is a sizable proportion of the life of a baby or a
young child. CA also marks the anniversary or end of a year of life and is misleading
in specifying the time since birth. Babies are identified as 1-year-olds or age 1 from
12 months through 23 months. This also is misleading because 1-year-olds are in
their second year of life after birth and also have had 9 months of life in utero.
These general comments on measuring age need to be kept in mind when
considering the passage of time during the early years of life.

General age periods are implied in terms such as infant and toddler. We shall use
babies to indicate individuals in their first two years of life after birth and young
children to indicate individuals from age 2 through age 7. These designations are
arbitrary on our part to maintain consistency. We shall use other terms less
definitively for other general age periods, including preschool years, early school
years, early and late childhood, and adolescence. Each of these terms will be given
general age limits when they are first used.

One problem in studying development is that we come to think of age as being
development, that age becomes an agent of change, perhaps even the agent of
change. It is easy to look at a graph of improved performance across age and think
that age determines or influences change. We must remember that time itself is not
causal and that age merely marks the passage of time or a period of time. Agents of
change, such as biological processes or social interactions, function during the
passage of time to determine or influence change. This means that we must
consider what is happening during a given period of time rather than view age as
the agent of change. To reiterate, age is merely time, and our problem is to identify
and understand the changes in movement development across time.

A DEVELOPMENT OF MOVEMENT CONTROL

CHAPTER

2 Early Movement Development: Birth to 24 Months

The development of movement control from birth to 24 months gives babies the basic control of their own movements, or the *control of self-movements*. Babies at birth have minimal control of their arms, legs, and head, and they cannot roll over, sit up, or in any way move from the position and location in which they are placed. Their most distinct movements are reflexes, such as grasping and sucking, which are sometimes necessary for survival. When babies initiate movements, rather than respond reflexively, they move their arms and legs in a seemingly random fashion without the precision and accuracy achieved later to control posture, locomotion, and manipulation. Children at 24 months have sufficient postural control to cope with many basic postural adjustments; they can walk and get around the environment reasonably well; and they can handle many objects. Children at 24 months, however, do not cope well with rapid self-movements and moving in relation to moving objects and other moving persons. They also are not yet self-sufficient enough to survive without the assistance of others.

The first and second years of life after birth are when the control of self-movements is established. From the rather diffuse and extraneous movements and the reflexes of the early months, sufficient control is established to produce distinct and reliable control of self-movements. These movement changes proceed from separate movements to more coordinated and adaptive movements, as seen when babies first walk with single, discrete steps and then are able to alternate their feet with distinct timing and spacing, followed by varying the walking pattern in relation to environmental conditions. Control of self-movements then is refined and varied to provide the repertoire of movements characteristic of older children, youths, and adults and can be used when moving in relation to moving objects and other moving persons.

A general expectation is that children at 24 months will have developed in a similar manner, although at different rates. That is, we expect all children at 24 months to sit, walk, turn a knob, and make similar movements characteristic of children of this age in all parts of the world. Progressions of change in specific movements also are expected to be similar, but the rate of movement development

21

may be quite different, in that some children will more rapidly perform these movements, whereas others will achieve them at a later age. There also will be differences in the quality of movement for children making the same movement. Movement development during the first 2 years after birth is reasonably universal in kinds of movements and progressions of change, though there are differences in the rate of change and the quality of movement.

Early movement development is the achievement of a basic level of postural control, locomotion, and manual control. Babies must gain control of posture as the foundation for locomotion and manual control. Without control of the head and the ability to stabilize the trunk, babies cannot sit or stand, much less walk, and cannot use their arms and hands to reach and grasp in an unsupported position. Postural control also is necessary in correcting for movements of body parts, because a simple reach of an arm or tilt of the head will disrupt body equilibrium and require a postural adjustment. Locomotion initially is moving with the body in contact with a surface, by rolling or otherwise squirming about. Arms and legs then become the propelling force, with upright postural control providing the opportunity for bipedal locomotion or walking. Many other locomotion problems must be resolved, including going up and down stairs, moving in water, and going over and under objects. Manual control begins with reaching for objects which soon can be grasped and held. Improved control of the fingers and thumb makes it possible to manipulate objects in many ways, including using both hands together.

Movements and Reflexes in Utero and After Birth

The normal gestation period for humans is 40 weeks, or approximately 9 months. Movement reflexes can be elicited in utero as early as the second or third fetal month after conception, and many of the reflexes observed at birth are present in utero by the fifth or sixth month. Pregnant mothers usually feel fetal movements during the fourth or fifth month and can differentiate some types of movement patterns.

Movements and Activity Level in Utero
Fetal movements become quite distinct in the last 3 months of pregnancy. Four types of fetal movements were charted by Walters (1964) who monitored the weekly reports of thirty-five pregnant mothers. Kicking movements made up 47 percent of the total number of movements reported, in comparison with 34 percent for squirming, 18 percent for ripples, and less than 2 percent for hiccups. Walters described kicking as a quick movement of the extremities to thrust or poke, whereas squirming is a slow movement to stretch, push, or turn. A ripple movement is a light and rapid wavelike movement going back and forth and up and down. Hiccups were defined as quick and convulsive rhythmical movements. The ripple movement reported by Walters was not noted in earlier studies and probably was included in earlier reports as kicking or squirming, which are the general movement patterns to be expected. No studies have determined whether some fetuses are kickers and others are squirmers and the relationships of movement style in utero to later developmental characteristics. The number of movements decreases during the ninth fetal month, perhaps in preparation for birth.

Walters (1965) followed fetuses in her 1964 study to examine the relationship of activity level in utero and development after birth, which was measured at 12, 24, and 36 weeks after birth, by using the observation scale devised by Gesell (Knobloch and Pasamanick 1974; see Box 2-2). Correlations were .3 to .5 for the total number of movements (activity level) in the seventh, eighth, and ninth fetal months and the total score on the Gesell observations at 12, 24, and 36 weeks. Correlations were slightly higher at a consistent level of .5 for the activity level and the Gesell motor subscale, which measures more total body movement. The results indicate that more active fetuses tend to develop more rapidly during the first 8 to 9 months after birth. This relationship is predictive only generally and to a moderate degree. More detailed analyses are needed to determine whether some types of movements in utero precede specific movement achievements after birth.

Some interesting techniques have been devised to measure neonatal, or newborn, activity levels in ways that could be useful in studying early movement development, such as wiring crib pads to measure the amount and direction of movement (Korner et al. 1974). Activity levels in utero and immediately after birth have been studied primarily in relation to levels of consciousness (sleep states), irritability, and similar concerns that do not contribute directly to an understanding of movement development (see Phillips et al. 1978 for examples).

Too much or too little activity may be a sign of distress, which means that there is a desirable, perhaps even optimal, range of normal and healthy activity. Extreme levels of activity become warning signs, whereas the midrange is satisfactory. The problem is to find the cutoff levels of too much and too little. Keep in mind that more is not always better and that predictions sometimes can be made better at the extreme levels than in the midrange. We may know with more certainty that an extremely high or low value for a measure indicates poor achievement on another measure than we can predict achievement from a midrange value.

Spontaneous Movements After Birth

Most young babies move their limbs and body in many different ways that do not seem purposeful or oriented to achieve a particular goal. They kick their legs, wave their arms, and rock their body, seemingly just to move and not to accomplish something. These appear to be spontaneous movements, rather than reflexive responses, and are general and diffuse. Very little has been done to describe them systematically until Thelen (1979) made extensive obvervations of babies during their first year of life after birth. Her observations provide an interesting starting point to study one aspect of changes in spontaneous movements.

Thelen studied what are called *rhythmical movement stereotypies*, movements of parts of the body or the entire body for several repetitions at regular, short intervals. This excludes the single and nonrepetitive movements that characterize most movement skills. Rhythmical movement stereotypies are abnormal in older children and adults; indeed, persistent rocking, swaying, and similar movements at older ages are associated with disturbed individuals. But young babies engage regularly in rhythmical movement stereotypies that they seem to enjoy, even though they seemingly achieve nothing beyond the movements themselves. Thelen observed twenty babies for 1 hour every other week from 4 to 52 weeks of age, in the home when the baby was awake and without changing the regular routine. She then analyzed approximately 500 hours of observations.

Thelen found a total of forty-seven different stereotypies. These movements were repeated at least three times at an interval of 1 second or less before they were counted as the occurrence of a rhythmical movement stereotypy. Nine of the eleven most frequently occurring stereotypies are shown in Figure 2-1, which parents and others who have watched young babies will readily recognize. Thelen found few stereotypies in the early weeks, but they increased to occur 6 percent to 8 percent of the observation time from 16 to 44 weeks. They then decreased to approximately 4 percent of the observation time during the last weeks of the first year. Thelen combined some of the movements into logical groupings, such as different types of leg kicking, and found that the age of onset and the age of peak activity level varied for the different groupings. This indicates that there may be some pattern of development that needs to be studied further.

Thelen's approach is one way to look at spontaneous movements that occur frequently during the first year. We do not understand the function of these movements, but they may be a means of communication and may be initial efforts to produce purposeful movements without sufficient control to approximate the intention. Thelen proposes several other possibilities, which will be discussed in Chapter 9.

FIGURE 2-1

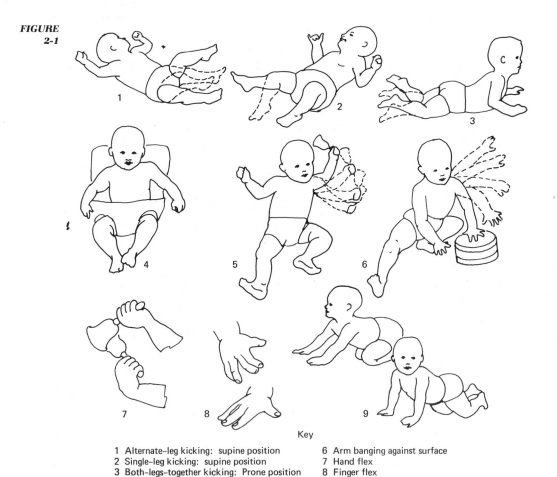

Key

1 Alternate-leg kicking: supine position
2 Single-leg kicking: supine position
3 Both-legs-together kicking: Prone position
4 Foot rubbing
5 Arm waving with object
6 Arm banging against surface
7 Hand flex
8 Finger flex
9 Rocking: hands-and-knees

Rhythmical movement stereotypes. (Reproduced by permission from Thelen, 1979.)

Reflexes

Newborns can produce many basic movement reflexes but have very little voluntary control of their movement or body posture. A reflex is a movement response elicited by a particular sensory stimulus, which can be light or sound, touch or pressure on a body location, or body position. Reflexes are expected to appear at a particular age, with some disappearing soon thereafter and others maintained throughout life. Reflexes at birth and during the first months after birth are evaluated according to intensity and quality and are used as developmental indicators (see Box 2-1). Reflexes should be in an expected range of intensity, with too brisk or too soft a reaction being an abnormal or negative sign. A lack of symmetry and incomplete reactions are qualitative signs of abnormality in some reflexes. Negative or abnormal signs are used as indications that specific aspects of the nervous

BOX
2-1

DEVELOPMENTAL INDICATORS

The newborn is evaluated in a number of ways at birth and in the days that follow in order to assess development status, particularly risk potential or possible developmental problems. Evaluation procedures of this type are used by medical personnel and psychologists as developmental indicators of problems that may require more detailed examinations. Reflexes are tested, spontaneous behaviors are observed, and specific test situations are arranged, as illustrated by the Gesell and other developmental scales described in the next section. A scale devised by Apgar (1953) will be discussed briefly to illustrate one type of developmental indicator.

The birth process, particularly the moment of emerging into a new environment, is a traumatic experience. The newborn now must breathe, which requires respiration movements to continue and constantly adjust to the oxygen demands of the internal systems. The womb's environment has given way to a larger and more complex environment.

The APGAR Scale is used at birth to determine whether a newborn may be at risk and need attention beyond normal birthing routines. The five items listed in Table 2-1 are checked visually 1 minute after birth. Each item is assigned a numerical value of 0, 1, or 2, using Apgar's criteria. If the total APGAR score is low, the newborn is considered at risk, and action is taken to deal with the danger signals. The five screening items are identified by an acronym that spells APGAR.

TABLE
2-1

Test Items in the APGAR Scale

Item	General Behavior or Characteristic
Activity	Muscle tone
Pulse	Heart rate
Grimace	Facial movements
Appearance	Skin color
Respiration	Breathing movements

Heart rate and breathing movements are basic indicators of a newborn's overall "life." Skin color can signal jaundice and other disease conditions. Muscle tone, if too flaccid or too stiff, may reflect problems in neuromotor development. The newborn's facial grimace is the contraction of facial muscles when responding to stimulation and producing a newborn crying expression. Abnormal signs in facial movement mean a lack of contractions or extreme contractions and asymmetry, such as more movement on one side than on the other side.

The APGAR Scale illustrates the type of initial movement development that is expected. Our example is limited because the scale's purpose is to identify life-threatening problems rather than assess movement development. We expect certain movement capabilities to be present and to be carried out within certain limits of the established movement pattern. Extreme differences in movement patterns and in movement intensity may indicate problems in movement development.

25

system may not be developing well. Several reflexes will now be described briefly to show their variety and how they might be involved in the development of movement control. The testing of reflexes requires professional training to provide an appropriate eliciting stimulus and to evaluate the response. But our descriptions here are general and do not deal with these problems.

The reflexes listed in Table 2-2 are arranged in the order of their first appearance in utero. Each of these, except sucking, normally disappears during the first year after birth. Rooting is a reflex that serves a functional purpose for a short period of time and then disappears when more adaptive means develop to provide a broader set of movement behaviors. Rooting is elicited by pressure on the cheek which results in the rooting or moving of the head toward the pressure. This serves as a direction finder to bring the mouth in contact with the nipple of a breast or bottle. Several months after birth, babies have sufficient voluntary movement control to locate a breast or bottle and move their mouths into position to feed, and so this rooting reflex disappears. If it did not, we would respond with a rooting movement whenever we felt a particular pressure on our cheek! The point is that many early reflexes must disappear or be placed under some higher control to be inhibited in order for more voluntary and adaptive movement control to develop.

Sucking is something of a compromise in that it will continue in our movement repertoire but will be under more voluntary control. Additional movements of the mouth are developed to enable us to drink, as well as suck in liquids, and to chew and eat solid foods. Rooting and sucking demonstrate the problem in discovering whether reflexes disappear, are suppressed, or become incorporated in voluntary movement control.

The palmar grasp is a familiar reflex to parents. When a finger is placed across the palm, infants and babies will flex their fingers and hold tight the adult finger. Parents are particularly pleased to show off their babies' strength by having them grasp their finger with both hands and be lifted up. About 5 to 6 months after birth, the palmar grasp diminishes and then disappears, to be replaced by more voluntary control of grasping. The more adaptive control of grasping includes opening the hands by extending the fingers and thumb prior to contact with an object, and the ability to release a grasp. This further shows the need for adapting the control of movement rather than being bound by a particular stimulus. Somewhat like a palmar grasp, a plantar grasp reflex can be elicited by pressure on

TABLE 2-2	The Appearance and Disappearance of Early Reflexes*		
REFLEX	GESTATIONAL AGE OF APPEARANCE (FETAL MONTHS)	POSTNATAL AGE OF DISAPPEARANCE (MONTHS AFTER BIRTH)
Rooting	2–3	3–4
Sucking	2–3	Persists
Palmar grasp	4–6	5–6
Tonic neck	6–7	6–7
Stepping	8–9	3–4
Placing	8–9	Up to 12, variable afterward

* Based on data reported by Taft and Cohen 1967.

the sole of a foot to produce flexion of the toes, but this reflex seems less important in tracing the development of movement control.

The tonic neck reflexes (TNR) cover many complex variations related to stretching the neck muscles and joints. The asymmetrical TNR is the position assumed by the legs and arms when the head is turned to the right or left. The leg and arm extend on the side of the head's turn and flex on the opposite side to look like the position of a fencer on guard. The head then is facing an extended arm which places the hand of that arm in view of the baby, which may be important in establishing eye-hand coordination. The difference in arm movements, in which one arm is extended and the other is flexed, may be useful in differentiating arm functioning for later coordination of arm movements.

Stepping and placing reflexes appear late in utero, and so after birth, a stepping movement can be produced when the baby is held upright and the sole of the foot is touched to a solid surface. A placing movement is the upright-held baby's lifting a foot when the upper part touches a surface, as if to lift the foot over an object. These reflexes suggest an effort at walking. Again, the reflexes must be inhibited, eliminated, or incorporated to enable the development of more adaptive movement control. But we still do not know how reflexive movements develop into adaptive movement control.

Reflexes often function together to help control more complex movements. Righting reflexes are an example in which a general set of reflexes develops into a system for maintaining postural control. These reflexes have not been identified and related systematically except to recognize that a complex network of reflexes is needed to maintain general body equilibrium in relation to gravity and the body's movements. Newborns cannot keep their heads in an upright position, much less control their bodies in a standing position and when moving. Righting reflexes are essentially responses to body position, often as created by body movements. These reflexes develop after birth, although some aspects may be present at birth, and they remain a fundamental part of our motor control system. Examples are given later in this chapter when discussing postural control.

Two questions are apparent in our description of reflexes. First, what is a reflex and, second, how do we progress from reflexive to voluntary control? It is difficult to distinguish clearly what a reflex is, as contrasted with an automatic response. The early-appearing reflexes described here are stimulus bound; that is, a certain stimulus will produce a certain movement response. Movements at a later age often are automatic, in that walking is a serial repetition of uniform movements that is usually not consciously controlled. The difference is that walking can be interrupted and adapted to conditions in the environment. But early-appearing reflexes are not adaptable because the response is attached or bound to the stimulus.

Between these two extremes of reflexes being stimulus-bound or automatic, there are other ways of thinking about reflexes. For example, righting reflexes are a type of reflexive movement that must function in relation to and in coordination with other movements and are needed to keep the body in equilibrium while participating as part of a larger movement operation. Righting reflexes must keep a child upright while walking, without bringing the body to a halt and interrupting the walking motion. In addition, subunits or parts of a larger movement are reflexes because they are fixed in what they can do, whereas the larger movement units must be flexible in order to accomplish the movement intention or plan. The point is that early-appearing reflexes are stimulus bound and will limit the subsequent development of movement control if not inhibited or incorporated, which leads to the second question of how we progress from reflexive to voluntary control.

The development from reflexive to voluntary control can be observed in a general, descriptive sense, but it is difficult to explain this change. Our comments here are limited to the observation that many early-appearing reflexes disappear and voluntary movements develop in order to function in a similar but more adaptive manner. Palmar grasp is an obvious example, in which the grasp reflex is limited to holding an object when contact is made with it, in contrast with the more flexible and adaptive grasping behaviors of anticipating when to grasp and when to release the grasp. Many early appearing reflexes disappear and cannot be elicited in the original manner, but others are known to reappear after a brain injury. These reflexes generally disappear again as the brain injury heals. This suggests that higher brain centers suppress or control these reflexes, but this still does not explain whether these reflexes become part of larger and more adaptive movements or merely are suppressed.

Progressions of Change

Early development follows an order or sequence that makes it possible to describe *progressions of change*. A progression of change is a list of specific achievements leading to an important general achievement, such as standing upright, walking, and reaching. We shall identify the *landmark achievements* in each progression that highlight the flow of early movement development. The age in weeks or months is given for many of these, indicating a general time relationship among them. Age, however, should be taken as approximate and only as indicating normative achievement, with considerable variation expected among individuals and across different groups. These progressions are intended to describe only patterns of change and are not meant to portray fixed and invariant sequences. Although babies tend to follow the same general pattern of change, there is considerable variation among them.

Progressions of change were compiled for postural control, locomotion, and manual control, from developmental scales prepared to assess individual babies and young children (see Box 2-2). A problem in using the data from these scales is that they are organized to analyze intellectual and personal–social development rather than movement. Movement is used to indicate other aspects of development, particularly during the first year, because babies during this time do not know how to talk, and so movement is the obvious and first behavior to be observed. Because movement behaviors are selected to represent other aspects of development, their observations and analyses often are insufficient to describe movement development. Thus the data from two developmental scales were rearranged for a more useful look at changes in movement behavior.

The Bayley Scales of Infant Development (Bayley 1969) and the Denver Developmental Screening Test (Frankenburg and Dodds 1967) were used to compile progressions of change for movement development. The Bayley Scales and the Denver Developmental are the most current sets of normative data for describing change during the first and second years. Each item in the two scales is given

BOX
2-2

DEVELOPMENTAL SCALES AND PROGRESSIONS OF CHANGE.

The early development of children has been traced in a variety of ways, including successive observations of the same babies in longitudinal studies, comparisons across socioeconomic and cultural groups, and extensive cinematographic analyses. Psychologists and physicians did most of this descriptive work, with the intention of explaining intellectual and personal-social development. A number of *developmental scales* were constructed to measure and assess babies' developmental progress during their first and second years of life after birth.

The behaviors selected for observation represent the normal progression of development as viewed by those who constructed the scale. Similar behaviors are included in the different scales to cover the first and second years, because these behaviors are common to the development of most individuals. Fewer and more varied behaviors are included for observation beyond the second year, and thus these scales are the most useful for assessment during the first and second years.

Some of the scales can be used to derive a total score in the form of a Developmental Quotient (DQ), similar to an Intelligence Quotient (IQ). But the main use of developmental scales is to assess the developmental status and progress of individual children. Professional training is required to administer and interpret a developmental examination, which usually is a lengthy procedure. Arranging a test environment is particularly difficult because babies cannot yet talk and may not interact well with an unfamiliar person.

Developmental scales were a natural product of the studies of children's behavior from 1920 to 1940. Gesell was the dominant figure in this work, and wrote many books on his observations at the Yale University Clinic of Child Development. Both Gesell and Amatruda in 1941 wrote a book on developmental diagnosis, which is the best overall summary of Gesell's work on infancy and early childhood. A second revision was completed in 1947, followed in 1974 by a third edition edited by Knobloch and Pasamanick. The developmental scale devised by Gesell and Amatruda has five subscales, called fields of behavior: Adaptive, Gross Motor, Fine Motor, Language, and Personal-Social. The original work of Gesell and his associates provides the basic performance information arranged in eight age groups from birth to 36 months. Five age groups are used for the developmental changes during the first year, followed by age groups for 18 months, 24 months, and 36 months. Most developmental scales, except some constructed recently (for example, Uzgiris and Hunt 1975), have similar subscales and a similar emphasis on the first year.

The Knobloch and Pasamanick edition (1974) is recommended as a systematic and careful description of early development. Each age group is described with a list of expected behaviors, drawings to illustrate important behaviors, and a discussion of growth trends. A 22-page growth trend chart in the appendix summarizes changes across ages in regard to body position (for example, supine, standing) and test object or type of task (for example, cube, chair, language, feeding). The developmental scale constructed by Griffiths (1954) also is recommended for her observations of 571 babies in London, on 260 behaviors during the first and second years, which extends the normative perspective beyond the American samples.

The Milani-Comparetti and Gidoni (1972) scale is useful for our purposes because it focuses on reflexes and early movement development, primarily as a screening test to identify babies with neurological and related disorders. In addition, an interesting graphic display of movement development observations of several movement tasks in the first year is provided by Zdanska-Brincken and Wolanski (1969). Their graphs show several behaviors, as well as the age in months for early, average, and late achievement. The graphic summaries we use in this chapter are similar, though are less detailed and cover a wider range of movements.

Two developmental scales were used to prepare the *progressions of change* for this chapter. The first is the Bayley Scales of Infant Development (Bayley 1969), the culmination of Bayley's lifetime of work assessing early development. Her study of motor abilities during the first 3 years was published in 1935 as the first monograph in a series published by the Society for Research in Child Development. The Bayley Scales, published in 1969, have 163 items in its mental scale and 81 items in its motor scale.

The normative figures are based on the testing of 1,262 children in fourteen age groupings, from 2 months through 30 months.

The second scale is the Denver Developmental Screening Test (Frankenburg and Dodds 1967). Because the earlier developmental scales varied considerably in the age assigned to the same behavior, test items from twelve developmental and preschool intelligence tests were used to standardize a new scale. The Denver Deveopmental thus has 105 test items which were administered to 1,036 healthy children ranging in age from 2 weeks to 6.4 years. The test items are grouped into the same categories that Gesell used, except that Fine Motor and Adaptive are combined. The usefulness of the Denver Developmental is limited to the first 2 years, because 76 of the 105 items are identified as expected achievements during this time.

Several items from each scale are listed in Figure 2-2 to illustrate how the normative data for each item are represented in the progressions of change used in this chapter. The age of achievement is taken as the age when 50% percent of the children at that age could do the movement behavior. Each item is placed in a rectangular frame and then arranged on an age line. The age of achievement is marked on the top line of the rectangular frame by a square for the Bayley Scale and a circle for the Denver Developmental. Both a square and a circle are present if the normative data from both scales are available and are included. The width of the rectangular frame indicates the variability or range of ages when individuals were able to do the movement behavior. For the Bayley items, the left-hand side of the rectangular frame indicates the age in months when 5 percent of the children did the movement behavior, and the right-hand side indicates achievement by 95 percent of the children. The range boundaries for the Denver Developmental are 25 percent and 90 percent. Although the range boundaries are proportionately smaller for the Denver Developmental, the overall picture of variability is not distorted by the difference in range boundaries between the two scales. Looking at the items arranged on the age line, the children in both samples could transfer a cube from one hand to the other at 5 months. A few children could make this exchange at 4 months, and all but a few children could do this by 8 months. Raking or scooping a pellet was achieved at 5 months in the Denver sample and at 6 months in the Bayley sample. Partial finger prehension was achieved at 7 months in the Bayley sample and thumb-finger grasp at 8 months in the Denver sample. These two items

FIGURE 2-2

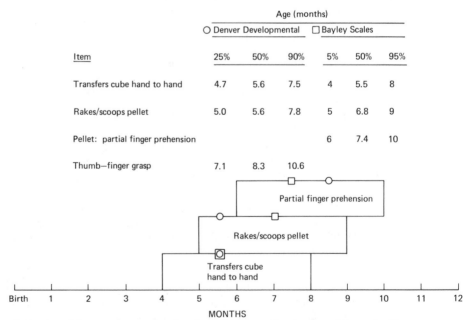

Illustration of the use of normative data from the Denver Developmental Screening Test (Frankenburg and Dodds, 1967) and the Bayley Scales of Infant Development (Bayley, 1969) to prepare a progression of change.

are labeled differently but seem to be the same movement of thumb-finger contact without true opposition of the digits' end points. These two items are identified in the top rectangular frame as partial finger prehension, showing how task labels sometimes were changed when combining data from the two scales. Many items included in the progressions of change were from only one scale because a comparable item was not listed in the other one.

an age in months to represent the age, or range of ages, when 50 percent of the children could do the movement behavior, as illustrated in Box 2-2. Each movement behavior is placed in a rectangular frame and is arranged on an age line to indicate median, early, and late ages of achievement. From several behaviors in the rectangular frames, a progression of change can be traced according to age of achievement and extent of individual variability. It is important to remember that the progressions and related ages of achievement listed throughout this chapter are only general indicators of change. Individuals and different groups may vary, but within the general flow of change represented by the set of movement behaviors included in a progression.

Body Control

Postural control and locomotion are two movement problems that the newborn must resolve. Both involve the control and movement of the entire body, which is our reason for including both under the title of body control, in accordance with the Gentile classification scheme presented in Chapter 1. Body control includes the Gentile categories of body stability and body transport, which we call, respectively, postural control and locomotion. The later development of body control cannot be observed in this simple dichotomy of postural control and locomotion, and thus, at older ages, it becomes necessary to look at changes in more specific types of tasks, such as running and jumping, which require the simultaneous control of posture and control of body movements. The early development of postural control and locomotion will be described separately, although using many of the same or similar movement achievements to portray their progressions.

Postural Control

General body position or posture must be controlled to some extent before the control of other movements is possible. Newborns lying on their back are supported by a surface, and so they can move their head and limbs without also having to control their postural position. But when placed on their stomach, their facedown position limits what they can do with their head and limbs, and when held by another person, they are placed in a variety of postural positions depending on how they are held. Some held positions enable babies to move their heads and arms, but other positions do not. An important achievement for babies is to control their own posture so that they can control other movements. A striking example is when babies can control their posture to move to an upright posture and then can move their legs in an alternating pattern to move forward, which also involves controlling their posture while moving forward. Postural control in this perspective underlies the control of all movements and so is part of all movements.

General Description. Three general progressions are listed in Figure 2-3 to describe the development of postural control during the first year of life after birth. Beginning with the lower left corner of Figure 2-3, babies in a prone position progress from momentarily lifting their head off the supporting surface to a push-up at 2 to 3 months, which extends their arms somewhat to lift both their head and chest. The important achievement in this progression is the control of the head, which is basic to all forms of postural control. A landmark achievement at 2 months is to be held while the holder is walking and to *keep the head steady, without support, while being moved.*

The second progression is to achieve and maintain an upright posture in a sitting position. Babies at 3 months can sit in a supported position and can keep their heads steady, but they cannot regain this control when they tilt to one side. Improved head control is noted when an adult pulls a baby from a supine, or back-lying, position to a sitting position and the head does not lag. Babies generally

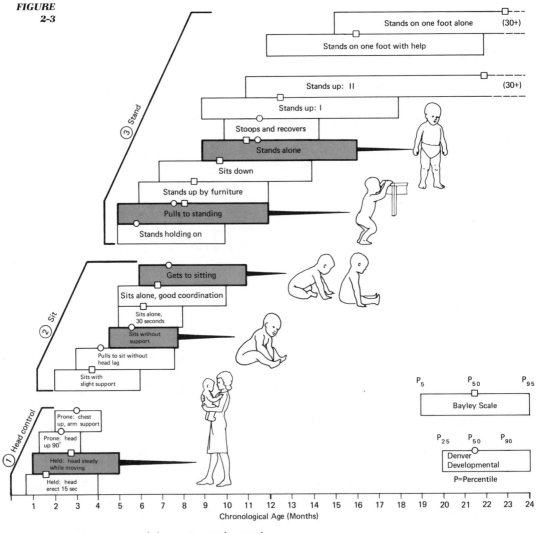

FIGURE 2-3

Progressions of change: Postural control.

can *sit without support* by 5 months, which is another landmark achievement for postural control and indicates a basic control of head and trunk, although only in a stationary position. As a culmination of this progression in control of sitting posture and another landmark achievement, babies at 7 months can *get to a sitting position* from a prone or supine position. This requires a change in posture as well as the maintenance of a posture. Babies at this time also can roll over to change positions from back to stomach and stomach to back, as noted in the locomotion progressions in Figure 2-5. Babies at 7 months can change body positions rather than being limited to the position in which they are placed.

When babies can maintain a sitting position, they soon can do other things while sitting, including turning their head and manipulating objects, which if attempted earlier would disrupt their equilibrium. Sitting activities also become part of other movements, such as leaning forward and then back and moving from a sitting position to a prone or a standing position. After achieving upright posture, babies then face the problem of sitting down, which includes moving from an upright position to squat or hunker down and stooping to pick up objects.

The third progression is to achieve and maintain a standing position. Babies can be held upright, with the many precursors of standing noted, but not until they are 5 to 6 months of age can they maintain a standing position while holding a support. Babies can *pull themselves to a standing position* at 7 to 8 months, which coincides with getting to a sitting position and rolling over. The sum of these achievements is another landmark in which babies can *change postural position* rather than just hold a position. The ability to change body position is the beginning of locomotion in which babies then can move from one place to another, however limited the actual distance may be. Another landmark achievement, which prepares babies for walking, is *standing alone* at 11 months. Babies now have achieved a full upright posture without assistance.

An important earlier achievement at 9 months is sitting down. We usually focus so much on getting up that we often overlook the problem of getting down in some manner other than falling down. Watching babies sit in a chair is an interesting movement to observe. The body must be lowered to a sitting position with the back to the chair, and so babies first will climb into the chair and from there get into a sitting position. Griffiths (1954) observed babies' various approaches to chairs and noted that they seated themselves at 22 months in the conventional manner of having their back to the chair. Another way of getting down was observed in the Denver Developmental when babies at 11 months could stoop to pick up an object and recover or return to an upright position. Sitting, stooping, recovering, and similar changes in body position reflect an increased flexibility in postural control.

Another interesting problem in getting to an upright position was observed by Bayley, who asked children lying on their back to stand up. She found three different ways of getting up, two of which are listed in Figure 2-3 as the last items of the third progression. Bayley observed that children at 14 months (I) got up by first rolling over to their stomach and then rising to a standing position. Children at 22 months (II) rolled only to their side before standing. The difference between rolling to a side position rather than to a stomach position probably indicates better postural control, because the side position is less stable. Better postural control is needed to begin the rise to a standing from a side position. The third position Bayley observed was not achieved unti 32 months, when children sat straight up to stand, without rolling to either side. The direct sit-up is

33

more complicated and may reflect movement-planning differences and increased strength more than improved postural control.

Progressions and landmarks in postural control are difficult to observe directly beyond the first year, because postural control becomes an integral and often inseparable part of all movements. Walking and running are locomotor movements requiring considerable postural control, as is true in more subtle ways for putting on trousers, using a spoon, and almost any other movement we can imagine. The control of all movements depends on the control of a postural position while the movement is being made. Babies at the end of their second year can walk quickly, run haltingly, do many interesting variations of sitting and walking, and do rudimentary forms of throwing and kicking. All of these achievements indicate improved postural control.

A detailed analysis of movements is needed to identify control of posture as a component of the overall movement. But because we do not have such a breakdown in measuring movement control, postural control is included in the overall measurement of movement control. An approximation of postural control is made by having individuals balance or control their body position in balancing tasks, with two examples listed in the top right-hand corner of Figure 2-3. Babies at 15 to 16 months can stand on one foot if given some support and at 22 to 23 months can stand momentarily on one foot without support. Balancing tasks of this type indicate postural control but do not measure it as part of other movements. Postural control, therefore, is viewed as more than balancing, and balancing in this view is only one kind of control of body position.

General Movement Problems. The early development of postural control can be seen as three general movement problems which are interactive and are not independently resolved. The first one is the need to *maintain a steady position* in relation to gravity. The progression in developing equilibrium was shown in Figure 2-3 as starting with control of the head and followed by control of the upper body in a sitting position and the whole body in the upright position. The solution to this movement problem is developing a complicated set of righting reflexes which maintain equilibrium when the body moves away from a position of stability.

Two righting reflexes are shown in Figure 2-4 to illustrate positive and negative reactions to movement (Fiorentino 1973). When the tilt board is moved in Pictures A and B, two different reactions are elicited. The positive action shown in Picture A is to counterbalance the tilt by moving the head up or away and spreading the arms and legs. The negative reaction is to go with the tilt, as shown in Picture B by the head and the left leg moving down in the direction of the movement. The upper bodies of the children in Pictures C and D have been moved to the side to determine whether the child is making some counterbalancing movements. The child in Pictures C moves the head away from the displacement and makes a hopping step with the right foot to maintain equilibrum. The child in Picture D goes with the movement as if passively allowing the external force on the upper body to occur without any counterbalancing movements. As might be expected from the progressions in Figure 2-3, positive reactions are expected on the tilt board at 6 months and for upper-body movement at 15 to 18 months. Counterbalancing movements to maintain equilibrium often are not as apparent as the reflexes illustrated here, because everyday movements are usually not as sudden a change in body position, and movement compensations are a combination or

FIGURE 2-4

Test conditions: Child is supine on board with arms and legs extended. Board is tilted to one side.

Normative expectations: Positive reactions are normal at about 6 months and continue throughout life. Negative reactions after 6 months are one indication of delayed re-flexive maturation.

Test conditions: Child is standing. Hold by upper arms and move to left or right side.

Normative expectations: Positive reactions normal at about 15–18 months and continue throughout life. Negative reactions after 18 months are one indication of delayed reflexive maturation.

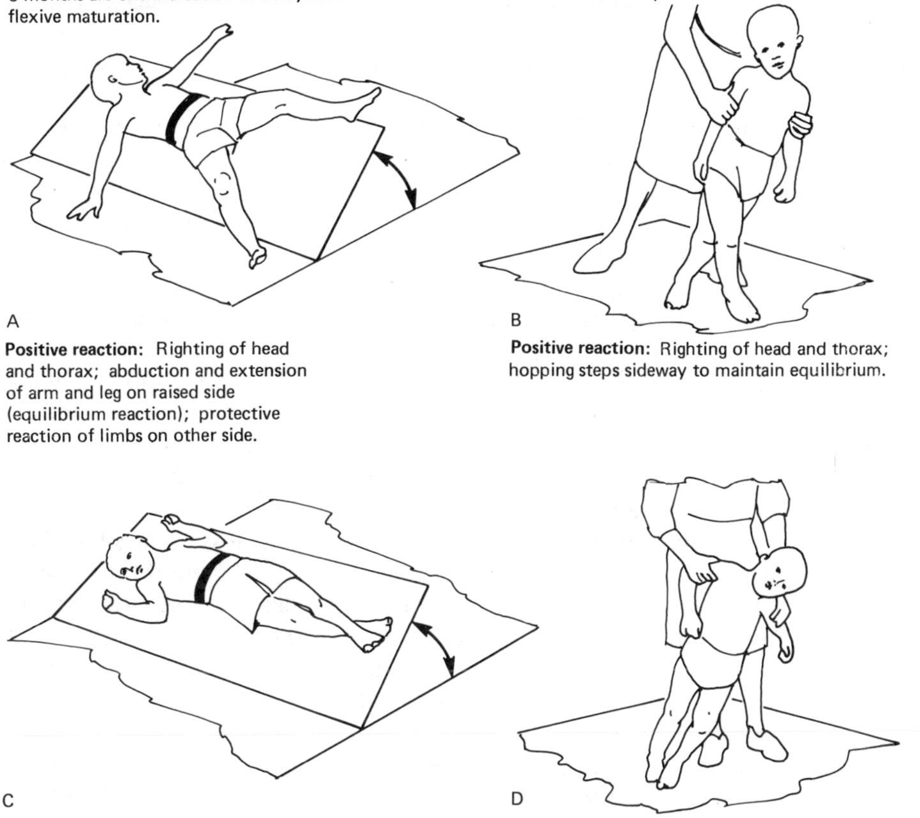

A

Positive reaction: Righting of head and thorax; abduction and extension of arm and leg on raised side (equilibrium reaction); protective reaction of limbs on other side.

B

Positive reaction: Righting of head and thorax; hopping steps sideway to maintain equilibrium.

C

Negative reaction: Head and thorax not righted; no equilibrium or protective reactions, although possible to have positive reactions in some body parts but not in others.

D

Negative reaction: Head and thorax not righted; no hopping steps.

Examples of positive and negative righting reactions. (Reproduced from M.R. Fiorentino, *Reflex Testing Methods for Evaluating C.N.S. Development,* Second Edition, 1973. Courtesy of Charles C. Thomas, Publisher, Springfield, Illinois.)

interplay of righting reflexes. Righting reflexes must continue to function throughout life, or difficulties will be encountered in maintaining a body position.

The second movement problem in postural control is *changing a position and achieving a new position.* This involves controlling body parts in what really is limited and noncontinuous locomotion. During the first months after birth, babies cannot change the position in which they are placed. They can make some minor adjustments in position from the third to the sixth month, after which they im-prove dramatically in their ability to change positions in many different ways. Establishing control of the head and upper body is a necessary but not a sufficient condition for changing position. Righting reflexes control various positions, in-cluding transitional positions when changing from a starting position to a new

35

position, but we now are talking about changing a position rather than just maintaining a position. Changing a position may be achieved in many different ways which require coordinated movements by the arms, legs, and head. Babies will move their limbs and head in a bewildering array of movements that seem intended to roll the trunk over, but they initially are not effective. When once successful in rolling the trunk over, limb and head movements soon can be used in several coordinated combinations to roll over whenever desired. Many other changes in body position become automatic parts of our movement repertoire. Thus, postural control requires more than righting reflexes to maintain equilibrium, and changing a position requires postural control as well as movement skill.

The third movement problem in postural control is how to *maintain equilibrium while moving* more continuously over a longer period of time. A more dynamic equilibrium is needed, as contrasted with the more static equilibrium in maintaining a position and changing positions. There is no clear difference between static and dynamic equilibrium except toward the extreme ends of a continuum ranging from static to dynamic. The principal distinction is that the continuous motion of the body over a period of time requires *motion stability* rather than position stability. Motion stability means that the body's movement can have either stable or unstable qualities, and it can exist even when the body positions at many points in the motion would not be stable if there were no motion. Taken the other way around, unstable body positions at rest can be maintained when the body is in motion. The body can be almost horizontal to the ground when skiing if there is sufficient motion stability to maintain it in this position. The speed of the overall motion serves to stabilize motion, provided that the body is kept within certain position limits. The use of speed to create stability seems contrary to our expectancy of going slower to make sure that a new movement can be carried out. Going slower makes many tasks more difficult, as can be seen in skiing slowly and riding slowly on a scooter or bicycle.

Babies need motion stability when trying to walk. They must move their body to place the center of gravity outside the base of support while establishing motion stability to maintain postural control. Using discrete stepping movements works against them because they must stop or limit the forward motion on each step, which means that they must use more force on each step to overcome inertia. A proficient walker keeps the body farther ahead of the center of gravity in order to minimize the resistance to forward motion. Running is an extreme form of walking in which the speed of forward motion is needed to maintain a body position that alternates from one foot touching the ground to both feet off the ground. Speed is necessary in movements to establish motion stability, but babies or novices of any age cannot initially use speed to control their posture.

Another consideration related to motion stability is that the mover must be able to control the momentum generated in a movement, a problem in forceful movements used to propel or strike objects. Considerable force is needed to throw or kick a ball, and the body often is in an unstable position. Throwing movements generate force to propel an object, which leads to the body's moving forward and out of equilibrium. Kicking a ball in however limited a manner means that the body is temporarily supported by one leg. Propelling and striking are discrete rather than continuous movements, but the problem of controlling momentum is similar in many respects to the problem of maintaining motion stability. The control of momentum seems to require a combination of maintaining or changing a position and maintaining motion stability.

A General Perspective. Postural control was first described as three movement problems, which we will now fit into two interlocking views. The first is that postural control is the *maintenance of a position*, which ranges on a continuum from static to dynamic equilibrium. The second is that postural control is the *changing of positions*, which ranges on a continuum from a single change to a continuing series or sequence of changes. The maintenance of a position in static equilibrium is our first developmental concern and is observed as the improved control of head position and the achievement of an upright posture to sit and stand. Babies then become able to change from one position to another, which includes rolling over, getting into sitting and standing positions, and sitting after standing. Then as these movements become a more continuous sequence of changes, dynamic equilibrium or motion stability is needed. Postural changes in a more continuous movement involve changes in body positions and locations while maintaining appropriate body positions. Walking and running require a change in space while maintaining a general body position. Throwing and kicking involve a change in position to generate the necessary propelling and striking forces while maintaining an overall position of stability. The development of postural control beyond the first year, then, is to make a continuous sequence of changes while maintaining motion stability.

Locomotion
General Description. Babies in the first and second months after birth are not mobile; they cannot change body position or move from one place to another. Later they become able, first, to move across the ground in a horizontal position and, second, to walk in an upright position (see Figure 2-5).

During their first 6 months, when babies are placed facedown (prone) or on their back (supine), they will remain in that position with little change in direction or location. When they are 2 to 3 months old, they can move slightly from a prone position to change the position of their head and push up with their arms (see Figure 2-3). They often move their arms and legs, but not in a coordinated fashion to move the body along the ground. During the early months, many of babies' movements seem intended to move their bodies along the ground or to roll their bodies over. Their knees come forward under the body, their legs are flexed and extended, and their head and trunk positions seem to be in position for a roll or a movement forward. All of this activity may produce small changes in the direction the babies face, but they remain in a prone position with little change in location.

Babies in a supine position can produce a great deal of movement in their arms and legs, because they are in a better position to move them than they are in a prone position. But babies in a supine position must get into a prone position before they can move away from their location. When placed on their side, babies during the first and second months can move to their back. By 4 months they can move from a back to a side position as a precursor to locomotion. When they move from back to side and side to back, the direction and location of their body may change somewhat.

Babies during their second 6 months after birth become mobile. This begins

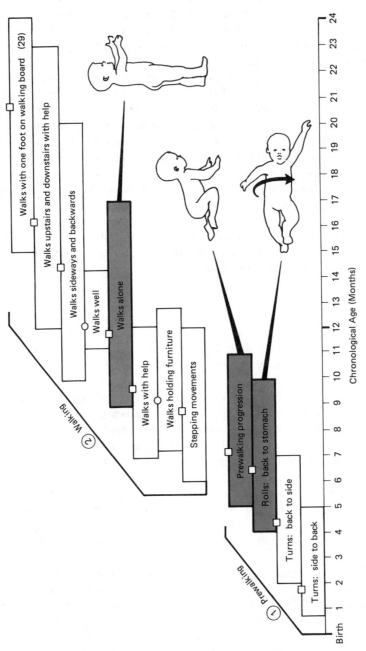

FIGURE 2-5 Progression of change: Locomotion.

with the landmark achievement at 6 months of *rolling over* from supine to prone, as well as in the reverse direction. Babies at this age also can pivot or turn in a prone position, a limited degree of locomotion that more properly is a change in position, but they now can change their location somewhat by a series of rolls and turns. In our description of postural control we noted that babies at 7 to 8 months can get themselves into a sitting and a standing position without assistance. All of these achievements give them the control of posture needed to become mobile, and they now can readily change almost any body position to place them in a position to move.

Babies at 7 months can *move forward in a prone position* which is the second landmark in this progression and the first true locomotion. Bayley calls this a prewalking progression, in which babies in a prone position make forward progress. Babies are quite variable in how they achieve forward progress. One movement pattern is some form of a *crawl* in which the arms are used to pull the body forward while the legs push. Babies may use their arms only, their legs only, or many combinations of arm-leg sequences. Their stomach and chest are on the ground or are elevated slightly. Although not a prone position, some babies move by sitting and scooting on their bottoms across the floor (Robson 1970). Many will use some form of a *creep* in which forward movement is made in an all-fours position. Palms and knees (down to toes) are the contact points, with the stomach and chest high off the ground. Babies will sometimes creep with only their palms and toes in contact with the ground, which raises their bottom higher in the air.

Arm and leg sequences in both crawling and creeping will vary markedly. One sequence is to use the arms to pull, followed by the legs to push. Two interesting limb movement sequences observed in both crawling and creeping are shown in Figure 2-6. The homolateral pattern is the leg and arm of one side alternating with the leg and arm of the opposite side, and the contralateral pattern is the right leg and left arm alternating with the left leg and right arm. There are many variations of these two alternation patterns, particularly in the timing among limb movements, which produces four separate movements rather than two limbs moving together followed by two limbs moving together. Much has been made of developmental sequences in crawling and creeping movements, but no careful observations have been reported to determine what babies do and the significance of not creeping or crawling. It seems more likely that locomotion on the ground takes many forms and that individual babies use a variety of them.

The second progression is the achievement of upright locomotion, in which *walking alone* is the landmark achievement. According to Figure 2-5, the general age of walking is 12 months, but reports of this age vary with the samples observed and the criteria employed. Malina (1980) summarized thirteen studies covering thirty sample groups, primarily in the United States and Europe. The mean or median age for all but one group ranged from 11.4 months to 14.5 months. The general expectation is that babies during the first 6 months of their second year achieve the rudiments of walking, which are refined considerably during the second 6 months of their second year.

When babies can pull themselves into a standing position, they soon can cruise, which is taking steps while holding onto the furniture or similar supports. They face the support and take single steps which generally are to the side. They then progress to taking steps forward in a true walk while holding someone's hands. Independent walking soon follows. The arms are held high and to the side, as if

39

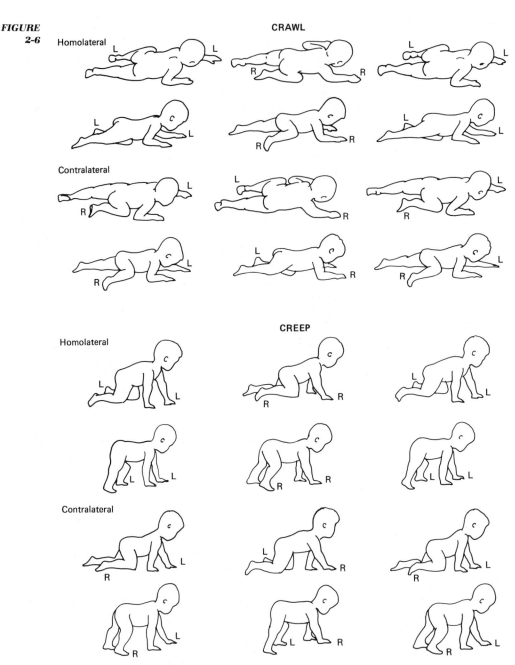

FIGURE 2-6

CRAWL

Homolateral

Contralateral

CREEP

Homolateral

Contralateral

Homolateral and contralateral patterns to crawl and creep.

providing some postural control in what is called the *high guard position*. Steps are discrete, with the feet placed quite wide apart. But leg movements then change to take steps more continuously and more directly ahead. The arms are lowered and are used in coordination with the movement of the opposite leg. One arm extends forward in unison with the extension of the opposite leg to produce the contralateral pattern characteristic of adult walking patterns. When babies achieve a basic level of independent walking, they seem to try it out constantly, as if using their new skill to enjoy moving and to explore a world they previously could see but could not contact.

The refinement of walking can be observed in many ways. Babies develop more control of their walking by being able to stop and change directions, although not rapidly. They soon can walk faster and in different ways, such as sideways and backwards, and they also begin to do something else while walking, such as pulling or pushing a toy. They master an elementary but stiff running movement by their second birthday. They also can walk up stairs with support, although only one step at a time to "mark time," in which both feet come to the same step before continuing one at a time to the next step. Steps also are climbed by crawling or creeping up and are descended by sitting on the steps to move down. This demonstrates a more elementary form of locomotion when upright locomotion on steps is difficult and perhaps more hazardous.

Analyses of Early Walking Development. Walking requires the resolution of a number of difficult movement problems which in many ways are created by the walking movements. The body in an upright position is less stable because the center of gravity is higher and the base of support is smaller than when on the ground in an all-fours or a prone position. Also, the center of gravity must be moved outside the base of support to produce forward motion. Motion stability must be established by moving fast enough to overcome or minimize the resistance to forward motion. Footsteps are placed more in line to reduce resistance to forward motion, which also reduces the base of support. Leg movements must be continuous rather than discrete, with a coordination of movement sequences and positions of arms, trunk, and head. The walker also must adjust to physical conditions, such as walking downhill on a wet pavement, and be prepared to stop and change directions in relation to environmental conditions. Walking becomes an automatic yet flexible movement skill by age 2 or 3, and each person establishes a style that often is recognizable to others.

The most intensive analysis of early development of walking was made many years ago by Shirley (1931) in cooperation with Boyd. A group of twenty-five babies was followed from birth to 2 years of age in a longitudinal study to gather medical, anthropometric, movement, and other data. Home visits were made weekly during the first year and biweekly during the second year to make the necessary observations and measurements. The magnitude of this project can be appreciated by noting that Shirley and Boyd made six to ten home visits each day for 2 years. Their movement observations concentrated on walking, including the development of postural control and prewalking locomotion as preparation for walking. A graphic record of walking was made by having the babies walk or attempt to walk on a length of unglazed paper after putting olive oil or powder on the soles of their feet to produce footprints. A total of 743 walking records (approximately 30 per baby) were produced in this manner, with the babies held upright in earlier, prewalking months to make a record of their leg movements. Individual analyses were made according to *walking age*, rather than chronological age, by taking the age of walking alone as a zero point and counting the walking age as the number of weeks preceding (−) or following (+) the week when the child walked alone. This offers an interesting record of walking behavior at comparable intervals preceding and following the achievement of walking alone, but this type of information is distorted when data points are averaged in relation to chronological age.

BOX
2-3

MOVEMENT BIOGRAPHIES

Shirley (1931) described the movement development of each of her twenty-five babies in the form of individual movement biographies, which include many bits of data from her observations along with her own extensive comments. Her interpretations and impressions are provocative and should help us understand babies' movement development in the larger context in which movement occurs. Excerpts are provided without comment with the hope that this sample will encourage you to read the original.

Harvey. At practically every test before he walked alone he stamped and patted most of the time. This trait fits in very interestingly with his other behavior; patting and slapping his stomach with good resounding smacks was a very favorite diversion with him before he was 3 months old, and swinging and banging and dangling toys was his characteristic reaction to the choice tests. At 72 weeks he inserted a hesitation step into his walking record; he stamped with his right foot, tossing his head and body to the left side, hesitated, stepped on his left foot, stamped with his right, and so on. Quite clearly this was not his method of walking to get somewhere but merely his way of jazzing up the dull old test. At 78 weeks he strolled leisurely; at 80 he ran to his brother; at 94 he fiddled along, making almost no progress; at 96, 98, and 100 weeks he slid, rubbed his feet on the paper, and refused to walk; and at 102 and 104 weeks he walked well. His record, more than that of any other child, reflects his mood of the moment and his general personality traits (p. 87).

Martin. Medieval bard might well have sung a lay to Martin's infant strength, his steadfast skill, his staunch, unswerving motor interests. As they watched him charge about the house, slaying such monsters as beset the path of twentieth-century babies, the examiners dubbed him "Infant Hercules." By 6 months he had tamed adults to be his derricks and his steeds; at 8 months he emerged triumphant from his conquest of furniture; and a few weeks later toys went down before his onslaughts. To Martin activity was no trivial play; it was his life's serious business, the labor in which he reveled. His favorite sport at 7 months was to grasp an adult's thumbs and be swung from bed to floor or jumped or dangled in mid-air. Chairs and tables early bore the imprint of his fingers; beds and sofas yielded to his prancing feet; big motor toys were his delight (p. 149).

Virginia Ruth. Although she was considerably advanced in motor development, Virginia Ruth was certainly the most independent child in showing off her accomplishments. If she were in the mood she rolled, crept, or walked with much enthusiasm; if she were not, neither love, in the form of her mother's coaxing, nor money, in the guise of enticing toys, could induce her to perform. She was an active baby, but, as her mother expressed it, she was a conscientious objecter. Her chief objection was at being handled, and even the everyday processes of being dressed and undressed aroused her wrath, which she displayed by screams with vigorous motor accompaniments (p. 152).

Winifred and Fred. Fred compensated for his lack of motor skill by jabbering. So marked were these motor and vocal differences between the twins at 10 months that older children in the family nicknamed the pair "Winnie Walker" and "Freddie Talker" (p. 156).

Walley. Slow in motor development. Walley's play was of the eager but inactive sort. He often struggled to get toys that were out of his range and did the usual amount of creeping and climbing, but like Fred and Renie May he spared himself motor activity and depended on adults to do for him the things his own legs could not do (p. 160).

Don. Although Don's motor performance was not in the least precocious it was strikingly individualistic and histrionic. Of all babies Don was the most ardently interested in playing with his toes and most eager bouncer. His delight in mimicry and buffoonery began to show up in his ninth and tenth months. His comedy was not for the sake of attracting an audience; for him it was spontaneous fun. To be sure, he enjoyed the attention it brought him. Not even the matter-of-fact scientific observers, much less doting parents and a 12-year-old brother comedian, could fail to stop work when this baby chose to favor them with an act. Like an actor sure of his audience and confident of his talents Don serenely did his number and then looked up for the applause he expected as his due and knew was forthcoming (pp. 161–162).

Shirley found four stages of walking development based on analyses of footprint data and related observations. Babies initially "patted" the paper in the form of pseudosteps in place while being held upright and neither stiffened their knees nor supported their weight. The second stage was standing with support. The age of onset correlated .8 to the age of walking alone. Shirley emphasized standing with support as the most important achievement in leading to walking alone. The third stage was walking when led or supported by both hands, followed by the fourth stage of walking alone.

Numerous analyses of footprints were made after the babies could walk alone. The width between their footprints decreased from 12 to 5 centimeters, and toe marks changed from toeing out to a more parallel alignment. Stride length increased in 4 to 6 months to be aproximately 20 centimeters, which is similar to adults when considered in proportion to leg length (see details in Chapter 3). Babies at first walked very rapidly: 180 to 200 footfalls per minute, compared with approximately 140 for adults. The overall picture for the Shirley babies is a change from short, rapid, toeing-out leg movements to longer and fewer strides taken more in line with the forward line of movement.

An unusual feature of Shirley's report is her descriptions of individual styles, such as the many walking variations observed in older babies who seemed to be playing, by walking in "fancy ways" (sideways, on tiptoe), and others who seemed bored and just walked off the edge of the paper. Shirley wrote a *movement biography* for each baby, describing individual walking progress (pp. 83–93) and what she calls motor play (pp. 148–164: gross motor activities observed during the home visits or reported by mothers). These biographies are highly recommended reading for a better appreciation of individual differences. Excerpts are presented in Box 2-3 to illustrate her insight and charm in describing individual differences.

Manual Control

The achievement of upright posture enables humans to use their arms and hands for the manual control of objects and other limb manipulations. Because arm and hand movements are used in such varied and complex ways, a general framework is presented in Table 2-3 to trace the development of manual control.

Manual control is a general movement classification for the arm and hand movements used to control objects. The arm and hand are the two primary body units, with their functions listed for each. The arm is a linkage system (upper arm, lower arm, and hand) that controls objects. Sometimes it is useful to consider the hand as a unit, so as to focus on the movements of the five digits and the

TABLE 2-3	A General Framework for Describing Manual Control
BODY UNIT	FUNCTION
Arm	Support
	Position
	Force
Hand	Grasp
	Manipulation

palmar surface. Using scissors to cut paper is a matter of controlling the digits to open and close the scissor blades: the arm linkage system provides the support necessary to use the digits and also positions the scissors in relation to the paper. Moving the arm to touch an object with a finger, however, is a matter of controlling the whole arm linkage system, with only a minor concern for controlling the one digit used to touch the object. The arm and hand are combined in any type of manual control and are separated here only for analysis and discussion. Further, manual control can be *unimanual* or *bimanual*, that is, using one arm to control an object or using two arms together, whether making the same or different movements. For now, our discussion will be limited to unimanual movements.

The first function listed for the arm is *support*, in which the arm linkage system is kept reasonably immobile in order to support the hand movements to manipulate an object. This is illustrated by the use of scissors. The second function of the arm is to *position the hand*, as when reaching to touch or grasp an object and when transporting an object held in the hand. The third function of the arm is to *generate and modulate force*. When an object, such as a doorknob or screwdriver, is held firmly in the hand, the arm linkage system moves it by rotating the wrist to turn or twist it. Pounding with a hammer and sawing require a firm hold on the tool, with force generated by coordinated movements in the arm linkage system. Propelling or throwing an object also requires the overall coordination of the arm linkage system in combination with digital movements to release the object. The generation and modulation of force in these examples vary from small to large amounts in single and repetitive movements.

The first function listed for the hand is *grasp*, which includes picking up and holding an object. It can be picked up either with the fingers scooping up the object or the fingers opposing the thumb to pinch it or with many variations thereof. When an object is held in the hand, we often describe the holding grip in terms of the functional control of the object. Holding an object, such as the handle of a hammer, in the palm of the hand is a *power grip* in which the handle is held tight to use the force in the arm linkage system to generate power in the hammer (Napier 1956). Holding of an object near the end of the digits and away from the palm is a *precision grip* which makes it possible to manipulate or change the object's position. A precision grip is useful in holding a pencil so that the digits can move it to write the letters of the alphabet. A second function of the hand is *manipulation*, in which fingers and thumb are used to change an object's position, as in using a pencil to write letters. The word *dexterity* often is used to indicate the degree of control of these digital movements. Manipulation also is involved when releasing objects, because digital movements are required to let go of them. Release seldom is considered in the manipulation of objects, but considerable control of digital movements is needed to release some objects in a skillful manner. Note that propelling an object requires releasing it, often with complex digital movements. This is particularly true when throwing to impart different types of spin to a ball.

Although we separate arm and hand for discussion purposes, most manual movement combine these body units and their related functions. A spoon must be transported and turned by arm movements while digital movements are used to help control the position of the spoon so as to be able to pick up food and place the spoon in the mouth. Arm movements generate force that is imparted to the ball, and digital manipulation is used at the release point to add force to and to control the ball's direction and rotation. Our perspective goes beyond this limited view of manual control as hand or digital control to achieve fine rather than gross motor skills. We include throwing and other forceful movements because they seem to be just another variation on the theme of arm-hand control.

Early Development

Three movement progressions are listed in Figure 2-7 to illustrate the early development of manual control. They overlap in many ways because a true separation of arm and hand control, as we have emphasized, is not possible. The first progression focuses on hand control in the ability to grasp, hold, handle, and release an object. The second is arranged to show changes in the arm linkage system to achieve greater spatial accuracy in hand placement. The third is a more functional view in terms of the achievement of self-help skills, which are an extension of the basic manual control described in the first two progressions.

In the early weeks, babies often hold their fingers together in a fist. They soon progress to having their hands open much of the time, but they cannot accurately place either hand in a particular location. Their random arm movements do seem at times to be oriented toward objects, even though they cannot reliably contact them. They can bring their hands together at about 2 months, which is some indication that they can use arm movements to place their hands in a desired location. They soon can grasp and manipulate objects. A landmark achievement at 3 to 4 months is to be able to *pick up a cube* (included in the first two progressions), which is the first successful reach and grasp of an object. The first grasp of a cube is without thumb opposition, and so the cube rests against the heel, or ulnar, side of the palm away from the thumb and is held there by the fingers and not by the thumb (see Figure 2-8). Children at 5 to 6 months progress to *thumb opposition*, in which the thumb opposes the fingers to pick up a cube, with little or no contact with the palm. During the fifth and sixth months, other indications of manipulative dexterity can be observed. Children crumple or rattle paper in what Bayley calls an exploitive way, and they rotate their wrist which increases their opportunities for manipulating objects. They also reach unilaterally rather than with both hands, and they transfer a cube from one hand to the other.

The grasping of smaller objects requires the opposition of the thumb with one finger. This is a landmark achievement at 9 to 10 months and is called a *neat pincer grasp*. This is preceded by raking or scooping up small objects and a partial finger prehension, or inferior pincer grasp, in which several fingers rather than one finger oppose the thumb. The importance of the neat pincer grasp and the complete thumb opposition in grasping larger objects is that a precision grip has been achieved and digital control of the object then is possible. The use of a palmar grasp, which is all that younger babies can do, is limited to holding an object in the palm without any way to manipulate the object. The control of thumb opposition marks the real beginning of the development of manipulative dexterity.

Another landmark achievement in manipulating objects is the *release of the object*, which occurs at 8 months (Knobloch and Pasamanick 1974). This achievement is often overlooked in the attention given to getting ahold of and handling an object. The crude release at 8 months is little more than opening the hand and letting the object drop. Later development of manual control requires considerable dexterity in releasing objects, as noted earlier in tasks such as placing an object in a particular place and throwing a ball.

In addition, children by their first birthday have sufficient digital dexterity to

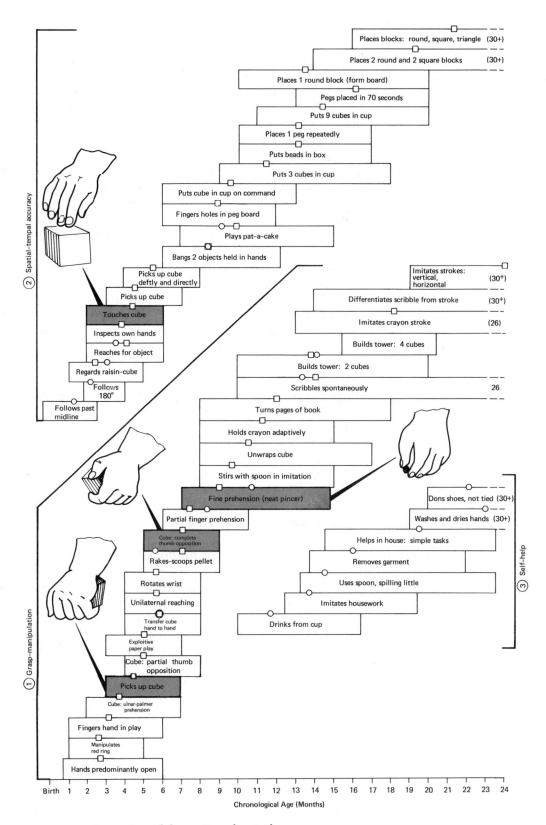

FIGURE 2-7 *Progressions of change: Manual control.*

46

stir with a spoon, unwrap a loosely covered object, hold a crayon in a position to scribble, and turn the pages of a book. During their second year, they can use a crayon to scribble and then make line strokes rather than scribbles. By their second birthday, they have sufficient control to make both horizontal and vertical line strokes. More precise control of hand movements also is observed at 13 to 14 months, in placing blocks on top of one another to build a tower of two blocks and, by 24 months, a tower of six to eight blocks.

The second progression concentrates on manual control movements using visual input to achieve greater spatial accuracy. Manual control clearly requires visual input to specify the environment and to participate in some aspects of monitoring and regulating arm–hand movements, because many arm–hand movements require considerable spatial accuracy. The visual and spatial aspects are heightened when arm-hand movements must be made in relation to moving objects, and so such movements are known as eye–hand coordination. Our examples here are limited to movements in a stable environment.

Young babies soon can follow past the midline and through 180 degrees in tracking a slow-moving object. They regard or scrutinize their own hand and nearby objects at 2 to 3 months. They can *reach and touch* an object at 3 to 4 months, which was noted earlier as a landmark achievement. Babies soon can pick up a cube and transfer it from hand to hand. All of these achievements indicate that babies at 6 months can position their hands accurately and easily. Examples beyond 6 months merely reveal further progress in different types of situations. Babies at 8 and 9 months are spatially more accurate in banging two cubes together and in bringing their hands together successively to play pat-a-cake. By their first birthday, they can accurately place their finger in a hole on a pegboard and can put three cubes in a cup. During their second year they can position pegs accurately and repeatedly and can place different shaped objects in their appropriate place in a form board.

The third progression is arranged to show the achievement of self-help skills. Because these skills require some dexterity in hand control, few are observed during the first year. Young babies may be able to feed themselves a cracker and hold their bottle or spoon or other utensil, but little else. When they acquire a precision grip, babies then have the movements to be used in feeding, dressing, and grooming. The skills listed in Figure 2-7 merely are some that may be expected. They may be more or less important and more or less taught in different child-rearing environments.

Many of the movements in self-help tasks require relating the object to the body in order to achieve an appropriate *spatial relationship*. This is demonstrated in putting the right shoe on the right foot and in bringing a spoon accurately to the mouth, which is not seen by the mover. Another problem in manual control is to *represent in movement* what we see. Babies watch someone use a broom and then they try to imitate what they have seen, or they look at a line and try to draw a line in the same direction. We have noted that spatial accuracy is an important control requirement to be mastered in placing the hand in a desired location and position, and we now add that spatial relationship and movement representation also are involved.

Reach and Grasp

The development of many aspects of manual control can be observed in reaching and grasping movements. Three general achievements are (1) differentiating reach

47

and grasp into recombinable movements, (2) improving reach in spatial accuracy and efficiency, and (3) modifying grasp from palmar to digital. These achievements occur during a 6-month period from 3 to 9 months after birth. Babies at their first birthday can control reaching and grasping and are able to pick up objects reliably and quickly. Manipulating or handling objects then becomes the next developmental problem to be resolved and will be described in Chapter 3.

Reaching and grasping are initially combined as a unitary or single movement pattern which later differentiates into two separate and recombinable movements (Bower 1979, 1982). Babies first reach with their entire body so that their trunk and both hands move toward the object. The fingers open as the reaching movement is begun, and they close when the arms are extended and near the object. This appears to be a single movement of reach-and-grasp which later becomes separate movements that can be combined into reach-then-grasp and grasp-then-reach. Thus, reaching for an object may not always result in a grasping movement, and grasping an object may be followed by reaching with the object held in the hand. Bower reported the separation of reaching and grasping as occuring between 4 to 5 months. Babies at 4 months were found to have a delay in hand closure of 450 milliseconds when the hand arrived at the object, indicating that the hand was moved into position but the grasp did not immediately take place. The pause in the grasp indicates that grasp is becoming distinct from the reach. The differentiation appears to be complete at 5 to 6 months, when babies will not grasp in a virtual-object situation. (A virtual object is an object without substance created in space by means of mirrors, lenses, or the like.) Younger babies will grasp the phantom object when their hand is in the object's spatial location, whereas older children will not complete their grasp without the contact of a real object.

Reaching accuracy in contacting an object is about 40 percent successful at 3 months, with few misses at 4 months (Bower 1979). Bower observed newborns reaching toward but seldom contacting objects. This reaching as orienting toward an object, Bower sees as disappearing at 1 month and appearing again at 3 months. Reaching also has been described as changes in the approach, or path, taken to reach an object. Halverson (1931) described babies' arm movements at 3 to 4 months as shoulder action, because they seemed to have very little movement in the elbow joint, thus making the arm more of a single unit directed by the shoulder. The backside of the hand often faced the object because the wrist did not rotate to bring the hand into a more prone position. The path of the arm also was analyzed by Halverson according to its direction and height above the object. Babies at 6 months used a more circular path, or an arc, to approach the object and at 8 months had a more linear or direct route. Younger babies lifted their hand up and came down on the object; older babies slid their hand on the table surface or lifted it slightly while moving forward, as if taking off in an airplane. Babies at 9 months approached the object directly at a low height in a smooth and easy movement. Bower (1979) also notes that younger babies reach in a single, ballistic movement without correcting for the object's location, whereas older babies make corrections in the reach pathway. Younger babies start over if they miss the object, rather than correct the ongoing movement.

The change from a palmar to a digital grasp was described by Halverson (1931) in a now-classic set of film analyses. Connolly and Elliot (1972) summarized these earlier analyses in a detailed review of hand function in primates and humans. Figure 2-8 is taken from their work to describe the hand and to illustrate this

**FIGURE
2-8**

Pseudo-opposition   True opposition   Neat pincer grasp

distal

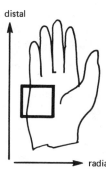

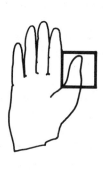

radial

Changes in grasping techniques. (Reproduced with permission from Connolly and Elliott, 1972.)

change in grasping technique. The thumb of the hand in humans can oppose the fingers to bring the thumb tip in contact with fingertip in what is known as true opposition. A pseudo-opposition is a limited version of opposition in which the thumb flexes against the side of the index finger and does not oppose the fingertip. Humans progress from no opposition to pseudo-opposition to true opposition. The hand also can be viewed as having a radial side (thumb side) and an ulnar side, which are named by the radius and ulna bones' location in the forearm. The palm of the hand then can be described as having a radial direction and a distal direction, as shown in Figure 2-8. When grasped, objects change in position to occupy a more radial and a more distal position. This places the object near the thumb and index finger rather than in the palm. The object then is not resting in the palm and can be handled better by the thumb and fingers. This shift in object position demonstrates the change from palmar to precision grip which allows more intrinsic, or digital, movements of the hand to manipulate objects.

Babies before 6 months were not observed by Halverson (1931) to have thumb opposition in grasping a cube. The thumb opposition observed at 6 months was a pseudo-opposition that became a true opposition at 8 months. The size and shape of objects may alter the age at which these changes are observed, but the order is the same. As expected, the ability to pick up a raisin or other small object comes later. The initial thumb-fingers grasp of a raisin is noted in some developmental scales as an inferior pincer grasp (pseudo-opposition of thumb and opposition to several rather than one finger). The neat pincer grasp of the thumb tip to the index finger tip is achieved at 9 to 10 months, as noted in the summary in Figure 2-7. As grasping shifts from palmar to digital, which is to a more radial and distal location of the object in the hand, the neat pincer grasp and general precision grip lead to more dexterity in handling and using objects. Wrist movements also contribute to the more precise handling of objects by rotation and flexion of the wrist in coordination with digital movements.

Babies at their first birthday can easily and efficiently pick up small objects of different shapes and with some precision can transport them to a particular location. Reaching and grasping now are separate movements that can be combined in many ways, with grasping done with the fingers used in opposition to the thumb which provides the base for manipulating objects.

Bimanual Coordination: Functional Asymmetry

Two hands often are needed or are used to do a manual task. Bimanual control can be both hands making the same movement or different movements, but it more often is each hand doing something quite different. Holding a bolt while twisting on a nut, buttoning a button, and tying shoelaces are examples of two hands collaborating while each is doing something different. The three tasks represent types of collaboration in three levels of difficulty. Holding an object with one hand and manipulating another with the second is at the first level and means that the first hand provides support while the second hand does the manipulating. Buttoning is at the second level of difficulty and requires the manipulation of cloth and button by both hands. Tying shoelaces is at the third level of difficulty, in which both hands manipulate the laces without the solid resistance of the material as a cue to regulating the movements. Shoelaces are flexible and do not have a stable form to provide an external resistance, whereas bolts and buttons are solid and stable in form. The adjustment of one hand movement in tying shoelaces is made in relation to the movement of the other hand, with the material providing very little useful information.

Bimanual control with each hand doing something different is described by de Schonen (1977) as *functional asymmetry*, because the asymmetry of movements is coordinated to be functional. Functional asymmetries in bimanual coordination are seen at 5 to 6 months when babies transfer a block from one hand to the other and hold a block in one hand while using the other to explore it. Another example is babies' reaching for a block resting on a person's hand, by using one hand to grasp and hold the hand, followed by the second hand grasping the block (Bresson et al. 1977). Both arms are in motion together, with one used to hold and support the other person's hand and the other doing the grasping. These are examples of the simultaneous and coordinated collaboration of the arms and hands in a functionally asymmetrical manner. Many of the achievements listed in Figure 2-7 for the second year are bimanual movements involving asymmetrical movements of the arms and hands. Analyze the bimanual movements involved in sweeping with a broom, washing and drying hands, and putting on clothes. Note also that the symmetrical coordination of arms does not appear until after asymmetrical coordination. Perhaps the first examples of symmetrical hand movements come at 8 months in banging two cubes together and playing pat-a-cake.

A basic problem to be resolved in the development of manual control is differentiating the two arm linkages so that they can be used *separately*. Equally important are the *simultaneous* and *coordinated* use of the two arms in symmetrical and asymmetrical movement patterns. The different functioning of the two arms is traced by de Schonen (1977) in regard to the asymmetrical tonic neck reflex (TNR). The asymmetrical TNR position is with one arm extended and the other arm flexed. The extended arm is described by de Schonen as an orientation or a pointing-reaching movement, whereas the flexed arm position contributes to postural control by coming to a position close to the upper body. The asymmetrical TNR is particularly strong in the first and second month after birth, for example, in turning the head to the right, perhaps to look at an object, which extends the right arm and flexes the left arm. As infants then follow an object moving slowly to their left, the left arm extends and the right arm flexes. The two arms move together in a fixed relationship to produce opposite movements that are fixed to the position and movement of the head. The two arms are differentiated, in that each does something different, but are coordinated—though not independent—in their movements.

Asymmetrical TNR diminishes and alters in the third month. The arms maintain the same flexion-extension opposition, but there is a wide variation in the extent of one arm's movement in relation to the other's, and the head position is not as important in determining the direction and amount of arm extension. The arms appear to be establishing some *independence* within the asymmetrical TNR in their relationship to each other and the head, which can be seen in the midline head position. Very little systematic arm use is noted in the midline head position until the third month, when infants may move one or both arms forward and bring their hands together in a midline position, rather than flexing one and extending the other. The hands may come together simultaneously, or one may arrive first and then be joined by the other. An important point, whatever the timing of the movements may be, is that both arms extend to reach forward, rather than one extending and the other flexing. The first independent use of each arm is seen in these midline movements.

The next change occurs in the fourth month when basic prehension is achieved in the form of a simple palmar grasp. The grasp is made with one hand and is quickly followed by the second hand also grasping the block or covering the first hand. The use of two arms in slightly delayed and somewhat asymmetrical movements is a sign of bimanual coordination of functional asymmetries. The two arm movements are coordinated and seemingly programmed together, in that the first arm reaches to grasp while the second arm reaches to cover the block or the first hand, and the second hand starts before the first hand arrives. But arm movements at this age are not fully independent, as illustrated by babies' dropping one block before they pick up another. It is as if they cannot hold with one hand and execute a grasping movement with the other.

Bimanual control is a matter of coordinating the two arm linkage systems, often while each system is making a movement different from the other. Functional asymmetry in bimanual coordination is established in a limited way at the end of the first year.

Chapter Summary

Movement development during the first and second years establishes the basic control of self-movements. The first months after birth are characterized by general movements and reflexes, in contrast with voluntary and adaptative movement control by the second birthday. The first and second years are when important movements are achieved and refined, which provide 2-year-olds with a good movement repertoire for postural control, locomotion, and manual control. Movements by age 2 become more continuous rather than discrete, and movement coordination is impressive in its sequencing and timing (phasing) of the movement components. Force can be monitored and regulated within broad limits, but not to the level of precision achieved in later years. Difficulties are encountered in controlling movement momentum generated in making a movement and in responding to open-movement situations, and so 2-year-olds can adjust to a variety of stable environmental conditions, but not when the conditions are variable or are changing.

Basic postural control is established during the first year by means of several landmark achievements: keeping the head steady (without support) while being moved, sitting without support, getting into a sitting position, changing postural position, and standing alone. Postural control is such an inseparable aspect of all movements that further development of postural control can be inferred only from achievements such as bending over, running, and riding a bicycle.

We presented a general perspective for thinking about postural control in which maintaining and changing positions were considered as a continuum ranging from static to dynamic equilibrium and single to continuing change. Motion stability in the form of maintaining dynamic equilibrium in a continuous sequence of postural changes, such as walking, is achieved to a limited extent by age 2, but babies have difficulty in controlling momentum generated when moving at a faster speed. The development of postural control beyond the first year is primarily improvement in controlling a continuous sequence of changes while maintaining motion stability.

The early development of locomotion was described in regard to two landmark achievements, rolling over and moving forward in a prone position, which precede the landmark achievement of walking alone. Obvious refinements in walking occur from 4 to 6 months after walking alone, in which the steps become more continuous and less widely spaced and the arms are lowered from a high-guard position and extended forward in unison with the extension of the opposite leg. The refinement of walking is seen in walking faster, changing directions, and performing fancy walks and in the functional activities of pulling or pushing a toy. Walking becomes more continuous and can be used in a variety of stable conditions, such as walking downhill and on different surfaces. Difficulties are encountered in controlling momentum generated in walking faster and when environmental conditions are variable or changing.

The early development of manual control was described in regard to three similar but important landmark achievements: picking up a cube, forming a neat pincer grasp, and releasing an object. These achievements necessitate the accurate placement of the hand at a desired location and the control of fingers and thumb in several ways to grasp and manipulate objects of different sizes. We offered a framework for manual control to distinguish between the functioning of the arm and the hand (including fingers and thumb). An early achievement is differentiating reach from grasp into separate but coordinated functions. Generally, spatial accuracy is achieved quite early. Digital dexterity soon follows in a shift from a palmar to a digital grasp and the achievement of a neat pincer grasp to pick up small objects. Digital dexterity improves rapidly when objects can be handled by the fingertips in opposition to the thumb. Babies at their first birthday can easily and efficiently pick up small objects of different shapes and can transport them with some precision to a desired location. Functional asymmetry in bimanual control also will have been partially established. The second year is the refinement of primary manipulative achievements by attempting tasks of daily living.

The major achievements in the early development of movement control can be summarized in 6-month intervals. The first 6 months is when the infant gains control of posture to sit without support; locomotion is limited to rolling over and spinning on stomach or back; and grasping becomes voluntary but undifferentiated. The next 6 months is when babies gain control of their posture to sit and stand, can get about on all fours or variatioins thereof, and can differentiate within a grasp to use their thumb in opposition to their fingers. The next 6 months (from 12 to 18 months) is a time of upright mobility and the initial use of utensils, and the final 6 months leads to faster, more reliable, and more varied mobility and the initial achievement of dressing and similar self-help skills.

Movement Development of Young Children: Two to Seven Years

Modifications and elaborations of earlier achievements lead to the development of a large repertoire of movement skills during the early years of childhood. This chapter will examine a 6-year period from age 2 through age 7, following young children from preschool through their early school years. At the end of this period, children should have good enough control of body movements to perform many fundamental play-game skills and many functional hand skills, although they will not use them very well in more open movement situations. They will continue to improve their control of body and limb movements beyond this period by increasing their level of performance and their repertoire of movement skills to cope with personal desires and situational requirements and conditions.

Descriptions of Change

The changes described in this chapter include general achievements that are similar in form to those described in Chapter 2. Two important differences are that young children's achievements become less definitive and more detailed analyses of movement mechanics and components now become important.

General achievements are the success in carrying out a movement task and the simple refinements and variations that follow. Examples are the initial achievement of upright posture and walking alone, followed by hands held lower, bending over, and changing directions. A list of general achievements provides descriptive information that can be ordered in different ways to trace changes in movement development, as we did in organizing the progressions of change in Chapter 2. Babies' and young children's achievements also include changes in movement mechanics, as illustrated by the lowering of arms in walking and the opposition of thumb and finger to achieve a neat pincer grasp.

Improved movement control, in turn, should make it possible to *vary a movement* or *use it in different ways*. Gutteridge (1939) recognized this in her four types of variations or uses: (1) moving faster and perhaps competing with oneself or another, (2) adding difficulties or taking chances, (3) combining one movement with others, and (4) using a movement in a larger context or situation. For example, while pedaling a tricycle, children might (1) go faster, (2) pedal with one leg, (3) wave to friends, or (4) ride to school. Pedaling a tricycle has been mastered to a point that the movement problem no longer is to make the tricycle go in the proper direction at a manageable speed, and so pedaling now can be varied and used in other movement situations. Many of the variations are clear indications of increased movement control, and the many uses of the movement in different situations are more subtle indications. Although the different variations and uses do not represent an orderly and sequential progression of change, they are useful indicators, especially in relating developing movers to different movement situations.

Movement mechanics change in a somewhat orderly and sequential manner as the control of a movement improves. Specific movement tasks during early childhood have been analyzed to trace changes in movement mechanics for angular relationships among body parts, accelerations and velocities of body parts, and similar measurements (Wickstrom 1975). These analyses show phases (sometimes labeled as stages) in the development of a movement skill. Phases in the development of play-game skills, such as running and throwing, indicate what certain body parts or segments are doing and the changes expected in each phase. An example is that children first walk with their feet wide apart and then progress to walking with their feet in line. Roberton (1977) emphasizes that change, however, does not necessarily proceed at the same rate in all parts of the body, that although there may be an orderly sequence of phases, there probably is considerable variation in the relationship and order of changes among the body parts. Roberton noted, as an example in throwing, that movement changes in the trunk can precede or follow changes in the legs or throwing arm. It is sufficient for our purposes to become familiar with the general patterns of change to be expected and recognize that individual variability is expected.

These analyses of movement mechanics document smaller and more precise amounts of change in body movements. This was illustrated in Chapter 2 by the analyses of arm movements to determine when babies have sufficient control of their arms to reach toward an object. But analyses are only descriptive tools and cannot explain why changes occur. Also, analyses are limited to changes within a specific movement, often with little application to other movements.

Movement components will be used as another way to trace changes in the development of movement control. Each movement can be defined according to the parts or components which must exist regardless of the level of achievement. When picking up a coin and placing it in a cup, the movement components are (1) picking up the coin, (2) carrying it to the cup, and (3) releasing it. Changes in each movement component can be measured in different ways to find similarities and differences among groups of children for each component. Older children may pick up the coin differently and in less time than younger children do, whereas they may carry and release it in the same way. This would point to change in a particular aspect or component of the movement, which in this example would indicate improved control of digital movements. If the difference were that younger children took more time to get their hands lower and closer to the cup at the point of release, this might suggest a difference in movement strategy.

The different forms of description, however, are alike in many respects, particularly that similar observations and measurements often are used, but for a different purpose. General achievements focus our attention on the total achievement, such as standing upright or riding a bicycle, and are quite visible indicators of change. We shall extend our observations to movement variations and different uses of a movement as we make more functional analyses of developing movers in everyday movement situations. Analyses of movement mechanics can be used to discern general patterns of movement changes, and analyses of movement components discover where changes occur in different aspects of a movement, suggesting what may be changing in its underlying mechanisms.

Body Control

The control of body movements was described in Chapter 2 as postural control and locomotion. We now shall examine six movement tasks that represent the development of body control during early childhood. The six tasks are walking, running, jumping, hopping, throwing, and balancing. Walking is our basic means of locomotion; running, jumping, hopping, and throwing are fundamental play-game skills; and balancing is a means of assessing one aspect of postural control. Other movements could be included, but much of the available descriptive information pertains to these six tasks. Besides, we are concerned here only with the basic control of body movements and not with the control of these movements in more open movement situations. For example, we shall discuss throwing as achieving control of throwing movements, without considering throwing to a partner who is moving or throwing while running.

As noted in our discussion of movement in Chapter 1, limbs and body parts must be properly coordinated in sequencing, timing (phasing), and spatial relationships. Appropriate force also must be generated to make the movements. Lack of strength generally is not a limitation because young children have sufficient strength to make most movements at a basic performance level. The problem more often is that too much force is generated, thus adding to problems in controlling the movements. A related concern is the need to move fast enough to make the movement easier, without going too fast and thus decreasing the time available to start subsequent portions of the movement sequence. Children not only must execute the movements but also must control the momentum they generate while moving fast enough to maintain their inertial advantage. This complex trade-off is seen in running, in which sufficient speed is needed to avoid coming to rest and having to overcome inertia to continue the forward movement. But running faster means more body control problems when turning or stopping. The development of body control thus requires coordinating the limbs and body parts in relation to the speed that can be maintained. Postural control is another consideration, in that the body control in all of the movements discussed in this section depends on postural control in the various ways suggested in Chapter 2.

Walking

Young children's walking becomes further refined in movement mechanics, along the lines described in Chapter 2. The legs and arms are alternated, and the feet are placed more in line to provide a less stable but more efficient walking pattern. The direct observation of changes in movement mechanics beyond age 3 or 4 are not useful because the changes are subtle and must be measured and analyzed with sophisticated procedures (Burnett and Johnson 1971a, 1971b). Walking, however, does improve in ways that can be noted in general terms. Walking can be varied to walk backwards, on tiptoe, and in funny ways. Walking becomes more automatic, and so children can walk and talk or walk while manipulating something in their hands. Walking can be done in different environmental conditions, such as walking up or down a steep slope, on slippery surfaces, and in the wind. Walking can be done at faster and slower paces and in step with another person.

There also are more detailed descriptions of changes in walking movements. Statham and Murray (1971) observed seven babies as they progressed from supported to independent walking. Their increase in stride length was small, but the babies walked faster and spent less time with one foot in contact with the ground. They also acquired more consistency in their overall movement pattern and in the component parts of each step cycle. Scrutton (1969) had children, ages 13 to 60 months, step into talcum powder before walking across the room and then measured their footprints in several ways in relation to their line of walk. Toeing out faded with age to have the heel-toe line of the foot more parallel to the line of walk. A step factor was calculated as a ratio of step length and leg length and showed only a minor increase from .71 at age 1 to .77 at age 4. Both absolute and relative changes in stride length were small in these two studies, the decrease in toeing out and the increase in consistency being the major changes that Scrutton identified.

Wickstrom (1977) summarizes other important changes in walking development, including a change from a flat-footed contact to a heel strike at contact, followed by a toe push-off and a decrease in hip flexion so as not to raise the thigh and knee as high. He stresses the achievement of a double-knee lock involving extension-flexion-extension during the contact period, as shown in Figure 3-1. The knee extends (lock 1) at heel strike, followed by plantar flexion of the foot and knee flexion until near midstance, and finishing with knee extension (lock 2) and heel raise during the push-off.

Stair climbing is a movement task that illustrates how children adjust their walking pattern to environmental demands and how the control of their walking pattern improves. Stair climbing resembles walking when one uses alternating steps to go up or down stairs. Before walking up or down stairs, children keep their center of gravity low and move up and down stairs in a sitting position or with crawling movements. When upright, children at first will need some support and hold onto a railing or the hand of another person. As expected, children in an upright posture can go upstairs sooner than they can go downstairs. Table 3-1 shows that children can walk upstairs, alternating feet, approximately 15 months sooner than they can walk downstairs, a considerable difference that is interesting to examine.

According to the findings of Bayley (1935) and Wellman (1937) summarized in Table 3-1, children first walk up and down stairs without support by marking time. They move one foot forward to the next step, then bring the other foot to the same step, and repeat the cycle of one step at a time. The discrete movement pattern of one step at a time soon becomes alternate stepping for going upstairs, but with the support of a handrail or the hand of another person. The first foot moves to the first step, the other foot moves to the second step, and a walking pattern is established. Each foot in the alternating pattern moves farther, and the body is in a less stable position when not putting two feet on the same step. These general changes in walking upstairs occur sometime the second year, with alternate stepping accomplished during the latter months.

**FIGURE
3-1**

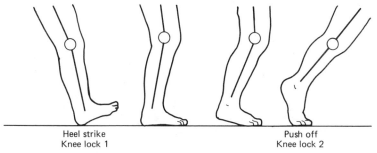

Heel strike
Knee lock 1

Push off
Knee lock 2

Knee lock at beginning and ending of stance phase when walking.

TABLE
3-1

Achievement of Stair-walking Patterns

STAIR-WALKING PATTERN	ASCENT AGE IN MONTHS	DESCENT AGE IN MONTHS	STUDY
Mark time without support	27–29	28–34	Wellman 1937
	24	24	Bayley 1935
Alternate feet with support	29–31	48	Wellman 1937
Alternate feet without support	31–41	49–55	Wellman 1937
	35	50	Bayley 1935

Descending stairs by marking time occurs at about the same time as does marking time to ascend stairs. Notice that alternating steps to walk downstairs without support does not occur until around age 4 (49 to 55 months). Wellman also reported that children did not use an alternating pattern to descend stairs, even with support, until 48 months. The differences in each study between ascending and descending stairs with alternating steps is minimally 15 months. The findings from the two studies do not match exactly by age in months, but the age differences for the patterns of change are similar. McCaskill and Wellman (1938) also found a similar ascent-descent age difference for climbing up and down a ladder with alternating steps.

Consider what must be done when walking downstairs with an alternating step pattern. One leg must be moved forward while the weight-bearing leg flexes to lower the body. The stepping leg reaches the step to become the weight-bearing leg, and the other leg must be moved from behind the body to go forward and down. If this sequence of movements is not controlled properly, the mover will fall forward. When walking upstairs, a similar movement sequence is used, except that the weight-bearing leg is in a flexed position and the back leg starts up and forward. The weight-bearing leg then extends, and the sequence continues in this manner. Walking downstairs is probably a more difficult movement to control because of the flexion of the weight-bearing leg to balance the body. Also, walking downstairs carries with it the possibility of falling, thus creating a potential harm that may be a deterrent to taking a step forward and down.

Stair walking illustrates the adjustment of the walking pattern to provide a means of locomotion over an uneven and sloping surface. Descending stairs requires a great deal of body control, which is barely within younger children's capabilities, whereas older children can descend stairs with a smooth stride and with little attention given to the task. The potential for harm in falling downstairs also adds a consideration beyond what are the capabilities of the neuromotor control system.

Running

Walking can become running in that arm-leg movements are used in a similar pattern to move the body forward. The principal difference is that while running, the mover is sometimes airborne (when both feet are off the ground), whereas while walking, one foot is always in contact with the ground. The beginning runner has many difficult movement problems to solve. Running requires moving in a way that will create less resistance to forward motion while maintaining a forward-moving equilibrium. Runners also must stop and change directions, as well as vary their speed.

A normative description of running is that some children begin to run at 18 months and most run by 24 months. Children attain a reasonably good running form by ages 4 to 6 (Fortney 1983), and so we become more interested in how fast they can run and how well they can use running in play-game activities. We also have analyzed in detail movement mechanics of running, particularly to discover the movement parameters of high-level adult performers (Dillman 1975). Wickstrom (1977) summarized a number of important changes in the movement mechanics of young runners, which will be used as the basis for our review.

The changes in running described by Wickstrom were based on cinematographic analyses, which we will present by comparing a beginning runner, Child A, with a more experienced runner, Child B. In Figure 3-2, the side view of Child A compared with that of Child B shows the increase in *length of stride* and the longer *period of nonsupport* that characterize development in running. Following the movement of one leg reveals another set of important changes in movement mechanics. The *support leg*, the leg in contact, of Child B becomes extended at takeoff in a forward direction, which places the body farther forward of the center of gravity. The leg now loses contact with the ground and must be brought forward

**FIGURE
3-2**

Child A   Child B

Child C   Child D

Sequence pictures to illustrate differences in movement mechanics for running. (Reproduced with permission from Wickstrom, 1977.)

as the *recovery leg* to regain contact with the ground. The backward position of the recovery leg progressively involves more flexion, and so the heel comes closer to the buttock as the leg moves forward. The forward swing of the recovery leg eventually brings the thigh and knee higher and farther forward. Notice also that the recovery leg at the point of contact with the ground comes more nearly under the center of gravity, thus reducing resistance to forward motion. Analyses have also followed the *path of the center of gravity*, which decreases in fluctuations up and down to become a smoother forward motion. Arms and legs fairly soon coordinate with the opposite arm and leg moving in unison. Individuals, however, establish idiosyncratic arm motions in running that are not useful in describing the general development of running form. The *time* characteristics of running change to have less time in contact with the ground, more time in the airborne or nonsupport phase, and faster leg movements.

Several additional points that need to be considered in the development of a running motion are difficult to observe in the simple drawings in Figure 3-2. The foot of a beginning runner's support leg contacts the ground with the full sole, which changes to heel-toe contact and then to contact only with the forward portion of the foot when running fast. Another important change in the bio-mechanics of the support leg is flexion after contact to maintain rather than interrupt forward momentum. A final point is that the forward thrust of a leg produces a rotary motion of the body's vertical axis which is countered by the forward thrust of the opposite arm. Changes in arm action serve to counter the rotary action produced by the forward leg thrust, even though individuals' arm actions vary considerably in style.

Four phases described by Seefeldt, Reuschlein, and Vogel (1972) summarize the changes in running form. Their four phases were derived from film analyses of approximately 150 children, ranging in age from 18 months to 8 years. The first phase is arms held high, short stride, little knee flexion, and foot contact with the full sole. The second phase is arms lower, stride longer, and more knee flexion. The third phase is arms low with counterrotary action, stride longer, and heel-toe foot contact. The fourth phase is arm-leg opposition, toe contact at faster speeds, and knee flexion of the support leg to maintain forward momentum. The four phases outline the overall pattern of change in movement mechanics, but there is considerable variation in the order of change among movement components.

Direct observation of an individual child running is difficult because the many body movements to watch occur quite rapidly, even with a beginning runner. We offer some suggestions to make it easier. Of particular importance initially is to watch only one body part, such as one leg or one arm, before trying to watch several in relation to one another. It is simple and inexpensive to film or videotape several children running and then practice observing them. Several points should be checked in observing a child running, which we shall do by using the picture sequences in Figure 3-2.

The beginning runner's feet will not be off the ground very far or very long, as seen in comparing the side views of Child A and Child B. Notice also the limited range of movement of the beginning runner's arms and legs, often with the arms held higher and not used in a forward-backward motion. The knee and thigh of the forward leg should go higher and more forward, with the foot strike coming more directly under the body. The arm movements become better synchronized with the leg movements to produce a pattern in which the opposite leg and arm extend forward and backward together. More forward body lean is expected. Now, look at the lower panels for a rear view of a beginning runner, Child C, and a more experienced runner, Child D. Child D's arms stay closer to the body, which can be observed by following the movements of the elbows. Look at the leg movements by following the heel movements, which come higher off the ground for Child D and do not rotate as far away from the midline of the body. Following the movements of one segment of a limb often is very informative and helps focus one's observations. In general, watch from the side to trace the leg movements, trunk lean, and arm-leg coordination, and watch from the rear to trace the movements of the elbows and heels.

Jumping

Jumping in the simplest sense is a single, discrete movement in which the body is propelled by the legs off the ground for a brief period of time. A jump may start with either a one-footed or a two-footed takeoff, and the landing may be on either or both feet. Stepping down from a step or similar platform is a form of jumping, in that the mover becomes airborne at some point when neither foot is in contact with the step or ground. Taking off with one foot and landing on the other is called a leap or a long step. A jump with a two-footed takeoff from a standing position can be made up (vertical jump) or forward (standing long jump). A mover may run and jump, generally with a one-footed takeoff, to jump for distance (long jump) or height (high jump). Jumping in these various forms becomes part of play-game activities, for example, when children jump to have a ball miss their feet in dodge ball, jump over a hurdle, or jump to rebound a basketball. Jumps also may be part of a movement sequence in activities such as jumping rope. A single hop is a jump that becomes hopping when several are made in succession. Hopping will be reviewed separately because it is a continuous rather than a discrete movement and several movement patterns can be analyzed as hopping variations.

The specific age of achievement for a particular jumping task varies across different studies, but the general pattern is consistent. Some of the variation is related to the test conditions and whether the age of achievement was calculated as a mean or median or by some other method. Stepping down from a step to be airborne briefly, which has been observed at 18 months (Hellebrandt et al. 1961), is usually the first type of jump to be executed. The step off has been studied both as a single-step and a two-footed jump down. A platform takeoff from two feet is a true jump, whereas a step down from one foot to the other is more properly a step, with gravity providing the opportunity to be airborne. The two-footed platform takeoff was not observed by Wellman (1937) until 33 months. In addition, children are less able to make a two-footed takeoff as the height of the step or platform increases, and so the fear of falling might also be part of the problem in jumping down from a platform.

A more important achievement, as well as a more sensible way to consider the beginning of jumping, is the *two-foot takeoff from the ground.* This starts as jumping up and down rather than forward or over an obstacle. The two-foot takeoff is a landmark achievement that can be achieved in rudimentary form near the second birthday and is the basis for the many jumping variations noted earlier. Jumping off the ground with two feet probably can be done earlier, as children then have the strength and coordination to flex their legs and extend them simultaneously. The difficult part is to control the body after takeoff, particularly when making several jumps in succession, as when standing in one place and jumping up and down. The landing must be controlled so as not to fall over or out of line if another jump is to be made. This is a good example of the point made in the introduction to this section, that a major problem in many movements is to control the force generated by the movement. The achievements in several jumping tasks are presented in Table 3-2.

The standing long jump (standing broad jump) is a good movement for observing the development of body control. The general task is to jump forward with a two-foot takeoff and make a two-foot landing. This is a discrete movement requiring a well-coordinated summation of forces to propel the body forward and to maintain postural control sufficiently when landing. The landing need not be elegant but must be controlled. Picture sequences of children making a standing long jump are shown in Figure 3-3. Although their goal was to jump as far as possible, we are concerned here with observing how they used their body parts to summate forces and to control the resulting movements of their body. This is a good task to observe because considerable coordination of limbs and other body parts is required, and the movements can be observed directly. Also, the standing long jump has been tested more than any other single task involving total body movement, thus providing a great deal of performance data and related movement analyses in published studies (see Chapter 4).

Table 3-3 describes Child A's jump to illustrate the analysis of movement phases and body parts. Its angular relationships, velocities, and similar measurements also could be studied, but the level of description in the table is sufficient for our purposes. Child A's jump has an adequate form to summate force, propel the body off the ground, and land under control. The legs are flexed and the arms are drawn back when preparing to jump. The arms are brought forward as the legs extend to form a straight body line at takeoff. However, the head does not stay up in midflight, and the arm and leg movements are not completely symmetrical. The legs are extended somewhat in preparation to land, and there is hip flexion to "sit down" when landing. The overall jump shows a coordinated sequence of movements with minor points of asymmetry and some incomplete movements.

TABLE 3-2	Level of Achievement for Several Types of Jumping Tasks		
	JUMPING TASK	AGE	STUDY
	From a step of 12 inches, jump a distance of		
	1. 4–14 inches	37 months	Bayley 1935
	2. 14–24 inches	39 months	
	3. 24–33 inches	48 months	
	Standing long jump on the ground		
	Mean = 20 inches	3 years	Morris et al. 1982
	27 inches	4 years	
	38 inches	5 years	
	43 inches	6 years	
	Mean = 35 inches	5 years	Keogh 1965
	42 inches	6 years	
	Jump over a string (2 inches high)	41 months	Bayley 1935
	Hurdle jump: Standing long jump over a bar		
	Mean = 14 inches	5 years	Keogh 1965
	17 inches	6 years	

**FIGURE
3-3**

Sequence pictures to illustrate differences in movement mechanics for jumping.

Child B's jump is a mixture of movements that often is characteristic of younger children's jumping. Child B goes into an extreme crouch with arms withdrawn to a point far behind the body. Leg and trunk extensions at takeoff are well co-ordinated and forward, but the arms remain behind the body. The legs are flexed in flight without extending, as if preparing to sit down while in midair. The arms come forward on landing, perhaps more with the forward momentum than as a

**TABLE
3-3**   **Analysis of Movement Mechanics for Child A in Figure 3-2**

	MOVEMENT PHASES		
BODY PARTS	*Preparation (Pictures 1–3)*	*Action (Pictures 4–6)*	*Completion (Pictures 7–8)*
Arms	Retracts and extends	Swings forward and extends to midline overhead, flexes and brings down	Remains in flexion and brings slightly to rear of midline
Legs	Moderate knee flexion	Complete knee extension at takeoff, quick flexion with feet to rear, some asymmetry of legs (Pictures 5 and 6)	Moderate knee flexion
Trunk Head	Forward lean of trunk, head somewhat upright (Picture 2)	Forward lean of trunk, head goes from upright to slightly down (Picture 6)	Moderate forward lean of head and trunk

63

purposeful movement. Overall symmetry is generally good. Child B seems to be making a great effort, yet is not effective in getting the arms involved and is overflexing the legs and hips. This child seemed to enjoy jumping and was very eager during the filming, making each movement with reckless abandon and without sufficient control of the force generated.

In contrast, Child C made an incomplete jump and did not put enough force into it. Preparation for the jump starts with a lean forward and the arms forward rather than back. The legs are not fully extended at takeoff, and the trunk is drawn up and back rather than forward. The arms rotate up and back while in midair and then come down by the time of landing. The feet are not far off the ground, and the legs are flexed for landing soon after takeoff.

Direct observations of jumping begin by watching the preparation to jump, which should be a general crouch, with the arms back and the body leaning forward. The takeoff should be a straight line of legs, trunk, and arms in a vertical-forward direction. The takeoff also should use both feet simultaneously, because a one-foot takeoff is merely a big step and not a jump. The legs should move quickly in midair to flex and then extend for landing, followed by flexion to "sit down." The arm movements may vary after takeoff, but the arms should come forward at landing. Look for the coordination of movement sequences to match the general sense of what has been described, as well as marked variations and asymmetry. Stepping with one foot, rather than jumping with two feet simultaneously, and arm movements out of synchrony with the forward movement are two obvious and important variations to check.

Hopping

A hop is a one-legged jump that children use in many play-game activities, such as skipping, galloping, and playing hopscotch. A hopper becomes airborne when one leg is flexed and then extended to lift the body off the ground. The same leg is used to contact the ground as the body comes down, and the sequence is repeated. Hopping is a series of discrete movements that are difficult to make continuously because the body is always propelled by the same leg. This means that the body comes somewhat to rest while the leg is being flexed in preparation for extension. Very good hoppers can minimize the time in contact with the ground to make the movement more continuous.

When first hopping, children propel their bodies too high by pushing too hard off the ground, as if unable to exert the appropriate amount of force. But propelling the body too high makes the landing recovery difficult, and the children then cannot prepare for the second hop without putting down the nonhopping leg for support. When first able to hop successfully, the nonhopping leg tends to be held forward, with the upper body leaning back as if providing some equilibrium in the overall postural control. The arms tend to be held high away from the body and extended somewhat, similar to arm use when first walking, and often are moved up and down as if flapping wings. Movement mechanisms change to having the nonhopping leg flexed, with the knee pointed to the ground and the heel to the rear. The arms are flexed and at the side, although this may vary. Finally, less force is used, with the hopping foot coming barely off the ground.

Hopping forward appears to be easier than hopping in place, because the momentum generated by each hop can be partially dissipated by moving forward. When first hopping forward, children often hop very quickly, as if trying to make as many as possible before they lose postural control and need to put down the other leg for support. This is another example in which too much force seems to be used, thus creating too much to be controlled. This also demonstrates that the less we are able to control parts of a movement sequence, the more difficult it is to sustain a movement sequence. The positive statement is that the better we can control the movement pieces, the easier it is to continue a movement sequence and make adjustments or alterations.

Achievements on several hopping tasks are summarized in Table 3-4. Children at 41 months can make a single hop on either leg and by age 5 can hop five times in place on either foot. Hopping soon becomes part of other locomotor movements such as skipping and galloping. Skipping is a sort of walking while hopping, in what can be described as a step-hop followed by a step-hop on the opposite leg. Step forward and hop on the right leg, and then a step and hop on the left leg. Most children can skip at age 5, with many skipping quite well at age 4. Galloping is pretending to ride a horse, in which one leg remains the lead leg. Step forward on the lead leg, jump into the air with both feet, land on the back leg, and step forward to continue the cycle. Galloping is an interesting coordination of leg movements, and most children can gallop at age 5.

Boys tend not to do hopping tasks of any kind as soon or as well as girls do (Keogh 1968b, 1969a). This is one of the most distinct gender differences in movement development before age 6. As an example, Keogh found that at age 5, 91 percent of the girls could skip five successive cycles, compared with 53 percent of the boys. Also, girls more quickly skip and hop smoothly and continuously, whereas boys often are more discrete and use more force in making jumping-stomping movements.

TABLE 3-4 **Age of Achievement for Hopping Tasks**

HOPPING TASK	AGE IN MONTHS	STUDY
Hop one time on either foot	41	Frankenburg and Dodds 1967 (Denver Developmental)
Hop on one foot:		McCaskill and Wellman 1938
1–3 hops	43	
4–6 hops	46	
7–9 hops	55	
10 hops	60	
Hop 5 times in place on either foot:	66	Keogh 1968b
Boys 67%		
Girls 90%		
Skip on one foot	43	McCaskill and Wellman 1938
Skip on alternate feet	60	
Skip:		Holbrook 1953
55 % successful	54	
80% successful	66	
Skip 5 continuous cycles:	66	Keogh 1968b
Boys 53%		
Girls 91%		
Gallop 5 continuous cycles:	66	Keogh 1968b
80% successful		

65

Throwing

Throwing is a general movement pattern used to propel objects. Throwing can be accomplished in so many ways with so many objects that it is difficult to isolate a basic pattern. Throwing can be a full-arm motion in an overhand, an underhand, or a sidearm movement or can be a partial arm–hand motion to toss or flip an object. Objects vary in size, weight, and configuration and can be held and thrown differently. The goal of throwing may be to achieve accuracy, force, distance, special flight characteristics, or a combination of effects. Throwing includes tossing a frisbee, shooting a free throw, pitching a coin, lobbing a ball, and throwing a stick. Throwing possibilities and variations, which are almost limitless, probably are influenced as much by our social-cultural environment as by our biological makeup. We shall limit our descriptions and analyses, however, to the single-arm, overhand throwing motion used to propel balls and similar small objects. Very little descriptive information is available to trace changes in other types of throwing motions.

The overhand throwing motion is a discrete rather than a repeated movement. The primary concern in the initial development of throwing is to achieve a general accuracy so that the object will land in a desired location, often in order for someone else to catch it. The thrower must resolve three movement problems. First, enough force must be summated through the arm linkage system and the trunk to impart force to the object. Second, a proper direction and flight path must be imparted to the object. Third, the thrower must contain the momentum generated in the throwing motion to maintain general postural control. The summation of force is achieved by using various segments of the arm linkage system in an appropriately ordered and timed (phased) sequence in conjunction with rotation of the trunk "back" and "forward." Proper direction and distance are achieved by releasing the object at an appropriate point and with appropriate forces acting upon it. Postural control is maintained by using movements in one part of the body to counter the force generated in other parts of the body and by moving the body parts in a way to provide a more stable end point.

If we observe babies as they approach their second birthday, they indeed can propel an object in a manner that resembles an overhand throw. Nonetheless, the object often does not go to the intended location and often is thrown too hard for a nearby partner to catch. That is, older babies have the rudiments of an overhand throwing motion, but they do not have enough control to propel an object to a desired location at an appropriate speed. Young children by age 3 can propel an object in the general direction of a target and for a distance of 5 to 10 feet, but they are not able to adjust or modulate the force sufficiently to make it easy for a partner to catch their throws.

The *throwing form* can be described as the early development of control of the throwing motion. (Accuracy, distance, and other performance outcomes will be considered later in Chapter 5). Four general phases in the development of the overhand throwing motion are shown in Figure 3-4, based on analyses by Wild (1938) of thirty-two children from ages 2 to 12. Wild's four phases should be viewed not as a fixed progression but rather as revealing some important changes. Young children at first throw with the arm only, as seen in the forearm extension in Phase I. They also use a "long arm" movement in which they bring the ball overhead and then forward without bending the elbow. The feet remain in place, the trunk does not rotate, and the body makes little forward movement. Young chil-

**FIGURE
3-4**

Phase I: The ball is thrown primarily with forearm extension. The feet remain stationary, body does not rotate, and there is a slight forward sway.

Phase II: Rotatory movement is added. The hand is cocked behind the head during the preparatory movement and the trunk then rotates to the left. The throwing arm swings around in an oblique-horizontal plane.

Phase III: A forward step with the right leg is added in a righthand throw. The step produces additional forward force for the throw.

Phase IV: Throwing arm and trunk rotate backward during preparation. A contralateral step moves body weight forward.

Sequence pictures to illustrate differences in movement mechanics for four phases proposed by Wild (1938). (Reproduced with permission from Wickstrom, 1977.)

67

dren can make the trunk and leg movements observed in more advanced overhand throws, but they apparently need to minimize their trunk and leg movements in order to maintain postural control. Fewer body movements also make it possible to throw in the intended direction, because fewer forces have been generated to disrupt the release.

Young children soon rotate their trunk, which means that the shoulder and hip turn to the rear on the side of the throwing arm and then come forward with the forward motion of the throwing arm (Phase II). The feet remain in place. Wild's phases III and IV include, first, a forward step with only the right leg during a right-arm throw and, second, a step with the left leg raised and extended forward during arm withdrawal and the right leg coming forward after the forward motion of the arm has been completed. Wild's phases indicate key points to observe, with the warning again that young children's throwing motions will look like combinations of the illustrations and may not progress precisely in the order indicated.

Phases III and IV show a much fuller involvement of trunk and legs, indicating that the children can contain the force they are generating. The step with the opposite leg provides a wider rotation to the rear by the shoulders and hip, which will lead to more force production and more stability at the end of the throwing motion. The follow-through of the throwing arm and leg on the same side provide a way to dissipate the force generated in the throwing motion. Flexing the opposite leg on the follow-through in order to lower the body also is important in maintaining postural control at the end of the throwing motion. A common observation is that girls are slower to reach Phase IV, and there are many who do not progress beyond Phase III, but few measurements have been made and reported to support this almost too obvious observation.

Phase IV pictures represent a more effective and thus more mature throwing motion in terms of generating force and maintaining postural control. Little attention has been paid to arm movements and object release, which are the key points in determining the object's direction and velocity. The throwing arm eventually will be drawn more to the rear, perhaps even into full extension, and the arm collapses as it comes forward to accelerate the speed of the object held in the hand. The movements of the wrist and fingers just before and during the release can be used to determine the extent of object rotation and to influence the direction and velocity (for example, baseball pitches that curve or "float" or are thrown slowly with a fast arm movement).

Roberton (1977) reported a more elaborate set of analyses which led her to suggest that the development of the component parts of throwing and other movements may proceed at different rates. This means that a movement's components also may not change at the same rate among different individuals, and so it may be useful to identify these components in order to trace the changes in them. Roberton calls arm movements and pelvic-spinal movements *components of the throwing motion*. Based on previous research, she then suggests five categories of change in the arm component and eight categories of change in the pelvic-spinal component, as shown in Table 3-5 in Box 3-1. Each category of a component presumably is ordered sequentially in a hierarchy of levels. Roberton limited her analysis to a group of first-grade children (ages 6 and 7), which limited the number of movement categories she might see, as younger and older children would need to be included to observe a full range of movement categories.

Roberton's data were reorganized to identify the six most common combinations

BOX
3-1

CHANGES IN THE MOVEMENT MECHANICS OF OVERARM THROWING

Roberton (1977) analyzed overarm-throwing movements to test some ideas about the stages of movement changes within a task. She uses the term *stage* to indicate an observable body configuration, with the expectation that all individuals will exhibit a common sequence of stages of change in their progress toward a more mature throwing motion. Each stage is a total body configuration including arm, leg, and trunk movements. Stages have been suggested in many aspects of development, but to cover a large area of change, such as shown in Piaget's stages of intellectual development. They probably should not be used to pinpoint change within a task, because the changes in one movement task clearly cannot be used to represent the broader change implied in the more common use of stages. Additionally, it is difficult to imagine that each person will exhibit the same overall body configuration or movement mechanics in establishing control of a particular movement. It seems more likely that there will be a general progression of change, with considerable variation in how and when parts of the movement will change. Roberton suggests that her findings support this last point of view. She states that "development within component parts may proceed at different rates in the same individual or at different rates in different individuals" (p. 55).

A total of 73 children (42 boys, 31 girls; ages 6, 7, and 8) were filmed from 2 locations while doing 10 overarm throws. Each throw was analyzed to describe movements for two *components* of (1) arm and (2) pelvis-spine. *Categories* were identified to mark changes in movement mechanics in each component. (See Table 3-5.)

TABLE
3-5

Definition of Movement Categories in Arm and Pelvic-Spinal Components for Throwing Movements of Children, Ages 6 and 7 (as reported by Roberton 1977)

Arm Component

Category	Definition
M	*Humerus oblique:* Humerus moves forward to ball release in a plane that intersects trunk obliquely above or below horizontal. (Elbow not traveling forward at shoulder height.)
N	*Humerus aligned but independent:* Humerus moves forward to ball release in a plane horizontally aligned with shoulders; appears to move independently of trunk action.
O	*Humerus in unison; no forearm lag:* Humerus moves forward to ball release in unison with trunk action in a plane horizontally aligned with shoulders.
P	*Humerus lags; forearm lags partially:* Humerus moves forward in a plane horizontally aligned with shoulders; lags slightly behind trunk.
Q	*Humerus lags; forearm lags fully:* Humerus moves forward in a plane horizontally aligned with shoulders; lags behind trunk.

Pelvic-Spinal Component

Category	Definition
A	*No trunk action:* Only arm is active in the throw.
B	*Extension and/or flexion of trunk:* Trunk action accompanies arm's forward thrust by flexing forward at the hips. Preparatory extension sometimes precedes forward hip flexion.
C	*Spinal rotation with pelvis stationary:* Upper spine twists away and then toward direction of force. Pelvis remains fixed and facing line of flight.
D	*Spinal-then-pelvic rotation:* Pelvis joins rotary movement after forward spinal rotation begins.
E	*Block rotation of trunk:* Spine and pelvis both rotate away from intended line of flight and then simultaneously begin forward rotation as a unit or "block."
F	*Block rotation plus lateral flexion of trunk:* Trunk tips laterally away from the ball with a block rotation trunk action.
G	*Differentiated rotation:* Pelvis precedes upper spine in initiating forward rotation. Child twists away from intended line of ball flight and begins forward rotation with pelvis while upper spine is still twisting away.
H	*Differentiated rotation plus lateral flexion of the trunk:* Lateral flexion of trunk away from the ball is accompanied by pelvic-spinal differentiation.

*FIGURE
3-5*

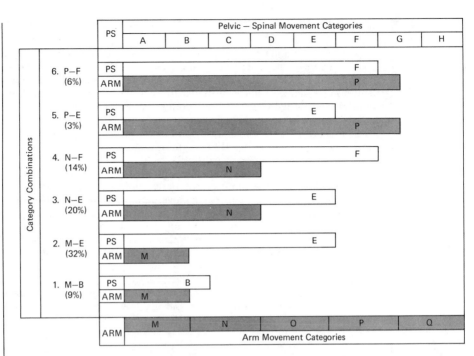

Combination of arm and pelvic–spinal movement categories for overarm throw by children, ages 6 and 7. (Refer to Table 3-5 for category definitions.) (Drawn from data reported by Roberton, 1977.)

Roberton found that some children were consistently in one arm category, though were more variable in the pelvic-spinal categories. This indicates some consistency in what a child's arm movements will look like, whereas pelvic-spinal movements may be more variable in a series of throws. Roberton then described the total body configuration according to the category for each component. The six most common combinations (covering approximately 84 percent of throws) are represented in Figure 3-5.

The Roberton study is limited because it filmed only a small age range and did not trace individual change over time. This means that some categories are not adequately represented, and we cannot know whether the categories in each component do change in the sequence suggested in Roberton's order. She recognized these limitations and used these preliminary analyses only to direct her next studies.

of component categories, as shown in Figure 3-5. The categories for each component are identified by letter in relation to the component scales at the top and bottom of the figure. Approximately 84 percent of the throws are included in the six combinations. In the first and second combinations (M-B and M-E), there is a considerable discrepancy in the pelvic-spinal movements for the humerus-oblique arm movements (elbow not traveling at shoulder height). Both simple extension or flexion of the trunk without rotation (M-B) and block rotation (M-E) were observed in the simple and probably the most basic arm movement (M). There is another discrepancy in the range of the arm movements (M, N, P), combined with block rotation (E) in combinations 2, 3, and 5.

The graphic representation of category combinations in Figure 3-5 is arranged so that the categories are sequential (A to H and M to Q), and each category within each component is equal in width. The category sequences, but not the category widths, must be as represented in the component scales at the top and the bottom of Figure 3-5 if there indeed is some fixed order of change within and among the components. This would indicate that the combining of movement components proceeds in an orderly and predictable pattern. Roberton's findings clearly do not demonstrate an orderly pattern of combining and recombining movement components within an overhead throwing motion.

Roberton's explanation of the variations in combinations of component categories is that each component develops at a different rate, and the variations noted in her analyses support this. Control in one component category may also permit the use of that component in another category. Postural control is needed before pelvic-spinal rotation can be done without disrupting the body position, and pelvic-spinal rotation in some form is needed before the arm can be withdrawn. That is, there may be some mechanical considerations determining arm movement, whereas other developmental constraints, such as postural control, may limit one or more components. Throwing can also be broken down into different components, such as withdrawing the ball, bringing it forward, and releasing and following it. These components focus on the movement pieces and their order, rather than on the anatomical parts of the arm and pelvis-spine. We might gain additional and different insights by analyzing the movements in different ways.

We have not described changes in movement mechanics in order to trace changes toward idealized movement forms, but rather to look for indications that young children are achieving better movement control. A general impression is that movements become easier, smoother, and more continuous, and fewer extraneous movements are observed. Also, movements involve a greater use of potential movement range, in contrast with a more limited use of body parts, as noticed in throwing with more trunk rotation, more arm withdrawal, and more follow-through of arm and trunk. Movements become more consistent, efficient, and effective by being more reliable, with fewer moving parts and achievement of more appropriate outcomes.

Balancing

Balancing tasks are used at about 30 months to monitor changes in children's ability to control a stationary and a moving body position. Children are asked to stand on one foot in various postures or to walk on a line or a balance beam. The achievements for these balancing tasks are listed in Table 3-6. Children can stand briefly on one foot by their second birthday, but not until 38 months can they stand for 5 seconds. Children at 23 months can walk on a line on the floor with their footsteps astride rather than on it, and at 27 months they can walk backward on the line in the same way. They can walk a circular path forward at 37 months with each footstep touching the line. Walking heel-toe is more difficult and is achieved only partially at 43 months walking forward and 56 months walking backward.

Standing and walking on a walking board or balance beam are more demanding tasks, with the difficulty level modified by changing the width of the board or beam. Bayley (1935, 1969) used a walking board with a width of 6 centimeters and a height of 10 centimeters off the ground. Children stood with both feet on the board at 24 months, attempted to take steps at 28 months, but did not walk with alternating steps until 38 months (Bayley 1935). The age of first steps on the walking board probably would have been several months lower in the 1969 study,

TABLE
3-6   **Age of Achievement for Balancing Tasks**

BALANCING TASK	AGE IN MONTHS	STUDY
Stand on one foot: Momentarily	22–23	Bayley 1969†
1 second	30	Frankenburg and
5 seconds	38	Dodds, 1967*
10 seconds	54	
Walk a line on the floor:		
Forward: General direction (astride)	23	Bayley 1969†
Backward: General direction (astride)	27	
Circular path: Forward	37	McCaskill and Wellman 1938
Heel-toe: Forward	43	Frankenburg and
Backward	56	Dodds 1967*
Stand on walking board:		
Tries to stand	18	Bayley 1969†
Both feet for a few seconds	24	
Walk on a walking board:		
With one foot on		Bayley 1969†
Attempts steps	28	Bayley 1935
Alternates steps partway	38	

* Denver Developmental Screening Test
† Bayley Scales of Infant Development

which consistently placed the age of achievement on balancing tasks several months lower than the 1935 study did. But the 1969 study did not test children after 30 months.

In summary, children at 24 months cannot hold a one-foot position more than momentarily, but they can walk astride a straight line. By their third birthday or soon after, they can stand on a walking board and take several alternating steps, and they are nearly 4 years old before they can walk heel-toe to follow a line on the floor. De Oreo (1976) suggests several levels of achievement in performing some beam-walking tasks, based on her observations of how children do them. More adept children will alternate their steps in walking the beam, whereas less adept children will shuffle or slide their feet without alternating them and will need the support of stepping off with one foot or taking the hand of another person. Observations of the kind suggested by de Oreo are useful in describing performance on balancing tasks.

The set of balancing tasks outlined in Box 3-2 were used with young school-children (ages 5, 6, and 7) to examine their ability to control their posture in various ways (Keogh 1969a). Rather than use the traditional categories of static and dynamic balancing tasks, a framework was formulated to select balancing tasks. Various kinds of postural control are needed in these tasks while staying in place and when traveling or moving. Staying in place can be to hold a position, to control a general position while making limited movements, and to make an explosive movement followed by holding a position. Postural control also is needed while traveling or moving in a certain way. Seven balancing tasks (sixteen test items) were selected to represent the four types of balancing tasks contained in this framework. See Table 3-7 in Box 3-2 for a list of the test items and performance results.

All of the test items, except the two involving walking backward, were passed by at least 50 percent of the boys and girls at age 5. The passing figure increased

ANALYSIS OF BODY CONTROL TASKS

Young schoolchildren's ability to control their limb and body movements was tested in relation to a framework in which, first, movements were made in place or at least in a limited space (Keogh 1969a). The body position was held, or a controlled or an explosive movement was followed by a held position. Holding a position is like the more traditional tests of static balance. The controlled and explosive movements both change and regain the body position, which is like our description in Chapter 2 of achieving and maintaining static equilibrium. Second, movements were made to maintain dynamic equilibrium while moving or traveling. This type of balancing task is often used in measuring dynamic balance. The tasks with a controlled or an explosive movement combine the traditional categories of static and dynamic balancing tasks.

A total of 270 children (ages 5, 6, and 7) were tested individually in a test session which took 15 to 25 minutes. Children were barefooted, which tends to make balancing more difficult than when wearing shoes, were allowed to keep their eyes open, and were allowed to move their arms and body, as long as the foot or feet in contact with the ground were not displaced or moved out of position.

The sixteen test items are listed in Table 3-7. The Heel-Toe Stand and One-Leg Stand had to be held for 10 seconds. The Heel-Toe-Touch was to touch the forward foot with both hands, return to an upright posture, and hold both hands on top of the head for 3 seconds. The Ring-over-Foot was to stand on one foot, place a 6-inch wooden hoop over the foot of the free leg and not move the support foot for 3 seconds. The Jump-Turn and Hop-Turn items were to jump the designated direction with a two-footed takeoff, land with two feet, and hold the landing position for 3 seconds. The Heel-Toe-Walk was ten steps, heel to toe, while keeping both feet on the line.

A second trial was given on each test item when a child did not pass the first time. Two points were given for passing the first trial, and one point was given for passing the second trial after failing the first. A maximum of thirty-two points could be scored by receiving two points for each of the sixteen items. The passing percentages for boys and girls at age 5 are listed in Table 3-7. The total mean scores are plotted by age and sex in Figure 3-6.

Body Control Framework and Percentage Passing at Age 5

Position		Task	Boys	Girls
In place	Hold	Heel-Toe Stand (R)	78	83
		(L)	83	87
		One-Leg Stand (R)	61	67
		(L)	52	70
	Controlled	Heel-Toe Touch (R)	57	72
		(L)	50	61
		Ring-over-Foot (R)	54	70
		(L)	76	76
	Explosive	Jump-Turn		
		Backward	80	80
		90°	85	91
		180°	50	57
		Hop-Turn		
		Forward	78	78
		Backward	13	46
		90°	53	52
Traveling		Heel-Toe Walk		
		Forward	65	87
		Backward	7	15

	Total mean score (standard deviation)		
	Age 5	16.2 (5.6)	18.6 (6.4)
	Age 6	21.9 (4.5)	24.8 (4.7)
	Age 7	26.0 (3.1)	27.8 (3.5)

FIGURE
3-6

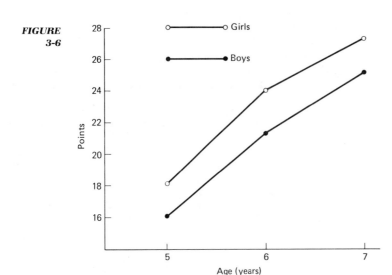

Total mean score for body control tasks by age and sex.

to at least 75 percent at age 6, except for walking backward, and only 58 percent of the boys successfully jumped and turned 180 degrees. Boys at age 5 had a better passing percentage than girls did only on hopping and turning 90 degrees. Girls had a significantly better total mean score at ages 6 and 7 and a larger, although not significantly better, mean score at age 5, as shown in Figure 3-6.

Young schoolchildren were very successful in the balancing tasks listed in Box 3-2. These tasks are similar to those used with younger children except that the test conditions required more time to hold a body position and used stricter criteria for success. The difference in difficulty level is revealed by the small number of children at age 5 who could successfully walk ten steps backwards, whereas the younger children in other studies were credited as successfully walking backwards if they walked in the general direction (Bayley 1969, Frankenburg and Dodds 1967).

Balancing tasks like those described in this section are useful through age 5. After that, these tasks offer little information, except that children can do them for longer periods of time while in unrealistic postures, such as standing like a stork for 30 seconds with one foot on the knee of the standing leg and the hands held on top of the head. Different types of balancing tasks are needed beyond age 5, and more importantly, we need to consider postural control rather than more variations of balancing tasks. The development of postural control can be seen in children standing with one leg on a scooter or skateboard and using the other leg to push, riding a bicycle, dodging a playmate, diving into a swimming pool, and other play-game skills in which the control of body posture is an important part of a movement skill.

Moving Slowly

An important and generally overlooked indicator of improved movement control is moving slowly, such as making a movement slowly rather than more rapidly and more forcefully. Initial efforts in making most movements tend to be too rapid and too forceful, with subsequent adjustments made to lessen the amount of force. Babies move their legs very rapidly when first walking and extend their arms too forcefully when reaching, so that they sometimes knock over objects. They soon learn to use less force to produce less abrupt and more precise movements and eliminate or minimize some aspects of the movement, such as not moving the trunk and head forward while reaching. Beyond these early adjustments to use less force more selectively, we tend to concentrate on using more force to move more rapidly and more forcefully in running fast, throwing far, and similar achievements. Moving slowly also requires a high level of movement control and is another indicator of improved movement control. Obvious examples are doing a forward roll slowly and riding a bicycle slowly.

Following this general line of thinking, Gipsman (1973) had two groups of children (mean ages of 4.5 and 6.8 years) do six movement tasks quickly and then slowly. She used the difference between the fast and the slow times to calculate a mean range of movement rate (RMR) for each task in order to measure the ability to control or vary the movement rate. The six tasks were walking a 30-foot curved path, rolling a large ball on the path, riding a tricycle on the path, drawing a line on the path (reduced to fit on a piece of paper), alternating hands to touch crayons in a line of boxes ("walking your crayons down the page"), and winding a 2-foot fishing line onto a reel.

The older children had higher RMR mean scores on all of the tasks, as shown in Table 3-8, but the mean differences were not significant for rolling the ball and riding the tricycle. The RMR mean scores more than doubled for the other tasks. There were no gender differences. The mean fast times improved, but only by a small amount compared with the much larger increases in the mean slow time. Thus, the increases in the RMR mean scores were primarily a function of improved control in making slower movements. The correlations of RMR scores for each pair of tasks ranged from .4 to .8, indicating something of a general ability to control movement rate. Other studies involving walking slowly and drawing slowly support the statement that children improve markedly from age 4 to age 9 in moving slowly (Constantini et al. 1973, Constantini and Hoving 1973, Maccoby et al. 1965).

Considerable care is needed in selecting the tasks to study moving slowly, as illustrated in Gipsman's observations (1973). When walking slowly, some older children shuffled while making sounds as if they were imitating trains, and others made high, exaggerated stepping movements while taking small steps. These

TABLE 3-8

Range of Movement Rate (RMR) Scores for Two Groups of Children*

TASK	YOUNGER (MEAN AGE = 4.5 YRS.)		OLDER (MEAN AGE = 6.8 YRS.)	
	Mean	*(SD)†*	*Mean*	*(SD)†*
1. Walking	8.1	(9.6)	20.9	(18.3)
2. Rolling a ball	12.3	(9.2)	22.6	(16.1)
3. Riding a tricycle	12.4	(9.7)	18.9	(13.7)
4. Drawing a line	6.1	(6.6)	25.9	(20.9)
5. Walking the crayons	2.0	(1.5)	6.3	(7.1)
6. Reeling a fishing line	13.2	(11.9)	25.4	(18.2)

* Based on data from Gipsman 1973.
† Standard deviations (SD) are large in proportion to mean scores, indicating that there are some extremely high scores, because low scores cannot be less than zero.

children continued to move rapidly or move a great deal, rather than making the same movement more slowly. That is, they changed the movement to take small steps, which was their strategy for moving slowly. These children simply found a different way to solve the movement problem, without having to move slowly. Notice that the movements are more fixed for riding a tricycle, drawing a line, and reeling a fishing line and provide a better test of moving slowly. It is important that the movement task require similar movements, whether moving rapidly or slowly.

The sizable changes in moving slowly occur in such a short age period that it likely involves more than just an improvement in the neuromotor control system. The stepping strategies used in walking show that children can solve this problem by altering the task and not really moving slowly. The children also improved greatly in drawing a line and reeling a fishing reel when made to do the same movement. Moving slowly seems to be a movement problem that includes improvement, not only in neuromotor control, but also in perceptual-cognitive skills that influence the production of movement. We shall examine this possibility in Chapters 10 through 13.

Manual Control

By their first birthday, children are reasonably proficient in separating reaching and grasping movements, and they can readily pick up objects by means of a power or precision grip. By their second birthday, they have well-coordinated movement sequences in the arm linkage system, are quite accurate spatially in placing a hand where desired, and are more dexterous in manipulating objects. In succeeding years, children become progressively more able to care for themselves, in feeding, dressing, and grooming themselves, which often are considered self-help skills. Children also use objects and materials to construct larger and different objects, as well as use tools of various kinds, including pencils and similar writing-painting tools, in addition to saws, hammers, screwdrivers, and wrenches. Normative data for self-help skills and construction tasks, including using particular tools, have not been gathered systematically and extensively. Perhaps this is just as well, because initial achievement in these movements is affected greatly by opportunity and expectations. For example, many of these movements tasks are considered social functioning and thus are observed as part of children's social development. Social expectations probably influence how a cup or spoon is held, and holding a cup or spoon in an expected or a different way probably influence the personal-social response, exemplifying a mover-environment transaction in which both mover and social environment will change.

Hand movements are used in such varied and complex ways, as noted in Chapter 2, that it is difficult to describe systematically their changes in control. We shall use the framework and terminology presented in Chapter 2 to analyze changes in manual control from ages 2 through 7, with normative data included when available. Manual movements require control of an *arm linkage system* and *digital manipulations* in *unimanual* and *bimanual* form. The *hand grip* may be *power* or *precision*, with the precision grip offering more *dexterity* in manipulating an object. The terms in italics are the basis for analyzing the movement problems that children resolve in order to establish control of different manual tasks. Additionally, we shall introduce three other ideas to help us think in broader terms about the nature of change in manual control.

The first of these ideas is the control of the object in *relation to the mover*, such as when wearing apparel is arranged and moved into the position in which the mover will wear it. The second is the control of an object to *represent in movement* what the mover perceives or imagines. Representing in movement is drawing what is seen, writing in symbols what one thinks, and the like. The third idea is that we develop *movement rules* and *movement strategies*. Rules are what we know about movements and their consequences, and strategies are how we can use different movements to accomplish similar outcomes. Knowing that an overhand throw produces a longer throw is a rule, whereas throwing underhand instead of overhand to have a more accurate control of distance is a strategy. We shall extend our thinking beyond normative expectancies and anatomical-bio-mechanical descriptions of movement change to speculate on the nature of change in manual control.

Self-help Skills

Dressing, grooming, and feeding require many types of movements, as shown by the self-help skills listed in Table 3-9. Frankenburg and Dodds (1967) report the general observations in the Denver Developmental Screening Test that children can dress with supervision at 32 months and without supervision at 42 months, but they do not indicate when children can use specific dressing skills. Knobloch and Pasamanick (1974), using data from Gesell's earlier findings, name 48 months as the age when children can dress and undress with supervision. They also note that children call pull on a single garment at 24 months, can put on their shoes at 36 months, and can lace them at 48 months. The normative differences in these two reports reveal the range in age of achievement expected for such general

TABLE 3–9	Age of Achievement of Self-help Skills		
	TASK	AGE IN MONTHS	STUDY
	Pulls on a simple garment	24	Knobloch and Pasamanick 1974
	Puts on shoes	36	
	Laces shoes	48	
	Unbuttons accessible buttons	36	
	Distinguishes fronts and backs of clothes	48	
	Dresses and undresses with supervision	48	
	Buttons up	36	Frankenburg and Dodds 1967
	Dresses with supervision	32	
	Dresses without supervision	43	
	Washes and dries hands and face	42	Knobloch and Pasamanick 1974
	Brushes teeth	48	
	Handles cup well	21	Knobloch and Pasamanick 1974
	Inhibits overturning of spoon	24	
	Feeds self, spills little	36	
	Pours well from pitcher	36	

skills. Some of the differences among these observations may be in the types of clothing and the type and extent of parental involvement.

Putting on garments is a dressing task that requires matching the garment to the proper body parts in an appropriate spatial relationship of garment and mover. A round-neck sweater may be pulled on backwards and be adequate, but putting on a jacket backwards or upside down will not. Knobloch and Pasamanick (1974) report that children can distinguish the fronts and backs of clothes at 48 months. Children at an earlier age may be able to hold and manipulate garments but not be able to arrange the proper spatial relationship between the garments and themselves. If the proper spatial relationships can be arranged, well-modulated movement control will be needed to place the body part into the garment with proper force and accuracy. This is seen in the difficulty in getting an arm to the end of a sleeve or a foot into a tight-fitting shoe. Putting on garments is a self-paced task that usually is bimanual and requires very little digital dexterity. The problem of putting on garments includes spatial relationships as part of the movement control.

Buttoning and tying a garment is quite a different task. Children are expected to button and unbutton at 36 months. Dexterous control of the fingers and thumb are required to get a button in or out of a hole and make the many movements to tie laces properly. Snaps, zippers, and similar garment closures also involve a fairly high level of bimanual dexterity. As a regular instructional activity during the early school years, children often are taught to tie their shoelaces.

Grooming is another self-help task, but one that uses tools or implements such as towels, brushes, and combs. Children can wash and dry their face and hands at 42 months and brush their teeth at 48 months. The movements often are serial or repetitive, such as rubbing or brushing for several strokes. Some dexterity of the fingers and thumb is required, as when using a bar of soap, but mainly involve arm-hand movements with the implement held in one position in the hand. Some movements are unimanual and others are bimanual. The main problem seems to be making repeated movements rather than dexterously using the fingers and thumb.

Feeding is a self-help skill that varies depending on the utensils to be used and social customs. Children at 24 months have some general control of holding a glass or cup and also can use a spoon to feed themselves, including preventing the spoon from turning over when bringing it to their mouths. Feeding activities of this kind are only generally successful. There is some spilling of food, a great deal of attention is required, and the movements are made in rather slow motion. Children at 36 months can feed themselves, again at a basic level of using different utensils, pouring into a cup, and the like. Data are not available regarding control of more intricate movements, such as using a knife to spread butter or cut while holding the food with a fork. Rosenbloom's and Horton's observations (1975) in watching young children (ages 1 to 4) use teapots to pour into cups exemplifies the type of movement analyses useful in describing the development of feeding skills. The older children were able to minimize shoulder and trunk movements when lifting and pouring, whereas the younger children moved their entire body, and the arm and hand not holding the teapot made associated movements. The teapot's path became a more direct and more continuous movement toward the cup and less a discrete set of movements to lift the pot high, bring it down to the cup, and then pour from it.

Many of the movements in feeding are unimanual and illustrate the development of control in one hand. Spatial-timing problems are minimal. The use of a spoon to eat cereal or soup illustrates the development of unimanual control: the spoon must be picked up, placed in the bowl, filled with cereal or soup, transported toward the face, and placed in the mouth. Placing the spoon in the bowl is not difficult, but the spoon must be gripped so that it can be filled. A natural and comfortable way to hold the spoon in the bowl is with the handle flat against the palm or the inside of the fingers in a power grip, which means that the wrist must be moved to place the bowl of the spoon in a horizontal position to enter the cereal bowl. It is more efficient to use a precision grip in which the fingers and thumb control the spoon and provide various ways to change the position of the bowl of the spoon. When the spoon is filled, the next problem is to keep it level until it is in the mouth. As the spoon comes up and toward the mouth, the body posture and arm-hand position must be adjusted to keep the spoon level. Children eventually learn to bring the spoon to their face while adjusting their fingers and thumb to compensate for the movement of their arm toward their face. The final problem is to place the spoon in the mouth, which cannot be seen by the eater. Younger children usually put some of the food in their mouth and some on their face.

Using a spoon is a complicated movement task requiring careful timing (phasing) of the hand's movements with the movements in the arm linkage system. Eating with a spoon is a self-paced task, although the eater may be in a hurry and will increase the rate of movement. Most eating tasks are unimanual and self-paced; the principal problem is to control and coordinate an extended sequence of arm and hand movements. Eating is using tools in a discrete movement for each bite or pour. Use of work tools requires serial or repeated movements, as when making repeated and often continuous pounding or turning movements.

Construction Skills

Developmental scales usually include tasks in which children must handle objects and materials in various ways to build or construct something. Children at 36 months can build a block tower that is nine or ten blocks high and at 42 months can use three blocks to build a bridge (Knobloch and Pasamanick 1974). Children at age 5 can do a more delicate bridge-building task, by placing one Cuisinaire rod across two upright Cuisinaire rods, which are narrow and not very stable (Keogh 1968a). Construction tasks of this type are self-paced and often require some dexterity in holding and manipulating the objects and materials to put them in place. The release of objects becomes important in more delicate tasks, such as using blocks or Cuisinaire rods to build towers or bridges.

Tools are used in many construction activities. A tool must be held correctly, and a particular spatial relationship must be maintained between the tool and an object. Children can use some toy tools by 24 months, and tools are included in instructional activities in the early school years. No formal testing of these skills has been reported, except as single items or anecdotal reports. Tool use often is a unimanual skill, although the other hand sometimes is used to hold or support the object or material. If the tool is used to create force, a power grip is used and the arm linkage system generates the necessary force while controlling the movement. A series of somewhat continuous strokes usually is needed, as when sawing or pounding. Errors in each stroke may create progressively greater correction problems for later strokes in the series. The force used when sawing must be enough but not too much, or the saw will bind in relation to the material.

79

Screwdrivers and wrenches are somewhat different in that they must be held in a proper relationship to the object being turned, and the turning movements often are discrete but are repeated rapidly. Construction tools require considerable accuracy in the arm linkage system's overall control of movements. Digital dexterity is needed only when using minimal force to make delicate adjustments and when using scissors and similar tools that require dexterity to control their moving parts.

Holding Grips: Writing and Drawing

Perhaps the most common tool use is writing or drawing, which involves holding an instrument to make marks on paper or similar material. The task is unimanual and requires considerable dexterity. The movements often are repetitive initially, as when scribbling or coloring, but eventually become more continuous in order to draw figures or write words.

Children at 16 to 18 months can hold a pencil or crayon and by age 4 have a large repertoire of holding grips. Changes in holding a pencil to draw were described by Saida and Miyashita (1979), who distinguished the four grip styles shown in Figure 3-7. A power grip of some form was the first style, as expected, in which the pencil was held across the palm and the arm linkage system was used to make the drawing movements. That is, the hand held the pencil, and the arm was used to move the pencil. Neither the elbow nor the wrist was in contact with the paper. The children then changed to a tripod grip with three styles noted.

The tripod grip is holding the pencil by the thumb, index finger, and middle finger. The tripod grip in any style is a precision grip that enables control of the pencil's movements by digital manipulation and wrist movements rather than arm movements. The first version of the tripod grip, in which the pencil often is held between two fingers rather than between the thumb and the index fingers, is called an incomplete tripod. It has many variations but does not fully meet the requirements of a tripod grip. The second version is a proper tripod grip without digital movements, in that wrist movements do not include the concurrent use of digital movements. This version is labeled a tripod posture because the tripod grip is used to hold but not to move the pencil. The third version is the dynamic tripod with a tripod grip and digital manipulation of the pencil.

The dynamic tripod grip marks the achievement of pencil control by the hand without using the arm linkage system to move the pencil. The Japanese boys and girls observed by Saida and Miyashita achieved a dynamic tripod grip at age 4. English children also achieved this landmark in manual control at age 4, but several months later than the Japanese children did (Rosenbloom and Horton 1971). Japanese girls were approximately 6 months ahead of Japanese boys. Many variations of a tripod grip are possible, such as holding the pencil against the first knuckles of the index and middle finger rather than the fingertips. Some variations offer a wider range of motion than others do, but the important consideration is that these variations enable instrinsic hand movements rather than arm movements to control writing or drawing tools.

Another analysis of holding grips was made by Connolly and Elliott (1972), who observed 3- and 4-year-old children using a paintbrush. The children were standing and using a brush to paint on paper attached to an upright easel. The paintbrushes were 12 inches long and one-half inch in diameter. The larger size of the brush and drawing in a vertical plan, make this task somewhat different from

**FIGURE
3-7**

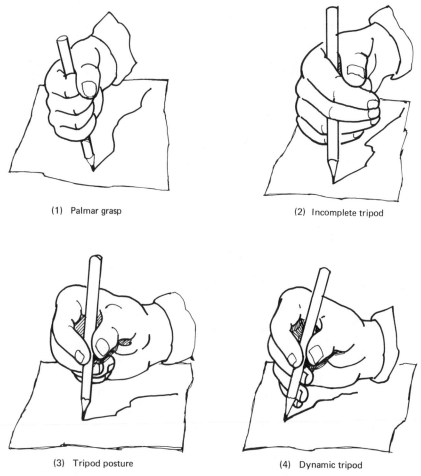

(1) Palmar grasp   (2) Incomplete tripod

(3) Tripod posture   (4) Dynamic tripod

Grip variations leading to dynamic tripod grip. (Drawn to represent grip variations observed by Saida and Miyashita, 1979.)

using a pencil to write on a horizontal desk top. The findings for using a paintbrush are similar to those for using a pencil: the children used a tripod grip 75 percent of the time but used arm movements to control the brush's movements. Only 12 percent of the movements with the paintbrush were made with the wrist and digital movements in a dynamic tripod grip.

The grips observed by Connolly and Elliott are presented in Figure 3-8. The adult digital grip was noted in 75 percent of the observations. Note that only the adult-digital and transverse-digital grips are precision grips. The others are power grips in which the paintbrush is fixed in the hand so that arm movements are needed to control its movements. The oblique-palmar and transverse-palmar grips are more obviously power grips because the paintbrush rests across the palm. The ventral, ventral-clenched, and adult-clenched grips do not rest in the palm, but the digits are clenched or fixed in a manner that precludes intrinsic hand movements. Note also that the thumb in these three grips is in pseudo-opposition, although more nearly in opposition for the adult-clenched grip.

Connolly's and Elliott's observations (refined by Moss and Hogg 1981) display a variety of anatomical configurations. But the function of the grip for power and

FIGURE
3-8

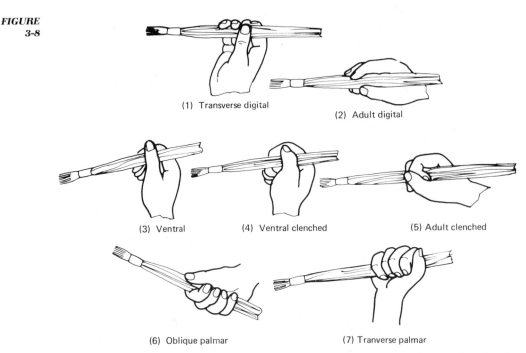

(1) Transverse digital

(2) Adult digital

(3) Ventral

(4) Ventral clenched

(5) Adult clenched

(6) Oblique palmar

(7) Tranverse palmar

Grip variations of 3- and 4-year-old children when painting on an upright easel. (Reproduced with permission from Connolly and Elliott, 1972.)

precision may be a more important distinction than the anatomical configuration. That is, the power and precision distinction may tell us more about the nature of manual control than does a description of different anatomical configurations of grips.

Drawing Lines and Figures

Children at 24 months can make circular, vertical, and horizontal lines that go in the appropriate direction but are quite variable in quality (Griffiths 1954, Knobloch and Pasamanick 1974). The order of difficulty tends to be that curved lines can be drawn before up-and-down lines, which come before horizontal or back-and-forth lines. Children first draw lines haphazardly and do not copy the lines shown to them, whereas schoolchildren can draw letters, which requires considerable digital dexterity. As noted earlier, a pencil or pen are first used with arm movements, whereas letters are written more precisely with movements of the digits and wrist. The manual control of a pencil is reasonably good by the early school years, when children can trace a maze in a pathway of one-eighth inch (Keogh 1968a).

Copying simple figures is a standard test item in most developmental scales and intelligence tests for young children. The general progression, with the approximate age expectancy in parentheses, is first to draw a circle (36 months), a cross (48 months), a square (54 months), a triangle (60 months), and a diamond (72 months) (Knobloch and Pasamanick 1974). Babies at 12 months can distinguish squares, triangles, and circles and by age 2 can fit them into form boards (Maccoby and Bee 1965). Children can make separate lines to draw these figures (Connolly 1968) and can use matchsticks to construct them (Landmark 1962, Wedell 1964) before they can draw them. The use of matchsticks is interesting because children begin with one matchstick and shift the position of the second until it is in place. The matchstick can be moved and checked again and again. Drawing with a pencil does not offer the opportunity to change line relationships except by erasing. The problem seems to be translating from perception into representation and not controlling the basic directional movements. The problem is planning and organization, not executing the movements.

Bimanual Control

An important type of bimanual control is the *functional asymmetry* noted by de Schonen (1977), in which the two hands make different movements in a coordinated and complementary manner. While one hand holds a piece of fruit, the other controls a knife to peel or cut it. Adults have a stable lateralization in this type of manipulation, as when one hand is used to hold a box of matches and the other strikes the match (Annett 1976). Additionally, the pattern of hand use is similar across adults, with more than 80 percent using the same hand for the same function. Children at ages 4 and 5 have established some stability in their lateralization of functional asymmetry, both across tasks and for individuals (Auzias 1975).

Very little is known about development of functional asymmetry in bimanual control, beyond the observation that it does occur and with a similar pattern of lateralization of hand use. Some bimanual tasks may vary as to which hand performs which function, probably when neither force nor precision is required. Also, it is not unusual for the left hand of an otherwise right-handed person to control the more precise aspect of the task. This occurs in dealing cards, in which the left hand slides one card forward on the top of the deck and the right hand grasps the card in a fixed digital position, with arm and wrist action used to distribute it. You can demonstrate this by reversing your hands in dealing cards: note that the main problem is sliding a single card forward out of the deck. Grasping and distributing the card generally can be done with either hand.

An interesting type of functional asymmetry is tying shoelaces, because the laces are soft, flexible objects that do not offer an externally consistent source of reference (de Schonen 1977). That is, the hands must adjust continuously in relation to each other's position and movements, whereas many manipulative tasks involve objects or tools that provide some regulatory or reference information. As an example, scissors are fixed to some extent in the range and direction of their movement, and their firmness is a constant. De Schonen notes that although apes can do many of the manipulative tasks that humans can and have been taught to untie laces, they have not learned to tie them. Untying provides some constant locations and pressures of materials, whereas tying is a much more open problem in the relationships between the two hands. Young children also have difficulty tying soft laces. They seem to lack some of the manipulative control needed in the hand's intrinsic movements, as well as the spatial organization needed to coordinate the changes in hand position.

There have been some observations of bimanual control in which the two hands perform the same movement. The terminology describing these dual movements is confusing, as they are basically symmetrical but may be opposite or the same in direction. When cranking two handles in a circular motion, the hands can move in opposite or the same directions. Try a simple experiment to see which combination of directions is easier and more natural. Point the index finger of each hand forward and move both fingers in a circle. Now reverse directions.

BOX
3-3

OBSERVATIONS OF BIMANUAL CONTROL

Elliott and Connolly (1974) discuss the organization of actions to produce outcomes that we recognize as movement skill. They offer some interesting analyses of the development of manual control before they present their study of bimanual coordination to observe movement sequences to analyze how children solve a movement problem.

A group of 24 boys and 24 girls (ages 3, 4, and 5) were tested on a marbleboard game manufactured by Brio and modified into the board layouts illustrated for Tasks 1 through 6 (see Figure 3-9). One knob tilts the board on one axis, and the other tilts the board on a second axis arranged at a right angle to the first. Each knob can be turned right or left and separately or together in eight combinations of hand movements. Imagine that you are seated with the box in front of you, as shown in Task 1, and that the marble is in the corner nearest to you. Turn the right knob to the right, and the board will tilt in that direction to move the marble in direction R. Starting again with the marble in your corner, move it in direction L by turning the left knob to the left. If you want the marble to move from your corner in the diagonal direction D, you must simultaneously turn the right knob to the right and the left knob to the left.

The eight hand movements can be divided into four *separate movements* and four *simultaneous movements*. The separate movements are merely the movement of the right knob to the right or left and the left knob to the right or left. The four simultaneous movements are the two opposite or mirror movements of both hands turning out or both turning in and the two movements in the same direction with both hands turning right or both turning left. A series of movements can be made by combining hand movements into a movement sentence. Looking again at Task 1, continue the movement in direction R with a left turn of the left knob, which will move the marble on the dotted path to D. The movement sentence is "right knob right; left knob left," a *successive movement* of first one hand and then the other. Notice that the *simultaneous movement* of both hands can be used to go directly (diagonally) to D.

The board can be modified to create different movement problems, ranging from the open board in Task 1 to the pathways to be followed in Task 6. The movement problem also can be changed by placing the marble in a different location. Try moving the marble directly to the hole in Tasks 2 and 3. A simultaneous movement is needed in both situations, but the hands move in an opposite direction in Task 2 and in the same direction (both knobs turn left) in Task 3. Successive movements can be used, as noted earlier, but the movement sentences will be different for the two situations. Tasks 4 and 5 are the same as Tasks 2 and 3, except that traps on either side of the opposite corner will catch the marble unless it rolls directly on the diagonal. If the marble lands in one of the traps, different combinations of knob movements will be needed to get it out and into the target corner. Task 6 has railings to mark a square path with holes at each corner. Successive movements must be made and timed to avoid the corner holes. The complete movement sentence is "right knob right; left knob left; right knob left; left knob right." Task 6 requires precise control of knob movements to keep the marble from rolling too fast, as well as making movement changes from one knob to the other at the appropriate time. Additionally, the second movement change from "left knob left" to "right knob left" is not a compatible change. Rather, the more natural and compatible change is to turn the next knob in an opposite direction.

You should discover that the fingers moved in opposite directions while making simultaneous circular movements. It generally is more difficult to move fingers or hands together in the same direction (both moving clockwise or both moving counterclockwise) than to move them together in the opposite direction. This has been demonstrated with different samples of schoolchildren and adults when using arm-hand movements to turn two cranks simultaneously (Jahoda 1976). Another way to demonstrate these simultaneous movements is to make the circular finger movements with the fingers pointed toward each other. Notice that there is a mirror pattern of movement for the opposite direction movements. It seems as if our neuroanatomical makeup is such that the natural and easier

**FIGURE
3-9**

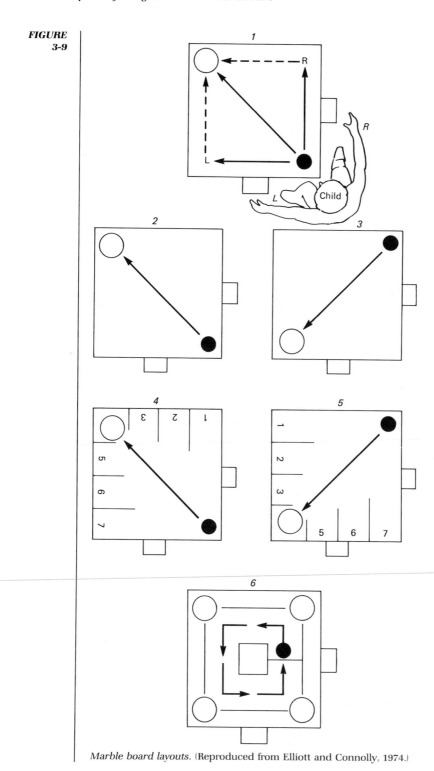

Marble board layouts. (Reproduced from Elliott and Connolly, 1974.)

pattern for symmetrical bimanual movements is to make opposite or mirror movements with the two hands rather than to make them in the same direction. Note that this does not apply to moving both hands while holding an object, such as a steering wheel. The hands then are yoked, and both must move in the same direction.

The movements just described are bimanual and symmetrical, as both hands make the same movement, whether in the same direction or as mirror movements going in the opposite direction. The study by Elliott and Connolly (1974), described in Box 3-3, shows how we can arrange movement situations to study different aspects of symmetrical bimanual control. Elliott and Connolly observed children using the Brio Marbleboard game in which two knobs were turned, separately or together, to tilt a board or platform to roll a marble. Many combinations of knob movements are possible, but the location of the marble in relation to the target or goal determines which movements must be made to make the marble move to the desired end location (see Figure 3-9). Look at the different board layouts, determine the knob movements that will move the marble to the desired end location, and note the knob movements that will not be useful. This type of apparatus offers a means of controlling the movement requirements in order to test many combinations of unimanual and bimanual control.

Knob or hand movements for the board layouts can be executed with *successive movements* of first one hand and then the other or with *simultaneous movements* of both hands. Various combinations are described in Box 3-3. Older children used simultaneous movements more often than younger children did when exploring the open board in Task 1 and in doing the diagonal marble roll in Tasks 2 and 3. Older children were better able to use a simultaneous (bimanual) movement, whereas younger children turned the knobs separately as successive (unimanual) movements. Opposite direction or mirror movements were easier for children of all ages, just as such movements were easier for both children and adults in turning handles in the Jahoda (1976) study. This can be seen in comparing Tasks 2 and 3. A simultaneous movement is needed in both tasks, but the hand movements are mirrored (both turn out) in Task 2 and are in the same direction (both turn left) in Task 3. More children did Task 2 with simultaneous movements, whereas many children did Task 3 with successive movements to roll the marble to a near corner before rolling it to the opposite corner (for example, the right knob turned left, and then the left knob turned left).

Task 6 was very difficult, as expected, because the task requires continuous movements and cannot be done successfully with discrete movements, whether successive or simultaneous. Children must anticipate when to make the next hand movement, and if they do not do it in time, the marble will fall in the hole rather than turn at the corner. Older children, as expected, were better able to anticipate and time the change in movements.

Elliott and Connolly demonstrated how the marble board's layouts can be modified to study different aspects of manual control. One finding is that making opposite or mirror movements, whether simultaneous or successive, is easier than making movements in the same direction. This is true for adults and seems to be characteristic of humans' neuroanatomical makeup, thus defining a constraint on our movement control.

Another difficult task for children in symmetrical bimanual control is the simultaneous release of objects by each hand. Some children from ages 5 to 9 released matchsticks, coins, or plastic disks one at a time rather than together when placing them in a box or on a peg (Keogh 1968a). Although the children were reminded to release the objects simultaneously, the tasks were timed and the children seemed more concerned with releasing the objects rapidly rather than simultaneously. Few daily tasks require rapid simultaneous release, which means that the development of this aspect of manual control probably is not very limiting. Improvement in rapid simultaneous release, however, is an indication of improved movement control.

Studies of associated movements, or asykinesia, provide some additional information about bimanual control in moving one body part without moving the others. Included as associated movements are mirror movements, such as turning the empty left hand to the left while turning a lid top to the right with the right hand, and nonspecific movements, such as extending the tongue and contorting the face while adjusting a knob with one or both hands. Extreme forms of associated movements have been documented as symptomatic of neural problems (de Jong 1967). A decrease in associated movements through childhood was proposed by Oseretsky (1923) and was part of his well-known test. Connolly and Stratton (1968) found a distinct improvement from ages 5 to 18 in making fewer associated movements in the tasks of pinching a clip with one hand, walking on the outside edges of the feet, and spreading the fingers of one hand. Girls at all ages made fewer associated movements than boys did. Associated movements are difficult to measure, as noted by Stott, Moyes, and Henderson (1972) when they decided to omit asynkinesia as a general category in their test of motor impairment. Although associated movements seem to decrease through childhood, no effort has been made to understand this progressive inhibition of extraneous movements in the development of movement control.

General Comments
We need to think more about the functional description of what occurs and what is possible rather than limit our observations to observed anatomical configurations. Connolly and Elliott (1972) view the anatomy of our hands as limiting what we can do but not as defining their functions. Many anatomical configurations can be used to produce movements that will differ somewhat, yet will have the same functional effect, and environmental circumstances will determine to some extent what we need to do and will do. Children in some societies do not need to use writing or drawing instruments. If they do, many grip variations are possible to provide a satisfactory outcome, but digital grips are better suited to precision outcomes. Detailed observations and analyses of grips according to anatomical configurations will show *how children handle an object*, but our observations and analyses will be incomplete without analyzing *what is to be accomplished*. We believe it is more useful to consider the function of grips as power and precision than to label grips according to their anatomical structure or configuration. The point is that we need to think functionally while using anatomical and biomechanical descriptions as empirical measures when needed.

A second point is that children develop *rules* and *strategies* in making movements. Rules are relationships or knowledges, and strategies are ways of doing. Rules are what we know, and strategies are how we do what we do. Beginning with rules, look at Tasks 2 and 3 for the marble board (Box 3-3), and consider what will happen if the right-hand knob is turned to the right. The marble in Task 2 will roll downhill to the right but will not move in Task 3. The marble ends at the same place in both situations, but the marble started in a different position in both situations. Children, as well as adults, must learn movement rules, or relationships, about the knob movements and the marble position. Movements then must be selected for the effect desired. *Movements cannot be made without being aware of the consequences.* This further supports our first point, that we need to think more about the functional description of what occurs rather than be limited to the biomechanical description that the knob was turned to the right and to the neuroanatomical description of digital placements and movements.

Movement strategy is demonstrated in an analysis of Task 6 which requires accurately anticipating when to execute the next hand movement. If not done in time, the marble will fall into the hole. If done too soon, the marble will hit the railing and not go around the corner. Older children, as expected, were better able to time the change in movements. Now consider how else the movement sequence could be executed, other than making two discrete movements of the right knob to the right and then the left knob to the left when the marble reaches the first corner. Quick alternating movements will keep the marble slowly rocking in place or moving slowly down the slope toward the corner. This is a different movement strategy to control the movement of the marble, which is used by more experienced and skillful players. The marble moves more slowly but more continuously. The strategy of one discrete movement followed by a second discrete movement will be effective in Tasks 2 and 3 to reach the opposite corner but will not be successful in Tasks 4, 5, and 6. A problem for younger children is that they may lack the precise movement control needed to execute the strategy. This is a common problem for novice performers of any age who may know what to do but are unable to carry out their plan.

Rules and strategies are embedded in the overall operations that control movement. They are not conscious acts in which the mover thinks, "Right knob right to start the marble right, and make the movements quick and in alternation, with the left knob turning left." But there do seem to be rules and strategies in the control of movement. The problem is to understand how the rules and strategies function and develop.

Control of Limb Movements

Another way to think about the development of movement control is to study the control of limb movements, because controlling body movements is largely a matter of controlling limb movements. Arm and leg movements are used to move the body and control objects, given that the control of the trunk and head help in postural control. Controlling limb movements, when separated from play-game skills and other movements described earlier in this chapter, offers a limited but useful perspective if the focus is on the general accuracy of control and not on speed and force. Limb movement tasks, such as alternately tapping the feet or opening and closing the hands, can be done for speed (Denckla 1974, Grant et al. 1973), but the first consideration is whether or not the movements can be done at all. The point is that improved control of limb movements is another indicator of the development of movement control. This general line of thinking was used in organizing a project to study the control of limb movements of children, ages 5 through 9 (Keogh 1968b, 1969a).

Limb Movement Framework

The first consideration in organizing our project was to limit the types of limb movements to be observed. Because our main focus was on control rather than speed and force, the limb movements needed to be repetitive movement sequences that children could make at their own pace without the need for fast or forceful movements. Also, the movements were not to be timed for speed and were not to be done in relation to external spatial-temporal demands. A limb movement framework (Keogh and Oliver 1968) was organized, and tasks were selected to represent the framework's dimensions: body position, limbs, and count pattern. The position of the body, whether seated, standing, or walking, requires different postural control which might influence the control of the limbs. The limbs are simply identified as two arms and two legs, although certain segments of each limb might be more or less involved and limbs sometimes provide support without being an active part of the movement. Limb control here is concerned only with the active movement of the limbs, and not with their support function. The limbs may be used alone or in combination with others in various ipsilateral and contralateral combinations. Count pattern refers to the number of movements made by each limb and can vary from a simple repetitive count of only one limb moving to two limbs alternating in a complex count pattern, such as one tap with one arm and two taps with the other arm.

Body position and limbs are arranged as the two dimensions of Table 3-10 in Box 3-4. Count pattern should be visualized as a third dimension within each cell. Limb movements were selected to represent the possibilities identified by the limb movement framework. Some of the cells in the scheme probably cannot be used in any meaningful form because tasks of this nature do not pertain to the general range of human movement patterns. Also, seated tasks can more easily be structured for the use of the hands and arms than for the use of the feet and legs, and the opposite is true for standing and traveling.

More than eighty separate test items were initially used to find a suitable set of movements to observe the control of limb movements. The limb movements for arms and hands included touching each finger separately with the thumb of the same hand, opening and closing the hands together and alternately, and clapping the hands and slapping them on the thighs at the same time and alternately. Tapping tasks were used to have children hold a pencil and tap the edge of a desk and tap their toes with their heels on the ground. Tapping was done with a single limb and in several combinations of hands and feet together and alternately. The children hopped in place and moved forward and also skipped. They made stride jumps to move their feet out and back as if doing a jumping jack and then added arm movements to do a jumping jack. Another form of stride jump was to start with one foot forward and the other foot back and then change foot positions while staying in place. Each movement was carried out for five cycles, such as tapping five cycles of once with the right and once with the left.

Performance Changes

Children from age 5 through 7 greatly improved their control of these limb movements, and girls were quantitatively and qualitatively better than boys were. Performance data for eighteen test items are summarized in Table 3-11 and Figure 3-10 in Box 3-4 to show these performance changes. The data for ages 8 and 9

**BOX
3–4**

STUDY OF LIMB MOVEMENTS

Two technical reports (Keogh 1968b, 1969a) analyze individual test items used to measure the control of limb movements. A framework was formulated for a variety of limb movement tasks and is outlined in Table 3–10, with the tasks listed as representing the limbs and body position used when performing them. As noted in the text, limb movements were selected to be repetitive, continuous, and self-paced, not made in relation to external temporal-spatial requirements and not requiring strength or stamina. These criteria eliminated tasks such as tapping for speed or in synchrony with an external beat, movement of hands and body to stay in target areas, and imitations of movements or gestures.

**TABLE
3–10**

Limb Movement Framework

Limb(s)	Body Position		
	Seated	Standing	Traveling
Arm-Hand	Finger Touch Hands Open-Close Hands Clap		
Leg	Feet Tap	Hop in Place Stride Jump: Legs	Hop Forward Skip
Arm-Leg	Feet-Pencil Tap	Stride Jump (Arms-Legs)	Walk-Clap

The 1968 report explored many test items to learn how well and in what ways children controlled their limb movements. *The changes from ages 5 to 7 were very striking, as were the many differences favoring the quantitative and qualitative performance of girls.* An important outcome of this study was the *observation of movement errors* collected

**TABLE
3–11**

Passing Percentages and Total Mean Scores for 18 Limb Movement Tasks (Keogh 1968b, 1969a)

Task	Pattern	Boys			Girls		
		Age 5	6	7	Age 5	6	7
Open-close hands	Separate	29	56	71	37	74	79
	Together	22	47	78	43	62	83
Clap-slap hands/thigh	2–1	38	73	86	70	90	91
	R/L	39	63	81	66	90	91
Feet tap	2–2	45	73	79	55	79	94
Tap pencil and foot	Right	46	78	90	59	86	93
	Left	57	67	83	46	77	84
	1–1	24	56	75	47	77	71
	2–2	3	5	14	14	18	34
Hop in place	Right	83	97	100	97	97	100
	Left	80	97	99	91	99	100
	2–2	3	10	48	16	45	69
Stride jumps	Out-back	34	77	86	75	92	94
	Jumping jacks	8	42	62	30	55	97
	Forward-back	17	40	70	74	86	94
Skip		61	88	89	86	91	98
Jump-clap	One	83	96	97	88	97	99
	Two	29	78	97	30	71	84
Total points	N	76	73	77	76	78.0	70
	Mean	11.5	20.2	25.0	18.0	25.4	28.6
	SD	5.4	6.4	6.0	7.0	6.4	5.5

as part of the performance record for each child on each test item. These observation notes commented on the nature of movement problems in controlling limb movements.

The 1969 report was an effort to create a test of movement control using a set of limb and body control test items. The test was not useful because the children improved considerably on the retests, but the general mean differences among age-sex groups were the same for the test and the retest data. (Data for the body or postural control test items were summarized earlier in the section on balancing.) A composite of the 1968 and 1969 data for selected limb movement test items is presented in Table 3–11 and Figure 3–10.

A group of 300 children (ages 5 through 9) from a school district in the Los Angeles area was tested in the 1968 test program. Another 270 children (ages 5 through 7) from a different school district in the Los Angeles area was tested in the 1969 test program. The data summarized in Figure 3–10 are for 450 children from the two school districts to cover only ages 5, 6, and 7. The children were within 3 months of their midyear birthday.

The limb movement test items were administered as described in Box 3–2. The mean scores in Table 3–11 and Figure 3–10 were derived by scoring two points for completing five cycles on the first trial, one point for passing the second trial after not completing the first trial, and zero points if not completing either trial. Eighteen test items were used and were combined for a total score of thirty-six possible points. Examiners scored each trial as pass or fail and marked an observation checklist to indicate the error noted when the child did not pass the trial. Additionally, comments were written to describe interesting and different movements observed on any trial, whether pass or fail. The jump-clap test item was included as an exception to making only repeated movements. Children jumped straight up with a two-foot takeoff and clapped once or twice.

FIGURE 3–10

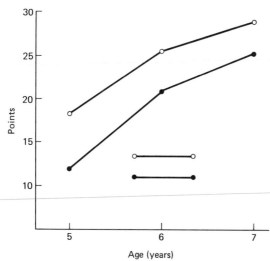

Mean scores for boys and girls for selected limb movement test items (Keogh, 1968b, 1969).

are not included because most of the test items were passed by 90 percent or more, thus indicating a test ceiling in which the test items are not difficult enough to differentiate how well individuals can control a limb movement, beyond the information that they can do it at a basic level. Children probably improve their control of limb movements at ages 8 and 9, but these test items are too easy for older children and are not useful beyond age 7. But care should be taken not to interpret a test ceiling as a lack of change or improvement (Keogh 1971).

Age and gender differences are clearly seen in Figure 3-10. Both boys and girls improved markedly from year to year with the girls' mean performance approximately 1 year better than that of the boys. The girls also were qualitatively better than the boys, as noted in the examiners' observations. The girls did not look at their movements as much, whereas the boys often looked at their movements, as if needing to see what they were doing and to think about the order of their movements. The girls generally were softer in their movements, whereas some of the boys splintered their pencils when tapping, slapped their hands when clapping, and pounded the ground when hopping. The boys more often jumped too far out in the jumping jack and then jumped their feet back together to collide in midair and upset themselves. The girls maintained an easier and quicker rhythm in their movements, and the boys made more discrete and halting movements.

Gender differences in early movement development have been checked for many tasks and many groups of children. Some differences have been noted, but they usually are small and often are not found in the next sample of children. The gender differences in the control of limb movements are the most distinct in movement development reported before age 7 or 8. Similar tasks have been used in several versions of the Oseretsky Test (Holbrook 1953, Sloan 1955, Stott et al. 1972), without such sizable gender differences. However, the limb movement tasks were tested in two different samples, using different groups of examiners (Keogh 1968b, 1969a). The mean performance differences were the same as were the observed differences in quality of control. Additionally, some of these tasks have been used in assessing individual children, always with the same results that the girls are better quantitatively and qualitatively.

The explanation of gender differences in the development of limb movement control may be that girls are biologically more mature than boys are. Girls reach puberty earlier and are more advanced in skeletal development and other indicators of biological maturity. The control of limb movements may thus be a general indicator of neuromotor control that would favor the biologically more mature girls. Another possibility is that these movements are culturally influenced and that girls are more likely to practice them. This might be true for children several years older, but girls younger than age 5 do not seem to be engaged more in movements that would lead to the development of the tasks used in studying the control of limb movements. Girls generally hop sooner than boys do, which supports the findings with the wider range of limb movement tasks. This is despite the fact that hopping is a gross body movement that often is claimed as something boys do better. Likewise, the rhythmical nature of the limb movements is something that often girls are thought to do better, but there are few data to support such a statement.

The progression in these limb movement tasks can be traced from the initial control of a single limb, as when tapping with a pencil or tapping with one foot, to combinations of limbs with complex count patterns. Control of an arm is observed before control of a leg to do the same task. Retests on these tasks within 1 to 4 days showed an increase in the mean value to approach a 1-year increase in the mean score. For this reason, these tasks are not useful items in a test battery. But, it is important that the differences among age-sex groups remained similar from the first to the second testing. Individuals maintained like positions within their age groups, as indicated by correlations of approximately 0.8 within age-sex groups. That is, the group means increased from the first to the second test session, but the high correlations indicate that high scorers on the first day were again high scorers the second day and that low scorers remained low scorers, although there scores did increase. When interpreting correlations, it is important to know that scores may increase and correlations may remain high if individuals stay in the same relative position within their group. Gender differences remained in the second testing, in that both boys and girls increased a similar amount. Although these movement tasks are not useful for conventional testing, because of the improvement between test sessions, they may be useful to distinguish individuals who readily perform tasks, as compared with those who need several trials to be able to do them (Ozer 1968).

Observations of Movement Errors

Observations of children's movement errors are a useful way to study movement problems to be resolved. A good time to observe movement development is when children first gain control of a movement. When children can make a movement, we do not learn much by watching it except that they can make it. What we are looking for is when they first can approximate the movement so that we can observe their efforts to solve the movement problem. Children at this time often are not successful, according to test criteria, but they make movements that can be analyzed in relation to the desired outcome. This allows us to analyze what Bruner (1970) calls the morphology of failure or what a person does when not quite able to do a task.

Children's movement errors when they did not successfully complete a movement task were recorded, as a means of forcing the examiners to judge more accurately when the movements were successful, because novice movers sometimes move in strange and different ways. A child may make a movement successfully, but the examiner may not mark the effort as such because it does not "look correct." The examiners also commented on unusual and interesting movements even though successful, and how children made a movement successfully but in a less elegant fashion.

An important observation is when a child seems to know that an error has been made, often indicated by comments ("Rats!" or "I goofed") or stopping to start over. Some children do not seem to recognize movement errors and keep moving until an examiner says "OK" or they stop because they think they did it right. An example is when a child counts to three while tapping five times. It is important to determine whether children know when a movement is correct or incorrect and what they think is wrong.

Lack of control of a limb movement takes various forms. Watch how young children tap one foot. They may pick up the foot and stomp, or they may rock from heel to toe and back, rather than keep their heel down. Several children did not move the front of their shoe off the ground, but their toes seemed to be wiggling inside, as if tapping. The other foot often moved as well, which was an error, or a lack of movement control, because the child could not isolate one limb without moving the other. Some children held one arm to their body as if to isolate the other limb that was supposed to move. They did this when tapping with one foot by holding the table with both hands and pushing down on the nontapping foot. It was as if they were preventing movement in the other body parts. All of these comments should help us think about what is involved in making a movement. The movement "message" should go only to the intended limb so that other body parts should not be included or should be inhibited.

The movement of the intended limb requires a carefully timed set of muscle contractions to produce a toe tap and not to pick up the foot to stomp, not to rock from heel to toe, and not to move the other limbs.

Alternating limbs to make the same single movement sometimes is switched after one or two cycles to moving the two limbs together. When opening and then closing one hand, followed by opening and closing the other hand, some children soon lapsed into opening and closing their two hands together. This happened when alternate foot tapping became simultaneous foot tapping. Some children also had difficulty in completely opening and closing their hands. They did about one-half of each so that their fingers stayed flexed but moved a bit open and a bit closed.

The footwork tasks of moving legs out-back or forward-back are interesting to observe. Some children, often boys, used too much force and got themselves in positions that made it difficult for them to continue the movement cycle. For example, they moved their feet so far apart that they could not make the reciprocal movement without stopping and moving one foot to shorten their wide-apart stance. If they used too much force when bringing their legs back together on the jumping jack, their feet collided in midair in what examiners called "ankle knockers." Some children did this and continued in spite of this problem. They clearly were making the task more difficult; yet somehow they had enough control resources to continue the movement.

The forward-back movement caused the feet to be exchanged in position, which in turn caused the body to turn from one side to the other and thus made the task difficult when a larger body turn was made. Some children could not make the exchange and instead produced a sequence of indescribable movements that would be a real challenge for someone to imitate. It was as if the back leg came forward in the air and then was put down beside the other leg, which stayed in place. Another sequence was the "walk-forward" movement, in which the forward leg stayed in place and the back leg came forward, and then the next foot was exchanged. The child walked forward one step at a time away from the examiner, who was expecting the child to stay in place.

An alternating hopping task, labeled the 2-2 hop, was analyzed and revealed some interesting movement errors. The 2-2 hop is hopping twice on one foot, then twice on the other foot, and continuing for five complete cycles of two hops on each foot. Children may do the task at their own pace, but they must not let both feet touch the ground at the same time. The girls were much better than the boys, to the extent of being about 1 year in advance, as shown in Figure 3-11. That is, 46 percent of the 6-year-old girls could do the 2-2 hop, which is the approximate percentage for the 7-year-old boys. A puzzling finding is that the girls reached a ceiling of 90 percent at age 8, whereas the boys in these samples did not reach a ceiling, even a year later at age 9. A few children might always have difficulty with a task, and so 90 percent or 95 percent is a ceiling or maximal figure. Approximately one-third of the boys at age 9, however, continued to have trouble with this task.

An effort was made in one study to identify problems in doing the 2-2 hop, by looking at the types of errors made and modifying the task so as to determine which parts of the task could be done (Keogh 1970). A total of 106 boys were tested within 3 months of their seventh birthday, at two different times, generally 2 days apart, on the balance hop, the count recognition-production, and the 2-2 hop. The balance hop was standing on one foot for three counts, hopping three

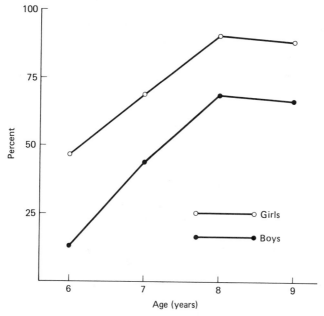

Composite plotting of percent passing 2–2 hop for designated age–sex groups.

times, and standing on the same foot for three counts. Count recognition-production was recognizing the number of pencil taps made by the examiner and producing the number of taps specified. Two trials of the 2-2 hop were administered on both the first and second days; two additional trials were given on the second day while holding the back of a chair for support. A performance summary is presented in Table 3-12.

Only 21 percent of the boys did the 2-2 hop on the first day. This is consistent with other findings that these boys were midway in age between the 6- and 7-year-olds reported in Figure 3-11. Another 15 percent were successful on the second day, which also is consistent with other findings and indicates that some

TABLE 3–12 Performance Summary of Seven-Year-Old Boys (N = 106) on the 2–2 Hop and Related Tasks

PERFORMANCE	N	COMMENT
Pass (N = 60; 57%)		
Did 2–2 hop on first day	22	Good performers
Did 2–2 hop only on second day	16	Need practice
Did 2–2 hop only with support	22	Need support
Fail (N = 46; 43%)		
Hop: Did not hop well on one foot	10	Poor hoppers
Count: Did not recognize and/or produce correct number of taps	5	Count difficulties
Hop/Count: Had both hop and count difficulties	7	Poor hoppers with count difficulties
Hesitation: Changed hopping leg by putting both feet on the ground	2	Not continuous
Performance difficulties not identified	22	Difficulties unknown

boys merely need some practice. A third group of twenty-two boys (21 percent) did the 2-2 hop on the second day, but only when holding the back of a chair for support. These boys could do the necessary movements, but they seemed unable to control the force they were generating. The support stabilized their body position and enabled them to produce the alternating hopping movements.

The remaining forty-six boys (43 percent) did not successfully do the 2-2 hop, even though given additional practice and support trials on the second day. Performance on the balance hop and the count recognition-production indicated that twenty-two boys in the failing group did not hop adequately on one foot and/or had difficulty in matching movements to counts. Count difficulties are subtle and easily might be overlooked, but hopping difficulties are more obvious. These boys could count, but they could not recognize the correct number of movements or sounds made by another person or the correct number of movements made by their own limbs. When they counted out loud, it was apparent that their verbal counts did not match the movements they were watching or making. Two boys could not maintain a continuous hopping movement, as they had both feet on the ground when changing from one leg to the other. They did this even when holding the back of the chair for support.

Specific movement difficulties were not identified for the remaining twenty-two boys in the group who did not do the 2-2 hop. This indicates that the movement performance was complex and that additional aspects need to be considered and/or more detailed analyses need to be made. But the movement errors made in the 2-2 hop and other limb movement tasks do demonstrate why some children cannot do them.

General Comments

Limb movements must be coordinated into a correct sequence with an appropriate temporal or phasing relationship. Children sometimes can initiate the appropriate movement sequence but cannot maintain the sequence beyond two or three cycles. All of their resources seem to be needed in this first approximation of the task. Their movements tend to be discrete rather than continuous, and the children often look at them as if they are consciously trying to organize each part of the sequence. They may be unable to maintain the movement sequence beyond two or three cycles because they "lose time" with each repetition and eventually do not have enough time to execute the next movement in the sequence. The movement sequences need to be organized and executed as a larger movement unit rather than as a series of discrete movements.

The amount of force must be appropriate, because excessive force creates additional movement problems. Children seem often to need to reduce their general and normal force, whereas adults often are concerned that children are not strong enough. Too much force in one part of a movement requires a sizable correction in the next part of the movement, which eventually leads to disruption or failure. Too much force also may create problems in postural control, as noted in many examples throughout this chapter, though we usually think of generating force and how can it be done to meet the movement task's spatial-temporal requirements. The problem initially may be how force can be inhibited either partially or totally. Inhibition in this sense may be the fundamental problem in movement development. All of the muscles of normal newborns work, but they must be used selectively in order to create the desired movement and the appropriate force. This means that many muscle fibers must be inhibited while trying to recruit the muscle fibers needed to create the movement. Inhibition may be difficult to achieve in early development and may be the key to the early development of movement control.

Chapter Summary

Young children develop good control of self-movements and have a large repertoire of movement skills by the time they finish the early school years. Their movements become more continuous and appear to be easier and smoother. They make fewer extraneous movements and go through a fuller range of motion. Their movements are more consistent, efficient, and effective. Simple observations of changes of walking, running, and many manipulation movements illustrate these general descriptions of change, as do the analyses of many movement skills. Young children also become able to do more things simultaneously and to achieve intended outcomes in many different ways. Gender differences begin to be noticed in both the quantity and quality of achievement.

One concern in this age period is developing force control. Young children become more proficient at modulating and varying force production in movements. They then can make more delicate and more precise movements and can adjust to task and situation requirements, such as needing to move slowly. Young children become more proficient at generating force more effectively by using movements to summate and transmit force, for example, in throwing. They also improve their postural control to control the forces generated in movements, which has the reciprocal effect of enabling more forceful movements. This also leads to some movements being less difficult because additional speed provides motion stability.

Manual control improves markedly during the preschool and early school years. Children at age 7 have a good repertoire of manual movements, including grip variations and numerous ways to combine arm and hand movements. The intrinsic movements of each hand provide dexterous control in handling objects, as when using drawing instruments. Older children can make power and precision movements with the same tool, whereas younger children often are limited to power movements. Functional asymmetry is well established to provide a wide range of collaboration between the two hands. The simultaneous release of objects is difficult for children to do, which brings our attention again to release as an important part of manual control. Some general neuroanatomical constraints may limit manual control skills, as noted in the difficulty encountered by children and adults in making bimanual movements in the same direction. Older children do quite well in self-paced manual movements, but they will improve considerably over the next ten years in movement speed and in timing their manual movements to external task requirements.

Change was described and analyzed from several perspectives to widen our view of movement development. Two general movement problems in manipulating objects were that young children have difficulty arranging objects in relation to themselves and when representing in movement a perceived or imagined figure. Young children seem able to control or do the many parts of these two general movement tasks, but they cannot put them together. We also pointed to the existence of movement rules and movement strategies that seem essential to the adequate development of movement control. Rules and strategies remind us that task and situation requirements, including a knowledge of movement conse-quences, must be considered in the production of movement, along with the constraints imposed by the neuroanatomical structures and systems.

In conclusion, movers encounter difficulty when the task and situation re-quirements exceed their resources. Young children become "overmatched" when they must move too rapidly and must do too much in too little time. This occurs particularly when executing a longer movement sequence, even when the move-ments are repetitive, and when doing several things at the same time. They also lack the resources for moving in relation to more variable conditions and move-ments of objects and other persons. Young children may be able to produce the necessary movements for the task and situation, but they often are not able to do so within the limitations of the spatial and temporal requirements.

Development of Spatial and Temporal Accuracy

Many everyday tasks involve moving our whole body or specific body parts in relation to the location and movements of other objects and other people. We move to chase or dodge another person, catch a ball, and take a dish of food as it is being handed to us. When driving vehicles, from scooters and bikes to automobiles, we must control the vehicle to stay in unison with or avoid others, whether it be other vehicles or other people. Our description of movement development to this point has been limited to children gaining control of their own movements, with only minimal recognition of environmental conditions. Such conditions obviously are present, but our main focus thus far has been on children establishing control of self-movements within a stable environment. Our emphasis in this chapter will be on the development of movement control in more open movement situations.

Younger children tend to be very late or very early in moving their body to the place where a moving object or a moving person is to be intercepted. When a ball is thrown directly to young children, their arms often close to capture the ball after it hits them. The same is true when swinging a bat at a thrown ball, in that some children will not start to swing until the ball reaches the place where it should be hit. Other children may move their arms as soon as they see the ball, so that their hands close too soon or the bat arrives too early. If the moving object is traveling rapidly, it may not be possible to solve the movement problem within the limited time available to predict an interception point, and then to move to the interception point at the appropriate time. To complicate matters, the movement situation may be continuous, and the moving object may make many changes in speed and direction, as when chasing another person or trying to stay in unison with another person.

Moving in a changing environment is such a multifaceted problem that no one movement task will capture the many aspects we need to observe and study. A general sense of the development of movement control in more variable and unstable movement situations can be obtained by tracing the development of performance in rope jumping, a common play-game skill that has many variations. Rope jumping progresses from the most basic performance of getting over a rope lying on the ground to successive jumps over a fast-moving rope. Several variations are shown in the movement sequences in Figure 4-1.

Young children trying to step over a rope lying on the ground will often step on it. When asked to run and jump over the rope, even though they are not yet able to make a running jump, children will display many interesting movement variations. Some children will run and stop and then will move up and down without lifting a foot off the ground, as if trying to jump. Other children will continue running while crossing over the rope, perhaps with exaggerated movements of arms, trunk, and head, again as if trying to jump, and will often step on the rope. Children who do jump over the rope sometimes make an exaggerated lift of the back leg after the forward leg has landed, as if not wanting the back leg to touch the rope. If the rope is held several inches off the ground, they may

FIGURE 4-1

Stepping over a rope

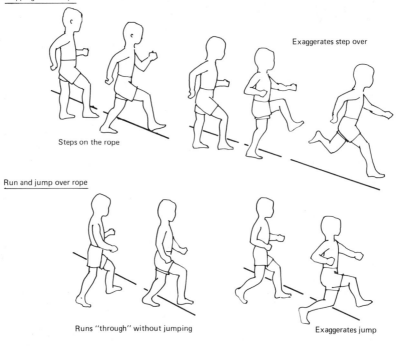

Exaggerates step over

Steps on the rope

Run and jump over rope

Runs "through" without jumping

Exaggerates jump

Bluebells: Jump over a low swinging rope
(not turning a full circle)

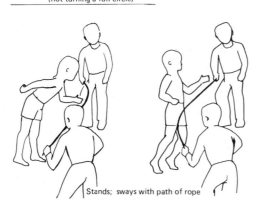

Stands; sways with path of rope

Sways with path of rope;
jumps as rope moves away

Side jump with rope turning continuously in a full circle

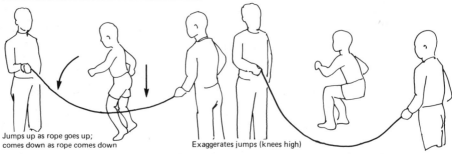

Jumps up as rope goes up;
comes down as rope comes down

Exaggerates jumps (knees high)

Movement variations in performing different rope-jumping tasks.

make similar but more exaggerated movements. These observations indicate that *children first must have sufficient control of their own movements before they can move in relation to external environmental conditions.* Even when moving in a stable environment, seemingly minimal environmental constraints will influence the type and quality of movement. This is particularly true when the mover has minimal control of self-movements.

The next variation is to have two people move the rope slowly back and forth, but not overhead, as done in the game of Bluebelles. Children now must jump over the rope at the proper time. If running to jump over it, young children will run through the rope or stop and try to step over it. It is interesting to have children stand in front of a slowly swinging rope and watch their effort to time their jump with it. Children will sway forward and backward in time with the rope. As it moves toward them, they will bend back and then forward as it moves away. After several cycles of swaying in time with the rope, they will step or jump forward as it moves away. They will either step directly on the rope or land short and be caught as it comes back toward them. Children thus must separate their jumping movement from the movement direction of the rope in order to jump when it is moving toward them rather than with them.

Children eventually will master a single jump over a rope slowly swinging through a full rotation, though they will have difficulty in making successive jumps. A problem in making a second jump is that the rope is now behind them and cannot be used as a visual signal or cue for making the next jump. Children soon learn to stand sidewise to the rope, enabling them to keep it in sight. However, jumping now is different and probably more difficult because the rope approaches from the side. Several single, discrete jumps may be made in succession with this sidewise strategy, but it is difficult to make more than three or four single jumps without being caught by the rope. The single jumps generally are large and do not leave enough time for the next jump. Jumping must become a more continuous set of smaller jumps, with a pace that matches the speed of the rope. Children often add an even smaller jump between two jumps over a rope in order to continue the movement.

Children finally become able to maintain a continuous set of jumps over a swinging rope, thus accomplishing two things. First, they gain better control of their own movements in order to make smaller jumps in a more continuous and rhythmical manner. Second, they know what the rope is doing without constantly watching it, which is critical for continuous jumping with a fast-moving rope. A jumping rhythm must be established to coincide with the rope's spatial and temporal path: a stationary rope creates spatial accuracy requirements, and a moving rope creates temporal accuracy requirements.

Our descriptions and analyses in this chapter will be organized around the two external requirements of *spatial accuracy* and *temporal accuracy* in the context of the framework presented in Chapter 2. We first shall review some important aspects of movement situation conditions to organize our thinking about development of movement control in more open movement situations.

Open Movement Situations

Movement situations can be analyzed according to the general movement classification framework presented in Figure 1-3. The interplay of mover conditions and environmental conditions creates spatial and temporal requirements, and therefore mover conditions, environmental conditions, and spatial-temporal requirements are the parameters of a movement situation and are arranged in Figure 4-2 as a slight modification of Figure 1-3. The upper border has been changed to identify the mover as stable or moving, rather than using Figure 1-3's labels of body stability and body transport. Our concern is the extent to which the mover moves into the physical environment and creates external requirements for spatial-temporal accuracy, because the mover constantly changes position in relation to objects and other people in the environment. If the mover remains stable by not moving into the environment, there will be fewer external requirements for spatial-temporal accuracy than when moving into the environment. The conditions of stable and moving are not separate but, rather, are on a continuum from stable to moving into the environment. The same is true for environmental conditions and spatial-temporal requirements, each of which forms a continuum, as shown in Figure 4-2.

The examples in the upper left-hand corner of Figure 4-2 are movement situations in which the mover remains in place, and objects and other people in the environment are stable unless acted upon by the mover. Jumping up and down, stepping over a rope, and swinging at a golf ball keep the body in the same

FIGURE
4-2

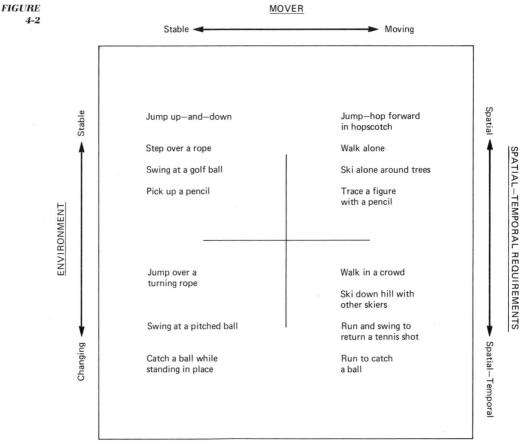

Movement situations in relation to mover–environment conditions and spatial–temporal requirements.

location without any need to adjust to the moving of objects and other persons. The physical platform, such as the ground, floor, or desk, also remains stable. These movement situations are *closed* because self-movements are produced in relation to stable environmental conditions with minimal external requirements. Some movement situations may require more attention to environmental conditions while preparing to move, such as deciding where to hit a golf ball and with which club, but spatial-temporal requirements during the actual movement are minimal because the environment remains stable.

Keeping the environment stable and having the mover move into it are more *open* movement situations. According to the examples in the upper right-hand corner of Figure 4-2, the mover creates additional spatial-temporal requirements by moving, because objects and other persons are thereby constantly changing their location. For example, playing hopscotch means moving into a stable environment with more spatial-temporal requirements than when jumping or hopping in place. Walking alone through a room or with other people standing still requires navigation around a series of obstacles. There are more spatial-temporal requirements than when walking in an empty room, but the increase is not sizable unless the task requires a high level of movement speed and accuracy, such as when skiing fast downhill around trees, which demands great control of self-movements while making rapid adjustments to avoid obstacles in the environment. Spatial-temporal requirements in a stable environment are principally spatial, except when speed creates temporal accuracy requirements. The range in temporal requirements is shown in the everyday task of walking around furniture in a room, as contrasted with skiing fast around trees on a steep slope.

Consider next the lower row of Figure 4-2 in which objects and people are moving in the environment, and keep in mind that the mover now must move in relation to the environment's temporal requirements. Movers may remain in place to jump a turning rope, swing at a pitched ball, or use their hands to catch a ball and may move into the environment to walk in a crowd of moving people, ski with other people, run to catch a ball, or return a tennis shot on the run. Spatial accuracy is required in each movement situation, but the speed of the ball, rope, and other people determines when the mover must move. Temporal constraints will be fixed when jumping, catching, and swinging if the movers want to intercept the ball or avoid the rope. Walkers and skiers have different options, such as stopping to let other people move past, but they must move in relation to other people when moving forward into a group of walkers or skiers.

Manual control movements do not fit as neatly into our analyses because segments of the arm linkage system usually are moving into the environment, although often for a limited distance. Additionally, body movements must be considered a part of the manual control movements, as they provide either a stable or a moving support structure from which the arm linkage system can function. Movers are more nearly in a stable condition when picking up a pencil than when tracing a figure with a pencil, but the distinction between stable and moving is not a clean one. The important point is that both movements are made in a stable environment. Manual control movements in a changing environment are easier to categorize in relation to mover conditions, as exemplified by catching while standing still, in contrast with catching while running.

A recent study by Hoffman, Imwold, and Koller (1983) analyzed movement situations along the lines we are discussing here. Children in the first, third, and fifth grades were placed in a moving seat to throw at a swinging target, as shown

FIGURE
4-3

Thrower
Stationary

Thrower
Moving

Target
Stationary

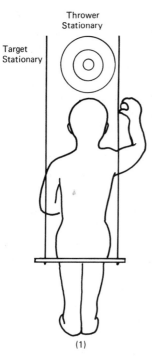 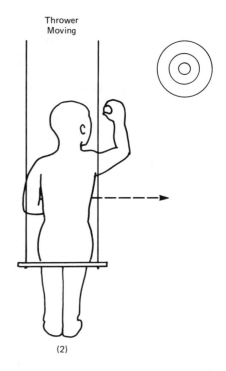

(1)

(2)

Target
Moving

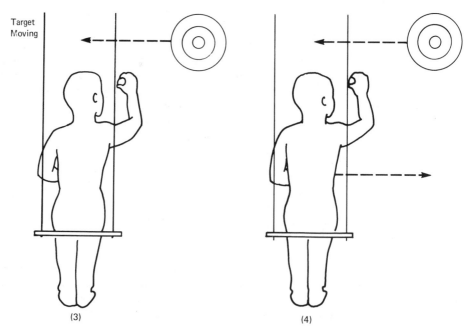

(3)

(4)

Throwing at a target in four conditions to illustrate movement situations varying from closed (1) to open (4). (Drawn to represent general test conditions used by Hoffman, Imwold, and Koller, 1983.)

in Figure 4-3. The four throwing conditions in the study matched the four general categories of mover-environment conditions listed in Figure 4-2: (1) seat and target both stationary, (2) seat moving and target stationary, (3) seat stationary and target moving, and (4) seat and target both moving. Children were the most accurate in condition 1 and the least accurate in condition 4. Their mean accuracy scores were similar for conditions 2 and 3 and were at an intermediate level of accuracy between conditions 1 and 4. The results show the general impact of increased spatial-temporal requirements on movement performance and mark a general continuum from closed to open movement situations.

We have analyzed movement situations in relation to mover conditions, environmental conditions, and spatial-temporal requirements in preparation for describing movement situations on a continuum from closed to open. This continuum is shown in Figure 4-4, with several movement situations marked in relation to mover conditions and environmental conditions. Movement situation A is very closed because both the mover and the environment are stable, whereas movement situations C and E are more open because the mover is moving more into the environment and the environment is changing more during the movement. Movement situations B and D show that movement situations become more closed or more open as one set of conditions remains the same while the other varies. Examples are in movement situation B, standing in place to reach for a pencil slowly rolling off a desk top and in movement situation D, running across the room to reach for the same slowly rolling pencil. Another example is with the mover staying in the same condition while the environment varies from stable to changing, perhaps when the mover is walking at a slow pace while reaching for a pencil resting on a table, in contrast with reaching for a pencil rolling very rapidly.

The representation in Figure 4-4 portrays only the general sense of a closed-

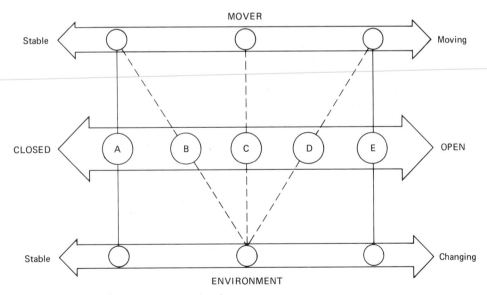

FIGURE
4-4

Continuum of closed–open movement situations.

open continuum and what might be important determinants: we cannot precisely calculate closed and open movement situations. Nevertheless, we find the idea of a continuum useful when trying to relate different pieces of information about movement development and when considering what may be important aspects of movement development. Of particular importance is that open movement situations involve more spatial-temporal requirements than do closed movement situations.

A stable environment requires varying degrees of spatial accuracy with few temporal requirements, unless more are created by moving faster. The mover determines the temporal requirements in self-paced movement situations. Fast movements by the mover can produce more temporal requirements, as when skiing fast downhill. A changing environment can have the same requirements for spatial accuracy as a stationary environment can, but temporal accuracy now is imposed by moving objects and other persons. Again, the mover can influence the temporal requirements by changing speed or moving in a way that will change the moving environment, such as walking directly at other persons to force them to change directions.

Spatial Accuracy

Spatial accuracy is required in all movements because the whole body or certain body parts must be moved to a particular spatial location and sometimes along a particular spatial path. The whole body or body parts also must be moved in an appropriate direction and for an appropriate distance, often with an appropriate amount of force and speed. We shall limit our discussion here to movement situations in a stable environment in which spatial accuracy is self-paced, temporal requirements tend to be few or can be determined by the mover, and the required degree of spatial accuracy varies according to the outcomes.

Play–Game Skills

Many of the play–game skills described in Chapter 3 require spatial accuracy, but not the temporal requirements of the more open movement situations. That is, the movement problem in the basic development of play–game skills is one of spatial rather than temporal accuracy. Our discussion here concerns single movements to strike and propel stationary objects and movements of the whole body into a stable environment. The striking and propelling of stationary objects are movement situations in which the mover and the environment are stable, according to our general framework. Movements of the body into a stable environment, which require an increase in spatial accuracy requirements, are shown in the upper-right corner of Figure 4-2.

A single arm movement is used in various ways to propel an object. Perhaps the most basic of these movements is striking a stationary object, which can be done by using the leg to kick or the arm to swat or by holding an implement to strike an object. Examples of these movements are kicking a ball held in place, socking a ball held in the other hand, and hitting a golf ball. Children must control the sequence of movements in the arm or foot linkage system and bring the limb or implement to the object's spatial location. Numerous movement errors can be observed in their initial efforts to strike a stationary object. They may miss the object or contact it away from the desired point. They also may contact the object before or after the limb movement sequence is completed, which lessens the force transmitted to the object.

Throwing is another way of propelling an object and is similar to a striking movement, except that the object is held and released, rather than hit, at the end of the sequence of limb segment movements. A thrown object is intended to move in a particular direction, often to land at a particular spatial location. The problem of spatial accuracy for the mover is the path of the limb and the point of release which combine to determine the object's flight path. Throwing is different from striking a stationary object, in that striking involves a visible point of contact on the object as the movement target, whereas throwing involves a nonvisible release point as the movement target. The sequence of limb segment movements, however, is similar in approaching the *point of contact* or *point of release*. Movement errors in throwing are similar to those in striking. Children will release the object too soon or too early, which is like missing the point of contact when striking; they also will move the arm in a direction that misplaces the release point or misses the desired contact point.

Children must solve three general movement problems when striking or throwing a stationary object. First, they must control the *sequence of their limb segment movements* while controlling their overall posture. Second, they must move their limb in a *direction and path* that will contact the object in the desired position or reach the desired release point. Third, they must *coordinate the sequence of limb segment movements in order to finish at the time of contact or release*. Control of the sequence of limb segment movements is control of the self-movements to summate force to be imparted to objects, as discussed in Chapters 2 and 3. The control of the direction and path of the limb movements and the time of contact or release are basic and initially difficult problems in fulfilling external requirements for spatial accuracy. Temporal accuracy is involved only in timing the completion of the sequence of the limb segment movements with the object contact or release point and does not deal with a moving contact or release point.

The three general movement problems are illustrated in Figure 4-5, with children using a bat to swing at a ball on the ground as if swinging a golf club. Child A draws the bat back and then forward in a sequence of arm segment movements intended to bring the bat into contact with the ball. Additionally, leg and trunk movements help summate the forces to be imparted to the ball and to control the posture. Child A has a good approximation of a striking movement and has sufficient control of self-movements to move the bat in a direction and through a path to contact the ball. But the bat contacts the ball when it is not yet at an optimal point in the swing to impart the proper direction and maximal force. The bat is late in "getting around" because the child's wrists have not yet uncocked or rotated. Notice with Child B that the arms and the bat are more nearly in line at the time of intended contact. Child A contacts the ball, but it is pushed to the side without much force; Child B has a potentially effective swing but misses the ball. Many combinations and variations of these two examples illustrate the difficulty in resolving the problems involved in propelling an object.

A fourth general movement problem overlays the others. If the object must be propelled a particular distance or at a particular rate, the mover must *modulate the amount of force* generated in the limb movement and imparted to the object. Children first must control their self-movements in order to propel objects in a general direction, and their play-game activities require that objects travel a par-

FIGURE
4-5

Child A

Child B

Sequence pictures to illustrate variations in striking movements and effectiveness in
contacting the ball. (Reproduced with permission from Wickstrom, 1977.)

ticular distance, often at a desired speed. Playing catch with a partner means
throwing a ball far enough but not too far, and fast enough but not too fast for
the partner to catch. Striking and throwing sometimes require putting an object
into or near a basket, hole, or similar target, as well as over or under goals, which
are ways in which the control of self-movements is used in play-game activities.
The general movement problem thus is to use the amount of force appropriate
to the situation.

Children can throw objects with some directional accuracy by ages 3 and 4,
but they often cannot control force well for distance or speed until later. By ages
3 and 4, children generally can strike a stationary object, as when kicking a ball
placed in front of them or swinging a small racquet to strike a ball placed on a
batting tee. Specific achievements in striking and throwing will vary depending

on opportunity and encouragement. A general expectancy is that children will enter school at ages 5 or 6 with the rudiments of striking and throwing, but without a good control of force for distance and speed. More importantly, they will not yet have enough control of these movements to cope with a moving environment.

Children encounter similar movement problems when their body moves into a stable environment, except they generally try to avoid rather than contact or propel objects. They now can change location, which then leads to the problem of *navigation*. This in turn requires spatial accuracy in relation to stationary objects or other persons. For example, walking must be directed spatially to avoid furniture, go through door openings, and generally navigate in the environment. Running has the same spatial accuracy demands, except that the body moves faster, thus limiting the time to change directions and correct movement errors. Propelling the body while riding a scooter or a tricycle also creates a navigational problem in addition to that of controlling the self-movements needed to propel the vehicle.

Young children handle the navigational problem quite well in a stable environment as long as they do not move too fast and thus decrease the time available to change directions and correct movement errors. Babies at first will not stop or change directions at the appropriate places, and they may run into objects and other people. This probably is more their inability to make the movement changes within the temporal requirements than their inability to deal with the navigational problem of matching body position to spatial requirements, which does not need to be precise in the same way that striking and throwing do. Babies can place their body in a general spatial location; the problem is to do it while moving. Moving into a stable environment probably is more of a problem of temporal accuracy than of spatial accuracy, particularly as the mover's speed increases.

Manual Control

Reaching and grasping are the starting point in tracing the development of spatial accuracy in relation to the external environment. As noted in Chapter 2, there is some controversy about when babies first can move a limb toward an object that is seen or heard. Bower (1979) argues that babies are born with the ability to move a hand in the general direction of what is seen or heard but subsequently lose it. When babies are 4 to 6 months old, they are reasonably accurate in contacting an object while trying to grasp it. This includes contact among body parts, such as reaching to grasp one's own feet and bringing the two hands together. Although not yet proficient in grasping and prehension, babies achieve an important landmark at about 4 months when they can *reach and place a hand on an object*.

Babies at 1 year can reach and grasp an object quite easily and can place objects precisely enough to put one block on top of another. The mechanics of reaching and grasping have differentiated sufficiently to reach out the arm and hand without also moving the body forward and an anticipatory use of the fingers to grasp without depending on contact with the object. Observations and analyses of this sort indicate that babies at 12 months are quite well developed in fairly precisely *moving a hand to a particular spatial location*.

Spatial accuracy requirements increase when the limb is moved while holding an object. The movement problem now is expanded beyond placing the hand in a particular location to *moving the hand into the environment*. Tasks like this include using a spoon or fork to pick up food and transport it to the mouth and pounding with a hammer. The task may be a single movement or a series of single movements, such as using a spoon to eat cereal. The task may require a continuous, repetitive set of movements, as when sawing a board or pounding a nail. When the movement is continuous, some internal timing (phasing) problems also must be resolved. More effective timing (phasing) of a sequence of limb segment movements minimizes spatial accuracy problems. For example, pounding or sawing in a consistent manner requires fewer spatial corrections, whereas less consistent movements lead to changes in the spatial relationships of limb and desired movement end points.

Babies in their second year begin to use objects as utensils and tools and so face a dual problem in controlling their movements to make the object move as planned. The object first must move to an appropriate location or through an appropriate pathway and, second, must be held and moved to accomplish the intended objective. A screwdriver must be placed in the slot on the head of a screw and then must be turned while held in the slot. The spoon must be put in the bowl and must be moved in order to get the food into the spoon. Then, the spoon loaded with food must be held level when moved toward the mouth and must be placed into the mouth, which cannot be seen by the mover. We described earlier the development of movement control to have the hands control the movement of a utensil or a tool. We now must also recognize the need for spatial accuracy.

Children between ages 2 and 5 become reasonably competent in using utensils and tools, if limited to single movements or a series of single movements. Spatial accuracy in these movements probably is less of a problem than is the control of the objects to achieve the desired effect. That is, controlling a spoon to prevent spilling its contents is probably more of a problem than the spatial accuracy needed to get the spoon into the mouth.

When movements must be continuous and rapid, children will have more difficulty with both spatial accuracy and control of the object or tool they are using. A pounding or sawing movement is reasonably simple as a single stroke forward and back, but when the speed of the strokes increases, it becomes more difficult to control their spatial accuracy. The faster repetition of the single strokes also places temporal constraints on the overall task, even though the movements are executed at a pace determined by the mover. A minimal speed often must be maintained in order to continue the movement, and so the mover may not be able to control the movements at the required minimal speed. Children generally are not able to make more continuous movements of this kind until ages 3 or 4.

Spatial accuracy also includes the problem of *relating objects to oneself*. The problem here is not the inability to move in a particular way, but to arrange an object in relation to oneself. When putting on clothes, such as a jacket, sweater, or pair of pants, the garment must be arranged so that the limbs and head can be placed inside it. A similar problem exists when placing a utensil or tool in relation to another object and oneself. Children must determine the appropriate arrangement of object and self. Controlling the required movements is not the problem because, for example, children can put on a slipover shirt, but they may put it on backward with the manufacturer's tag on the front instead of the back. The outcome is more obvious and more limiting when putting an arm into the wrong sleeve of a jacket.

Another spatial accuracy problem is making a *movement represent what is seen or imagined*, particularly when copying a figure and writing words. Children can carry out all the requisite actions of recognizing a figure and drawing the necessary lines long before they can copy a figure.

Temporal Accuracy

External requirements for temporal accuracy are created when the environment and/or the mover is moving and at a faster speed. Temporal accuracy means timing self-movements to the place and time of external events, that is, coinciding the self with objects and other people to stay in unison or to intercept or avoid them. Examples are trying to stay in time with a partner and the music while dancing, trying to intercept or tag another player, and trying to avoid being tagged by another player. The rules of the game add to the temporal accuracy requirements in an abstract and invisible way, by indicating what we should do and when we should do it, such as keeping the ball or throwing it to a partner who is ahead of the runner. Children before age 3 will be limited in coping with temporal accuracy requirements but will show great improvement from age 3 to age 10.

We shall describe these changes in temporal accuracy separately for body control and manual control. There is little information available on changes in temporal accuracy for body control tasks, although these are the types of movements used most often in play-game situations. Nevertheless, only casual observations are needed of children running to catch a ball, dodging other players, and similar play-game situations in order to be impressed with their improvement in open movement situations during the early school years.

Body Control

Watching a young child move to pick up a rolling ball illustrates the temporal accuracy requirements of moving into a moving environment. As shown in Figure 4-6, a child will first take Path A and move directly to where the ball is seen, which will place the child behind the ball as it rolls on. The child then turns in the direction in which the ball is moving and tries to catch up with it when it stops. When the child recognizes "being late," he or she may use Path B and try to head off the ball by running to a place in front of it and waiting for it or approaching it "upstream." The child eventually will take Path C to move in a straighter line toward the ball, but ahead of where it first was viewed. We can expect similar movement errors when examining other movement situations involving higher levels of spatial and temporal accuracy, except that the movement errors will vary according to the spatial-temporal requirements.

Improvement in dealing with increases in temporal accuracy requirements is demonstrated in a study by Leavitt (1979), who measured the speed of boys and young men when ice-skating through a 50-foot course with pylons placed at 10-foot intervals. These ice-hockey players, ages 6 to 20, were timed, first, for skating as fast as possible on alternate sides of the pylons and, second, for skating as fast as possible while stick-handling a hockey puck without losing control of it. Figure 4-7 summarizes the mean performance times by age for the two skating conditions. The speed of skating improved by age groupings, and the 6- and 8-year-olds were alike, but they were slower than the 10- and 11-year-olds, who were alike but slower than the 14 and 20-year-olds, who were alike. As expected,

FIGURE
4-6

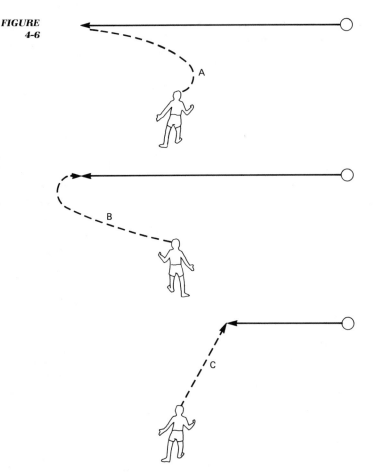

Different movement paths used to intercept a rolling ball.

the mean time for each age group was higher when stick handling because the moving skater had to stay in contact with the moving puck. The important finding is that the stick-handling mean times for younger boys increased much more than those for the older skaters, showing the impact on the younger boys' performance when the task was changed to require them to deal with moving objects.

Skating for speed among the fixed pylons is a movement situation in which the mover enters into a stable environment, as illustrated in the upper-right corner of Figure 4-2. As the mover goes faster, the requirements for temporal accuracy increase because less time is available to make each change in direction. These requirements again increase when a puck must be moved and handled while skating among the pylons. The movement situation now is more open in the sense shown in the lower-right corner of Figure 4-2 and toward the right of the closed-open continuum in Figure 4-4. If the puck is well controlled, the demands on the mover can be reduced because he or she has sufficient resources to cope with the spatial-temporal requirements, as discussed in Chapter 1. However, younger boys probably cannot control the puck well, which means that their lower level of movement control is not sufficient for coping with the high levels of spatial-temporal requirements. We can see something of the magnitude of their difficulty by looking at the size of the difference in mean times when comparing

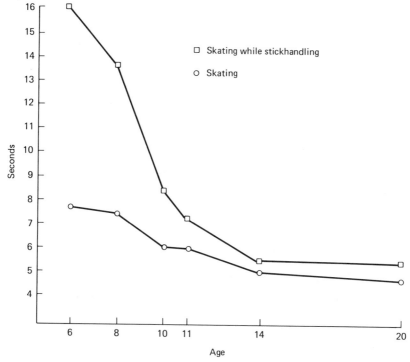

Time to skate a 50-foot course. (Drawn from data reported by Leavitt, 1979.)

skating only and skating while stick handling. Younger boys took 6 to 8 seconds longer and essentially doubled their time when stick handling; older boys and young men added less than 1 second to their mean time.

Skating while stick handling also adds a second task to be executed concurrently with the first task of skating. This in turn leads to an increase in movement control requirements because the mover must do two things rather than one, and the two tasks may not be compatible, at least not at first. Skating may lead to arm movements made in coordination with leg movements, whereas stick handling requires that the arms be used separately to control the stick and puck, so that they reach and turn separately from the legs. The Leavitt study shows that younger boys have a relatively greater loss in performance when temporal accuracy requirements are increased. Our analyses indicate the movement problems to be resolved, but more studies are needed to isolate the contributing factors.

Changes in moving to intercept a moving object when vision was limited were studied by Williams (1973). She had children stand under a large canvas "roof" and watch a ball projected in the air by a tennis-ball boy, as shown in Figure 4-8. They could see the ball's initial flight path until the canvas blocked it, and it landed silently in a net above the canvas. They were asked to move quickly to the spot where they could catch the ball if it came down. All of the children moved in the correct direction, but the younger children (grades 1, 2, and 3) had a mean error of 22 feet in locating the projected landing spot, compared with the older children (grades 4, 5, 6) who had a mean error of 2.5 feet. The younger children knew the correct direction but were unable to use the limited flight information to be in an area where it would be possible to catch the ball.

**FIGURE
4-8**

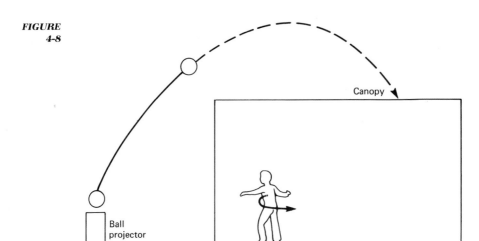

*General representation of ball projected to land on overhead canopy with child
moving to spot where he thinks ball will land* (Williams, 1973).

Williams commented on the certainty with which the children moved to what
they thought would be the landing spot. The younger ones moved very quickly
in the correct direction of the ball's flight, but well beyond where it would have
landed. Williams observed that the older children made quite different responses.
The fourth graders were very good in locating the probable landing place, but
they took a long time to make the judgment. They knew where the ball was going,
but they would not have arrived in time to catch it. The fifth graders were a little
less accurate than the fourth graders were but moved quickly to the probable
landing place. The sixth graders were both quick and more accurate. The older
children all knew where the ball was going, but the fourth graders could not use
that information as quickly as the sixth graders could. Although more precise
measurements and analyses are needed to verify Williams's observations, her report shows the development of knowing something about the moving environment
and then being able to use that knowledge within a time constraint.

One difference between stick handling and catching is that stick handling involves a continuous and changing set of interception points to keep the puck in
motion, whereas catching has only one interception point. Stick handling might
be successful for several contacts of stick and puck, but errors can accumulate
to increase the temporal accuracy requirements as the movement progresses.
Catching requires a similar set of adjustments to get the body and hands into
the appropriate location to intercept the ball, but catching is more of a single
movement, even though occupying an extended period of time before the ball is
in a position to be caught.

It is impressive that older children and adults can perform adequately in movement situations that are far more complex and demanding than anything we
have described and analyzed. We know that children improve markedly in dealing
with moving, and so it seems likely that there are some major developmental
changes in their ability to receive, interpret, and use information about moving.
Movers often increase their temporal accuracy requirements by going faster, doing
two tasks concurrently, and moving more continuously, but they can minimize
these requirements and can maintain an adequate level of performance by better
controlling their own movements. Nonetheless, events in the environment may

increase temporal accuracy requirements in ways that movers cannot directly influence. The speed and path of objects and other persons often are controlled by others, and game-play rules may be imposed by others. Movers must improve their skills in "reading" or knowing the environment, and they must improve their skills in using their knowledge of the environment to cope with increasingly complex movement situations.

Keeping Time

Temporal accuracy in controlling hand and arm movements may be divided into keeping time and coincidence timing. *Keeping time* is maintaining a temporal pattern in a continuous set of movements. The temporal pattern may be regular or irregular and may be established by the mover or may match an imposed temporal pattern. *Coincidence timing* is matching a mover's position to the changing position of an object or another person. The task may be to intercept or avoid the object or other person or to match its movements. Coincidence timing always is concerned with moving in relation to the moving of others, as when tagging or dodging others, catching a ball, and guarding an opponent. Keeping time and coincidence timing are different aspects of the problem of coping with temporal accuracy requirements. Keeping time is a more limited and regular set of movements, without the unpredictability of coincidence timing. Keeping time also is the ability to maintain a temporal pattern in a movement, often in relation to an imposed temporal pattern, whereas coincidence timing is the ability to move in relation to others' moving.

Moving to keep time with an external signal or beat often requires only a minimal spatial accuracy of movements, such as when tapping hands or feet to stay in unison with a sound or light signal or reproducing a practiced pattern without the presence of sound or light. Keeping time is executing a movement sequence with a particular temporal pattern. A simple example of reproducing a temporal pattern is pushing a telegraph key for a designated amount of time and then releasing it for a designated time in order to produce an on-off pattern. Gardner (1966) found that children from ages 5 to 12 were equally accurate in reproducing a single time interval, such as holding a key down for 0.5 seconds. When making an on-off pattern, such as on for 1.0 seconds, off for 0.5 seconds, and on for 2.0 seconds, there was a significant increase in temporal accuracy from ages 5 to 12 (Rosenbusch and Gardner 1968). The older children seemed to use the relationships among the time or movement intervals to improve their sense of temporal accuracy for separate intervals when done in a sequence. Each interval may become a reference point for the next interval in order to create a pattern of proportional relationships among interval durations. Thus, the whole may become more accurate than the sum of its parts.

Holding or releasing a movement for a period of time is not a normal part of everyday rhythmical movements which have a more frequent and continuous exchange. An interesting study was done many years ago by Jersild and Bienstock (1935) to measure young children's ability to keep time to music. A player piano was arranged to provide the music, which was played at several tempos. Children, ages 2 to 5, and adults were filmed in two conditions of walking to the music and beating time with their hands. The films were analyzed to measure the accuracy of leg and hand movements in matching 50 beats of the music. A percentage of accurate beats was computed for 400 beats and included the accuracy of hands and feet at all tempos. The accuracy percentages increased steadily from 21 percent at age 2 to 48 percent at age 5 and 85 percent for the adults. Younger children improved considerably in their temporal accuracy, with even more improvement after age 5. An interesting finding was the trend of better accuracy at the faster tempo of 136 beats per minute. The finding of less movement accuracy at a slower tempo is similar to observations that coincidence timing may be less accurate at slower speeds.

A study by Wolff and Hurwitz (1976) offers additional information about the accuracy of rhythmical movements and indicates that girls may be more accurate and less variable than boys are in doing several finger-tapping tasks. Alternate finger tapping was first done in time with a metronome for 15 seconds, and then each child tried to keep the beat for 45 seconds without the metronome. A second condition was to begin tapping in time for 15 seconds with the metronome and then to try to maintain the beat for 45 seconds when the metronome shifted to another beat. The first condition was to keep the beat going after the metronome signal stopped, and the second condition was to maintain the beat despite an interfering beat. Performance was measured both in deviations from the number of taps that should have been made in the 45-second intervals and the tapping variability around the rate which was done. Five-year-olds had large deviation scores, were quite variable in trying to keep a steady pace, and were so disrupted by the interference that no difference and variability scores were reported for them. Deviation and variability scores decreased (improved) steadily from age 6 to age 16. In both tapping conditions, girls to age 10 and sometimes beyond were more accurate than boy were in matching the expected beat, and the girls were better in holding a steady or less variable beat.

Keeping time to an external event and the consistency of the movement rate seem to improve greatly around age 6 and steadily beyond that age to adolescence or the early adult years. Younger girls may do somewhat better than boys do at the temporal aspect of keeping time. But the movement tasks described thus far have not involved spatial accuracy in making the movements follow a specified pathway and come to a specified end point at a proper time.

Smoll (1973) devised the apparatus shown in Figure 4-9 to measure both temporal and spatial accuracy in repeating movement. The movement begins with the arm at the side, and the aim is to raise the arm forward to shoulder height into a fully extended position and then to return it to the side position. The arm movement continues in this manner as a forward-and-down swinging movement. Smoll had someone hold the handle of a metal arm which was arranged to move in the forward-and-down movement, with several ways to provide a time signal and a target height for the forward movement. The apparatus was wired to record the movement's various temporal and spatial aspects.

Smoll (1974b) found that children improved steadily from age 5 to age 11 in both spatial and temporal accuracy, as shown in Figure 4-11. Constant error (CE) decreased in a linear fashion with no sex differences. (See Box 4-1 for a discussion of absolute error (AE), constant error (CE), and variable error (VE), including some limitations on the measurement of spatial accuracy.) The negative values for the CE scores indicate that the children were behind the beat, which placed them below the target height. Smoll (1975) also found that the children were less variable with age in holding a steadier pace, as measured by VE. The tempo or beat signal interval was varied across trials in another study, without any significant differences among the three tempos, although the sizable mean differences in CE scores show an increase in spatial accuracy as the tempo decreased in speed from 0.8

**BOX
4–1**

MEASUREMENT OF SPATIAL AND TEMPORAL ACCURACY IN A RHYTHMICAL MOVEMENT

Smoll (1973) saw that rhythmical movements had been measured mainly for tasks requiring temporal accuracy, such as finger tapping, without any demands for spatial accuracy. Movements were not made in relation to a target, which requires spatial accuracy, depending on the target's size. He argued that movements generally require both spatial and temporal accuracy and that we need to study movements that use both. Smoll constructed the apparatus shown in Figure 4–9, which has the subjects move the lever arm from the down position to the forward position indicated by the target height. The apparatus is wired to record the lever's movement and position. A noise or light signal can be given to indicate the movement beat when the lever is at the target height. Spatial and temporal accuracy can be measured as errors in the lever arm's deviation from the target height at the time of each beat signal.

The task is an arm swing from down to forward and back to the down position. The pathway is fixed by the lever arm. A forward-and-down movement is one cycle in a repetitive and limited movement pattern, and the tempo or speed of the beat can be changed from one trial to another and within trials. The spatial location of the target height also can be varied between and within trials. The apparatus can be modified to measure leg movements and simultaneous movements of two or more limbs.

Error Measurements

If the movement objective is target accuracy, performance will be measured as errors of space and/or time in relation to the target. The extent of movement error can be calculated in several ways, as illustrated in the recorder tracing in Figure 4–10. Beginning with the lever arm in the down (D) position, the tracing in the lower-left corner of Figure 4–10 moves upward to show its movement toward the target height (H) which is to be intercepted at the time of the beat signal (B). The lever arm in this tracing was late in arriving at H for beat signals 1 and 2 and was on time for beat signal 3. Looking now at the distance from the target height, the three lever arm movements at the finish (high point) were short, at target height, and long.

The three lever arm movements demonstrate some of the problems in selecting an appropriate measure of spatial and temporal accuracy. The first lever arm movement is both late and short. The second lever arm movement is spatially accurate but late,

**FIGURE
4-9**

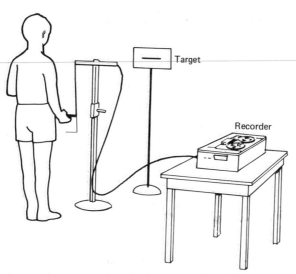

A general representation of an apparatus devised by Smoll (1973) to measure spatial and temporal accuracy in making a repeated movement. (Reproduced with permission from Smoll, 1973.)

FIGURE
4-10

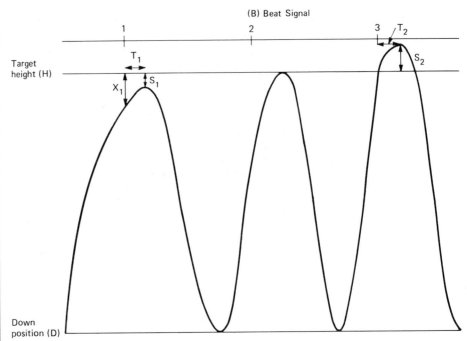

Simulated recorder tracing of lever–arm movements on the Smoll (1973) apparatus to illustrate measures of spatial and temporal accuracy.

whereas the third arrives at the target height on time but continues beyond it. We now face the problem of how to measure short-long and late-early. If we measure in relation to the beat signal, X_1 represents the distance as short, which also can be translated to time as late. If the concern is whether the total movement is short or long, this can be measured by S_1. Another temporal measure (T_1) indicates whether the movement's end point is early or late in relation to the beat signal. The measurement of spatial and temporal accuracy becomes even more complicated when the movement pathway is not fixed, as when throwing for accuracy, for the projectile can vary to each side, as well as long or short, when trying to hit a moving target.

A negative error indicates that the lever arm was below the target height at the beat signal; that is, the arm movement was late in arriving. A positive error indicates an early arrival. Early and late arrivals often are described, respectively, as undershoots and overshoots.

In his various studies Smoll used X_1 as the spatial accuracy error and T_1 as the temporal error. As noted above, X_1 also indicates the temporal error at the beat signal. It would be useful to know S_1 in order to have a more complete picture of the movement error. Several forms of error should be reported, because readers may have different questions or concerns.

Error Scores

Three different error scores often are calculated for any particular form of error measurement and are used so extensively throughout the remainder of the text that we shall take time here to define each one. First, error scores can be averaged without inlcuding their plus and minus values. This is *absolute error* (AE), which is the average or mean error from the target. Second, error scores can be averaged with plus and minus signs, thus indicating error direction. This is *constant error* (CE), sometimes called algebraic error. AE shows how close, on the average, an individual or a group is to the target, but without an indication of being early or late. CE is useful in naming error direction but can be misleading when the average values approach zero.

Error scores may be quite high, with a nearly equal number of plus and minus error scores to produce a low CE score (Example 1). Error scores also can be quite low, which also produces a low CE score (Example 2). Although CE measures error direction, it often does not tell the size of the error. Very large CE values, however, tend to have error scores that are mostly positive or mostly negative, which produces a CE score similar in size to AE (Example 3). AE scores are generally more useful when describing level of performance because they tell us how close, on the average, performers came to the target (Example 1). Newell (1976b) points out that performers try to get close to the target, which means they focus on AE.

	Example 1	Example 2	Example 3
	+10	+1	−5
	−10	+1	−5
	+6	+1	−3
	−6	+1	−3
Constant error (CE)	0	+1	−4
Absolute error (AE)	8	1	4

A third error is *variable error* (VE), which tells how variable an individual or a group of individuals is in terms of their own mean performance. VE is calculated by computing the variability of each person around his or her own mean performance and then computing the average intraindividual variability for the group. One individual, or one group, may consistently have a low VE score but a high AE score, indicating a consistent inaccuracy, by being at the same general location away from the target (Example 3). VE is a useful indicator of accuracy because increased consistency is one aspect of improvement in movement control.

There is some controversy about the use of AE, CE, and VE for statistical analyses in experimental studies (Schutz and Roy 1973, Newell 1976b) because the three error scores are not independent. CE and VE are statistically independent and combine to determine AE in most situations. Readers should be aware of this controversy when considering certain sets of experimental evidence and related analyses.

FIGURE 4-11

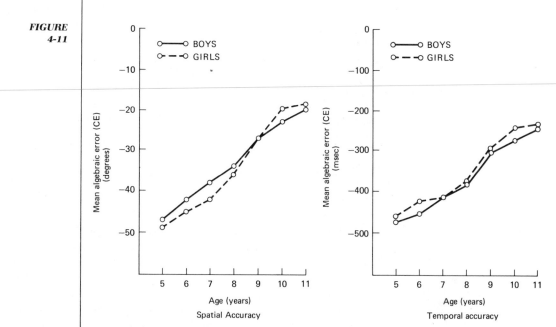

Mean algebraic error (CE) for spatial and temporal accuracy on the Smoll apparatus as a function of age (Smoll, 1974b). (Reproduced with permission.)

Results

Smoll (1974a, 1974b, 1975) used his apparatus to conduct several studies to measure children's spatial and temporal accuracy. He reported the CE error scores shown in Figure 4–11 (Smoll 1974b) for children, ages 5 to 11, making sixteen consecutive arm swings with an auditory stimulus of 50 milliseconds in duration and occurring at a 0.9-second interval to mark when the arm was to be at the target height. The CE scores for both spatial and temporal accuracy were negative, which means that the children generally were late. As noted earlier, spatial and temporal accuracy measure essentially the same thing, but in different units. That is, 5-year-olds were approximately 500 milliseconds late, which placed them 50 degrees below the target height (or approximately 30 milliseconds and 3 degrees for each of the sixteen arm swings). If late in time, they must be low in height. The CE scores in the Smoll report indicate the size of the error, because most of the error scores probably were negative. Nevertheless, it would be useful to have the AE scores in order to determine more accurately the size of the error scores.

seconds to 1.1 seconds to 1.4 seconds (Smoll 1974a). Thomas and Moon (1976) analyzed the error scores of 5-year-olds, using the Smoll apparatus. They found that children in a self-paced condition were no different from those trying to match an external time signal and that the mean error scores for boys and girls were not significantly different.

Children performing on the Smoll apparatus showed a steady, linear increase with age in their ability to stay in unison with an external event. Their spatial accuracy improved, but the spatial demands of the Smoll apparatus were minimal, because the direction of movement was fixed and only the extent of the movement was involved. Spatial accuracy also needs to be studied for its accuracy at the termination of the forward swing, rather than being limited to spatial error at the time of the expected temporal accuracy.

The tasks and studies pertaining to keeping time are limited to regular, external requirements that create an expected pattern of movement without the changing environmental demands that we shall examine next. The principal finding is that children improve substantially in spatial and temporal accuracy related to keeping time, but we do not have performance data and analyses to penetrate much deeper into this general finding. Girls may be somewhat better than boys are in some aspects. Younger children may be able to manage simple rhythms, whereas older children may be able to use differing count patterns and time intervals to improve their overall rhythm. Tempo may be a factor, particularly because each of us may have a preferred movement tempo.

Coincidence Timing

Coinciding one's own movements to the movements of an object or another person occurs in two ways. First, the mover tries to intercept a moving object or another moving person; second, the mover tries to match self-movements to movements in the environment. *Interception* involves a single coincidence point, and so the mover or an object propelled by the mover comes to a place occupied by a moving object or another moving person. For example, ball skills require interception, such as catching a ball, passing a ball to a running partner, and kicking a moving ball. *Continuous matching* has the mover maintain a consistent position in relation to the ongoing and changing movement path of a moving object or another moving person. Examples are dancing with a partner or guarding an opponent. The important distinction is that the interception is a single coming together, whereas continuous matching is the ongoing maintenance of a moving, spatial relationship. The distinction is somewhat artificial but is useful in tracing the development of movement control in more open movement situations.

Early Development of Interception. Babies at their first birthday are reasonably accurate and quick in reaching and contacting stationary objects. They also can move into the environment and can somewhat control moving relationships, such as banging blocks together and playing pat-a-cake. Babies have reasonably good spatial accuracy in relation to stationary objects, and they can cope to some extent with moving.

We now need to examine interception when the moving of objects and other persons is not controlled directly by the mover and there is a longer time period in which the mover must track the moving in the environment while moving appropriate body parts to intercept the object or other person. Interception can be divided into two general achievements. First, the mover must be able to look at a moving object or another moving person and know where the moving target is going and when it can be intercepted. Second, the mover must be able to move to the interception point and arrive at an appropriate time; that is, if the mover knows what the moving target is doing, he or she can use this information to create the necessary movement control. The general expectation for babies at their first birthday is that they can intercept a slow-moving target with their hand while seated. This is an important achievement that indicates that the basics for moving in a moving environment are in place, even though children must develop further before they can deal with the more rapid requirements of moving in play-game and other movement situations.

A set of reports by von Hofsten (1979, 1980, von Hofsten and Lindhagen 1979) documents the early development of interception. The general picture is that babies at 4 months can track moving objects and can move an arm ahead of the target pathway to intercept the object; that is, they can anticipate the future location of a moving object and can lead the object to make an interception. The perceptual skill of specifying what the moving object is doing seems reasonably well developed by 4 months. But the control of the arm at 4 months is not well developed, in that arm movements are inefficient even when on target. This means that interception seems to improve more as a function of better arm control than better perceptual development.

Von Hofsten's three reports cover one study, in which the efforts of eleven babies to intercept a moving object are summarized (see Box 4-2). Observations were made of the object moving at three speeds and when stationary. The babies were tested at 3-week intervals, from 15 weeks of age to 36 weeks of age. The interception of the moving object is shown in Figure 4-12 for one baby at 21 weeks. The babies' success in interception is presented in Figure 4-13. Approximately 90 percent of the reaches at 15 weeks were successful, in that the moving object was touched. By 18 weeks, approximately 45 percent of the reaches were touches, and another 45 percent were grasps in which the baby got ahold of the object. The proportion of grasps continued to improve in subsequent weeks. An important point is that only 10 percent of the reaches were misses throughout this time period. Babies could intercept the moving object at 15 weeks, but they could not also grasp the object until 18 weeks.

The observation that babies *can intercept a moving object* at 15 to 18 weeks (4 months) is a major landmark that coincides with the age when babies can reliably

BOX
4-2

THE INTERCEPTION OF MOVING OBJECTS BY YOUNG BABIES

The interception of moving objects by eleven young babies was studied by von Hofsten and described in three reports. The first report (von Hofsten and Lindhagen 1979) contains the procedures and basic analyses and the more general descriptions of interception accuracy. The second report (von Hofsten, 1979) contains analyses of the number, duration, and direction of segments of arm movements during reaches. The third report (von Hofsten 1980) is concerned with the movement segments' spatial and temporal accuracy during reaches. The three reports should be read as a single study that we shall call the von Hofsten study.

An important aspect of the von Hofsten study is that each baby was observed at 3-week intervals. This provided a *longitudinal* look at interception of a moving object, rather than a *cross-sectional* look, which would be the observation of different babies at each age period. Longitudinal observations make it possible to trace an individual's change. Cross-sectional observations provide a mean score for each age so as to form an average pattern of change. An advantage of longitudinal observations is that individual change can be studied. A disadvantage is that it takes a long time to collect the observations. Another limitation of longitudinal studies is that children may move or otherwise be lost as part of the sample. Cross-sectional observations can be collected at one time, but individual change cannot be studied. Longitudinal studies usually study young babies because change occurs rapidly and often needs to be traced for only several months. Many of the studies of Gesell, Bayley, and others were longitudinal to cover several months or several years.

Von Hofsten conducted his study because earlier studies of reaching had been limited to reaching for a stationary object. Additionally, he wanted to analyze reaching in a variety of ways that would show how young babies change. Von Hofsten suggested that the interception of a moving object has three interrelated aspects. First, one must perceive motion. Second, hand motion must be coordinated with object motion, which means starting the hand motion in time to reach the intercept point. Third, the hand must move to an intercept point ahead of where the object is seen when the reach is initiated. Von Hofsten used this perspective to identify the types of analyses he needed to make. We have analyzed the task requirements somewhat differently here, but our point of view is quite similar.

Von Hofsten's study is important in providing a comprehensive set of observations and analyses to demonstrate that *babies can intercept a moving object quite well by 4 months.* He also offers many ways to describe and analyze the changes occurring as reaching for a moving object becomes more accurate both spatially and temporally.

Subjects. Eleven babies (six female and five male) were observed individually at 3-week intervals, beginning at an age of 12 to 24 weeks. The observations continued until 30 weeks and were followed by a final observation at 36 weeks.

Test apparatus. The babies sat in a chair in a slightly reclined position. The object to be intercepted was a wooden fishing lure (with hooks removed) attached to a metal rod that moved horizontally across the front at the babies' nose height. The lure was colorful and attractive to them. Two TV cameras recorded two views of their movements, as illustrated in Figure 4-12. Measurements were made on the video recordings at 100-millisecond intervals to provide the data for von Hofsten's many analyses.

Experimental conditions. Eight experimental conditions were observed for each child at each test session. The object was moved at three velocities of 3.4, 15, and 30 centimeters per second and was placed motionless in front of the baby. The object was varied to be 11 or 16 centimeters from the baby's eyes when directly in front. Thus, there were four velocities (including rest = 0 centimeters per second) and two distances. The object was started randomly from one side and then was moved horizontally back and forth until the baby grasped it. The object was moved back and forth until three reaches were made or until it had passed six times in front of the baby. The object was stopped in front of the baby at the end of each motion condition to let the baby reach for the object at rest.

Reaching. An elaborate system was used to classify the babies' movements as different types of reaching and nonreaching. If a movement was determined to be a reach,

**FIGURE
4-12**

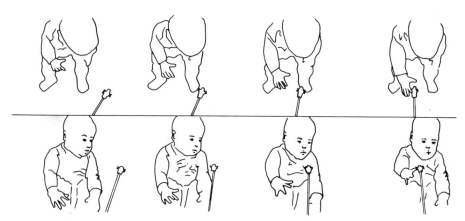

Two views of a successful reach of a moving object (30 cm/sec) by a baby at 21 weeks.
(Reproduced with permission from von Hofsten, 1980.)

whether or not successful in touching the object, it was included in the analyses of reaching movements. Nonreaching movements were judged as not directed to intercepting the object and were included in the analyses only to find the proportion of reaching efforts among the total of all movements.

Movement segments. Reaching movements were analyzed into units of movement which von Hofsten labeled as movement elements and we shall label as *movement segments.* An acceleration or deceleration within a single arm movement is called a movement segment. If the arm changes acceleration at a particular point in a movement pathway, this will indicate a change in the control messages that can be considered as initiating a new segment of the movement. A direct reach to a moving object might have only a single acceleration and be a single movement segment that crashes into the moving object. It is more likely that two movement segments are needed in an efficient and effective reach, first, to accelerate toward the moving object and, second, to decelerate when nearing the target. A number of accelerations and decelerations will be needed if steering a variable course toward the target. Von Hofsten used this idea of adjustments in velocity to mark the beginning and ending of movement segments within the total reaching movement. Velocity was derived from the distance traveled by the base of the index finger from one reading to the next of the two video recordings at 100-millisecond intervals. Acceleration was defined as the difference between two velocities.

Accuracy of movement. Separate movement segments were analyzed in relation to their direction of movement and the location of the moving target. One measure was a simple observation of whether or not the movement segment was moving away from the path of the moving object. A second measure was a comparison of the hand's movement direction with the best interception point. These measures were used to examine the baby's effort to move ahead of the moving object rather than directly to its current position.

reach and contact a stationary object. Both of these achievements indicate that babies at 4 months can see an object and can use that visual information to move their hand to contact or intercept it. We do not know what visual information is needed to specify the location and movement of an object, nor do we know how the motor control system uses that information to create a reaching movement that spatially and temporally will bring the hand to coincide with the object's location. The von Hofsten study demonstrates that babies can intercept a moving object at 4 months, which means that some aspects of intercepting a moving object are in place at an early age. Additional findings from the von Hofsten study

FIGURE
4-13

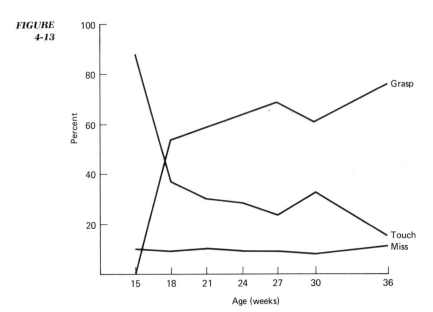

Percentage of total number of reaches which were miss, touch, or grasp.
(Reproduced with permission from von Hofsten and Lindhagen, 1979.)

suggest that the visual-perceptual aspects of interception are better developed at an early age than are the motor control aspects.

The graphs in Figures 4-14 and 4-15 trace changes with age in the length and duration of reaching movements as general indicators of reaching efficiency. Babies contacted the moving object in 90 percent of these reaching movements, and so we know that their interception efforts were successful. According to Figure 4-14, the younger babies moved their hands in a path that was approximately 3.5 times as far as the most direct path to intercept the target. They reduced the relative length of their movement path to 2.0 at 24 weeks and 1.5 at 36 weeks, and so they were moving more directly to the intercept point. An interrelated finding in Figure 4-15 is that it took them less time as they grew older. Von Hofsten noted that the reaching movements at 24 weeks were straighter and had fewer zig-zag and round-about movements. Also, there was less variability among the children as well as within their individual reaches. Notice that for both the relative length and the time of movement path, the reaching movements were more direct and took less time at the faster target velocities. The major finding, when all measurements in the von Hofsten reports are taken into account, is that babies can intercept a moving object at 15 to 18 weeks, even though their arm movements are not well controlled. Babies show considerable improvement in their control of arm movements by 24 weeks, with more refinements by 36 weeks.

Each reach was analyzed further to describe changes within the reaching movement. Hand velocities and accelerations were measured, as described in Box 4-2, to calculate the number of movement units or segments in each reaching movement. Reaching directly to the object should require fewer movement segments than should a movement path that has many changes in direction and velocity. As seen in Table 4-1, babies at 15 weeks made only 22 percent of their reaches with one or two movement segments, in comparison with 75 percent at 36 weeks of age. Von Hofsten also looked at each reach to isolate reaches with

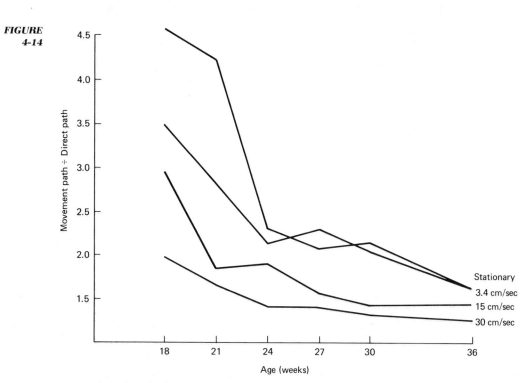

Mean relative length of movement path as a function of age for each velocity condition. (Reproduced with permission from von Hofsten, 1979.)

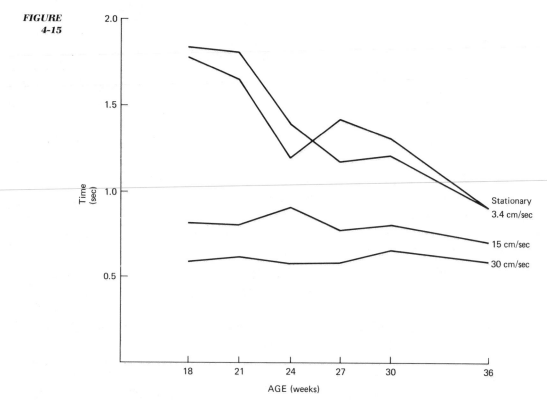

Mean time of reaching movements as a function of age for each velocity condition. (Reproduced with permission from von Hofsten, 1979.)

TABLE 4–1	Changes with Age in Reaching Movements[*]						
	AGE (WEEKS)						
	15	18	21	24	27	30	36
Percentage of reaches with only one or two movement segments	22	37	38	61	60	62	75
Percentage of reaches with one or more movement segments directed away from target trajectory	61	46	43	22	14	17	4

[*] Based on data from von Hofsten 1979.

one or more movement segments turned away from the target path. Babies at 15 weeks made 61 percent of their reaches with this type of inaccuracy, and at 36 weeks they reduced this figure to 4 percent. Using more elaborate analyses of duration and direction of each movement segment, von Hofsten showed that the first segments increased in time and accuracy toward the interception point, indicating a better initial control of the reaching movement. In summary, older babies could begin an accurate movement toward the interception point and needed only one additional adjustment to make the interception. They also arrived at the interception point ready to make the additional movements needed to grasp the object. Von Hofsten found in various analyses, too, that movement segments were directed ahead of the object, thus demonstrating that babies were aware of the need to "lead" the moving object.

The findings from the von Hofsten study indicate that the problem in interception for the younger babies is control of the arm. The babies at 15 weeks could intercept the moving object, even with an inefficient arm movement that did not take a direct path, and the babies at 36 weeks were quite efficient in following a direct path to the moving target. Von Hofsten made additional analyses of the hand's path and found considerable vertical changes at earlier ages. He suggested that the vertical changes may be a matter of imprecise adjustments to gravity while in motion and described the arm movements at younger ages as an instability in arm control.

Another of von Hofsten's observations is that babies, as shown in Figure 4-12, watched the moving object and did not look at their hand. This means that visual information can be used in the motor control system to produce an appropriate reaching movement without needing to watch the hand. That is, there is coordination at this early age between what the eye sees and what the hand does. Young babies watched only the target object rather than shifting their visual focus back and forth from object to hand. Babies may look back and forth when gathering information, but it was not necessary in the reaching movements observed by von Hofsten. This general observation needs replication, along with more detailed analyses of eye movements related to object and hand position.

Reaching generally was more accurate at faster speeds, as noted earlier in Figure 4-14 for relative length of movement path. Von Hofsten reported similar findings in other movement analyses. The shorter the time that is available to make the interception at faster object velocities, the less time there will be to take a longer-reaching path and adjust the reaching movement. But babies at the younger ages were able to intercept at higher velocities with only a slightly higher percentage of misses. It is possible that the two faster velocities of 15 and 30 centimeters per second forced them to respond more directly. Von Hofsten observed that babies in the 3.4 centimeters per second–condition sometimes touched the slow-moving object, as if playing with it, before they followed and grabbed it. Perhaps some of the movement adjustments at the lowest velocity and the stationary position were playful or exploratory approaches to an object that could be contacted when desired. It would be useful to separate the movement analyses to compare the differences between the two higher velocities, which require a more direct reaching movement, and the two slower conditions, which provide time for "fooling around." Our comments do not alter the general finding that young babies can intercept moving objects, but rather, they suggest a higher level of achievement at slower velocities to do more than is strictly required.

An additional consideration is whether babies reached for the moving object with the contralateral hand (opposite the side of the object's starting point) or the ipsilateral hand (nearest the object's starting point). Considering only the two faster velocities, the ipsilateral arm must be moved rapidly and directly to intercept the moving object before it gets away, to the extent that babies using an ipsilateral reach generally had to chase the moving object. More time is available when using the contralateral limb, and the hand needs only to come forward to be ahead of the moving object (see Figure 4-12). Von Hofsten reported that 82 percent of the reaches were contralateral at 30 centimeters per second and were 64 percent and 40 percent, respectively, at 15 centimeters and 3.4 centimeters per second. These percentages did not change appreciably across age or within test sessions. Young babies apparently recognize that they need to use a reaching movement that will provide more time to intercept the object. Von Hofsten also noted that babies seemed to prefer one arm to use in reaching, which means that they had to let the object go past their face in order to get it in the desired position for a contralateral reach with the preferred hand. All of this argues that young babies are quite developed in many of the basic aspects of reaching and interception.

Later Development of Interception. Many movement situations involve moving a limb, usually an arm or hand, to intercept a moving object. This is done directly to intercept a moving object and indirectly to propel an object, such as a ball, at a moving target. A study done many years ago by Hicks (1930) examined the improvement of younger children, ages 3, 4, 5, and 6, in throwing at a moving target and is useful in analyzing movement problems to be resolved. A large circular target (48 inches in diameter) was rolled along a trackway. The center of the target was adjusted to the shoulder height of the child, who stood 5 feet away from the center of the trackway. The target moved slowly at 3 feet per second down the 8-foot trackway. The child was told to throw a small ball (2.25 inches in diameter) at the green center (7 inches in diameter), which made a noise when hit. Each throw was scored as the number of inches away from the center. Hicks was interested in the practice effects over an 8-week period, but the gains were small and were not significant when compared with a control group. We shall describe the control group's performance to indicate changes with age in throwing accuracy.

Hicks found a large increase in throwing accuracy, with the 3-year-olds having a mean absolute error (AE) of 18 inches off center, compared with 8 inches for the 6-year-olds. Variability in standard deviation was similar for the three younger groups, whereas that for the 6-year-olds was much less. The findings are limited by the control group's small size (N = 30) and the lack of more sophisticated statistical analyses. But there was a distinct increase in throwing accurately at a moving target during these early years.

Children stood opposite the center of the trackway with the target center 48 inches away. They had ample time of approximately 1.3 seconds to throw before the target center arrived directly in front of them. Hicks found that rather than wait until the target was in front of them, the children threw when it had traveled approximately one-half of the distance to the middle of the trackway. They tended to throw ahead of the target, and so two-thirds of the throws hit left of center. But the target was moving quite slowly and 96 percent of the throws were right-handed to a target coming from the right and often at an angle to the right. Different target locations and directions at faster speeds might present different interception problems relative to leading or throwing ahead of a moving target.

Another interesting finding was that 88 percent of the throws were overhand, wheres an underhand throw or lob might be more successful for this type of reasonably simple accuracy throw. Approximately two-thirds of the throws were low on the target, which indicates that the children held the ball too long before releasing it.

A study by Bard, et al. (1981) offers some descriptive information about other aspects of spatial and temporal accuracy when throwing at a target. Children, ages 6 to 11, stood 2 meters away from a target apparatus that produced a stationary or a moving target (coming from right or left and traveling 75 or 150 centimeters per second). Spatial and temporal accuracy were measured for three test conditions: (1) throwing at a stationary target, (2) pressing a button to intercept a moving light at a designated point, and (3) throwing at a moving target. As expected, the children were spatially more accurate when throwing at a stationary target (Figure 4-16, Test 1), but their mean performance in throwing at a moving target (Test 3) was only slightly worse. The pattern of mean improvement with age was also strikingly similar for both target conditions. The temporal error for intercepting a moving target (Figure 4-17) was markedly less for pressing a button (Test 2) than for throwing (Test 3). The overall findings illustrate the need to look at different aspects of coincidence timing. Children at all ages were more accurate in knowing when a moving object was nearing a given location (button pressing), but they were not much less spatially accurate in throwing at a moving target than at a stationary target. Throwing in either target condition involves spatial and temporal requirements not present in button pressing.

The findings from the studies of Hicks (1930) and Bard and colleagues (1981) confirm our general expectation that children improve in the temporal accuracy required to intercept moving objects. We now need to examine temporal accuracy in relation to different kinds and levels of requirements, such as the speed and location of the mover and moving targets. We also need to measure components of the movement and its outcomes, such as the time and speed of movement release and the relationship of those spatial and temporal errors around the point of interception. The existing data are limited, but we shall present several studies to show the current approaches to some of these questions.

Two common laboratory tasks in which a moving object must be intercepted are described in Box 4-3 as part of the description of two studies. One task is pushing a metal doughnut down a rod to intercept and knock down a cartoon figure moving at right angles to the rod (Wade 1980). The other task is intercepting

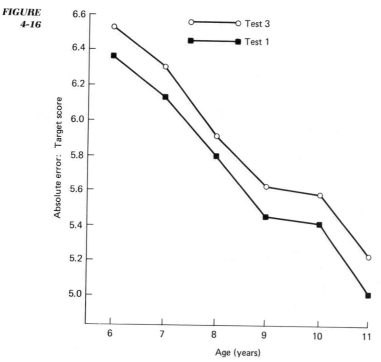

FIGURE
4-16

*Spatial error when throwing in Test 1 (stationary target) and Test 3
(moving target).* (Redrawn from graphic data reported by Bard,
Fleury, Carriere, and Bellec, 1981.)

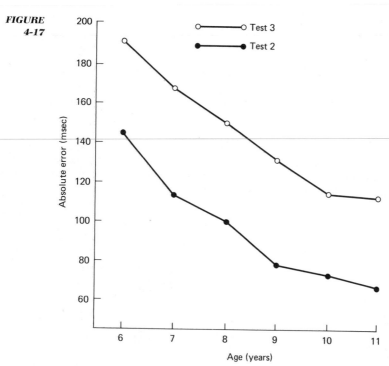

FIGURE
4-17

*Temporal error for interception of a moving target in Test 2 (button
press) and Test 3 (throwing).* (Redrawn from graphic data reported by
Bard, Fleury, Carriere, and Bellec, 1981.)

BOX
4-3

INTERCEPTION OF A MOVING TARGET

Dorfman (1977) and Wade (1980) both measured children's coincidence-timing accuracy, but in two quite different ways. Dorfman had his subjects move their hand to an interception point, whereas Wade had his subjects propel an object to an interception point. Each study also included a test condition in which vision was limited. But we shall not be concerned with the findings from the limited vision conditions until we examine the role of vision in movement development in Chapter 11.

DORFMAN STUDY

Dorfman has an interesting discussion of timing and anticipation in movement skill execution that is worth reading.

Subjects were 20 males and 20 females in each of 6 age groups (6 to 7, 8 to 9, 10 to 11, 12 to 13, 14 to 15, and 18 to 19; total N = 240). An oscilloscope was used to project a moving target dot that the subject tried to intercept ("hit") by moving a slide to control the movement of a cursor dot. The apparatus was similar to an electronic or TV-screen game. The target dot traveled vertically from the top left of the oscilloscope at a constant velocity of 10.88 centimeters per second, with a total travel time of 700 milliseconds from start to intercept point. The cursor dot, controlled by the subject, moved horizontally. The spatial relationship between the target and the cursor dots remained constant, but the starting points of the target dots were shifted slightly to change the interception coordinates. The time to intercept (700 milliseconds) remained constant, as did the distance to intercept, but the location (coordinates) of the intercept on the oscilloscope changed.

Each subject had 60 trials. When the target dot reached the intercept point, the display was "frozen" to indicate the *relative* position of the target dot and cursor dot. For trials 41 to 60, the target dot was masked or blocked out after 90 milliseconds (1 centimeter of travel distance on the oscilloscope). The subject then had to move the cursor dot to intercept without a visual reference (610 milliseconds without sight of target dot).

WADE STUDY

Wade was concerned primarily with errors of anticipation in spatial-temporal accuracy as a possible difference between normal and retarded children. He reported two experiments to examine separately the variations in target speed (Experiment 1) and length of viewing time (Experiment 2). We are concerned here only with the performance of the normal children.

Subjects in experiment 1 were 41 normal children selected from 3 age groups (ages 7 to 9, 9.5 to 11.5, and 12 to 14) and 41 retarded children matched by chronological age. For experiment 2, 39 different normal children were selected from the 3 age groups and were matched by chronological age with 39 different retarded children. The task was like a shooting gallery in an amusement park with children pushing an aluminum doughnut down a steel rod mounted at right angles to a trackway. The target was a cartoon figure which moved from right to left on a 5-foot trackway (152.4 cm).

Each child in both experiments was given ninety trials. Three target speeds were used in Experiment 1: 1 foot per second (30.5 centimeters per second), 3 feet per second (91.4 centimeters per second), and 5 feet per second (152.4 centimeters per second). This provided three viewing times of 5.0, 1.7, and 1.0 seconds. Thirty trials were given at each target speed, and the order of the target speed presentations was counterbalanced over subjects within each group. Experiment 2 involved only the middle target speed of 3 feet per second, with the viewing time controlled by blocking one-third of the trackway (1.27 seconds of viewing time) or two-thirds of the trackway (.63 seconds of viewing time). Forty-five trials were given at each viewing condition, and the order of presentation was random. The two experiments made several manipulations of the target speed and the viewing time, with different children as subjects in the two experiments.

COMMENTS

The interception task in the two studies is similar: making a quick and probably a ballistic movement to intercept the moving target. Little adjustment, if any, can be made in the movement once either the aluminum doughnut or the hand lever has been pushed. The movements are different, as the Wade movement propelled an object to intercept and the Dorfman movement moved the limb to intercept. Both tasks include important aspects of everyday movement situations, such as throwing a ball to a moving partner or using a hand to intercept and catch a ball thrown by someone else.

Spatial accuracy was minimized in the Dorfman and Wade tasks by fixing the paths of the moving target and the interception object or hand. This arrangement enabled temporal accuracy requirements to be studied without the intrusion of many spatial accuracy requirements. But other studies are needed to examine the interplay of spatial and accuracy demands and will require different movement tasks and different measurements to determine spatial and temporal adjustments in the initiation and execution of interception movements. *Adjustments in interception movements* can be used to indicate the *nature of adjustments* in the underlying motor control system. The study described next in Box 4-4 shows some measurements of adjustments in interception movements, also in a task with few spatial accuracy demands.

An interesting feature of the Dorfman task is that it is not a direct interception of a moving object. The hand guides a lever that move a dot on a screen, rather than the hand directly intercepting a moving object, as when catching a ball. The distance moved by the lever in this type of task often is not the same distance moved by the guided dot, although there usually is a proportional relationship, such as Dorfman's four units of lever distance for one unit of guided dot distance. Another potential influence on performance is added when a translation intervenes between the movement of the hand and the movement of the guided dot. Younger children may have difficulty with this translation, however it is accomplished. Also, there may be more difficulty in relating the hand movement to the movement of an object on a screen or in similar display modes.

The time available to intercept is a consideration that was nicely contrasted in the two studies. Interception in the Wade task was directly manipulated in Experiment 1, with the subjects needing to wait in all conditions before pushing the aluminum doughnut. Interception in the Dorfman task was fixed for 700 milliseconds from the appearance of the target dot on the oscilloscope. Younger children's reaction time generally is 300 or more milliseconds, compared with 200 milliseconds for older children and adults (see the reaction time data in Chapter 5). This means that very little time was available, particularly for younger children, to accelerate the lever and make an adjustment. It was difficult in the Dorfman task to arrive much ahead of the target dot, and so a useful strategy might be to go as fast as possible. Thus, the interception task must test the ability to control movement speed in relation to target speed. If the target dot moves too quickly, the subjects must proceed as fast as they can; if the target moves too slowly the subjects can move near the interception point and wait for the target to arrive. Neither of these extreme target speeds is a useful test of the ability to intercept a moving target, and it is not clear whether the time constraints in the Dorfman task were a useful test of ability to intercept a moving target, as the subjects may have needed only to move as quickly as possible.

Our discussion is intended to point up important methodological considerations in studying coincidence timing. Any study will have limitations because its conditions are arranged to study only one or two aspects, while minimizing the other aspects influence. This means that a series of studies is needed to study the many considerations we can identify in coincidence timing. We have suggested that time constraints are important, that movement adjustments need to be measured, and that both spatial and temporal requirements must be examined. Another consideration is to measure separately the ability to read the spatial-temporal cues in the movement environment and the ability to use the spatial-temporal information to move appropriately.

a moving dot on an oscilloscope, by moving a handle that controls a cursor or an interceptor dot, somewhat like a TV game (Dorfman 1977). The two tasks are essentially ballistic, as a single movement is made to propel an object or move a handle to intercept a moving target. Movement direction is fixed in both situations because the doughnut is fixed on the rod and the lever moves horizontally in a fixed position. Spatial accuracy requirements have been minimized in order to focus on temporal accuracy.

The general finding for the two studies was a steady decrease in interception error as the children grew older. From ages 6 to 9, the boys were better than the girls in the Dorfman study; Wade did not report boy-girl comparisons. Children of all ages in both studies improved their performance with practice, as noted by a decrease across trials in both absolute error and variable error.

Wade found that younger children were quite early in intercepting the moving target, in contrast with older children, who were late. The children in the Wade study had to wait from 1 to 5 seconds, depending on the speed of the target, before pushing the metal doughnut. The younger children pushed too soon, as if they pushed when they first saw the target move. But the older children waited too long to push, waiting until the target was at the interception point before they pushed, without recognizing how much they needed to lead the target. Dorfman reported that all of the children were late, with the older children being less late or closer to intercepting the target, which took 700 milliseconds to travel to the interception point. The mean reaction time to start moving the lever after seeing the target dot first appear is 300 or more milliseconds for the younger children, in contrast with 200 milliseconds for the older children and adults (see the reaction time data in Chapter 5). It seems likely that the children in the Dorfman study were late to the interception point because they did not have enough time to catch up with the target dot, whereas the children in the Wade study had to delay their response until the target was approaching the interception point. The conditions in the Wade study provide a better test of whether or not children are early or late in arriving at the interception point.

The target's speed was varied by Wade, with the expectation that the slower speed of 1 foot per second, which provided 5 seconds of viewing time, would be the easier task and would produce smaller errors and less variable performance than would the faster speeds of 3 feet per second (1.7 seconds of viewing time) and 5 feet per second (1 second of viewing time). But the children were less accurate and more variable at the slower target speed, with their performance generally better at the middle target speed. Wade speculated that there may be an *optimal target speed* for children in a coincidence-interception situation, that slower or faster target speeds may not match as well with their perceptual abilities. A developmental possibility is that there may be a shift in the optimal target speed for coincidence-interception functioning and/or a widening of the range of optimal target speeds.

A recent study by Shea, et al. (1982) supports an optimal or desired speed of moving targets. They also measured changes in the speed of the intercepting limb during the interception task in order to describe differences in adjusting the limb to the target speed. The apparatus and experimental conditions are described in Box 4-4. The task was to move the right hand to the left to follow a moving light path and to arrive at the end of the pathway simultaneously with the moving light, which traveled at six different speeds selected at random. The light path did not start moving until the hand moved in the direction of the end point, which eliminated the movers' need to respond to a starting signal. After the hand and light were moving, adjustments needed to be made during the movement to have the arrival of the hand at the end point coincide with the arrival of the light. Spatial accuracy demands in this type of task are minimal because the hand moves in a general direction without changing and the end point is not precise.

132

**BOX
4-4**

ANALYSES OF MOVEMENT SEGMENTS IN A COINCIDENCE-TIMING TASK

Shea and his associates (1982) looked at the accuracy of coincidence timing in relation to the time available to process information. The target speed was varied in order to manipulate the processing time, with the general and expected finding that adults and older children needed less processing time. Shea and his associates made some interesting analyses of arm movement changes that are useful in looking at changes in movement control.

Three groups of 15 subjects each were tested (ages 5 and 9, and college freshmen; no designation of sex). The subjects faced a table with their right hand on a microswitch start button. A Bassin stimulus runway (Lafayette Instruments 50575-R) was positioned parallel to the edge of the table to define a movement pathway from the start button to a small end-point barrier (68.4 centimeters from the start button). When a subject moved the right hand off the start button, the lights on the Bassin stimulus runway were activated to create a light path moving from right to left and ending at the barrier. The subjects saw the light path moving from near their right hand to the barrier; their task was to contact the barrier when the light path arrived. Their arm movement continued beyond the barrier so that they were not trying to stop it. Note that the movement of the right hand initiated the movement of the light path, so as to eliminate the initial reaction time that would be needed if the subjects did not move until the light path was activated. After their initial movement, the subjects had to adjust their arm movement speed to the speed of the light path.

The light path was controlled to move at one of six velocities: 671, 894, 1,118, 1,341, 1,565, or 1,788 centimeters per second. The time durations for each velocity were, respectively, 1019, 765, 612, 510, 437, and 383 milliseconds. Each subject did trials at each light path velocity, for a total of sixty trials randomly presented. At the end of each trial, the subjects were told the direction and extent of their error.

Coincidence-timing accuracy was measured by the conventional method of milliseconds early or late to calculate the AE and CE scores. The velocities of the six segments of each arm movement also were measured, by placing photocell timers at five equidistant points along the light path. The hand's movement interrupted the first photocell at one-sixth of the distance from the start switch to the end barrier. The fifth photocell was placed at five-sixths of the total distance, and the end barrier was the sixth measurement point. The time taken to move from one point to the next was designated as the *segmental movement time.* This means that the smaller the segmental movement time is, the faster the movement will be and that the larger the segmental movement time is, the slower the movement time will be. Because the hand begins at rest on the start switch, the first segmental movement time naturally will be longer (slower). After the hand is in motion, adjustments must be made to match the light path velocity or somehow bring the hand and the light together at the end point. The segmental analyses provide a number of ways to find out when the adjustments are made and their extent. One disadvantage of the segmental analyses in this study is that the adjustments that occur during the segment are not identified. That is, we have only six data points, whereas additional data points might be useful for a more continuous look at the movement changes. This probably is not a serious disadvantage in this rather limited movement.

Also, the hand moves through the end point and does not grasp or catch an object.

Shea and his associates found the expected result that interception accuracy improved with age for the three test groups, who were 5-year-olds, 9-year-olds, and adults. Accuracy tended to decrease as velocity increased, presumably because the movers had less time to process the information required to determine the speed of the moving light and adjust the speed of their moving limb. The mean absolute error scores (AE) for each of the stimulus velocities are presented by age group in Figure 4-18. Notice that the AE increases for each group as the

FIGURE
4-18

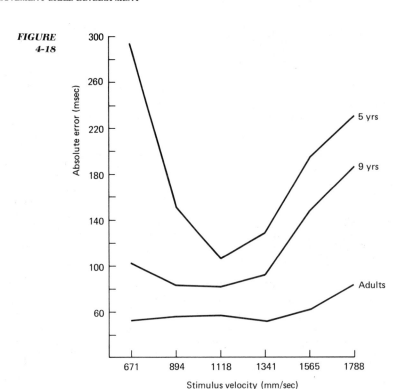

Mean absolute error at six stimulus velocities for three age groups.
(Reproduced with permission from Shea, Krampitz, Northam, and
Ashby, 1982.)

two higher velocities are encountered. The increase for adults is small, whereas
those for the two groups of children are larger and quite similar.

Notice also that the curve for the younger children is U-shaped and indicates
poorer accuracy at slower and higher velocities, with better accuracy at a moderate
velocity. This is the pattern of performance suggested by Wade—movers may be
better tuned to or more compatible with a particular range of target speeds. As
children develop, they may expand their compatability range to deal equally well
with many target speeds. This seems to be true for adults until the target speed
increases to a point at which there is not enough adjustment time, as seems to
occur with the fastest velocity in Figure 4-18. There is some indication that the
older children began to increase their error time at the lower range, which might
extend to a U-shaped curve if slower target velocities were included. There does
not seem to be an indication that the midpoint of the optimal range might shift
with age.

All of this has been speculation to indicate that target velocities need to be
considered as a possible influence on interception accuracy. One problem in
these findings is that the total traveling time, or processing time, was not kept
constant and was not sufficient in some test conditions. The seemingly optimal
target velocity for 5-year-olds in Figure 4-18 is 1,118 millimeters per second, which
is approximately 2.6 miles per hour. This is a very slow speed for target speeds
in everyday play-game activities. A more important consideration may be that
the light path moving at 2.6 miles per hour travels for only 612 milliseconds before
arriving at the end point, thus providing only 612 milliseconds for movers to

134

process the required information and make the required adjustments. Shea and his associates were interested in limiting processing time, and their manipulation of velocity and processing time suited their purpose. We now need to determine the extent to which children can achieve temporal accuracy at various target velocities without constraining their processing time.

The speed of hand movements was monitored in the Shea study by arranging photocell timers along the light pathway. The hand's movement interrupted the light beams of the photocell timers to measure the time between the six equal segments of the light pathway. In Figure 4-19, segmental movement times are plotted for each stimulus velocity by age groups. The 5-year-olds' segmental movement times decreased progressively from segment 1 through segment 3, which is an increase in the velocity of limb movement. Notice that the velocities during segments 1, 2, and 3 were the same for each of the moving light's six velocities. Beginning with segment 4, limb movement velocity was adjusted to be slower (more time) for the slowest stimulus velocity. The children in this age group accelerated their limb to its peak velocity at the midpoint (segment 3) of the light pathway and then slowed it, as if now recognizing the slow speed of the moving light and the need to lessen their own speed. It is interesting to note that the 5-year-olds arrived quite early for the slowest stimulus velocity. They made a correction to slow down after segment 3, but not soon enough or slow enough to let the moving light catch up.

A common pattern of adjustments was made by the 5-year-olds for the remaining five stimulus velocities. The limb continued to move in segment 4 at the same fast velocity reached in segment 3, followed by some minor adjustments in segments 5 and 6. These younger children arrived late at the interception point for the four faster stimulus velocities, which means that they should have moved their limb more quickly rather than more slowly. Limb speed was maintained and accelerated in segment 6 only for the fastest stimulus velocity. Approximately 460 milliseconds had elapsed by the end of segment 4, which did not leave much time for adjustments. As noted earlier, it would be useful to observe the adjustments at these faster velocities over a longer pathway that provided more processing time to make them.

The 9-year-olds and the adults both made an initial adjustment during segment 3 and a second adjustment during segment 6, which is an increase in velocity after a leveling or slowing of velocities during segments 3, 4, and 5. Both of these groups used the same starting strategy that the 5-year-olds did of accelerating at a similar rate and then adjusting to the velocity of the moving light. Only 250 milliseconds elapsed before the adults initiated an adjustment during segment 3, compared with 310 milliseconds for the 9-year-olds. This indicates a general improvement in processing time, particularly between ages 5 and 9, as the 5-year-olds required 460 milliseconds before making an adjustment. The second adjustment by the 9-year-olds during segment 6 further indicates a similarity in processing speed between the older children and the adults. The adults, however, appeared to have better control of adjustments, as seen from their smoother and more consistent changes between change points.

Measuring the adjustments in hand control is one way to monitor and analyze the control of hand movements during interception tasks. A movement strategy was observed in accelerating the limb at a similar rate until it could be adjusted to the velocity of the moving light. Older children and adults have a similar pattern of adjustment, which may be controlled by adults more consistently. Younger

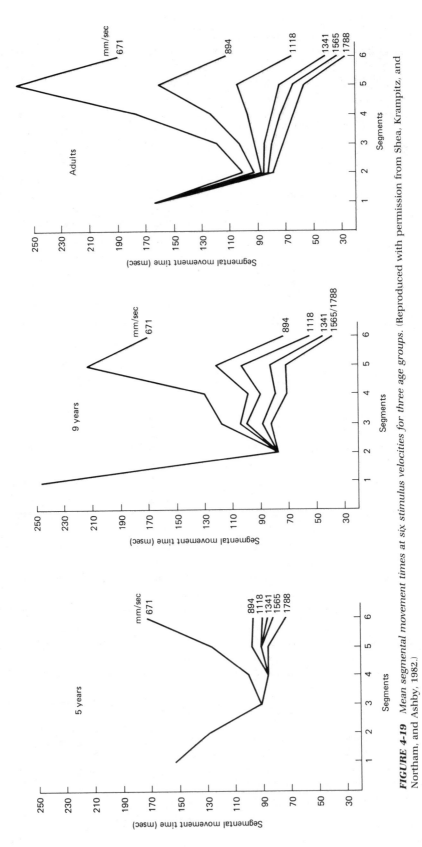

FIGURE 4-19 Mean segmental movement times at six stimulus velocities for three age groups. (Reproduced with permission from Shea, Krampitz, and Northam, and Ashby, 1982.)

children take much more time to adjust, as might be expected, and the time constraints somewhat limit their opportunity to make a second adjustment. Changes in time constraints and modifications to measure acceleration at more points along the pathway would help us understand the adjustments that younger children can make and the precision of their control. Interception conditions could also be changed to examine changes in the positions of the mover and the moving target for alterations in the target pathway and in the interception approach. Spatial accuracy could be included, as well.

Continuous Matching. A continuous matching, or a coincidence of the hand and the moving target rather than a single interception of a moving target, is our second type of coincidence timing. Although many everyday movements require a more continuous matching of self-movement with the moving of others, we have very little descriptive information for movement tasks of this nature. The pursuit rotor apparatus has been used some with children and provides the only empirical results we can offer. This apparatus requires the continuous tracking of a moving target, whose path can be varied in speed and shape. The task is similar to trying to keep a finger above a particular location on a moving phonograph record. Time-on target (TOT) is a standard performance score, but other scores can be obtained to show when a person is on target, as a means of determining movement strategies. For example, a person unable to keep up with a fast-moving target may wait at one point on the path and score a few milliseconds as it goes by, rather than chase it around the path. Counts can be made to pinpoint where in the pathway a person is on target and the length of each on-target period.

The early study by Ammons, et al. (1955) demonstrates a consistent increase in TOT from age 9 to age 18. A rather fast speed of 60 revolutions per minute (1 per second) was used, and the percentage of time on target was less than 10 percent for younger children. Boys had a better mean TOT than girls did, with small differences at earlier ages compared to means which were more than double those of girls at ages 17 and 18. Girls peaked at age 15 and leveled off, whereas boys had a linear increase from age 9 to age 18. Children at all ages improved with practice.

Younger children, ages 5 to 10, have been tested with slower speeds of 15 to 45 revolutions per minute (Davol, et al. 1965, Davol and Breakell 1968, Horn 1975). Results from Davol and colleagues (1965) are summarized in Figure 4-20. TOT increased with age and was better for the slower speed of 33 revolutions per minute. College students tested at 33 revolutions per minute had a mean TOT of 530 seconds out of a possible 600 seconds, compared with third-grade children (approximately age 8) who had a mean TOT of less than 60 seconds.

The inability of younger children to stay on target for even 10 percent of the total test time of 600 seconds is a dramatic illustration of child-adult differences when continuously tracking a moving object. Adults approach 90 percent on an on-target time at a slower speed of 33 revolutions per minute. Target speed again raises the problem of time available to process the information needed to perform the task. We need to observe the performance of younger children at speeds that enable them to stay on target for a longer period of time. This would indicate the speeds that are within their range and whether certain speeds are more compatible with their movement capabilities. We also could analyze their movement components to identify their movement adjustments, from which we could infer

FIGURE
4-20

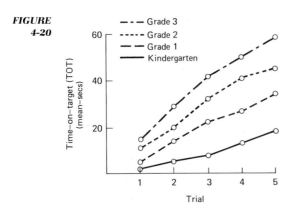
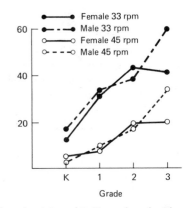

Rotary pursuit performance of children in kindergarten and grades 1, 2, and 3. (Reproduced with permission of authors and publisher from: Davol, S.H., Hastings, M.L., & Klein, D.A. Effect of age, sex, and speed of rotation on rotary pursuit performance by young children. PERCEPTUAL AND MOTOR SKILLS, 1965, 21, 351–357, Figures 2 and 3.)

something about their movement strategies. We presently know only that younger children do not do well in matching their movements to a continuously moving target, but we do not know at what level of speed they can function more adequately and how they try to stay on target.

Chapter Summary

Children before age 3 have limited success in open movement situations. But they are reasonably good by age 3 in moving in a stationary environment, as long as they have sufficient time to make movement alterations and the task does not require delicate force control and multiple movements. Fundamental achievements in more open movement situations are observed in many ways during the preschool and early school years. The outcomes are not at a high level of performance, but the first achievements are impressive because they subsequently become commonplace in open movement situations with very high levels of spatial-temporal requirements. The younger children in Williams's study (1973) could not accurately locate where and when the ball would come down, but they did run in the correct direction. Children in this time period begin to approximate what they later can do smoothly and seemingly effortlessly. This is an important time period because movement control in more open movement situations now becomes visible in ways that would be useful to study. Rudiments of this type of movement control are in place quite early, as noted in the von Hofsten reports (1979, 1980, von Hofsten and Lindhagen 1979). We need to look further at basic achievements of this kind and study the later appearance and refinement of movement control in fundamental achievements in more open movement situations. Unfortunately, we have very little descriptive information of any kind to use in documenting and analyzing these changes.

Improvement of movement control in open movement situations is striking during the elementary school years: even casual observations indicate the better performance of children ages 10 to 12 in comparison with that of children ages

5 to 7. Laboratory measurements confirm the magnitude of the improvement on different types of coincidence-timing tasks. Children continue to improve beyond these early school years, although we do not know when the maximal mean performance levels are achieved. Based on performance data presented next in Chapter 5, it is reasonable to guess that youths at age 14 are similar to adults in their mean performance levels in many open movement situations. The general picture is that there are very large improvements from ages 6 to 10 which continue at a slower rate to age 14, when mean performance levels approximate those of young adults. This statement applies only to open movement situations in which strength and endurance are not involved significantly.

Some gender differences have been reported that indicate that young girls keep time better and at a steadier pace. A similar finding was reported in Chapter 3 for young girls making repeated limb movements better than young boys did (Keogh 1968b), but we do not know whether these differences continue beyond the early school years. Younger and older boys are better on some coincidence-timing tasks in which children intercept a moving object or continuously match the position of a moving object. All of these findings regarding gender differences in open movement situations are tentative, because boy-girl comparisons are not reported in many studies, and we do not have the volume and variety of descriptive data needed to deal with this very broad issue.

Moving adequately in an open movement situation requires the mover to read the internal and external surrounds and to produce movements that relate to these readings. This is a general statement of the perspective we set forth in Chapter 1. In this chapter we indicated that young babies can read some movements in the physical environment and can respond adequately in some limited but clearly open movement situations, which means that the rudiments of movement control in open movement situations are in place at an early age.

We also described the difficulties that young children encounter in moving in open movement situations when they are rapid and continuous and involve multiple movements. They may be able to make the same movement if done in separate parts at their own rate, which would indicate that they can read their surrounds and respond adequately if the movement is simple and spatial-temporal accuracy does not need to be precise. As more movements need to be made simultaneously and continuously, their resources may not be adequate for coping with higher levels of spatial-temporal requirements. This reasoning points to an increase in processing requirements that children may not be able to handle. Movement situation conditions and related spatial-temporal requirements thus create a load to be handled by the internal processing systems. If the processing systems become overloaded and cannot carry out their functions, then they become a weak link in movement production. This occurs even when as adults we try to do too much in too little time. Therefore, one possibility for younger children is that their processing systems cannot function rapidly enough to handle the volume imposed upon them, which is a temporal constraint because a given amount must be processed in a specified time. Another possibility is that younger children's processsing systems cannot do some of the things required of them, even if given sufficient time. We noted difficulties in spatial relationships involving one's own position and in using movement to represent what is seen or imagined. These and similar difficulties may be inadequacies in sensory-perceptual development or in the translation of perceptions into movement.

An interesting developmental possibility is that there is an optimal target speed for coincidence-timing tasks. It seems reasonable that human systems are preadapted or biased to function better in certain types of environmental conditions, which include rate, intensity, and similar qualitative characteristics. Sensory-perceptual development has been studied in various ways to examine this issue, but not in relation to movement control.

B | DEVELOPMENT OF MAXIMAL PERFORMANCE

CHAPTER
5 | *Normative Comparisons*

Movement development beyond the early school years often is traced through normative performance data. Children, youths, and young adults have been tested in different movement tasks to establish norms and to make age-related and sex-related comparisons. These comparisons provide general descriptions of change for movement tasks that require maximal performance in closed movement situations. The level of achievement for these movement tasks is influenced by strength and participation experiences, and thus we shall discuss them before examining the descriptions of normative change.

The ability to generate force is a basic requirement of most movement tasks in which the performer is asked to move as fast as possible or propel an object as far as possible. This involves the *effective use of strength* in a movement skill which is more than the strength registered on a dynamometer or demonstrated in lifting or holding a heavy object. The performer must summate and direct force effectively. Children can become better at these movement tasks if they have more strength to draw on and more skill to summate and direct it. Some children may have an advantage in producing force, in the structural and functional features of their biological makeup, such as size and muscle mass. Training also can greatly affect strength and force production.

The influence of *participation experiences* pertains to what individuals are allowed and encouraged to do, that is, the nature, extent, and quality of involvement in movement activities. Some quite young children may swim, and others may ride horses, ski, or participate in other sports. Some children may be very active, but not in organized movement activities, and others may not be active at all. Social values, as transmitted through family members, peers, and others, will influence what an individual does and the way it is done. Social influences may come directly through parental rules and guidelines and less directly but very powerfully through sex roles.

Our review of normative change is a description of age-related and sex-related changes. Age-related changes are related to age only through the agents of change functioning over a period of time: age is only the passage of time and not an agent of change.

We shall call sex-related differences *gender differences*, a term that should remind you that being female or male is only a designation, just as age represents only the passage of time. Normative gender differences often are found when comparing the mean performances of females and males on closed movement tasks requiring maximal force production. Biological differences following puberty provide males more potential for force production, and differences in participation experiences also favor males, who are encouraged and rewarded for maximal force production. Females, however, now have more opportunities and support for developing their potential in these movement tasks.

Normative performance data have been reported for a variety of movement tasks, but these tasks have not been grouped into categories or types. Our review of these data generally is arranged according to body movements and manual movements. Many of the data describe performance on several play-game and balancing skills; there are fewer normative data available detailing the diverse character of manual movements. Reaction time and strength are included, even though not within the general meaning of movement tasks or skills, because they are important to the production of speeded and forceful movements. Individual change for several play-game skills also is contrasted with the group patterns of change in normative analyses.

Play-Game Skills

The three play-game skills of jumping, running, and throwing are used to demonstrate performance changes with age and differences between boys and girls. Three general graphs show mean performance changes with age. The preparation of the three graphs, which combine the performance data from seven studies reported between 1960 and 1968, is described in Box 5-1. Jumping is reviewed in more detail because more performance data have been collected on the standing long jump than for any other play-game skill.

Jumping

Composite curves for the mean performance scores of boys and girls on the standing long jump are presented in Figure 5-1 for ages 7 through 17. The general patterns of change for boys and girls are similar to the composites of earlier studies prepared by Espenschade (1960). Data from several European studies and other American studies are summarized in Table 5-3 to demonstrate that *similar patterns of change for boys and girls across ages have been found in different regions and in different time periods.* Notice that the mean values reported for the boys, ages 7 through 17, in the major study by Clarke (1971) match almost exactly the composite mean values. The mean values are somewhat higher for the normative data reported for the California (1981) boys and girls, but the patterns of change are similar.

The mean values for the boys and girls in Figure 5-1 increase 3 to 5 inches per year from age 7 through age 11, and the boys jump 3 to 5 inches farther, on the average, than the girls do, at each age. Performance on the standing long jump improves steadily during these years, with the boys' mean values approximately 1 year ahead of the girls'. The pattern of change after age 11 is quite different. The girls' mean scores level off, whereas the boys' continue to increase until age

BOX
5-1

COMPOSITE PERFORMANCE CURVES

The seven studies listed in Table 5-1 were used to prepare composite performance curves for jumping, running, and throwing for a 10-year period from age 7 to age 17. Each data set involved the testing of a substantial number of children with well-defined and similar test procedures. The data sets were reported between 1960 and 1968, which eliminates the possibility of performance scores varying among data sets because the children were of different generations. Each data set included both boys and girls, because regional differences in mean performance scores are quite common for play-game skills. If a regional bias exists, so that the children from one region have higher or lower mean performance scores than do the children from another region, a composite will be biased by including only girls or only boys in one or more of the data sets. The composite mean scores used here to construct the performance curves for the three play-game skills may be biased by not being based on sets of national norms. But the composite performance curves generally represent the changes across age and the differences between boys and girls.

TABLE
5-1

Summary of Seven Data Sets Used to Prepare Composite Performance Curves

Study	Children	Tests and Related Information
Keogh 1965	1,171 Ages 5 to 11 Santa Monica (California)	12 tests: Run, throw, jump, hop, balance, grip strength; age-sex comparisons; summaries of performance data from related studies; measurement comments
Malina 1968	1,396 Ages 6 to 11 Philadelphia	7 tests: Run, throw, jump, strength; mixed longitudinal data
Peacock 1960	2,800 Ages 7 to 15 North Carolina	7 tests: Run, jump, throw, kick, grip strength
Washington 1965	2,100 Ages 6 to 12 Washington	5 tests: Run, jump, strength; normative data for state of Washington
AAHPER 1965	8,000 Ages 10 to 17 United States	7 tests: Run, jump, throw, strength; national normative data
California 1966	4,600 Ages 10 to 18 California	6 tests: Run, jump, throw, strength; normative data for State of California
Fleishman 1964	2,000 or more for each test Ages 13 to 18	14 tests to cover 9 factors; percentile norms and age-sex graphs

The three data sets reported by Keogh (1965), Malina (1968), and Peacock (1960) are the work of a single investigator conducting a study of age-related and sex-related differences. The other four data sets are normative reports in which large numbers of children were tested to prepare state or national norms. The normative reports used larger and more representative samples, and the single investigator's reports have the advantage of more direct and often personal control of data collection.

The composite curves were prepared by calculating a composite mean performance score for boys and girls at each age. The seven data sets and composite mean performance scores for jumping are listed in Table 5-2 to illustrate the general procedure. The data sets overlap at ages 10 and 11 to provide six mean or median scores for calculating a composite mean score. The calculation of a composite mean is only an approximation, because different numbers of children were tested in the different data sets, and the mean scores were averaged with the median scores. The approximations do, however, show the change. Notice that the patterns of change in each data set are quite similar, although at a higher or lower absolute level of performance within different data sets. This means that the boys and girls in one study may have jumped better or worse, but their pattern of change across age was similar to that of the boys and girls in the other studies.

TABLE 5-2

Composite Data for Standing Long Jump Performance (Inches)

Study	Data	Age (Years)										
		7	8	9	10	11	12	13	14	15	16	17
Boys												
Keogh 1965	Mean	49	55	57	61	67						
Malina 1968	Mean	46	50	54	56	59						
Peacock 1960	Mean	47	51	53	57	60	63	68	74	77		
Washington 1965	Mean	44	47	50	54	57	59					
AAHPER 1965	Median				60	62	66	70	76	81	85	87
California 1966	Mean				58	60	66	71	78	82	83	85
Fleishman 1964	Median							68	74	82	85	85
	Composite Mean	47	51	54	58	61	64	69	76	81	84	86
Girls												
Keogh 1965	Mean	49	50	53	57	62						
Malina 1968	Mean	43	47	50	52	56						
Peacock 1960	Mean	42	46	48	51	56	56	61	62	62		
Washington 1965	Mean	41	44	47	50	53	53					
AAHPER 1965	Median				55	58	60	60	63	64	64	65
California 1966	Mean				55	56	65	65	67	66	66	65
Fleishman 1964	Median							60	60	60	61	63
	Composite Mean	44	47	50	53	57	59	62	63	63	64	64

The composite for running was made according to the number of feet per second. Running time could not be used because the running distance varied from 30 to 50 yards, and there is a problem in converting to feet per second when dash distances are different, because children probably run at a different rate of speed during the start, middle, and finish of a dash. Again, the composite mean scores are adequate for general age and sex comparisons. The composite curves for throwing were based on six data sets, because throwing for distance was not included in the Washington (1965) test program.

15 and somewhat beyond. The mean difference between boys and girls increases from 3 inches at age 12 to 19 inches at age 15 and 22 inches at age 17. Individuals may continue to improve with intensive and specialized instruction, but the general performance differences for the age and sex groups will be the same. Male performance seems to level off at age 17: the jumping performance of young adult males (AAHPER 1965, Keogh et al. 1965) has been measured at the same mean level of the composite curve.

Another way to look at performance changes across ages is through the relative amount or percentage of change in a particular time period. Both boys and girls improve approximately 45 percent in their mean performance on the standing long jump during the 5-year period from age 7 to age 12. The curves for the boys and girls are parallel and increase at a similar rate, even though the boys have higher mean scores at each age. The percentages of change are quite different

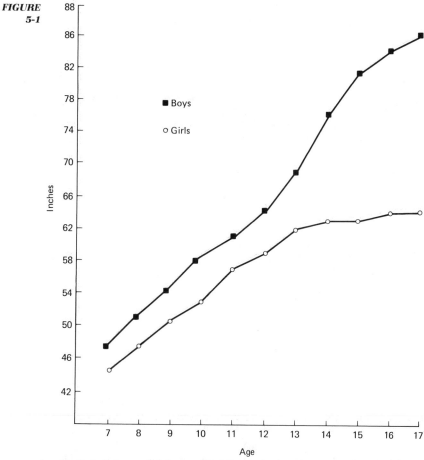

FIGURE 5-1

Standing long jump performance changes with age for boys and girls, ages 7 to 17, based on composite mean values in Table 5-2.

for the 10-year period from age 7 to age 17 when boys increase 83 percent and girls increase 49 percent. The percentages of change for the various play-game skills will also be compared for a general perspective of change across skills, as each skill differs in what might limit or enhance the relative amount of change over time.

Comparisons among mean performance scores sometimes may be misleading if we do not consider how much *overlap* exists among the groups being compared. Normative data from the California (1981) report were used to prepare Figure 5-2. Scores at the tenth, fiftieth, and ninetieth percentiles are plotted for boys and girls at ages 11, 13, 15, and 17. This provides the midpoint (median) and the general range for each age-sex group. According to the median scores, the boys improved markedly during this age period, whereas the girls leveled off. Notice that at age 11 and age 13 the boys had a higher median score than the girls did, but there was a considerable overlap of the two distributions at each age. This means that many girls at age 11 and age 13 jumped as far as the median distance for the boys of their age, with the reverse being true, that many boys did not jump as far as the median jump for the girls of their age. There is also a considerable overlap when comparing children between the two age groups. Many of the 11-year-olds jumped as far as the median distance of the 13-year-olds, even though the 13-year-olds had a higher median score. There is a minimal overlap between distributions when comparing 17-year-old boys with 17-year-old girls and 17-year-old boys with 11-year-old boys. We can say that most 17-year-old boys jumped farther than did most 17-year-old girls and most 11-year-old boys.

Graphic and tabular summaries describe group (mean/median) performance but do not indicate individuals' performances. The general expectations for ages 7 through 11 are that mean performance will increase steadily each year and that boys will have higher mean values than girls will at each age. However, some individuals at these ages perform more like children of the opposite sex or like children who are 1 or 2 years older or younger. The boys' mean performance continues to increase up to age 17, in contrast with the leveling off of the girls' mean performance. Few young women jump as far as do the young men of the same age. Few boys at age 11 jump as far as any young adult males do, whereas many girls at age 11 jump as far as the mean distance for young women.

Some performance data have been reported for young children doing the standing long jump, but it is questionable whether all young children try to jump as far as they can. A range of performance data is listed in Table 5-4, which is summarized here to show the improvement in several kinds of jumping tasks. Bayley (1935) had children jump from a step rather than from the ground, and they achieved a distance of 4 to 14 inches at 37 months and 24 to 33 inches at 48 months. Although the actual distance jumped is confounded by starting from a step, the children in the Bayley study improved their jumping distance by approximately 20 inches over 1 year. This is not unexpected, as a jump of 15 to 20 inches should be possible as soon as the basic takeoff is achieved with some amount of forward body lean. A more appropriate performance base line is a standing long jump on the ground. Children's mean jumping distance was measured as improving from 20 inches at age 3 to 43 inches at age 6 (Morris et al. 1982).

Jumping over objects to "high jump" is similar to jumping forward, except that the jumper must propel the body up and over rather than forward. Bayley (1935) reported that children were 41 months old before they could jump over a string 2 inches above the ground. A hurdle jump has been used as a jumping task in which the child stands in front of a high-jump bar or hurdle and tries to jump over it from a standing position with a two-footed takeoff (Keogh 1965). This is like making a standing long jump over a high-jump bar. Children at age 5 jumped 12 to 15 inches, which is approximately knee-high. This is considerable improvement in performance during the 2-year period during which Bayley first noticed their ability to make a high jump. The vertical jump, another kind of upward jump, has been analyzed for older children and young adults (Wickstrom 1977). The vertical jump is a jump straight up to touch or grab something, much as is done in rebounding a basketball or spiking a volleyball. Poe (1976) found that children at about 30 months could jump and touch a ballon held overhead but that individual differences were so great that it was meaningless to characterize the movement patterns of these young jumpers, who apparently found a number of ways to jump to touch an object. The same caution is needed in accepting younger children's performance scores as normative or representative, because the variations in testing conditions and in the children's motivational states make it difficult to obtain meaningful and consistent performance scores.

146

TABLE 5-3. Standing Long Jump Performance (Inches): Comparative Data for European and North American Children

STUDY	COUNTRY	7	8	9	10	11	12	13	14	15	16	17
Boys												
Composite (Table 5-2)	United States	47	51	54	58	61	64	69	76	81	84	86
Clarke 1971	United States	46	52	56	58	62	64	69	75	79	85	88
California 1971	United States				59	63	67	70	76	81	84	86
California 1981	United States				59	64	68	72	78	82	85	88
AAHPER 1975	United States				59	62	65	69	74	80	84	86
Canada 1966	Canada	44	48	52	54	58	60	64	70	74	79	82
Keogh 1966	England	42	46	48								
	Great Britain							71	75	79	83	
Stakionene*	Lithuania		46	52	57	60	64	67	71	80	83	87
Teply*	Czechoslovakia						60	63	64	71	76	81	84
Pieron*	Belgium							71	75	81	84	
Girls												
Composite (Table 5-2)	United States	44	47	50	53	57	59	62	63	63	64	64
California 1971	United States				56	59	62	65	65	65	65	66
California 1981	United States				56	60	64	66	66	67	67	67
AAHPER 1975	United States				56	59	60	63	64	65	63	65
Canada 1966	Canada	43	46	49	52	55	56	58	59	61	62	60
Stakionene*	Lithuania		46	47	52	56	60	63	65	69	69	69

* Second International Congress about the Physical Fitness of Youth, Prague, 1966.

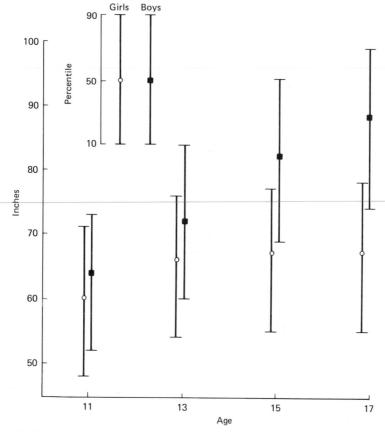

FIGURE 5-2

Distribution overlaps for standing long jump of boys and girls, ages 11, 13, 15, 17. (Drawn from data reported by California, 1981.)

147

TABLE
5-4

Age of Achievement for Several Types of Jumping Tasks

JUMPING TASK	AGE	STUDY
From a step of 30 cm (12 in.), jump a distance of		
10 to 35 cm (4 to 14 in.)	37 mos.	Bayley 1935
36 to 60 cm (14 to 24 in.)	39 mos.	
60 to 85 cm (24 to 33 in.)	48 mos.	
Standing long jump on the ground		
Mean = 51 cm (20 in.)	3 yrs.	Morris et al. 1982
69 cm (27 in.)	4 yrs.	
97 cm (38 in.)	5 yrs.	
109 cm (43 in.)	6 yrs.	
Mean = 89 cm (35 in.)	5 yrs.	Keogh 1965
107 cm (42 in.)	6 yrs.	
Jump over a string 5 cm (2 in.) high	41 mos.	Bayley 1935
Hurdle jump: Standing high jump		
Mean = 36 cm (14 in.)	5 yrs.	Keogh 1965
43 cm (17 in.)	6 yrs.	

Running

The speed of running a dash has been measured in a number of studies. Composite curves for the mean performance scores of boys and girls are presented in Figure 5-3 to cover ages 7 through 17. The length of the dashes varied from 30 to 50 yards. Times were reported in tenths of a second and have been converted to feet per second as a common basis for comparison. Children were timed from a standing start, which means that their initial reaction time and acceleration

FIGURE
5-3

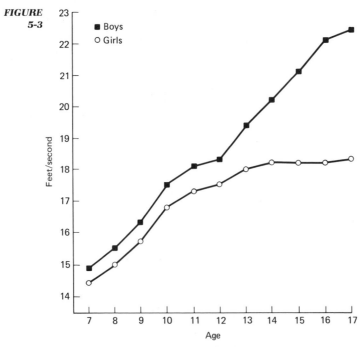

Performance changes with age on timed dashes for boys and girls, ages 7 to 17, based on composite mean values. (See Box 5-1.)

are included in these data. Some investigators, such as Glassow and Kruse (1960), used a running start to time runners from 5 yards beyond the starting line to the finish line. Although it is preferable to use a running start and eliminate initial reaction time and acceleration, a standing start was used in most studies. Mean performance data from different studies naturally cannot be meaningfully compared unless the same timing procedure is used.

The general patterns of change for the timed dashes are similar to those for the standing long jump. The increase up to ages 11 or 12 is essentially linear, followed by a leveling off for girls and a continuing increase for boys. Boys consistently have better mean performances than girls do up to ages 11 or 12, with a considerable overlap in distributions at each age. The mean difference between boys and girls at age 17 is sizable, with very little overlap in distributions. The composite means at age 17 are 22.0 feet per second for boys and 18.0 feet per second for girls. Transforming these figures to time for a 50-yard dash, the mean times at age 17 are 6.8 seconds for boys and 8.3 seconds for girls. The mean times for a 50-yard dash at age 11 are 8.3 for boys and 8.7 for girls. It is obvious that the mean times differences at age 11 are much smaller than those at age 17. Also, the mean time for boys at age 11 is the same as that for girls at age 17.

Both boys' and girls' performances increased 23 percent during the 5-year period from age 7 to age 12. Boys continued to improve and had an increase of 49 percent in the 10-year period from age 7 to 17, whereas girls had only a slight improvement beyond age 12. The change for both boys and girls averaged just less than 1 foot per second/per year from age 7 to age 12.

Throwing

The general skill of throwing has been measured most often as the distance that children can throw. There are many problems in obtaining distance scores that can be compared across studies because procedural differences can bias throwing performance. Procedural considerations are the size of the ball, style of throw (underhand or overhand), and starting position (stationary or running up to the throwing line). But the differences between age and sex groups are so large that the procedural differences do not affect the general pattern of change summarized in Figure 5-4. Boys begin at age 7 with a composite mean distance that is greater than the girls' and increases progressively to be more than double the girls' mean throwing distance at age 17. A similar pattern of change was reported in a summary of five studies of ball-throwing velocity by younger children, ages 4 to 7 (Roberton et al. 1979). Boys at age 4 had a greater mean throwing velocity and had greater yearly improvements. The overall patterns of change for boys and girls are similar to their jumping distance and running speed, in that boys increase until age 16 or 17, whereas girls level off at an earlier age. The patterns of change are different, as boy-girl differences became greater at each age, in contrast with a constant difference in the early years for jumping distance and running speed.

The percentage of change across ages is somewhat misleading for throwing distance, as boys begin at age 7 with a much larger mean score. Both boys and girls increase threefold in their mean throwing distance from age 5 to age 12. These proportional changes are very large compared with jumping distance and running speed. Girls as well as boys increase relatively more in throwing distance than in other skills. This probably indicates more learning and refinement of the throwing motion, as well as greater strength. Boys increase approximately 60 feet in throwing distance beyond age 12, whereas girls level off with a small mean

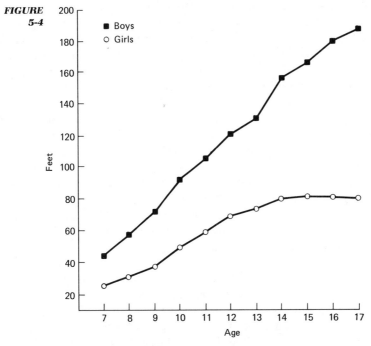

Performance changes with age in throwing for distance for boys and girls, ages 7 to 17, based on composite mean values. (See Box 5-1.)

increase of 10 to 15 feet. Group variability increases noticeably from early to later ages which indicates that some children have even greater increases with age than noted for their sex groups and that others have quite small increases.

Throwing skill also has been measured for accuracy, but test procedures vary so much that the data cannot be summarized across individual studies. The pattern of change cannot be described beyond the general statements that children improve with age in throwing accuracy and that boys generally are more accurate (Gardner 1979, Keogh 1965, Peacock 1960). One important limitation is that the distance to a target creates a strength problem for younger children, while being too close for older children. Another problem is that a large number of throws are needed to obtain a reliable estimate of an individual's level of performance.

Balancing

A variety of tasks have been used to measure balancing skill. Walking on a beam and maintaining a balanced position on a stabilometer are the two tasks that have been used most often and that we shall use to show the general patterns of change in balancing skills. Both tasks require maintaining equilibrium, first, while walking on a narrow path and, second, while standing on an unstable platform. No other tasks have been used often enough to compile a general picture of change during the 10-year period from age 7 to age 17.

Walking beams of different widths have been used to measure this type of balancing skill. Variations in test procedures have influenced performance scores. Children can walk better on walking beams with their shoes on than with them

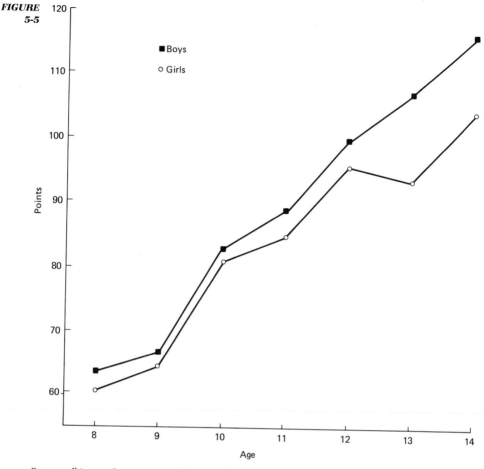

FIGURE 5-5

Beam walking performance as a function of age. (Drawn from data reported by Heath, 1949 and Goetzinger, 1961.)

off, and the task is less difficult when they take large steps rather than walk heel to toe. Additionally, there are no standards for length of beams, number of trials, and scoring system. Data from the studies of Goetzinger (1961) and Heath (1949) are combined in Figure 5-5 to show the general change in beam walking from age 8 to age 14. The same beam widths and test procedures were used in both studies, and the results were similar in the two samples. Boys and girls had a similar pattern of improvement with age, except that girls' mean performance did not increase from age 12 to age 13. The overall pattern of change was uneven from year to year, with smaller mean increases from age 8 to age 9 and age 10 to age 11. Keogh (1965) also found a similar pattern of uneven change from age 5 to age 11. The mean differences between boys and girls were small in these studies, with the boys slightly better in Heath's and Goetzinger's studies and the girls slightly better in Keogh's study. The overlap between the distribution for boys and girls is large at all ages.

Using a stabilometer as a balancing task is described in Box 5-2. Figure 5-6 summarizes results from a study by Bachman (1961) for mean performance scores of boys and girls on the stabilometer at 2-year intervals from age 7 to age 25.

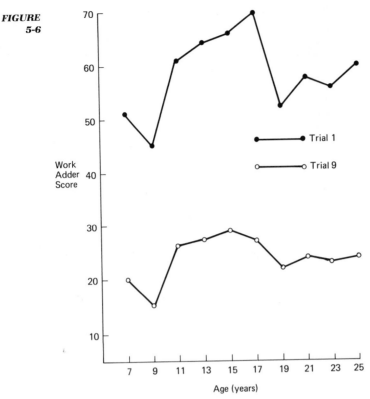

Stabilometer performance for ages 7 to 25. (Drawn from data reported by Bachman, 1961.)

Bachman tested eight boys and eight girls at each age from 6 to 26 and reported their mean scores for 2-year intervals, beginning with ages 6 and 7 and continuing to ages 24 and 25. Each 2-year group is identified in Figure 5-6 by the older age in the group, beginning with age 7 and continuing to age 25. Each person did ten trials. Work-adder mean scores were reported only for trial 1 and trial 9 and are plotted for boys and girls across ages in Figure 5-6.

Each age group improved markedly from trial 1 to trial 9. The grand mean score for all performers was approximately 60 on trial 1 and decreased to approximately 20 on trial 9. There were not significant gender differences in this overall improvement, and individuals of all ages improved their stabilometer performance in a small number of trials.

Bachman's more important finding is that the *mean performance tended to decrease as the children increased in age.* Balancing skill, as measured by performance on the stabilometer, did not improve with age, which is contrary to performance on walking beams and the play-game skills reviewed earlier in this chapter. Performance did improve with practice, as seen when comparing the mean performances of age-sex groups on trials 1 and 9. Older children, however, on both trials had larger mean scores or were no better than younger children. Although Bachman does note the older children's poorer performance, this contradictory and confusing finding has been accepted without comment in other reviews of movement development. The trend of lack of improvement in older children's stabilometer performance was replicated when Eckert and Rarick (1976) found no age and gender differences among children ages 7, 8, and 9. When testing only boys, Anooshian (1975) reported an increase in mean work-adder score from ages 6 to 9 and no difference from ages 9 to 12.

The older children's performance on the stabilometer probably is due to their heavier weight, because a heavier child will cause the platform to move more rapidly, thus creating a more difficult movement problem to resolve. This possibility is discussed in Box 5-2. Several lighter-weight children in the Anooshian study moved the platform to a horizontal position and stood for the remainder of the trial, looking around the room. Anooshian obtained a correlation of .36 for age and work-adder score, indicating that older children tend to have higher (poorer) work-adder scores. When weight was partialled (removed mathematically from the calculation), the correlation of age and work-adder score was − .51. This indicates that *older children tend to have lower (better) work-adder scores if their weight is held constant.* The task of maintaining an in-balance position on an unstable platform must be similar for each performer before age, sex, or other performer characteristics can be compared. Anooshian's analyses indicate that stabilometer performance improves with age, which seems reasonable, but we need performance data on a stabilometer adjusted for apparatus stiffness and performer weight to determine age-sex differences more completely.

Performance data for beam walking and stabilometer do not present a clear picture of the balancing skills of boys and girls from ages 7 to 17. It seems unlikely that balancing skills deteriorate or do not change during this 10-year period, as shown with existing stabilometer data. Performance on walking beams increases during this age range, which is a better general indicator of change in balancing skills. But performance data for walking beams are quite limited, whereas performance data for the stabilometer can be gathered in a variety of ways and can be separated to analyze *performance components.*

The scoring procedures and analyses that Anooshian (1975) used, as described in Box 5-2 and illustrated in Figure 5-8, indicate some of the possibilities. He was able to trace continuous changes in platform movement to demonstrate what each performer was doing, rather than being limited to a single outcome measure of amount of total board movement (work-adder score) or time in balance. Anooshian found two different *movement strategies* of (1) *quick alternations* in platform direction and (2) leg opposition for *braking* the platform's movement as it moved in one direction. Quick alternations is a movement strategy similar to the quick alternations of hand movements used to control a marble moving through a maze, as used by Elliott and Connolly (1974) and discussed in Chapter 3. Stability and control can be produced by keeping the platform in motion, whereas braking is an effort to achieve minimal movement by having the force in one leg counteract the force in the other. Wade and Newell (1972), using similar procedures and analyses, found another strategy in which performers seemed to be trying to keep the platform at an angle rather than having their feet at the same level. This could be to provide a discrepancy to work against rather than to bring the balance information to zero. We are limited at the moment by measurement problems in equating the levels of task difficulty, but analyses of performance components for the stabilometer are a promising source of developmental information.

BOX
5-2

STABILOMETER

The stabilometer is a test instrument devised by Henry (1956) and used extensively in learning studies with adults and to a lesser extent with children. A person stands on a platform resting across or suspended below an axle (see Figure 5-7). The suspended platform is the preferred version because a platform resting directly on the axle is very difficult to control and generally produces unreliable measures. The stabilometer's sensitivity can be altered by changing the suspension length and the friction component (at the suspension joints). A more stable platform and a less difficult movement task would be produced by increasing the length of the suspension (Thomas et al. 1974) and increasing the friction component.

The task while standing on a stabilometer is to keep the platform from touching the side boards. The distance to the side boards determines the angle that the board can tilt before touching them. The angle of tilt generally is 10 degrees in each direction. Performance has been measured as time in balance (not touching a side board), number of contacts, and amount of platform movement (measured by a work adder). These scores are collected by wiring the apparatus to register the number and length of contacts and the movement about the suspension joint (word-adder score). Examples of stabilometer test procedures can be found in the studies of Ryan (1965), Singer (1965), and Welch and Henry (1971).

Work-adder and similar scores measure stabilometer performance as a single output score. Wade and Newell (1972) used a potentiometer attached to the suspension joint to monitor board position and to provide multiple measures of stabilometer performance (also see Newell and Wade 1974). They created the possibility of analyzing changes in performance components to identify movement strategies. As an example, when the platform was "in balance" (minimal platform movement), the platform often was at an angle and not level. Individuals seem to achieve a balanced or stationary position by placing one foot lower than the other, rather than having them even. Having a discrepancy to work against may be a way to gather more information and provide a better sense of being in balance.

Anooshian (1975) followed Wade's and Newell's idea of having the potentiometer output recorded on a polygraph. A sample of the graph output is presented in Figure 5-8. A trial begins with the platform resting on the side board under the performer's left leg. This is seen in M1 as a straight line at the top of the graph readout. When the

FIGURE
5-7

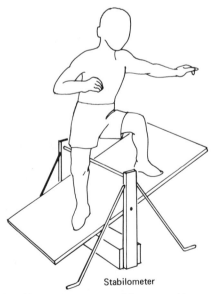

Stabilometer

Child in position on a stabilometer with right side (foot) in contact with support structure.

154

**FIGURE
5-8**

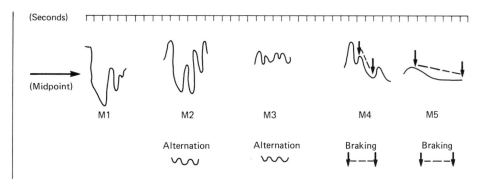

(Seconds)

(Midpoint)

M1   M2   M3   M4   M5

Alternation   Alternation   Braking   Braking

Examples of two movement strategies when trying to remain in balance. Board moves
to the right when line goes down and moves to the left when the line goes up. See Box
5-2 for further explanation of movement strategies.

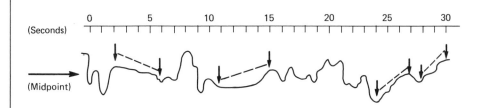

(Seconds)

(Midpoint)

Graph readout for 30 seconds of stabilometer performance : Note long breaking periods
(↓ - - -↓) from 3 to 6 seconds and 11 to 15 seconds, followed by slow alternations and
ending with 2 long breaking periods.

*Analysis of movement components and identification of two movement strategies during
stabilometer performance.* (Reproduced from Anooshian, 1975.)

board moves from the left contact toward the right contact, this is seen in M1 as a
downward movement of the pen. The change in board direction is recorded by a change
in pen direction. Anooshian found several types of board movement which are different
movement strategies to control the position of the platform. The first is an alternation
or oscillation strategy, as shown in M2 and M3, in which the board is moved back and
forth. Note that M2 is an alternation across the platform's balance point, whereas M3
is an alternation to the left of the balance point. M3 keeps the platform in the off-
balance position observed by Wade and Newell (1972) and clearly is in better control
than M2 is; yet both use a similar movement strategy of *alternation.*

The second movement strategy observed by Anooshian is called *braking* which is
an effort to slow down a movement in one direction rather than to change directions.
With the platform moving to the right, as shown in M4, the performer first changed
directions and then slowed or braked before changing positions again. A better example
of braking is shown in M5. The distinction between alternation and braking is that
alternation occurs within 1 second. If there is no change in direction in this time, the
platform will contact the side board unless some braking action is used. The Anooshian
procedures and analyses examine the components of stabilometer performance, and
a 30-second record is shown at the bottom of Figure 5-8 to illustrate alternation and
braking movement strategies.

The stabilometer can measure balancing performance, but its sensitivity must be
standarized before performance or learning results can be compared among different
studies. An important and overlooked point is the friction component at the suspension

joints. A stiff joint makes the platform quite stable and the task quite easy, and so the stabilometer should somehow be calibrated to various degrees of stiffness. The changes of stiffness then could be used as a treatment condition, or level of difficulty, at a known level of stiffness. The performer's weight also must be taken into account. A lighter performer will not displace the platform as rapidly as the heavier performer will and thus will not have the same movement problem to resolve. Therefore, the stiffness of the apparatus (length of suspension arms and friction component at the suspension joints) and the weight of the performer must be considered. Bachman's finding (1961), that *children decrease with age in performance on the stabilometer*, is not sensible and probably is a matter of older children's facing a more difficult movement problem because they weigh more. All stabilometer studies are confounded to some extent by the unequal task difficulty for individual performers. Descriptions of change with age are particularly confounded by the performer's weight.

Speed of Manual Movements

The speed of manual movements has been measured in various ways, ranging from the time needed to do specific tasks or skills, such as stringing beads or moving pegs, to the time needed to respond to single or multiple stimuli. We shall describe three patterns of change in the speed of manual movements: (1) specific movement tasks or skills requiring manipulation to sort or construct objects; (2) tapping a single digit or hand; and (3) reaction time and movement time in making a limited movement. This progression will take us from a broader look at speed in doing a movement task to a narrower view of limb movement speed.

Manipulation Tasks

Many manipulation tasks have been used to assess adults' potential to do industrial jobs. Tasks of this nature are also used to test the speed of children's manual movements. These tasks can be picking up an object and placing it in a container or on a peg and putting objects together to construct a larger unit. Objects are manipulated, rather than just held, and both unimanual and bimanual movements are included. Examples of these tasks are picking up matchsticks or pennies and placing them in a container, picking up washers and placing them on a peg, and stringing beads on a lace.

The speed of moving pegs from one row to another is described in Figure 5-9 for children from ages 3 to 15 (Annett 1970). These performance data illustrate a basic pattern of change seen in studies using similar tasks. Gains are larger during the earlier years, with quite small changes beyond age 10. The same negatively decelerating curve for children, ages 3 to 8, was reported for a composite score of moving pegs, placing toothpicks in a styrofoam ball, stringing beads, and tapping with one finger (Schulman et al. 1969). Other examples of performance data for manipulative tasks are the use of the Purdue Pegboard by Costa, Scarola, and Rapin (1964) and Gardner and Broman (1979) and a variety of tasks used by Keogh (1968a) and Stott, Moyes, and Henderson (1972). Sattler and Englehardt (1982) analyzed Gardner's and Broman's (1979) Purdue Pegboard data and found that the girls were significantly faster than the boys on 17 percent (15 of 88) of the comparisons covering different types of hand use across an age range of 5 to 16 years. Annett found no gender differences, and other studies have reported few sex differences. Small and occasionally significant differences have been found between boys and girls, but not consistently favoring one or the other.

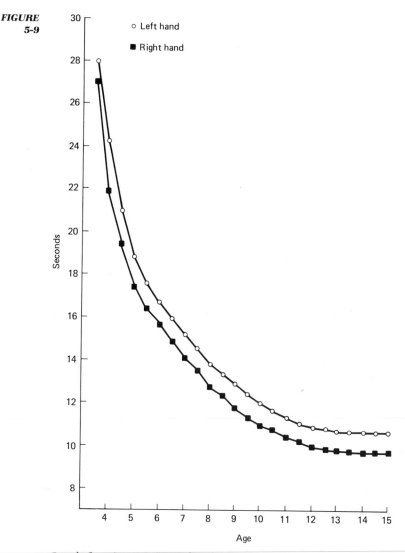

Speed of moving pegs. (Reproduced with permission from Annett, 1970.)

A limitation of most performance data is that a single score is obtained that represents total achievement without indicating how the performer produced the outcome. Connolly (1968) analyzed several performance components for children doing a peg task, similar to the one Annett used, to study change beyond the knowledge that children improve in speed as they grow older. Connolly had children, ages 6, 8, and 10, move twelve pegs from one row to a parallel row of twelve target holes 8 inches away, as shown in Box 5-3. Four sizes of target holes were used so that the task could be changed from having the peg just barely fit to having it fit easily. Connolly measured the total time to move the twelve pegs and also four component times: (1) grasp (2) carry, (3) release, and (4) return.

As expected from what we know from other studies, the older children were faster in overall time, and all of them were slower as the size of the target hole became smaller. Connolly looked beyond these findings to find out where the changes occurred within the four component times. Grasp time, as shown in

**BOX
5-3**

ANALYSIS OF PERFORMANCE COMPONENTS

In a paper on the processes underlying movement skill development, Connolly (1968) reported a study in which the components of performance scores were examined to find changes in movement skill development and to *infer changes in movement strategies*. The task was to transfer twelve pegs from one row to a parallel row of twelve target holes 8 inches away. This type of task is used quite often in studying adults' manual control peformance. Three groups of children (boys and girls ages 6, 8, and 10) were tested on four sizes of target holes (0.26, 0.36, 0.49, and 0.74 inches in diameter and always 0.25 inches deep), using pegs of 1.25 inches in length and 0.24 inches in diameter. A peg was a tight fit in the smallest target hole and was a loose fit in the largest hole. Each child was given three trials per day at each target size for 5 consecutive days, which is fifteen trials per target and sixty total trials.

A system of electrical circuits was arranged to measure automatically four *components of movement time.*

1. *Grasp time.* Time from when the peg was touched to when it was pulled away from contact with the positioning hole.
2. *Carry time.* Time from leaving the positioning hole to contact of the peg with the target hole.
3. *Release time.* Time from initial contact with the target hole to release of the peg in the target hole.
4. *Return time.* Time from release of the peg in the target hole to contact with the next peg to be transferred.

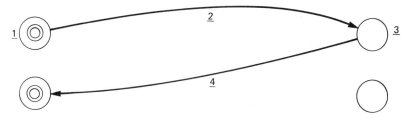

Each trial meant transferring twelve pegs, and so the score for each component was the sum of twelve movements. That is, if a child had a grasp time of 0.02 seconds for each peg, the total grasp time for the trial would be twelve times 0.02, or 0.24 seconds. The total performance time for each trial was the sum of grasp time, carry time, release time, and return time (see results in Figure 5-10).

Connolly suggests that the size of the target hole is part of a *perceptual load* that influences movement speed. A smaller target increases the spatial accuracy requirements in placing the peg in the target hole and is the more obvious meaning of an increase in perceptual load. An interesting finding is that there was a small but significant increase in the return time as the target hole *increased in size*. The children presumably were concerned that the peg in the larger target hole might fall over, and Connolly observed that they hesitated after placing it in the larger hole. Thus, we want to keep in mind that perceptual load might be influenced by many considerations, which in this case included "looking ahead" and "looking back."

Figure 5-10, was signficantly faster for 10-year-olds than for 8-year-olds, who were significantly faster than 6-year-olds. Grasp time did not change as the size of the target was changed. Connolly observed that the younger children sometimes readjusted their grip as if their initial effort was not adequate for carrying and releasing the peg. The faster grasp time for the older children indicates that manipulative skill in the form of digital dexterity helped them improve their performance speed.

Carrying time decreased with age and target size. There were no significant

158

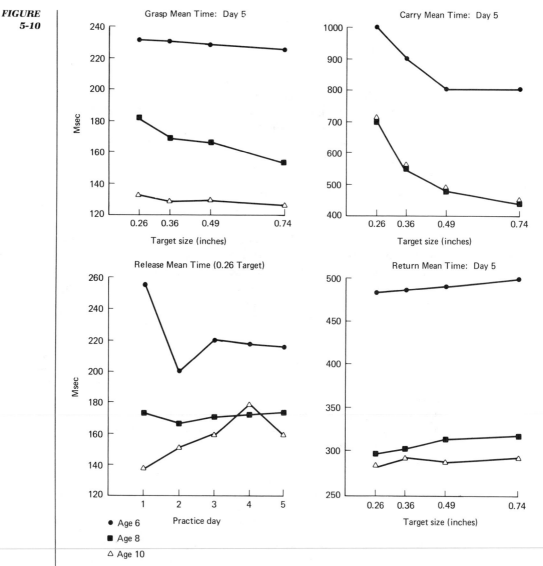

*FIGURE
5-10*

Performance component mean times for a peg-moving task. (Reproduced with permission from Connolly, 1968.)

differences between the 8- and 10-year-olds, who both had significantly lower mean scores than the 6-year-olds did. Connolly observed a "bombing" strategy by younger children, who lifted the peg up, moved it over the hole, and seemed to sight down to the hole. These were discrete movements, in contrast with Connolly's observation that older children made a more continuous movement in the form of an arc.

The release and return times are less clear-cut and are somewhat confusing. The older children were much better than the young children, with the 8-year and 10-year-olds often not significantly different from each other. But the release times were quite variable and did not change with target size or with practice. The return times increased slightly and significantly as the target size increased. The larger targets seemed to pose the problem that the peg might not stay in the hole. Connolly observed that children of all ages seemed to make an effort during release to make the peg stay and seemed to hesitate while returning, as if checking on the peg they just released.

Connolly also reported that individual release times were quite variable and that group mean comparisons were erratic across target and trial conditions. He observed children using different movement strategies for positioning the peg, such as coming in more vertically or approaching at an angle to hit the side of the hole and then straightening the peg. It is interesting that 10-year-olds increased their release times from day 1 to day 5, perhaps in trying different ways to resolve a difficult part of the movement task.

Connolly's component analyses and related observations suggest some ways to look beyond the total performance score. Three aspects of movement control seem to contribute to faster performance on a task of this nature. First, manipulative dexterity is part of some phases of the overall movement and probably improves with age. Second, movement speed may be a matter of how the movement is made, such as up and down or in a more direct arc to be less discrete and more continuous. Third, the task's perceptual requirements will determine how some phases of the movement are accomplished. The primary perceptual requirement for this task is the target hole, which can be of various sizes. This accuracy requirement seemed to affect release and return, as well as carrying.

Tapping speed

The speed of tapping is shown in Figure 5-11 as an average of the mean number of taps in 10 seconds for each hand and each foot (Knights and Moule 1967). The increase is reasonably linear in contrast with the speed of moving pegs (Annett 1970), in which there were larger increases for younger children and leveling off after age 10. No gender differences were found by Knights and Moule. The mean differences between hand and foot speed were significant, but quite small in size to favor hand speed. The correlations of speed of dominant hand and dominant foot for two different test sessions were .58 and .70. The slightly slower foot speed and moderately high correlation between foot and hand speed has been found in other studies of movement speed. Denckla (1973) measured digital speed in another way by having younger children, ages 5, 6, and 7, repeatedly touch their thumb to their index finger and successively touch each finger to their thumb. She found an increase in speed with age and found girls faster in successive finger-thumb touches. The pattern of change for tapping speed and digital speed is a steady increase to at least age 15, with a similar level of speed expected for arm and leg tapping.

Movement strategies were suggested by Connolly, Brown, and Bassett (1968) in a study of tapping speed. Children, ages 6, 8, and 10, tapped back and forth between two circles with a 1-inch radius and centers 5 inches apart. The girls tapped faster than the boys did, and the older children tapped faster than the younger children did. All of the children improved with practice, but the older children (ages 8 and 10) improved more than the younger children did. The children making the fewest taps were described as "wasting time" in two ways: they lifted their pencil in a high arc when moving between circles, and they tended to look from target to target in time with the pencil's movement (verified in a study by McCracken 1983; see Chapter 11). They seemed to treat the task as a series of discrete movements, whereas the children with the larger tapping scores

**FIGURE
5-11**

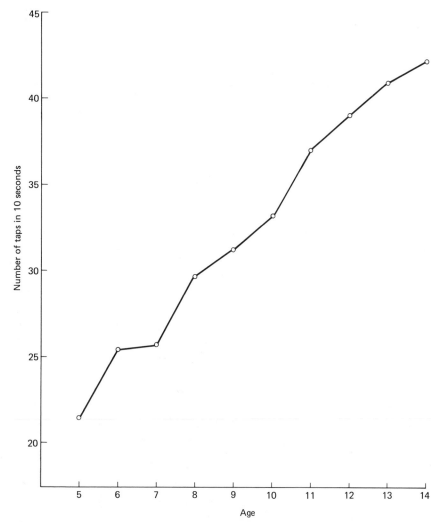

Mean number of taps in 10 seconds averaged across feet and hand movements. (Drawn from data reported by Knights and Moule, 1967.)

watched one circle and moved the pencil in a low arc. These observations are similar to those made by Connolly in the peg-moving task.

Reaction Time and Movement Time

Movement speed has been isolated to some extent from accuracy and other perceptual requirements by having individuals make simple movements in relation to a single stimulus. It is necessary to separate overall movement time into reaction time and movement time, which we have done in Figure 5-12. The total performance time to make a movement includes both the time needed to prepare for the movement and the time that the limb or body part actually is moving. The reaction time (RT) is the preparation time, and the movement time (MT) is when the movement first can be measured up until the movement task is completed. The total performance time is the sum of RT and MT.

Reaction time and movement time are usually measured by having a signal or

FIGURE
5-12

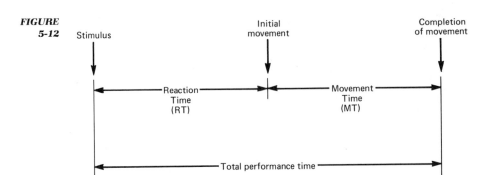

Division of total performance time into reaction time (RT) and movement time (MT).

stimulus indicate when an individual should make a movement. RT is the time from the signal's appearance to the initial movement, which often is lifting a finger off a key or switch. MT is the time from the movement's onset to its completion by reaching to touch a plate or turn a switch. An athletic example is when runners in a race are given a verbal signal of "go" or a visual signal of a hand dropped. RT is the time it takes to hear or see a signal and start the movement; MT is the time from a runner's first movement until the runner crosses the finish line. RT is an important part of the time for a short race, but not for a long race. RT is very important when driving a vehicle, as in how long it takes from the time that a driver sees another car or person until the foot starts to move to the brake pedal or starts to reverse the bike pedal to stop the bike. Analyses of RT and MT become quite complicated in ongoing activities, such as dribbling a ball while responding to what partners and opponents are doing, because the movement situation becomes a continuous series of reaction times and movement times.

RT and MT vary according to the task. Reaction time is called either *simple RT* or *choice RT*: simple RT is responding only to one signal, and choice RT means that one or more of several signals can appear. If a movement is to be made when a bell rings, simple RT will include both detecting the sound of the bell and initiating the movement. When several signals are possible, such as a move to the right when the blue light appears and a move to the left when the yellow light appears, choice RT means detection and initiation time plus discrimination and decision time. The performer must detect the signal, discriminate whether it is blue or yellow, decide in which direction to move, and initiate the movement. RT will increase as more choices are involved, because more information must be processed.

Reaction time will increase as uncertainty increases. Uncertainty can be decreased by reducing the number of choices and making the choices more predictable. In many situations, we realize that signals appear in a predictable order, as when waiting for red, green, and yellow signal lights at an intersection. The lights appear in a particular order and with a set time spacing, as well as in time-order relationships with the signal lights on the nearby streets. When in a familiar situation, we know what is likely to come next, and so we can reduce the number of choices in order to create a simple reaction time situation. We do this by anticipating what will happen next. If we are wrong, we may cause a problem, as when walking down the street and stopping to let another person pass, who also stops to let us pass. RT is a function of uncertainty and how much information must be processed before the movement can be initiated.

Movement time will vary according to the movement task. If the movement must cover a long distance, MT quite naturally will be greater if the speed of the body part is the same for the shorter and the longer movement. The actual speed of the movement also depends on the degree of control required to make the movement. If more accuracy is required during the movement or as an end product, the movement speed will decrease and MT will increase. Tapping in a large square with a pencil can be done more rapidly and in less time than can tapping in a small square or on a line. Movement speed when doing the same task can be increased as the mover becomes better at making the movement; thus MT is a function of distance and accuracy.

With this background, we shall look at performance changes with age for some limited movement situations. Although RT has been measured extensively with adults, there are not enough performance data available to compile a composite graph of changes with age for children. One problem is that girls have not been measured sufficiently to provide a stable picture of their performance changes. Selected data are listed in Table 5-5 to illustrate the mean values for simple RT that have been reported. Data from a recent study by Thomas, Gallagher, and Purvis (1981) are plotted in Figure 5-13 to show the general pattern of change.

Different investigators report different absolute values for young children, but the general pattern of change is a proportionately large decrease in simple RT during early childhood. The mean values for young adults in each of the studies, except Carron's (1971), are approximately 200 milliseconds. We can expect that children age 6 or younger will have a simple mean RT of 350 or more milliseconds. Surwillo (1971) reported a mean of 712 milliseconds for boys at age 4, with a consistent improvement to 231 milliseconds at age 16. He also summarized earlier studies which also reported a much larger simple mean RT for younger children compared with that for young adults.

Procedural differences in warning or alerting signals and the stimulus signal may explain some of the mean differences among the studies, but the *simple RT for young children is much greater than that for older children and young adults.* This is an important child-adult difference, because young children in many movement situations simply may not have enough time to respond and to process information in correcting and changing movements.

TABLE 5-5. Comparative Data for Simple Reaction Time Means (milliseconds)

STUDY	SEX	6	7	8	9	10	11	12	13	14	15	16	17	18	19	20 to 24	to 30
Hodgkins 1963*	Male	345						190				200				170	185
Hodgkins 1962	Female	343						222				225				203	214
Fulton and Hubbard 1975	Male				245		212		214		208		195				
	Female				235		218		214		200		202				
Henry 1961	Male			275				214						191		192	188
	Male			295				226						202		208	198
Carron 1971	Male			396			313			236			246				
Thomas et al. 1981	Male			370	330		288		249					200			
	Female			438	363		324		277					227			

* Estimated from a graph.

163

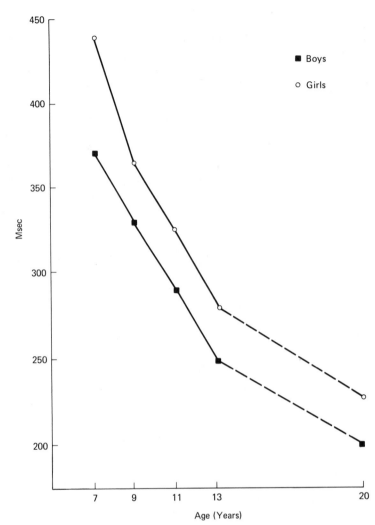

FIGURE
5-13

Simple reaction time means for boys and girls as a function of age.
(Reproduced with permission from Thomas, Gallagher, and Purvis, 1981.)

The pattern of change in Figure 5-13 shows a consistent gender difference, with boys approximately 2 years ahead of girls. However, Fulton and Hubbard (1975) did not find a gender difference from age 9 to age 17, and Hodgkins (1962, 1963) did not find a gender difference among young children. Standard deviations are large at earlier ages, which means that there is a great deal of overlap, even in the boy-girl differences reported by Thomas and colleagues (1981). Young adult males seem to have lower mean simple RT values than do young adult females, but the mean differences are only 10 to 30 milliseconds and are not important in most movement situations. Simple RT increases beyond age 30, with male-female differences disappearing by about age 60 (Hodgkins 1963).

The pattern of change described here for finger movements has been reported for the simple RT of other body parts (Birren and Botwinick 1955; Fulton and Hubbard 1975) which are only slightly slower than for finger and hand movements. Simple RT mean scores for retarded persons are much slower and more variable

(Baumeister and Kellas 1968). The mean scores for retarded adults are more like those for normal young children, and the standard deviations for retardates are three or four times larger. Choice RT was reported for ages 8 to 84 by Noble, Baker, and Jones (1964), who found the same pattern of change described here for simple RT. They found females as peaking in mean performance at age 16 and males at age 20. They also noticed an increase in choice RT beyond age 30, with male-female differences lessening to a point of convergence around age 60. In summary, both simple and choice RT improve greatly during the early years, followed by a gradual decline. Male-female differences exist in the early through middle adult years, but the differences are reasonably small in absolute value.

Movement time (MT) obviously improves substantially during the early and middle years of childhood, in that overall movement speed improves greatly during these years in making the manual movements reviewed earlier in this section. More direct evidence is given in several of the studies listed in Table 5-5, in which descriptions and analyses of MT scores were made in conjunction with RT scores (Fulton and Hubbard 1975, Henry 1961, Hodgkins 1962, 1963). It is not possible to be more specific about absolute and relative amounts of change in movement time because movement tasks are quite different and cannot be directly compared. Mean differences favoring males were noted in each of the studies, although without a clear indication of how early an age at which to expect significant male-female differences. Henry reported that the female mean MT was 22 percent slower than that for males when taken across the entire age range he tested.

RT and MT are not correlated in most movements (see Henry 1961), which means that a fast reactor is not necessarily a fast mover, and vice versa. This is an important point to consider when studying movement situations in which RT may be an important part of overall movement speed, such as stopping or turning a vehicle to avoid an accident. Although RT by definition is not movement, movement speed in many movement situations must be separated into RT and MT.

Strength

Strength is an important consideration when studying maximal performance. Early movement development is gaining control of the motor system to achieve a particular movement, and sufficient strength usually is available. The problem is to control the force that can be generated. Later development is generating and controlling the high levels of force needed to move faster and farther. Children's strength at older ages helps increase their levels of achievement, but it is difficult to relate strength to levels of achievement in particular movement skills. A high level of strength does not necessarily mean that it can be used effectively to produce a higher level of achievement.

Strength usually is measured with dynamometers and tensiometers to record the force output of isometric contractions. Individuals push or pull to exert force on a fixed plate or wire, such as squeezing a hand dynamometer or trying to extend a leg constrained by a wire. The force registered in the hand dynamometer or the tensiometer attached to the restraining wire is used to measure the strength of the muscle groups involved, by selecting a movement that uses these groups and by arranging to monitor the force changes. We need to remember that measuring muscle tension in this way does not indicate the extent to which a person can summate force to produce more functional strength in jumping, throwing, or similar movement tasks. Our summary of strength changes during the 10-year period from age 7 to age 17 is limited to isometric force production.

Grip and arm strength are summarized in Figure 5-14 for age and sex, based on testing 82 percent of the residents in Tecumseh, Michigan, between 1962 and 1965 (Montoye and Lamphiear 1977). Notice that the changes in *relative strength* and *absolute strength* (strength divided by body weight) were quite similar for arm and grip strength. For grip strength, boys initially had slightly higher absolute mean scores, with gender differences pronounced from age 14 onward. Men at age 20 had an absolute mean grip score that was more than twice the mean score for women. Mean grip strength scores relative to weight show the same difference between men and women, beginning at about age 14. The absolute scores for men were more variable by age 14, but there was very little overlap in distributions between men and women at age 20. These results are typical of other findings, except that the absolute values may differ from study to study depending on sample differences and instrument or test-procedure differences. The mean values for girls may be equal or slightly higher than those for boys for ages 9 to 11, as girls are entering puberty but boys are several years away from it. Greater mean

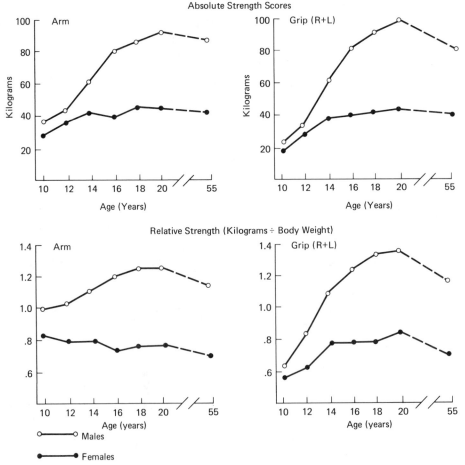

FIGURE 5-14

Absolute and relative strength of men and women in Tecumseh (Michigan) Study. (Drawn from tabular data reported by Montoye and Lamphier, 1977.)

strength scores also have been reported for newborn boys on measures of grip and a prone head reaction taken at approximately 30 hours after birth (Jacklin et al. 1981).

The most extensive study of strength in childhood was part of a longitudinal project conducted by Clarke (1971) in Medford, Oregon. The Medford Study was limited to boys and included a wide range of anthropometric and performance measures. The mean changes across age are summarized in Figure 5-15 for a cable-tension strength test that combines measures of shoulder flexion, shoulder inward rotation, hip flexion, knee extension, and ankle plantar flexion. The strength measures for younger boys were made at yearly intervals for 44 boys from age 7 to age 12 (Jordan 1966). The strength measures for older boys were taken at yearly intervals for 111 boys from age 12 to age 17 (Bailey 1968). The mean strength score more than doubled (132 percent) between age 7 and age 12 and then doubled (101 percent) again between age 12 and age 17, making an increase of 362 percent from age 7 to age 17. Similar proportional increases were reported for left grip and back lift (312 percent from age 8 to age 17) and for right grip strength (393 percent from age 7 to age 17).

Strength increases threefold to fourfold for boys in the 10-year period from age 7 to age 17. Although fewer data are available to describe strength changes for girls, they probably double their strength from age 7 to age 12 and have a sub-stantial increase beyond age 12. Males have higher mean strength scores, pre-

FIGURE 5-15

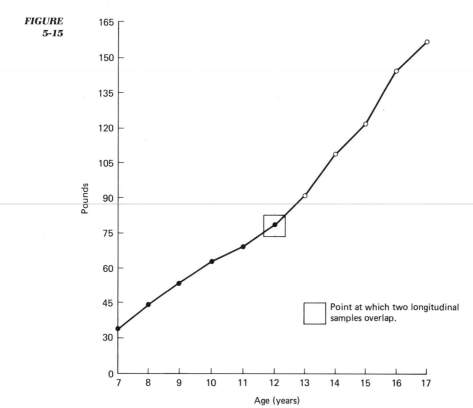

Point at which two longitudinal samples overlap.

Mean cable-tension strength scores for two longitudinal samples in the Medford Growth Study. (Redrawn with permission of Prentice-Hall, Inc., Englewood Cliffs, N.J., from H. Harrison Clarke, PHYSICAL AND MOTOR TESTS IN THE MEDFORD BOY'S GROWTH STUDY, © 1971, p. 189.)

167

sumably from birth, with mean differences increasing by age 20 so that there is little overlap between men's and women's strength scores. The strength changes described here include only measures of isometric strength, without any measures of strength as part of movement skills. Strength is quite variable within individuals and among groups, can increase greatly with training, and can decrease with inactivity.

Gender Differences

Gender differences in favor of males have been found in most of the normative comparisons reviewed in this chapter. As noted in the introduction, these gender differences likely are due to biological makeup and participation experiences. These two major influences will be considered in several ways in Part II. At this time, we want to present two illustrations of the potential impact of participation experiences as related to sex roles.

Our first illustration concerns the effort that individuals must make when attempting to produce a maximal performance. Fleishman (1964) conducted an extensive study of movement abilities, including a national sample of adolescents who were asked to make a maximal performance on a number of strength and skill tasks. Figure 5-16 summarizes the mean performance scores of boys and girls on two strength measures. Grip strength changes were linear for boys and girls from age 13 through age 18; boys had higher mean scores at each age and increased at a more rapid rate. This finding is similar to the normative strength changes noted earlier. An important point is that girls doubled their mean strength score during this 5-year period. Now look at the mean score changes for holding a half sit-up. Boys maintained a steady figure of approximately 60 seconds, whereas girls *decreased* steadily from almost 60 seconds at age 13 to nearly 20 seconds at age 18.

How can we explain this decrease in girls' strength for one task and their increase in another task? Begin by thinking about what a half sit-up is. The upper body is raised off the ground and is held in that position as long as possible. Why would an individual's ability to do this decrease? One possibility is a loss of strength in the abdominal muscles, but everything we know indicates that individuals become stronger during these years, as seen with grip strength and other strength tasks. A more reasonable explanation is that during these years it becomes less important to girls to do this task, particularly when physical discomfort is involved.

The normative changes in holding a half sit-up is a good illustration of motivation and is not an adequate description of normative changes in abdominal strength. The motivational state is sex related and likely is a product of experiences occurring in the context of our society's sex roles. This illustration is obvious, whereas others are not, but we must consider that many gender differences are greatly influenced by sex-related experiences.

Our first example points to negative influences that serve to increase gender differences. The opposite consideration is to offer girls participation experiences similar to those for boys and see if the gender differences decrease. Although we cannot do this in controlled experiments, we can look at gender differences during time periods in which participation experiences change. This means that we must look in retrospect at differences in normative comparisons across an ex-

**FIGURE
5-16**

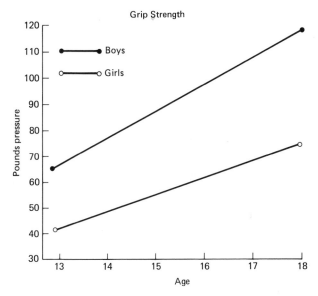

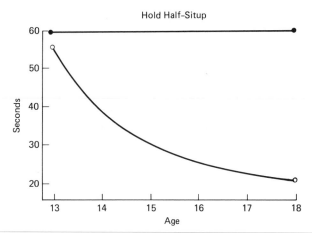

Boy-girl comparisons on two strength measures. (Redrawn with
permission from E.A. Fleishman, *The Structure and
Measurement of Physical Fitness,* Prentice-Hall, Inc., Englewood
Cliffs, N.J., 1964.)

tended time period. Such comparisons obviously are confounded by many variations in social conditions, but we can get a sense of their effect.

Girls in recent years have had more opportunities and more encouragement
to participate in movement activities, although not as fully and positively as boys
have. Recent normative comparisons (California 1981) follow a pattern of gender
differences similar to that of earlier normative comparisons. We need more data
and more careful analyses, however, to detect difference changes. A recent analysis
by Dyer (1977) of recognized world and national records indicates that gender
differences at very high levels of achievement are decreasing.

Dyer's findings are shown in Figure 5-17. Yearly world records for track and
swimming, and national British records for cycling were examined. The mean

169

**FIGURE
5-17**

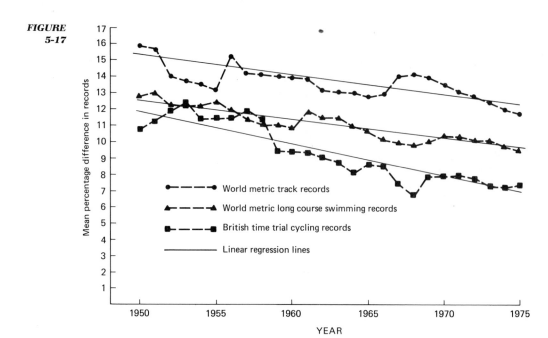

Relative differences between means of female and male recognized records for each year from 1950 to 1975. (Reproduced with permission from Dyer, 1977.)

percentage differences favored males from 11 percent to 16 percent in 1950 and decreased in 1975 to 7 percent to 13 percent. Dyer projected that the mean differences would approach zero in 60 to 130 years. But the reductions in mean differences may eventually be limited by a match between event requirements and females' and males' biological characteristics. Our concern here is that gender differences have been reduced, which points to the influence of participation experiences, even though we cannot specify their nature, extent, and quality. Dyer's approach shows how changes in gender differences for normative data can be made. Although it seems reasonable that gender differences in maximal performance should decrease, we do not have enough appropriate normative data to make the necessary analyses.

Individual Change

Descriptions of change in movement development are primarily descriptions of group patterns of change, as very little information is available to outline individual patterns. The main problem is that movement development data are mostly cross-sectional, whereas longitudinal data are needed to chart individual patterns of change. Longitudinal studies are time consuming and are limited by many methodological considerations, including loss of subjects, effects of retesting, and problems in analyzing gain scores in changing distributions. Nonetheless, several longitudinal studies have been made of performance on the play-game skills included in this chapter. A brief summary of the results offers the little we do know about the stability of individual performance over time and individual patterns of change.

Longitudinal Studies

Longitudinal studies of movement development have been made more often with babies because the changes are more distinct and more rapid, and a natural setting can be used more often. Much of the earlier investigators' work was longitudinal to observe general movement achievements of a small number of babies at weekly or monthly intervals. Recent longitudinal studies with babies have focused on more limited and finer-grained analyses of movement, such as the reaching-interception movements studied by von Hofsten (1979). A continuous and detailed measurement approach now is advocated in longitudinal descriptions of early development (Tipps et al. 1981).

The results from the five longitudinal studies listed in Table 5-6 will be used to describe individual change in several play-game skills. Children were tested in each study for at least 3 years, with intervals between test sessions varying from 6 months to 1 year. Each study included a test of throwing distance or velocity, and all but one (Halverson et al. 1982) included a timed dash and a standing long jump. The studies of Glassow and Kruse (1960) and Keogh (1969b)

TABLE 5-6 Longitudinal Studies in Which Play-Game Skills Were Tested for at Least 3 Years

STUDY AND SUBJECTS	TESTS	GENERAL DESIGN AND OTHER INFORMATION*
Espenschade (1940)		
Ages: 13 to 17	50-yard dash	Initiated 1934
85 boys, 80 girls	Standing long jump	One group: grade 8
Oakland, Calif.	Jump-reach	Tested at 6-month intervals
	Distance throw	for 4 years
	Brace Test	
Glassow and Kruse (1960)		
Ages: 6 to 14	30-yard dash	Initiated 1953
123 girls	Standing long jump	7 groups: started at different
Madison, Wisc.	Throwing velocity	grade levels
		Tested yearly for 3 to 6 years
Rarick and Smoll (1967)		
Ages: 7 to 12, 17	30-yard dash	Initiated c. 1953
25 boys, 24 girls	Standing long jump	One group: grade 1
Madison, Wisc.	Throwing velocity	Tested yearly for 6 years,
	Strength tests	then again after an
		interval of 5 years
Keogh (1969b)		
Ages 6 to 11	30-yard dash	Initiated 1963
57 boys, 57 girls	Standing long jump	2 groups: age 6, age 8
Santa Monica, Calif.	Distance throw	Tested at 6-month intervals
	50-foot hop	for 4 years
	Grip (right + left)	
Halverson et al. (1982)		
Ages: 6 to 13	Throwing velocity	Initiated 1972
22 boys, 17 girls		One group: kindergarten
Madison, Wisc.		Tested yearly for 3 years,
		then again after an
		interval of 5 years

* Group indicates age or grade when group first was tested.

started with more than one age group, which extended the age range but meant that each child was tested for only part of the age range indicated in Table 5-6. These longitudinal studies, except Espenschade's adolescence study (1940), focused on the early and middle school years. Also, Rarick and Smoll (1967) and Halverson and colleagues (1982) held a final test session after a 5-year interval to provide a longer age interval between the initial and final test sessions. Three of the studies were done in Madison, Wisconsin, and two were done in California. The Keogh study is described later in Box 5-4 to provide some detail on measuring individual patterns of change.

Individual change for the children in these studies is outlined here in two ways. First, the *stability* of individual performance is determined by the correlations between the test sessions. The higher the correlation is, the more stable the relative level of performance of individuals for the time period will be. Second, and only for the studies of Espenschade (1940) and Keogh (1969b), *individual patterns of change* are described by plotting separately individual children's performances, rather than plotting the group's mean performance. The correlations provide a statistical summary of stability, which is a group average and conceals individual patterns of change. The graphs show individual patterns, but it is difficult to compare and summarize them. Each way of looking at individual change is useful, but each is limited in relation to what the other provides.

Stability

The stability of individual performance is the extent to which an individual maintains the same *relative position* for two test sessions, even though others increase, perhaps even decrease, in absolute performance score. An individual maintains the same relative position when changing the same amount as the group mean change. If most individuals maintain approximately the same relative performance level for two test sessions, the correlation will be higher than when many individuals change their relative performance level. However, a correlation is a summarizing statistic, and some individuals may be more or less stable than indicated by the size of the correlation. Also, summaries of large numbers of correlations are general pictures of stability and do not apply to everyone. This again means that some will be more stable and others will be less stable than indicated by a correlation or a group of correlations.

Two groups of correlations have been taken from the longitudinal studies summarized here. First, the correlations between adjacent test sessions (for example, tests sessions 1 and 2, 2 and 3, and 3 and 4) are summarized in Table 5-7 as a short-term view of stability. Second, the correlations between early and late test sessions are summarized in Table 5-8 as a long-term view of stability.

Short-term stability is summarized in Table 5-7 for test intervals of 6 and 12 months. As expected, the correlations generally are high because only a small amount of change takes place in such a short time period. A total of 190 correlations are listed for jump and throw combined, with more than 40 percent of the correlations being .8 or larger and approximately 10 percent being less than .6. Boys had somewhat higher correlations in the Keogh study, whereas girls appeared more stable in the Espenschade study. The correlations for the timed dashs were lower in the Espenschade study and quite high in the Glassow-Kruse study. The general picture is that children maintained similar relative performance levels on these tasks over a short time period, but the size of correlation for type of task and sex group varied among the studies.

TABLE 5-7 **Size and Number of Correlations for Adjacent Test Sessions (6-month and 1-year intervals)**

| | SIZE AND NUMBER OF CORRELATIONS | | | | | | | |
| | *Boys* | | | | *Girls* | | | |
TASK/STUDY	$<.4$	$.4/.5$	$.6/.7$	$.8+$	$<.4$	$.4/.5$	$.6/.7$	$.8+$
Jump								
Keogh (1969b)	0	1	13	12	0	4	15	7
Glassow and Kruse (1960)					0	0	10	12
Espenschade (1940)	0	3	10	0	0	1	7	3
Throw								
Keogh (1969b)	0	0	5	21	1	6	17	2
Glassow and Kruse (1960)					0	4	5	7
Espenschade (1940)	1	3	5	4	0	0	0	11
Dash								
Glassow and Kruse (1960)					0	0	6	13
Espenschade (1940)	2	5	6	0	0	4	5	0

TABLE 5-8 **Correlations by Test and Sex Across Years for 3 Play-Game Skills**

| | | TEST | | |
STUDY	AGE PERIOD (YEARS)	*Jump*	*Throw*	*Dash*
Boys				
Rarick and Smoll (1967)	7 to 12	48	50	39
	8 to 12	53	31	42
	9 to 12	66	48	46
	7 to 17	60	28	18
	8 to 17	56	14	14
	9 to 17	70	38	-07
Keogh (1969b)	6 to 9	54	71	57
	8 to 11	75	73	76
Halverson et al. (1982)	6 to 13		43	
	7 to 13		37	
	8 to 13		62	
Espenschade (1940)	14 to 17	40	62	29
Girls				
Rarick and Smoll (1967)	7 to 12	71	12	92
	8 to 12	71	53	83
	9 to 12	76	46	78
	7 to 17	50	12	56
	8 to 17	80	25	70
	9 to 17	70	20	77
Glassow and Kruse (1960)	7 to 12	74		70
	7 to 11	56		87
		66		82
	7 to 10	70		81
		65		68
Keogh (1969b)	6 to 9	73	46	39
	8 to 11	46	69	45
Halverson et al. (1982)	6 to 13		77	
	7 to 13		84	
	8 to 13		85	
Espenschade (1940)	14 to 16	68	84	49

173

Long-term stability is summarized in Table 5-8 for test intervals of 3 to 10 years. The study of Rarick and Smoll (1967) has the most comprehensive coverage in terms of yearly data from age 7 to age 12 and a final test session at age 17. Again, the correlations vary considerably in size among studies, which means that a number of studies are needed to compile a general picture of long-term stability. The standing long jump has the most consistent set of correlations, with all but a few values in a range from .5 to .7. The correlations for girls are slightly higher overall, but boys have similar or higher values in many comparisons.

The correlations for throw and dash range from quite large to quite small, with many contradictions in gender comparisons among the studies. The correlations for the throw are low for the boys and girls in the Rarick and Smoll study, high for the girls in the Espenschade and Halverson studies, and above .6 for the boys in the Espenschade and Keogh studies. The correlations for the dash are high for the girls in the Rarick-Smoll and Glassow-Kruse studies and low for the boys in the Rarick-Smoll and Espenschade studies and are above .7 for the boys in the Keogh study.

The general picture for long-term stability is that correlations can be quite high across reasonably long time periods, but it is not unusual to find low correlations and quite different correlations among studies. Girls generally were more stable in these longitudinal studies, although boys were as stable or more stable for some task intervals. There may be methodological considerations that contribute to the rather variable pattern of results for long-term stability. It is not easy, however, to sort out the effects of different examiners, different scoring procedures, and the like without conducting a series of longitudinal studies. The best we can do at the moment is recognize that we do not have a clear picture of stability of movement performance over an extended time period. This is particularly true when considering that we do not have longitudinal data for different types of movement tasks.

Individual Patterns of Change

Individual patterns of change have seldom been documented systematically, and there are many problems in compiling such a representation. One problem is that there are no conventional procedures, particularly to summarize individual patterns of change into similar types of groups. General impressions of individual change have been recorded in comments about individual children, and some detailed records and comments are available, as illustrated by Shirley's movement biographies (1931) and the analyses of changes in movement mechanics (Halverson et al. 1982). Espenschade (1940) prepared what is probably the most extensive set of individual descriptions of changes in movement development. Her descriptions were organized according to biological maturity, with extensive comments about relationships to other aspects of the development of the boys and girls who were part of the Adolescent Study conducted at the University of California. Data and analyses from the Keogh (1969b) study are described in Box 5-4 and are used here to show individual patterns of change and some of the difficulties in studying them.

Individual change includes both *absolute (raw score) gain* and alterations in *relative level* or position within a group. Individual children generally increase or gain in absolute level of performance score over several years, but the amount of change between test sessions may vary considerably. The pattern of change for an individual also should be viewed in relation to that of other children in

BOX
5-4

INDIVIDUAL CHANGE IN MOVEMENT PERFORMANCE DURING EARLY SCHOOL YEARS

Individual change in movement performance was studied as part of the Santa Monica Project. The first year of the project was a normative test program conducted in the school year of 1963–1964, with thirteen movement tasks and 1,171 children in kindergarten through the sixth grade (Keogh 1965). The subjects for a longitudinal test program to examine individual change were selected from all 6- and 8-year old children who had been tested in November 1963 and who were available for testing in May 1964 (Keogh 1969b). Fall and spring test sessions were repeated for the children in the longitudinal test program through eight test sessions to cover 4 school years, ending in May 1967.

The children were grouped by age and sex to form four groups: boys 6 (B6), girls 6 (G6), boys 8 (B8), and girls 8 (G8). A total of 210 children were tested at the first and second test session, which was reduced to 114 at the eighth test session. The children were ages 6–0 to 6–11 or 8–0 to 8–11 at the first test session and were 9–6 to 10–5 or 11–6 to 12–5 at the eighth test session. The longitudinal test program spanned 4 school years but actually only 3.5 years from the first to eighth test session.

The children completing the final test session were somewhat above the norm on school achievement data. The mean score on the Lorge-Thorndike Intelligence Test for the B8 and G8 children was 110 when tested in the fifth grade. The mean grade placement on the Iowa Test of Basic Skills was 4.3 for the B6 and G6 children, with an expected mean grade placement of 4.1 at the time of the test. The children were in two elementary schools in the Santa Monica (California) Unified School District, with surrounding residential areas classified as 2 (School R) and 4 (School G) on a socio-economic scale of 1 (high) to 6 (low) (Meeker 1964). Approximately 90 percent of the children were Caucasian. The 96 children who did not complete the longitudinal test program were compared with the 114 children included in the final analyses. Appropriate age-sex groups were compared on ten measures (age, height, weight, and seven movement performance scores) taken at the second test session. Only two of forty comparisons were significantly different, which indicates that there were no systematic differences on these measures between the dropouts and the survivors.

The selection of tests for the longitudinal test program was based on tests used in the normative test program which met certain criteria for the description of change. Because the purpose of the longitudinal test program was to describe individual change, tests were needed which had well-defined patterns of mean increases across the early school years. Distributions needed to be well balanced and with adequate group variability so that standard scores could be used. Also, the tests could not impose ceilings, real or artificial, that would result in poorly balanced and changing distributions.

A set of seven tests was selected and used in the eight test sessions, but only four tests proved to be useful for longitudinal analyses according to the criteria. The four tests used for describing individual change were standing long jump, ball throw for distance, 50-foot hop for time, and grip strength (hand dynamometer: sum of right and left grips). The beam walk, beam balance, and 30-yard dash were administered in each test session but were not used in studying individual change. The beam tests had a ceiling of a maximum number of steps (30) to walk and a maximum number of seconds (60) to balance. Most children reached the maximums on the third or fourth test session. The mean changes for the 30-yard dash were erratic, and the range of scores was limited in relation to the measurement unit of one-tenth of a second. The beam tests and 30-yard dash can be used to determine group mean changes, if the ceiling and limited score range are kept in mind, but individual change cannot be detected well with these tasks. This illustrates one of the difficulties encountered in planning and conducting a longitudinal study.

The children were brought to the test area in groups of six to ten. Each child was tested individually, except that the children were run in pairs in the 30-yard dash. Each test session was completed in 20 to 25 minutes, and the test procedures are described in the report of the normative test program (Keogh 1965). Within-day reliability figures were .9+, except for some correlations of .8 for the 50-foot hop and grip strength.

Group data were used to calculate correlations for each test across all combinations

FIGURE
5-18

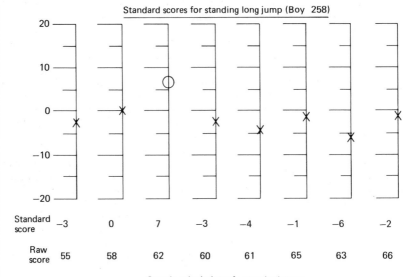

Stability scores for Boy 258

Test	Standard scores for test sessions								Range	Stability Score
	1	2	3	4	5	6	7	8		
StBJ	−3	0	(7)	−3	−4	−1	−6	−2	−6 to 0	6
BTh	5	9	11	(2)	4	5	8	10	4 to 11	7
50 Hop	2	(8)	3	−3	0	1	0	1	−3 to 3	6
Grip	(−16)	−3	−5	−15	−9	−6	−2	−6	−15 to −2	13

Standard scores for standing long jump (Boy 258)

Standard score	−3	0	7	−3	−4	−1	−6	−2
Raw score	55	58	62	60	61	65	63	66

Sample calculation of a standard score

$$10 \left(\frac{\text{Boy's score–group mean}}{\text{Standard deviation}} \right)$$

$$10 \left(\frac{55 - 56.9}{6.8} \right) = 10 \left(\frac{-1.9}{6.8} \right) = -3$$

Conversion of performance scores to standard scores and calculation of a stability score for Boy 258 (Keogh, 1969b; see Box 5-4 for explanations).

of the eight test sessions. Some of these correlations are listed in Tables 5-7 and 5-8. These correlations show *group stability*, the extent to which individuals maintain a relatively similar level of performance in the group during a designated time period.

A simple procedure was used to measure *individual stability* in the range of standard scores across the test sessions. Each performance score for each child was converted to a standard score so that 1 standard deviation was 10 points and the mean score was 0. A sample calculation of a standard score and a complete set of standard scores for Boy 258 are presented in Figure 5-18. Boy 258 jumped 55 inches in the first test session and had a standard score of − 3 based on a group mean of 56.9 and a standard deviation of 6.8.

The range of standard scores for each task was converted to a *stability score* by calculating the difference between the lowest and the highest standard score after the most discrepant standard score was removed. If a child's general level of performance is to be judged over time, removing a very discrepant score will give a truer picture for a child who otherwise was not variable, though not altering the picture of a very variable child. The most discrepant score for each task is circled in Figure 5-18. The standard scores were limited to 2 standard deviations (−20 to + 20) because an extreme standard scored beyond −20 or + 20 does not change the general assessment of level of performance as very poor or very good. The stability scores appear more stable by excluding the most discrepant score and limiting the standard scores to a range of −20 to +20. The purpose was to determine the general level of stability over time and not to predict individual scores. Variability at one point in time and fluctuations at extreme levels do not alter a general pattern of change, even though we cannot define it in more precise mathematical terms.

Boy 258 had a stability score of 6 for the standing long jump, based on seven standard scores ranging from −6 to 0, compared with a stability score of 7 for the ball throw, based on seven standard scores ranging from 4 to 11. His performance level was different for the two tasks, in being below the mean for jumping and above the mean for throwing, but he had a similar level of stability for the two tasks and also for hopping. Boy 258 was more variable on grip strength, with a stability score of 13.

The mean stability scores for the four age-sex groups on the four tasks were around 10, with standard deviations of 3 to 4. As another way to describe the level of stability, the distributions were inspected to find a cutoff score that included a substantial number of children for each task. Approximately 75 percent of the stability scores were 12 or less, as shown for the different groups in Table 5-9. The boys were somewhat more stable than the girls, who had low percentages for the G6 group on throwing and hopping and for the G8 group on grip strength. Using a cutoff of 15, more than 85 percent of the stability scores were included for each group on each test.

TABLE
5-9

Percentage of Children with Stability Scores of 12 or Less (Keogh 1969b)

		Task			
Group	N	Jump	Throw	Hop	Grip
Boys 6	26	69	85	65	88
Boys 8	31	84	94	77	71
Girls 6	28	86	54	39	82
Girls 8	29	77	83	79	59
Boys	57	77	90	72	79
Girls	57	75	68	60	70
Total	114	76	79	66	75

the appropriate age, sex, or regional group. A child might have a steady rate of absolute improvement, though not matching the pattern of group change. Stability, therefore, can be viewed from different and sometimes conflicting perspectives.

Individual and group performance curves for the standing long jump are plotted in Figure 5-19 for the Boys 8 group in the Keogh (1969b) study to show absolute and relative views of individual change. The average of adjacent test sessions was used as the plotting score to smooth out individual performance scores. Thus, the first plotting point is the average of the scores for the first and second test sessions; the second plotting point is the average for the second and third test sessions; and so on. The group mean increased at a constant rate, except for a smaller increase between the first and second plotting points. The five boys maintained the same relative position to one another and were stable in this respect, even though Boy 258 "lost ground" to the others.

The overall impression in Figure 5-19 is stability, in that each boy stayed within

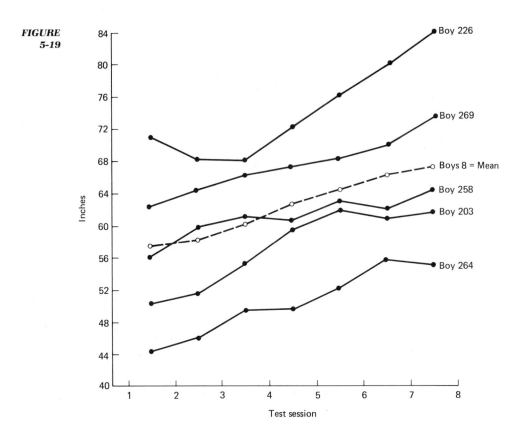

Individual performance curves for standing broad jump using averages of adjacent session scores (B8 Group: Santa Monica Project, Keogh, 1969b.)

a *general level of achievement.* A teacher or other professional interacting with these boys during these 4 school years would see the level of each boy's jumping achievement as stable, even though each varied within a level of achievement ranging from the high-level performance of Boy 226 to the low-level performance of Boy 264. Several different patterns of change are seen in the shape of individual performance curves. Boys 269 and 264 were quite stable in having a reasonably constant rate of gain, and they approximated the group pattern of change. Boy 226 decreased in absolute score in the early sessions but kept the highest position and then surged in later sessions to score much higher again in absolute score. Boy 203 also had a period of considerable absolute change counterbalanced by a period of no absolute change. Boy 258 stayed around the group's mean, with a small decrease in relative position. These are only general observations which are difficult to verify or test so that unequivocal criteria can be used to place individual patterns of change into types or groups. Individual performance curves also were selected to show easily recognized and orderly patterns of change. Some of the individual patterns of change were quite erratic and difficult to group with other individual patterns.

A simple procedure was used to define individual stability, that is, the extent to which an individual stayed within a similar level of achievement. The procedure is described in Box 5-4 and is illustrated in Figure 5-18. A *stability score* was calculated to find the width of the range of standard scores, or the width of the relative level of achievement, on a task across the eight test sessions. According to Figure 5-18, Boy 258 had a stability score of 6 for the jump. His performance was quite stable in that his relative performance level for each test session of the jump was in a narrow range of six standard scores (.6 unit of standard deviation). Notice that he had low stability scores of 6 and 7, respectively, for the throw and hop, but that his level of performance was somewhat different for each. He was consistently just below the mean on the jump and consistently above the mean between .4 and 1.1 units of standard deviation for the throw. Stability scores show the extent of similarity in standard scores across test sessions but do not indicate the level of achievement. Boy 258 was more variable on grip strength, as indicated by his stability score of 13, and his level of performance was below the mean, which can be discovered only by looking at the standard scores.

Given this way of looking at individual performance, what can be said about individual stability? On each of the four tasks, as shown in Table 5-9, many children had stability scores of 12 or less which indicates that the width of their general level of achievement was 1.2 or fewer units of standard deviation. A few children were more variable than this, but many were less variable, as approximately 50 percent of the stability scores were less than 10. The problem remains to decide what should be used as a criterion level or cutoff for identifying stable and un-stable. A stability score of 5 seems quite stable, and an argument could be made for 10, as a general level of achievement (good, average, poor) probably includes a range of 1 standard deviation. How much further should a stability criterion be extended? All that we can say now is what the Santa Monica children did within the limits of their performance. Our opinion is that many children were quite stable in relative performance level on individual tasks, but others might not view a stability score of 12 as stable.

Matters become even more complicated and interpretive when considering stability across a set of tasks. The stability scores of Boy 258 in Figure 5-18 show that he was quite stable on three tasks, even though his absolute level of per-formance was somewhat different for each. That is, he had a consistent profile on the three tasks across the eight test sessions, but his grip strength scores were not as stable. The Santa Monica data provide some sense of what individual change looks like, and we have commented on some problems in getting beyond the simple descriptions presented here.

Stability of individual performance can be quite high for both short and long time periods, but there can be considerable variation from one study to the next. Also, the data summarized here are limited to three play-game skills of jumping, running, and throwing, and we do not know whether the data represent other types of movement skills. Individual stability for short periods of time likely will be quite high because only a small amount of change is expected. That is, in-dividuals must be quite stable in order to maintain the same relative level of performance if little or no change occurs. Individual stability over a longer period of time is difficult to summarize, because the results among the studies vary. Girls tend to be more stable than boys, although contradictions to this general statement are easy to find, and results within some tasks vary in different studies. Individual stability usually is estimated from a correlation or other group statistic, which means that many individuals will be quite different from the group estimate. Individual stability scores (Keogh 1969b) provide a more direct idea of the range of individual performance, suggesting that a considerable number of individuals stay within a certain level of achievement.

Chapter Summary

Normative data for a variety of movement tasks were presented to trace changes in movement proficiency from the early school years to the early adult years. The movement tasks represent more closed movement situations and efforts to produce maximal output scores. Reaction time and strength were included as important aspects in the production of speeded and forceful movements.

The general picture is that movement performance improves markedly during these years, meaning that mean scores will double and even quadruple or will decrease by similar proportions for tasks in which proficiency is measured by a decrease in the performance score. The absolute amount of improvement is greater in the earlier years up to ages 10 or 12 for reaction time and many manual movements. The mean changes in play-game skills and strength continue to later ages, particularly for males. Changes in the components of performance scores were described as a way to study the nature of change in these movement tasks. Changes in movement strategies can be inferred from changes in component scores, as demonstrated by alternating and braking strategies in stabilometer movements and discrete and continuous strategies in moving pegs.

Boys' and girls' mean performance differences do not follow a consistent pattern across the normative data reviewed. Small and occasionally significant mean differences on manual movements and balancing tasks favor first one and then the other. The mean reaction times clearly are smaller (faster) for young adult males and perhaps for young boys, but the mean differences are fairly insignificant for most movement tasks. Young boys have small and significantly better mean performance scores on play-game skills. These differences become quite large during adolescence when the mean performance scores for girls tend to level off, though they continue to improve for boys. A similar pattern of mean differences is expected when comparing the strength of boys and girls, except that the girls' mean scores continue to improve during adolescence, but at a lesser rate than the boys' do.

An important qualification for the many statements about age and gender comparisons is that distributions sometimes overlap to the extent that many individual children perform more like the comparison group than like their age or sex group. However, boy-girl mean differences on strength and some play-game skills become sufficiently large by late adolescence that few girls score better than any but the lower scoring boys.

Individual patterns of change are more difficult to describe and analyze. Some simple descriptions of individual patterns of change were presented, but we do not have the analytical methods to go beyond individual "pictures" of change. Perhaps we need to make even more detailed descriptions of individual change and link change to what individuals do to be competent in their environments. Individual change also should include change across different types of movement achievements. Although this compounds the difficulties noted in studying individual change for one type of movement achievement, we should view individuals' movement development as larger and more general achievements rather than as a set of unrelated achievements.

Our review of normative data merely confirms that movement performance improves considerably from when we are young children to when we are young adults. But it is difficult to synthesize the many individual findings into a comprehensive set of substatements that specifies change in the different types of movement achievements. This leads to thinking about what may be underlying abilities or aptitudes, which might provide a way to organize and describe the many known achievements.

6 | *Movement Abilities*

Movement abilities can be thought of as underlying aptitudes that suggest general traits or qualities. These traits presumably determine the level of performance in similar movement situations and function throughout an individual's lifetime. We all think and speak of abilities when we use terms such as agility, coordination, dexterity, rhythm, speed, and balance, and we often describe people in terms of ability, such as having good eye-hand coordination or poor dynamic balance. If movement abilities could be identified and studied, we would understand individuals' movement makeup, rather than just knowing their performance level for a long list of movement situations. Although there is little evidence for a concise and comprehensive set of movement abilities, a review of efforts to study movement abilities can be useful in thinking about movement development (Noble 1978).

An ability is an inference derived from observing performance consistencies across similar kinds of movement tasks. This means that an individual consistently performing at the same level on several movement tasks indicates that a basic trait or quality is responsible for the consistent level. An ability can be quite broad, as when saying that an individual is athletic, or can be more limited, as when saying that an individual has poor arm speed. An ability or a combination of abilities should predict levels of performance across a number of movement tasks. Although inferred and not directly measureable, abilities can be quite useful in thinking about movement performance and movement development.

The primary difficulty with abilities is that they eventually must be measured in order to test the relationships and predictions suggested by their existence. Abilities may be proposed in a structure or framework, but performance data are needed to evaluate them. Abilities imply performance across a number of situations, which means that studies of abilities must cover many situations and many people. The enormity of such undertakings makes it unlikely that many abilities can be identified and tested in one study or set of coordinated studies.

Two issues are involved in studying the development of movement abilities. One is identifying children's movement abilities, and the other is the extent of changes in these abilities. Identification obviously must be accomplished before changes can be studied. Very little evidence regarding these two issues is available, which means that our review must be general.

Factor Analysis

The basic approach to identifying abilities and testing related predictions uses factor analysis, which is a mathematical procedure for determining the extent of commonality or similarity among tests. Each cluster or grouping of like tests is viewed as representing a factor or an ability. The process begins with the investigator's preparing a tentative list of what seem to be important movement abilities. Several movement tasks are then selected to represent each ability. A sample of people is tested on each of the movement tasks; all combinations of performance scores are correlated; and the correlations are analyzed to see how the tasks cluster or group. Each cluster is a factor identified by the nature of the clustered tasks, and is labeled by the investigator. A factor analysis leads to identifying those *factors* that *represent abilities.* We shall discuss a study by Fleishman (1964) to demonstrate factor analysis as an analytical procedure.

Fleishman conducted an extensive project to find "components of physical proficiency." He began by reviewing previous studies in which factor analyses and other correlational data for movement tasks were reported. He then formulated several broad ability areas, as listed in Figure 6-1, which seemed to be defined by his summary of existing data. The terminology for ability areas and factor labels is a problem because different investigators often use different labels to identify the same cluster of tasks or use the same label to identify clusters with different tasks. Fleishman's review thus was useful in establishing a consistent terminology to summarize the work to that time.

Fleishman found that the strength area had the most consistent set of factors reported in the literature. He proposed three abilities of explosive, dynamic, and static strength. A complex set of abilities was arranged in hierarchical form to describe a general area of flexibility-speed. Fleishman then suggested the interrelationship of abilities, whereas most investigators had listed them without considering how they might be interrelated. He also defined three new areas: balance, coordination, and endurance.

These areas and related abilities, as shown in Figure 6-1, formed a framework that Fleishman then set out to test. Remember that an ability can only be inferred and cannot be measured directly. If an individual has a high degree of consistency in performing several movement tasks, we can infer that he or she has an ability

FIGURE 6-1

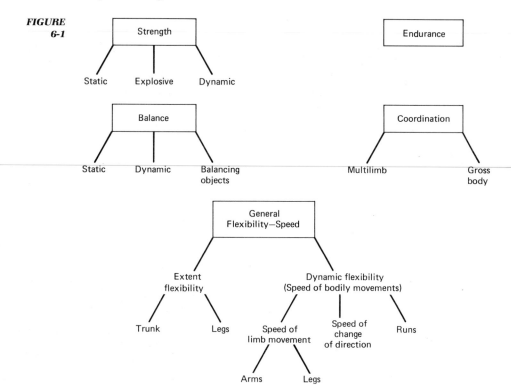

Abilities structure hypothesized by Fleishman (1964).

that determines the consistent level of performance. This inference is stronger when many individuals are consistent across all of these tasks. This means that some individuals are consistently good, others are consistently average, and still others are consistently poor. With this view of abilities in mind, we can consider how Fleishman tried to identify abilities.

His next step was to select several movement tasks, each of which seemed to require the same movement ability for successful performance. Beginning with the three strength abilities, Fleishman chose several tests that had been used in previous studies and also included several new tests, to determine whether he could extend and clarify the sense of each ability. For example, he included flexion and extension movements in dynamic strength movements of arms and legs to determine whether dynamic strength might be separated into subabilities related to body part and type of movement. Fleishman then tested 201 male navy recruits on thirty movement tasks (Study 1). Selected results of his factor analyses are listed in Table 6-1 to illustrate factor analysis loadings and to examine the match to Fleishman's proposed strength abilities listed in Figure 6-1.

There are many ways to calculate a factor analysis, depending on the particular mathematical model selected and the related analysis rules. Any factor analysis defines the mathematical levels of the relationships among tests. A level of relationship is the loading of a test to a particular direction or vector in space. Each test is mathematically located in space and has a different loading, or relationship, to different vectors. By grouping tests with high loadings on a particular vector, we can find those tests that best represent the vector. Because these tests have something in common, we now can think of them as representing a factor. If the loadings are high, the factor will be more robust then when the loadings are low. Additionally, Factor A will be more distinct if tests loading high on Factor A do not load high on other factors. The next step is to name or label the factor, by looking at the high test loadings on the factor and using the nature of the tasks to formulate a description. It is important to note that the factors are labeled by the viewer. The viewer should thus not accept the factor labels as fixed. Anyone can and should help name factors.

Fleishman found five factors in his factor analysis of the strength tests (Study 1), which are summarized in Table 6-1, with the tests listed if the loading is .40 or higher. The factors are not named, and you may want to try your hand in the game of naming the factor. Compare the results in Table 6-1 with Fleishman's proposal in Figure 6-1 that strength area includes three abilities of dynamic, static, and explosive strength. Fleishman argues that Factors 1, 2, and 3, respectively, are dynamic, static, and explosive strength. His factors seem robust and somewhat distinct, because the loadings are reasonably high. Notice that there are some tests that load on both Factors 1 and 2 (pull-ups in 20 seconds, rope climb in 6 seconds, 50-yard dash). Factors 4 and 5 have only three tests, each with loadings above .40, and should be considered accordingly.

Strength probably is more complex than Fleishman's general factor structure, but his analysis of strength shows how one begins with a proposed, or hypothesized, set of abilities and how factor analysis is used to evaluate them. Fleishman found a reasonable match for his proposed strength abilities, with further work needed to refine his findings.

Fleishman did a second study with different subjects to evaluate his proposed abilities of flexibility-speed, balance, and coordination. He tested 204 male navy recruits on thirty test items. Factor analysis identified the six factors summarized

TABLE 6-1. Factor Loadings*

STUDY 1†			STUDY 2†		
Factor	*Test*	*Loadings*	*Factor*	*Test*	*Loadings*
1.	Pullups (to limit)	81	1.	Dodge run	69
	Pullups (20 sec)	78		Figure-8 duck	68
	Pushups (to limit)	74		Shuttle run	63
	Bent arm hang	73		Grass drill	62
	Dips (10 sec)	70		Circle run	59
	Pushups (15 sec)	68		Arm circling	52
	Hold half-pushup	68		Plate tapping	39
	Rope climb (6 sec)	67			
	Dips (to limit)	63	2.	One-foot lengthwise	
	Squat thrusts (30 sec)	45		balance (eyes closed)	72
	50-yard dash	44		Two-foot cross	
				balance (eyes closed)	64
2.	Hand grip	72		One-foot cross	
	Arm pull	71		balance (eyes closed)	54
	Medicine ball put			Two-foot cross	
	(standing)	71		balance (eyes open)	53
	Weight	70		Railwalking (eyes open)	44
	Trunk pull	59		One-foot cross	
	Push weights-arm	51		balance (eyes open)	38
	Medicine ball put				
	(sitting)	44	3.	Lateral bend	58
	Height	42		One-foot tapping	58
				Block transfer	56
3.	Shuttle run	77		Squat, twist, touch	53
	50-yard dash	75		Bend, twist, touch	50
	10-yard dash	70		Leg circling	48
	Standing broad jump	66		Soccer dribble	32
	Vertical jump	64		Board dribble	30
	Softball throw	54			
	Rope climb (6 sec)	41	4.	One-foot lengthwise	
	Pullups (6 sec)	40		balance (eyes open)	64
				One-foot cross	
4.	Leg lifts	47		balance (eyes open)	55
	Hold half-situp	45		Stick balance	33
	Leg raiser	43		Two-foot cross	
				balance (eyes open)	32
5.	Pull weights-arm	50			
	Push weights-arm	44	5.	Abdominal stretch	55
	Push weights-feet	43		Twist, touch	49
				Toe touching	39
			6.	Ball balance	47
				Two-foot tapping	46
				Plate tapping	44
				Arm circling	39
				Two-foot lengthwise	
				balance (eyes closed)	33
				Two-foot lengthwise	
				balance (eyes open)	31

* Based on data from Fleishman 1964.
† Loadings of .40 and above for Study 1; loadings of .30 and above for Study 2 (sign and decimal point omitted).

in Table 6-1 for Study 2. Loadings of .30 and above are included for a more complete picture of test loadings. The factors are left unnamed so that you may participate further in the game of naming the factor. The loadings in the second study are not as high as those in the first study, and the factors are more difficult to label. Notice also that there is not a good match for the proposed abilities listed in Table 6-1, which is a problem in identifying abilities, even with well-planned and reasonably comprehensive studies.

Factor analyses of movement performance have been done primarily to study the movement abilities of adult males, often in regard to military job requirements, such as predicting who will be successful in different phases of pilot training, with very little research done after 1970. The publications of Guilford (1958) and Fleishman (1966) are a useful starting point in tracing the research before 1970. Bechtoldt's critical review (1970) is an important reference when considering the extent to which factors (abilities) predict performance and learning.

Children's Movement Abilities

Children's movement abilities have not been studied systematically until recently in a series of studies directed by Rarick. We shall call these studies the Rarick Project, which is described in a book by Rarick, Dobbins, and Broadhead (1976). We first shall comment briefly on other research studies.

General Review

There have been a number of factor analyses of children's movement performance, but often as single efforts by the investigators without any further work by them. Many of the studies, too, are quite limited, with few tests and children and a confounding of age by including a wide range of ages in a single factor analysis. Because children's mean performance on movement tasks generally improves with age, correlations among tests will be increased and will bias the analyses that use the correlations. As well, some studies emphasize the relationship of movement performance and perceptual-cognitive performance in order to examine school-learning problems, which limits the scope of the movement abilities being studied. The most common approach has been to use factor analysis as a means of examining the structure or composition of a movement performance test. The general finding is that factor analyses of movement performance tests have not matched well with the abilities proposed for children by those who constructed the tests. A recent study by Krus, Bruininks, and Robertson (1981) demonstrates this.

Bruininks (1978) revised the Oseretsky Test (Doll 1946, Sloan 1955) into the Bruininks-Oseretsky Test of Motor Proficiency, with eight subtests and forty-six test items. Each subtest was selected to represent a "dimension of motor ability." The test was administered to a carefully selected national sample of 765 children, ages 4 through 14. Factor analyses were performed on the total sample, as well as on three age groupings of age 4, ages 5 to 9, and ages 9 to 14. The results were similar enough across the four analyses that only the factor analysis loadings for the total sample were reported, as shown in Table 6-2. Notice that more than half of the test items (25 of 46) have loadings of .3 or more on Factor I. This

TABLE 6-2 **Factor Analysis Loadings* of Test Items on the Bruininks-Oseretsky Test of Motor Proficiency†**

SUBTEST ITEMS	I	II	III	IV	V
Subtest 1: Running Speed and Agility	.55				
Subtest 2: Balance					
1. Standing on Preferred Leg on Floor			.48		
2. Standing on Preferred Leg on Balance Beam			.61		
3. Standing on Preferred Leg on Balance Beam—Eyes Closed			.35		
4. Walking Forward on Walking Line		.36			
5. Walking Forward on Balance Beam		.49			
6. Walking Forward Heel-to-Toe on Walking Line		.50			
7. Walking Forward Heel-to-Toe on Balance Beam			.54		
8. Stepping Over Response Speed Stick on Balance Beam			.54		
Subtest 3: Bilateral Coordination					
1. Tapping Feet Alternately while Making Circles with Fingers					.41
2. Tapping—Foot and Finger on Same Side Synchronized	.39				
3. Tapping—Foot and Finger on Opposite Side Synchronized	.47				
4. Jumping in Place—Leg and Arm on Same Side Synchronized					.57
5. Jumping in Place—Leg and Arm on Opposite Side Synchronized					.68
6. Jumping Up and Clapping Hands	.62				
7. Jumping Up and Touching Heels with Hands		.48			
8. Drawing Lines and Crosses Simultaneously	.68				
Subtest 4: Strength					
1. Standing Broad Jump				.59	
2. Sit-ups	.64				
3a. Knee Push-ups (For Boys Under Age 8 and All Girls)				.58	
3b. Full Push-ups (For Boys Age 8 and Older)				.51	
Subtest 5: Upper-limb Coordination					
1. Bouncing a Ball and Catching It With Both Hands		.72			
2. Bouncing a Ball and Catching It With Preferred Hand		.67			
3. Catching a Tossed Ball with Both Hands		.56			
4. Catching a Tossed Ball with Preferred Hand	.67				
5. Throwing a Ball at a Target with Preferred Hand	.49				
6. Touching a Swinging Ball with Preferred Hand		.53			
7. Touching Nose with Index Fingers—Eyes Closed		.41			
8. Touching Thumb to Fingertips—Eyes Closed		.54			
9. Pivoting Thumb and Index Finger		.49			
Subtest 6: Response Speed	.57				

TABLE 6-2 **Factor Analysis Loadings* of Test Items on the Bruininks-Oseretsky Test of Motor Proficiency† (Continued)**

SUBTEST ITEMS	FACTOR				
	I	II	III	IV	V
Subtest 7: Visual-motor Control					
1. Cutting out a Circle with Preferred Hand	.50				
2. Drawing a Line Through a Crooked Path with Preferred Hand	.35				
3. Drawing a Line Through a Straight Path with Preferred Hand	.65				
4. Drawing a Line Through a Curved Path with Preferred Hand	.37				
5. Copying a Circle with Preferred Hand	.36				
6. Copying a Triangle with Preferred Hand	.49				
7. Copying a Horizontal Diamond with Preferred Hand	.51				
8. Copying Overlapping Pencils with Preferred Hand	.61				
Subtest 8: Upper-limb Dexterity					
1. Placing Pennies in a Box with Preferred Hand	.69				
2. Placing Pennies in Two Boxes with Both Hands	.60				
3. Sorting Shape Cards with Preferred Hand	.76				
4. Stringing Beads with Preferred Hand	.70				
5. Displacing Pegs with Preferred Hand	.67				
6. Drawing Vertical Lines with Preferred Hand	.65				
7. Making Dots in Circles with Preferred Hand	.78				
8. Making Dots with Preferred Hand	.64				

* Decimal point omitted.
† Reprinted with permission of authors and publishers from: Krus, P.H., Bruininks, R.H., & Robertson, G. Structure of motor abilities in children. PERCEPTUAL AND MOTOR SKILLS, 1981, 52, 119–129, Table 6.

includes all of the manual control items (subtests 7 and 8), many limb movements from other subtests, and some body movements. This grouping of test items is difficult to interpret and label. The other factors are more distinct, but the test items within subtests 2, 3, 4, and 5 load on different factors. This means that subtest 2 is two factors rather than one, as is true for subtests 3, 4, and 5. In summary, one large factor captures much of the essence of the test, and each subtest, as arranged by Bruininks, is not a factor or an ability. What is needed next is a rethinking and an adjustment of the theoretical structure, followed by further testing and related analyses, to sharpen our view of children's movement abilities. The study of Krus, Bruininks, and Robertson is a useful first step, but a coordinated sequence of such steps is needed before we can expect definitive results. Our brief review reveals the enormity and complexity of searching for abilities and the need for a systematic program of research if abilities are ever to be identified.

A serious problem in the search for children's movement abilities is that very few of the studies propose a structure of abilities that would be useful to direct subsequent work. Also, there must be some recognition of change when a structure of abilities is viewed developmentally. A paper by Meyers and Dingman (1960) begins considering change in abilities. They reviewed existing tests and related

TABLE
6-3

Psychomotor Abilities Hypothesized for Young Children*

ABILITIES	AGE OF EMERGENCE (YEARS)	MOVEMENT TASK EXAMPLES
Whole body		
Postural balance	1.5	Beam walking, toe balance
Dynamic balance	1.5	Hop-skip, jump-balance
Impulsion	2.5	Standing long jump, kick
Coordination	2.5	Hurdle jump, cable jump
Flexibility	3.0	Toe touch
Strength	3.0	Grip, leg abduction
Hand-eye		
Static precision	3.0	Steadiness (aim), tracing
Dynamic precision	3.0	Rotary pursuit, circle dotting
Reaction time	3.0	Simple, choice
Dexterity	3.0	Tweezer use, cube stacking
Speed	4.0	Finger-dot tapping

* Based on data from Meyers and Dingman 1960.

performance data and hypothesized seven domains or areas in order to create a structure of human abilities for preschool ages. Whole body movements and hand-eye movements are their two movement domains, with hypothesized abilities listed under each, as shown in Table 6-3. The interesting feature of their proposal is that they indicated the approximate age when they expected each factor to emerge. When studying the development of movement abilities, we must realize that abilities may emerge and change. As noted earlier, this imposes the double difficulty of identifying abilities and tracing emergence and change. The ages of emergence suggested by Meyers and Dingman do not seem compelling, but just recognizing them is an important feature of their proposal.

Rarick Project

The project directed by Rarick is the most comprehensive factor analytic view of children's movement performance (Rarick et al. 1976). The Rarick Project was conducted, first, to describe a factor structure and, second, to describe person-clusters, or typologies. The factor structure was derived by the process used in the Fleishman study to find out how tests group or cluster. A second set of analyses was made to discover the grouping or clustering of persons who have similar performances across the factors and, thus, represent a type of mover. The two types of analyses identify test-clusters and person-clusters, and we can infer from them what the types of abilities and persons might be.

Test clusters. The Rarick Project began by formulating an ability list and selecting tests for each. As shown in Table 6-4, forty-six tests were used to represent twelve abilities. The tests include seven measures of physical size and body composition (Abilities 11 and 12), seventeen measures of strength, endurance, and flexibility (Abilities 1, 2, 3, 5, and 10), eight measures of manual control (Abilities 6 and 7), and fourteen measures of body control (Abilities 4, 8, and 9). Five tests involving running, jumping, and throwing are listed in Abilities 2 and 5 as strength and endurance, whereas others might consider these tests as measures of body control. The Rarick Project included a variety of tests that were carefully pretested and well administered. Note that the Rarick Project includes in one study the

TABLE 6-4 **Hypothesized Abilities: List for Rarick Study with Tests Identified for Each Ability***

1. *Static muscular strength*	7. *Manual dexterity*
Grip strength right	Minnesota Manipulative
Grip strength left	Purdue Pegboard
Elbow flexion	2-Plate tapping
Elbow extension	Ring stacking
Knee flexion	Golfball placement
Knee extension	
	8. *Static balance*
2. *Explosive muscular strength*	Bass test
Vertical jump	Stabilometer
Standing broadjump	Stork stand
35-yard dash	
Bicycle ergometer (10 sec)	9. *Dynamic balance*
(with resistance)	Railwalk forward
Bicycle ergometer (10 sec)	Railwalk backward
(without resistance)	Railwalk sideways
Softball throw (velocity)	
	10. *Flexibility*
3. *Muscular strength-endurance*	Toe touch
Situps	Spinal extension
Trunk raise (held: time)	Spinal rotation
Leg raise (held: time)	Lateral spinal extension
Bicycle ergometer (90 sec)	
(with resistance)	11. *Body fat*
	Triceps skinfold
4. *Gross body coordination*	Subscapular skinfold
Scramble	Abdominal skinfold
Mat crawl	
Tire run	12. *Body size*
	Biacromial breadth
5. *Cardiorespiratory endurance*	Biiliac breadth
Physical work capacity (PWC_{170})	Height
150-yard dash	Weight
6. *Limb-eye coordination*	
Pursuit rotor (40 RPM)	
Target throw vertical	
Target throw horizontal	

* Based on data from Rarick et al. 1976.

general types of tests used by Fleishman (1964) in his two studies. The Rarick Project had fewer tests than Fleishman's two studies did but examined the relationships among measures of physical size, body composition, strength, endurance, flexibility, manual control, and body control.

The Rarick Project's main concern was to compare the movement factor structure of normal and retarded children. The forty-six tests were administered to 145 normal children, ages 6 through 9, and 261 retarded children divided into younger (ages 6 through 9) and older (ages 10 through 13) age groups. Our summary will focus on the normal children. The test data were correlated separately for boys and girls, with age partialled to remove the possible confounding effect of the 4-year age span within each of the age groups. Six factor analyses then were calculated separately for boys and girls by using three different types of analytical models, with an orthogonal and an oblique solution for each. Different factors may be found by using different analyses, which made it possible to find factors that consistently appear, regardless of the analysis being employed.

Table 6-5 lists the six *Comparable Common Factors* (CCF) identified for the boys and girls in the Rarick Project. These factors had three or more tests with loadings of .40 or higher and were found in at least four of the six factor analyses. The loadings in Table 6-5 are an average of the three orthogonal solutions, giving a general sense of the loadings' magnitude. These factors offer the strongest definition of the clustering of the tests used in the Rarick Project.

A general inspection of the factors for boys and girls indicates a distinct similarity. The similarity of each factor was tested by calculating the cosines between factor axes to provide the agreement cosines listed for each factor in Table 6-5. Although not a correlation coefficient, an agreement cosine indicates the similarity of a factor for boys and girls in u .ch the same way. Notice the strong similarity for all but CCF 2 (cosine = .73) and CCF 6 (cosine = .69). The overall similarity is quite impressive. Remember that the level of performance may be quite different, with boys generally having higher mean performance scores, but the factors for boys and girls are very much the same. The factors for mentally retarded children, analyzed separately for younger and older boys and girls, were similar, although not to the extent for normal boys and girls. *A major finding in the Rarick Project is the similarity of factors identified for children, regardless of sex and intellectual level of functioning.*

According to the factors in Table 6-5, CCF 1 had many test loadings above .40 for what appears to be strength and body size, as listed for hypothesized abilities 1, 2, 3, and 12. Notice that strength did not divide into several factors, and endurance did not appear as a separate factor. CCF 6 included some of the tests proposed as explosive muscular strength, and the distinction seems to be that CCF 6 is body control or coordination to run and jump, whereas CCF 1 is limited to force production with few coordination problems to solve. This may be strength as a more direct output (CCF 1), compared with strength as an indirect part of maximal performance in more skillful movements (CCF 6). Note that a body composition (fat or dead weight) factor was identified in CCF 4, as was proposed in hypothesized ability 11. The three highest loadings in CCF 4 did not relate to strength or skill in CCF 1 and 6, as might be expected, considering the maximal strength and force outcomes being measured.

Manual control was identified in CCF 3 in essentially the way listed in hypothesized ability 7. We use manual control to label this factor because it includes manipulative dexterity and some visual-spatial control, as discussed in Chapter 3. Throwing skills of accuracy and distance were the primary definers in CCF 2 which the Rarick Project called Gross Limb-Eye Coordination. Further examination of this factor is needed to determine whether it goes beyond throwing as a general skill to include other aspects of limb-eye coordination, as listed in hypothesized ability 6 (pursuit rotor). Balancing tasks grouped somewhat together on CCF 5, with static and dynamic balance not separated, as listed in hypothesized factors 8 and 9. The lack of separation is consistent with other findings discussed in Chapter 3.

The overall power of the Rarick Project can be seen in the six analyses accounting for an estimated 72 percent of the total variance for boys and 68 percent for girls. The reverse of this is that approximately 30 percent of the total variance was not attached or not related in describing factors for these tests and participants. Nevertheless, this is quite good when considering the difficulty of accounting for all of anything. The tests in the Rarick Project were varied and were

TABLE   **Comparable Common Factors (CCF)***
6-5

FACTOR (AGREEMENT COSINE)	AVERAGE LOADINGS†	
	Boys	*Girls*
CCF 1. Strength—Power—Body Size (.95)		
Bicycle with resistance	87	68
Height	85	47
Knee flexion	84	61
Grip strength right	80	64
Bi-acromial breadth	78	57
Weight	75	
Grip strength left	73	62
Knee extension	73	58
Elbow flexion	68	69
Bicycle without resistance	70	50
Elbow extension	66	65
Bicycle ergometer total		66
Physical working capacity (170)		53
CCF 2. Gross Limb-Eye Coordination (.73)		
Target throw horizontal	80	60
Target throw vertical	79	42
Softball throw	72	68
Mat crawl	60	
Tire run	52	60
CCF 3. Fine Visual Motor Coordination (.97)		
Purdue Pegboard	78	68
Minnesota Manipulative	72	75
Ring stacking	70	73
Golfball placement	65	58
2-Plate tapping	65	54
Tire run	62	
Pursuit rotor (40 RPM)	57	
CCF 4. Fat or Dead Weight (.95)		
Abdominal skinfold	94	88
Subscapular skinfold	92	91
Triceps skinfold	82	86
Weight	49	77
Bi-illiac breadth		66
Bi-acromial breadth		57
Scramble		51
CCF 5. Balance (.89)		
Railwalk sideways	‡	67
Stork test	57	55
Railwalk backward	‡	58
Railwalk forward		58
Target throw vertical		50
CCF 6. Leg Power and Coordination (.69)		
Scramble	53	47
35-yard dash	‡	81
150-yard dash	‡	74
Vertical jump		70
Standing broadjump		58
Mat crawl		‡

* Based on data from Rarick et al. 1976.
† Average of three orthogonal solutions with decimal point omitted. Blank indicates that two or more of the three loadings were less than .40.
‡ Only two of three loadings were .40 or above.

analyzed in a rigorous, multiple fashion. The proposed ability structure was not verified in the subsequent analyses, but it was a useful starting point for selecting a preliminary set of tests. Considerable work now is needed to carry the obtained factors further, as suggested in some of our comments. The most important finding is the similarity in factors identified for boys and girls.

Person-clusters. A second type of analysis was made in the Rarick Project to identify person-clusters, to make a graphic profile of relatively homogeneous groups of subjects. Using the factors identified for a group, the children's scores

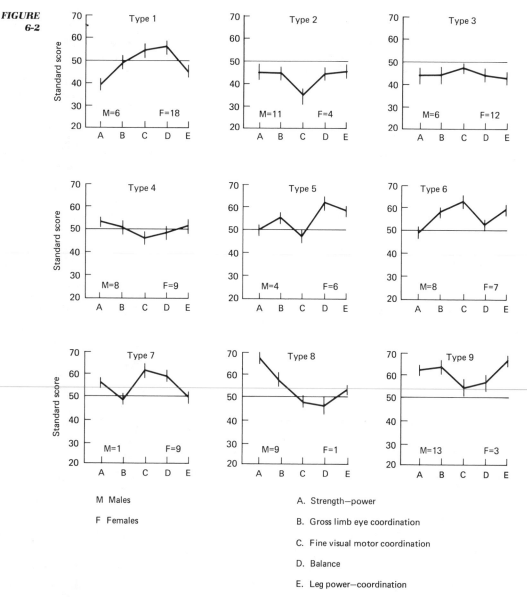

FIGURE 6-2

M Males

F Females

A. Strength—power

B. Gross limb eye coordination

C. Fine visual motor coordination

D. Balance

E. Leg power—coordination

Motor performance typologies for boys and girls. (Reproduced with permission from Rarick, Dobbins, and Broadhead, 1976.)

in that group were converted to standard scores for the tests used to define CCF 1 through 6, except that CCF 4 (fat or dead weight) was omitted. Level of performance in the form of a standard score was used to place a score of one child on one test in relation to those of all other children in the group. A profile was constructed for each child to describe the relative level of performance on each factor. A series of analyses was made to cluster or group individuals with similar profiles for the five factors. This is shown in Figure 6-2 for the nine typologies for normal boys and girls in the Rarick Project. Type 1 was characteristic of 6 boys and 18 girls. Using the factor labels in Figure 6-2, Type 1 children had low strength-power scores, were average in gross limb-eye coordination, were above average in fine visual-motor coordination and balance, and were marginally low in leg power-coordination. Types 2 and 3 were low in all factors, whereas Type 4 was average, and Type 9 was above average in all factors. All but 10 of the 145 boys and girls were placed in one of the nine person-clusters.

Typologies give a different view of factors or abilities because they refer to individuals rather than tests. One warning is that a different set of person-clusters or profiles should be expected if this type of analysis is carried out separately for boys and girls. Combining boys and girls into one analysis will alter the standard scores if their means and distributions are not similar. This is illustrated in Type 8, in which eight boys and only one girl are found to have quite high strength-power and gross limb-eye coordination (throwing accuracy and distance), with average performance in the other factors. The reverse is true in Type 7, in which nine girls and only one boy are identified. It would be useful to place individuals in a typology within their gender group.

Chapter Summary

Normative performance data were reviewed in Chapter 5 with the conclusion that we need to synthesize and organize the vast amount of rather unrelated movement performance data into some form of conceptual order. One approach has been to think of abilities as underlying aptitudes determining the level of performance in similar movement situations. The use of factor analysis was reviewed as a procedure for identifying factors and inferring the existence of abilities. We stressed that researchers must begin with a hypothesized set of abilities to be tested and adjusted in a sequence of studies, including a demonstration that factors (abilities) can predict achievement in a variety of situations.

Nothing definitive can be stated at this time, because the search to identify children's movement abilities has not been conducted extensively and with sufficient rigor. Adult males' movement abilities have been reliably identified, although with rather limited applications. The Rarick Project (Rarick et al. 1976) is a starting point with a good preliminary structure and a good first set of findings, but other studies of children's movement abilities provide very few organizing structures and little useful test information. An important finding in the Rarick Project is the similarity of factors for boys and girls, even though their mean performance levels generally are quite different. This finding needs to be replicated and tested at many age levels. Another important contribution is the recognition of person-clusters in addition to test-clusters. The clustering of profiles should remind us that factors only identify abilities, whereas we also need to study how levels of abilities are combined in individuals to represent different types of movers.

The search for children's movement abilities has been limited primarily by the lack of systematic and continuing efforts. Part of this is the enormity and complexity of this line of research. Also, most studies to date have focused on other issues, such as test validations and perceptual-motor learning problems, which provide information about children's movement abilities only as a secondary and not as a continuing concern. A serious conceptual limitation is that single performance scores are used in factor analyses. It would be interesting to use component scores, such as the four component scores in Connolly's (1968) peg-moving task, which are combined and lost when using a single performance score. Different test conditions, such as the size of the target hole, also should be included, because component scores sometimes are affected differently. Analyses become more complicated with the addition of component scores and different test conditions, but we should learn more about abilities, with many ways to measure each movement effort, and not be limited to a single outcome measure. Another consideration is that the maximal effort is measured in most movement tasks, whereas the establishment and refinement of movement control should be the focus in the early years. This means that different movement tasks must be used and that measurements must reflect the initial control of movement rather than the maximal output, along the lines of the limb movement tasks described in Chapter 3.

Without being able to identify children's movement abilities, we cannot study their changes, but we can offer some comments for consideration. In general, abilities usually become more complicated with age, which requires examining movement factors at different ages. Analyses across several age groups by Krus, Bruininks, and Robertson (1981) were said to be similar, but no test of similarity was reported in the way that the factors of boys and girls were compared in the Rarick Project (Rarick et al. 1976). Many movement factors have been found for adults, which means that the movement factors for children also must be numerous or must increase in number with age. If movement factors indeed exist and change with age, we need both cross-sectional and longitudinal analyses to study changes.

A particularly difficult problem in studying change in movement abilities is measuring movement performance. This was discussed earlier in measuring components of performance scores and initial control of movement, rather than maximal output. Matters become more complicated when recognizing that the same measurement often cannot be used at different ages. For example, walking is not a useful measure during the first year, is a primary descriptor in the second year, and is progressively less useful in subsequent years. We need the same or similar measures when studying change, which is a problem encountered when studying any aspect of human movement and is something that can be only partially resolved by finding similar rather than the same movement measures.

Identifying children's movement abilities does not seem very promising at the moment, and understanding their development is even more remote. This does not mean that movement abilities do not exist, but we need to explore different approaches to the existence of abilities and the changes within and among them.

C | *SUMMARY AND COMMENTS*

7 | *Nature of Change*

Changes are particularly noticeable and dramatic earlier in life, as well as reasonably similar in progression, if not in rate, among individuals. Early movement development follows a general order or sequence that is similar for babies in all parts of the world, although the rate of development for the age of specific achievements may vary considerably for individual children. Thus, we expect babies and young children to walk and handle objects in a similar progression of improvement, but some will do so sooner than others. Later movement development is less orderly, in that considerable variation is observed in what individuals do and how they move to perform similar movement tasks. The following descriptive summary will elaborate the nature of change in earlier and later development. We also shall comment on limitations and problems in describing and analyzing change.

Descriptive Summary

Self-movements must be controlled to some extent before they can be used in a changing environment. Babies at their second birthday have a basic control of posture, locomotion, and manipulation. The major achievements in controlling self-movements are standing upright, walking, reaching, and grasping. Refinements and variations are achieved by the early school years, and so younger school-children have a large movement repertoire that is well adapted to more closed movement situations. Their movements are more consistent, more continuous, more accurate, and better coordinated, with fewer extraneous movements. They have better motion stability and can do more things simultaneously. Force is better modulated, and spatial accuracy is quite good when moving in a stable environment. The force generated in producing movement also is better controlled and creates fewer related problems.

Young babies soon can move in a changing environment, but only in very limited movement situations. They can read the environment to grasp a slowly moving object, even though their control of arm-hand movements is not yet very accurate. But children in their early school years have considerable difficulty in open movement situations that are continuous and limited in the time available to cope with spatial-temporal requirements. Even older children have difficulty when abstract requirements, such as game rules and game strategies, are involved. Younger children are limited in some respects by their lower level of movement control, which increases the magnitude of their movement errors and also their movement control requirements, because they must make larger movement adjustments than do movers who make smaller movement errors. Younger children's movement control is adequate when spatial accuracy requirements are not too great, abstract requirements are low, sufficient time is available to do the movement task, and simultaneous movements are not involved. Younger children are limited in how much and how fast they can process environmental and movement information, as well as in what they can process. They also have fewer movement knowledges (rules) and movement strategies, which means they do not have as many options in solving movement problems.

Maximal performance scores increase noticeably by the early adult years in measures of force, distance, and speed. The speed of manual movements and reaction time improve substantially during the early school years, followed by a lesser rate of change for older children and youths. Forceful movements, including strength measures, tend to increase at a steady rate of change until a mean peak performance is reached soon after the pubertal years. Mean performance scores sometimes vary quite substantially when comparing age groups from different geographical regions, but the patterns of change across age are quite similar.

Gender differences are negligible until the early school years when mean differences in performance levels are consistently reported for some movement skills, although the differences at these ages are not very substantial in absolute amount. Small but significant mean differences in the speed of manual movements have been reported, but with no consistent pattern to favor boys or girls. The mean reaction time tends to be faster for boys and clearly is faster for young adult males, although the size of the mean difference is not important in most movement situations. Younger boys have better mean performance scores than younger girls do for play-game skills and strength, but there is considerable overlap in boy-girl distributions. Mean performance score differences for these maximal performance measures become larger by the end of the pubertal years, and so there is little overlap in the score distributions of young men and young women. There is some evidence that gender differences on maximal performance measures are decreasing, because girls are becoming more involved in movement activities.

Movement abilities, as underlying aptitudes, have been hypothesized in various ways, but little has been done to identify children's movement abilities systematically and comprehensively. If movement abilities exist, even though not yet specified for children, it seems likely that they change with age to become more complex. It would be useful to go beyond identifying movement abilities to profile individuals and trace individual changes in movement abilities. Measurements and analyses also are needed to examine changes in components of performance scores rather than be limited to single performance scores.

Group patterns of change for a specific movement task across ages often are similar for different groups, but absolute levels of performance may be different among groups. That is, rates of change appear to be similar among groups, but the age of initial achievement and the level of achievement may be different. Patterns of change also are similar across some movement tasks, as noted for a more consistent rate of change in forceful movements (play-game skills and strength), in contrast with large increases during earlier years, followed by small increases in later years for speeded manual movements and reaction time.

It is difficult to get beyond these general statements about group patterns of change because very large amounts of data and sophisticated statistical analyses are needed to look further. A particular group, or *cohort*, may have a different pattern of change because important events in the surround may strongly influence both the rate of change and the level of achievement. For example, children in the depression years of the 1930s lived in a different personal-social-cultural environment from that of their off-spring, who enjoyed the affluence of the 1950s or 1960s. Girls in both generations were surrounded by different attitudes toward participation in physical activity. Another possibility is that children living in the same time period may have similar diets, similar climates, and other similar conditions in their surround to form a cohort, in contrast with children living in a different set of conditions. Also, an individual might be a member of several cohorts, depending on the criteria. A problem in studying the development of cohorts is that they can be formed and reformed according to the investigator's interest. Nevertheless, it is important to recognize that the group patterns of change discussed throughout Part I are general representations which surely are *different in level of achievement for some cohorts*. We must find out if the cohorts differ in their overall pattern of change, which leads us to ask: *Is there a change in kind in addition to a change in quantity?*

Individual differences in movement development are obvious but have not been carefully documented. Babies follow similar progressions of change with different individual rates of change, as illustrated in Shirley's movement biographies (1931). Group variability measures of performance scores reveal the rather sizable differences in level of individual performance to be expected in any group of children. The ability profiles in the Rarick Project (Rarick, et al. 1976) are an interesting visual representation of individual differences. The problem remains that very little is known about individual patterns of change and stability.

General Perspectives of Change

The development of movement control has been viewed primarily as achieving control of self-movements and moving in a changing environment. From this perspective, the nature of change is that early movement development is establishing control of self-movements, whereas later movement development is using self-movements in changing environments that involve progressively greater requirements for spatial-temporal accuracy. Early movement development is gaining control of movement production to have the appropriate body parts move in an appropriate sequence with an appropriate amount of force. Later movement development is refining and extending movement control to create the spatial-temporal accuracy appropriate for the existing movement situation. Movement control in closed movement situations is needed to some extent before it can be used in similar but more open movement situations.

Other perspectives of change need to be considered, given that each is merely a way of organizing descriptions of change. We shall present two more perspectives, with the reminder that all perspectives overlap and intermingle. Perspectives are not correct or incorrect and are not explanations in competition with one another, but are a different way of looking at the same thing differently.

Consistency and Constancy

Another way to regard the general nature of change is that movement development involves the solution of two major movement problems of consistency and constancy (Keogh 1975, 1977). The first movement problem is developing *movement consistency* in order to have a *reliable set of movements* for coping with everyday, recurring movement problems. Young movers have minimal movement control, and they cannot consistently repeat an intended movement. Initial attempts to grasp an object or hold the head upright illustrate a lack of movement consistency. Lack of consistency, in turn, is characterized by too much movement, unnecessary movements, and variability in sequencing and timing (phasing) within a movement. Movements become more consistent and refined and in time are modified to produce a more elegant solution to a movement problem. Consistency in a basic and comprehensive movement repertoire provides the building blocks that can be used to develop more complex movements. An important difference between younger and older movers is that older movers have a greater movement consistency in controlling more limited and more complex movements. The development of movement consistency is the first major achievement needed by young movers.

The second movement problem is developing *movement constancy*, which is the *flexible use of movement consistencies* in a variety of movement situations. When a movement can be made with sufficient consistency, the mover must learn to use and then to vary the movement in solving various movement problems. Constancy is recognizing and using similar situations and responses and requires flexibility in both perceptual and response organization. The mover must recognize the need to "catch," whether seeing a person making a throwing movement with a round object or seeing a piece of paper about to be blown off a desk. The mover then must be able to catch, whether sitting down or standing upright. The same movement may be used to catch the ball and the falling piece of paper. The mover may also use quite different catch movements in both situations, often depending on considerations such as the mover's initial position and the importance of catching the object. Older movers will have more ways to move, and they will know more about mixing and matching movement solutions and problems.

Consistency and constancy are twin concepts conceived as transactional, as each alters the state of the other. It seems obvious that a sufficient consistency level must exist before a movement can be used flexibly, and achieving movement consistency should lead to movement constancy. It also seems likely that developing movmement constancy can help improve movement consistency. Children's play activities exemplify the difference between consistency and constancy and the existence of both in the same general situation. Children at play often repeat a movement many times, as well as "play" with it by making it in different and unusual ways. Repetition should lead to a more consistent movement performance and a better knowledge of the movement. Playing with a movement is the flexible use of it and an achievement of movement constancy. Some children play solo catch for long periods of time by throwing a ball against a wall and catching it as it rebounds. The solo player can modify the play by throwing to the same place but varying the catch hand, often as part of an imagined set of events. The player can also use the same general catching movement but vary the throwing movement to create a different rebound. The point is that children establish an extensive repertoire of reliable movements that can be used flexibly and adaptively. These general achievements are the development of movement consistency and movement constancy.

Competence

Describing change in the development of movement control has been limited to specific achievements, with very few ways of describing movement environment interplay beyond our analyses and comments. Achievements are measured primarily according to movement mechanics and performance scores and do not help us see a whole person in the complete surround. Achievement needs to be measured and studied in a broader perspective of effective participation or *competence* (Connolly and Bruner, 1974). This is a functional rather than a skill perspective that tells whether a person is *effective* in a situation. Babies may be effective, thus competent, even though they are not skillful in more traditional performance measures. Babies may find many different ways to cross a room and examine an object, though vary markedly in their level of achievement on specific locomotor skills. Shirley's movement bibliographies illustrate competent behavior without a correspondingly high level of movement achievement, including Walley's competence in "getting adults to do for him the things his own legs could not do." We all know other examples in which individuals are good movers but not successful participants. Competence implies that an individual can adapt and adjust to get the job done.

Competence also implies the transactional interplay of movers and environments, particularly that movers can change environments rather than limit the interplay to the environment's changing the movers. The impact of individuals on their environments is most obvious in social interactions in which babies and mothers both help determine and change their social interaction (Ainsworth and Bell 1974). Changes in individual perceptions are well documented and can lead to changes in environments. One example is a baby's changing view of the world in both direct and abstract terms. A newborn usually lies face up or face down with a limited view of the immediate surround. The view changes considerably when a baby changes to an upright posture and becomes mobile, although visual input is from the knee to the belt height of adults, whose faces generally must be seen with an upward look. Changes in physical growth, added to increased mobility, offer a visual perspective from a different position. Abstract perceptions of the world expand to include imagined physical and social surrounds that have not directly been viewed. All of this is to emphasize that as the mover changes, the environments must change in how the mover reads movement situations and helps create movement tasks.

Competencies often are used in a rather limited sense when compiling a list of tasks as goals to be achieved in an educational program or as criteria for job selection and promotion. Specific behaviors are stated as criteria for achievement. An example of a general competence is to be "water safe," which is defined in a list of competencies (criteria), such as entering a swimming pool from the side and staying afloat for 10 minutes. Notice that competencies are only a general mastery of "can do" at a specified level of performance.

Our concern here is with competence in more general terms, although we shall also consider more limited, specific competencies. One problem is that general movement competencies must be defined before the development of competencies can be studied. White and Watts (1973) resolved the problem of identifying developmental competencies by making extensive observations of young children.

They then asked experienced professionals to examine the observational data and point out important social and nonsocial competencies. An involved set of analyses and discussions led to the identification of eleven classes of behaviors characterizing young children as competent.

1. To get and maintain adults' attention when appropriate.
2. To use adults as resources.
3. To express affection and hostility toward adults.
4. To assume control (leadership) in peer-related activities.
5. To follow the lead of others.
6. To express affection and/or hostility toward peers.
7. To compete.
8. To resist distractions.
9. To empathize.
10. To praise oneself and/or show pride in one's accomplishments.
11. To involve oneself in adult role-playing behaviors or otherwise express the desire to grow up.

The social competencies listed by White and Watts are broad, but they provide a more functional sense of development than does a listing of specific achievements. We need a similar list of movement competencies to identify and study movement change in broader terms. Consistency, constancy, and competence are offered as different views of change in the development of movement control.

The Nature of Change in Developmental Functions

Our discussion to this point has concentrated on different ways to characterize change. Descriptions of change also can be separated into two general concerns: change in developmental functions and change in individuals. This is an important distinction discussed by McCall (1979) and credited to Emmerich (1964). *Development functions* are the constructs being studied, such as movement speed or throwing accuracy, which vary considerably in the scope of their intended coverage within the area of movement development. *Individual change* is related to the pattern of change in a developmental function and may be extended to include individual patterns across several developmental functions. A simple illustration of developmental function and individual change is provided in Figure 5-19. The group pattern of change, shown by the plotting of group mean scores across test sessions, describes change in the developmental function of jumping. Individual patterns of change are shown by the performance curves plotted for each of five boys.

Developmental function and individual change are not independent. The measurement of a developmental function is the average of many individual performance scores at a series of points in time. The importance of an individual pattern of change is in comparison with the pattern of change for the developmental function. Thus, change in a developmental function is an average pattern of individual change, and an individual pattern of change must have a reference point, which is the pattern of change for the developmental function.

Our discussion pertains to developmental functions as the *general constructs we use to represent a conceptual sense of movement development*. The patterns of change summarized in Part I chart developmental functions, even though not explicitly stated in most cases. In some cases, change is described simply because obvious changes, such as walking and grasping, occur. At some point we must consider what these changes mean to developmental functions, and so we must identify and study developmental functions more systematically in order to describe the nature of change in movement development.

Levels of Description: Norms and Components

Assuming that several developmental functions have been found, each must provide information about change over a period of time. Two ways to describe change are as norms and components. This is an overly simplified division, but one that is useful in examining change in developmental functions.

The order and rate of change are noted in specific achievements and levels of achievements across a set of age points for more general performance outcomes. Much of what is presented in Part I is normative in its progressions of change and summaries of changes in performance level. Normative data offer common and often functional expectancies about changes in movement behaviors. Normative descriptions of order and rate of change help us understand better the nature of change, but only at a superficial level based on general preformance outcomes.

Movement sometimes is analyzed in order to study changes in movement and performance components, which shows where changes occur in the movement and the movement situation. As noted, this is an inferential process in which component changes are seen as indicating changes in certain aspects of the motor control system or other systems that help produce movement. The approach continues to be normative in looking for the order and rate of change, but the emphasis is on changes within components of what is observed and measured, rather than on general performance outcomes.

The different levels of description may be viewed as different levels of analysis. Each can be limiting. A strictly normative approach, as illustrated by the data summaries in Chapter 5, is a general and quite narrow analysis of the order and rate of change. We get better as we get older, to a point, and we can do more complex things. But a component analysis of a movement may be so limited that we cannot formulate useful inferences about how movement development is changing. This is exemplified by the detailed and almost microscopic analyses of movement mechanics in play-game skills in Chapter 4. Although each level of analysis can be useful, *we need many sources of information and many variations of both levels of analysis when studying change.* Additionally, we must describe and analyze in relation to an overall perspective of movement. We must be prepared to modify and perhaps radically change our perspective as we learn more, but there must be a perspective to direct our information gathering and to provide a basis on which the information is organized and tested. Our general perspective, as presented in Chapter 1, is to think about movement problems to be resolved in relation to controlling self-movements and moving in a changing environment. We also view movement in relation to the control of body movements and limb movements.

General Illustration: Reaching–Grasping–Intercepting

An important set of movement skills requires using the arms and hands to obtain and manipulate objects. Reaching is transporting one or both hands to a spatial location; grasping is using the digits of one or both hands to hold an object; and intercepting is transporting one or both hands to coincide with the spatial location of a moving object. For our purposes, reaching, grasping, and intercepting are three developmental functions whose pattern of change we shall describe and analyze. We shall simplify our illustration by ignoring the manipulation of objects, the continuous coinciding with moving objects, and other aspects of manual control that might be studied as developmental functions.

Reaching and grasping in the early months are organized as a single movement and later become two movements which can be carried out separately in a co-ordinated pattern of movement. Children can easily reach and grasp stationary objects by their first birthday. But many grasping variations are observed in the following years, particularly in holding writing instruments and other tools. Some interesting experiments provide a components analysis of change, such as the presentation of virtual objects to observe the conditions that elicit a grasping movement (Bower 1979). The normative descriptions of the order and rate of change catalogue the expected changes which then need to be examined at a components level of analysis to identify the conditions related to these changes. Simple reaching and grasping are not worth following much beyond the first year, because these basic movements become part of other developmental functions, such as manipulating and intercepting objects.

Intercepting a moving object adds the spatial and temporal requirements discussed in Chapter 4 to reaching for a stationary object. That is, picking up a pencil rolling on a table is reaching to place the hand in a spatial location to grasp the pencil before it falls off the table. Interception uses other developmental functions, including grasping in this example, with the need to read a moving environment and produce a movement that is spatially and temporally accurate. We do not have sufficient normative data to describe the order and rate of change, but we do know from everyday observations that young schoolchildren improve in intercepting moving objects in play-game skills such as catching, striking, chasing, and being chased. The component analyses summarized in Chapter 4 indicate that babies at 4 months can read slow movements in the environment to intercept objects, even though their control of hand movements is not very adequate. But young children have considerable difficulty with rapid movements and more continuous movement situations. This leads us further in our study of change in this developmental function to consider the role of vision in controlling movement and the need to improve processing skills, both of which will be examined in Part II.

The need for many sources of information and the use of both levels of description are clearly seen in this illustration. We also tried to demonstrate that descriptions of change lead to additional questions and concerns, including identifying and conceptualizing developmental functions in different ways.

Identifying and Describing Developmental Functions

Part I traces change through tasks, such as reaching, grasping, walking, throwing, and the like. This is a matter of convenience because it is easy to gather normative data from and make component analyses of tasks that have similar movement patterns or purposes. We want to emphasize the need to think in terms of developmental functions, rather than descriptions of changes in an endless number of tasks. Reaching and grasping, as used in our illustration, really are too narrow in scope to be developmental functions, but manual control is too large an aspect of movement behavior to treat as a single developmental function. A developmental function must have sufficient scope but be of a manageable size in order to serve as a developmental function. Intercepting moving objects might be an appropriate choice as a developmental function in terms of scope and size.

In studying movement development, developmental functions will be redefined as we learn more and have different concerns. As we accumulate more descriptions and analyses, we shall shift our thinking away from tasks and level of performance to how the movement is produced. An example is our suggestion that the role and use of vision and the processing of information be considered in producing movement and, therefore, in developing movement control. We should identify developmental functions according to vision and processing rather than types of movements or types of tasks. Our focus then will be on developing mover resources for coping with task requirements and situation conditions. This will shift our perspective as we learn more about developmental change and think more about changes in mover resources.

One consideration in trying to measure change in developmental functions is that movement tasks and situations are not the same as individuals develop. We necessarily must describe movement behaviors across a period of time, which means that the movement tasks and situations should have a similarity or *equivalence* across the designated time period. Equivalence is an obvious and a complex problem that we have mentioned many times in tracing the development of movement control from the early months through the early school years. Many basic achievements in the first and second years cannot be followed directly and easily in subsequent years. For example, reaching and grasping become part of manipulating and intercepting. In the terms we have been using, are the spatial-temporal requirements similar or equivalent when tracing the development of movement control needed to reach and grasp a stationary object through to manipulating it and intercepting a moving object? It seems likely that reaching and grasping must be achieved to some extent before manipulating and intercepting can be successful, but it also seems likely that additional and quite different aspects of the movement production systems now are important. More precise control of digital movements is demanded, and the mover must be able to read the environment in more dynamic and continuous ways. Additionally, the mover's resources change, which further confounds the issue of equivalence. Thus developmental functions must be redefined as we trace change across the longer time periods.

Conceptualizing Change and Development

A key point in conceptualizing development is that individuals qualitatively differ in how they do things. An example given in our introductory chapter is thinking in abstract rather than concrete terms. Movement examples are making a continuous movement out of a series of discrete movements and represesenting in movement what is seen or imagined, as when copying figures. We must find out when movers' resources change qualitatively to enable them to do things differently.

General representations of qualitative and quantitative change are placed side by side in Figure 7-1 to illustrate periods of change. Quantitative change is shown on the right to represent a normative change. The pattern of change may vary, but the change can be described as the rate of improvement for the entire period

FIGURE
7-1

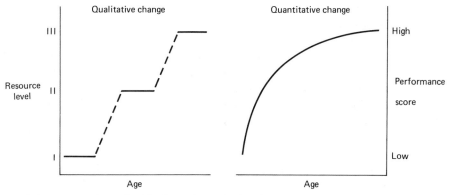

General representations of qualitative and quantitative change.

of time or portions thereof. Qualitative change is shown as a change in resource level to indicate that a mover achieves a higher and different level of resources. A transition between resource levels is marked with a dotted line. The shift might be from a concrete to an abstract level of thinking or from a discrete to a continuous organization of movement. Qualitative changes in resource levels presumably affect quantitative changes in performance scores, although not directly, as implied by placing the two figures side by side.

The transition between resource levels is when the resources change. Development in the most basic sense occurs during transitional periods, and so our study of transitional periods must begin by confirming the existence of two or more resource levels. Individuals must be identified as being in one resource level and approaching a transitional period and then must be studied during the transitional period. This simple time schedule for studying change is exceedingly difficult to accomplish, but it offers a general sense of what needs to be done.

The time that an individual is at a particular resource level is what others have called a *developmental stage.* Examples are Piaget's intellectual stages of development and Erikson's stages of man. Stages often are viewed as fixed and invariant sequences, but there probably are individual variations that combine stages or resource levels. Stages in movement development when movers are qualitatively different have not been pinpointed.

Our descriptions of change in Part I are organized according to developing control of self-movements and developing movement control in changing circumstances. These are not stages of movement development, nor are consistency, constancy, and competence, but are perspectives for looking at the development of movement control as what movers need to accomplish. We use these perspectives to help us consider movement development. We now need to conceptualize change in movement development as change in resource levels, analogous to the stages proposed in other areas of human development, although we do not believe that there are fixed sequences to be found. Our point is that we do not know very much about how change occurs in movement development, which requires a change in how we conceptualize movement development. Part II discusses how change in movement development occurs, although at this time we can only point to possible changes in resource levels, without proposing stages or explanations to be tested.

Chapter Summary

Our descriptions of change in movement development are limited to quantitative descriptions of change, which range from normative performance scores to analyses of movement mechanics. Throughout Part I we tried to look at change in more qualitative terms by emphasizing what little is available to describe component changes and by discussing movement problems to be resolved. This leads us to think about changes in the mover's resources, rather than about changes in achievement levels for specific movement tasks. What we are suggesting is a radical change in perspective to get away from the tasks and to begin to think about the movers. But we shall continue to be interested in tasks as indicating what movers can do, and so we must continue to describe movement, but for different reasons and in more effective ways.

PART TWO

INFLUENCES ON CHANGE

The descriptions of change in Part I led to many comments and speculations on how change occurs and what influences change. We shall examine some of these possibilities in Part II. As noted at the end of Chapter 7, this is merely description at another level. The best that can be done now is to identify general influences on change and speculate on what might be specific mechanisms of change and how they might function. The general influences are the environments of the inner and outer surrounds portrayed in the movement situation in Figure 1-1, with the different environments providing the organization of the chapters in Part II.

Our emphasis in Part II is on the aspects of the inner surround that seem to affect movement development most directly. Personal influences in the inner surround and social influences in the outer surround are important, but probably in less direct ways. Personal values and social conditions are more likely to influence what a person chooses to do and the extent of involvement. That is, personal-social influences affect participation experiences that limit or enhance movement development. Personal-social influences in this respect have an indirect effect on movement experiences.

The general issue in Part II is the influences on change in movement development. A number of possibilities are identified and discussed separately for three general influences: biological structures and systems, sensory–perceptual systems, and processing capabilities. An important point is that each agent of change may make a different contribution to different aspects of movement development and at different ages.

A | BIOLOGICAL STRUCTURES AND SYSTEMS

CHAPTER
8

Biological Changes Toward Maturity

An individual's biological makeup provides the structures and functions directly responsible for producing movement. Bones are held in place by different kinds of tissue and are moved by muscle contractions that are organized and directed by neural impulses. Oxygen taken from the atmosphere is transported to the muscles for use in energy production. Most of the body's systems participate in some way, such as providing information, regulating particular operations, or eliminating waste products. Our concern in this chapter is biological change toward maturity in those aspects of our biological makeup that are important to movement development.

Newborns change almost as we watch them, to become bigger in overall size and different in body proportions. Similar changes in internal organs and systems, although not directly visible, can be measured in ways that help us "see" internal biological changes. As a starting point for considering biological changes leading to a mature state, some changes are *structural*, and others are *functional*. Physical features may change to create a change in structure, in contrast with a change in how an organ or system functions. Organs, such as the brain and heart, will change in structure to be larger as well as different in the interconnections of units within each organ. Functional changes mean that more can be done or done differently, such as the control of lower neutral units by higher brain centers, a decrease in heart rate, and an increase in amount of oxygen transported. The distinction between structure and function is not always clear-cut, but it is useful when trying to understand biological change.

Our review of biological change toward maturity covers the period from conception to *biological maturity*. Individuals are expected to change in somewhat similar ways to reach a time when each biological organ or system has and is *a complete, fully functioning structure*. At that time, an individual is mature in this aspect of biological change. The rate and age of maturity vary among the many biological organs and systems, and so each aspect of biological change must be described separately.

Maturity can be identified with some certainty for structural changes, whereas maturity of most functional changes is less certain, because functional maturity often is difficult to separate from achievements related to the functioning of the organ or system. Although size, myelinization, and similar structural features of the brain are difficult to measure, the end point of change, or maturity, in each is recognized when there are no more changes in the physical measures taken to represent these structural changes. Maturity of functioning, however, often must be inferred from related rather than direct achievements. For example, one indication of the brain's functional maturity is lateralization, in which one hemisphere controls a general type of behavior. At present, lateralization is difficult to measure, except by inference based on hand use, speech, spatial perception, and related achievements. More direct measurements of lateralization likely will be possible as technical advances are made. The example of lateralization also shows that both the structural and the functional maturity of an organ or a system are multi-faceted and involve maturity of many structural features and functional outcomes.

Biological change is used in the title of this chapter, although others might call this topic physical growth. We chose biological change to imply a broader sense of change toward maturity because growth too often is limited to structural change, particularly size. Our emphasis is on functional change because it has more impact on the development of movement control.

A framework is presented in Figure 8-1, showing three areas of biological change that are important to movement development: *bones* (skeleton), *tissues* (body composition), and *systems*. Bones and tissues provide the basic body structure for size and form and are measured as linear and proportional dimensions. The length of major bones determines linear size and body proportions, with muscle, fat, and other tissues filling out the shape of the bony structure. Muscles are lean tissue and are the means of moving bones and creating movement. The neuro-

FIGURE 8-1

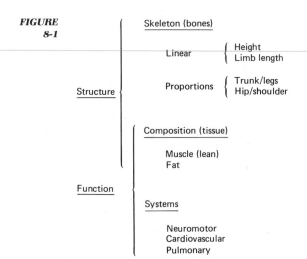

Selected aspects of biological changes toward maturity with important influences upon movement development.

209

motor system is the coupling of nerves and muscles to control muscle activity, and the cardiovascular and pulmonary systems service the neuromotor system's energy needs, primarily oxygen transport and related metabolic needs.

Structural Changes

Change in height has been described and analyzed so extensively that we shall present it first and in more detail than the other structural changes. Analyses of change in height also provoke many of the questions encountered in describing other aspects of structural change, and height is a useful alternative to chronological age as an indicator of general biological maturity.

Height

Change in height during the growing years is obvious in even casual observations and is the simplest measure of structural growth, although it requires careful measurement procedures to gather useful data. Tanner (1981) compiled a comprehensive record of the study of human growth (auxiology) in which he found that height was the basic measurement of structural growth from the time of the Greeks to the present. He lists many reasons why height measurements were recorded, including the identification of people before signatures and pictures were available, selection of military personnel for processional and fighting purposes, and medical-social concerns related to the employment of children. Tanner's historical review is an interesting account of the origins of major issues and related findings, such as daily and seasonal variations in growth measures and growth rates, secular (generation) trends, catch-up growth following interruptions related to trauma and illness, and explanations of growth as body heat (temperature), temperament, and other proposed causal factors. He also discusses the major longitudinal studies of structural growth in the United States and Western Europe. Our review of height growth follows his writings, including an earlier book on growth at adolescence (Tanner 1962).

Patterns of Change. Newborns are 18 to 22 inches in length (height) at birth, which is an amazing amount and rate of change in the 9 months since conception. Children grow to one-half their mature height by age 3 and to two-thirds their mature height by age 6. The general rate of height change can be divided into four periods, as shown in Figure 8-2. The rate of height change is very rapid from conception through birth to age 3. There is a slow but consistent rate of change from age 3 until the onset of puberty, when there is another period of rapid height change accompanied by dramatic changes in body proportions. Small increases in height occur after the end of the pubertal period. Full height usually is achieved by age 20 or soon after. Until puberty, boys on the average are slightly taller than girls. There is a large overlap, though, with some girls taller than boys

FIGURE 8-2

A general representation of four major periods of rate of height change with general comparisons of male (M) and female (F) average heights.

210

of average height at the same age and some boys smaller than girls of average height at the same age. Girls on the average enter puberty 2 years earlier than boys do, and the age at onset of puberty is quite variable among individuals. This means that height comparisons between boys and girls during puberty can differ within different samples and at different chronological ages. Men on the average are 4 to 6 inches taller than women are, with much less overlap than during the developing years.

Changes in height can be graphed as *distance* or *rate*, as shown in Figures 8-3 and 8-4 which summarize the first longitudinal study on record (Tanner 1981). A French nobleman, Count de Montbeillard, measured the height of his son at 6-month intervals from birth to age 18 between 1759-1777. Tanner explains the calculations and plottings of the data and notes a gap in the measurements from age 10.0 to 11.5, which no one can explain. The general shapes of the two curves approximate findings from many later studies in different parts of the world. The distance curve in Figure 8-3 merely indicates the height, or distance, achieved at each age. Montbeillard's son was a bit more than 50 centimeters (20 inches) at birth and was approximately 185 centimeters (72 to 73 inches) at age 18, tall even by modern standards. The rate of height change can be seen by the changes in the slope of the distance curve, but a better view of rate of height change is shown in Figure 8-4.

The rate of height change, which Tanner calls *height velocity*, is the amount of change per unit of time. The rate in Figure 8-4 is calculated as a rolling, yearly

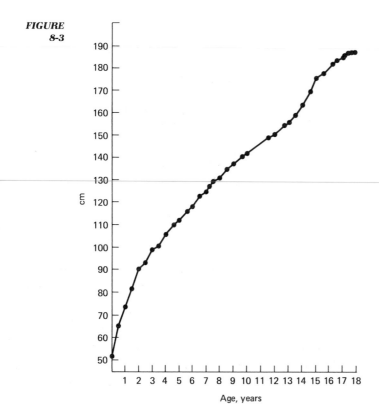

FIGURE 8-3

Height of Count de Montbeillard's son, 1759–1777.
(Reproduced with permission from Tanner, 1981.)

211

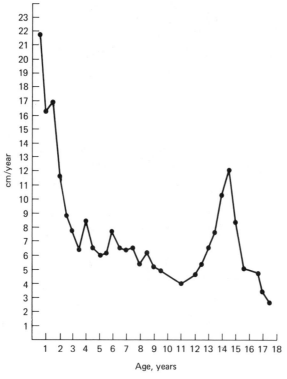

Rate of height change of Count de Montbeillard's son, 1759–1777. (Reproduced with permission from Tanner, 1981.)

velocity, by plotting 1 year of change at each 6-month interval. This means that the first plotting point at 0.5 years (6 months) is the increase from birth to 12 months, the second plotting point at 1.0 years (12 months) is the increase from 6 months to 18 months, and so on. Each plotting point overlaps with adjacent plotting points to remove *seasonal effects* in which height tends to increase more in summer and less in winter. From the general shape of Figure 8-4, we can see the four periods identified in Figure 8-2. The change is very rapid until age 3, followed by a slower and more consistent rate of change until the rapid change at puberty. The fourth period of minimal or no change marks the achievement of mature stature.

Notice that the *rate of height change decreases from birth to age 3* but that the absolute rate (amount of increase) is large compared with that at other ages. The rate of height change for Montbeillard's son decreased from 22 centimeters per year in the first year (plotting point at 0.5 years) to 9 centimeters per year in the third year (plotting point at 2.5 years). The rate of height change beyond age 3, until the decrease in rate preceding puberty, was 6 to 8 centimeters per year. The rate then increased to a peak height velocity of 12 centimeters per year during puberty. The rate of height change for Montbeillard's son varied from nearly 9 inches in the first year of life to 2 to 3 inches each year during the slower-growing years, followed by an increase of approximately 5 inches during 1 pubertal year. A decrease in rate, as seen at age 11, marks the onset of puberty, and the *peak height velocity* (age 14) is a marker that is used to represent the maximal rate of height change during puberty.

FIGURE
8-5

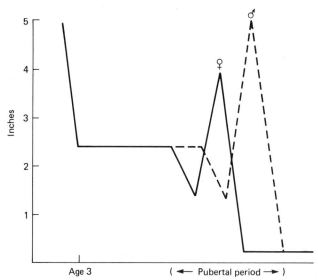

A general representation of rate of height change for girls and boys.

A general representation of the rate of height change for boys and girls is presented in Figure 8-5. Rate and age will vary considerably for individuals and different samples, but the general pattern of change for boys and girls will approximate the two curves. The decrease in rate that marks the onset of puberty is that the legs continue to grow, but the trunk slows its growth for a period of time, as if the body is preparing for the pubertal changes that occur primarily in the upper body. The increase in leg length, with proportionately less change in trunk length, produces a "leggy" look which often is quite noticeable, to the embarrassment of the growing youth.

The rate of change is similar for boys and girls up to the onset of puberty for girls, with boys on the average being slightly taller. Girls enter puberty approximately 2 years earlier than boys do and tend to go through the pubertal period in less time. Boys not only enter puberty later, but they also generally have a higher peak height velocity and a somewhat longer pubertal growth period. Boys are 4 to 6 inches taller than girls when they reach mature height, because they grow for several more years and slightly more during their pubertal years.

General Influences on Mature Stature. There are a number of genetic and environmental influences on the height achieved at maturity. Siblings tend to be similar in height because they have similar genes and usually share a similar environment. The correlation of mature heights of identical twins is .9, compared with .5 for fraternal twins and nontwin siblings (Bloom 1964). Tanner (1962) reports correlations of approximately .5 for the heights of parents and the mature stature of offspring. The larger correlation for identical twins points to genetic influences as the major determinant of mature stature.

Gender is an important part of genetic influence because males, on the average, are taller at maturity than females are. But female-male comparisons must be made within reasonably common gene pools. Height varies considerably in different gene populations, and so women in one gene population may be taller on

213

the average than are men in another gene population. Too, people in industrialized societies are increasingly mobile, which makes it difficult to select appropriate samples for female-male height comparisons. Tanner (1981) summarizes many earlier studies in which the samples of males and females for each study were from a reasonably common gene pool and the men on the average were taller than the women at maturity in all comparisons. General conclusions are that mature stature is very much determined by the genetic codes transmitted by parents and is related to gender.

Tanner also points out those environmental factors that affect mature stature. Nutrition, climate, and socioeconomic conditions have been identified as contributing to *secular trends*, which are changes noticed across time. Different generations or cohorts will achieve different mean heights or will have different rates of height change which sometimes can be attributed to environmental factors. (See Roche 1979 for a summary of secular trends in human growth, malnutrition, and development.) We generally think of secular trends as increases, but Tanner cites instances in which these have been decreases, seemingly related to times of war, economic depression, and similar extreme environmental events. Environmental factors need to be quite substantial in "weight" (for example, severe malnutrition or superior health services) in order to have an impact. Deprivation also seems to have more of an influence than enrichment does. The mean height changes between generations are small in absolute value and can be reversed in subsequent generations.

Individual Patterns of Change. The rate of height change to this point has been presented as a group or mean change in relation to chronological age. But individual children mature at such different rates that chronological age often is a misleading indicator of change. As shown in Figure 8-6, the form and intensity of height change during puberty is underestimated when viewed in relation to

FIGURE
8-6

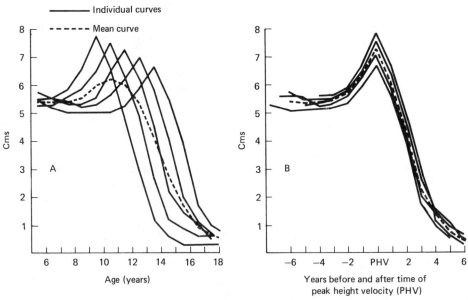

Two views of individual and mean rate of height change during pubertal growth period, plotted in relation to (A) chronological age and (B) peak height velocity. (Reproduced with permission from Tanner, 1981.)

chronological age. Individual rates of height change are plotted to the left in relation to chronological age, with the mean rate of change shown by the dotted line. Individual rates of change in the graph to the right are plotted in relation to the *peak height velocity*. Rather than chronological age, age now is years before and after the time of peak height velocity. Individual curves are strikingly similar, and the mean in the graph to the right is a better representation of their similarity. Notice in the figure to the left that earlier-maturing individuals have slightly larger increases at the time of peak height velocity, which is offset to some extent by the longer growing time of later-maturing individuals.

Individual Stability. Bloom (1964) examined stability and change in human characteristics, with height as a basic model, because height data have been reported so extensively and height probably is among the more stable human characteristics. Bloom defined stability as consistency from one point in time to another. He wanted to know if individuals maintain a similar position in a group over time, even though everyone is changing. If a child is tall when younger, will he or she be tall when older? Bloom estimated stability by the correlation of height at one age to height at a later age.

One of Bloom's main points is that *height is more stable when there is less change.* He illustrates this with what he acknowledges is an obvious and absurd question: What is the correlation of height measurements for a sample of people measured at age 20 and again at age 40? The correlation should be close to 1.0 because no change is expected and each person should have the same height measurement at both ages. We also expect a high correlation for height measurements taken at ages 7 and 8, because children change only a small amount and thus cannot be very different after 1 year. The converse is that measures of stability (correlations) will be smaller when individual change is greater; that is, when there is a long time interval with a slow rate of change or a large rate of change in a short time interval. Bloom stresses the *amount of change* as the most important consideration, because the larger the change is, the more opportunity there will be for individuals to change positions in the distribution.

Bloom carries his point further to state that stability is a function of the proportion that a growth characteristic at time A is of the growth characteristic at time B. Stated for height, he proposes that the square of the correlation is equivalent to the proportion between two height measures taken at time A and time B:

$$r^2 = \frac{\text{Mean of height at time A}}{\text{Mean of height at time B}}$$

An example is the correlation of height at age 3 (time A), when children have achieved approximately 50 percent of their mature height, to mature height at age 18 (time B). The stability correlation should be approximately .7, because $r^2 = .50$ in Bloom's equation. Bloom offers much evidence to support his point that *stability increases as less change is likely.* He also demonstrates that stability is erratic during times of great change, particularly when individuals go through a change period at different times and different rates. This means that stability will be more tenuous when one or both measurements are taken during puberty.

Bloom brings our attention to the amount of change during the period of time in question. His primary concern was to identify the influences on change, by studying height and other stable characteristics when individuals encountered extreme environmental conditions. He concludes that *environment will have the greatest influence during a period of rapid change and the least influence during a period of slow change.* Injury, disease, starvation, and similar extreme conditions will retard height growth more during the early years and puberty when there is more change to be affected.

Body Proportions

Individuals grow bigger from birth to the early adult years, by becoming taller and increasing the length of limbs and trunk and the width of hips and shoulders. Body dimensions not only increase in size but also at different rates to produce changes in body proportions. These proportional changes are shown in Figure 8-7, with body pictures at different ages adjusted in order to maintain the same height. Looking first at the newborn in the third picture from the left, the head is one-fourth of the total body length, and the legs are a little more than one-fourth of the total body length. All parts of the body grow, but the body proportions at mature height (right-hand picture) change so that the head becomes one-tenth of the total body length, compared with nearly one-half for the legs. Body proportions change more rapidly in utero, as seen in the changes from the second fetal month through the fifth fetal month to birth.

Some proportional changes in body breadth are shown, but they do not represent changes in girth. Notice that the head width approaches the shoulder and hip width at birth, whereas the head width of adults is only one-third of their shoulder width. Shoulder width from birth is greater than hip width, with males' shoulder/hip ratio increasing more than females' during puberty. Some proportional changes in girth can be inferred from these pictures, because a marked change in width also is a change in girth. Thus, the change of the head girth is proportionately smaller than that of the chest girth. The proportion of thigh girth to hip girth changes from quite small before birth to larger at birth, which is followed by a decrease that changes to an increase in the adult years.

FIGURE 8-7

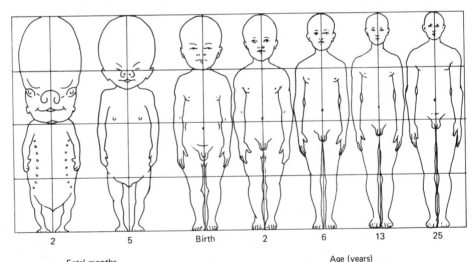

Changes in body proportions with age. (Reproduced with permission from Tanner, 1981, as copied from Stratz, 1909.)

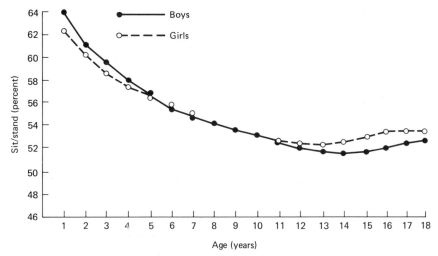

FIGURE
8-8

Ratio of sitting height (sit) to full standing height (stand) from age 1 to age 18. (Reproduced with permission from Bayer and Bayley, 1976.)

Trunk-leg Ratio. The length of the legs, trunk, and head can be measured to monitor proportional changes in body segments that contribute to height changes. The major change occurs in the legs and trunk, with the head contributing only a small amount of absolute increase from birth to the early adult years. The legs grow at a more rapid rate, as shown in Figure 8-8 by the decrease in the ratio of sitting height to standing height. Sitting height is measured as the height from the seat of the chair in which a person is sitting to the top of the head. This measures the change in trunk and head, to be compared with a full height measure that includes leg length. Sitting height is more than 60 percent of standing height in the early years and decreases to a little more than 50 percent at mature height. The change in leg-trunk proportions also can be seen in Figure 8-7.

Gender differences exist at birth and in the early years, with girls slightly longer legged in comparison with their upper-body length. Girls may be biologically more mature and, thus, slightly "ahead" in the ratio decrease shown in Figure 8-8. The reverse occurs during puberty, when boys become slightly longer legged in comparison with their upper-body length.

Hip-shoulder Ratio. Hip girth is less than shoulder girth at all ages, as shown in Figure 8-9, although hip girth increases in comparison with shoulder girth. There are no gender differences until age 7, when the hip-shoulder girth ratio increases for girls and levels off and later decreases for boys. The ratio at age 18 is quite different and is a noticeable gender difference in body proportions.

Body Composition
Bodies are composed of several kinds of tissues, with our primary concerns being muscle, as lean tissue, and fat. It is difficult to try to describe the changes in each type of tissue and in lean–fat proportion. Both muscle and fat bulk can change considerably in a short time, depending on exercise and diet. Tanner (1962) describes several ways to measure lean and fat, including X rays to measure bone, muscle, and fat, and skin-caliper measurements of skinfolds to measure the width of fat tissue surrounding a muscle. Body composition is difficult to measure well,

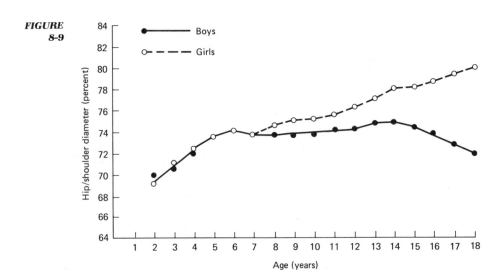

*FIGURE
8-9*

Ratio of bicristal (hip) diameter to biacromial (shoulder) diameter from age 1 to age 18. (Reproduced with permission from Bayer and Bayley, 1976).

and longitudinal data are sparse. Our brief review highlights several points, with the recommendation that Tanner and others should be consulted if you want to pursue the topic further.

General patterns of the rate of change for bone-muscle and fat are shown in Figure 8-10 for boys and girls. Bone-muscle measurements were derived from X rays of the calf and skinfold measurements were used to estimate subcutaneous

*FIGURE
8-10*

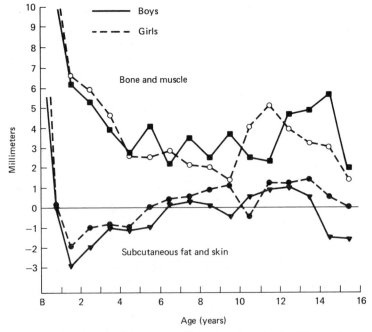

Velocity curves from birth to age 16 of bone-muscle and subcutaneous tissue (fat and skin). Measurements taken from X rays at the maximum diameter of the calf. (Reproduced with permission from Tanner, 1962, as drawn from data reported by Lombard, 1950, and Stuart and Sobel, 1946.)

fat. Although the two measures are breadths (widths) and not cross-sections, Tanner (1962) notes that they adequately approximate the relative amount of tissue composition.

The general patterns of change are somewhat similar, except that there is a greater rate of gain for bone and muscle. This means that babies are relatively fatter than children are. Additionally, there is a loss in fat, rather than a gain, from age 1 to age 5 or 6. Children beyond age 6 have very small gains in fat, with boys losing fat during part of their pubertal growth period. The rate of change for bone and muscle resembles that for height, and the rate of change for bone and muscle decreases to a more steady rate from age 4 until the onset of puberty. Girls' rate of change increases during puberty, as does the boys', who have a

FIGURE 8-11

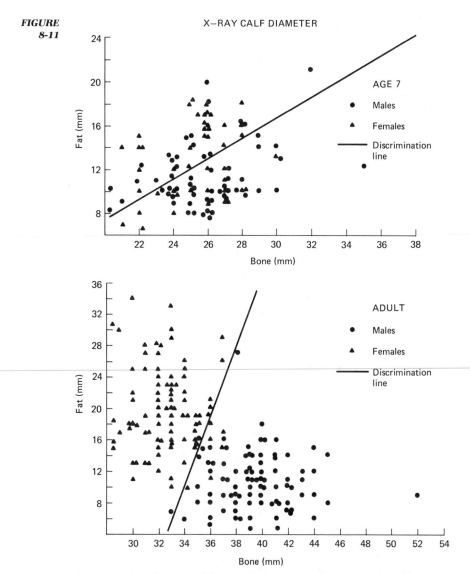

Discrimination of males and females by fat and bone diameter in the calf at age 7 and for adults. The amount misclassified to either side of discrimination line is 38 percent at age 7 and 5 percent for adults. (Reproduced with permission from Tanner, 1962.)

slightly higher peak muscle-bone rate of change. Looking across the full age range in Figure 8-10, boys overall have a higher rate of change for bone and muscle and a lower rate of gain for subcutaneous fat. The overall effects are that children progressively increase their ratio of muscle to fat and boys have a higher ratio of muscle to fat at maturity than girls do.

Another view of gender differences in body composition is shown in Figures 8-11 and 8-12. Bone and fat measurements derived from X rays of the calf were plotted in relation to one another, as illustrated in the scatterplot in Figure 8-11 for children at age 7 and for adults. A discriminant function was calculated to

FIGURE 8-12

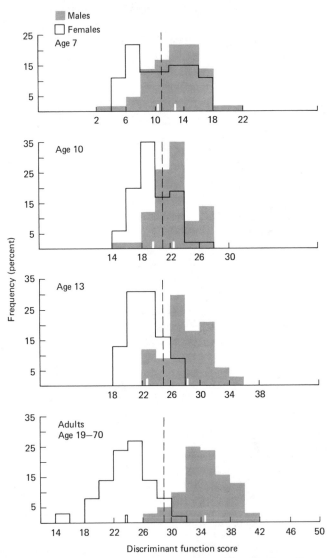

Discrimination of males and females by fat and bone in the calf at selected ages. The amount misclassified to either side of discrimination line is, from youngest to oldest, 38 percent, 29 percent, 14 percent, and 5 percent. (Reproduced with permission from Tanner, 1962, as drawn from data by Reynolds, 1949.)

220

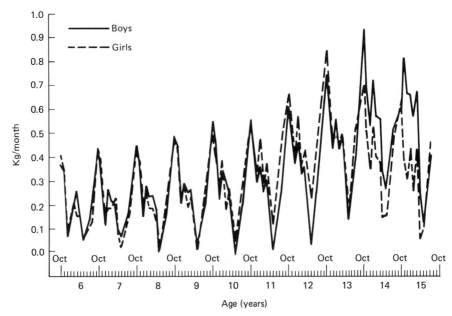

Seasonal variation in weight gain for boys and girls. (Reproduced with permission from Palmer, 1933.)

find the line that best separated males and females. A count then was made to determine how many individuals were misclassified, which means that females appeared on the male side of the line, and vice versa. Misclassification was nearly 40 percent at age 7 and only 5 percent for adults. Female and male distributions are shown in Figure 8-12, with the discriminant function line drawn vertically. This shows, at each age, the overlap and extent of misclassification. Tanner (1962) noted that this type of analysis had been done for other growth characteristics and reported that misclassification for shoulder-hip width was about 10 percent for adults.

A consideration in all aspects of growth is that there may be seasonal variations, as shown in Figure 8-13 for boys' and girls' weight gain. The rate of weight gain is larger during October and smaller during April or May. The opposite is true for height changes, with larger gains in height during the warm months and smaller ones in the cold months. Seasonal variations in weight are matched with those in muscle and fat.

Physique

Differences in body build are noted informally when, to describe general tissue composition, we say that a person is lean, muscular, or round. We refer more to structural proportions when describing a person as stocky or long- or short-waisted. Although differences in body build often are quite obvious, it is difficult to measure body build in a way that captures the many aspects involved. Physique is not body size, in being large or small in length and mass, but is a composite of proportional relationships among sizes of body parts and measures of body composition.

Various ratios of height and weight provide simple and quick estimates of physique. Bayley and Davis (1935) used the ratio of weight/(height)^2 to measure a lateral–linear relationship during the first 3 years. Another ratio is the Ponderal Index, in which height is divided by the cube root of weight. Wetzel (1941, 1943) devised a grid based on height and weight for seven different growth channels that represent different body builds. Children are measured at regular intervals with the expectation that a change in growth channel will indicate a change in health status. Ratios of height and weight obviously are quite limited estimates of physique, but they have the advantage of using readily available measurements and simple calculations. Malina and Rarick (1973) discuss other ratios of height and weight, including some of their limitations.

More elaborate systems of describing physique have been devised, often with the idea that body build is indicative of personal behavior. Sheldon's somatotype classifications (Sheldon and Stevens 1942, Sheldon et al. 1954) are the best known and most widely used identifications of body build. The Sheldon method is a complex rating of three standardized photographs in combination with a Ponderal Index score. Three components are rated separately on a 7-point scale from 1, as least indicative, to 7, as most indicative. The three components are *endomorphy*, *mesomorphy*, and *ectomorphy*, suggesting the embryonic tissues of endoderm, mesoderm, and ectoderm. Endomorphy implies a softer, rounder body build, in comparison with the better-defined musculature and balanced body proportions of mesomorphy and the leaner, linear dimensions of ectomorphy. Each component contributes to the total physique makeup, and so there is a continuum of physiques rather than three separate categories. As an example, a somatotype rating of 6-2-2 (endomorphy-mesomorphy-ectomorphy) refers to an *endomorph*, with only minor expressions of mesomorphic and endomorphic characteristics. Ratings of 2-6-2 and 2-2-6 refer, respectively, to a *mesomorph* and an *ectomorph*. Many individuals are combinations: 4-5-2 is an endomesomorph, and 2-5-4 is an ectomesomorph.

An important limitation of Sheldon's somatotypes is that the ratings are organized to classify adult males and are not appropriate for women and children. Most women are endomorphic in Sheldon's ratings, and children change markedly in the characteristics being rated. Parnell (1954, 1958) modified Sheldon's method so as to derive a physique description that can be used at any age for any individual, rather than being defined according to the body characteristics of adult males. Parnell rates three components of *fat*, *muscularity*, and *linearity* to describe what he calls a phenotype. Another modification was made by Heath and Carter (1966, 1967), with considerable data collected to study physique and high-level athletic performance.

Factor analysis has been used in searching for general dimensions or components of physique, but Malina and Rarick (1973) concluded that the findings are not definitive. An important caution is that each factor analysis is limited to the measurements included in the analysis. Quite different measurements often are used in different studies, and so it is not possible to compare across studies and to have a comprehensive view of physique dimensions in a single study. Two sets of findings are listed here to indicate what might be physique factors or dimensions.

Five factors were found for young men and women by Tanner, Healey, and Whitehouse (see Tanner, 1964) when using X-ray measurements of bone, muscle, and fat in addition to anthropometric measurements. The five factors were skeletal frame size, limb bone width, limb bone length, muscle width, and fat thickness. Barry and Cureton (1961) found three factors for prepubescent boys, ages 7 to 11, when using anthropometric measurements and photographic ratings. The three factors were ponderosity (transverse dimensions and fat), lankiness (vertical dimensions and attenuated extremities), and leg-trunk development (disproportionate development of legs and trunk). The findings from these two studies point to the difficulty in establishing factors for a comprehensive view of physique. Tanner's and his associates' five factors do not match well with Barry's and Cureton's three factors, partly because they used different terms and also somewhat different measurements with subjects of different ages. The findings from factor analyses, however, suggest that physique dimensions or components may be more complicated than Sheldon's and others' more general components.

Our discussion of physique to this point has been limited to how physique can be described. An even more difficult problem is describing changes in physique during the growing years. An obvious limitation is the lack of a well-established and acceptable method of physique classifications that can be adopted for use with children. Malina and Rarick (1973) summarize evidence that points to more similarity of parents and children in linear (height), as compared with breadth and girth dimensions. Parnell (1958) reported that approximately 75 percent of forty-five children followed their parents' physique pattern in terms of his phenotypic ratings.

All of this suggests an expected genetic link but still leaves us with the problem of describing physique changes during the growing years. Proportions change for body measurements and tissue composition, which makes it difficult to organize a scheme for physique classifications at one age that is appropriate for a later age. Malina and Rarick (1973) summarize evidence that points to a consistency in physique components for individuals during short intervals of 3 or 4 years, except during adolescence. But there is no evidence showing consistency in physique from the early years to maturity. This is a particularly difficult problem because the physique during the early years is quite different in its proportions or ratios at later ages. A reasonable proposition is that individual physique, as we now conceive and measure it, is mostly genetically determined. If so, an individual's physique changes during the growing years should follow a predictable course, even though we have not yet found a means of tracing these changes in relation to the individual's mature physique.

Boys and girls probably have similar physiques from birth through the prepubertal years because they are similar on many separate measures of body proportions and body composition. Males, however, are bigger after puberty, and there are noticeable differences in female-male comparisons after puberty on many structural characteristics. As noted earlier, the overlap or mismatch is often less than 10 percent when classifying adults as female or male on measures such as hip-shoulder width and lean-fat ratio. This means that female-male differences in physique changes must be recognized when describing patterns of change.

Individual and gender differences in physique clearly exist at maturity, and changes in structural characteristics are expected for individuals during their growing years. Difficulties in conceptualizing and measuring physique limit us when trying to describe the development of physique, and so we must be critical and careful when considering the relationship of physique to movement development.

223

Functional Changes

Functional aspects of biological changes are limited here to systems that might influence the development of movement control. We shall consider the development of the nervous system first and at some length because it provides the basic control of movement. Our review will be general to cover a broad and technically complicated area of study that is not yet well linked to direct observations of movement control. The development of physiological functioning for oxygen transport and related metabolic needs is the second topic in this section. Physiological functioning of this kind is related more to endurance than to movement skill, but the neuromotor system depends on these physiological resources in order to function.

Nervous System

The nervous system extends to all regions of the body and participates in all body functions by gathering, organizing, and transporting information. The cerebral cortex is the structural top of the nervous system and is the functional head of the nervous system in its responsibility for higher-order processes. At the other end of the structural-functional scale is the individual neuron that combines with other neurons to transmit neural signals. There are other neural structures between the cortical and neuronal levels to form the full nervous system. A general representation of several important neural structures is shown in Figure 8-14. Areas of importance are the spinal cord, hindbrain, and forebrain. The spinal cord contains nerve fibers in the spinal roots, spinal nerves, and their branches. The hindbrain contains the medulla, pons, midbrain, and cerebellum, and the forebrain is dominated by the cerebral hemispheres which contain the cerebral cortex.

Structural Changes. The neuron is the basic cellular structure of the nervous system, with the nerve impulses traveling along the neurons to transmit information. Information is relayed from one cell to another via the synapse which is a junction between two cells. Information is transmitted throughout the nervous

FIGURE 8-14

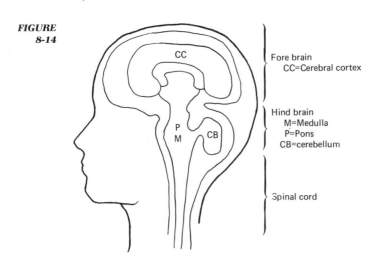

A general representation of selected neural structures.

224

system by the neurons and their synapses. The axon, which is the part of the neuron along which the nerve impulses travel, is surrounded by a sheath of fatty material known as myelin. One of the functions of myelin is to insulate each axon from its neighbors, thus avoiding confusion in the messages passing down each one.

Neurons develop over a long time, with different ones forming at different times. Rodier (1980) has graphically summarized the sequence of neurogenesis in a set of drawings that illustrate the variability within and across neuroanatomical regions. Neural conduction velocity changes quite dramatically in the early months to add to the functional complexity of early neural development. Thomas and Lambert (1960) reported ulnar neural conduction velocities as increasing from 30 meters per second at birth to 50 meters per second at 9 months and reaching 60 meters per second at 3 years to match the performance of adults.

The brain at birth is approximately 25 percent of the weight of an adult brain. This proportion is 50 percent at 6 months, 75 percent at 2.5 years, and 90 percent at 5 years. Contrast this with the weight of the whole body, which at birth is about 5 percent of the weight for young adults and at 10 years is about 50 percent. The *rate of growth* in brain size is near its maximum at birth, and children by 6 years of age have achieved almost all of their adult brain size (Kessen et al. 1970). The percentage of total brain volume for different parts is shown in Figure 8-15. The midbrain, pons, and medulla occupy 8 percent of the total volume at 3 months fetal age, but by birth this has fallen to 1.5 percent. From 1 to 10 years, the per-

FIGURE 8-15

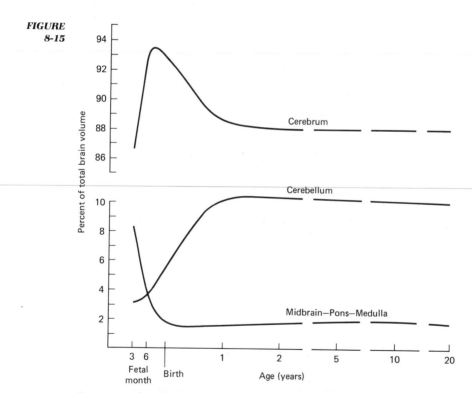

Percentage of total brain volume for cerebrum, cerebellum, and midbrain-pons-medulla from third fetal month to adulthood. (Reproduced with permission from Tanner, 1978, as drawn from data reported by Dunn, 1921, and White House Conference, 1933.)

centage increases slightly again because of fiber tract growth. The cerebrum increases in percentage in utero and then decreases as the cerebellum increases in relative size.

Much of the early growth in brain size and weight can be attributed to myelinization, which is complete at birth in all of the cranial nerves, except the optic and olfactory, and is absent in nearly all of the cerebral neurons. Much of the myelinization in the brain takes place in the first year of life, as shown in Figure 8-16, but myelinization in some parts of the nervous system continues into the pubertal growth years.

The process of myelinization has been the most extensively examined index of neural growth. Before myelinization, neurons have slower transmission rates, are prone to fatigue, and are limited in their rate of repetitive firing. The relative rates of myelinization in different areas of the brain give a rough idea of when these areas reach adult levels of functioning (Bronson 1982). Both sensory and motor pathways begin myelinization 5 to 6 months before birth. In the sensory system, subcortical afferents are in a relatively advanced stage of myelinization by birth, but the pathways in the neocortex begin the process only at or shortly before birth. A similar sequence is found in the motor system with, for example, the pyramidal tract which is the major efferent pathway from the motor cortex, beginning myelinization a month before birth and achieving full myelinization by the end of the first year.

FIGURE 8-16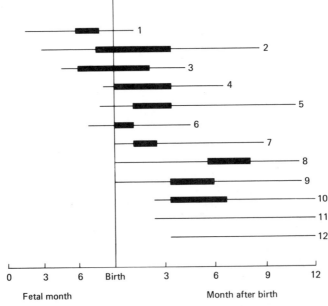

The beginning and end of myelinization-gliosis in different parts of the neural system. The process is maximal during time shown by broader lines. The parts in order are: (1) Auditory nerve; (2) internal capsule; (3) pyramidal tract (mid-olivary level); (4) pyramidal tract (crus cerebri); (5) optic tract; (6) cerebellar subcortical: central; (7) cerebellar subcortical: peripheral; (8) cerebral subcortical: central; (9) striae of striatum; (10) corpus callosum; (11) cerebral subcortical: occipital; (12) cerebral subcortical: frontal. (Reproduced with permission from Dodgson, 1962.)

226

The human cerebral cortex is identifiable at about 8 weeks following conception, after which it gradually increases in width. All nerve cells present in adults are thought to be formed during the first 20 or 30 weeks in utero, and subsequent development is from cell differentiation, axon and dendrite growth, and myelinization, with only a few new nerve cells appearing. The cortex at birth is functioning but is poorly organized. There is considerable growth after birth in the structures just noted, including marked changes in both surface areas and fissurization, especially during the first year (Tanner 1970). There is considerable debate as to the extent that environmental conditions can influence brain maturation and organization. From comparisons of premature with normal full-term infants, it seems that most of the changes in cortical activity are related to age rather than environment; that is, early neural development is primarily a matter of biological maturation. But extreme environmental conditions, such as malnutrition, can influence neural development, and there are times when the neural system is more vulnerable to disease and injury.

Tanner (1970) notes that the much quoted cephalocaudal law is more likely to be caudocranial for development in the nervous system. That is, instead of the central nervous system's developing from head to tail, neural structures develop in the opposite direction. The midbrain and spinal cord regions are the most advanced at birth, followed by the pons, medulla, cerebellum, and finally the cerebrum. As a final comment on structural changes, the rate of change is quite different among the many neural structures. As examples, each cerebral lobe has its own rate of development, each area in each lobe has its own developmental rate, and each area's layers have different rates of development.

Functional Changes. Bronson (1982) notes the usefulness of the gross distinction between the subcortical (spinal cord, brain stem) and the neocortical (cortex) systems, especially at the neonatal period. At the time of birth, human infants are in a transition period in which cortical influence is marginally present or about to emerge. Based on an extensive review, Bronson argues that newborns are largely influenced by the better-developed subcortical systems, and the emergence of neocortical influence is reflected in early changes in infant behavior. Thus in the early postnatal period, reactions such as reflexes, which require only subcortical control, should be more readily elicited; second, in reactions requiring neocortical participation, there should be a wide range of individual differences; and third, there should be a rapid postnatal advance in motor abilities as neocortical control starts to provide a more complex level of neural organization.

An example of functional development in the higher centers is the differentiation of function between the right and left hemispheres. Because of their physical separateness and the results of some early split-brain experiments, it has been customary to view the different hemispheric functions in dichotomous terms. Analytic processing in the left hemisphere, versus Gestalt or holistic in the right, is an example. These rigid dichotomies have been questioned (Henderson 1982), although it is clear that different processing functions are preferred by each hemisphere.

The left hemisphere of adults generally contains mechanisms for speech, whereas the right hemisphere specializes in spatial relations (especially visual cues). In Chapter 10 we shall discuss handedness and eyedness in relation to hemispheric specialization, but language is the ability most often studied. Human

227

language is controlled by the left hemisphere, and so individuals who have suffered damage in the left hemisphere are more likely to show language deficits than are patients with damage in the right hemisphere.

There are many questions regarding the two hemispheres' specialization of function, such as when specialization or lateralization of function occurs. Some have argued for a propensity for lateralization at birth, with lateralization by 5 years of age (Hiscock and Kinsbourne 1978). Others feel that hemispheric lateralization does not begin until 5 or 6 years of age. What is relatively clear is that it is practically complete by 10 to 12 years of age. Much of the evidence comes from studies of aphasia, in which recovery is much more common below ages 10 to 12 than at older ages. It is as though the brain is relatively plastic in the early years, and so speech function can be taken over by the right hemisphere. After about 12 years of age, however, the prognosis is poor.

Sensory development is another illustration of neural development, because the sensory systems basically are neural networks. This is particularly true for the kinesthetic system (described in Chapter 10) which provides sensory information for the neuromotor system. Proprioceptors and spindles are found in the muscles of the tongue and eye during the fourth fetal month. Carmichael (1970) reports work by Mavrinskaya (1960, 1962), who studied the correlation of development of skeletal muscle nerve endings with the appearance of motor activity in the human fetus, showing that the primitive sensory motor nerve endings are present at 7 to 8 weeks in utero and are functional by the eleventh week. Sensory and motor endings arise simultaneously and are basic to the developing fetus's reflexive movements. Carmichael concludes that the study of prenatal behavior in humans and lower animals indicates that proprioceptors in muscles, tendons, and possibly joints are functional before birth and by that time are among the best organized receptor fields for the initiation and control of behavior.

Myelinization develops rapidly during the first year and more slowly up to pubescence. Myelinization seems to occur in functional units carrying impulses to specific cortical areas that are myelinating at the same time as those carrying impulses away from these areas to the periphery. Structure and function seem to be interrelated in a complex manner. For example, fibers associated with auditory stimulation myelinate as early as the sixth fetal month and continue to myelinate up to 4 years of age. The visual system starts to myelinate later, just after birth, but myelinization then is completed very quickly. If we relate these comparisons to function, audition is analyzed at subcortical levels in utero and becomes cortical after birth through a slow development. Vision is not needed in utero, but its development must proceed rapidly after birth to provide a functional system in a short period of time. Audition can function adequately with the slower rate of myelinization, whereas visual development requires a more rapid rate of myelinization at a particular time. Myelinization is related more to functional units than to neuroanatomical regions.

There are two clear divisions of neural development in the first 2 years of life after birth. First is an order in which the various areas of the brain develop, and second is an order in which the body functions associated with these areas develop. The primary motor area, for example, is the most advanced, followed by the primary sensory area, and gradually development spreads out from these areas. Within the motor and sensory areas, the nerve cells controlling movements of the arms and upper trunk develop ahead of those controlling the legs. Although the motor cortex develops earlier than the other neural areas do, the legs remain the last to develop in the motor cortex. By 2 years of age, the primary sensory area has caught up with the primary motor area, and the association areas have developed further, but other areas are still immature.

In summary, the human brain undergoes both quantitative and qualitative changes from conception to maturity. The brain grows bigger and increases its number of cells, folds, and fissures; myelinization occurs; and the amount of water decreases. The brain also changes in function, as illustrated by hemispheric lateralization, which is complete by ages 10 to 12.

Physiological Systems: O_2 Skills

The physiological changes important to muscular activity are centered on intake, transportation, and the use of oxygen. The cycle is to take air into the lungs, extract oxygen from the air, transport it through the cardiovascular system to muscles and other functional units, and gather carbon dioxide for transport back to the lungs, where the cycle continues by expelling carbon dioxide and gathering additional oxygen. This is a simple and superficial description of the route taken by oxygen to supply a necessary commodity in the energy operations of muscular activity. A number of important oxygen "skills" are necessary, including the ability to take in large amounts of air, transport large amounts of oxygen, and exchange large amounts of oxygen at places where needed. These O_2 *skills* are functions of the pulmonary and cardiovascular systems. It is thought that O_2 skills improve from birth to maturity and that boys and girls are similar until the pubertal years, when boys improve their O_2 skills more than girls do.

Vital Capacity. Respiratory ability is measured in a number of ways, with vital capacity as a representative pattern of change. Vital capacity, which is maximal expiration following maximal inspiration, is shown in Figure 8-17 for boys and

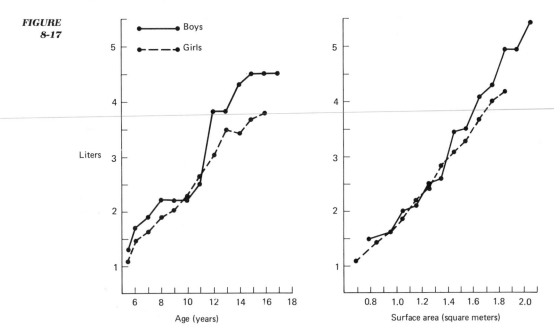

*FIGURE
8-17*

Changes in vital capacity in relation to age (left) and body surface area (right). (Reproduced with permission from Ferris, Whittenberger, and Gallagher, 1952, and Ferris and Smith, 1953. Copyright American Academy of Pediatrics 1952 and 1953.)

girls in relation to age and body size (surface area). Both boys and girls increase at a similar rate to about age 12, when boys improve at a faster rate to have an approximately 20 percent greater vital capacity at age 20. Because males are larger at maturity than females are, their increased vital capacity might be merely a matter of greater size with relatively the same vital capacity. This seems to be the case in the prepubertal years, when boys are slightly larger and have a slightly larger vital capacity. Girls enter puberty earlier than boys do and so are similar in size at ages 11 and 12 and have a similar vital capacity. According to the right-hand graph in Figure 8-17, however, boys have a larger vital capacity than girls do when their body size (surface area) is greater. Vital capacity is related to body size, with no gender differences until the older ages, when body sizes are larger for both boys and girls. Males at maturity are both larger than females and have a larger vital capacity in relation to body size.

Heart Rate and Blood Pressure. The mean resting (basal) heart rate decreases from 15 to 20 beats per minute from the early years to age 10, as shown in Figure 8-18. Boys and girls are similar until age 10, when boys continue to decrease and girls level off. Pulse pressure increases in the early years, as heart rate decreases, to provide more pressure per pulse for fewer pulses per minute. Pulse pressures increase during the pubertal years, with girls leveling off at age 13 while boys continue to increase, as shown in Figure 8-19. Males at maturity have more pressure per pulse for fewer pulses per minute than females do. Systolic blood pressure, as shown in Figure 8-20, rises steadily during childhood. During the pubertal

FIGURE 8-18

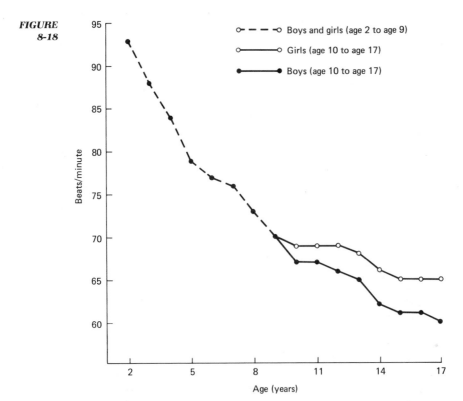

Mean basal heart rates for boys and girls from age 2 through age 17. (Drawn from data reported by Iliff and Lee, 1952.)

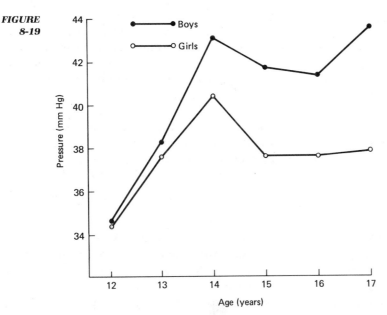

FIGURE
8-19

Mean pulse pressure of boys and girls, ages 12 to 17. (Drawn from data reported by Shock, 1944, taken in six-month intervals and subsequently averaged for each year.)

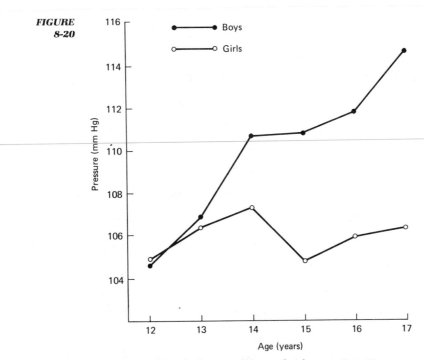

FIGURE
8-20

Mean systolic blood pressure of boys and girls, ages 12 to 17. (Drawn from data reported by Shock, 1944, taken in six-month intervals and subsequently averaged for each year.)

231

years, girls' systolic pressure increases less than boys' does. There is very little change in diastolic blood pressure during the pubertal years and thus, the changes in pulse pressure during these years are in systolic blood pressure, which is related to greater basal stroke volume. Finally, blood volume increases from birth to maturity, with boys and girls having similar blood volume until the pubertal years, when boys' volume increases more than girls' do.

Red Blood Cells. A greater blood volume means a larger number of red blood cells to transport more oxygen to the muscles and to carry more carbon dioxide away from the muscles. The general pattern of change is shown in Figure 8-21. As expected from the changes in blood volume, boys and girls have a similar pattern of increase until the pubertal years, with males increasing noticeably beyond age 12, when girls level off.

Basal Metabolic Rate. Changes in basal metabolic rate (BMR) are shown in Figure 8-22 for boys and girls, ages 2 to 15. BMR, which is heat produced per square meter of body surface, declines continuously from birth through the early adult years into the older years. Boys have a slightly higher BMR at all ages, which decreases in loss during the pubertal years, though girls continue a similar rate of decline. Tanner (1962) suggests that males' higher BMR is related to their greater muscle mass as well as hormonal differences.

In summary, O_2 skills improve to provide a greater supply of energy resources for muscular activity. Boys and girls develop at a similar level and rate until puberty. Mature males tend to have better O_2 skills in intake, transport, and use of oxygen.

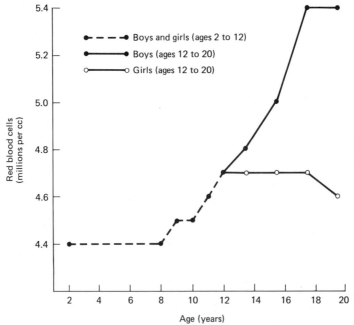

Mean number of red blood cells for boys and girls, ages 2 to 20. (Drawn from data reported by Mugrage and Andresen, 1936, 1938.)

FIGURE
8-22

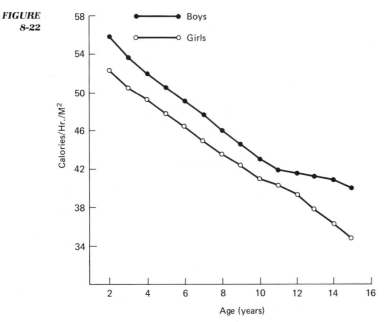

Changes in basal metabolic rate (BMR) for boys and girls, ages 2 to 15. (Drawn from data reported by Lewis, Duval, and Iliff, 1943.)

Pubertal Changes

Boys and girls are alike in most biological characteristics before puberty, although they are quite different in many biological characteristics after puberty. Changes during the pubertal years are quite important in regard to increased potential for fitness and strength, which are needed for high-level performance in some movement skills. Although we mentioned many pubertal changes in our review of structural and functional changes, we now bring them together as another way of looking at biological change toward maturity. Because individuals go through puberty at such a wide range of chronological ages, we will look at changes in regard to several measures of pubertal age, as ways of adjusting individuals to a common growth time, rather than using chronological age as a base-line measure of age. We shall first describe some of the more visible (secondary) sex changes that occur during puberty.

Secondary Sex Changes

The secondary sex changes in Figure 8-23 are listed in relation to chronological age and pattern of height change. The onset and completion of some changes are marked with a range of chronological age to illustrate individual variability. For example, pubic hair is rated on a scale from 1 to 5 for amount and texture, with an average rating of 2 for girls at age 11 and for boys at age 12. Note that girls range in chronological age from 8 to 14 for a rating of 2, with boys ranging from 10 to 15. Similar ratings and age ranges are noted for breast development and first menstrual flow, or menarche, for girls, and changes in testes and penis for boys. The pattern of height change at puberty, called height spurt, provides

FIGURE
8-23

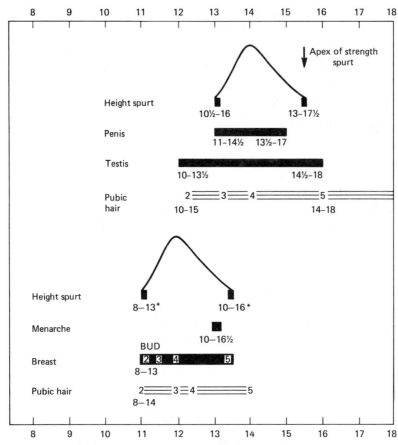

Range of ages for onset and completion of selected pubertal changes. (Range of ages for onset and completion of height spurt for girls is from data reported by Faust, 1977.) (Reproduced with permission from Tanner, 1962.)

a general means of marking the onset and completion of puberty. Notice that menarche occurs late in puberty and really marks the beginning of the completion of puberty. The rate of strength increase tends to come near the end of puberty, probably because some time is needed to incorporate and use the biological changes, such as the increase in muscle mass, to produce strength (Asmussen 1973).

Girls undergo their pubertal changes approximately 2 years earlier than boys do and also go through the pubertal years in a somewhat shorter time. Add the wide range of ages at which individuals enter puberty, and it becomes obvious that individual difference is the rule rather than the exception in pubertal changes in relation to chronological age. When children become teenagers at age 13, many girls are completing their puberty, whereas most boys are just entering it. This means that a teacher in a classroom of 13-year-olds is looking at a group of young women and older boys.

Structural and Functional Changes

Adjustments have been made to represent biological changes during puberty in ways that remove the confounding effect of individual variations in maturity level as related to chronological age. An example is the alignment of individual rates of height change on peak height velocity, as shown earlier in Figure 8-6. Another way is shown in Figure 8-24 in the four graphs of rate changes of selected structural features. Tanner (1962) used data from Shuttleworth (1939) and made a number of adjustments to compare the patterns of change for boys and girls. He began by including only boys with peak height velocities between ages 14 and 15 and girls with peak height velocities between ages 12 and 13. This provided comparable samples of boys and girls who were at relatively the same level of maturity within

FIGURE
8-24

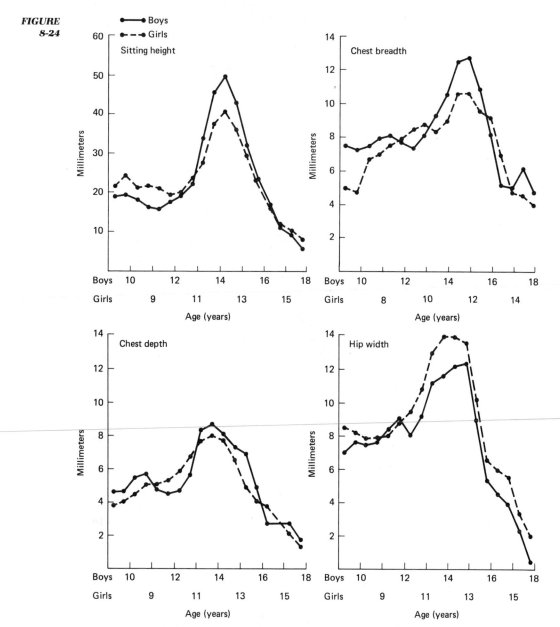

Comparison of patterns of pubertal structural changes for height, chest breadth, chest depth, and hip width. Peak height velocities for boys were at ages 14 or 15 and for girls were at ages 12 or 13. (Reproduced with permission from Tanner, 1962, as drawn from data reported by Shuttleworth, 1939.)

their sex group. That is, Tanner eliminated earlier- and later-maturing boys and girls and then aligned the patterns in relation to peak pubertal changes, with the chronological age base lines adjusted accordingly. Notice that the base-line adjustments are similar in each graph, except that the changes in chest breadth occur a bit earlier for girls.

Tanner's comparisons demonstrate the similar patterns of change for boys and girls when adjusted for level of maturity. There are differences in absolute amount of change, as noted earlier for boys' gaining more height and wider chests and girls' gaining more hip width. Yet the patterns of change are strikingly the same in the times of rises and falls in the curves and the overall lengths of the pubertal change period for these structural functions.

Malina (1978) arranged several measures of boys' body composition in relation

FIGURE 8-25

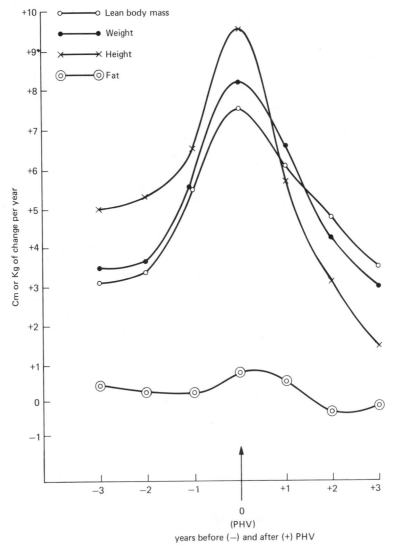

Changes in body composition and weight relative to peak height velocity (PHV) for boys, ages 10 to 17 (N = 40). (Reproduced with permission from Parizkova, 1976.)

236

to peak height velocity, by using data from Parizkova (1976). This makes it possible to look at the timing of changes among measures, as shown in Figure 8-25. Notice that there is very little change in body fat, and the changes in lean body mass (LBM, or muscle) and weight are the same. The patterns of change for weight and LBM coincide with the pattern of change for peak height velocity, although Malina notes other findings that are not as well timed as these are. Nonetheless, there is an overall coincidence among these changes during puberty.

Faust (1977) made extensive analyses of the pubertal height growth of the girls in the California Adolescent Study (Jones 1939) to derive a procedure for marking the onset and end of pubertal height growth, as shown in Figure 8-26. Onset (b) and end (d) are the first points on either side of the peak height velocity when the rate in height growth falls below an individual's 5-year average rate of height gain. A prepubertal (b - 3) period and a postpubertal (d + 3) period also are marked. Faust provides a different age base line, which is ordered in relation to four developmental points (b - 3, b, d, and d + 3). Her age base line with four developmental points is used in several comparisons to demonstrate another way to look at pubertal changes.

The rate of height gain for two girls is shown in Figure 8-27 to show early and late development. Girl 316 ends her pubertal height growth period before girl 401 enters hers. Changes in shoulder-hip ratio are shown in Figure 8-28 to cover the 3 years before the onset of pubertal height growth (b - 3) to the 3 years after the end of pubertal height growth (d + 3). The time of onset (b) to the end (d) varies in numerous ways, as we have seen, and so the time from b - 3 to d + 3 is approximately 8 to 10 years. The shoulder-hip ratio that Faust reports is the inverse of the hip-shoulder ratio in Figure 8-9. The proportional increase in boys' shoulder width is seen as an increase in the ratio in Figure 8-28, with girls decreasing because of a larger proportional increase in their hip width.

Faust's age base line for developmental points adjusts children to a common growth marker (height) and better portrays the relative time and the magnitude

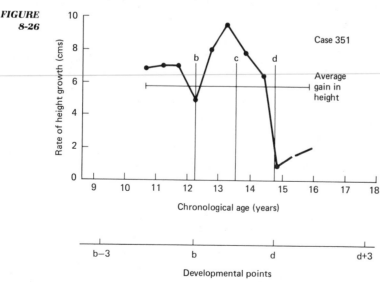

FIGURE 8-26

Individual curve for rate of height change to illustrate four developmental points used by Faust (1977). (Reproduced with permission from Faust, 1977.)

*FIGURE
8-27*

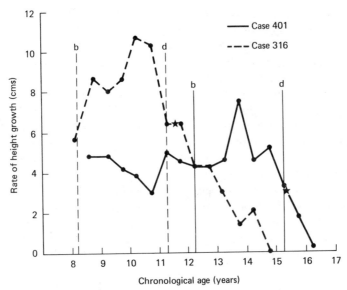

Differences in timing of pubertal growth period in height. Early-developing girl reached end of growth period (d) before late-developing girl reached onset (b). (Stars indicate menarche.)
(Reproduced with permission from Faust, 1977.)

of change. Another example is her comparison of the rates of change in sub-cutaneous tissue, as shown in Figure 8-29. Girls increase slightly in rate through the time period, in contrast with boys' more steady rate of change, and girls have a higher rate of change (increase) at each developmental point. Notice also the decrease in overlap from b - 3 to d + 3. A puzzling finding is that boys do not decrease to a negative (loss) rate, as noted in other studies. It is possible that the dip to a zero or negative rate from point b to d is concealed by having plotting points that are several years apart. But Faust's developmental points are very useful in describing general patterns of change during an important period of change.

*FIGURE
8-28*

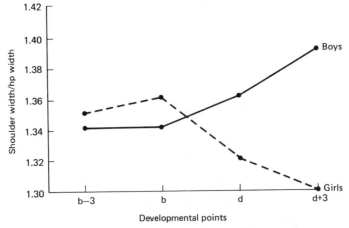

Gender differences in mean shoulder width/hip width ratio at four developmental points. (Reproduced with permission from Faust, 1977.)

238

**FIGURE
8-29**

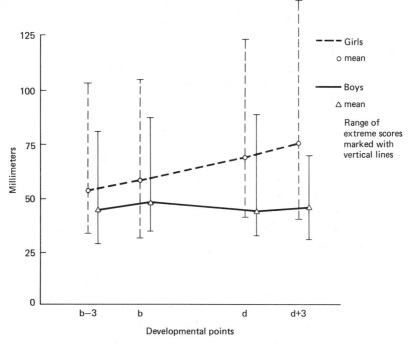

Gender differences in subcutaneous tissue with extreme scores and mean values plotted at four developmental points. (Reproduced with permission from Faust, 1977.)

Shock (1946) put together the interesting arrangement of girls' physiological changes shown in Figure 8-30. He used menarche as the focal age point and covered a time period of 9 years, 3 years before and 6 years after menarche. Both heart rate and basal metabolic rate continue to decrease after menarche, whereas systolic blood pressure levels off almost precisely at menarche.

The patterns of biological change during puberty are quite similar for individuals

**FIGURE
8-30**

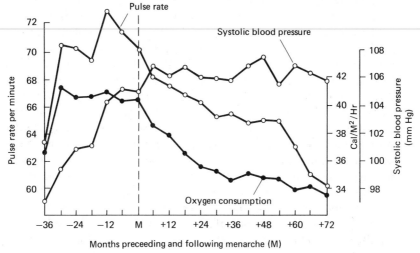

Physiological changes for girls in relation to menarche. (Reproduced with permission from Shock, 1946.)

when considered in relation to level of maturity, or what might be called pubertal age. Additionally, those biological systems that serve a common function seem to develop uniformly, as demonstrated by the similar timing among patterns of change when adjusted to pubertal age. Although gender differences in patterns of change are quite striking for many aspects of pubertal development, both females and males improve their resources substantially for maximal movement performance.

Maturity

Our principal concern in our review of biological changes has been progress toward maturity, whose general criteria are that the structure is complete and fully functioning. It should be apparent by now that maturity is an elusive and changeable state depending on which biological change is being described and what the criteria for maturity are. As noted earlier, it is easier to identify structural maturity than functional maturity, although it is difficult to obtain some structural measures. We shall examine some structural measures of maturity that are used to label individuals as early, average, and late maturers. These measures are useful in studying the relationship of level of maturity to many movement performance achievements. We shall first look at the differences in rate of maturity for different types of biological change.

General Maturity Differences

Differences in the rate of maturity among several aspects of biological change are shown in Figure 8-31. These are structural changes in size, with maturity marked as size at age 20. The curves are different from the distance and rate curves used to this point, in that they represent the percentage of postnatal development from birth to maturity (age 20). Each curve begins at zero and ends at 100 percent. The brain and head grow rapidly in the early years, to achieve 90 percent of their growth beyond birth by ages 6 or 7. General growth, which includes many of the biological changes we are reviewing, is not yet at 50 percent by age 6. Remember that these percentages describe the proportion of growth from birth to age 20 and do not consider the amount of growth achieved in utero.

The reproductive system grows very little until the pubertal years, when growth is very rapid. We also know that the reproductive system is not functional until pubertal changes occur and that functionally the reproductive system matures very rapidly to provide the potential for procreation. But women do not become functionally mature until later, at a better time to bear children. We do not know the precise chronological age, but we do know that first children born to very young or very old mothers are more at risk in their subsequent development. Also, women decline in procreational potential to the point that their reproductive system is nonfunctional, whereas men can maintain their procreative potential to some degree throughout their lives. Thus, functional maturity often cannot be defined and measured with the clarity and precision we desire, and there is considerable variation in maturity states for men and women.

The pattern of lymphoid change also points out the differences in maturity among biological changes. The lymph system increases in size and function during the pubertal years in order to serve the pubertal change processes, which are primarily biochemical and hormonal in nature, and then decreases in size and

240

FIGURE
8-31

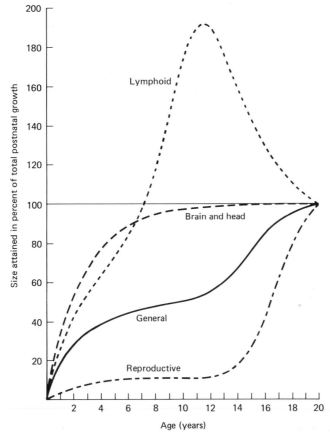

*Growth curves of different parts and tissues of the body. All the
curves are plotted as percent of total gain from birth to 20 years,
so that size at age 20 is 100 on the vertical scale. (Lymphoid:
thymus, lymph nodes, intestinal lymph masses; Brain and head:
brain and its parts, dura, spinal cord, optic apparatus, cranial
dimensions; General: body as a whole, external dimensions (except
head), respiratory and digestive organs, kidneys, aortic and
pulmonary trunks, musculature, blood volume; Reproductive:
testis, ovary, epididymis, prostrate, seminal vesicles, Fallopian
tubes.)* (Reproduced with permission from Tanner, 1962, as
redrawn from Scammon, 1930.)

function. This means that maturity for the lymph system more properly should
be recognized as occurring at an earlier age, with a decrease occurring more
rapidly than for other biological changes.

Earlier examples showed differences in maturity rates and difficulties in establishing age of maturity. Vision was noted as developing very rapidly in the first
year of birth, in contrast with audition which developed considerably, in utero,
with a longer and slower development after birth. Matters become complicated
if we extend our view of mature visual functioning to include perceptual aspects
of vision, in addition to visual acuity, focal length, and the like.

There is much concern also about what happens to biological changes when
change mechanisms are disrupted. Change might slow down or stop, perhaps
becoming a permanent disruption. If the interference is removed, how much can
growth be restored to make up for lost growth? That is, how much *catch-up*

growth will there be? There is evidence that body systems make an effort to catch up, as seen by accelerated growth rates after interruptions by disease or injury (Tanner 1962). Recalling Bloom's ideas regarding stability and change (1964), he suggests that more is lost and not regained when disruption occurs during times of rapid change. If a proportion, such as one-half, is regained during the catch-up period, the final loss will be greater if the initial loss is greater. There is much to be learned about catch-up growth, beyond knowing that the body does try to accelerate growth during catch-up periods.

Individual Level of Maturity

We often want to specify the level of maturity for an individual, such as how far an individual has progressed toward maturity and how an individual compares in level of maturity with others. Measures of distance and rate might indicate that an individual is nearing maturity, even though he or she is relatively late in reaching it. Another individual of the same chronological age might be an early maturer who has already reached maturity. Chronological age often is used in the early years as a general estimate of biological maturity, but it measures only the passage of time and not biological change.

Skeletal or bone maturity is measured by X raying bones and studying the bones' growth centers. If a growth center is open, the growth will continue, whereas it will cease when the growth center closes. X rays of the hand often are used to estimate *skeletal age* (SA) or bone age, because the hand's many bones offer many growth centers to rate. Standards have been established from X rays of children at many ages, meaning that on the average they are expected to have growth centers of the size and shape seen in the X ray selected as the standard for that age. There are several ways to use these standards, as explained by Tanner (1962), but the general idea is to specify the level of maturity for skeletal development. When an individual is measured as having a particular skeletal age, we compare skeletal age with chronological age to determine whether an individual is early or late in skeletal maturity. All people, whether they are early, average, or late maturers, do reach a point of complete skeletal maturity. That is, a point is reached when everyone has the same skeletal age because there is a ceiling or maximum score when all growth centers are closed.

Girls are more biologically mature than boys are until they reach a chronological age when both are mature. This is shown in Figure 8-32 for the skeletal maturity of the hand. Skeletal maturity in this illustration is measured in score units, rather than skeletal age, but the consistent difference in favor of girls is clear. Tanner (1962) estimates that boys' mean skeletal age is approximately 80 percent of that of girls of the same chronological age from birth until near the time of maturity. The reverse statement is that girls are 20 percent more advanced in skeletal maturity than boys are. The absolute difference at age 1 is about 2 months and at age 10 is about 2 years.

Individual variability in level of maturity can be considerable. Tanner (1962) states that the standard deviation for the skeletal age of the hand increases from 4 months at age 2 to 1 year at puberty. Clarke (1971) reported standard deviations for boys of approximately 1 year at each age from 7 to 17. Using a standard deviation of 1 year, the variability of skeletal age for boys at age 10 is represented in Figure 8-33. Approximately two-thirds of the 10-year-old boys have a skeletal age ranging from 9 to 11, and one-third have a skeletal age of less than 9 or more than 11. Boys at chronological age 10 have a range of four or more skeletal years,

FIGURE
8-32

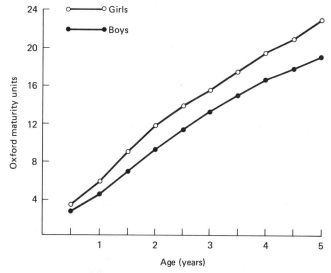

Skeletal maturity of the hand for young boys and girls.
(Reproduced with permission from Acheson, 1954.)

which shows the magnitude of individual variability in the rate of biological change. If we include 10-year-old girls, who are 20 percent more mature than boys are, the range in skeletal ages for children at age 10 will be around 6 skeletal years.

Level of maturity can be assessed in other ways by choosing a particular biological characteristic and establishing norms or standards to mark progress toward maturity. *Peak height velocity* is used in several ways to provide a point around which maturity in stature can be defined and measured. This includes Faust's (1977) developmental points which can be used to chart height age before (b - 3) and after (d + 3) peak height velocity. Specific occurrences, such as menarche and other pubertal changes, can be used similarly to identify a level of maturity around which earlier and later development can be marked. Another example is that tooth appearances (eruptions) are used to calculate dental age.

FIGURE
8-33

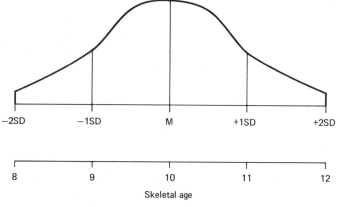

A general representation of variability of skeletal age for boys at age 10.
(M = mean; SD = standard deviation.)

243

An important limitation in using these maturity measures is that we must wait until they occur. Also, we must make a series of observations or measurements over a period of time if we want to have pre- and postmarkers, such as Faust's b - 3 and d + 3. These measures of level of maturity can be quite useful for research purposes, but they are not convenient and simple means of estimating the level of maturity at a particular time. Although skeletal age can be used at a single time to estimate level of maturity, considerable professional skill is needed to obtain useful measurements, and subjects now are not as willing to have X rays taken unless they have a medical problem. Measuring level of maturity is even more difficult when trying to assess more functional aspects, as noted for the functioning of the reproductive system and as would be expected for determining the level of personal and social maturity.

We often are concerned with the development of individuals who seem to be *late maturers* or *early maturers*. Despite the many problems encountered in measuring level of maturity, extreme levels can be established with more assurance than can levels in the middle range of maturity. This is because a specific score or age is not needed; we need only to find those who are *beyond* a particular score or age. From Figure 8-33, we could identify all of the 10-year-old boys from -2 standard deviations to +2 standard deviations as being within a normal range (sometimes labeled as within normal limits, or WNL). Late maturers then would be those with a skeletal age of less than 8.0, and early maturers would have a skeletal age of more than 12.0. This would mark 2 to 3 percent as being late maturers and 2 to 3 percent as being early maturers. Thus, designations of late and early are arbitrary and depend on our judgment of where to place a *cutoff*. A less extreme cutoff in this example would be to choose ±1.5 standard deviations, which would establish the normal limits as 8.5 and 11.5. Assuming a normal distribution, the less extreme cutoff would identify 7 to 8 percent as late maturers and 7 to 8 percent as early maturers. Another method of identifying late and early maturers is to make a percentage cutoff, for example, of the lowest 10 percent and the highest 10 percent. Extreme designations, such as early and late, are in the eye of the beholder, which means that we must check the basis for such designations to determine whether they match what we will accept as appropriate cutoff points.

A general representation of rate of maturity in relation to chronological age is shown in Figure 8-34 for boys' skeletal age and pubertal development. Late and early maturers for skeletal age were chosen as being 20 percent behind or ahead of mean skeletal age. According to chronological age 10, the average maturer is skeletal age 10 in comparison with skeletal age 8 for a late maturer and skeletal age 12 for an early maturer. A similar comparison with other chronological ages should find a 20 percent lag or acceleration for the late and the early maturer, respectively, with skeletal age matching chronological age for the average maturer. This demonstrates that early maturers take 4 to 5 fewer years to reach skeletal age 20. Furthermore, early maturers tend to go through the pubertal growth period in a shorter time than late maturers do.

Our representation of pubertal development is based on a 4-year period of pubertal development, which underestimates early-late differences and is conservative. Note that the early maturer finishes puberty at a time when the late maturer is entering it. An actual comparison of this difference was shown earlier in Figure 8-27 for an early-maturing and a late-maturing girl.

*FIGURE
8-34*

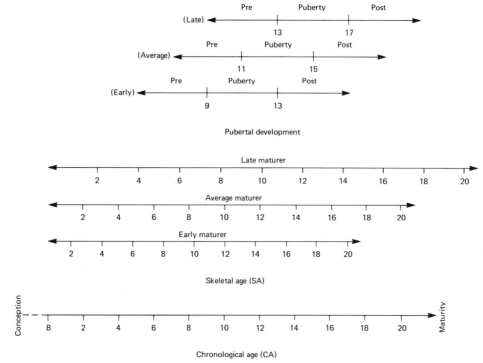

General comparisons of different rates of maturity for skeletal age and pubertal development of boys in relation to chronological age.

Chapter Summary

Biological change toward maturity was reviewed in relation to the structural and functional aspects of skeletal, tissue, and system changes. The rate and age of maturity vary greatly among the many different biological characteristics, and so maturity must be defined and described separately for each. With this limitation in mind, some general patterns of change can be defined.

The neurological system matures quite early so as to provide the basis for the early development of movement control. The development of some functions, such as brain lateralization, may not be complete until later years, but the neurological system is mature in most respects by the early school years. The rate of change varies among different parts of the neurological system and seems related more to functional need than to structural order. The rate of change also varies within a particular area of the brain, seemingly to serve one aspect of movement before another. For example, the neural development of arm and trunk movements in motor and sensory areas occurs before the neural development of leg movements in the same areas. Also, sensory and motor areas develop in relation to each other in ways that reflect their roles in specific aspects of movement control.

The pattern of height change provides a general pattern of change for body size and some aspects of muscle functioning. These changes go through four periods, beginning with rapid early development and followed by a consistent

245

period of change until puberty. The third period during puberty is rapid and produces important structural and functional changes. The fourth period is a time of little or no change when individuals reach a mature state. Changes across these four periods are quite substantial and lead to an increase in body size, changes in body proportions, an increase in muscle/fat ratio, and changes in cardiorespiratory functioning to provide more oxygen as energy for muscular activity. These changes are unified and so have a greater potential for producing forceful movements.

Individuals vary greatly in maturity state when measured by skeletal age, peak height velocity, and similar measures. It is possible to label individuals as early or late maturers by using one or more of these measures, but individual patterns of change for height are quite similar when adjusted to an age base line reflecting maturity level. Individual patterns of change for other biological characteristics have not been described in sufficient detail to make comparisons of this type.

Gender differences before puberty have minor implications for movement development, except that girls are approximately 20 percent more mature than boys are in many of the biological characteristics described here. Changes during the pubertal years lead to males' being larger and potentially stronger than females are. Strength potential is related to males' having more muscle mass and increased cardiorespiratory functioning. Individuals vary so much in their chronological age of entering and completing puberty that developmental comparisons of any kind are confounded from chronological ages 10 to 18 by the individual's pubertal state.

This chapter reviewed change toward maturity for body size, proportions and composition, and neurological and cardiorespiratory functioning. Although variability is the rule for different biological characteristics and individuals, there is an underlying organization and order that seems to reflect functional development. We noted this in our summary statements about changes in neurological development being related to the early development of movement control and changes in body makeup and muscle functioning being related to the later development of speeded and forceful movements. Although we cannot capture this complex organization and larger order, there appears to be an overall unity that is lost when looking at smaller pieces of the total picture.

9 | *Biological Changes and Movement Development*

The biological changes discussed in Chapter 8 were selected for review because they seemed likely to be related to changes in movement development. We now shall consider the extent to which these changes in biological resources can influence changes in movement development.

A general but unrefined expectancy is that movement development improves as biological changes occur; that is, children move better as they grow older. Our problem is to find those aspects of biological change that are related to changes in movement development. There is no one simple solution to such a broad and complex topic, and the best that can be achieved at the movement, for all but the narrowest question or prediction, is to establish some guidelines for thinking about biological changes and movement development and related expectancies or predictions.

An important first step is to decide which aspect of movement development is being considered and at what level of performance. Is it early mastery and initial refinement of movement control or maximal performance of a movement skill? Each is important, depending on the interests of the person asking the question, but we must be careful to limit our concerns and not confuse one for the other. Most of the thinking and research has been directed toward maximal performance of specific movement skills and strength; very little has been done to study biological changes in relation to early mastery and refinement of movement control. But thinking and findings regarding maximal skill performance and strength often are taken as covering all of movement development. We shall separate these concerns in order to clarify what have been vague inferences about movement development.

Figure 9-1 shows major concerns in how biological changes may influence movement development. The list includes the many changes in lean (muscle) tissue, O_2 skills, and the like discussed in Chapter 8. Movement development is the division used in Part I. We shall deal separately with the development of movement control and maximal movement performance and then shall conclude by discussing the level of maturity.

Early Development of Movement Control

The development of movement control has been described as the control of self-movements and moving in relation to changing conditions. The early development of control of self-movements is largely the development of the neuromotor system, whereas the later development of moving in relation to changing conditions is the development of perceptual-cognitive abilities. We shall concentrate on neural development and control of self-movement and examine perceptual–cognitive development and more open situations in later chapters.

In the final analysis, the neuromotor system is directly responsible for producing movement. It is difficult, though, to specify its constituent parts and limits, because

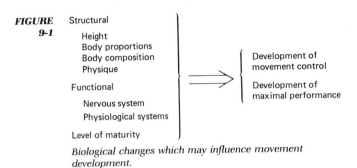

Biological changes which may influence movement
development.

the neuromotor system has interrelationships with essentially all of the body's physiological systems. Even within the nervous system, it is difficult to separate the neuromotor system from other neural systems or parts, which means that we generally will be speaking of changes in the neural system rather than confining our discussion to the neuromotor system.

An important limitation is that early movement functioning often is used to estimate the adequacy of other aspects of development, including neural development. That is, holding the head upright, reaching and grasping an object, and similar achievements are used to indicate adequate development of the neural, vestibular, visual, and other biological systems, as well as adequate development of perceptual, cognitive, and social functioning. Reflexes, in particular, are used to check on certain aspects of neural development, thus producing a circularity that is difficult to avoid, because we do not have other convenient measures of neural development.

General Relationships

Despite recent advances in developmental neuroanatomy and neurophysiology and in descriptions of behavioral development, there are many problems in establishing causal relationships between neural and behavioral development (Parmelee and Sigman 1982). One problem is the degree to which environmental stimulation influences changes in neural development. Also, Parmelee and Sigman believe that there historically has been a tendency to overestimate the amount of behavioral change that could be accounted for by a corresponding change in brain development. They note that up to 1 month before normal birth the fetus seems relatively unaffected by external sensory input. As it reaches 34 to 36 weeks in conceptual age, its nervous system develops to a level that enables it to be more interactive with the environment. In their review of current work, Parmelee and Sigman take the viewpoint that behavior is limited in utero by neurophysiological development but that behavioral development is influenced more and more by the environment during infancy.

From birth to 4 months there are changes reflecting a rapid organization of inhibitory and controlling mechanisms. They include sustained sleep of greater than 4 hours, more organization of sleep states with a doubling of quiet sleep, a closer association of EEG patterns with sleep states, a sharp decrease in crying during waking hours, a suppression of primitive reflexes, an increase in alertness, and the rapid development of a social smile. The most dramatic changes take place from 4 to 8 weeks after normal birth, which seems to be a particularly sensitive period for environmental influence.

After the early months of life following a normal birth, many variables are present in both neural and behavioral development. For example, as noted by Parmelee and Sigman, concept generalizations depend less on identifiable structural changes in the brain in terms of synaptic or dendritic growth than on the integration of previous sensory perceptions. Therefore, after the first few months of life, it becomes very difficult to relate neurological changes directly to movement and other behavioral development. But there are methods that can be used to look at some aspects of this relationship, though we should note that other factors may also be in operation.

Reflexes

Early reflexes were discussed briefly in Chapter 2 in examining their role in movement and describing changes for selected reflexes. We noted that some reflexes disappear (or at least are suppressed) and that others remain active throughout life. Reflexes in the form of more automatic movements also become part of the development of voluntary movement control. The grouping of reflexes has recently been proposed as a means of explaining how individuals can perform an infinite number of complex movements involving several different muscle groupings. Easton (1978) argues that reflexes form the basis of voluntary control to produce purposeful coordinated movements. Reflexes ae preorganized, complete, stereotyped acts, whereas voluntary movements are flexible and variable. To be used in voluntary movements, reflexes must be smoothed and tuned by interactions with other reflexes and by signals from higher centers. Easton has studied how this tuning takes place by examining movements in cats.

McGraw (1963) proposed a four-stage view of the reflexes fading into voluntary and more adaptive control. Stage 1 is the appearance of the reflex, which continues to function until the central nervous system (CNS) develops sufficiently to inhibit lower (spinal) control of the reflex. Stage 2 is the CNS's inhibition of the reflex, followed by Stage 3 in which the CNS assumes voluntary control of the movement. Stage 4 is the integration of the reflex into larger movement patterns.

Palmer grasp was used by McGraw to demonstrate her four stages. Stage 1 is that appropriate pressure on the palm will elicit the flexion of fingers and thumb to produce a palmer grasp until 3 to 4 months after birth. Inhibition by the CNS in Stage 2 will produce extension of the fingers and thumb or very little response of any kind when a baby feels pressure on the palm. Voluntary control is achieved in Stage 3 so that a palmer grasp will be produced when appropriate, without pressure on the palm. This can be seen when the fingers extend in anticipation of grasping before contact is made with an object. Stage 4 is more difficult to observe and comes when grasping becomes useful in a variety of situations and in combination with other movements.

McGraw has no empirical support for her statement that a reflex becomes part of later movements. But her descriptions through the first three stages suggest a general progression from a reflexive response, which often is flexion, to inhibition that produces extension or very little movement and then to voluntary control when a baby anticipates the need for movement rather than being bound to the eliciting stimulus. Reflexive to voluntary control in McGraw's terms can be described as progressing from flexion to extension to anticipation. This is an overly simplified sequence, but one that explains generally the change from reflexive to voluntary control.

249

Spontaneous Movements

Spontaneous movements were discussed in Chapter 2 in regard to a type of movement very common in young babies. Thelen, Bradshaw, and Ward (1981) note that spontaneous movements may be precursors to later development in much the same way that reflexes may provide a basis for the later voluntary control of movement. For example, they point out that reflexive stepping has been considered as the developmental precursor to walking, whereas spontaneous kicking shows a spatial and temporal structure like that of mature locomotion in humans and other species and also may be a developmental precursor to walking.

Well-coordinated kicking begins at around 1 month, increases in frequency up to 7 months of age, and then declines with the onset of crawling and walking. Thelan and colleagues videotaped eight full-term babies from 4 to 6 weeks of age and used frame-by-frame analyses. The repetitive cycle of flexion and extension in the hip, knee, and ankle joints was morphologically much like the cycle of a single leg movement in mature locomotion, both for spatial and temporal characteristics. Mature locomotion has two distinct temporal phases: (1) the swing phase when the foot is off the ground and the body is moving forward and (2)

 FIGURE 9-2

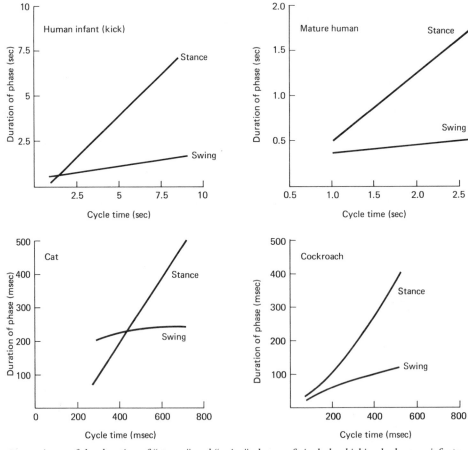

Comparisons of the duration of "stance" and "swing" phases of single-leg kicking by human infants to duration of stance and swing phases as step cycle time increases in mature humans, cats, and cockroaches. (Reproduced with the permission of Thelen, Bradshaw, and Ward, 1981.)

the stance phase when the foot is on the ground and the body is moving forward over the stance foot. As the walking speed increases, the stance phase decreases in duration, but the swing phase remains constant or increases. Thelen and colleagues equated various parts of the spontaneous kicking action to the swing and stance phases and then compared them with locomotion in the mature human, cat, and cockroach. The results presented in Figure 9-2 show the similarity of the time durations. As the cycle time increases (*slower* walking), stance time increases; swing time is only marginally affected by cycle time.

Spontaneous kicking is different from reflexive walking in that there is no input from either weight-bearing changes or tactile feedback from the feet. Kicking therefore may be controlled by a central motor program or central pattern generator. Thelen and colleagues conclude that both spontaneous kicking and early reflexive stepping may be foreruners of mature locomotion. They view kicking as manifesting a central patterning of the limbs and reflexive stepping as reflecting a system that modifies or tunes movements to environmental specifications.

Control of Muscle Groups and Motor Units

Electromyography (EMG) has been used to examine the control of motor units and muscle groups. EMG can provide information about the force, number, sequencing, and timing of muscle groups, as well as indirectly provide evidence regarding individual motor units that control specific muscles; that is, it describes motor control functioning rather than movement behavior.

For motor control to be effective, muscle groups must be both *excited* and *inhibited*. In voluntary movements, the timing of the inhibitory processes affects the starting and stopping of a movement and contributes to its smooth production. Gatev (1972) examined agonist and antagonist inhibition in the biceps and triceps muscles of three groups of children: Group I, ages 1 to 2 months; Group II, ages 7 to 9 months; and Group III, ages 2.5 to 3 years. Gatev found three patterns of agonist-antagonist relationship. First were extension movements without antagonist inhibition; second was delayed inhibition, when antagonist inhibition occurred after agonist excitation; and third was anticipatory inhibition, which is the mature form of antagonist inhibition occurring before agonist excitation. The percentages of children demonstrating the three types of inhibition are shown in Table 9-1. Group I was primarily without inhibition, whereas Group III had anticipatory inhibition in 59 percent of the experiments.

EMG techniques were used by Simard (1969) to examine the ability of children from 2 to 12 years of age to control individual motor units. All demonstrated gross

TABLE 9-1 **Percentage of Occurrence of Types of Inhibition for Different Age Groups***

| | | NUMBER OF EXPERI- MENTS | TYPES OF INHIBITION | | |
GROUP	AGE		*Without inhibition*	*Delayed and simultaneous*	*Anticipatory*
I	1–2 months	65	83	17	—
II	7–9 months	32	72	25	3
III	2.5–3.0 years	97	21	21	59

* Based on data from Gatev 1972.

control in that they were able to activate, as well as rest, designated muscles. With training, it was possible for 90 percent of the children to isolate a single motor unit after a delay of 5 minutes after the practice time. After the children could carry out this delay task, they were asked to isolate the single motor unit again while the opposite limb was being used in another movement. The children were asked to drink from a cup held by one arm while trying to activate a single motor unit in the rhomboid muscle in the opposite arm. Greater proficiency was demonstrated by 7- to 9-year-olds, with children below age 3 not able to perform the task. Success increased from 30 percent at ages 4 and 5 to 50 percent at age 6 and 70 percent at ages 7 to 9. The low and variable numbers at each age make the exact percentages a little suspect, but the trend is interesting.

Muscle Synergies

Another way to think about the development of motor control is in regard to muscle synergies, which Gelfand proposes as the fundamental explanatory unit in motor control (Gelfand, et al. 1971). A synergy is a synchronization of motor neurons, resulting in an overt movement pattern, that provides coordinated movement involving multiple joints and limbs. Bernstein (1967) proposed that synergies exist in a hierarchical system of motor control, with the higher centers prescribing the sequence of patterns executed by the lower-level centers. The higher centers do not directly control the muscles, thus freeing them for organizational control.

An interesting possibility, put forth by Bressan and Woollacott (1982), is that the development of movement control can be explained as the development of synergies. They begin with Fiorentino's (1981) proposal that reflexive behavior has three levels of maturation, progressing from spinal and brain-stem synergies that control static posture, through midbrain control of synergies that affect sitting and crawling behavior, to cerebral and cerebellar control of synergies for upright locomotion. Bressan and Woollacott call this the *preadaptive phase* of movement development, in which new synergies are attributed to the maturation of the nervous system. In the *adaptive phase*, individuals between the first and fifth years develop appropriate synergies that allow for the selection of movements to fulfill intentions. During the adaptive phase, the synchronization of muscle synergies into coherent action represents the means to achieve desired outcomes in a movement situation.

The development of the synchronization of synergies is linked by Bressan and Woollacott to Jewett's and Mullan's (1977) Movement Process Category System, which was formulated for curriculum decision making. The seven processing levels proposed in the Jewett–Mullan system is reorganized into three subphases for the adaptive phase of skill acquisition, which is an individual's gaining control over the requisite synergies. The first subphase is *skill construction*, in which the synergies are first automated. Bressan and Woollacott believe that during this subphase, neural control begins in the cerebral cortex, and control is shifted to the cerebellum or brain stem when the synergies are automated: a progressive shifting of control among neural centers toward a decreasing need for conscious involvement. The second substage is *skill stabilization*, in which the automated synergies are accommodated and refined. They believe there is no appreciable difference in the neurological location of synergy control, but the cerebral cortex now is abailable to deal with a range of environmental information, and with this comes the development of the capacity to adjust the synergies in response to environmental changes. The refining of synergies reduces the number of muscle units activated in the muscles by a synergy. Bernstein (1967) calls this "mastering redundant degrees of freedom." The third subphase is known as *skill differentiation*, in which collections of synergies are modularized and automated. Synergies become sufficiently automated for the cerebellum and lower neural centers to control performance in both dynamic and static environments. The cortex is involved even less than during skill stabilization. Synergies now can be employed creatively by individuals in situations and contexts not previously experienced. Individuals can vary, improvise, and compose.

Bressan's and Woollacott's ideas depend in part on the motor control concepts of the principles of least interaction and relative complexity of synergies. The principle of least interaction is the disposition of the neurological system to control synergies by means of the lowest possible neural center in order to free the higher centers for task analysis and synthesis. The relative complexity of synergies is the concept that because new synergies to some extent build on old synergies, there must be time for the old synergies to be constructed, stabilized, and differentiated before establishing new ones.

Development of Maximal Performance

The most common way of studying biological changes and movement development is through the maximal performance of specific movement skills. The normative summary of play-game skills in Chapter 5 considers these movement skills, which are primarily closed skills involving body control and not manual control. Movement tasks of this kind require a high level of force production to create speed or impart force to objects (including one's own body), which means that a functional use of strength is important.

In fact, the functional use of strength is so important to producing maximal performance in closed movement skills that it must be recognized as a major consideration. Throwing for distance demonstrates the need for functional strength in an effective summation of force. The analyses of throwing in Chapter 3 indicate how the ordering and timing of movements among arm and trunk segments lead to a more effective summation of force. Jumping for distance requires the same functional use of strength, but to propel the body rather than an object. Running for speed is somewhat similar, except that the movements are repeated in a series of coordinated movements of body parts to propel the body forward. More force could be generated in these movement skills if children were stronger and if available strength could be effectively used. This means that "skillful" summation is limited by children's ability to create muscular tension. The converse is that additional strength in creating greater muscular tension is not useful unless the movement parts are coordinated to summate the potential available in the muscles. The desirable combination is "strong" muscles and "skillful" coordination to achieve maximal force output appropriate to the task requirements.

We next shall review the relationships among structural changes and development of maximal performance involving the functional use of strength. Because these relationships tend to be greater at the upper and lower ends of distributions, we shall examine performance extremes separately, and we shall end with some general comments on the development of fitness and strength in relation to more functional biological changes.

General Relationships

The development of maximal performance has been studied primarily in terms of structural changes, except for the development of muscle in relation to functional strength. The principal finding is that structural differences among children of the same chronological age cannot predict maximal movement performance as defined here. Few of the measures of height, body proportions, body composition, and physique for children at age 6 correlate substantially with their maximal performance scores for running, jumping, throwing, and similar movement tasks. Malina and Rarick (1973), in a critical review of related literature, concluded that "performance in motor skills during elementary school ages is largely unaffected by body build and constitutional factors, *except at the extremes of the continuum*" (p.150, italics added). They acknowledge that physique and related structural characteristics can limit or enhance performance but are not good predictors of maximal performance scores (also see Malina 1975).

Some of the findings from the Medford Growth Study (Clarke 1971) are presented in Tables 9-2 and 9-3 to show the relationships among biological measures and movement performance. The Medford Growth Study annually tested boys in an Oregon town from 1956 through 1968. The Cable-Tension Strength Test in Table 9-2 is the average of eleven strength measures. The reaction times and movement times in Table 9-3 are a conventional arm-hand movement to touch a target in

TABLE 9-2 Relationship* of Cable-Tension Strength Test to Measures of Maturity, Size, Physique and Movement Performance for Boys in the Medford Growth Study†

MEASURE		CHRONOLOGICAL AGE				
		7	9	12	15	17
	(N =)	(113)	(175)	(278)	(343)	(272)
Maturity						
Skeletal age		34	24	40	56	15
Structure (size)						
Height		44	34	43	49	21
Weight		48	35	53	59	46
Leg length		41	25	35	30	11
Arm girth		52	34	50	54	46
Physique						
Endomorphy		01	15	28	03	07
Mesomorphy		37	27	33	42	35
Ectomorphy		−20	−18	−31	−22	−39
Movement performance						
Standing long jump						
Distance		37	38	30	44	25
Distance × weight		59	52	65	70	53
Shuttle run (60-yd.)‡		49	51	29	31	29

* Pearson product-moment correlations with decimal point omitted.
† Based on data from Clarke 1971.
‡ Sign reversed.

TABLE
9-3
Relationship* of Simple Reaction Time (RT) and Movement Time (MT) to Measures of Maturity, Size, Strength, and Movement Performance for 13-Year-Old Boys (N = 65) in the Medford Growth Study†

MEASURE	BODY MOVEMENT		ARM-HAND MOVEMENT	
	RT	MT	RT	MT
Maturity				
Pubertal assessment	14	06	00	00
Structure (size)				
Height	22	−05	−02	18
Weight	11	15	00	12
Hip width	15	06	00	21
Chest girth	05	21	−04	12
Upper arm girth	03	18	04	−04
Strength				
Cable-Tension Strength Test	−07	−19	−11	−16
Movement performance				
Standing long jump	−18	−42‡	01	−35‡
Shuttle run (60-yd.)	24	48‡	14	43‡

* Pearson product-moment correlations with decimals omitted.
† Based on data from Clarke 1971.
‡ Significant at .05 level.

response to a stimulus light and a body movement from a standing position to move forward 10 feet and touch a target.

Looking first at Table 9-2, body size and muscle size (arm girth) correlated .3 to .6 with strength. This probably is a matter of more muscle mass for boys with larger body structures, because when measuring strength in a more direct outcome (cable-tension), muscle mass is more important in force production than in a skilled movement. Physique and maturity correlations with strength were at a lower level and were a more erratic set of values. This is a complicated set of relationships, because more mature children presumably have acquired more of their muscle mass, and the three physique ratings are based partly on estimates of muscle mass. Notice that skeletal age correlated higher (.40 and .56) with strength during the pubertal years (ages 12 and 15), when early maturers probably were acquiring muscle mass at a higher rate than late maturers were. Mesomorphy (well-defined musculature) correlations also were positive, in comparison with negative correlations for ectomorphy and low positive correlations (neutral) for endomorphy. But for the most part, the physique and maturity correlations were low (.3 or less).

The Cable-Tension Strength Test correlated .3 to .5 for jumping and running, which need force production to achieve maximal distance and speed. The importance of strength is emphasized when correlations increased to .5 to .7 for jumping performance times weight. For example, two boys at age 7, weighing 60 pounds and 70 pounds, would score 300 points and 350 points, respectively, for jumping the same distance of 50 inches. The boy weighing 70 pounds must generate more effective force to jump the same distance, which is a more functional use of strength, but the heavier boy generally has more muscle mass.

Correlations with reaction time and movement time in Table 9-3 show the *lack of relationship* of structural characteristics to movement performance *when force production is minimal.* Reaction time, which is the time taken to initiate a movement, did not correlate significantly with level of maturity, size, and strength. Movement time also did not correlate significanlty with these structural characteristics, probably because the arm-hand and body movements were so limited that the generation of force was not critical. Notice that MT correlated .3 to .4 with jumping and running, which presumably indicates a skill not related to strength.

In the introduction to this section we said that the functional use of strength is a major consideration in maximal performace. Muscle mass, therefore, becomes important in concert with skill in summating force. Various structural characteristics and level of maturity may be related to maximal performance because they reflect muscle mass and functional strength. To confirm this, we need more direct measures of muscle mass and more functional measures of strength, and we also should analyze movement skills more carefully when studying strength and force production.

Results from a study by Rarick and Oyster (1964) are presented in Table 9-4 to illustrate how we can untangle some of the measures we have been discussing. Second-grade boys, ranging approximately 2 years in chronological age (mean = 8.3 years), were measured on the age, structural, strength, and performance characteristics listed in Table 9-4. *Zero-order correlations* were calculated in the conventional manner of correlating chronological age to ankle extension, then to knee extension, and so on. The eight measures of strength (except for shoulder strength) correlated .5 to .7 with age (chronological and skeletal) and size (height and weight). Throwing velocity correlated .3 to .5 with age and size, whereas jumping distance and running speed correlations were lower (.1 to .3). This is how these characteristics usually are presented, as we did for the findings from the Medford Growth Study.

TABLE 9-4. Relationship of Structural and Maturity Measures to Strength and Movement Performance of Second-Grade Boys (N = 48)*

| MEASURE | ZERO-ORDER CORRELATIONS† | | | | THIRD-ORDER PARTIAL CORRELATIONS† | | | |
| | Age | | Size | | Age | | Size | |
	CA	SA	Ht	Wt	CA	SA	Ht	Wt
Strength								
Ankle extension	52	60	72	73	28	22	14	27
Knee extension	63	51	73	67	38	− 09	36	14
Hip flexion	58	56	53	48	32	26	17	− 07
Hip extension	64	57	66	61	37	12	24	− 06
Wrist flexion	61	54	68	63	34	04	28	09
Elbow flexion	65	63	74	71	36	15	30	14
Shoulder medial rotation	21	35	40	43	− 07	10	09	14
Shoulder adduction	57	43	53	54	37	− 05	06	20
Movement performance								
Standing long jump	25	25	26	08	10	20	30	− 33
Throwing velocity	53	48	49	35	23	27	26	− 25
30-yard dash‡	28	32	19	07	12	30	08	− 23

* Based on data from Rarick and Oyster 1964.
† Pearson product-moment correlations with decimal omitted.
‡ Signs reversed

CA = Chronological age
SA = Skeletal age
Ht = Height
Wt = Weight

The problem with using zero-order correlations is that the correlation between two measures (A and B) may reflect their relationship to other measures (C and D). Notice that ankle extension strength correlates .72 and .73 with height and weight, respectively. We know that chronological age and skeletal age also correlate somewhat with ankle extension strength (.52 and .60, respectively) and probably with height and weight. This means that we are overestimating these four correlations of age and size with strength. Rarick and Oyster took their analyses a step further by calculating *third-order partial correlations* in which the influence of three of the measures of age and size were partialled, or removed, while calculating the correlation of the fourth measure with strength. An example is that when the relationship of skeletal age, height, and weight was removed (partialled), the correlation of chronological age and ankle extension strength decreased from .52 to .28. Even larger decreases were found when calculating correlations in this way for skeletal age, height, and weight. Third-order partial correlations in Table 9-4 are a better estimate of structural and maturity measures to strength and movement performance than are zero-order correlations, which most often are reported.

Looking now at the third-order partial correlations, chronological age correlated .3 with all but one measure of strength, in contrast with the other partial correlations which were mainly 0 to .2. Another way to view these two sets of correlations is that these four measures of age and size have a substantial relationship with strength when confounded with one another (zero-order correlations); each measure taken alone (third-order partial correlation) is not predictive. It also is likely that each of these measures is only secondary and reflects muscle mass or other considerations. The net result, as stated by Malina and Rarick (1973), is that level of maturity and structural characteristics are not related substantially to strength during the prepubertal years.

Third-order partial correlations of age and size with movement performance, as shown in Table 9-4, are usually less than .3. Notice that the correlations for weight are negative, indicating that weight is a handicap, although not a great one. Rarick's and Oyster's analyses demonstrate the need to untangle cumulative and secondary relationships. They found low and often nonsignificant correlations which seem typical when describing relationships among structural biological characteristics and movement performance.

Despite the generally neutral findings, structural differences probably are important to maximal performance for the movement skills we are reviewing here. The problem seems to be in matching specific structural characteristics to specific task requirements. For example, it seems too much to expect that a general measure of physique will predict a specific movement achievement. But the general physique category of mesomorphy does combine the body proportions and composition that should contribute to better performance in many play-game and athletic skills. We should analyze task requirements more carefully to find specific aspects of physique that contribute to maximal performance. We also need to include functional characteristics, which may be more important. Asmussen (1973) stresses strength as a skill in its own right, along the lines of our recognizing the functional use of strength. This means that we must find ways to assess the coordination of movement parts, which leads us back to the development of movement control. Some individuals probably are better equipped than others are to coordinate movement parts in summating force, although they can make great improvement with good instuction. Our comments here do not change our conclusion that structural differences among children of the same chronological age do not predict maximal performance.

Extremes in Level of Biological State and Performace

In regard to very high or very low levels of biological state, extreme structural and functional differences may predict level of performance. An obese child has more body weight to move and has proportionately less muscle mass; a mal-nourished child lacks muscle mass and is deficient in those energy systems that support muscle activity. The impact of extreme structural and functional differences is easier to imagine and is probably more predictive when the potential is to *limit performance.* Injury and disease may limit movement potential, although individuals sometimes can compensate by moving in alternative ways. Loss of a limb alters structure, and a neural impairment, such as cerebral palsy, alters function. Movement potential is limited substantially in both examples. The extent of the limitation depends on the availability and use of other resources.

The *enchancement of performance* is less predictable because many factors contribute to a high level of performance. One way to think about enhancement is to reverse our perspective and look at individuals who are high-level performers, rather than to start with individuals who are at a high level in structural and functional characteristics. Tanner (1964) found well-defined differences among athletes in different events in international competitions. High jumpers had longer legs relative to their trunk length; weight lifters were taller and heavier, with a larger muscle mass in relation to the size of their limb bones; and sprinters were relatively short and muscular, with relatively larger limb muscles in relation to their bone size than was found for other runners. Malina and colleagues (1971) reported similar differences among women in different track and field events.

Differences are so striking for some types of athletic events and games that only casual observations are needed to identify some of the characteristics, such as the height of gymnasts compared with that of basketball players and the weight of football players compared with that of badminton players. High-level perform-ance in some types of physical activity does require certain structural and func-tional characteristics, but it is misleading to think that an individual with the biological characteristics of an international performer can actually become an international performer. Ambition, motivation, and opportunity also are important. Nonetheless, individuals without the specified biological characteristics are not likely to succeed at a high level, particularly if they differ markedly in important characteristics.

Another consideration when studying extreme groups is to determine how extreme is extreme. Our examples of international-level performers and injury-disease conditions make up groups that are less than 1 percent of the population. If the cutoff were 10 percent, the relationships with performance probably would not be very large. An example is identifying "small" 6-year-olds, on the basis of being in the lower 10 percent for height, and studying their maximal performance in play-game skills. It is not likely that 10 percent is extreme enough as a cutoff point to limit the effective use of strength for maximal performance. Also, the selection of "better" performers in the upper 10 percent will not likely identify a group with common structural and functional biological characteristics. Extreme really must be extreme to expect predictions or similarities, but there is not a fixed cutoff point to guide us.

258

Fitness and Strength

Fitness has a variety of meanings when applied to human movement. We shall confine it here to exercise or work fitness as generally used in studying exercise physiology. Strength often is included as an aspect of fitness, as we shall for convenience here. Exercise as physical activity will increase work fitness and strength if an individual completes an appropriate number of repetitions in combination with various loads or resistances. The lack of exercise will lead to a decrease in fitness and strength. Although training effects confound analyses of developmental changes, our comments are appropriate for children who are physically active within a similar, normal level of activity.

Another consideration for fitness, as we are using the term, is that such measures refer to biological functioning and not movement skill performance. O_2 skills and similar measures are how exercise or work fitness is assessed. Thus, changes in O_2 skills measure changes in fitness. O_2 skills range from direct measures of exercise functioning, such as vital capacity, to measures of contributing components, such as number of red blood cells. We include fitness in our discussion of maximal performance because it pertains to maximal peformance, although not in terms of movement skill.

The general pattern of change in fitness is that children steadily increase their O_2 skills, which contribute to the *potential* for improved fitness. Level of fitness can vary noticeably among children at a particular age, because they vary in their activity level, but their potential for fitness improves with chronological age. Physiological changes during puberty also greatly enhance fitness potential, particularly for males.

Strength should be considered in two ways. First, strength can be the direct and primary outcome, as when exerting pressure on a dynamometer or lifting a certain amount of weight. Second, strength can be part of a movement skill when using it functionally to contribute to maximal performance, as when going faster or imparting force to objects. We know that children improve their strength in both respects to have larger grip strength scores, greater running speed, and longer jumping distances. An important contributing factor must be the absolute and relative (to weight) increases in muscle mass. Again, muscle mass increases particularly during the pubertal years, with males having greater absolute and relative increases. Strength potential improves with chronological age, and level of strength can change when participating in appropriate physical activities.

Our comments to this point have pertained to changes in O_2 skills and muscle mass as primary contributors to fitness development and strength development, respectively. Other aspects of biological change also may contribute, but probably to a minor degree. Structural changes create a larger and differently proportioned body. There is little in these changes that should affect fitness development, except that older children have larger bodies to move. Extremely large children and those with very different proportions may be at a disadvantage when participating regularly in physical activity, but structural differences must be quite extreme to affect fitness development. Although strength is related to body structure in some respects, the relationship is more a matter of muscle mass and the effective summation of force. Height and weight correlate moderately to direct measures of strength, and endomorphs and mesomorphs tend to be stronger than ectomorphs. Each of these structural charcteristics means having more muscle mass, whether it is a larger body or a physique classification that reflects more muscle mass.

Biological changes in the nervous system must be related to fitness development and strength development, because neural transmission is part of the contributing systems. But there does not seem to be a direct impact. Level of maturity should have an important influence, because a more mature individual should have better-developed physiological functioning and more advanced muscle development than should a less mature individual of the same chronological age.

Level and Rate of Maturity

Level of movement development should be related to level of maturity, because a more mature individual should have better-developed personal resources. Also, early (more rapid) maturers tend to be mesomorphic and endomorphic in physique, which gives them a potential advantage in speeded and forceful movements. Very little useful information is available, however, on the relationship of level of or rate of maturity and level of movement development.

Longitudinal Studies

Several longitudinal studies of pubertal changes have included analyses of development of maximal movement performance and strength in relation to level of maturity. The general purpose was to follow individuals during a period of rapid change when relationships to level of maturity might be more visible. Most of this information was collected many years ago, but the approaches and findings are a useful starting point.

The first study is the set of longitudinal analyses made by Espenschade (1940) as part of the Adolescent Study conducted at the University of California (see Table 5-6). Level of performance on the 50-yard dash, distance throw, and Brace Test were plotted in relation to level of maturity, as shown in Figure 9-3. Level of skeletal maturity was measured by X ray readings and was scored on a point scale. The scores of 29 to 35 in Figure 9-3 cover the higher level of skeletal maturity when boys and girls are approaching full maturity in skeletal development. Boys' and girls' chronological ages vary greatly at each point. Performance changes in Figure 9-3 are shown in relation to level of skeletal maturity and not in relation to chronological age.

The patterns of performance change are not consistent in Figure 9-3. There is very little change with increased skeletal maturity for the 50-yard dash, in comparison with the consistent increase by boys in the distance throw. Boys with a higher level of skeletal maturity have higher scores on the Brace Test, whereas the girls' scores are lower. The Brace Test is a series of "stunts" that emphasize control of movements rather than maximal force production. Espenschade's approach is an interesting illustration of how we might look at level of maturity in relation to level of performance. But the results do not show clearly the nature of this relationship. Espenchade observed that extreme levels of maturity for boys seemed related to their levels of performance and that no late-maturing boys scored consistently high on movement performance and no early-maturing boys scored consistently low on movement performance. The best clue from the Expenschade analyses is that there may be a relationship between rate, rather than level, of maturity and level of performance.

Rate of maturity in relation to strength was analyzed by Jones (1949), whose findings are shown in Figure 9-4. He gathered information on the same children

FIGURE
9-3

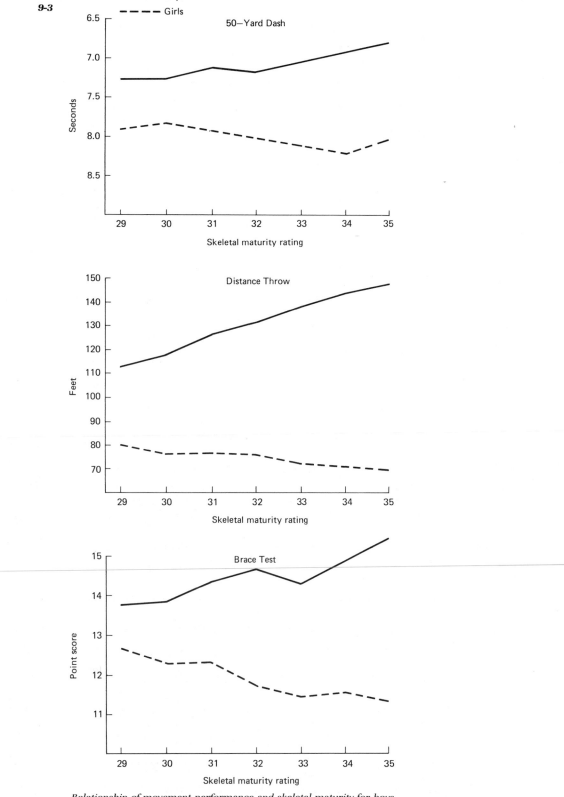

Relationship of movement performance and skeletal maturity for boys
and girls approaching full skeletal maturity. (Reproduced with
permission from Espenschade, 1940.)

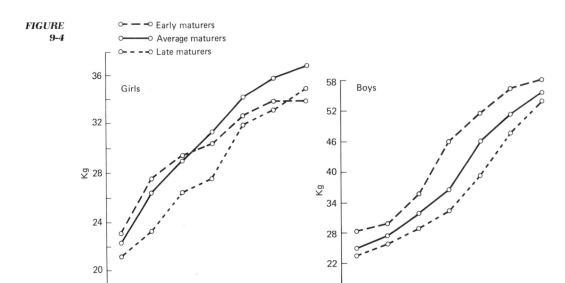

Grip strength (right hand) scores for early, average, and late maturers. Girls were classified on the basis of age at menarche; boys were classified on the basis of skeletal maturity. (Drawn from data reported by Jones, 1949, in six-month intervals which were averaged within each year to plot scores at yearly intervals.)

from age 11 through age 17 as part of the Oakland Growth Study at the University of California. Early-maturing boys, as measured by skeletal X rays, were stronger throughout these years in comparison with average and late-maturing boys. But the same pattern of change was not true for girls. Early-maturing girls were stronger during their earlier years, but the differences among early, average, and late maturers were minimal by age 15. Early maturers might have an advantage in strength measures because they enter puberty earlier and their muscle mass increases sooner. Findings from the Jones study show that for boys, their rate of maturity, when considered at extreme levels, may be related to their level of performance.

The third longitudinal study is the Medford Growth Study (Clarke 1971), discussed in Chapter 5. Clarke's approach was to study the characteristics of high-level performers. He found that successful athletes in interschool sports (grades 5 and 6 through the senior year in high school) were more mature in skeletal age than their peers were. These male athletes also were superior to their peers in body size, strength, and movement performance. Note that the Clarke's comparisons start with the high-level performer rather than the level or rate of maturity. Clarke's findings imply that high-level performers are likely to be early maturers, although some early maturers may choose not to enter athletic competition, and some late maturers may be successful athletes despite their late maturity. The findings from each of these longitudinal studies support the possibility that there may be relationships among extremes in maturity and movement development, but there is little information about these relationships across the full range of maturity and movement development.

262

General Considerations

The rate of change in relation to maturity and the age of achieving maturity varies noticeably among the many aspects of our biological makeup. As noted earlier, we can measure level of maturity for selected biological chacteristics, but we cannot single out one level of maturity for all aspects of biological change. Chronological age, through a convenient indication of level of maturity, is not useful except to mark the passage of time. Skeletal age, peak height velocity, and similar measures are appropriate for certain purposes, yet often are too general. Microscopic measures of change, such as dendritic growth in a specific neural area, can precisely measure level of maturity but cannot be easily related to movement changes. There is no easy solution when trying to choose an appropriate measure of maturity, but a first step is to consider the appropriateness of maturity measures when reading research reports and proposed explanations.

The other side of the coin is to measure movement changes in a way that would match maturity and movement, and thus we must use changes in movement components rather than general achievements and general performance scores. Longitudinal measures also are needed to trace maturity and movement relationships, with an emphasis on the development of movement control rather than maximal performance.

The distinction between level and rate of maturity also must be kept in mind. The level of maturity for a biological characteristic indicates the level of development for a particular resource at a particular time. The rate of maturity makes a comparison across time and in relation to other individuals and has been the general maturity concern in regard to studying early and late maturers. The level of maturity, if well measured, would be a more definitive approach, because we could match changes in movement development to the level of the development of resources. The distinction between level and rate leads to two questions: What is the relationship of resource level and movement development? And how is movement development enhanced or limited when the developmental rate in a resource is rapid or slow?

Chapter Summary

We organized our brief review around, first, the early development of movement control and, second, the maximal performance of forceful movements. The early development and initial refinement of movement control seem to be determined largely by the development of higher-level neural control centers, which organize movement into larger and more adaptable packages. Reflexes and spontaneous movements are the prominent observable movements in the early months. Higher-level neural centers develop later than do more peripheral aspects of the nervous system, which seem to control reflexes and spontaneous movements. As the higher-level neural centers develop, they begin to establish some degree of control over the lower levels of neural control. We do not know exactly how the different levels of neural control change in their organizational relationships, but there appear to be substantial changes that must increase the potential for a more complex and adaptable organization of movement.

We described the general changes in the control and organization of muscle groups and motor units. These changes in more basic units of the neuromotor system lead to anticipatory inhibition and the organization of muscle synergies. We reviewed a proposal in which the development of muscle synergies were nominated as a primary level of the development of movement control. This proposal also included the changing roles of higher-level neural centers in the organization of synergies. We now need more detailed descriptions and analyses to evaluate propositions such as these and to generate competing explanations.

The development of maximal performance involving the functional use of strength has been studied in relation to many biological characteristics. One conclusion is that the structural differences among children of the same chronological age do not predict maximal performance. A limitation in studies of this issue is that the biological and performance measures have been too general to reveal much of a relationship. Many measures are needed to predict performance, with task requirements matched more carefully to the biological characteristics of interest. An example is the strong relationship generally obtained for performance on strength or exercise fitness tasks and measures of muscle mass or O_2 skills. It is more difficult to find such relationships for movement skills, even for maximal performance of forceful movements.

An important qualification is that extremes in level of biological state may be quite predictive of extreme levels of performance. Extremes may serve both to limit or enhance, as often seen in individuals who achieve a high level of performance. They tend to have common biological characteristics, particularly those that pertain to a high level of performance in the specific movement task. Particular biological characteristics may be helpful and almost necessary to achieve a world-class level of performance, but no set of biological characteristics is likely to be sufficient without the addition of certain personal-social qualities.

Very little of the studies reviewed in this chapter can help us understand change, as their designs have not been arranged to describe and analyze relationships among changes in resources and movement development. A longitudinal study could do this, but few of the existing ones have examined changes in resources, except as rate of change in early and late maturers. An exception is Espenschade's analyses (1940), in which she studied level of maturity (skeletal age) in relation to movement performance. Movement skill needs to be measured in some different ways with a better rationale for the potential match between biological characteristics and movement development. Cross-sectional studies also can be used but do not usually focus on what is happening at a particular level for a particular resource in relation to particular changes in movement development. The overall approach has been too general and has not stressed change in resources and movements. This may account for some of our inability to confirm that changes in biological resources contribute to changes in movement development.

B | SENSORY-PERCEPTUAL SYSTEMS

| *Sensory-Perceptual Development*

The central theme of our text has been that an individual moves in an environment in order to resolve a movement problem. When explaining the movement solution, any analysis must take into account the natures of the movement problem and the mover in the environmental context. We have shown how children's movement problems change from those of self-movement control, with gravity being the constraining environmental factor, to moving in relation to objects and other persons, with spatial and temporal requirements increasing in importance. The development of sensory and perceptual abilities helps children acquire knowledge of their bodies and their movements and specify the environment in order to cope with spatial and temporal requirements.

Sensory and perceptual development have been studied from many points of view. Our presentation necessarily will concentrate on those aspects that are most relevant to the development of movement control. We shall emphasize two uses of sensory and perceptual information in the development of movement competence. First, sensory and perceptual information provide the basis for movers to *know their bodies* and *know their movements*. Second, sensory and perceptual information are used to *specify the environment*. In a general sense, we must have information about what our body can do and is doing and what is and is not happening in the environment. That is, we develop a body knowledge system and ways to specify the environment that provide the information needed to select, plan, execute, and evaluate our movements.

The chapter will be organized around kinesthesis and vision as the two primary sensory modalities providing the body-knowledge system and specifying the environment. Each will be described in terms of *sensory functioning*, which is the collection of information, and *perceptual functioning*, which is the meaning or understanding an individual attaches to the sensory input. Different kinds of energies impinge upon a sensory receptor, and the individual selectively monitors and transforms them into meanings or understandings. Development occurs both in how such information is collected (sensation) and in the meaning or understanding (perception) of the sensory input. Our principal concern will be perceptual development in kinesthesis and vision to deal with the meanings and understandings that may be important to the development of movement control.

The development of kinesthesis is of crucial importance to movement skill production. It can be thought of as knowledge about the body and its parts and movements without reference to vision or verbal cues. It is often described as the "feel" of the movement which provides preparatory, ongoing, and terminal information about it. At a basic level, babies and young children become able to differentiate their own bodies from the environment, recognize and know their body parts, recognize their positions in relation to one another, and know their movement functions. The kinesthetic system also specifies body position and movement through a network of receptors. Kinesthesis, as a sensory and a perceptual system, is the body-knowledge system that provides the mover with knowledge about body parts and their functions and specifies body position before, during, and after movement.

The development of vision also is important in movement skill development, mainly to impart environmental information to the mover. At a very basic level, vision specifies the environment's spatial coordinates. For example, we locate a chair as behind, in front of, or to the side of a table; we recognize that an object is farther way, nearer, bigger, or smaller than another object. Vision provides *spatial information* to set the scene in which the movement will take place. If objects or people are moving in the environment, vision provides *temporal information* about changes in locations as they occur and as they are predicted to occur. Vision also is used to *monitor movements*, especially when precision is required and when there is adequate time for visual information to be used. Another use of visual information is after the completion of movements in order to observe the *effects of movements* and determine whether the intended goals were achieved. Visual information helps specify the environment and control and evaluate movement.

Development of Kinesthesis and Body Knowledge

A traditional definition of kinesthesis refers to a person's knowledge, without the use of vision, about positions and movements of the body and its parts. Though accepting this general and more popular sense of kinesthesis, we want to present it as the development of *body knowledge*. We shall use body knowledge as the term for what we know about our body and its movements. Body knowledge develops by finding out more about body parts and their functions, recognizing directions on the body, and establishing a hand preference. Some of these achievements are movements, such as hand preference, whereas others are knowledges to be used in movement.

Sensory Receptors

Kinesthesis is not a single sensory system, in the sense that vision is confined to the sensory information gathered through one set of sensory receptors. Rather, kinesthetic information is gathered through a number of quite different sensory receptors to provide knowledge about the body's position and movement. We shall study five types of sensory receptors and the contributions of each to kinesthetic information, although we cannot document their developmental progress and precise involvement in the development of body knowledge.

Numerous sensory receptors, which are located in the muscles, tendons, bones, and moveable joints, respond to mechanical distortion. Mechanoreceptors found in skeletomuscular structures are stimulated by joint movement and changes in muscle length and tension and are often called proprioceptors. Proprioceptors code the parameters of joint position and movement (direction, rate, and duration of movement), and they provide information about muscle length and tension. The coded information is relayed both to centers that consciously recognize joint movement and muscle tension and to centers in which sensory signals can influence motor output. This sensory information is used at all levels of the nervous system, including the spinal cord, cerebellum, and cerebral cortex.

Sensory receptors convert one form of energy, mechanical distortion, into another, bioelectrical. It is thought that the mechanical distortion of unmyelinated sensory endings leads to an enlargement of the membranes' pores, making them more permeable to small ions such as sodium. The current generated when the sensory ending is mechanically distorted is called the *generator potential*, and it is unique to the sensory ending. Once this generator potential reaches a critical level or threshold, the electric current triggers a nerve impulse. The rate at which each successive nerve impulse is triggered is related proportionately to the size of the generator potential. The number of impulses per unit of time is the frequency code of the receptor, which can signal the strength and location of a single stimulus.

If a stimulus is applied to a receptor for a long period of time, the frequency code will begin to decline, in a process known as adaptation. Some mechanoreceptors adapt slowly, thus providing a stable frequency code for an extended duration (5 minutes to over 2 hours), and others adapt quickly (1 minute to less than 1 second). Slow and fast-adapting receptors together provide information about the onset, intensity, and duration of the stimulus. We cannot detail the mechanisms of neuromuscular control, mainly because we have almost no developmental evidence, but we shall survey some of the receptors and their contribution to kinesthesis. These include vestibular receptors that are not part of the mechanoreceptors in skeletomuscular structures but are important in knowing the head's position and movement.

Joint receptors. Nerve branches are distributed in the joint capsule, fibrous cartilage, hyaline cartilage, and articular fat pads, with the receptors being divided into four main categories based on their morphology, location, and physiological characteristics. Three types function as mechanoreceptors, and the fourth is part of the pain receptor system. The first three provide information about joint movement and position as they respond to the mechanical stresses applied to the nerve ending, as described in Table 10-1. Responses can be classified by location, and joint receptors fall into the two categories of slow- and rapid-adapting receptors. *Slow adapters* respond to both joint position and joint movement, with each receptor having an activation range from 15 to 25 degrees over which it is excited. Joint positions outside this range have no effect, and the receptor remains silent. Within the excitatory range, the receptor has a characteristic frequency rate for different angles. Movement within the activation range produces a transient discharge that quickly declines to a steady state determined by position. *Rapid adapters* are excited by a rapid joint movement in any direction and adapt rapidly when the movement stops. Speed is generally a critical parameter, and

267

TABLE 10-1 **Proprioceptive Information Available from Joint Receptors**

MOVEMENT PARAMETER	TYPE OF RECEPTOR	
	Slowly Adapting	*Rapidly Adapting*
Joint position (static)	Differential adaptation rates to joint positions within excitatory range	Cannot differentiate
Direction of movement	Differential transient response to movement in opposite direction	Cannot differentiate
Speed of movement	Frequency of transient response related to movement rate; rate of adaptation differs with movement	Different threshold to movement rate

units appear to have different thresholds. Joint receptors offer the following information to higher neural centers:

1. Static position of joint.
2. Onset, duration, and range of joint movement.
3. Velocity and acceleration of joint movement.
4. Pressure and tension on joint structures and joint torque.
5. Pain in joint structures.

Tendon Receptors. Golgi tendon organs (GTO) are located predominantly at muscolotendinous junctions and less frequently wholly within the tendon. The GTOs' nerve endings are compressed when tension is placed on the collagen fascicles. When the muscle is relaxed, there is no tension on the loosely packed collagen fibers and no compression of nerve endings. However, when the muscle stretches or contracts, the collagen fibers are pulled together to compress the nerve endings. Most GTO endings are extremely sensitive to contractile tension placed on the collagen fascicles, which constantly monitor muscular tension and give that information to the central nervous system. Each GTO probably samples the tension levels of several different motor units, and the combined response from all participating receptors provides detailed information concerning the state of the contraction.

Pacinean Corpuscle. These ellipsoidal structures are located in the various connective tissues, such as subcutaneous tissue, fascia of muscle and tendon, and periosteum. The pacinean corpuscles are very responsive to the slightest compression, and because of their location in the connective tissues surrounding bone and muscle, they can signal pressure caused by muscular contraction. They adapt very rapidly to maintained pressure and have no frequency code to signal different intensities of contraction. But each pacinean corpuscle has a distinct threshold, and the nervous system can use the range of stimulated receptors to determine the magnitude of the pressure.

Muscle Spindle. The muscle spindle is an unusual structure in that it is both an auxiliary motor unit and a sensory organ that combine to regulate muscle

**FIGURE
10-1**

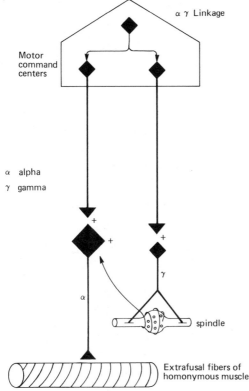

α γ Linkage

Motor
command
centers

α   alpha

γ   gamma

γ

α

spindle

Extrafusal fibers of
homonymous muscle

*Alpha–gamma coactivation. Motor command
centers link descending signals so that alpha and
gamma motoneurons are coactivated during each
contraction.* (Drawing reproduced with the
permission of J. L. Smith.)

stiffness. It is located in somatic muscle between the muscle fascicles and parallel
to the extrafusal fibers (see Figure 10-1). It consists of a variable number of intrafusal
fibers surrounded by a connective tissue capsule which is continuous with the
connective tissue of the extrafusal fiber fascicles. These intrafusal fibers are in-
nervated by fusimotor neurons, also known as gamma motoneurons. Contraction
of the intrafusal fibers does not add appreciably to the gross muscle tension
produced by the extrafusal fibers, because the intrafusal fibers are few in number
and small in size compared with the extrafusal fibers. On the other hand, the
fusimotor neurons influence gross muscle contraction via the circuit called the
gamma loop. Activation by the gamma motoneurons has a triple effect at the
spinal level. First, a proprioceptive code is sent through the ascending pathways
to the cerebellum and cerebral sensory cortices. Second, alpha motoneurons of
the same muscle are facilitated. Third, alpha motoneurons of the antagonistic
muscle are inhibited.

The spindle as a motor and sensory mechanism is part of a theory of neuromuscular control known as alpha-gamma coactivation, which states that all muscular contractions are controlled by independent but cooperative signals to the
target muscle's alpha and gamma motoneurons. Because of these cooperative
signals, the spindle can be passive or active during gross muscle stretch, which
means that it can respond to the length of the muscle but does not always do

so. When the spindle is passive, its output is related in a near linear fashion to the length of the passive muscle; that is, it follows the muscle. When the spindle is active, the spindle discharge is a result of both the true muscle length and the rate of gamma activation. In effect, the spindle is set by the gamma motoneuron to expect a certain amount of muscle stretch for an activity, such as walking. Muscle action for walking takes place via the alpha motoneurons, and spindle activity is a result of muscle stretch plus what has been set by the gamma motoneurons. If the muscle stretch is greater than expected, as in missing a step while walking downstairs, the spindle will fire its Ia afferents (see Figure 10-1) which link with the alpha motoneurons and in turn adjust the muscle action. This is the spindle working as a *sensorimotor* organ. Because of its unique sensorimotor properties, the spindle has become an important part of current theories of motor control.

Vestibular Receptors. Vestibular receptors are located in the membranous labyrinth which is filled loosely in the bony labyrinth of the skull's temporal bone at the internal end of the external auditory canal. There are two types of receptor organs in the vestibular labyrinth: *cristae* in the semicircular canals and *maculae* in the utricle. Cristae can detect acceleration-deceleration and the direction of rotary head movement, but they cannot detect head position or the constant velocity of head movement. These receptors are very important to occulomotor reflexes, in which eye movements are matched to head movements. Maculae detect the position of the head relative to gravity and help in righting reflexes.

Comments. The functions of sensory receptors described in this section are summarized in Table 10-2. The body is wired in an intricate and interlocking manner to produce position and movement information from many sources. Specific functions can be pinpointed, such as detecting the acceleration of head movements and detecting and regulating muscle stiffness, but we do not know

TABLE 10-2 **Function of Kinesthetic Sensory Receptors**

RECEPTOR	TYPE	FUNCTION
Type I (Ruffini)	Joint mechanoreceptor	Slow adapting to joint movement and position
Type II (Pacinean)	Joint mechanoreceptor	Fast adapting to rapid movement in any direction
Type III (Golgi)	Joint mechanoreceptor	Slow adapting to joint movement and position
Golgi tendon organ (GTO)	Tendon mechanoreceptor	Fast adapting to muscle contraction and stretch
Pacinean corpuscle	Connective tissue mechanoreceptor	Fast adapting to muscle contraction pressure
Spindle	Sensorimotor organ	Regulates muscle stiffness through muscle length and gamma bias; provides information about muscle length
Cristae	Vestibular receptor	Detect acceleration-deceleration and direction of rotary head movements
Maculae	Vestibular receptor	Detect head position in relation to gravity

270

how the more specific functions are combined or used in more complete movements and in adjusting to different movement situations. Also, as noted earlier, we do not know what developmental changes to expect in individual receptors and in the combined use of the information they provide. The sensory receptors described here are the sensory basis of kinesthesis.

Kinesthesis: Acuity and Memory

Kinesthesis generally is measured as discrimination *acuity* in detecting differences or matching quantities, such as location, distance, weight, force, time, speed, and acceleration. The stimulus to be detected or matched is usually present, and so only acuity is measured. If the stimulus is removed after presentation, then kinesthetic *memory* will also be measured. Kinesthetic acuity and kinesthetic memory are measured mainly as the extent to which individuals can discriminate stimuli or reproduce a movement. *Discrimination* confirms that a difference exists and judges its amount. Simple examples are comparing the weights of objects and the location, distance, and speed of limb movements. *Reproduction of movements* is used to indicate that a person remembers certain kinesthetic information, such as the location, distance, and speed of a previous movement by accurately repeating it. It is difficult to separate specific aspects of kinesthesis because kinesthesis and movement are not simple functions. Many laboratory procedures have been devised in efforts to isolate specific aspects.

Kinesthesis can be measured in terms of space, force, and time, and these variables can be analyzed in active, passive, and constrained movements. *Active movements* are measured by requiring subjects to reproduce a movement they set as a criterion. Typically, blindfolded subjects will actively move a distance and then try to reproduce the movement. In *passive movements*, the experimeter moves the subject's limb, and then the subject tries to reproduce the movement. In a passive situation, the subjects receive less information during the criterion movement than when they actively set the movement criterion, because only sensory and no motor information is available in a passive movement. Between passive and active modes are *constrained movements*, in which the subjects actively move but are stopped at a predetermined location. This allows the experimenter to control the distance traveled and the location of the stop. These three types of measurements are often compared to evaluate the efficiency of afferent versus efferent information in a given movement. For example, a task could be performed by using each of the three movement modes. If active movement is superior, the subjects presumably are benefiting from efferent or motor output information. If there is no difference among the movement modes, then sensory information is dominant.

Many different kinds of kinesthetic judgments can be measured, as illustrated in Table 10-3 for making kinesthetic judgments about a limb movement's spatial properties. The movement mode can be active, passive, or constrained to have subjects judge when a movement starts, how far it goes, and where it stops, as well as discriminate these features among a series of movements. Similar judgments are needed to measure kinesthesis in other situations involving weight, force, speed, and related body and movement information.

Changes with age for both acuity and memory in the same subject sample were reported in the two studies described in Box 10-1 (Lazlo and Bairstow 1980, Bairstow and Lazlow 1981). In the first study (1980), children at each age from 5 to 12 and a group of young adults were tested in an active movement mode on the

*BOX
10-1*

KINESTHESIS IN ACTIVE AND PASSIVE MOVEMENTS

Recent studies by Laszlo and Bairstow (1980, Bairstow and Laszlo 1981) illustrate the measurement of kinesthesis in two ways. On the runway apparatus shown in Figure 10-2, the subjects were required to hold an object (car, toy animal, or lever) in each hand and simultaneously move them up a different runway. The two runways were set at different angles. After the two objects had been moved up and down, the subjects had to indicate which runway (or object) went up higher. This task was designed to measure kinesthetic acuity independent of kinesthetic memory. The second task used the stencil apparatus shown in Figure 10-2 and required the subjects to remember a pattern on a stencil. They first traced in the stencil, after which it was rotated and the subjects had to reorient the pattern back to its original position. Twelve patterns were used on the stencil apparatus, except for ages 5 and 6 for whom only four patterns were used. In both experiments, the apparatus was covered by a cardboard box so that the subjects could not see it. The box was used instead of a blindfold because many children objected to being blindfolded. The 1980 study was done in an active movement mode, in contrast with the use of a passive movement mode in the 1981 study. Children ages 5 through 12 were tested in both studies, whereas adults were tested only in the 1980 study when the active mode was used.

Kinesthetic acuity on the runway apparatus improved steadily until age 8, as shown in Figure 10-3, when they were approaching the adults' mean performance. Lazlo and Bairstow noted that also some 6-year-olds performed at this level.

Kinesthetic memory, as measured on the stencil pattern test, was relatively less developed than kinesthetic acuity was. Children at ages 5 and 6 had such difficulty that they were tested on only four of the twelve stencil patterns. Mean error scores decreased considerably from age 7 to age 12, but adults (tested only on the active movement mode) had much lower mean error scores (see Figure 10-4). The general pattern of change for *kinesthetic memory* was a steady improvement with age through to the adult group. This is in marked contrast with the pattern of change for kinesthetic acuity, in which children by age 8 were approaching the adults' mean performance level.

The pattern of change was similar for the active and passive movement modes. There were no significant mean differences on either task at any age between females and males, nor were there any differences between right-handers and left-handers. The correlations between the tasks were low for each group.

*FIGURE
10-2*

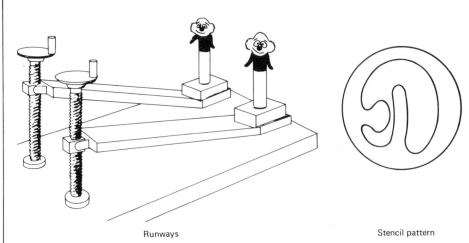

Runways   Stencil pattern

General drawings of equipment used to measure kinesthetic acuity (runways) and kinesthetic memory (stencil pattern). (Reproduced with permission from Bairstow and Lazlo, 1981.)

FIGURE
10-3

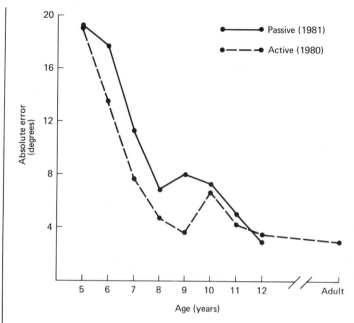

Mean absolute error of kinesthetic acuity as measured by
discrimination of difference between angles of runway apparatus for
active (Lazlo and Bairstow, 1980) and passive (Bairstow and Lazlo,
1981) movement modes. (Reproduced with permission from Bairstow
and Lazlo, 1981.)

FIGURE
10-4

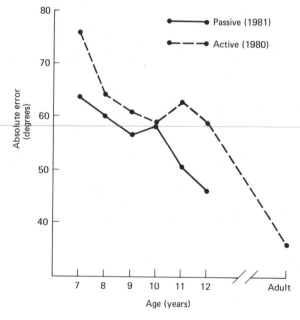

Mean absolute error in kinesthetic memory as measured by
orientation of complex movement patterns for active (Lazlo
and Bairstow, 1980) and passive (Bairstow and Lazlo, 1981)
movement modes. (Reproduced with the permission of
Bairstow and Lazlo, 1981.)

273

TABLE
10-3

Kinesthetic Judgments of a Movement's Spatial Properties

KINESTHETIC JUDGMENT	EXAMPLE
Threshold	When did the limb start to move?
Extent	How far did the limb move?
Location	Where did the limb stop moving?
Discrimination	Does this limb movement differ from the previous movement in how far it went? Where it stopped?

runway apparatus and the stencil pattern apparatus shown in Figure 10-2 and described in Box 10-1. The second study (1981) had children perform in a passive movement mode. Kinesthetic acuity in both studies approached adult levels by age 8, though kinesthetic memory had not reached an adult level at age 12.

Another measurement technique, used by Connolly and Jones (1970) and others, is to present a criterion in one sensory modality and reproduce it in the same or a different modality. Connolly and Jones had their subjects draw a line without vision and then reproduce it without vision. This is a kinesthetic-kinesthetic (K-K) condition to test kinesthetic memory. Having subjects draw a line without vision and then visually select the length of the line is a K-V condition. V-K and V-V conditions also can be tested to examine different aspects of intersensory integration, which will be discussed later in this chapter. On the K-K condition, Connolly and Jones (1970) found a reduction in memory error from age 5 to age 8, with very little difference among 8-year-olds, 11-year-olds, and adults. Sugden (1980a) used a lever-positioning task as another way to measure kinesthetic memory. Nine- and 12-year-olds approximated adult performance levels and were much better than 6-year-olds. Smothergill (1973) reported that in the kinesthetic localization of a finger, there were only slight differences among adults, and 6- and 10-year-olds, when no memory was involved. However, adults were better than children when a response delay was introduced that required kinesthetic memory.

We have very little direct information about the kinesthetic acuity and memory of very young children. But from age 5 to about age 8, there seems to be a substantial increase in performance as measured by a reduction in error. Acuity seems to improve faster and earlier than memory does, perhaps because memory is more complex, as it uses acuity and memory functions. A general representation of the differences in the rate of development of kinesthetic acuity and memory is shown in Figure 10-5. Information from studies using more complex research designs will be covered later in the chapter when discussing visual-kinesthetic integration.

Body Knowledge

Movement is made in a three-dimensional world whose central reference point is the body, which means that knowledge about the body is a necessary part of movement. As children grow, they must establish *body knowledge* in many ways and must continuously adjust and calibrate it. A general achievement of babies and young children is becoming able to differentiate between themselves and their environment. They come to know their body boundaries and to recognize

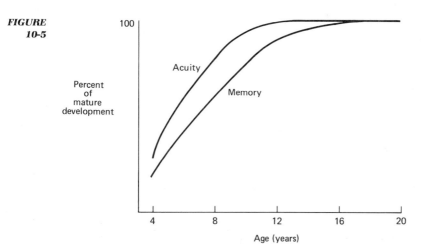

**FIGURE
10-5**

General representation of percent of mature development of kinesthetic acuity and memory.

themselves as separate from objects and other persons. Part of this body knowledge is functional, such as a physical knowledge of separateness, and part is affective, such as knowing that one has an existence in thought and emotion. The sum of this physical separateness and identity of self provides a basis for the body to be a reference point in the environment.

We shall divide body knowledge into two parts. First is the *functional knowledge* of knowing body parts and their functions and dimensions of external space in relation to body dimensions. Second is an *affective knowledge*, how one feels about one's own body. We shall limit our discussion here to functional knowledge because it is more directly related to understanding the development of movement control. A summary of achievements in the functional development of body knowledge is presented in Table 10-4 which was compiled from several sources. The achievements are divided into four areas.

Knowledge of Body Parts. The knowledge of body parts and their functions can be considered as having three levels. First is *procedural knowledge,* when children show an understanding of their body parts by using them appropriately. For example, babies will reach and pick up objects with their hands, thus demonstrating that they have procedural knowledge in knowing that their hands are the most useful parts of their body for performing this act. Second is the *recognition* of what these parts are. In response to "Show me your hands," babies will look at their hands or raise them. Third is the *verbal identification* of these parts. In response to a person touching a body part and asking, "What is this?" children will correctly state, "This is my arm." Very early in life, babies will reach for objects on their right side with their right hand, indicating a basic procedural knowledge. Before they are 18 months old, they can show or touch major parts of their body: eyes, nose, ears, hands, and feet. As they grow older they can recognize other parts, such as elbows and knees, and identify body parts verbally. Ilg and Ames (1964) report that at 5 years, 80 percent of children can verbally identify eyes and 50 percent eyebrows, which increases to 70 percent at 7 years. By age 5 or 6, 70 percent of boys and girls can accurately identify major body parts (eyes, ears, hands, knees) and are only slightly less accurate in identifying

TABLE 10-4. General Achievements in the Functional Development of Body Knowledge

AGE IN YEARS	IDENTIFICATION OF BODY PARTS	LATERALITY	DIRECTIONALITY	LATERAL PREFERENCE: HANDEDNESS
0–2	Begin to "show" major body parts (eyes, nose, ears, hands, feet)			Preference changes during first year depending on task
2–5	80 percent identify eyes 50 percent identify eyebrows	Left-right discrimination, no better than chance Ages 4–5: realization that left and right are on opposite sides of the body; unsure of which is which	Very little knowledge of directionality	Ages 3–5: increase in right-handedness
5–7	Ages 5–6: 70 percent identify all major body parts Age 7: 70 percent identify minor body parts (elbows, wrists, heels)	Consistent in response whether right or wrong Age 7: mistakes are infrequent	Age 6: mirror and imitate movements Age 7: begin to use body as directional reference of object, but still subjective	Handedness may shift or be inconsistent
7–12	Ages 8–9: mistakes are rare	Beyond ages 7–8: identify all left and right body parts	Age 9: make objective directional references Age 10: identify right and left of person facing them Age 12: begin to use natural reference systems	Ages 9–10: right-handedness stabilizes for approximately 80 percent Right-eyedness increases Ages 10–11: right hand-eye preference increases

276

minor body parts (elbows, wrists, heels). Mistakes in identifying body parts are rare at ages 8 and 9.

Laterality. Closely associated with the knowledge of body parts is children's perception of sides of the body, which we label as laterality. As they grow older, children realize that their body has two sides, with two hands, two eyes, two legs, and so on. The corresponding parts are similar in size and shape but occupy different positions on the body. Laterality is thought by many to be an important foundation on which the delineation of other spatial dimensions is built.

Laterality in the simplest sense means that babies and children know that two body parts are similar but are on opposite sides of the body, even though they do not recognize and cannot accurately use the words "right" and "left" to label the two sides. The simple knowledge of *sideness* is a perceptual distinction, whereas the attachment of right-left labels is more of a cognitive distinction to create general directions that apply, eventually, to spatial dimensions. Babies make the perceptual distinction quite early, in that they will use their two hands independently but in a coordinated manner, as we have described functional asymmetry in bimanual control. That is, they will use one hand to hold a cube while using the other to explore it or to bring another cube to bang on the first one. They can interchange the function of their hands, and they can use both hands doing the same movement. As well, they recognize that they have two hands and know that each is in a different position on their body.

The more cognitive distinction of right and left to label body parts is assessed initially by observing children's behavior when asked to "show me your right leg" or "touch your left knee with your right hand." There is considerable variability in the ages when children can accurately identify and use right and left body parts, which can be explained by the informal and formal instructions to which children have been exposed and by differences in testing procedures. Despite the wide range in individual achievement, the cognitive distinction of the body's right-left dimension is generally only a chance response before about age 5, in contrast with an accurate response by ages 7 or 8 (Belmont and Birch 1963). The general progress in distinguishing right from left begins when children realize that right and left are opposite sides of their body, but they do not know which is which. They then identify rights and lefts, but they may be reversed and always wrong in regard to some or all body parts before they become consistent and accurate.

Belmont and Birch (1963) confirm the progression of laterality development just described. They used seven measures of right-left discriminations of body parts and found that 95 percent of the children over 7 years of age responded correctly to all seven questions, whereas only 69 percent of those under 7 years of age could do this. Long and Looft (1972) reported similar results when using a battery of 125 items to measure both laterality and directionality of children ages 6 to 12. Children at age 6 had an accurate knowledge of body parts and could easily discriminate betweeen right and left by age 7 or 8.

Directionality. Children also must establish a sense of direction in the space around them, including labels such as right-left, up-down, and forward-back. We call this knowledge of dimensions of external space *directionality*, which children often organize in relation to their position. For example, when looking at a house, we see a car parked on the left. If we change our position to view it from the back of the house, the car will now be on the right as we look at it. Or when we give directions to someone for finding a place of interest, we often use our body as a reference point, because if we do not, the instructions may be ambiguous. We say, "If you are traveling toward the beach, the camera store will be on your left." Of course, when leaving the beach, it will be on the right. Because there are no invariant spatial references in external space, children begin with their own body as a reference to the dimensions of external space. Eventually, they are able to do this without consciously referring to their own body.

Long and Looft (1972) found that children at age 6 are aware of vertical and horizontal identification of up-down and are able to imitate or mirror many movements made by the experimenter. Children at age 8 begin to relate body laterality to other objects, in that they start to use their body for the directional reference of another object in one position (for example, "The book is on my right"). But if the children change position, they will not change their reference position. Thus, children can make judgments that are not egocentric but are still subjective. By age 9, children base their answers on objective directional relationships. For example, when they change their position to the opposite side of a table, they then see a book as being on their left. They can also follow directions based on two directional references (for example, "Draw a triangle at the *bottom left-hand* corner of the paper"). By age 10, children can correctly specify the right and left of a person facing them. By age 11, they are able to judge correctly that certain objects are adjacent to other objects, even when they are opposite the table containing these objects. Finally, by age 12, children begin to use natural reference systems (for example, "The sun sets in the west").

Children progress from a subjective and egocentric perspective toward a more objective view of space. Piaget and Inhelder (1956) see this transition from an egocentric to a decentered laterality as progressing in stages that culminate with the children's using natural frames of reference based on permanent areas and invariant points of reference, such as horizontal-vertical, east-west, and north-south positioning. Long and Looft show these progressions to be gradual, with sizable changes at around ages 7 and 8 and a slower but continued increase through age 12. The culmination in a well-organized spatial knowledge is an important perceptual-cognitive organization of the visual world. Body knowledge seems to be a significant aspect of the early organization of spatial knowledge, because it is an essential reference.

So far, we have discussed several general achievements in the development of body knowledge. First, children acquire a knowledge of their own body surfaces and body parts. Second, they recognize and then verbally identify their body's symmetrical structure. Third, they understand and can verbalize spatial directions without having to locate objects and places in relation to themselves. The order of appearance does not indicate a fixed sequence in which one achievement determines the next one. Rather, body and spatial knowledges probably develop independently in many respects, but knowledges of body and space seem to become interrelated in many ways and probably facilitate each other. We shall now turn to hand preference, which becomes a basic part of our movement behavior and is another functional part of our body knowledge.

Lateral preference: Handedness. A universally observed behavior is that humans use one of their eyes, hands, or feet in preference to the other. When we kick a ball, aim a gun, write our name, or cross our legs, we favor one side of our body over the other. Preference sometimes is labeled as dominance to suggest the prevalence of one of the cerebral hemispheres in controlling the preferred eye, hand, or foot. If children develop a preference for an eye, hand, and foot on the same side of the body, they are said to have pure dominance. If any one of the preferred body parts is on the opposite side of the body, the children are said to have mixed dominance. We shall use the word *preference* for preferred use and shall not use the word *dominance* except when referring directly to control by the right or left cerebral hemisphere. We shall focus on hand preference, or handedness. The comprehesive review of Harris (1983) and the analytical comments of Wolff (1981) need to be consulted for a more complete review of this seemingly simple but actually complex phenomenon of handedness.

Limb preference is measured by observing how children perform a variety of movements, such as writing, reaching for objects, using a spoon or scissors, and throwing and kicking a ball. Eye preference can be observed when looking through a telescope or aiming a gun. Considerable care must be taken in observing preferred use. Variations in task presentations may favor one side or the other, such as when handing an object to babies to observe which hand is used in reaching, and a number of tasks must be observed and at different times. We also must remember that many hand movements can be made reasonably well with either hand if the requirements for accuracy and speed are minimal, as when opening some doors or carrying small objects. Most humans at any age are somewhat ambidextrous in using the nonpreferred hand when convenient or necessary. We stress that preference is just that and does not mean that the other hand is not used and is not useful.

Hand preference can be observed during the first year after birth but will change in a short time. That is, preference seems to exist and change quite early in life. Seth (1973) observed babies from 5 to 12 months of age and found a marked preference for the left hand from 4 months through 7 months. He filmed the manipulation of objects such as a cube and a bell and found in the early months a tendency for the left hand to predominate over the right. Also, babies had a better success rate with their left hand than with their right hand. There was a shift, however, in the later months when babies used their right hand more and with a higher success rate.

Anderson and McDonnell (1979) also report a change in hand preference during the first year, but in a different pattern of change than that observed by Seth. They found that future right-handers had a left-side preference until 12 weeks and were ambidextrous from 12 to 20 weeks, followed by a lateralization in the direction of right-side preference. McDonnell (1979) suggests that the lack of agreement among researchers may be related to whether the types of activities studied were reflexive or voluntary. Although the pattern of change has not clearly been defined, it seems that hand preference is present and can change during the first year of life.

Hand preference has not been studied in the second and third year of life after birth, although we do know that most children by age 3 will show a right-hand preference for many everyday activities and that there will be some changes in hand preference until about age 10. The ages and percentages will vary depending on the task being observed and the preference criteria being used. The lateral preferences for several sensory and movement functions are listed in Table 10-5.

Right-hand preference was observed for 68 percent of young children, ages 3

**TABLE
10-5**

Lateral Preference for Several Sensory and Movement Functions

SENSORY-MOVEMENT FUNCTIONS	PREFERENCE	PERCENTAGES* BY AGE (YEARS)								
		3–6	5	6	7	8	9	10	11	15–19
Hand	Right	68	87	60	75	75	82	79	83	81
	Left	26	5	12	4	10	12	21	6	14
	Mixed	6	9	28	21	15	6	0	11	6
Foot	Right	77	83	88	89	80	88	79	83	82
	Left	13	9	8	7	15	12	21	11	11
	Mixed	11	9	4	4	5	0	0	6	8
Eye	Right	55	44	52	43	60	41	57	78	66
	Left	6	31	20	21	15	24	29	6	9
	Mixed	40	26	28	36	25	35	14	17	25
Ear	Right	53								70
	Left	7								5
	Mixed	40								25
Hand-eye	Right		39	36	36	50	41	78	67	
	Left		31	16	14	15	24	8	6	
	Mixed		31	48	50	35	35	14	28	

* Percentages in first and last columns are from Coren et al. 1981; percentages in middle columns are from Belmont and Birch 1963.

to 6, and increased to 81 percent for young adults in the study reported by Coren, Porac, and Duncan (1981). The right-hand preference percentages for ages 5 to 11, as reported by Belmont and Birch (1963), fit well into the middle years not reported by Coren and his colleagues. Jenkins (1930) and Keogh (1965) also found that more than 90 percent of young schoolchildren threw right-handed. The overall picture is that the preference for the right hand increases during early childhood to be approximately 80 percent by age 9 or 10.

Foot preference is similar, except in hopping. Both Jenkins and Keogh found that approximately one-third of the children did not consistently use the right leg when hopping 50 feet as fast as they could. Keogh further found that only 71 percent of the children used the same leg for hopping when doing two different tasks, one to hop 50 feet for time and the other to hop for accuracy in a series of marked squares. Some investigators have observed that hand preference may change during the early school years and may not be consistently the same for some individuals until about age 10. The same probably is true for leg or foot preference. Both Jenkins and Keogh reported that only 65 percent and 67 percent of the children used the arm and the leg on the same side of the body to throw and hop, respectively, another indication of differences in individual preferences for limb use. Notice in Table 10-5 that many children and young adults have a left or a mixed preference for the use of one eye or one ear. This carries over to a similar proportion of left and mixed preference of hand and eye until ages 10 and 11, when Belmont and Birch report an approximately 70 percent right preference for both.

Hand preference to this point has been limited to unimanual tasks in which one hand or the other, but not both, will be used. As noted earlier in Chapter 3, Annett (1976) found that more than 80 percent of adults use the same hand for the same function, such as holding the match box in the left hand while holding the match in the right hand when lighting it. Auzias (1975) observed that children at ages 4 and 5 became more consistent in their hand preferences in bimanual tasks. Bruml (1972) examined hand preferences for bimanual tasks requiring one hand to hold the object while the other moved, as when threading beads. She found that children from ages 5 to 11 increasingly kept one hand stable while the other hand moved, rather than having both move, and the right hand was more and more the moving hand.

A question pertaining to laterality is whether the establishment of preference has any effect on other skills. Kaufman, Zalma, and Kaufman (1978) addressed this by trying to relate hand preference to right-left awareness, mental ability, and motor coordination. They compared groups with and without established preference. Two age groupings were formed, with ages 2 to 4 as the younger group and ages 5 to 9 as the older group. Significant mean differences favored the preference-established children in the younger group for both cognitive and motor measures, whereas no differences were found in the older groups. However, a significant relationship between preference and right-versus-left awareness was reported for the older group. Normally we acquire preference between the ages of 5 and 9, and so we could argue that the younger group showed precocious development. If that were true, we could also argue that children who establish preference precociously may be brighter and better coordinated than those who have not yet established preference. By contrast, children who establish preference within the normal age range do not seem to have any advantage on cognitive and motor tasks. Kaufman, Zalma, and Kaufman did advise caution in interpreting their results but added that preference may be a variable that can contribute to the psychological assessment of a child.

An interesting phenomenon is that left handers seem to have a smaller between-hand difference than right handers do. In other words, for left handers, the difference between performing a task with the preferred, as opposed to the non-preferred, hand is smaller. Peters and Durding (1978) investigated this developmentally to evaluate the explanation that left handers living in a right-handed world use their nonpreferred hand more than do right handers. Peters and Durding argue that if this is the case, the differences for children should be larger than those for adults. A study of five hundred elementary children showed, however, that this was not the case. Left-handed children showed a significantly smaller between-hand difference than did right-handed children, and this did not change with age.

Why do humans prefer one side to the other? The genetic, learning, and pathological antecedents of human handedness have been examined, and Hicks and Kinsbourne (1976) concluded, after reviewing much of the evidence, first, that there is little to suggest that handedness is learned. But if learning is a reason, then we should find cultures in which left-handers predominate. We also should see an increase with age in the incidence and degree of right-handedness in right-handed cultures. Hicks and Kinsbourne report that indirect evidence, such as paintings, suggest that across cultures, people have been predominantly right-handed since prehistoric times. Recent studies have found a general invariance in handedness from childhood through young adulthood. Second, Hicks and Kinsbourne note that there are some pathological conditions associated with left-handedness, including an increased frequency of left-handedness in mental retardation, epilepsy, cerebral palsy, stammering, developmental aphasia, articulating apraxia, and learning disorders. But the relationship between handedness and dysfunction is very complex and certainly is not directly connected. Indeed, most left handers do not have any noticeable pathological disorders, and most persons with disorders are right-handed. Finally, Hicks and Kinsbourne support a genetic hypothesis for the genesis of handedness, with the warning that although the evidence for this is strong, the appropriate genetic model is far from clear.

We noted earlier that preference is related to cerebral dominance. In this case, being dominant means that one hemisphere controls a particular function. The general expectation is that the left hemisphere controls the facility for speech and language, whereas the right hemisphere controls various spatial operations. It is not relevant to detail the research concerning the roles of the two hemispheres, except to note the relationship between cerebral dominance and handedness. Right-handers will control speech in the left hemisphere, as will most left-handers. There does seem to be a relationship between cerebral dominance and handedness, but it is complex. It has often been stated that consistent preference—right-handed, right-eyed, and right-footed—is preferable because it reflects complete left hemispheric dominance. Mixed preference, on the other hand, may indicate inadequate cortical development and, like left-handedness, has been associated with various perceptual, cognitive, and motor dysfunctions. Yet there is little direct evidence to support a causal relationship.

Development of Visual Perception

Vision is our principal and most comprehensive means of specifying our environment and provides a display to represent the part of the environment in our visual field. Reading the visual display becomes the general problem in visual-perceptual development. Individuals need to find and know specific objects and their spatial and temporal relationships. They need to perceive objects as parts and wholes and be able to combine them into larger configurations and patterns. They also must be able to see into the environment and perceive distance and depth and detect and follow movement.

Early Development

The eye approximately doubles in size between birth and maturity, with great variability in the growth rate of different parts of the eye. All of the visual structures are intact at birth, but many of them are immature. The fibres of the optic nerve at birth are myelinated, but with a thinner nerve sheath than in the adult. Estimates of the completion of the myelinization of the optic nerve range from 3 weeks to 4 months. The visual neural pathways and the visual cortex are functional at birth and continue to mature beyond birth (Cohen et al. 1979).

Visual acuity in the first month of life has been measured by contrast sensitivity in discriminating black–white stripes (width measured in minutes of arc) from a uniform field of the same average luminance (Atkinson and Braddick 1982). Acuity improves from 30 minutes of arc at birth to 15 to 20 at 1 month, improving steadily to 6 months. Myelinization of the optic nerve continues after birth and could be a variable affecting the quality of transmission up the optic nerve, thus influencing visual acuity. The acuity levels estimated for newborns are about twenty to thirty times lower than adult levels. However, this may not be as much of a handicap as it appears, because a high level of acuity is necessary only for tasks involving great distances or fractions of a millimeter, neither of which are of great importance to newborns.

TABLE 10-6. Aspects of Visual-Perceptual Development Important to the Development of Movement Control

1. Object perception	*2. Depth perception*	*3. Perception of movement*
Constancy	Absolute distance	Detect
Shape	Relative distance	Track
Size	Distance cues	Predict
Location	Binocular parallax	
Object relationships	Motion parallax	
Part-whole	Optical expansion	
Figure-ground	Perspective	
Field dependence-independence		

Studies by Fantz (1958, 1961, 1965) provide convincing evidence that newborns of under 5 days can make selective visual responses, thus implying the presence of some visual sensitivity. The level of sensitivity depends on a number of factors, such as the pupillary reflex which seems to be present at birth. Monocular adjustment and binocular focusing are other factors, and although there are divergent opinions as to the time that binocular fixation first appears, it does seem to occur in the first 2 months of life. At birth, the eyes' nerves and muscles do not work together smoothly, although the principal nerves begin developing 3 weeks after conception. Newborns at 2 or 3 days will follow a moving light, albeit jerkily, with their eyes shifting abruptly from one focal point to the next. Within 2 months, children have binocular vision with smooth and quick convergence of the eyes, plus other developments which result in clear images for both near and far objects. Accommodation of the lens to change focal length is fixed in the early weeks, thus making babies more farsighted, but it soon becomes more adjustable. Near-point vision is established at about 9 inches, which is a comfortable reading distance when holding a printed page. But near-point vision later retreats or extends into space, thus creating the need for reading glasses.

Vision in the sense just described is well developed by 2 months of age and may reflect the change from subcortical to neocortical control, as outlined in Chapter 8. Neocortical control also is a determining factor in visual-perceptual development, which is more complex and elusive and extends into the early years of childhood. Many obvious and interesting changes in visual-perceptual development can be observed quite early. Babies begin to recognize faces that were previously undifferentiated and they no longer reach for objects that are out of reach. We now shall review three aspects of visual-perceptual development, which are listed in Table 10-6.

Object Perception

Newborns see objects as things and do not see the space between them as things. That is, they extract objects for their visual attention rather than space from the visual display. When an object becomes known, it becomes recognizable as that object from whatever angle it is viewed. The object will have a constancy in that it will remain the same shape, even though the retinal image has changed. Constancy is established also for size and location. If we approach a stationary object in our visual field, the object will retain the same shape, appear to be the same size, and maintain the same location, even though our retinal image grows bigger and the object changes position on the retina.

Constancy is an important perceptual attribute that applies to many, if not all, of our perceptual skills. We become able to *recognize different sensory input as having the same perceptual meaning.* We have noted the occurrence of perceptual contancy for the shape, size, and location of objects. Perceptual constancy is needed also for kinesthetic and other sensory input, such as recognizing an upward movement of your arm from different starting positions and recognizing your name when spoken by different people.

Size constancy for objects was reported by Bower (1966) for babies at 6 weeks when they attended to the actual size of cubes rather than their retinal image size. The perceptual judgment of object size is influenced at later ages by background cues of color, texture, and gradients (Wilcox and Teghtsoonian 1971, Yonas and Hagan 1973). Three-year-olds were not influenced by background cues, whereas 7-year-olds were somewhat influenced, and adults were markedly influenced. Object-size constancy develops quite early, but size perception later is affected by cues from the larger context in which the object is viewed. Thus, visual perception changes in complexity by using additional cues to alter what earlier was a stable perception of object size.

Position or location constancy is a complex and puzzling phenomenon. An object will be projected on different parts of the retina when the eyes move and the head is stationary, but the object is seen as staying in the same position in relation to the viewer. Bower (1982) argues that the nose provides the stabilizing reference point by determining the body position in relation to the object. When the eyes move, both the object and nose are projected onto the retina. If the relative positions of the object and nose do not change, there will be no indication of change in the object's position.

Object relationships also become important in using parts of objects to construct and know more about objects and recognizing individual objects among many. This includes recognizing both the parts and the whole object, using part of the object to recognize the whole, extracting an object from a group, and organizing objects into a total picture.

Object relationships are developed in a variety of ways that enable us to know and use an object beyond its own identity. *Part-whole relationships* within and among objects enable us to organize visual information in different ways. We may perceive objects as the object itself, or we may identify parts of the object without perceiving the whole. Elkind, Koegler, and Go (1964) had children look at figures of people formed by various kinds and arrangements of fruit. Children at ages 5 and 6 saw the pieces of fruit or the figure of a person but seldom reported seeing both. Older children of 8 and 9 tended to see both the fruit and the people, but not at the same time. Children at age 9 described the picture as a person made of fruit, thus indicating that they simultaneously perceived both the parts and the whole.

Objects also must be perceived in relation to other objects in order to organize perceptually the whole visual display. Thus *figure-ground* perception has been studied to examine how and why some objects become figures and others become the background. Figure-ground relationships are changeable and complex, but young babies have sufficient perceptual development to identify people and objects as separate from the background. Stationary figure-ground relationships in everyday situations do not seem to limit the movement control of babies and young children. But this does not mean that they will cope well with the more difficult figure-ground tasks used to study more complex aspects of figure-ground development, as when shown figures embedded in a pattern of colored dots.

Perceptual organization also is studied as *field dependence* and *field independence* in order to discover the extent to which an individual is influenced by or is dependent on the field or background. As noted earlier in regard to the influences of background on object-size constancy, we are affected more by surrounding information as we develop. Witkins's rod-and-frame test (Witkins et al. 1962) has been used in various versions to assess field dependence and independence. Subjects sit in a chair in a dark room and initially are shown a vertical rod mounted in the middle of an upright square frame. The rod and frame are lighted, but nothing else in the room is visible. The experimenter can tilt the chair, rod, and frame in various combinations and then ask the subjects whether they and the rod are vertical. Field-independent persons will judge verticality according to their body position, whereas field-dependent persons will judge verticality by the relationship of the rod to the frame. Other tests of field dependence and independence have been devised, with the common findings that young children are more field dependent and adults are more field independent. Field dependence and independence also are viewed as a cognitive style, in which individuals have either a more global (field-dependent) or a more analytical (field-independent) approach to problem solving.

Object perception develops in complex ways that we have described briefly in relation to constancy and object relationships. Constancy provides the general perception of recognizing a visual feature as the same, even though it is projected differently onto the retinal image. Various object relationships enable us to organize visual pictures differently. Babies and young children seem to perceive more isolated features, as noted with object constancy, whereas older children and adults use more of the visual display's surrounding features. More flexibility in organizing our visual world is possible when not bound by specific features.

Depth Perception

The perception of depth is another much-studied aspect of visual perception. Depth perception enables us to recognize that the glass of water is too far away to reach, the boy is farther away than the girl, and the man is bigger than the dog, even though the man looks smaller because he is 200 yards farther away. These various distance judgments are grouped under the general title of depth perception, which requires both absolute and relative judgments of distance. Throwing a ball to a partner requires an absolute judgment of distance, whereas determining whether a partner or an opponent is nearer is a relative judgment of distance.

The judgment of *absolute distance* is used in many everyday tasks, such as reaching and grasping an object or tossing a ball to another person, and we do them quite easily and often with rather limited visual information. As Bower (1982) notes, it is difficult to study the development of perception of absolute distance. Performance errors may be caused by poor distance perception, poor use of distance information to organize the motor response, or poor control in the execution of the motor response. However, we know that babies at 4 months are reasonably accurate in reaching and contacting both stationary and slow-moving objects. A general expectation is that young babies know the absolute distance of objects within reasonable limits but that their motor control is not very precise.

The ability to judge *relative distance* requires using a number of visual cues. One is *binocular parallax* which comes from possessing two eyes that are a distance apart. Each eye receives a slightly different retinal image, or visual picture.

This can easily be demonstrated by extending your arm and pointing your index finger at an object across the room. Open and close each eye, one at a time, and you will notice that your finger is pointing at the object when one eye is open but not when you are looking with the other eye. Also, you can stand near the corner of a building so that you can see around the corner with one eye but not with the other. The visual system integrates the two retinal images into one visual picture, with the two retinal images providing distance and depth cues. A developmental consideration in binocular parallax is that adults' eyes are twice as far apart as newborns' eyes are, which means that an ongoing recalibration is required throughout the growing years.

Motion parallax is another visual cue in which objects on the retinal image are displaced or "moved" when the head turns or is moved. The amount of retinal displacement of objects is a function of their distance and direction from the point of focus, as illustrated in Figure 10-6. The direction and rate of retinal displacement indicate the objects' relative distance. Motion parallax is not subject

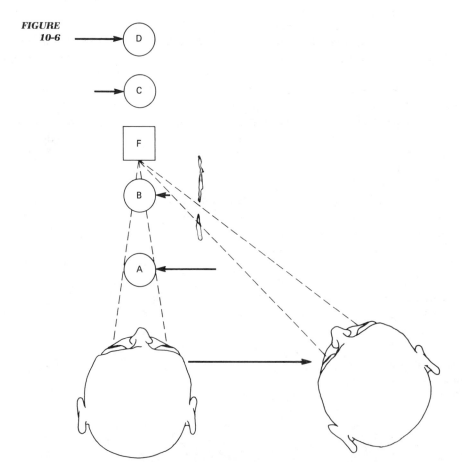

FIGURE 10-6

Motion parallax occurs when the eyes remain focused on a fixed point (F) while the head turns or is moved. As the head is moved to the right, objects A and B, which are nearer to the head than the fixation point, move in the opposite direction (left). Objects C and D, which are farther from the head than the fixation point, move in the same direction as the head (right). Objects farther away from the fixation point (A and D) appear to move faster and farther than objects nearer to the fixation point (B and C).

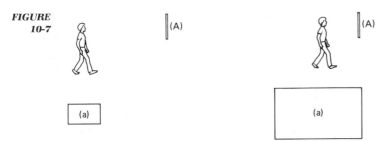

**FIGURE
10-7**

The retinal image (a) of an object expands as a person moves
toward the object itself (A).

to the same growth problems as binocular parallax is, because changes in retinal image, as a function of head movement, are independent of physical growth changes.

Another visual cue for distance is *optical expansion*, which occurs whenever the distance between the perceiver and another person changes, as shown in Figure 10-7. If an object's retinal size increases by one-third when we move toward it, we will know that the object now is one-third closer. Optical expansion, as well as optical contraction, specifies proportional changes from the starting point, rather than distance in absolute terms. Relative distance also can be judged by perspective, or what is called *painter cues*. Linear perspective and density gradient are shown in Figure 10-8 to illustrate the perspective cues that artists use to gauge distance and depth. There are similar perspective cues in our retinal images which are important in judging distance and depth.

Cues that specify relative distance seem to be present very early in life. Binocular parallax is present in babies at 5 months, but its development from then to adulthood is largely unknown. Motion parallax is present at 2 months, perhaps earlier, and by the end of the first year, differences of 5 inches can be discriminated. Few attempts have been made to study developmentally the perception of absolute distance. With children, ages 8, 10, and 12, and college students as subjects, Degelman and Rosinski (1979) found all ages able to estimate accurately the relative

**FIGURE
10-8**

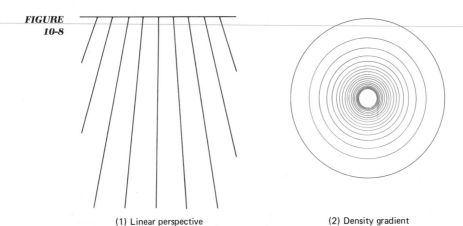

(1) Linear perspective   (2) Density gradient

Relative distances in drawings and paintings can be suggested in many ways.
Illustrated here are (1) linear perspective, in which the decrease in distance
between lines suggests an increase in distance, and (2) density gradient, in which
the increase in the density of lines suggests an increase in distance.

287

distance in a task requiring them to state which of two objects was closer. But in an absolute distance task requiring the subjects to match a criterion distance, their judgments became more consistent with age.

Children's depth perception sometimes is studied as part of a general examination of spatial perception. In one such study, children ranging in age from 5 to 12 were asked to estimate distance on a variety of tasks (Smith and Smith 1966). The children were as accurate as the adults except when the experimenter limited their vision, though they also improved with age in the limited vision condition. Younger children may need visual cues that are redundant and not needed by older children and adults. Results from another study were that younger children, age 5 to 10, greatly overestimated distance, compared with the estimates of 12-year-olds and adults (Harway 1963). In summary, babies soon can use cues to judge relative distance, whereas their ability to estimate absolute distance improves until approximately age 12.

Development of depth perception has been studied in some interesting experiments which we will briefly review. In 1960, Gibson and Walk carried out their famous "visual cliff" experiment. Babies at 6 to 14 months were placed on tables with a sheet of glass for the top. One-half of the table had a checkerboard pattern on the underside of the glass. The other half had the same kind of pattern several feet below the glass to create the illusion of depth. The babies were placed on the table and encouraged to crawl to their mothers at the other end. But they would not crawl over the "cliff," even with coaxing, and Gibson and Walk concluded that they could indeed see depth. Gibson and Walk used this experiment with many different animal babies and observed the same reluctance to move across the "cliff." An important finding is that depth perception is functional when human and other animal babies become mobile, presumably to help them avoid real cliffs and other places from which they might fall. (See Richards and Rader 1981 for a current review of other explanations and related data.)

Another technique used to analyze young babies' distance perception is to study their responses to approaching objects. This methodology is based on the reasoning that if babies do nothing when an object approaches, it is because they do not see the changing distance between them and the object; but if they do respond, it is because they have detected something. White (1971) dropped objects from 2, 7, and 12 inches toward babies lying on their backs. A plexiglass shield stopped the objects and eliminated changes in air pressure. Defensive blinking was recorded by means of electrooculography. Although some babies at 2 to 5 weeks blinked in response to the 12-inch drop, it was not until 9 to 13 weeks of age that 50 percent of the infants blinked on 70 percent to 80 percent of the trials. More recently, Petterson, Yonas, and Fisch (1980) used preterm, full-term, and postterm babies of the same chronological age, as well as similar techniques and found a consistent increase with age in the probability that an approaching object would evoke a blink. The response levels increased from 16 percent at 6 weeks to 45 percent at 8 weeks and 75 percent at 10 weeks. The finding that postterm infants blink more frequently at an approaching object than preterm or full-term babies do, strongly argues for a maturational rather than a learning explanation of the development of defensive blinking. Bower (1977) and Bower, Broughton, and Moore (1970) claim that defensive behaviors can be seen after the second week of life. They observed defensive behaviors of eyes widening, head retracting and the hands blocking the face from approaching objects, but not the blinking response. Even though Bower's claims have been difficult to replicate, it is clear that babies early in life can discriminate an approaching object from a stationary or a receding one.

Perception of Movement

When objects start to move in the environment, children are faced with more and more visual problems to solve. They must *detect* motion and *track* moving objects as well as *predict* their future locations. When an object is moving, they also must use all of the visual skills needed when the environment is stationary and do so more continuously. The object is no longer a static picture of a moment in time; it is constantly changing and thus requires continuous perceptual re-organization. For example, we must be able to know that other persons are walking, must be able to keep them in sight, and must be able to know where they will be in another few steps.

Young babies seem able to determine the direction of moving objects relative to themselves. As described earlier, Bower, Broughton, and Moore (1970) found a defensive response to an object moving toward young babies, and Ball and Tronick (1971) did not find a defensive response when the object was on a miss path. These studies together show that motion and direction are perceived at an early age. One of young babies' general achievements is to track objects moving in larger areas. In the first weeks of life they can follow an object through a small arc, and during the early months they can make a flexible visual pursuit through larger areas. This goes hand in hand with accurately perceiving objects at an increasing distance from the observer. Thus, young babies can detect motion and can track slower-moving objects.

The ability of young babies to predict the future location of a moving object is difficult to study. An ingenious study of tracking behavior by Mundy-Castle and Anglin (1969), as reported in Bower (1982), offers some interesting observations. The experimental apparatus is shown in Figure 10-9, in which an object is shown moving in order from porthole 1 to portholes 2, 3, and 4. At around 12 weeks, babies showed a simple place-to-place tracking ability, even though the object disappeared behind the board when going from hole to hole. They anticipated its appearance in each porthole by simple eye movements, including a horizontal eye movement (A) from porthole 2 to porthole 3. A little later, however, the babies began to look up and over between portholes 2 and 3 (eye movement B), as though they were following the trajectory they thought the object must have been following in order to get from 2 to 3. With an increasing time delay between portholes 1 and 2, their eye movements indicated that they predicted the interpolated trajectory to be higher and steeper (eye movement C). This demonstrates that babies knew that the object should travel in a trajectory and recognized its speed by moving their eyes along with it. The studies of von Hofsten (1979, 1980; von Hofsten and Lindhagen 1979) presented in Chapter 4 also support babies' ability by at least 4 months to track and predict the path of a slow-moving object.

A problem encountered with a fast-moving object is that less time is available to identify and track it, as well as to predict when and where it will arrive at a landing or interception point. Very little is known about children's coincidence-timing skills except that they seem to improve with age, because the children improve their coincidence-timing performances with age (see Chapter 4). However, movement control accuracy is confused with visual-perceptual proficiency in most of these studies. One study shows how we might study the visual-perceptual skills needed in knowing about moving objects. Cratty, Apitzsch, and Bergel (1973)

289

FIGURE
10-9

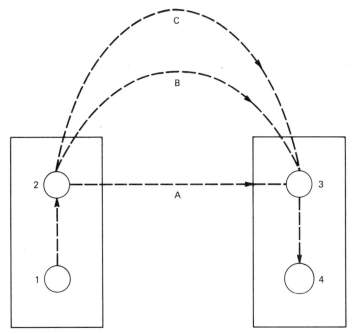

Eye movements of babies when tracking objects in an apparatus used by Munday-Castle and Anglin (1969). Objects appear in order in portholes 1 through 4 to simulate movement.

tested children between ages 5 and 12 on three measures of dynamic visual acuity. The task was to identify targets traveling at various speeds on a horizontal path across a screen from left to right. As shown in Figure 10-10, dynamic visual acuity decreased as the target speeds increased, and it was at the fastest target speed (120 degrees per second) that the age differences were the greatest. The young children could deal quite well with the slower speeds, but the fastest speed led to greater mean differences between the younger and the older children. There were also significant sex differences at all target speeds in favor of boys.

Individuals thus seem to devise *knowledge rules* that guide their visual perception. We call these knowledge rules because individuals know things about their environment and themselves without needing to experience them directly and completely. An example is knowing that objects continue in motion, even though they disappear behind something. The object's speed and trajectory also are known and are used to anticipate when and where the object will reappear.

Knowledge rules related to the visual perception of movement are illustrated in the study of Bower, Broughton, and Moore (1971), who performed a series of experiments showing that babies at 3 to 4 months could identify a moving object from rules related solely to the object's movement speed, whereas older babies used additional rules related to other features of the object. In the first experiment, babies watched an object approach and then move behind a screen. When it was time for it to reappear, a different object emerged and continued on the same path at the same speed. Babies at 3 to 4 months continued tracking as if nothing unusual had happened, but babies at 5 months looked back for the original object. In the second experiment, the object moved behind the screen and then re-emerged, but much sooner than expected if the speed had been kept constant. All of the babies made a rapid eye movement to catch up with the object, but

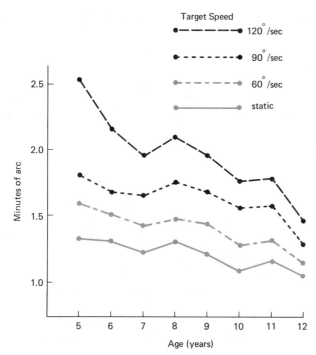

FIGURE
10-10

Mean dynamic visual acuity scores by age and target speed.
(Drawn from data reported by Cratty, Apitzsch, and Bergel, 1973.)

they then looked back to the exit point on the screen. They apparently thought that a different object had appeared. The change in speed in the second experiment apparently violated the rule that the object should have the same speed at exit that was seen at entrance. When the rule regarding movement speed was obeyed, as in the first experiment, only the older babies used the additional rule, that the object should look the same at the entrance and at the exit. With increasing age, babies learn more about moving objects and their properties, and they begin to make accurate predictions based on these knowledge rules. The idea of knowledge rules also can be applied to other aspects of visual-perceptual development.

Visual–Kinesthetic Integration

Visual and kinesthetic development have been described separately to this point, and so we now need to consider the functioning of the two sensory systems together. When moving in almost any circumstances, both visual and kinesthetic information are useful and usually necessary, as the development of movement control probably depends very much on the development of an interplay between vision and kinesthesis, as well as that among other sensory systems, but to a lesser extent.

Newborns clearly can recognize *intermodal equivalences*, that information gathered in one sensory modality is equivalent to that gathered in another, although there are serious methodological and design considerations that can confound the interpretation of findings (Meltzoff and Moore 1983). One way of testing an intermodal equivalence is to have 4-week-old babies suck on a pacifier that either is smooth or has small nubs on the protruding end and then remove it and observe the extent to which they attend to a picture of a smooth or a "nubby" pacifier. Meltzoff and Borton (1979) found that babies attended more to the picture matching the pacifier they had been sucking. Thus the babies seemed to recognize the visual information that was equivalent to the tactual information. In a different experiment, babies at 2 to 3 weeks were able to imitate adults' lip, mouth, and tongue movements (Meltzoff and Moore 1977). This is an impressive finding, because the babies created a movement (for example, tongue protrusion) to match what they saw, even though they could not see and probably never had seen their own "matched" movement. This means that they translated visual information into an equivalent body movement and implies an existing equivalence in kinesthetic information about their tongue movement and visual information about the adult's tongue movements.

The evidence regarding further development of intermodal equivalences (or what at older ages often is called cross-modal matching) is contradictory and ambiguous. Cross-modal matching was studied by Birch and Lefford (1963, 1967) who had children, ages 5 to 11, make "same-different" judgments on geometric forms presented in one modality and matched in another. The modalities were visual, haptic (active manual exploration), and kinesthetic (manually guided by the experimenter). In all conditions, errors decreased as age increased. Birch and Lefford argued that improvement was the result of increasing efficiency in intersensory (intermodal) integration. They did not consider the possibility, suggested by Bryant (1968), that improvement in intrasensory (intramodal) functioning may help improve intersensory performance.

Connolly and Jones (1970) compared intrasensory and intersensory development. Children (ages 5, 8, and 11) and adults were presented visually or kinesthetically with straight lines of varying lengths and then were asked to identify or reproduce the line length in either the same or a different modality. This provided the following experimental conditions:

PRESENTATION	REPRODUCTION	EXPERIMENTAL CONDITION
Kinesthetic	Kinesthetic	KK Intrasensory
Visual	Visual	VV Intrasensory
Kinesthetic	Visual	KV Intersensory
Visual	Kinesthetic	VK Intersensory

Errors declined in each of the four conditions as age increased. KK and VV were equal, and both were more accurate than KV, which in turn was more accurate than VK. Connolly and Jones explained this order as the need for an extra translation in the intersensory conditions (KV ad VK), to shift from one modality to the other. The asymmetric effect of KV being more accurate than VK in the intersensory condition was explained as information being lost in the less stable kinesthetic memory. But the asymmetry of KV and VK reproduction seems to occur only when visual information of the surrounding area is available, which tends to refute Connolly's and Jones's explanation (Newell et al. 1979). This does not detract, however, from their finding in all conditions of a decrease in errors with increasing age.

Millar (1975a) suggests that the differences between kinesthetic and visual input could be important. As one possibility, visual inputs are a simultaneous, single display, whereas kinesthetic inputs are sequential and come from many sources. Millar also proposes that intersensory development is related to the development of better processing strategies, which are discussed in Chapter 12. Goodnow (1971) suggests that we need to abandon our search for the simple relationships in V-K and similar cross-modal matching procedures and argues that we should instead focus on what and how each sensory modality contributes. Task or situation requirements may favor the contributions of different modalities, as well as depending on the ability to combine different sources of information.

It is clear that with increasing age children become more proficient at integrating visual and kinesthetic input, in that they are better able to make cross-modal judgments. Why this happens is not clear, and so we need to think about the contributions of modality information and the dynamics of weaving together different sources of information. We also do not know how intersensory functioning affects the development of movement control. Earlier accounts suggested the development of intersensory integration as a basis for skilled performance. Jones (1982) rightly criticizes this view as being too general and maintains that we should not assume that all skills must necessarily have something in common.

Chapter Summary

The functioning and development of kinesthesis and vision were reviewed to provide some background for examining movement development in relation to perceptual development. We began with the premise that kinesthesis and vision are the basic sensory and perceptual systems for knowing our bodies and our movements and for specifying the spatial and temporal requirements of the environment. We concluded that babies by their first birthday have acquired the basics. Their general achievements in reaching and grasping demonstrate that they have some knowledge of body movements and can read basic aspects of their visual display, including tracking slow-moving objects. Babies become less bound by specific stimuli and become better able to use surrounding sensory-perceptual information.

Kinesthesis is an accumulation of input from many sensory receptors, which makes it difficult to characterize kinesthetic development. Changes with age have not been measured for the specific sensory receptors involved in kinesthesis, such as joint receptors and muscle spindles. Kinesthetic acuity and memory, as measured by the discrimination and reproduction of movements, improves noticeably until about age 8. Kinesthetic acuity in these test conditions does not improve much beyond age 8, in contrast with kinesthetic memory which improves to age 12 and beyond.

Body knowledge is the general term we used to cover the many things that we know about our body and our movements, presumably by means of kinesthesis. Our review was limited to functional knowledge, which can be summarized as three general achievements. First, children establish a knowledge of their own body surfaces and body parts. Second, they recognize, and then verbally identify, the symmetrical structure of their body. Third, they understand and can verbalize spatial directions without having to locate objects in relation to themselves. These general achievements occur interactively and not in the fixed sequence implied by the order of listing.

Lateralization, preferring to use of one of a pair of body parts, is a general development that occurs in many ways. It is most often studied through hand-edness, which shifts and may be erratic early in life but eventually becomes a right-hand preference for more than 80 percent of people in all parts of the world.

Visual development, in contrast with kinesthetic development, has been studied extensively and in clever ways to identify and describe many different aspects of visual perception. Object perception and depth perception are important aspects of more static visual displays, whereas the perception of movement is important when objects and people in a visual display are moving. Most of the abilities required for visually specifying the environment are reasonably well developed in babies by their first birthday. They can see depth and distance, can differentiate between objects approaching from those moving away, are able to judge accurately the size of an object, can track a moving object, and can predict the motion variables of speed and trajectory. We also know that many of these abilities continue to improve during childhood.

Visual-perceptual development leads to extracting more from the visual information collected by the visual system. The early development of constancy for shape, size, and location leads to the recognition that different visual input can have the same perceptual meaning. The development of object relationships to organize visual pictures occurs in several ways, which take longer to develop though offer more perceptual flexibility and adaptability. Distance and depth must be judged in absolute and relative terms, with accuracy in absolute judgments improving throughout childhood. Various visual cues are used in judging distance and depth. The basics of perception of movement develop quite early for detecting motion, tracking moving objects, and predicting the future location of moving objects. Older babies and young children seem to have adequate visual development when spatial and temporal requirements are limited, but they encounter difficulties when movements of objects and persons are rapid and occur in complex situations.

CHAPTER 11

Vision and Development of Movement Control

Kinesthesis and vision obviously function in some combination as part of an overall system to produce movement. The seemingly simple movement of reaching to touch a moving object requires visual information to locate the object and kinesthetic information to locate the limb, followed by the coordinated use of both to aid in bringing the limb to an interception point. We now shall consider the relationship of kinesthetic and visual development to development of movement control. We should examine the separate contributions of kinesthesis and vision to the development of movement control and then study their influence when functioning together. We shall limit our discussion, however, to visual development because very little information is available about the development of movement control in relation to kinesthetic development. But at several points we shall be able to include some aspects of kinesthetic development and movement development.

The framework for our analysis of vision and movement separates the solution of a movement problem into three steps, and we shall analyze five general movement tasks in order to discover possible developmental difficulties in these three steps. We then shall discuss one developmental change and one developmental issue which capture much of what seems important in understanding vision and development of movement control.

Three Steps in Solving a Movement Problem

The solution of a movement problem can be viewed as having the three steps shown in Figure 11-1. First, sensory-perceptual systems *specify* the movement situation, particularly to read or know the current status of the body and the environment. Second, sensory-perceptual information is used to *select* the movement to be made and to *generate* response specifications. Third, the neuromotor system functions to *execute* the movement. The complete operation involves processing information within and among the three steps, as suggested by the dotted line around them. The picture in Figure 11-1 is only a general representation and does not identify and model the functioning of the many perceptual and motor processes that have been proposed in the control of movement.

Step I is specifying, or reading, the body and the environment. The sensory-perceptual systems must determine a number of things about the body and the environment in preparation for movement. The position of the body and body parts must be known, because the movement preparation and execution may change, for example, if reaching for an object while standing rather than sitting and if facing the object rather than having the object to the right or the left. The tension state of the muscles and other body conditions and the location, size, and even composition of the object also must be known, if, for example, reaching to pick up a rose by its thorny stem. More complex and abstract information also may be useful, as when trying to anticipate the consequences of events and the

FIGURE
11-1

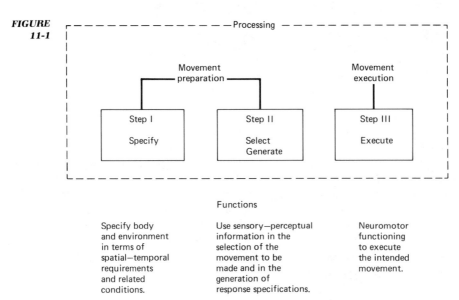

Three steps in the solution of a movement problem and the general functions of each.

intentions of others. Kinesthesis and vision provide the basic sensory input needed to control movement. We indicated earlier some of the important perceptual information provided by these two sensory-perceptual systems.

Step II is using the sensory-perceptual information to plan a movement. It is easy to describe in general terms but difficult to study and know in concrete terms. Select and generate are two important aspects in translating sensory-perceptual information into movement. Many things are involved in selecting a particular movement to be carried out in a particular way to solve a movement problem. The decision may be deliberate, although we usually are not consciously aware of our movement decision process, such as when seeing the size of an object and deciding to reach for it with both hands or when lying down and deciding to roll over rather than sit up to reach for the telephone. Nonetheless, a decision is made to solve a movement situation in a particular way, and that decision is a movement plan. Sensory-perceptual information specifies the body and the environment, and the knowledge of body-environment conditions helps formulate the movement plan, as does the store of information available from prior experiences and the different ways to interpret and use it.

The use of sensory-perceptual information becomes more obscure when considering how motor program specifications are generated to produce a movement appropriate for the prevailing body-environment conditions. Although we do not know how motor programs are put together, it is thought that we select a general motor program, such as reaching, that can be modified to meet the movement situation's perceived requirements. If the decision is to throw an object, the motor program specifications must be adjusted to the body-environment conditions specified by the sensory-perceptual information. For example, a thrower must use less force and perhaps a higher trajectory if throwing to a nearby partner. When the partner reaches for the moving ball, motor program specifications must be adjusted to match the direction of the reach to the anticipated interception point. One issue, which has not been resolved, is how the motor program specifications are adjusted to the body-environment conditions. Sensory-perceptual information must be available to identify the existing conditions, and the movements clearly are modified in relation to the mover's perception of them. But we do not know how movers use this sensory-perceptual information to generate and adjust motor program specifications.

Step III is executing the intended movement, by a coordinated sequence of muscular contractions controlled by the neuromotor control system. If an appropriate motor program has been selected, corrections can be made during and/ or after the movement to match more closely the situation conditions. Ongoing corrections made during the movement are part of Step III. Corrections made after the movement is completed really are part of Step I, in that body and environment conditions are specified in preparation for the next movement, whether this movement is immediately repeated or not attempted until a later time. Step III is limited to when the movement takes place, and its main concern is how well the neuromotor system can carry out a movement and ongoing movement corrections.

The three steps in solving a movement problem also can be viewed as two movement phases. The first phase is *movement preparation,* and the second phase is *movement execution.* Movement preparation is selecting a movement plan and generating response specifications which necessarily uses the body-environment conditions specified by the sensory-perceptual systems. The first phase combines Steps I and II to consider what happens before the movement is initiated. The second movement phase is Step III and is the actual execution of movement.

General Movement Tasks

We now shall consider what babies and children do on five different movement tasks in which the role of vision has been studied to some extent. Each task will be analyzed according to developmental changes as related to the three steps in solving a movement problem.

Reaching for Stationary Objects
The early development of reaching and grasping was described in Chapter 2, and we noted that reaching and grasping initially is a single movement before becoming two separate movements of reaching and grasping. Babies at 4 months begin to reach accurately and by their first birthday are both quick and accurate.

Early Development. One line of study has concentrated on the early development of visuomotor coordination in relation to the development of spatial knowledge. Lockman and Ashmead (1983), in a major review, found several asynchronies or differences in the ages at which different aspects of a type of behavior develop. Precise adjustments in arm-linkage control precede hand-finger control when measured in relation to object features, such as size, orientation, distance, and direction. Babies demonstrate a knowledge of the spatial properties of manual displacement sooner than they do a knowledge of locomotor displacements. They also establish spatial relationships between themselves and objects sooner than between objects and objects. These asynchronies all should be considered when studying other aspects of early reaching for objects.

Another line of study has concentrated on the role of vision in the early development of hand movements. Bower (1979) identifies two reaching phases that illustrate possible changes in the role of vision in changes in reaching and grasping. He describes Phase I reaching as a single movement with no differentiation between reaching and grasping. Vision seems to elicit a reaching-and-grasping movement and to control hand closure or grasping, but it does not seem to control hand transport during the reaching portion of a movement. Bower describes Phase II reaching as a differentiated movement in which reaching and grasping are independent movements, rather than the reach always ending in a grasp. The use of vision in Phase II changes, so that hand closure is tactually controlled and hand transport is visually controlled.

Bower reported that Phase I reaching was observed in the 4 weeks immediately after birth and then disappeared, to be observed again at 16 to 20 weeks (4 months). Phase I is reaching for objects, although babies have little success in contacting them. *This early reaching is a general orientation toward an object*, which was measured by McDonnell and Abraham (1978) by using signal detection theory. The signal was a change in the position of a target, and the distribution of arm movements over time in response to this target in an initial position was considered as the noise distribution. The distribution of arm movements in the new position constituted the signal plus noise distribution. The signal was either a red ball or the mother's face placed close enough to be reached. Videotape recordings measured whether the orientation of the hand movements actually changed in response to an alteration in the signal's position. The signal-noise analyses indicated that the limb movements were oriented to the visual targets and that there was substantial improvement from 3 to 8 weeks. The reaching of newborns (5 to 10 days) was reported by von Hofsten (1982), who believes that a rudimentary form of eye-hand coordination exists at birth, but with the primary function of attention rather than manipulation. Another finding of interest is that many of the components of later reaching were observed in young babies (9 to 23 days) but were uncoordinated (di Franco et al. 1978). The review by McDonnell (1979) is a comprehensive and critical look at the issues and complexities in studying the early development of visuomotor coordination.

Bower reported that Phase I reaching disappeared after 4 weeks and reappeared at 16 weeks, which contrasts with the maintenance and improvement observed by McDonnell and Abraham. Bower also noted that Phase I reaching could be maintained with a careful presentation of objects and believes that the lack of success in reaching during the early weeks leads to a decrease in reaching activity. Whatever the pattern of reaching activity in the early weeks may be, babies are able to reach and contact stationary objects at 4 months.

Bower reports Phase II reaching as beginning at about 20 weeks. Each reach then includes both contact and grasp, and so grasp now is differentiated from reach in two ways. First, the grasp is delayed when the hand reaches the object. Second, the grasp is elicited by tactual contact with the object rather than by visual control. Tactual control is demonstrated when older babies reach for a virtual object (one created by light projection) and do not grasp the phantom object when they cannot touch it. Babies in Phase I reaching will grasp at the virtual object, indicating that the sight of the object elicits the grasp. Bower points out that younger babies will grasp an object placed in their hand but that physical contact is not necessary.

Phase II reaching is visually guided, which explains why older babies reach more accurately than do younger babies, whose reaching does not seem to be corrected by visual feedback in the same way. This was demonstrated by Dunkeld and Bower (1978), who placed prism spectacles on babies to displace objects in their visual field. Both object and hand were displaced the same amount and were still seen in the same relationship. Babies in Phase II reaching maintained their reaching accuracy, whereas babies in Phase I reaching became less accurate. Babies in Phase II reaching presumably were visually monitoring both object and hand because they maintained their reaching accuracy. Babies in Phase I adjusted their hand to the object's displaced position, as if they used the kinesthetic (and real) information about their hand and did not have or ignored the visual information. In addition, corrections in Phase I reaching were made after the reach was completed rather than during the reaching movement.

Bower reversed the game to give an advantage to younger babies, by eliminating the use of visual control (Bower and Wishart 1972; Wishart et al. 1978). Babies were shown an object with the lights on and then with them turned out just before they initiated a reach. Younger babies (5 months) were more accurate when reaching in the dark than were older babies (7, 9, and 11 months), as if the younger babies did not need to use visual control of their reaching movement.

Lasky (1977) found that babies after 5 months needed visual evidence of their hand movements to maintain their reaching accuracy, whereas younger babies did not. He tested babies in two reaching conditions of directly viewing an object with their hand in sight and viewing a virtual object with their hand concealed by the mirror used to create it. As shown in Figures 11-2 and 11-3, babies at 5 and 6 months were quite successful in contacting and retrieving the object when it was in direct view, but they were no more successful than babies at 4 months were when reaching for the virtual object with their hand concealed. Lasky suggested that older babies expected their hand to be in their visual field and seemed confused when they could not see it. This could be a *disruption* in addition to a need to monitor hand control.

FIGURE 11-2

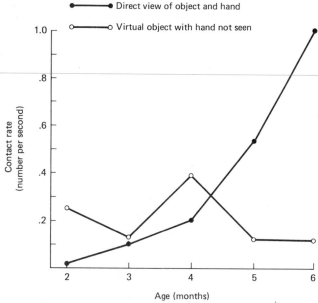

● ● Direct view of object and hand
○ ○ Virtual object with hand not seen

Age (months)

Contact rate (number per second)

Contact rate when reaching for an object during different visual conditions. (Drawn from data reported by Lasky, 1977.)

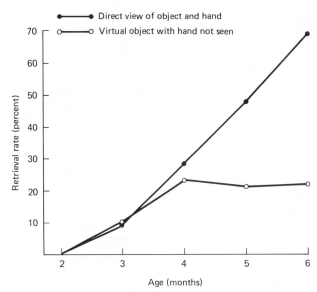

*FIGURE
11-3*

Retrieval rate when reaching for an object during different visual conditions. (Drawn from data reported by Lasky, 1977.)

The many analyses of Phase I and Phase II reaching indicate that babies change noticeably in the early months. They initially have no ongoing visual control of an undifferentiated "reach-and-grasp" which is not very accurate. Reaching becomes accurate at 4 months, with a more differentiated reach-then-grasp. Reaching beyond 4 months becomes progressively more visually controlled to include corrections during the reaching movements.

The overall success in reaching and contacting an object indicates that babies are able to accomplish some of each of the three steps in solving this general movement problem and by 6 months clearly use visual information about their moving hand during a reaching movement. Bower suggests that older babies merely process and use visual information that has always been present and believes that an increase in processing skills is needed to enable young babies to use vision in the control of hand movements.

Later Development. Two experiments by Hay (1979) chart the changes in the use of visual information during the reaching movements of children ages 5 to 11. The first experiment required reaching to point at a target when the children could not see their arm. Three types of reaching movements were observed.

Type A: Ballistic reaching with a very sudden braking near the end of the reaching movement; most of the distance covered at a fast and uniform rate of speed.
Type B: Early braking to reduce or even abolish the movement's initial ballistic phase.
Type C: Initial ballistic phase with a smooth, sometimes two-stage braking; points to feedback used later in the movement.

The percentage of each type of reaching movement is shown in Figure 11-4 as a function of age.

FIGURE
11-4

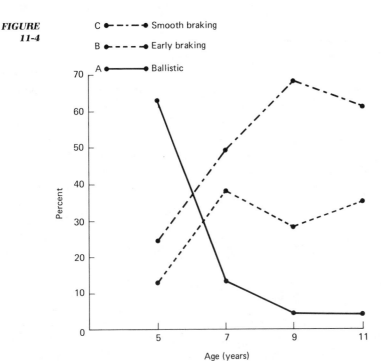

C ●— - —● Smooth braking

B ●- - - -● Early braking

A ●———● Ballistic

Percentage of three types of reaching movements as a function of age. (Reproduced with permission from Hay, 1979.)

Type A reaching movements predominated at age 5, thus indicating that the movements were direct, stable, and stereotyped. A marked change occurred at age 7, when Type B or Type C was characteristic of almost 90 percent of the reaching movements. Children now were braking their reaching movements earlier rather than waiting until near the end point. Type A reaching disappeared almost completely by age 9, when Type C reaching became predominant. Hay concluded that reaching movements at age 5 were ballistic and open loop because they did not use feedback control. Feedback started to be used at age 7 and at first was a hindrance. Children at age 9 were better able to move, locate their hand kinesthetically, and then coordinate the kinesthetic information with their visual information regarding the location of the target.

Hay's second experiment investigated the extent to which children, age 5 to 11, completed a reaching and pointing task with normal vision and when looking through prisms. When wearing prism spectacles, they initiated their movement to the right of the real position, and as their hand came into the visual field after the movement began, they could make adjustments. Children at age 5 made their corrections late, often when the movement had ended. Their lack of movement guidance confirmed that their reaching movements were performed ballistically. At age 7, they made their corrections earlier, and at ages 9 and 11, they used visual guidance to make a relatively smooth change later in the movement.

Hay proposes that at first children may not use visual information to help ongoing movement control and that when they do begin to use it, they may overuse it, which leads to a disruption in performance. A balanced or optimal use is achieved when corrections are made at fewer and more efficient times in the movement. This sequence of change suggests an improvement in Step III to use visual information to execute the movement more effectively.

There is another example of overusing visual information in a study by Mc-Cracken (1983), who filmed the eye movements of two groups of boys (ages 6 and 10) as they tapped rapidly back and forth between two circles. Try tapping back and forth while also looking back and forth at where you are tapping. The yoking of eye movements to hand movements will greatly limit your tapping rate. A more effective strategy is to look at one target or between the two targets and inter-mittently check your accuracy with a quick peek. Looking at each target as it is being tapped is an overuse of vision, at least for large targets that allow for con-siderable movement variation.

McCracken used three sizes of target circles (1, 2, and 3 inches in circumference; 5 inches between the circle centers). A different set of boys in each age group did twelve trials of 5 seconds each. An eye movement index (EMI) was calculated by dividing the number of eye movements in a trial by the number of taps. Thus, the EMI is 1.0 for eye movement on each tap and 0.5 for eye movement on every other tap. As shown in Figure 11-5, the older boys improved their mean EMI scores on each circle size, in contrast with the younger boys who did not change significantly during the twelve trials. Notice that the younger boys moved their eyes on nearly every tap of the small circle, whereas the older boys quickly adjusted to the small circles and did not look more often than the younger boys did at the large circles.

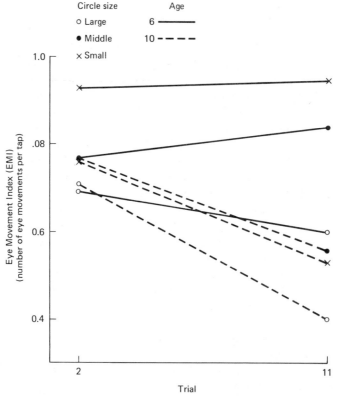

FIGURE 11-5

Mean EMI scores for early and late trials on a continuous tapping task. (Drawn from data reported by McCracken, 1983.)

In summary, an interesting general progression in the use of vision appears to be characteristic of both babies and young children. Vision initially is not used for the ongoing control of hand movements. Later it does help control the movement, but perhaps in a disruptive manner. A balance is achieved even later when children can flexibly choose when to use vision, which may be a progression in many aspects of movement development. When presented with a novel situation, children may make a movement without using all of their sensory-perceptual resources. They then monitor their movements too often but finally are able to use their sensory-perceptual resources more selectively and effectively. In regard to the three steps in solving a movement problem, children seem able to specify (Step I) the environment(s) and select (Step II) the general response, but they seem to have problems in generating (Step II) appropriate response specifications and correcting (Step III) movement errors.

Interception of Moving Objects

The use of visual information to intercept a moving object requires reaching plus coinciding or timing body movements with target movements. Von Hofsten's movement analyses (von Hofsten 1979, 1980; von Hofsten and Lindhagen 1979) were reviewed in Chapter 4 to demonstrate that babies clearly have this system in place to intercept moving objects. These analyses indicate that the major improvement from 4 to 8 months is related to better control of the limb movement. Using a similar setup with more detailed analyses of limb movements in relation to target movements, von Hofsten (1983) argues that babies move their arm with the target while moving toward the target path. That is, instead of reaching to a fixed interception point, as proposed in most analyses of how interception occurs, von Hofsten suggests that the limb movement will be directed to a meeting point with the object if the tracking system correctly matches the object's physical velocity. This means that the reach is made in reference to a coordinate system fixed to the moving object and not to the static background. However the theoretical views may differ, babies seem capable enough in Steps I and II, but they need to improve in Step III.

Although babies can intercept a slow-moving object, young children have great difficulty in coping with rapid, simultaneous events in a moving environment. As noted in Chapter 4, younger children are much less accurate than older children are when moving to where a ball may be caught, ice-skating while stick handling a puck, and intercepting or continuously matching a moving light path. We also know that younger children have more difficulty in "reading" road traffic and in knowing when it is safe to cross a street (Hoffman et al. 1980). The problem seems to be that more information must be processed, and this must be done in less time and on time.

Interception difficulties also may be related to inadequacies in movement adjustments or corrections (Step III). Shea and his colleagues (1982) found that all children and adults initiated the interception movement of arm and hand similarly, by moving fast, but younger children did not make a correction as soon as older children and adults did. Adults also seemed to make smoother corrections similar to the older children observed by Hay (1979).

A study by Alderson (1974) provides a look at adequacy of movement control during the interception (catching) of an object. Alderson filmed fifteen boys (ages 7, 10, and 13) making a one-handed catch of a ball projected by a ball-throwing machine. As shown in Table 11-1, catching success increased from 7 percent at

TABLE
11-1

Percentages of Several Measures of Catching Success*

AGE	CAUGHT	CONTACTED	CONTACTED ON TARGET†
7	7	77	61
10	45	97	79
13	83	100	73

* Based on data from Alderson 1974.
† On target means 1 inch above or below the optimum contact area on the inside of the metacarpo-phalangeal joint.

age 7 to 83 percent at age 13. Alderson further analyzed catching attempts and noted that even the youngest boys were able to get their hand in place to catch, with 77 percent success in contacting the ball with the hand. The youngest boys often (61 percent) were on target, that is, were contacting the ball within 1 inch of the optimum contact area. An analysis of flexion of hand movements indicated that each age group had the same flexion time but that the 7-year-old boys started their flexion 10 to 15 milliseconds later than the older boys did. Although the younger boys could get their catching hand in place, they could not begin flexion to coincide or be "on time" with the movement of the ball. The problem for younger boys in catching seems to be in adjusting their motor responses to the environmental conditions and not in reading the environmental conditions.

Another possibility is that *younger children may need more visual information,* even though they may not use the information very effectively. This follows from Hay's suggestion (1979) that children may at first overuse visual information and later may use this information more selectively and at better times. Another of Hay's observations is that visual information may be used too soon, as if it were used when available rather than at a later and more appropriate time in the movement. Hay observed this in Type B reaching, when corrections were made early to interrupt rather abruptly the initial movement rate, rather than waiting to interject a smoother change later during the reaching movement. It is as if younger children cannot wait to use their visual information. Part of this may be because they know that they do not have much time, and so they do it as soon as they know something needs to be done. This temporal pressure may produce an immediate and often a hasty response.

Some limited evidence to support these speculations is provided in several studies in which the path of the moving target was partially occluded. Williams (1973) allowed children to see only the initial portion of the ball's flight and asked them to move to the place where the ball would land. The younger children responded quickly and overran the landing spot by more than 20 feet. The children in the middle years of her sample were quite accurate but slow and seemed to be checking their "calculations." These children clearly could not have arrived at the landing spot in time with the ball. The older children were accurate and unhurried, and Williams judged them to be in time with the ball's projected arrival. The younger children seemed to use their information too soon and in haste to establish direction, but not to determine location. These younger children may also need more viewing time to gather more information, whereas the older children can gather the necessary information more quickly or can get by with less.

Limiting visual information sometimes leads to a relatively larger decrement in younger children's performance, when compared with their performance with complete visual information. Dorfman (1977) reported a relatively greater increase in absolute error (AE) for younger children trying to intercept a dot moving in a straight line when the dot disappeared after a brief view of its speed and direction (see Box 4-3). Wade (1980) also found that younger children had a relatively greater loss if part of the target pathway was concealed when pushing a steel doughnut to intercept the moving target (see Box 4-3). As shown in Figure 11-6, the mean AE scores for the older children (ages 12 to 14) changed from 4 centimeters when viewing the entire target pathway to 9 centimeters when viewing two-thirds of the target pathway. Comparable changes in mean AE scores were from 5 to 12 centimeters for the middle-age children (ages 9 to 11) and from 6 to 20 centimeters for the younger children (ages 7 to 9). The younger children were also quite variable across trials and were considerably ahead of the target, thus indicating that they had moved too soon. The younger children seem more to need visual information in that they have a relatively larger decrement in performance when this type of information is limited, and they seem to be quicker in using the available information. It as if they are committed to use visual information but do not know when to use it. Another consideration, noted earlier, is that experimental manipulations of vision may be disruptive. Older children and adults, however, seem able to handle such disruptions and to function effectively with less visual information.

Wade (1980) suggested that some target speeds may better match people's visual capabilities. This possibility was discussed in Chapter 4, in which Shea and his associates (1982) found an optimal range for young children. If an optimal range does exist, it should be narrower for babies and young children, with the possibility that the range and the focal or mean speed could change. This type of devel-

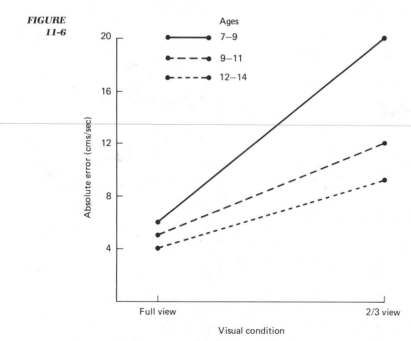

FIGURE 11-6

Mean absolute error with full and limited vision to intercept object traveling at 91.4 cms/sec. (Estimated from graphs in Wade, 1980.)

opmental change would indicate a change in Steps I and II, in which the basics for interception would be modified to be better suited to a particular range of motion speeds in the environment.

Force Control

Vision also helps determine the amount of force that a movement requires. This is apparent when considering that it is force in appropriate amounts that determines important aspects of spatial and temporal accuracy. If a movement is made in the correct direction, the amount of force then must be correct in order to reach a specific location, whether to grasp a stationary object or intercept a moving object. However, it is not easy to study the role of vision in force control because force is so intertwined in all aspects of movement control. Two examples that suggest the role of vision in force control are anticipating an object's weight in order to set the correct amount of muscle tension and determining the amount of force required to propel an object an appropriate distance.

In a series of ingenious, videotaped studies, Bower (1982) described babies' development in anticipating an object's weight before touching it. When presented with a heavy object when 6 or 7 months old, the baby's arm dropped and then compensated by adjusting muscle tension to bring the arm back to its starting position. This indicated that the baby did not anticipate the object's weight. Babies at 12 months anticipated the object's weight by the second presentation and at 18 months anticipated the weight of objects they had not grasped. In effect, older babies were able to look at the size of an object and predict its weight. Bower then tricked the older babies by giving them large objects made of a lightweight material. Older babies overestimated the weight by applying too much muscle tension, so that their arms flew up in the air. When they grasped a small, heavy object, their arms dropped as if they were not applying enough muscle tension. Bower (1982) points to the older babies' errors as evidence "that accommodation is now anticipatory for all objects that can be serially ordered in some visible dimension which covaries with weight" (p. 176). It is clear that older babies are able to predict an object's weight purely from visual information and that they use this information in producing movement force.

Using vision to determine the force needed to propel an object was examined in two sets of studies, by having children push a toy car down a trackway to a designated target. The studies are described in Box 11-1. The trackway fixed the direction of the toy car so that children had only to determine the force needed to propel it to the target. The trackway was covered in some of the test conditions to determine whether other information in the form of verbal knowledge of results (KR) and kinesthetic memory of previous trials could be used effectively when visual information was limited.

A general finding was that children needed more visual information than did young adults, as shown in Figures 11-7 and 11-9. The lower line in both figures is a base-line performance level when pushing the toy car with a full view of the trackway. When looking at the upper line when the trackway was covered, the young adults maintained their same general level of performance, in contrast with the children, who were much less accurate, even when given KR in some form at the end of each trial. Notice the similarity in the two sets of curves, except that the younger children in the Whiting and Cockerill (1972) study had a relatively greater loss. The younger children in the UCLA studies were approaching a maximal error ceiling when the trackway was covered, and so their potential for error

306

was not adequately measured. If the trackway were longer, it is likely that they would have had even greater difficulty on the UCLA apparatus when their vision was limited, as it would increase the possible error range.

Several sources of information might be useful in producing an appropriate amount of force to push a toy car close to a target. Distance can be specified by visual observation of the target or a related reference point, and information about previous efforts can be used to adjust subsequent efforts. The children in the UCLA studies apparently could not use the visual cues provided on the tunnel and could not use the verbal KR from a previous trial. The adults performed the same in all of the conditions, which argues that they were able to use any of the available sources of information, whereas the children needed direct visual information. The trackway cover on the UCLA test apparatus was modified in Study III (Carter 1980) to have a roof that could be tilted to provide end-point vision of where the toy car stopped (see Figure 11-8). The children in this limited vision condition performed as well as the children who pushed the toy car without a trackway cover. This is in contrast with the children with end-point vision in the Whiting and Cockerill study, who had larger error scores than did the children with a full view of the trackway. But they did not have the visual cues provided by matching the tunnel colors to the trackway colors. The general conclusion is that children apparently need more information than adults do to produce what is for them an appropriate amount of force, and they particularly seem to need direct visual information.

An interesting finding in UCLA Study III was that children and adults performed similarly when transferred to a condition eliminating all information except kinesthetic feeling and memory. Children and adults practiced with the trackway either uncovered or covered and with end-point vision provided and then transferred to a condition of minimal information in which the trackway was covered and no KR was provided. The results for the last twelve practice trials and the first twelve transfer trials are shown in Figure 11-10. Both the children and the adults practicing with the uncovered trackway significantly increased their mean errors when transferring to the minimal information condition, whereas the children and adults practicing with a covered trackway and verbal KR maintained their mean level of performance. The pattern of results for the adults is consistent with the findings for adults on a lever-positioning task (Adams et al. 1977).

The children's maintenance of performance with minimal information is impressive, because the children in UCLA Study I were not able to maintain their performance level on the covered trackway, even though they were given verbal KR at the end of each trial. A possible explanation for the maintenance of performance level with minimal information is that the children's attention was directed to pertinent task requirements needed in the transfer condition. The children and adults practicing with the covered trackway were asked in each of the UCLA studies to estimate where the car stopped before they were given endpoint vision or verbal KR. The performance estimate may have directed their attention to their kinesthetic information, which was the primary information available and needed during the no-KR condition. A similar finding was reported by Hogan and Yanowitz (1978). Children who were asked to estimate their performance on each trial were better able to maintain their level of performance than were children who did not make an estimate. But the children using a covered trackway in Study II could not achieve an appropriate level of performance, even though they were asked to estimate their performance and then were given

BOX
11-1

FORCE CONTROL IN DIFFERENT VISUAL CONDITIONS

Two sets of studies are described with the earlier set of two studies done by Whiting and Cockerill (1972, 1974) and the later set of three studies done at UCLA under the direction of Keogh. The task in each of the five studies was to push a toy car on a trackway to a designated target. The car's movement direction was fixed by the trackway, and the pushing movement was ballistic. There was little that could be done to alter the pushing movement because the alignment of the body to the apparatus was standardized in each study. Thus, each participant in each trial used a similar ballistic arm movement, and the amount of force to be exerted was the primary judgment to be made in producing the pushing movement. Visual input was an obvious source of information in deciding the amount of force to use. The children and adults also were given verbal knowledge of results (KR) or end-point vision of where the car stopped on some trials when their vision was limited. And they always had their own kinesthetic memory of current and previous efforts.

These studies illustrate ways to examine the importance of different sources of information in producing an appropriate amount of force. It also is possible to study this type of force production by having subjects push against a rigid object engineered to register the force imparted to the object. But younger children may not understand this more abstract sense of force production in which nothing moves or a moving dial on a gauge is not perceived as related to pushing a stationary object. Pushing a toy car on a trackway offers a more realistic sense of force and effect. Perhaps even more important, most children like the task and are eager to continue, even after many trials.

WHITING AND COCKERILL STUDIES

The task in the first study (1972) was to push a Fletcher Trolley (board with wheels) forward and up an inclined plane for a designated distance. A tunnel covered the trolley and the pushing hand, but the trolley could be seen as it came out of the short

FIGURE
11-7

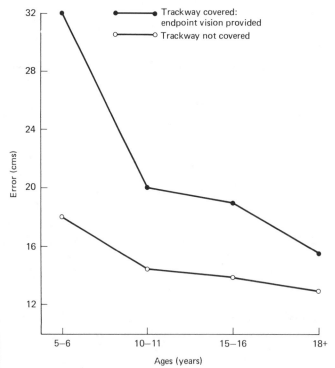

Mean absolute error scores by age in two visual conditions when pushing a toy car to a target. (Reproduced with permission from Whiting and Cockerill, 1972.)

tunnel and went up the inclined plane. In a second test condition, a black screen was placed between the subject and the pointer marking the target. The subjects saw the target pointer before the black screen was lowered, they pushed the trolley with the screen in place, and they then were shown where the trolley stopped.

The subjects were twenty males in four age groups: 5 to 6, 10 to 11, 15 to 16, and 18 plus (total N = 80). Ten males in each group pushed the trolley with the inclined plane in sight, and ten in each group saw the target and trolley only before and after it was pushed. Each subject did 5 trials or pushing attempts at five different target distances presented randomly (total trials = 25). The performance was measured as centimeters of error between the front end of the trolley and the target distance. The mean error scores for each age group are plotted by test condition in Figure 11-7.

A second study was made to determine whether the subjects were more accurate in pushing the trolley when looking at the target or their hand. The subjects were twenty males in three age groups: 6 to 7, 10 to 11, and 19 plus (total N = 60). The apparatus was modified to remove the tunnel and have the subjects stand at the side of the inclined plane to push the trolley from right to left. They wore elastic headbands with a cardboard blinker. They were instructed to place the blinker on the right side of their face and watch the target or place the blinker on the left side and watch their hand. The two target distances were 200 centimeters (long) and 100 centimeters (short). Each subject underwent forty trials of a random presentation of visual and distance conditions. Each group was more accurate in the long distance when watching the target, but there were no significant differences for visual condition and age in the short distance.

UCLA STUDIES

A similar apparatus was used in the three studies at UCLA, whose purpose was to determine the visual input that children needed to estimate force production. Some results from these studies have been summarized by Keogh (1981). The children's vision was limited in some trials by using a tunnel to cover the trackway. The tunnel and trackway were marked in matching color bands, as shown in Figure 11-8, to help the subjects visualize the trackway rather than conceal it by a screen or a blinker. With the tunnel in place, the children and adults could not see the target, but they could see the color bands on the tunnel as distance cues. Verbal KR or end-point vision were provided in some test conditions when the tunnel was in place, to determine whether force production could be adequately produced by using other sources of information.

Children and adults pushed a "hot wheels" car down a trackway to a designated target, which always was the middle color band at approximately 100 centimeters. The toy car was pushed from right to left while facing the trackway. A pushing block was used in Studies I and II in which the right thumb was placed on top of a wooden house and the fingers of the right hand were used to push a block that propelled the toy car. This pushing procedure was replaced in Study III to have children and adults grasp the toy car and push it down the trackway. A tunnel was placed over the trackway during some trials in Studies I and II to prevent the children and adults from seeing where the car stopped and to conceal movement of the car down the trackway. The

FIGURE 11-8

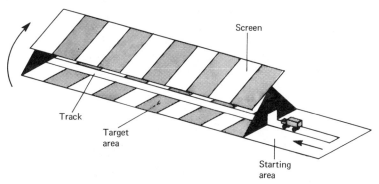

Trackway and cover used in UCLA Study III (Carter, 1980).

tunnel was modified in Study III, as shown in Figure 11-8, to be a sloping roof that could be tilted when necessary to provide end-point vision of where the car stopped.

Study I (Keogh, 1978)
The base-line data for performance on this task were gathered for an approximately equal number of boys and girls at ages 6, 8, and 10 (total N = 123). Each child had twenty-four trials with the trackway uncovered on the first day and then returned another day for twelve trials with the trackway uncovered, followed by twenty-four trials with the tunnel in place. KR was provided at the end of each trial on the second day by pointing to the color band on the tunnel where the car stopped and stating the color. Children wore earphones in which white noise was played to mask the noise of the car moving down the trackway. Each age group improved its mean performance across the twenty-four trials on the first day and quickly achieved the final peformance level of the first day during the first set of trials on the second day. The transfer condition of limited vision with verbal KR tested their ability to *maintain performance* without direct visual information. Children at all ages increased their mean error score on the transfer condition and thus were not able to maintain the performance level they had established during the practice trials.

Study II (Burton 1979)
The transfer condition of Study I was used as an initial practice condition to determine whether an adequate level of performance could be achieved with only verbal KR provided. The subjects were ten males and ten females in four age groups (7, 9, 11, and 19 to 26). Each individual was tested on one day and in the same test order of twenty-four trials with the tunnel in place and verbal KR provided, followed by twelve trials with the tunnel in place and no KR. The children's performance on the opening set of twenty-four trials was very poor (see Figure 11-9). Comparisons with the last set of twelve no-KR trials were not meaningful because the children were not able to *establish* an adequate level of performance when the KR was provided.

FIGURE 11-9

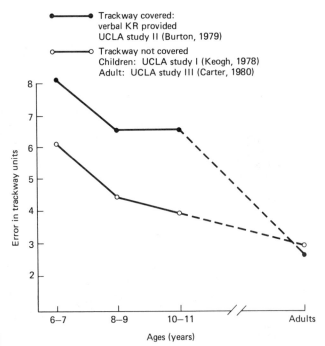

Mean absolute error scores by age in two visual conditions when pushing a toy car to a target. (Practice trials 1–24, UCLA Studies. See Box 11-1.)

Study III (Carter 1980)

The apparatus was modified in several ways to help the children perform more satisfactorily on the task. A hinged roof on the tunnel made it possible to show them where the car stopped. This provided end-point visual information while continuing to conceal the car moving down the trackway. The pushing block was removed to allow the subjects to push the car, which perhaps better indicated the force exerted and better simulated the normal pushing of a toy car. No earphones were used, and the trackway was padded underneath to reduce the sound of the toy car moving down it. Twenty males were tested in four age groups (6, 8, 10, and 20 to 24). Only males were included to have more homogeneous test data, as the females' test performances tended to be poorer and more variable in Studies I and II. One-half of the subjects in each group had forty-eight trials with the trackway uncovered. The other subjects underwent forty-eight trials with the tunnel in place. The roof was tilted back at the end of each trial to show where the toy car had stopped. Both groups then had twelve transfer trials with the tunnel in place; verbal KR and end-point vision were not provided. The general results are shown in Figure 11-10 and are discussed in the text.

FIGURE
11-10

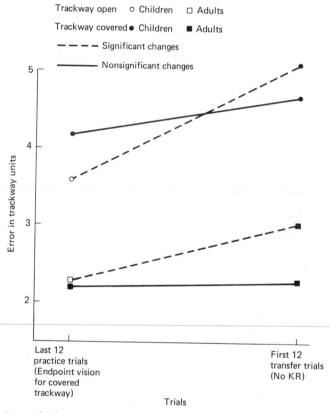

Mean absolute error scores for children and adults in relation to visual conditions and KR in UCLA Study III (Carter, 1980).

verbal KR. Therefore we must consider whether an individual is in a state of establishing control of a movement (practice trials) or has some mastery of it that must be maintained when the information conditions change (transfer trials).

When considered in relation to the three steps proposed for solving a movement problem, children needed more visual information than adults did in Step II to generate force specifications of a pushing movement. Children were less able to use related visual information, such as the color bands on the trackway cover, and adults apparently used other information when their visual information was limited. Another difficulty in Step II is that the availability of visual information may limit the use of other information. This attentional overpowering by vision appears to be a difficulty for adults as well and will be discussed further in the concluding section. Determining how much of which visual information is needed when seems endless, but it is sufficient to note that children generally need more visual information than adults do. Our problem now is to understand when and how children progress to needing less visual information.

Postural Control

The control of posture has been studied in some interesting ways that suggest an interplay of vision and kinesthesis in controlling movement. Proposals by Lee (1978) provide a general background for reviewing these studies. He suggests that three types of information are necessary for planning and controlling movement. First, *exteroception* is information that indicates external objects and events in the environment. It details the layout of the external environment so that an act can be planned accordingly. Vision is the main system in performing this function. Second, *proprioception* is information that specifies the positions and movements of the body parts in relation to the body. This information, which often is called kinesthesis, is used in the control of movements. Third is *exproprioception*, a new term, which means obtaining information about body movement, position, and orientation relative to the environment. Exproprioception is used both in planning and controlling movement. Lee's proposal is different in that he introduces exproprioception to recognize the need for information about environment and body in relation to each other, whereas exteroception and proprioception separate the environment and body. Lee summarizes the functions of these three types of information as planning for exteroception, control for proprioception, and planning and control for exproprioception.

Lee argues that not only is vision the most powerful exteroceptive sense but it also functions as a proprioceptive and an exproprioceptive sense. Vision specifies the environment and then acts as an overseer in the control of movement by helping formulate patterns of action and tuning or preparing other perceptual systems. Vision acts as a *proprioceptive check* by intermittently monitoring to correct for drift in other sensory systems. Lee uses the example of playing a musical instrument, such as a violin, which becomes an extension of the body. In the early stages of learning, players use vision both exteroceptively to watch the teacher and proprioceptively to monitor their hand and finger movements. An accomplished player's movement control is taken over by mechanical proprioceptors (joints, muscles), which frees vision for reading music and planning the activity. Without vision, however, mechanical proprioceptive control tends to drift and is monitored intermittently by vision. Lee also presents anecdotes to illustrate the pervasive involvement of vision with other sensory systems. An everyday skill like running over uneven ground is no problem during the day, but in the dark with limited vision it becomes a movement that jars the whole body. Vision in this case prepares the traditional proprioceptors to accept an irregular surface, as noted also by Turvey (1977).

The exproprioceptive functioning of vision is more difficult to conceptualize. The idea is that visual information plays a major role in planning and controlling movements that require an adjustment to the environment. Control of posture requires this type of adjustment and is the main way of examining this line of thinking.

Lee and Aronson (1974) tested toddlers (babies who had just started to walk) in a room that could be moved forward and back in a rhythmical and irregular pattern. When moving the room forward and back, they found that toddlers compensated by swaying with the room and they often fell over. The swaying of the room apparently caused the toddlers to think that they were swaying. Lee and Lishman (1975) extended this study by examining the relative effectiveness of vision and kinesthesis in controlling balance in different types of stance. They used three different stances and found that vision was not only essential to each stance but that it also furnished more sensitive information than kinesthesis did, even in normal standing.

Lee and Aronson (1974) argue that the movement of the room produces an optic flow pattern at the retina which provides information about the movement of the body relative to the environment. They further state that vision's exproprioceptive functioning prevails over vestibular and mechanical proprioception in babies who have recently learned to walk. Butterworth and Hicks (1977) ask whether this is because standing is so unstable for toddlers that their vestibular and mechanical proprioception are not powerful enough to maintain control, so that visual control develops with standing, or whether postural control that occurs earlier than walking also depends on vision. In other words, does visual-exproprioceptive control come about with the unstable two-footed stance, or is it present earlier? Two experiments were performed using an apparatus similar to Lee's and Aronson's moving room (1974). In the first experiment, standing stability was compared under two conditions of discrepant visual information in a group of babies who had recently learned to walk. The results replicated Lee's and Aronson's, and the forward and backward movement of the visual field produced a greater loss of postural control than did its lateral movement.

In the second experiment, postural stability in a seated position was tested in an older group of babies (mean age = 15.8 months) who could stand unsupported and a younger group (mean age = 10.9 months) who could sit but could not stand unsupported. For both groups of babies, discrepant visual information produced a loss in stability of seated posture, but the amount of sway was less for the seated posture than for the standing posture. Butterworth and Hicks regard these results as evidence that vision does not acquire its exproprioceptive function as a result of learning to stand. They also reject Lee's and Aronson's suggestion that postural control is the preference of one type of feedback over another. Rather, they suggest that postural control depends on a congruence among different indices of postural stability. Because sitting seems to be a more stable posture than standing is, the lesser effect of the moving visual field may indicate for a seated baby that a discrepancy between kinesthetic and visual information is less critical in maintaining postural stability.

A related question is whether focusing on a stationary object also provides visual-exproprioceptive information for children, because Lee and Lishman (1975) reported that adults decreased their postural sway by focusing on a nearby object. Children, ages 7 and 11, were tested by Zernicke, Gregor, and Cratty (1981) on five different standing positions, with and without looking at a fixed visual target. Lateral and anterior-posterior deviations were recorded on a force platform. Looking at the fixed visual target had little effect on anterior-posterior postural stability but did have a significant effect on lateral postural stability. Both groups of children improved in lateral steadiness during two-foot stances while looking at the target, but only the older chidren improved their performance on the more difficult one-foot stand. Even though Lee and Aronson (1974) found that anterior-posterior stability in 18- to 16-month-old children can be influenced by movement in the visual field, it seems that looking at a fixed visual target is not as useful for controlling anterior-posterior stability as for controlling lateral postural stability. Developmental differences became apparent during the one-foot stance when older children could effectively use the visual target.

The cumulative findings from these studies support the case for a substantial role for visual information in postural control, and Zernicke's and colleagues' 1981 study demonstrates that children's ability to use this information differs with age. Visual involvement in controlling posture is present before an infant walks, changes qualitatively during childhood, and is a pervasive influence through adulthood. It is impressive how well and how early vision and kinesthesis participate in controlling more stationary postural positions. We now need to learn about their functioning and development in controlling less stationary and more rapidly changing positions, particularly in maintaining motion stability.

Representation in Movement

We noted in Chapter 3 that young children have difficulty in representing in movement what they see or imagine. An example is the perceptual discrimination of shapes long before the same shapes can be copied. The larger issue is how action is organized and produced to represent thought. Forman (1982) notes that this issue can be approached from different and often nonrelated perspectives, particularly if the focus is on action *or* thought, rather than action *and* thought. The concern in this chapter is that representation in movement appears to be a Step II problem in solving a movement problem. If we can demonstrate that children can read the environment and produce the necessary parts of a movement, then the difficulty must be in selecting the appropriate movement and perhaps in generating appropriate specifications for the motor program. Because the research in this particular area is quite limited, we can do little more than present some descriptions of change and some explanatory speculations.

Connolly (1968) tested children (ages 4, 5, and 6) to describe changes in visual perception, movement control, and copying skill. The children were asked to match shapes to a test figure, draw lines in the orientation required in test figures, draw the test figures, and construct the test figures with matchsticks. All of the children were able to recognize (match) the test figures and draw lines in vertical, horizontal, and oblique planes. No failure in copying figures could be attributed to their inability to recognize the figures or to inadequate control of the required movements. The children's construction skill was approximately 1 year ahead of their drawing skill. Connolly concluded that the construction-drawing difference was related to differences in task requirements. The construction task provided a greater opportunity to use visual information continuously, because the children could repeatedly refer visually to the test figure and then adjust the matchsticks. In the drawing task, children could not easily alter their drawing after it was started. But construction with matchsticks allowed children to copy the figure one part at a time, whereas drawing required starting with a complete movement plan that could be checked during movement but could not be easily changed.

Writing letters and words is an even more complicated movement problem,

314

because both *form* and *orientation* must be reproduced, and often in a continuous sequence of movements. Lurcat and Kostin (1970) tried to isolate form and orientation in letter writing, by having children (ages 4 to 10) reproduce the cycloids and spirals shown in Figure 11-11. More than 90 percent of the first-grade children were able to reproduce both the cycloids and the spirals. There was great improvement from kindergarten (50 percent success) to first grade, which probably was related to the first-grade children's having received handwriting training. Correct orientation was not exhibited by a high percentage (75 percent) of children until the second and third grade for the cycloids and even later for the spirals. Thus, the younger children could produce the form, but not the orientation to these shapes. Lurcat and Kostin looked also at reproduction using different combinations of visual and kinesthetic (hand-tracing) information. The relative importance of visual and kinesthetic cues was related to the type of figure being reproduced. Copying the cycloid depended more on kinesthetic cues, and copying the spiral depended more on visual aids.

The many descriptions and comparisons of children copying figures clearly indicate that younger children have great difficulty in this type of representation in movement. Maccoby and Bee (1965) suggested a "number of attributes" hypothesis in arguing that one must use many more attributes of a figure when organizing the parts of a figure into a whole for copying than for recognition or discrimination. This is similar to Connolly's argument that drawing must be done as a totality, in contrast with construction being done one part at a time. The difficulty, from our perspective, is somewhere in the translation of perception to movement, which is stated by others as thought to action. We cannot offer much

FIGURE 11-11

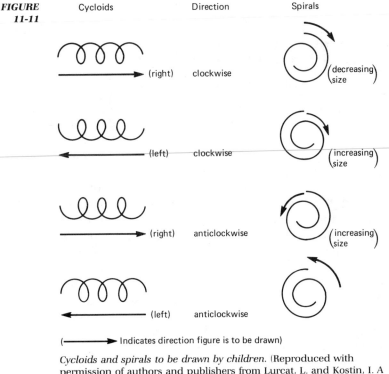

(⟶ Indicates direction figure is to be drawn)

Cycloids and spirals to be drawn by children. (Reproduced with permission of authors and publishers from Lurcat, L. and Kostin, I. A study of graphical abilities in children. PERCEPTUAL AND MOTOR SKILLS, 1970, 30, 615–630.)

more at this point except to note that this aspect of movement control develops rather late, in comparison with the many achievements occurring in the first and second year of life after birth, and is important to functioning in more highly developed societies.

A Developmental Change and a Developmental Issue

Babies quite soon can reach and accurately contact both stationary and slow-moving objects, which indicates that they have a basic competence in the three steps we have been using to analyze the solution of these movement problems. Young babies seem to be more limited in Step III, in that they do not control their movements precisely. But young children also have considerable difficulty in coping with rapid, simultaneous events in a moving environment and in selecting a movement plan and generating movement specifications for more stable movement situations. Reading or specifying the body and the environment seem not to be important limitations for young children, whose principal problems appear to be in Steps II and III.

Two major points are proposed to help us think further about these general findings. First, there appears to be a developmental change in the *role of vision*, along the lines suggested by Hay (1979). This pattern of developmental change helps organize a confusing and somewhat contradictory array of descriptive findings. Second, there is an unresolved developmental issue in the *use of visual perceptual information* in Steps II and III.

Role of Vision

Visual information seems to be needed more by children at certain periods in the development of movement control, but it seems to be *related more to situation than to age*. Young babies apparently do not initially "see" their hands when reaching, but they soon become visually aware of them to the extent that they expect to see them (Bower 1979, Lasky 1977). Corrections of hand movement with visual input are not effective until several months later. Hay (1979) reported a similar sequence of change for children ages 5 to 11. The general pattern is to ignore visual information or to use it to correct after the movement, followed by an ineffective overuse that eventually becomes more selective and appropriate. We propose that this is a general change in the role of vision, which is related more to movement situation than to age. That is, the role of vision must be adjusted to the movement situation conditions and occurs in a *general progression from minimal use to overuse to selective use*. If the movement situation is simple enough in relation to the mover's resources, the progression will not be noticeable. But if the movement situation is new or sufficiently different and demanding (that is, taxes the mover's resources), we can expect this progression of change in the role of vision in the development of movement control.

There seems to be a period in the development of movement control in different types of movement situations when visual information is needed and seemingly overused. Adults and older children can use other sensory-perceptual information to make a movement or can use less visual information. But younger children without vision cannot generate an appropriate force to propel an object and need almost continuous vision to perform alternate tapping movements between two circles. Visual information in this period also is used too rapidly and too much in correcting movements, as if the mover cannot delay using the information to make corrections at a later point in the movement. The more selective and flexible use of vision is observed in a variety of ways, which are really just the reverse of what happens when vision is needed and overused. Less visual information is needed, and visual monitoring is intermittent rather than continuous.

We should not, however, think of the role of vision as changing in an age-related progression. Rather, we should think of a similar type of developmental change occurring within different movement situations. Younger children seem to need more visual information and overuse it more, and they may take longer to use it flexibly and selectively, but this progression of change also characterizes the change in the role of vision within a movement situation. The need for vision and overuse of vision is determined in each situation, with a lesser effect across ages.

Use of Visual Information

The three steps in solving a movement problem will be reviewed in order to find major limitations in the development of movement control in relation to that of vision. Step I, specifying the body and environment, does not seem to be a limitation except when needing to read too much in too little time. There also may be some difficulties in perceptually specifying larger spaces and rapid changes of self and objects within a space, such as when running to catch a fly ball and riding a bicycle on a street with moving cars and pedestrians. Although we have few data to isolate what might be called dynamic visual perception, the problem seems to be too much to read in too little time. By the second or third year, visual development seems adequate to cope with a small number of simple, self-paced events. But there are very real limitations when more things happen faster. This may be more of a problem of improving processing efficiency than not being able to specify body-environment conditions. The additional information load and time constraints may also be disruptive, in pressuring the overall processing system, which may then be hasty and inefficient.

Step II is the two interrelated functions of selecting a movement plan and generating motor program specifications. Selecting a movement plan is not a major limitation in that babies' and young children's movements are purposeful and generally appropriate. That is, they seem to be doing what they want to do, even if they do not always do it gracefully and skillfully. An exception is when copying figures that we described as representing a visual image or an imagined image as movement. Young children have considerable difficulty in selecting an appropriate movement plan for copying figures, and they often recognize that their product is not adequate. There seems to be a similar problem in deciding what to do when in regard to game objectives and rules. For example, in a game of dodge ball, the child with the ball can throw it at a player on the other side or can throw it to a partner who is in a better position to throw it at an opponent. Movement selection becomes a problem when the movement is part of a larger situation and involves strategy options. Movement selection often is a direct decision, in that the movement is the major outcome, as when dancing, or produces the major outcome, as when throwing a ball to a partner. When movement becomes the tool or means to accomplish a larger and less direct outcome, many other factors enter into the selection process. It is sufficient for our purposes to state that selecting a new movement plan is not a major limitation unless there are strategy options that can be selected to produce an outcome in different ways.

The generation of motor-program specifications appears to be a problem in producing a skilled outcome, which was noted when younger children had difficulty in pushing a toy car without full visual input. They seemed unable to use other information in the form of verbal KR and kinesthetic knowledge to generate the force specifications of the pushing movement. The problem for younger children and less experienced performers was described earlier in regard to the need for visual information. Older children and more experienced performers are capable of using other information sources, apparently including memory of previous movements and verbal information from others. The direct use of visual information to generate motor program specifications also improves with age. Older performers do better than younger performers when both have a full view of car and trackway. But the generation of movement specifications seems adequate quite early and merely improves with age and experience to become more precise. The important point is that other sources of input become useful. Part of this may be an earlier dependency on visual information, and part may be an improvement in the ability to use other sources of information. The latter seems particularly important in using verbal information from others and less direct clues, such as the responses or reactions of others who look startled or surprised when they watch a child riding a bicycle toward a closed gate.

Step III has been discussed mainly as making ongoing corrections to achieve better movement control after the movement plan has been selected and the initial specifications for the motor program have been generated. Visual information is used in these ongoing corrections, as demonstrated in the changes in postural control when the room was seen to move. Visual information was also used in quite different ways to help correct hand movements when vision was limited or distorted. Indeed, visual information at times seems needed and overused.

Chapter Summary

The major limitations in using vision in the development of movement control are in the generation and correction of movement control and in the need and overuse of vision at particular times. We discussed the need and overuse of vision and found a progression of change within movement situations and somewhat across ages. We view this progression as a developmental change in a broad, descriptive sense. The use of vision in generating and correcting movement control is a developmental issue, as it identifies an important set of relationships to be studied in trying to understand the development movement control. The generation and correction of movement control are parts of the neuromotor control system and are not easy to isolate for study.

Throughout this chapter we noted the processing of information as part of the three steps in solving a movement problem, by using processing as the border in Figure 11-1 to surround the three steps. This means that visual input is processed to create visual information and that selection, generation, and correction in movement control mean processing visual information to use in movement control. We found increases in processing load, time available, and time needed as limiting the use of visual information in movement control.

C | PROCESSING INFORMATION

12 | *Development of Processing Abilities*

The performance of any movement requires processing body-environment information. Whenever sensory stimuli from any source are organized and used, we are processing information. Specific aspects of processing are studied separately, but we can speak of processing as all operations in which we analyze, organize, and use sensory stimuli. Processing requirements can increase in amount and complexity when continuously using multiple and related inputs. The *time available to process* becomes shorter as events occur more rapidly and as the *time needed to process* becomes greater, which tends to be true for younger children who process slower. We also recognize that information may be analyzed, organized, and used differently to adjust to changes in processing requirements. Developmental changes in processing skills lead to better ways of coping with processing requirements in movement situations.

The example of jumping rope, used in Chapter 4, illustrates the increase in processing requirements as movement tasks become more complicated and more continuous. Children at first have difficulty in making a single jump over a rope lying on the ground, but they progress to maintaining a continuous, rhythmical jumping sequence in relation to a rope swinging continuously and rapidly. They can stand in different positions, sideways or head-on to the rope, can have others jumping with them, and can have the rope change speeds while they are changing their foot patterns. The more complicated and more continuous movements obviously create a more complicated set of body-environment relationships to be processed, and a greater amount of more complicated information must be processed in less time. The continuous full jump-rope movements also increase the processing requirements because of the need to plan ahead, or anticipate, without a stopping point to prepare for the next movements in the sequence. Processing requirements increase substantially in this respect for movements in a more open situation involving less predictable environmental conditions, such as when children turn their own jump rope and move around the playground in which other children are moving and must be avoided. Children improve greatly in their ability to process very large increases in body-environment information.

In this chapter we shall examine the development of processing abilities in preparation for studying in Chapter 13 the development of movement control in relation to the development of processing abilities. Processing information is how people acquire, retain, and transform knowledge. They come to know something, can retain it for future use, and can alter and combine it in order to know more. Processing in the production of movement means that between any initial sensory stimulation and the final movement, information is transformed in a variety of ways. Individuals seek information from the environment and perform on it numerous operations that affect the movement. Implicit is the notion that "knowing" will affect "doing," that perceptual discriminations and cognitive decisions will influence movement production.

The three steps described in Chapter 11 are our general representation of the processing used to solve a movement problem. Processing information is needed to specify the body and the environment, select a movement plan and generate appropriate motor program specifications, and correct movements as they are executed. Processing information is an integral and necessary function in all aspects of a movement's preparation and execution. Faust and Faust (1980, p. 10) describe this as processing to "reconstruct incoming sensory information while transforming it successively from the level of sense receptors through levels in which recognition is appraised, meaning is extracted, task-specific operations are performed, and overt acts may be planned, directed and executed."

When a child is attempting to catch a ball, we can observe the ball, the child, and the act of ball catching. But these observations tell us little about what the child does to produce the movement. We cannot see the rules that govern the behaviors we observe. Estes (1978, p. 2) summarizes this dilemma by stating that we "need factual accounts of what the individual is doing between the initiation of the observed stimulus context and the ultimate observable responses indicating that the individual has obtained information or solved a problem." We must know how the information is processed in preparation for the movement and during the movement.

Two processing concerns will be the focus of our discussion of the development of processing abilities. The first is an individual's *processing capacity* or limit, and the second is the general nature of *processing skills.* It is obvious from our jump-rope example and everyday observations that children improve markedly in being able to process more information in a shorter time. Thus, younger children's processing systems can more easily be overloaded, whereas older children and adults can process more information before their processing systems become overloaded. This very simple view of processing capacity or limit is true in general terms, but it is deceiving if we think of our processing systems as just processing faster and faster. It is more likely that we process differently and more effectively. Our processing skills improve and in some cases may change. Younger children may lack particular processing skills, which limits the amount they can process in a given time. As a simple example, younger children may process information that older children will disregard and thus will have to do more because they cannot set aside irrelevant information. Capacity now becomes a more complicated idea when individuals are processing different information, perhaps in a different way, but the end result is the same, that some individuals process more quantities of pertinent information.

General Processing Systems

We view processing as a necessary part of the three steps we listed for solving a movement problem. This is a broader perspective than is generally taken by cognitive psychologists, whose work has been focused on *knowledge processing*, which is concerned with what people know and how they know it. Less attention has been given to *action processing*, in which processing is part of doing. Some models of how individuals might process information will be reviewed to illustrate how psychologists have thought about knowledge processing that can be used to think about action processing, which is our main interest.

Psychologists applied system analysis work to behavioral rather than engineering systems, as exemplified by Shannon and Weaver (1949). They compared human processing to computer operations in which information is encoded, stored, transformed, retrieved, and acted upon and used the mathematical basis of information theory to make quantitative predictions about behavior. In essence, information theory is a system of measurement, with the amount of information dependent on uncertainty. *If more uncertainty exists in a particular situation, then more information will be present and require a longer processing time.* For example, a ball thrown at a constant speed has less information each time it is thrown than does one that varies in speed. Similarly with spatial directions, a ball that always comes to the right contains less information than one that may come from either the right or the left.

Information in information theory terms is represented by the formula $H = \log_2 n$, where H is information, and n is the number of equiprobable alternatives in a given situation. The unit of information in this equation is a *bit*, which is a contraction of the computer term *binary digit*. In any given situation with a specified number of alternatives, the presentation of one bit of information will halve the alternatives. The often-quoted example is drawing one of eight numbers out of a hat. If one is told that the number is even, then that person has been given one bit of information that reduces the number of possible alternatives to the four even numbers, out of the whole set of eight numbers. The speed at which responses are made in this type of situation is measured and reported in bits per second. The information requirement (usually called *demand*) for a problem is a function of the amount of information present and the time available to process it.

Information theory has influenced our thinking about processing in two ways. First, human processing often is described and conceptualized in computer language and computer analogies, which stems informally from the increased presence of computers in our lives and formally from the language and concepts of information theory. Second, the measurement techniques associated with information theory have been used directly or have been the basis for deriving many additional measures of processing. The impact of information theory on the many ways in which processing has been studied has been substantial, and it is important to recognize this. But there are many other models and theories, of which information theory is only one, and so should not be used as a general term to denote all views of information processing.

Models

Various processing models have been formulated to represent individuals' processing activities. Models are representations, descriptions, or analogies to help us visualize something that cannot be directly observed; they deal with how information is transformed as it passes through a processing system. Information enters through one or more of the sensory systems and can come from external sources, as indicated by the environmental display in Figure 12-1, and from internal sources, which include body knowledge of muscle tension and limb position and information generated internally through ideas and feelings. Information is transformed in many ways to make the input meaningful to the individual and to make the decisions needed to act upon the existing conditions as perceived by the individual. The transformations provide the impetus for the effector system to select a plan of action. The effector system produces a movement within the processing system's information constraints, and an action takes place within the context of the existing environment.

Models of processing usually include both *structural components* and *control operations*. Structural components are permanent features of the model, and control operations are procedures performed within and among the structural components. Most processing models include the construct of *memory* as a structural feature. Memory is shown in Figure 12-1 as an underlying base to indicate the need in a general processing system for the storage of information for each processing function. Memory is being able to recognize something as familiar or known and to make a movement in a similar manner without each time having to construct it anew. Information must be stored in some way to make it possible to act further on past information. Memory and processing are not located in one neuroanatomical location but, rather, within and across neural networks. Our diagram includes boxes showing different types of functions, but this does not mean that they are confined to a certain neuroanatomical location.

Control operations regulate how information is processed. The computer analogy is that a general processing system has structural or hardware components that are operated upon by software or control operations. There must be hard-

FIGURE 12-1

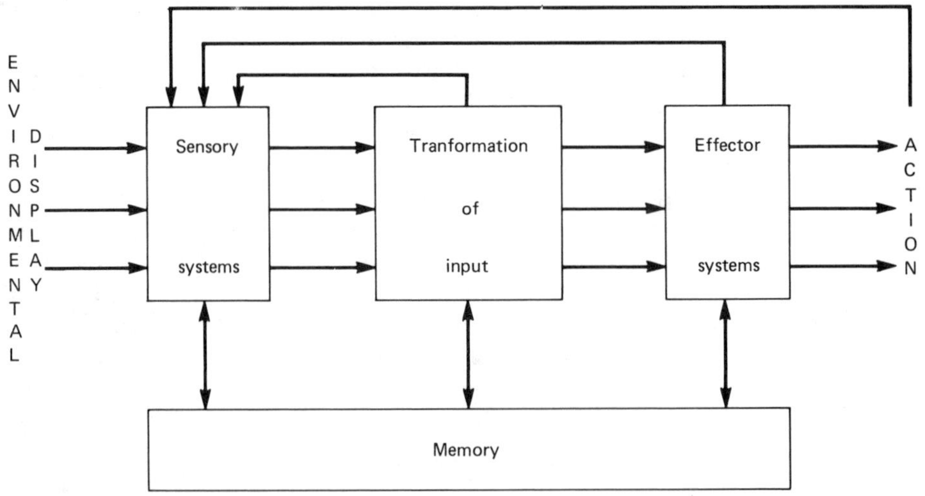

A general processing system.

ware—perhaps the hardwire or neural system in humans—that functions in relation to the instructions or commands called software. Considerable effort has been made to understand the human control operations in processing information. Examples are the organization of information into larger units or chunks and the rehearsal of information to facilitate recall. Control operations are not identified on the diagram but should be viewed as the programming of a general processing system.

Another aspect of a general processing system is *attention*, which has several meanings for processing. Our focus will be on attentional capacity: how much information may be processed in a specific time. Looking at our diagram and thinking about the elaborate networks that comprise a processing system, it is not difficult to imagine that attentional capacity can easily be overloaded in specific functions and in general. We shall now look separately at memory, control processes, and attention.

Memory

Most information models include a memory, which is seen as a structural feature in the processing system. This is complicated by the fact that memory often is broken down into permanent structural features and changing control operations. Structural features are assumed to be independent of age, with young children having the same structural features as adults do, but control operations vary according to the child's developmental level.

Multistore Model. Atkinson and Shiffrin (1968) present a multistore view of memory, with information flowing from the sensory register's structural components to a short-term store and finally to a long-term store, as shown in Figure 12-2. They identify three types of memory which are assumed to have different characteristics. The sensory storage system has a large capacity, yet is short in memory duration, probably up to a maximum of 2 seconds. Very often we can keep a visual image of many objects, but only for a brief period of time. The short-term storage system has a small and limited capacity with a duration, according to different researchers, of up to 60 seconds. We can look up a new telephone number, remember it, dial it, and have our conversation, but forget the number

FIGURE 12-2

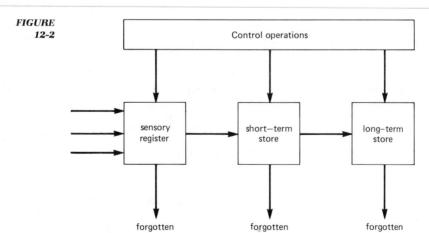

A multistore model of memory.

afterwards. Finally, there is a long-term storage system that has a large capacity and is relatively more permanent. Functional strategies, such as chunking and rehearsal, organize and direct the information flow among the memory system's various structural components.

The length of time that information may be retained is a key distinction among the three memory stores. Two theoretical explanations for this loss of information are spontaneous decay and interference. Decay theory assumes that when something is learned, a memory trace is formed that decays spontaneously, thus providing less discrimination between memory traces. Interference theory views forgetting as being due to competing responses between the criterion task and tasks that have been learned before or after the criterion task. These theories do not seem to be mutually exclusive, and the loss of information may be a combination of both. Atkinson and Shiffrin (1968) state that the information in the short-term store is held in auditory, verbal, or linguistic codes and that information loss is due to decay or displacement by other input. On the other hand, the loss of information in the long-term store can be due to interference and the temporary inability to retrieve the information.

Levels of Processing Model. In contrast with a multistore view of memory, Craik and Lockhart (1972) argue that separate components of memory may be too rigid a system if everyday tasks of memory are to be adequately explained. They propose that memory is better viewed as levels of processing and define memory as the processes performed on information to be remembered. No permanent structural features, as in the multistore models, are specified, with the accuracy of remembering being totally a function of control operations.

Processing is done at various levels, starting with "shallow" sensory processing and progressing to "deeper" abstract and semantic levels. Depth of processing is an elusive characteristic, usually defined as the meaningfulness extracted from the stimulus. Meaningfulness requires more time for analysis and results in better retention. For example, words are remembered better if some meaning is attached to them, than they are as just the physical characteristics of the size of the letters. Naus, Ornstein, and Hoving (1978) note that a levels-of-processing approach is similar to the Soviet view of memory, which stresses meaningful interaction with any stimulus. Although attractive, the levels-of-processing approach is not without its critics (Eysenck 1978), and difficulties arise when trying to find suitable criteria for the concept of depth of processing.

Craik's and Lockhart's original proposal has been elaborated (Craik 1979), as displayed in Figure 12-3. Depth is no longer seen as a simple continuum from shallow to deep levels without accounting for the information's physical, phonemic, and semantic characteristics. Memory effectiveness also is determined by the elaboration and distinctiveness of the processing, the consistency of the conditions under which the information was originally encoded and later must be retrieved, and the congruity of the processed event with the processing system. Battig (1979) adds multiple and variable processing and contextual interference as additional considerations in effective memory. By this, he means that processing can be done in more than one way and that increased interference or difficulty during the original acquisition, particularly with changes in contextual conditions, will improve recall. Battig and Shea (1978–1980) state that an item or event is more likely to be remembered if it has been processed deeply, elaborately, distinctively, congruently with context and retrieval conditions, in multiple and variable ways,

FIGURE
12-3

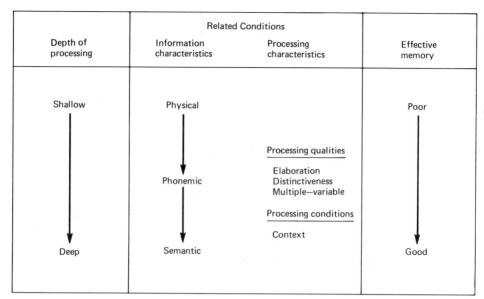

Levels of processing and related conditions which are proposed as determiners of effective memory.

and with high contextual interference and variety. These are a bewildering array of conditions which are difficult to measure and test, but the idea of levels of processing is that we should focus on how information is processed and the meaningfulness of the processing.

Control Operations

The two memory models present what are seemingly different views of memory, but both approaches argue for some type of control operations. A multistore approach emphasizes structural components that are run by various control operations. The levels-of-processing approach stresses the operations used to analyze information. A multistore view holds that these control operations work on the structural components of the sensory register and the short-term and long-term stores. Proponents of levels of processing argue against structural components with set characteristics, maintaining that differences in retention are due to the depth of processing which is a function of how an individual processes in relation to existing conditions and the meaningfulness of the processing.

In their multistore model, Atkinson and Shiffrin (1968) see control operations as adaptable and individually determined. Each person has a level of competence and a past history of experience and circumstances associated with the particular task. Hall (1980) notes that control operations in the sensory register are limited because of their short time span and supports the contention that selecting the sensory modality is the most important function of the control operations at this level. The short-term and long-term stores hold things for a longer time to allow a greater variety of control operations.

Control operations in the storage, search, and retrieval of information have been examined in both short-term and long-term memory studies. An example of a control operation is rehearsal, in which information is overtly or covertly repeated or made the focus of attention. Rehearsal presumably functions to strengthen the memory trace, thereby preventing decay so that the information is not lost and can be transferred to the relatively long-term store. Another control operation is the search procedure or strategy used to find and retrieve information. It also is argued that executive control operations are needed to determine which control operations to use and when they will be used.

Craik and Lockhart (1972) found that the more processes or control operations that are performed on information, the deeper the processing and the better the retention will be. Physical features first are analyzed, followed by more detailed phonemic and semantic examinations. We noted earlier that the depth of processing involves a variety of more elaborate and more distinctive processing. The different analyses and differences in processing all require control operations, although these are not specified in the various statements about levels of processing. Naus, Ornstein, and Hoving (1978) note that it is difficult empirically to differentiate ideas about control operations in levels of processing from those proposed in a multistore position. The investigators of multistore control operations have outlined a more specific set of control operations, particularly in processing strategies, and have provided more research data. Levels of processing is a more recent idea, and it remains to be seen how control operations will be specified and tested.

Our brief review of control operations in these two memory models indicates the importance of control operations to each position, with the multistore research literature providing more of the specific ideas and research data. We remind you that the focus in both models is on knowing, remembering, and forgetting, whereas we are mainly concerned here with processing that leads to and is part of action. Nevertheless, memory models and related control operations are a useful starting point in thinking about a general processing system.

We also need to consider the distinction between structural features and control operations in memory and in a general processing system. One concern is whether development changes are changes in structure or in control operations, or a combination of both. Thus far, structure and control operations have been differentiated, like separating memory and other parts of the processing system into hardware and software. Although we can make this distinction in our theories and models, it is difficult to do so in more empirical terms. We shall encounter this distinction throughout our review of processing development and believe that it is useful to think about it and similar issues, even though it is not always necessary to resolve them.

Attention

Attention as a concept sees the whole processing system as having structures and control operations that use attention as needed. Everyday tasks involving attention as processing capacity are common. For example, a list of four items is quite easily attended to and processed in order to be remembered. But if this list is increased to fifteen, it is unlikely that an individual will have enough processing capacity to remember them. It also is possible to perform two tasks at once as long as the total amount of processing capacity available is not exceeded. But if the tasks' attentional requirements exceed the available capacity, one or both tasks will be interrupted to some extent. Our particular concern, therefore, is attention as a processing capacity, and we want to know how processing capacity changes with age.

Earlier views of processing assumed that attention could be allocated only to one operation at a time, and with this came the notion of a "bottleneck" in the processing system in which information "queued" up to be processed. The concept of a single processing channel was that each stage or component in the processing system was capable of only a single operation at any one time. The early arguments centered on where the bottleneck was situated in the system. Broadbent (1958) argued that it occurred just before or at the perceptual mechanism, whereas Deutsch and Deutsch (1963) and Welford (1968) placed it at the response selection mechanism.

The single-channel view of processing, with a bottleneck placed somewhere in the system, has been superceded by the view that a total amount of attention is available to be used by any part of the system as required. The amount of attention or processing capacity is limited, but it is a general capacity and not one in which there is a convergence of demands on a particular process to create a bottleneck. Tasks can be performed simultaneously, provided that the capacity available to the individual is not exceeded by that required for each task: there is a limited amount of capacity available that can be variably allocated to the different components of the processing system. The amount of attention available is seen as a pool or reservoir that can be allocated to the parts of the processing system that are in need, as shown in Figure 12-4. There is a fixed amount in the reservoir, and limitations of performance because of attention are due to processing requirements exceeding this fixed amount. The amount required depends on the task and the individual. Kahneman (1973), a proponent of this viewpoint, states that the important issues are what makes an activity need more or less attention, which factors control the amount of capacity available at any one time, and what are the rules of the allocation policy.

Attention often is referred to as processing capacity or processing space, which implies that processing takes place in an area with measurable dimensions. This is not true in the same way that the volume of a box can be measured, but a general sense of capacity can be observed as the number of items that can be remembered. Another way to study attention requirements is to have subjects do two tasks simultaneously in a *dual-task paradigm.* Changes in performance from doing the task alone to doing it simultaneously with another task indicate the attention required for the single task and the processing priority of the two tasks. The dual-task paradigm is one way to study the general issues that Kahneman raised.

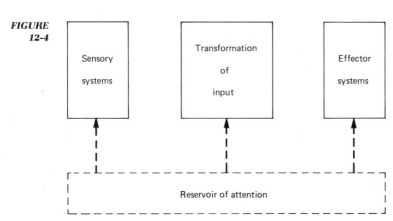

FIGURE 12-4

Sensory systems

Transformation of input

Effector systems

Reservoir of attention

Variable allocation of attention.

Development of Processing Skills

Memory and attention obviously change throughout our lives, but it is not simple to describe and analyze these changes. Children become more capable of processing larger and more complex types of information, and more simultaneously and more continuously. Children not only increase their ability to process more, but they also seem to be able to process in different ways.

There is much literature on memory development, but we shall use only one model to represent the general issues. Our discussion of attention will be limited and disjointed because attention is so embedded in the study of other aspects of human behavior that it is difficult to extract a general view of it.

Memory

Multistore and levels of processing are presented as general models of memory, but they are not developmental models, even though they have sometimes been used to discuss memory development. Brown (1975) approaches memory as *knowing* rather than as remembering and forgetting, which shifts the general focus to what people know and how they come to know it. Brown outlines three kinds of knowing:

(a) *Knowing*: Our knowledge base, which is our semantic memory and provides a dynamic knowledge system underlying all cognitive activity.
(b) *Knowing how to know*: Our repertoire of processing skills.
(c) *Knowing about knowing*: Our metamory or knowledge about our own memory.

Brown organized a model to show some of the aspects of change in developmental memory.

Knowing. Brown notes that most of what we know and remember about our world comes from a continuous interaction with a meaningful environment to produce a knowledge store, or *knowledge base*. General features of events are retained in what Brown calls *semantic memory* which provides *more meaningful knowing*. She also recognizes that we process information related to particular events, or episodes, such as reading the letters on an eye chart or reading a list of nonsense syllables in a laboratory experiment, and that such *less meaningful knowing* may be retained as *episodic memory*. The episodic–semantic distinction is a continuum from more specific to more general knowledge of events, with the idea that the more semantic memory is, the more useful it will be.

Brown uses children's memory for narratives to illustrate the general development of knowing. She points out that preschool children can reconstruct meaningful narratives to provide the gist of a story but have problems with the sequence of events. They later become better at retelling stories and can use meaning to produce the most probable order of events. Here the children are not just remembering a copy of events; they are also using their semantic knowledge of the world to *reconstruct a course of events*. The meaning in their knowledge base aids in retrieval and, more importantly, in the use of what is known. The development of semantic knowledge also is essential to the use of episodic memory. Lindberg (1980) found that adults restricted in their use of their large semantic knowledge base performed no better than young children did on episodic tasks. But when allowed to use their semantic knowledge base, adults were substantially better than young children. In a similar vein, Perlmutter and Myers (1979) studied the development of recall in 2- to 4-year-olds and found that the older children performed better than the younger children did, even though they used no strategies. Perlmutter and Myers suggested that the difference was related to an increase in general semantic knowledge.

Craik's and Lockhart's levels-of-processing approach (1972) is compatible with the idea of knowing, in that information processed at deep semantic levels is better remembered than is information processed at shallow physical levels. Owings and Baumeister (1979) used a levels-of-processing approach and found that the semantic, phonemic, and physical levels of processing affected children's memory performance in the same order as it did adults', with better memory associated with greater depth of processing at the semantic level. They suggest that knowledge increases with age and affects memory by increasing the possibilities for *relating new information to what is already known.*

Memory viewed in Brown's broad perspective is difficult to separate from intelligence. A Piagetian view of memory holds that overall cognitive development is responsible for memory development (Piaget and Inhelder 1973), that memory is not just a copy of events but is a continuously changing *constructive process, with the individual actively organizing the material to be remembered.* For Piaget, understanding, knowing, and remembering are inseparable parts of intelligence. As children's general operational levels change, so does their ability to remember meaningful events.

Knowing How to Know. Brown uses the term *knowing how to know* to describe the *development of control operations,* particularly strategies, for deliberate memorization. Brown (1978) reviewed the literature on processing strategies and memory development and came to three conclusions. First, the developmentally young, that is, children who are chronologically or mentally young, are deficient in using strategies. They do not seem to use rehearsal and similar strategies spontaneously. Second, developmentally young children can be trained to use some strategies, which has been confirmed in studies on both normal and retarded children. Third, these trained processing skills tend to be abandoned unless they are actively used.

Four general types of control operations that differ in children and adults have been proposed by Chi (1976). Lack of *rehearsal* by children before the age of 5 has been documented on several tasks as leading to inferior performance. A second process is *naming,* which Chi defines as attaching a verbal label to a visual stimulus. It was thought that naming was a precursor to rehearsal, but a deficiency in naming can take place in isolation and does not preclude subsequent rehearsal; thus, a lack of rehearsal cannot be attributed to a lack of naming. Chi also notes that adults typically *group* and *recode* information, whereas young children do not. Finally, she proposes that children differ in *long-term memory attributes,* especially in the complexity of their knowledge base. These differences seem to be the absence, rather than the presence, of a recognizable chunk of information, the size of each information chunk, and its accessibility. Chi stresses that the knowledge base available in long-term memory will greatly influence the type of operations performed in short-term memory. She recently formulated a learning framework for the development of this knowledge base (Chi and Rees 1983).

Differences between children and adults also have been found in the memory

329

retrieval process. Kobasigawa (1977) notes that the retrieval process requires both a memory search and an "acceptance decision," that the appropriate information has been retrieved. The memory search may be simple or may require complicated search strategies, depending on whether the items are still active, whether classification is necessary, and whether time is limited. The acceptance decision has many complications, including the level of accuracy desired. Older children are better able than young children are to conduct a thorough and systematic memory search and make better acceptance decisions.

A developmental change in strategies for obtaining information was suggested by Wright and Vliestra (1975), who saw the change as a shift from an *exploration* mode to a *search* mode. Exploration is spontaneous, somewhat random, and short in duration. Search is characterized by planning and reflection and is related more to informational needs than to stimulus qualities. The shift from exploration to search probably is related to changes in overall cognitive development.

In regard to the overall development of processing strategies, Flavell (1970) believes that children may not use available strategies because of what he calls production and mediation deficiencies. A *production deficiency* is an inadequate use of control operations which can be remediated by adequate training of the required strategy. A *mediation deficiency* can be observed when children are trained to produce the required strategy but cannot use it to mediate or help in doing the task. A strategy must be produced and then must be used as a mediator. Deficiencies may occur in either production or mediation. Turning this reasoning to a positive direction, Flavell believes that children develop from producing strategies without using them spontaneously, to using them more spontaneously and effectively. He also believes that this pattern of change is related to both age and situation. That is, developmentally young children may use strategies spontaneously and effectively in a simple situation, but not when more complex strategies and situations are required.

Knowing About Knowing. Children's knowledge of their own memory develops in that they become better able to evaluate situation requirements and discover more about their own memory operations. Adults know that is harder to remember twelve rather than four items, and they consciously know how they change their strategies for remembering. They may group the items by common characteristics or in relation to an artificial ordering system, such as assigning numbers to each item. Adults also know other things about how they go about knowing. They know that they have a repertoire of strategies and if they have a preferred approach, such as dividing the information or the problem into two groups before analyzing it further. They also may know that they retrieve or remember on the basis of how they code the information for storage, such as being aware that "it begins with a 'B' " or "it is very large and soft" when verbally describing their search for something in memory. Children seem to know less about their knowing.

Knowing about knowing is often labeled *metamemory*. In their studies of metamemory, Kreutzer, Leonard, and Flavell (1975) found that as they grew older, children recognized that older children studied differently and remembered better. Younger children seemed to be *aware* that familiarity and similar abstract properties affect the retrieval of information, whereas older children seemed to *know* this. As early as kindergarten, children can verbalize about memory being affected by study time, number of items, and knowing that it is easier to relearn a forgotten activity than to start on a totally new task. All of this knowing about knowing improves with age.

An unresolved issue is how, if at all, metamemory is related to improvements in memory. Cavanaugh and Borkowski (1980) found that metamemory improved with age but that metamemory-memory correlations were not significant within each grade level. Good metamemory is not predictive of good memory, but this does not mean that changes in metamemory are not related to changes in memory. As Cavanaugh and Perlmutter (1982) state, the concept of metamemory is poorly defined because of the lack of distinction between memory knowledge and executive memory processes. They argue that only the former is metamemory, that more definitive tests are needed to monitor specific types of change in metamemory in relation to certain aspects of memory development. Thus, metamemory seems to improve with age, but we do not know what impact it has on memory.

Brown's Developmental Model of Memory. Brown's (1975) developmental model of memory is organized around three issues that we have touched on in our discussion of her views of knowing. First, she distinguishes between episodic and semantic memory, which we described earlier as being on a continuum from specific to general and somewhat from less meaningful to more meaningful. Second, tasks may or may not require processing strategies (control operations) to be carried out efficiently. The more strategies a task requires, the more developmental changes we can expect to observe. Third, strategies may not be used because of a production or a mediation deficiency, both of which may change with age and situation. Brown emphasizes that each of these three issues is a continuum and not a dichotomy, as they often are viewed. Her model is presented in Figure 12-5 as a flow chart for a chain of decision events.

FIGURE 12-5

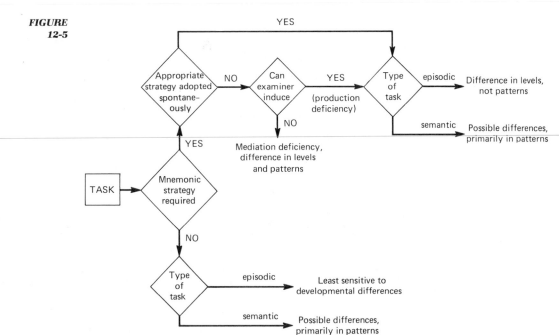

A developmental model of memory proposed by Brown (1975). (Reproduced with permission from Brown, 1975.)

Brown sees two types of developmental changes, which she calls level differences and pattern differences, and are observed as outcomes related to memory processes and are listed at the several end points in the flow chart. *Level differences* are developmental differences attributable to developmental stage or chronological age. Thus, the performance of 12-year-olds might be different from that of 10-year-olds on a particular task, in that the 12-year-olds' mean score will be better in an absolute sense and also might be less variable. *Pattern differences* are developmental differences in which specific task variables interact with developmental stage or chronological age. For example, a pattern difference is reflected in the type of strategy used by different age groups. Not only are the groups different in an absolute sense, but they also are different in how they operate on information. The analogy of ANOVA (analysis of variance) main effects and interaction effects has been used to illustrate level and pattern differences. Level differences are differences in the main effect of a developmental stage, whereas pattern differences are interactions of the developmental stage and task variables. Brown stresses that developmental differences might not be expected in some situations, and so neither level nor pattern differences would be predicted.

Working through the model, we begin with the task. The first decision point is whether or not a mnemonic (memory) strategy is required. If the answer is no, the next decision will be to determine the type of task. An episodic task that does not need a memory strategy will be the least likely to show developmental differences. If the task is more semantic but does not require a memory strategy, developmental differences may be observed in pattern differences. Thus, Brown is predicting the type of developmental differences related to strategy requirements and the meaningfulness of the task and context. Pattern differences might be expected for nonstrategic, semantic tasks, but no developmental differences would be expected for nonstrategic, episodic tasks.

If the tasks require a memory stategy, this will lead to the upper portion of the flow chart. When an appropriate strategy can be adopted spontaneously, we can expect to find developmental differences on episodic tasks in levels but not in patterns. Semantic tasks may not show developmental differences, but any that occur would be pattern differences based on the interaction of a particular task with a developmental stage. The trend is that episodic tasks will show developmental differences in levels and only if a strategy is required, whereas semantic tasks will show fewer developmental differences and principally in patterns. The meaningfulness of semantic tasks minimizes the strategy requirements and leads to a complex interaction of task and developmental stage. The lack of meaning in episodic tasks requires more strategies but leads only to differences in levels and only when strategies are used.

Most of the studies on the development of strategies have been performed in episodic situations in which deliberate memorization takes place. We noted that in these episodic situations, as they grow older, children are better able to name, group, recode, and rehearse in order to acquire and retain information and to make systematic searches and decisions when retrieving information. But often in everyday life we come to know with less conscious recourse to strategic behavior.

Young children acquire knowledge through an active interaction with meaningful problems in the environment which reduces the need for some of the strategies identified and studied in episodic situations. Brown points out that few memory studies have been done outside her strategic-episodic category and calls for experiments to study the other categories. In some ways this request has been answered, but we are still a long way from establishing the interactive effects of her three types of memory: knowing, knowing how to know, and knowing about knowing.

Attention

We stated earlier that attention often is viewed as having a limited processing capacity that can be allocated as needed to any part of the processing system. It seems logical that attention allocation will show a developmental trend, because improvement in allocation requires selecting a task's relevant variables. The concept of selective attention often is investigated in dual-task or time-sharing paradigms in which a central task and a secondary task are performed separately. Then when the tasks are performed simultaneously, any differences between them indicate how children allocate their limited processing capacity. In a series of studies by Hagen and his associates (Druker and Hagen 1969, Hagen 1967, Hagen and Fisch 1968), performance on the central task improved with age, but performance on the secondary task did not or sometimes declined. This indicates that younger children allocated their available attention somewhat equally between the two tasks. Older children seemed to recognize the importance of the central task by allocating more attention to it, as indicated by their improved performance on it. Conroy and Weener (1976) supported these findings, in that central task learning increased with age for both auditory and visual presentations, whereas secondary task learning declined at the oldest age level for both auditory and visual tasks. Similar findings by Dusek (1978), Hale and Alderman (1978), and Lane (1979) confirmed this. Simon (1972) reviewed this literature and postulated a fixed fund of attention. In his view, the structural limits of attention cannot be increased or diminished, but they can be reallocated. As they grow older, children become more adept at controlling the allocation of their attention, by adopting deliberate, though not necessarily conscious, strategies.

Wickens and Benel (1982) state that capacity allocation, or what they call time-sharing efficiency, improves with age and pinpoint four possible sources of improvement.

1. *Automation*: Performance on one task stays the same with less attention used, thus making processing resources available for doing a concurrent task.
2. *Expanding resources*: A structural increase in capacity.
3. *Functional differentiation of resource reservoirs*: The existence of more than a single capacity, so that two tasks interfere with each other only to the extent that they draw from the same reservoir.
4. *Attention deployment skills*: The use of strategies (control operations) as a functional means of processing more information.

Wickens and Benel tentatively conclude that the developmental differences for dual tasks are mainly due to automation and attention deployment skills.

Manis, Keating, and Morrison (1980) also found that cognitive processes involved in a task compete for limited central processing capacity. They argue that age changes in cognitive performance may be the reason for improvements in the efficiency and flexibility of capacity allocation to the involved processes. This can occur without changes in the amount of capacity available. Using a dual-task paradigm with letter matching as a primary task and an auditory probe as a secondary task, they found a decrease from second graders to adults in the amount of capacity allocated to less complex processing. As the task became more complex, the adults allocated more capacity, but they still used less than the sixth graders did, who in turn used less than the second graders did. It seems, therefore, that as they grow older, children become better able to control the allocation of available attention or capacity, and these age differences are related to the stage of processing. But what accounts for this increasing ability? The reasons that children become more proficient at using this limited capacity are at the very heart of their development of processing ability.

Our earlier distinction between structural components and control operations provides two different points of view as to why older children are better at using available processing capacity. The first suggests that there is an actual structural increase and that developing processing ability is a function of this increase in actual capacity. The second attributes this development to more sophisticated strategies and control operations that allow the handling of more information. Connolly (1970) agrees with the latter, stating that "capacity is not so much built into the apparatus as it is built into the strategy the child is using." A different approach was taken by Pascual-Leone (1970) in his theory of cognitive operators, more commonly known as neo-Piagetian theory, which indicates that structural changes are responsible for this increasing ability.

Neo-Piagetian theory (Pascual-Leone 1970, Pascual-Leone and Smith 1969) attempts to explain why children pass through Piaget's developmental stages. It combines the concept of limited capacity, which increases developmentally as a function of maturation, and cognitive style to determine what affects maximum capacity usage. Central to the theory is the notion of schemes, which are units containing factual or procedural knowledge. The activation of these schemes is determined by "M-power" (mental power) which is limited in capacity. M-power increases linearly with Piaget's developmental stages, as shown in Table 12-1, and is dependent on maturation and general experience. M-power is conceptualized as structural and often is called structural M space, or Ms space. To explain why individuals with the same Ms space may not always behave in the same way, Pascual-Leone offers the concept of functional M space (Mf space), which represents the amount of potential Ms space typically used, thus labeling individuals as high or low M processors. The theory predicts that children with different structural mental space (Ms space) will process at different levels and that those with the same Ms space can be differentiated by their functional M space (Mf

TABLE 12-1   **Predicted M-Capacity in Relation to Piagetian Substages and Chronological Age (CA)**

PREDICTED MAXIMUM M $(e + k)$	PIAGETIAN SUBSTAGES	CA
$e + 2$	Preoperational: Last substage	5–6
$e + 3$	Concrete operation: Low	7–8
$e + 4$	Concrete operation: High	9–10
$e + 5$	Formal operation: Introduction	11–12
$e + 6$	Formal operation: Low	13–14
$e + 7$	Formal operation: High	15–16

space). Thus, the theory posits structural capacity growth, with the differences within Ms space levels being attributed to functional variables.

Neo-Piagetian theory seems to be alone in proposing actual structural growth in a child's processing capacity, and it has its critics. Chi (1976) states that what appears to be a structural limitation in children is actually a deficit in their processing strategies and processing speed. Most researchers agree with Chi, who believes that children's qualitative processing differences account for their developmental changes. She points out that on tasks evaluating such parameters as rate of information loss, there is no difference between children and adults. There were, however, substantial differences in the utilization of control operations, such as rehearsal, grouping, and recoding, plus differences in the content of long-term memory or knowledge base.

Processing Speed

We now will look at processing speed as an important and a practical outcome. Movement situations often have time constraints, which means that better processing speed is needed during both movement preparation and execution. In many movement tasks, processing speed may account for most of the performance differences between children and adults. We shall look at changes with age in processing speed to consider what seems to influence processing speed, what are child–adult differences, and how processing speed can be improved.

Processing Load and Processing Time
Processing speed is the rate at which information is processed. Speed or rate is calculated as the amount of information processed in a certain time, which often is stated as bits per second, in line with our earlier description of information load calculated in information bits. Processing speed thus is the information load processed per second, which can be measured by a variety of techniques.

Reaction time is the basic measure of processing time, on the assumption that reaction time reflects the time needed to process information. If the information load is known, the processing speed will be the information load divided by the reaction time. The classic statement of the relationship between information load and reaction time was made by Hick (1952), in what has become known as Hick's law: Reaction time increases linearly as information load increases, when load is specified as the logarithm of the number of alternatives to calculate the bits of information. Hick added +1 to the number of alternatives because there is an added unit of uncertainty if subjects do not know when the stimulus will appear.

Hick's work was extended by Hyman (1953), who varied not only the number of choices but also the sequential dependencies and the probabilities of their occurrence. As with Hick's experiment, the relationship between information load and reaction time was again linear, thus implying processing strategies. For example, a four-choice reaction time task with equiprobable stimuli and a fixed foreperiod has an information load of 2 bits:

$$H = \log_2 n$$
$$= \log_2 4$$
$$= 2$$

But the same four-choice task, with the alternatives changed until the probabilities of their occurrence become .6, .2, .1, and .1, has only 1.57 bits of information transmitted:

$$H = pi \log_2 \frac{1}{pi}$$

where p is the probability of stimuli i occurring. The implication is that by assigning probabilities, which is a transformation of information, individuals can reduce their processing time.

As early as 1868, Donders (reprinted in 1969) tried to differentiate within reaction time the decision processes of choice and discrimination. Donders's experiments did not totally succeed, but a more recent series of experiments by Sternberg (1969, 1975) is a useful approach to discovering different decision processes within reaction time. Sternberg's paradigm deals with memory scanning, in which subjects are presented with a list of items followed by a single probe item and must state whether or not the original list contains the probe item. In effect, the subjects must scan their memory and compare the probe item with the items in the list. Their time to respond is measured, and latency or delay increases linearly as the list lengthens. Each additional item on the list prolongs the search by 35 to 40 milliseconds, which led Sternberg to conclude that the memory search proceeds serially. Different subjects and list materials have been used, and the same linear relationship is still found. Another finding is that it takes as long to decide that a stimulus is present as it does to decide that it is not. In other words, even if the item appears early in the list, an exhaustive search will still take place.

Both the Hicks-Hyman and Sternberg paradigms tell a similar story. Increase the number of choices and the time for processing will increase; reduce the number of alternatives and the processing time will decrease. What is really happening is that the predictability is increasing or decreasing, first, by changing the number of options or choices and, then, by altering the probabilities and sequence of the remaining options. The amount of information is changed in these several ways and leads to a change in processing speed. If individuals are presented with eight response choices that must be made at speed, the first strategy is to eliminate those alternatives that they know, from previous experiences, will not apply. The response choices might thus be limited to five alternatives. Probabilities can be assigned to the two choices most likely to occur, the two choices not very likely to occur, and one choice as the least likely to occur. The information load thus has been reduced by eliminating some of the alternatives and assigning probabilities to those remaining. Less information now must be processed, which leads to a faster processing speed. Although processing errors can be made when less likely responses occur, the information load often must be reduced so as to be able to cope with large amounts of information in a limited time.

Changes in Processing Speed with Age

Children's reaction times have been measured in various situations, and the results have been reasonably consistent in the general patterns of change graphed in Figure 12-6. First, as expected, there are absolute performance differences, with children becoming faster as they grow older. Second, Hick's law has been confirmed, with reaction time rising linearly as the amount of information to be processed is increased. Third, the regression line defining the relationship of infor-

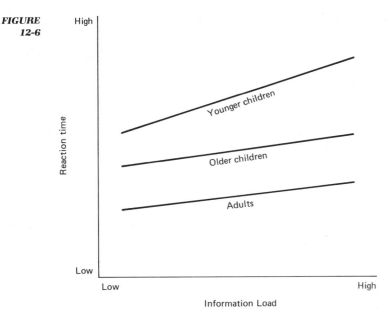

A general representation of increases in reaction time as information load increases.

mation load and reaction time for young children often has a steeper slope. Young children are not only slower in an absolute sense, but for higher information loads, they also require relatively more processing time.

Connolly (1970) performed four experiments investigating reaction time in adults and children ages 6, 8, 10, 12, and 14. He used a card-sorting task to vary the information loads from one to three bits and included simple and choice reaction time situations using relevant and irrelevant stimuli and stimulus variation. Hick's law was confirmed, and the slopes of the regression lines were usually steeper for the younger age groups. Connolly found two transition ages when large performance differences were observed. One was from age 6 to age 8, and the other was from age 14 to adults. Other results indicated that selective filtering mechanisms were poorly developed in younger children, because irrelevant stimuli had a smaller effect on older children. Connolly argues that more than one mechanism is involved and that many simultaneous developmental changes take place to produce a faster processing speed.

Another way to think of processing speed is to measure the time needed to process a particular amount of information, rather than to ascertain how much can be processed in a particular amount of time. Surwillo (1977), using differences between simple and choice reaction times, estimated that 5-year-olds take nearly three times as long as 17-year-olds do to process 1 bit of information. On his card-sorting task, Connolly (1970) measured processing speed by dividing the amount of information per card by the decision time per card. This varied from 1.69 bits per second for 6-year-olds to 4.07 bits per second for adults, to approximate the relative size of the difference that Surwillo reported.

Processing speed also was measured by Fairweather and Hutt (1978), who tested children ages 5 to 11 and adults on two-, four-, and eight-choice tasks. Again, reaction time decreased as age increased and increased as the number of choices increased. Younger children found the four- and eight-choice tasks differentially

337

more difficult than did older children and adults. The reaction time increase is thought to represent difficulties in stimulus selection and response selection. Fairweather and Hutt argue that the response selection accounts mostly for the developmental change. Interestingly, they found that girls were consistently faster than boys were, which they attributed to underlying physiological parameters, such as girls' more rapid maturation and their greater degree of hemispheric plasticity.

We noted earlier that if probabilities could be assigned to stimuli in reaction time paradigms, then the amount of time for processing could be reduced (Hyman 1953). It is possible that children are slower than adults because they are less able to use advance information in parallel with ongoing responses. Kerr, Blanchard, and Miller (1980) investigated the ability of children and adults to use the information that one item provides about the most probable subsequent event in a partially predictable reaction item sequence. The results showed that children used the sequence probability information quite successfully and in parallel with other processing. But the children had larger recovery times when the expected event did not occur. Although the children performed more slowly than the adults did, their processing trends were the same, except that the unexpected upset children more than it did the adults.

The proposition that with age children increase their speed of processing has been well supported. But we must be careful not to think of processing speed as a unitary factor, because the speed of detection, recognition, decision making, movement, and their components may change at different rates over the course of development. As an illustration, Bisanz and Resnick (1978) examined two different aspects of visual processing speed. The first they called *localization*, which is selecting certain information while rejecting what is not to be processed. The second they called *identification*, which is processing information that has been located. Localization speed increased between the ages of 8 and 12, with no further increase; identification speed increased from age 8 to 10 and then remained stable. Bisanz and Resnick concluded that processing speed is not a unitary factor and that different types of processing speed may not increase linearly with age.

Another consideration suggested by Wickens (1974) is that there may be both central and noncentral reasons that account for child-adult differences in processing speed. Attentiveness, incentive, and practice are noncentral factors, which Wickens recognizes as important, but he cites the work of Elliott (1972), who controlled for noncentral factors and still found pronounced changes with age in processing speed.

Following Wickens's (1974) suggestion that noncentral factors might have a differential effect on subjects of differing ages, Nicolson (1982) examined simple reaction time when the incentive was varied, in 4-, 10-, and 20-year-olds. Reaction times became faster with increasing age, but there was a differential age response to the various incentives. Visual feedback helped the youngest subjects most, but they were unable to use a speed-error tradeoff strategy. This strategy, nonetheless, was used by adults and meant increasing the speed of response as the display speed increased (a spaceship moving across a video monitor). Thus, when the display was slow and there was little danger of missing, the adults responded safely with relatively slow hits, but they speeded up when the display was fast, in order to have fast hits or misses. These trends were not seen in 4-year-olds. Finally, all ages responded faster after they had missed the target, whereas only the 4-year-olds were significantly slower following a hit, indicating the disincentive it provided. Nicolson argues that the experimental manipulations have clear differential age effects, but they cannot be the whole cause of improvement in response speed with age, because of the lack of overlap between 4-year-olds and adults.

Reduction of Processing Time

Processing speed can be deceptive because the processing load can be variable and elusive. The amount of information to be processed is found by analyzing the choices or decisions present in the situation. Yet, we have noted many ways in which individuals can reduce the number of decisions, so as to lighten their processing load, and can make small changes in the situation, so as also to reduce the amount of information to be processed. Processing effectiveness thus can be increased if processing time can be reduced to make processing time available for other processing requirements.

Perhaps the most obvious way to reduce processing time is to *increase certainty*, which in processing terminology is called *redundancy*. The less we know about incoming stimuli, the more processing time we will need to analyze and organize this uncertain input. When input is known or easily recognized, less processing time is needed. Also, the larger and more varied our knowledge base is, the more likely it is that we will need less processing time, because we will know more of what we encounter. Another aid is to arrange to make our movements in a familiar situation in which we will have more redundant or certain input to process. For example, children must process a large amount of input when first riding, pedaling, and steering a bicycle. But their overall processing time can be reduced by being in a familiar area that is level, has no other moving objects in sight, and does not require a precise control of movements to drive through gates and avoid obstacles.

Better processing skills also save processing time because more information is processed in less time. Examples are the use of expectancy probabilities to focus attention and processing time on the events most likely to occur, and the ability to process input in larger units or chunks. Improved movement performance also may save processing time because less movement information may be created in more efficient movements and we know better what to expect.

Reducing processing time is a useful way to think about developing processing abilities. Processing speed focuses our attention on processing faster and faster without considering how we improve our speed and how we process information. If we can save processing time, then we do not necessarily need to process faster. The importance of focusing on the reduction of processing time is that it pertains to how processing abilities change and improve.

Direct Perception

At the beginning of this chapter, we presented a traditional view of information processing in which individuals must "work" on available sensory input in order to use it. This view is called *indirect perception* by Michaels and Carello (1981), who offer an alternative view of *direct perception* in which perceiving and doing are directly linked, without the need for complicated processing operations.

Basic to any view of perception is what information is available to individuals, how is it obtained, and how is it used. Michaels and Carello believe that indirect perception deals with these questions in several ways. First, it assumes that the senses have an impoverished view of the world. Therefore, processing or transformations must take place in order to make meaning out of the display. Second, because of this impoverished view of the world, the stimulus input from the environment must be processed. Perceptual and cognitive operations must therefore intervene constructively, by detecting, selecting, attending, remembering, and decision making. Third, perceiving is the sampling of sensory input and is limited to one moment in time. Perception is in the present, and the present is a discrete moment, which creates the problem of how to relate one time sample to another. Indirect perception performs this function, with memory as the internal mechanism. Fourth, perceiving and acting are different entities in indirect perception. The environment is seen, elaborated, and transformed by the individual to establish a basis for acting. The movement is then made by using any one of a number of control systems.

The idea of direct perception evolved from Gibson's (1966) work on perception, to provide very different ways of answering these questions. Gibson begins by using *information* to denote a structure that specifies an environment to an individual. Information is not defined as single-instance images or stimulus patterns waiting to be transformed, as the processing theorists stipulate, but as complex structures of higher-order patterns of stimulation over time. Stimulation specifies the environment, and no elaboration is needed. This means that in direct perception, perceptual richness comes with the structure (information), whereas in indirect perception, perceptual richness can be obtained only through elaborations performed by processing operations.

Information in a Gibsonian view is composed of *events* rather than objects isolated in time and space. Perception is not limited to the present instant captured by a retinal snapshot, and the information and the events it specifies last over time. Thus, perception is continuously knowing the environment. Michaels and Carello (1981) outline two differences in the concept of time between the direct perception and the information-processing viewpoints. First, direct perception does not distinguish among past, present, and future. Perception is unfolding events, rather than snapshot instances, which blurs any distinctions among past, present, and future. Second, absolute time has little value to direct perception theorists. Events are their unit of analysis, and they are determined by space and time. Perception is the continuous detection of information that can describe or specify an event of unlimited temporal extent. Figure 12-7 shows the distinction between indirect and direct modes of perceiving events and stimuli.

An important consideration in direct perception is the assertion that in order to study movement in the environment, the minimal system of analysis must be a coalition of mover and environment. This is similar to our perspective in Chapter 1 in which we discussed a movement situation as the interplay of mover and environment to create a movement task and a movement solution. Direct perception, however, does not involve the processing operations suggested as necessary in our analyses of movement situations. Two important concepts of invariants and affordances are offered in direct perception to explain the coalition of mover and environment.

If patterns of stimulation persist over time and space and do not need embellishment, then stimulation will be invariantly tied to the environmental source. *Invariants* or stimulation patterns that do not change over time and space underlie the persistent properties of the environment that an individual knows. An example

**FIGURE
12-7**

Indirect Perception

The ball flight is seen as a succession of occurrences, each with its own stimulus.
The batter must put the separate occurrences together to form the total ball flight.

Direct Perception

The ball flight is seen as one event, such that information occurs over time
and coexists with the event. The batter has only to detect the event as
specified by the environment.

Indirect and direct modes of perceiving a ball pitched to a batter.

is the perceptual constancy outlined in Chapter 10, the phenomenon in which
the perceived properties of an object, such as size, remain constant, even though
the retinal image changes. An indirect approach says that the organism uses
mediating processes to compensate for the changing image size. For direct perception, the answer lies in the properties of the stimulation which has an invariance accompanying the objects' persistent properties. Within the changes in
stimulation there are invariant patterns that provide the basis for perceptual constancy. Michaels and Corello (1981, p. 40) state that "invariants come from the
lawful relations between objects, places, and events in the environment . . . and
the structure or manner of change of patterns of light, sound, skin deformation,
joint configuration and so on." Invariants specify objects, places, and events in
the environment and are necessary for any information to be specified. But environmental invariants are not sufficient without considering the individual.

The individual is necessary because not all invariants are ecologically significant
enough to permit or guide adaptive behavior. Also, an individual's activities make
available additional information. The integrating concept is that of *affordances*
to denote behavior permitted by the environment. Affordances are what the environment means to an individual and describe an environment with reference
to an individual. Gibson (1977, p. 67) calls an affordance "a specific combination
of the properties of a substance and its surfaces with reference to an animal."
Affordances are what a situation offers to an animal or person. For example, when
the properties of an object are seen as rigid, level, extended, and at "knee height,"
an individual recognizes that the object affords sitting. The separate properties
by themselves do not afford sitting; it is only when they are seen together that

the affordance is recognized. This can be appreciated by changing only the property of "knee height" so that the same object now affords leaning with the hands at shoulder level for a 3-year-old, affords crawling under for a baby of 9 months, and affords landing for a bird. The concept of affordances has been extended to a larger match of species and environment called a *niche*. Humans fit into particular niches that contain affordances relevant to humans. Other animals will fit into different niches; thus air affords flying for birds but does not do so for humans. Turvey, Shaw, and Mace (1978) characterize a niche as when "a situation or an event *x* affords an activity *y* for an animal *z* if only, and only if, *x* and *z* are mutually compatible."

An example adapted by Walder (1981) from Turvey (1977) describes a movement activity from a direct perception point of view. A soccer ball is passing a player and affords interception. In the player's field of view, the soccer ball is projected as a constantly changing pattern onto the optic array. The player's visual mechanisms detect those characteristics in the field of view that change over time and those that do not. The former specify the ball in terms of distance, speed, and projected path, and the latter identify the object as a soccer ball and as an object to be intercepted. To someone unfamiliar with soccer, it might afford interception with the hands rather than the feet. Babies and young children would detect characteristics that change over time, but probably less efficiently than older children and adults would. Invariant characteristics, however, might not afford interception.

We have outlined direct perception as an alternative theory of perception that does not involve processing information. This means that an environment's perceptual richness is obtained directly, without the need for intervening perceptual and cognitive operations to elaborate sensory input. Direct perception focuses on the larger occurrence of events and how the change and lack thereof in sensory displays lead to the recognition of invariants. It sees the mover and the environment as a coalition in which the environment affords certain behaviors. The theory of direct perception has been used to suggest new and radical explanations of how movement is produced, and we recommend its careful study as a contrast with more established points of view.

Chapter Summary

At the beginning of this chapter we asked how the ability to process information develops in children. This question is really part of a much larger issue of how perceptual-cognitive abilities develop. We have been selective in our presentation, with an eye to models and findings that can be applied to the development of movement control.

A general and quite obvious point is that children improve both quantitatively and qualitatively in their ability to process information. Older children and young adults are quantitatively better in processing more in less time and in processing better in continuous and multiple (simultaneous) situations than are young children. Qualitative distinctions are apparent, because older children and young adults are better at using control operations, which enables them to plan ahead and use different strategies, such as search, selection, and rehearsal. The general payoff, as processing ability improves, is that individuals can participate more adequately in situations in which more things happen more rapidly and more continuously. Viewed in another way, individuals have available more processing time to permit them to enter more complicated and more rapidly occurring situations.

Processing speed and control operations were separated for instructional purposes, whereas they are merely two ways of looking at the same phenomenon of improvement in processing ability. Processing requirements can be reduced by ruling out alternatives, recognizing larger chunks or pieces of information, and employing other, more advanced uses of control operations. This means that less processing time is needed and that processing speed is improved. Reducing processing time was suggested as another way to view the development of processing ability, because this focuses our thinking on how processing changes and improves with age. Two ways to reduce processing time are to increase certainty (redundancy) and improve processing skills.

Information processing was defined in general terms as the way in which individuals attain, retain, and transform knowledge. Memory, control operations, and allocation of attention were discussed from different perspectives to consider how processing occurs. We examined Brown's perspective (1975) of knowing as the core of the development of processing ability. She states that an individual's knowledge base at any point in time provides what is known and can be recognized with minimal processing time, and what can be used to deal with unknown occurrences. She sees developmental change as level differences and pattern differences which are related to the need for processing strategies and episodic or semantic memory and to limitations on the use of strategies because of production deficiencies or mediation deficiencies.

Processing is a complicated function that has been studied in many different ways. The radical approach of direct perception was reviewed in the final section to provide an alternative view in which processing operations are ignored in favor of a more direct perceptual relationship between the individual and the environment. We currently do not have a clear and detailed understanding of how individuals read their environments and use their readings in producing movements; the best we can do for now is to keep the general themes in mind as we consider next the development of movement control in relation to the development of processing abilities.

CHAPTER 13

Information Processing and Development of Movement Control

Movement skill development depends, in a variety of ways, on increased processing skills. Development of sensory-perceptual systems and processing capabilities was detailed in previous chapters and will now be related to development of movement control. Additionally, we will examine selected issues in motor control to consider information processing in movement execution.

Processing Information

As they grow older, children develop more proficient processing abilities. This proficiency encompasses skills in memory, attention, and general processing abilities, together with better performance when speed is required. Children also develop strategies that aid in attaining, retaining, and transforming information. These strategies and their appropriate use become part of children's knowledge base and allow them to approach tasks differently and to process more quickly and more efficiently. In short, older children possess more processing resources.

Spatial and temporal accuracy requirements of movements increase the processing load in a number of ways, including the need to make a more precise movement and to coincide movements and external events. Also, a mover must make continuous corrections, which are more of a processing problem for the poor mover who creates large movement errors to be corrected. The mover's resources can be exceeded when needing to process too much information, as when reading complex and abstract situations, making continuous, simultaneous, and precise movements to coincide with external events, and correcting accumulated movement errors.

General Processing Abilities

Recognizing that processing abilities increase with age and noting again the interplay of environment and individual, it is logical to assume that tasks have processing requirements that match or are congruent with the processing abilities of some children more than for those of other children. Put another way, children at a particular level of processing ability will find some tasks just demanding enough, whereas other tasks will be too easy, and still others will be too difficult. This reasoning was used by Temple and Williams (1977), who classified the information-processing characteristics of a group of children and then measured their performance and learning on tasks with different information-processing requirements. They hypothesized that the children would perform at a higher level and would learn more quickly if their information-processing abilities matched the information-processing requirements of the movement tasks.

A group of sixty sixth-grade children was divided into high, middle, and low processors of visual and proprioceptive information. The processing tests for vision included static and dynamic depth perception, embedded figures, and mirror tracing and for proprioception included movement reproduction, static and dynamic balancing, and stabilometer performance. Each child was tested on a pursuit rotor as a task using both vision and proprioception and then was assigned randomly to either a moderate proprioceptive task requiring performance on an obstacle course or a high proprioceptive task using the same obstacle course with specific targets to touch, thus making the movement requirements more precise.

On the pursuit rotor, both the high visual and the high proprioceptive processors had better scores than did the middle processors, who in turn had better scores than the low processors did. There were no differences in obstacle course performance in regard to the processing levels, except that the high proprioceptive processors had better scores on the obstacle course with specific targets to touch. The rate of task mastery or learning did not vary in regard to the processing level, but there was some indication that the level of task mastery was higher when the processors were matched to the task requirements.

This type of study does support the notion that matching processing abilities and task requirements should produce the best results, but it does not offer any substantive theory as to how processing abilities function in relation to task requirements. One attempt to do this has utilized neo-Piagetian theory (Pascual-Leone 1970) which predicts children's performance on the basis of certain aspects of their general processing ability. The theory evolved from cognitive studies, but more recently it has been used in studying movement development. As outlined in Chapter 12, a task is first analyzed for demand on mental capacity, which Pascual-Leone calls M-demand, from Piaget's substages of intellectual development (see Table 12-1). Children are viewed as differing in *mental space* structure and function. On the one hand, between age groups, the children will differ on *structural mental space* (Ms), and so those with higher Ms spaces will perform better on those tasks that demand a higher Ms space. On the other hand, within age groups, the children are differentiated according to *functional mental space* (Mf space), and so children classified as high Mf processors should perform better than low Mf processors on tasks commensurate with their Ms space.

A major difficulty in testing neo-Piagetian theory is measuring Ms space and Mf space and the task's M-demands. The work of Todor (1978, 1979) is described in Box 13-1 as an example of how M-demand has been analyzed for a movement task. The measurements of Ms and Mf space are described in Todor's papers, but his cited sources should be consulted for a more complete description. Todor's findings and analyses offer preliminary support for the idea that processing abilities, in the form of Mf (functional) space, are important when M-demands are similar to available Ms (structural) space. Thomas and his associates (Thomas and Bender 1977, Gerson and Thomas 1977, 1978) reported findings from similar experiments that support the predictions of neo-Piagetian theory. They used a variety of tasks, including curvilinear positioning and stabilometer balancing, and suggest an unidentified cognitive strategy for the retention of task relevant cues as a possible explanation for increased Mf space.

Not all studies have supported the predictions made by neo-Piagetian theory. Connell (1980) tested eighty children (ages 5 to 8) on simple and choice reaction time, short-term memory, and schema learning. She found that Ms and Mf space were of more value in explaining performance and learning differences on tasks requiring more complex processing. The predictions did not hold for simple reaction time or short-term memory tasks; predictions for choice reaction time and schema learning, however, were found, but they were not definite. Connell discusses some of the issues in applying neo-Piagetian theory to movement skills.

**BOX
13-1**

A NEO-PIAGETIAN ANALYSIS OF TASK REQUIREMENTS AND MOVER RESOURCES, AS RELATED TO MOVEMENT PERFORMANCE

The work of Todor (1978, 1979) shows how a movement task's M-demand can be analyzed into its constituent schemes. Todor used a modified Rho task, which is moving a crank handle around to a bumper, letting go, and moving the hand forward to knock down a target, as shown in Figure 13-1. Todor analyzed effective performance on the task as using three schemes: (1) movement to the target, (2) knowledge that the hand is open, and (3) location of the target. The least efficient strategy, which should produce the slowest movement, is one in which the three schemes are chained together as three separate, consecutive movements: rotate, open the hand, and move to the target. This *movement strategy* has an M-demand of only 1. Chaining two or more movements together involves more complex movement strategies and increases the M-demand to M = 2 or M = 3.

Todor used neo-Piagetian theory and his analysis of M-demand for the Rho task to make several predictions:

1. Children at ages 5 and 6 (Ms = 2) do not have sufficient Ms (structural) space to integrate the three parts of the Rho task (M-demand = 3).
2. Children at age 7 and older (Ms $\geq$ 3) do have sufficient Ms space to integrate the three parts of the Rho task (M-demand = 3). However, the movement strategy they use will depend on their Mf (functional) space.
3. The more that Ms space exceeds the task's M-demand, the less influence that Mf space will have.

Subjects were 114 children, ages 5 to 12. Mf space was measured by using two Piagetian tasks. Thirty trials were given, with the mean of the last five trials used to represent the final performance. Latencies were recorded for four component parts of the Rho movement: reaction time, the time to move through the circular phase and hit the bumper, the length of the delay caused by hitting the bumper, and the time from hitting the bumper to knocking down the target. These performance times were analyzed to define the extent to which the movement was integrated. Todor used cluster analysis to find four performance groups or typologies. One cluster of children was superior to all the others in more efficiently mobilizing the three schemes. Table 13-1 breaks down by age group this cluster's composition.

The percentage of children exhibiting the mature profile increased almost in a linear fashion. Some younger children, presumably with less Ms space, achieved the most efficient mobilization of the three schemes. Todor reported that these higher-achieving younger children had better Mf scores than did their agemates, a possible reason for their better use of their Ms space,

Todor argues that his findings support his hypotheses. Ms space seems to limit the younger children in performing the Rho task in a more integrative manner, whereas

**FIGURE
13-1**

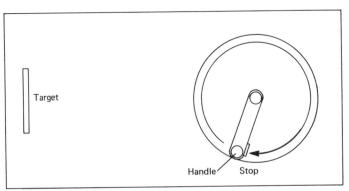

Rho task in which the subject grasps the handle, turns it clockwise to the stop, releases it, and moves forward to touch the target.

346

the older children's increased Ms space is sufficient to achieve the movement integration without considering the level of Mf space. The critical test of Todor's position is that the children in the middle age period have sufficient Ms space but will vary in their achieving movement integration of several schemes, depending on their Mf space. His findings are in the direction he predicts for the middle age period.

Todor presents some interesting ways to measure and analyze the constructs of Ms, Mf, and M-demand. We now need replications and variations of this paradigm to test the strength of these propositions and to look further into these findings.

TABLE 13-1	Efficient Task Integration by Age Group*	
		Percent with
	Age	*Mature Profile*
	11–12	100
	9–10	79
	7–8	42
	5–6	9

*Based on data from Todor 1978.

She points out that there are difficulties in separating the two mental spaces, and she questions whether the tests for Ms space really tap a structural capacity uninfluenced by control processes (Mf space). It is difficult to assign schemes to movement tasks, especially when the environment and performer are moving.

High- and low-processing groups both within and between ages have been compared on a variety of movement tasks. Both neo-Piagetian theory and other methods, such as the one used by Temple and Williams (1977), have had some success in relating children's general processing abilities to their performance on selected movement tasks. The argument that there are general processing abilities on which children can be differentiated and which then can be used for prediction purposes on movement tasks is very attractive. A general processing ability is not unlike Brown's (1975) category of memory called "knowing," but there seems to be a difference in the way each is used. Brown's knowing is the general knowledge that gives children a base and background to approach a variety of tasks. A general processing ability, though similar, has been used more often on a specific task for predictive purposes. As a methodological approach, it is a good idea to classify subjects by their processing abilities rather than by their chronological age; yet because of their global nature, general processing abilities are difficult to unravel. The main flow of research is now geared toward uncovering task-specific control operations or strategies rather than underlying general abilities. The application of Pascual-Leone's theory to movement behavior is an interesting attempt to explain the development of increasingly mature processing abilities. But the lack of clarity of some of the concepts and difficulties encountered in testing the theory indicates that our immediate task is to define and study control operations that are explicitly or implicitly part of all of the processing approaches to movement behavior.

Memory

In Chapter 12 we stated that children's memory improves with age as a result of their greater overall knowledge, their increasing use of strategies, and their growing awareness of memory. There is every reason to believe that the same concepts apply to movement. However, important though memory must be to movement,

347

the study of memory and movement has been confined to quite a narrow perspective. Studies have been limited primarily to a multistore view of memory in regard to movement performance and adults' learning, with relatively few studies of children. Work with short-term memory paradigms, though, has given us some insights into the memory processes involved in movement.

Studies of short-term motor memory (STMM) have usually been of blindfolded subjects making a criterion movement by moving an arm a designated distance on a linear or curvilinear track (see Figure 13-2). The criterion movement can be performed in active, passive, or constrained movement modes (as for the kinesthetic measurements in Chapter 10). After returning their arm to a starting position and waiting a certain length of time, the subjects attempt to reproduce the criterion movement. The waiting time is varied to provide different lengths of retention intervals in which the subjects must keep the criterion movement in memory. Retention intervals may be unfilled to allow them to concentrate on and presumably *rehearse* the motor memory of the criterion movement, or they may be filled with a second task to be done as a way of trying to disrupt the retention of the memory of the criterion movement. Because the subjects are blindfolded, they receive only proprioceptive information about the criterion movement. Vision sometimes is available, but it is limited because environmental

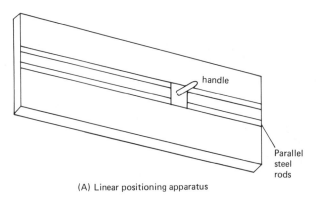

(A) Linear positioning apparatus

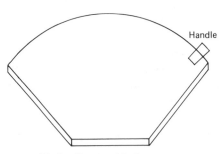

(B) Curvilinear positioning apparatus

Limb positioning apparatuses. Both apparatuses can be used with the same experimental paradigm. Subjects perform a criterion movement in an active, passive, or constrained mode, while blindfolded or with environmental cues concealed or masked. After a period of delay, which can be filled or unfilled, subjects are asked to reproduce or recognize the criterion movement.

348

cues must be masked when the subjects are not blindfolded. Schmidt (1982) explains that this general methodology was common in the early and middle 1970s but is seldom used today because researchers want to advance beyond slow, stereotyped movements and the retention of sensory information. Nonetheless, the research in this earlier time added substantially to our understanding of motor control.

Researchers initially questioned whether STMM followed the same laws as verbal short-term memory did. Their early findings somewhat contradicted the verbal studies, with Adams and Dykstra (1966) and Posner and Konick (1966) failing to find the rehearsal of movement tasks over an unfilled retention interval. Verbal memory, but not motor memory, was differentially affected by the difficulty of the second task used in the filled retention interval. Some of the earlier inconsistencies, however, were explained by the finding that different encoding processes were used for different reproduction cues, particularly location and distance cues. Location cues are those from the final location where the limb movement finishes; distance cues are concerned with how far the limb travels in space. Probably the most comprehensive study of these cues was by Laabs (1973), who found that location information was retained during an unfilled retention interval, whereas distance information decayed over a 12-second period, whether or not rehearsal was allowed. Laabs proposed two types of STMM: one in which proprioceptive information could be coded as long as there was access to the central processing space for rehearsal or other use of other control operations, and one in which proprioceptive information was lost spontaneously. The review by Laabs and Simmons (1981) provides a current and critical view of STMM studies.

There have been only a few studies of the development of movement memory in children, and these have been concerned mainly with mnemonic strategies, such as rehearsal. Sugden (1978, 1980a) examined the development of rehearsal in the visual-motor and motor memory of normal and mentally retarded boys. The two studies are described in Box 13-2, and the general pattern of results for normal children is shown in Figure 13-3. Sugden's studies confirm that on visual-motor and motor tasks, as on verbal tasks, a characteristic feature of immature memorizers is the lack of spontaneous use of control operations, such as rehearsal. Immature memorizers include both normal children who are young in age and mentally retarded children who are young in mental functioning.

Reid (1980b) also found evidence for rehearsal by 10- and 16-year old normal children on a STMM task, with retarded children not showing evidence of rehearsal. In a second study, Reid (1980a) attempted to aid memory in retarded children by teaching them a mnemonic strategy. The teaching was successful, with retarded children being more acccurate in an instructional condition than in a noninstructional condition. Reid suggested that the problem was a production deficiency, as discussed in Chapter 12, because training resulted in improved performance.

Kelso and colleagues (1979) allowed mentally retarded children to select their own movement to reproduce, rather than having the experimenter fix the movement criterion. In a series of three experiments, they found rehearsal in 12-year-old mentally retarded children, which was shown when performance in a rest condition was better than performance after an interpolated activity. They suggested, therefore, that active involvement in producing the criterion movement aided retention and might help overcome a production deficiency. Reid (1980a)

BOX
13-2

REHEARSAL IN SHORT-TERM MOVEMENT MEMORY (STMM)

Sugden (1978, 1980a) used a linear positioning task to investigate the development of rehearsal in short-term movement memory (STMM). The first study (1978) was conducted with full vision, but visual cues were eliminated by having only the lever handle visible in a plain, unmarked test area. Vision was limited in the second study (1980a) by a blindfold. Sugden tested visual-motor (1978) and motor memory (1980a).

A different group of normal boys, ages 6, 9, and 12, was tested in each study. Mentally retarded boys, matched for mental age, were tested only in the first study (1978). The task was to reproduce a criterion distance (20, 25, 30, or 35 centimeters) performed in an active movement mode. After making a criterion movement, one of four test conditions was used before reproduction of the criterion movement was attempted. The time interval between the criterion movement and the reproduction movement was 10 seconds or 30 seconds, and the boys were asked either to do nothing (rest) or to count backwards (interpolated activity). Conditions were randomized so that each boy attempted to reproduce a criterion distance after a 10-second rest, a 10-second period of interpolated activity, a 30-second rest, and a 30-second period of interpolated activity.

The interpolated activity of counting backwards was adjusted to have a boy count backwards by ones if a pretest indicated that this was difficult and demanding. Some boys counted backwards by threes because counting by ones or twos did not seem to occupy enough of their processing capacity. Boys in the rest condition were not interrupted and were free to rehearse the information just gathered while making the criterion movement. The 30-second time interval created the possibility of memory loss or decay, as compared with a 10-second time interval.

The pattern of results for absolute error for the normal boys in the two studies is shown in Figure 13-3. The pattern for variable error was similar, with no trend for constant error. The pattern of results also was slightly better for the visual-motor task of positioning the lever with vision on an unmarked apparatus than for the motor task of positioning the level while blindfolded.

Notice that the 6-year-old normal boys had similar mean error scores in the interpolated activity condition of counting backwards and in the rest condition of no secondary activity. This contrasts with the older normal boys, ages 9 and 12, who had

FIGURE
13-3

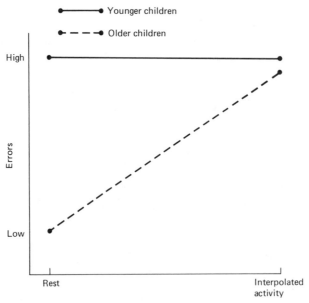

A general representation of the development of a rehearsal strategy in normal children when doing a visual–motor or a motor task following two different retention interval conditions.

lower mean error scores during the rest condition. The inference is that the older boys rehearsed during the rest conditions to improve their performance, whereas the younger boys did not rehearse, because the interruption of the interpolated activity did not decrease their performance.

The boys were asked at the end of their participation how they tried to reproduce the movement. This was an effort to study their metamemory or what they knew about how they remembered something. The 12-year-old boys were able to tell the experimenter the methods they thought they were using to remember the criterion movement. But the metamemory responses of the 6- and 9-year-old boys did not differ from each other and were not informative. Although no metamemory changes were noted between age 6 and age 9, this does not necessarily mean that changes were not taking place. A possiblity is that boys at age 6 and age 9 knew more about their memory processes than they could verbalize.

Retardates were tested only on the visual-motor task. They were not different from normals on the interpolated activity condition, and their performance did not improve on the rest condition. This indicates that like 6-year-old normal boys, they were not rehearsing. The retardates at all ages did not answer the metamemory questions in meaningful ways.

noted, however, that the retarded children in these experiments were instructed to remember the movement's end location and suggests that they may have been directed unintentionally to rehearse and, thus, may not have been spontaneously producing a rehearsal strategy.

Movement memory for location and distance was tested in a large-scale environment, by having children (ages 4 to 12) jog (run) through a course and then recall the location or distance of an event (Thomas et al. 1983). Location information appeared to be more automatically encoded than distance information was. Effortful processing, such as rehearsal, seems to be needed for distance information. The spontaneous use of strategies to remember distance also increased across age. The results from the two experiments in this study are similar to the findings from the arm-positioning movements in laboratory studies.

Another strategy in movement memory was suggested by Corlett and Dickinson (1983), who found that older children sometimes could use a strategy of "directed forgetting" to block out irrelevant movement information when trying to reproduce a movement. Based on a series of studies of tactile and movement memory in blind and sighted children, Millar (1974, 1975b, 1978) concluded that strategies are indeed used in memory for movement. She believes that the children's use of these strategies depends on their access to central processing space.

From the few studies of children's memory for movement we can make several general conclusions. First, very young children seem to have few and unsophisticated processing strategies. The acquisition of processing strategies seems to be a developmental process, but strategies sometimes can be taught. Second, crucial to the effectiveness of these strategies is access to central processing space; if this is denied, the strategies will not be spontaneously produced, and the developmental differences will be minimal. Finally, the use of these strategies by mature memorizers leads to improved performance.

The research on memory described thus far has been on short-term memory paradigms. These are relatively easy studies to design, and their confounding variables are easier to control than in studies of memory over long periods of time. As a result, we have less information about movement tasks involving long-term memory (LTM). The work on long-term memory with adults has shown movement tasks to be particularly resistant to decay. Fleishman and Parker (1962), for example, tested subjects on a compensatory tracking task at 9, 14, or 24 months after the original practice session. There was no appreciable loss in performance, even after 24 months. The relative permanence of achievement on continuous tasks is confirmed by everday observations of movement tasks such as swimming and cycling. But there does seem to be evidence that forgetting on discrete tasks is considerable (Neumann and Ammons 1957). Schmidt (1982) thinks that this is because discrete tasks contain more verbal-cognitive components than continuous ones do and that verbal-cognitive components are more quickly forgotten than motor components are. Schmidt also asks what the retention characteristics would be of a discrete task that is highly motor rather than verbal-cognitive.

The study of children's long-term retention of movement tasks presents quite formidable research design problems and an interesting paradox. The main difficulty is the intermingling of learning and development. For example, if 6-year-old children were limited to a period of 3 weeks to learn to ride a bicycle, they probably would be reasonably proficient in riding and controlling it, except when going fast in a rapidly changing environment. But what would happen if these children did not ride a bicycle again for 5 years? On the one hand, they would lose a great deal: 5 years with no practice, on top of a short practice period resulting in only a moderate level of achievement. On the other hand, 11-year-olds have much more going for them than 6-year-olds do. They have a larger movement vocabulary, have more strategies that can be used more efficiently, and have more experience with a wider range of movement tasks and movement situations. Over this period of time it is very difficult indeed to study retention and related memory functions. An obvious possibility is to use shorter time spans to lessen the impact of development, but the shorter the time span is, the less one will be able to assess long-term retention. Longitudinal studies with different practice experiences is another possibility, but such studies are extremely expensive and difficult to control.

Processing Capacity

A basic tenet of most views of processing is that there is a limited capacity that can be variably allocated as needed. Developmental changes in capacity limitation and capacity allocation also are expected. Both of these concepts apply to the whole processing system and affect the execution of and the preparation for movement and provide a division in our review of processing capacity as related to the development of movement control. We have seen that access to central processing space is crucial to the use of memory strategies, and later we shall detail its importance in the execution of movement.

Capacity Limitations. The system's capacity limitations are discussed in Chapter 12 in regard to the various ways to measure processing capacity. The general expectation is that an increase in information load will lead to the use of more processing time. Processing time is measured as reaction time if the information is needed to initiate or prepare for a movement and as movement time if the information is required to execute a movement. Reaction time is a function of uncertainty related to the number of stimuli and response choices to be identified and organized before a movement is initiated. Movement time is a function of movement distance and movement accuracy, in that the variation in distance and accuracy requirements will change the information load related to the control of movement. The motor system's capacity to function at different information loads has been studied extensively in regard to movement time. A small set of studies of children is a starting point for examining the development of the motor system's capacity.

Fitts proposed in 1954 that movement time varies in relation to movement distance and accuracy. His formula for this relationship has been tested and supported in so many conditions that it now is called Fitts law. Modifications have been proposed (Welford 1968), and Sheridan (1979) questioned whether any simple formula can account for the complexities of human movement control. But the data and analyses from studying Fitts Law have been of great benefit in studying processing requirements during rapid movements. Fitts law is explained in Box 13-3 along with two methods for measuring the motor system's capacity.

The general findings for the movement speed of children doing reciprocal and discrete tapping tasks are shown in Figure 13-4. The index of difficulty is the part of Fitts law representing the extent of difficulty in changes in movement amplitude (distance) and target width (accuracy). Movement time, as expected, is less for adults at any level of difficulty, and older children have smaller movement times than younger children do. Children's and adults' movement times increase as difficulty increases, because more information must be processed to control movement over a longer distance and/or control movement accuracy to contact a smaller target. An important and unresolved question is whether children have relatively greater increases in movement time as level of difficulty increases. Group B is one possibility in which younger children are slower, but the increases in processing requirements are not relatively more difficult for them. Group A is a second possibility in which increases in processing requirements are relatively more difficult for them, as if younger children are less able to adjust to the larger processing loads. That is, the capacity of their motor system may be limited so that larger processing loads are relatively more difficult for them than for older children and adults.

Two ways of defining and measuring the motor system's capacity are described in Box 13-3. The first measure of capacity is the amount of information use per unit of time, which is the index of difficulty (ID) divided by movement time, or ID/MT. Younger children clearly have less capacity in this absolute sense of information used per second, because their movement time is larger at each level of difficulty. The older children (Group C) also use less information than the adults (Group D) do at each level of difficulty. Sugden's findings (1980b) are listed in Table 13-2 to show the increase in capacity with age for both serial (reciprocal) and discrete (single) tapping tasks. There was little overlap between ages, and each group stayed within a narrow range on both tasks. Twelve-year-olds at their maximum capacity values overlapped the adults' minimum levels on both discrete and serial tasks, as reported by Fitts (1954) and Fitts and Peterson (1964).

The second measure of capacity is the reciprocal of the slope of the regression line, or 1 / b. This is the capacity to adjust to increases in processing loads, which addresses the important and unresolved question we posed earlier. Note that a larger value for 1 / b indicates a greater capacity for adjusting to increases in processing loads. The findings from two studies (Salmoni and Pascoe 1978, Sugden 1980b) are presented in Table 13-3 to illustrate the differences in findings for younger children. The values for 1 / b differ in the two studies because of the length of the trials and other procedural differences. The important concern is the value of 1 / b among the groups in each study. Group values are quite similar in Sugden's study, indicating that the slopes of the regression lines are similar,

BOX
13-3

FITTS LAW AND THE CAPACITY OF THE MOTOR SYSTEM

Adults' movement time was determined by Fitts (1954) to vary in relation to movement distance and movement accuracy. Fitts law states that more movement time is needed to move farther and touch a small target than is needed to move a shorter distance and touch a larger target. Its formal statement is $MT = a + b \log_2 \frac{2A}{W}$, where A is movement amplitude (distance), and W is target width (accuracy). The terms a and b in Fitts law are constants, with a being where the equation line crosses the Y (vertical) axis and b being the slope of that line. Recall that the amount of information in reaction time is $\log_2 N$, where N is the number of choices. The amount of information in Fitts law is defined by $\log_2 \frac{2A}{W}$. Distance to travel (A) and width of the target (W) are the variables that determine the amount of information present in the execution of a movement task. Another way to express Fitts law is that movement time (MT) varies linearly with the logarithm of the index of difficulty $(\log_2 \frac{2A}{W})$. The index of difficulty is the information load for a movement that has been shown to vary in relation to movement amplitude and target width.

Different combinations of amplitude (A) and width (W) are listed to illustrate how the index of difficulty (ID) changes in relation to changes in A and W.

A	W	2A/W	ID
8	4	16 / 4 = 4	2
4	2	8 / 2 = 4	2
8	2	16 / 2 = 8	3
8	1	16 / 1 = 16	4

ID is 2 when A is 8 and W is 4, because $2A / W = 4$ and $\log_2 4 = 2$. If A is reduced to 4 and W to 2, ID will not change. A smaller target width of 2 will increase MT, but this is counterbalanced by reducing the movement distance. ID increases to 3 when A increases to 8 and W remains 2. ID is further increased to 4 by keeping A at 8 and decreasing W to 1.

Fitts law has been tested most often with a reciprocal tapping task in which a person taps back and forth between two targets for a designated time. Apparatuses have been constructed to make it possible to vary amplitude and width, as well as automatically record tapping counts and errors. Other movement tasks have been used, such as fitting pegs into hoies or placing washers over pegs (Langolf et al., 1976). Single, discrete movements also have been tested by measuring MT for a single tap rather than for a series of reciprocal tapping movements. The pattern of findings is shown in Figure 13-4 and is discussed in the text.

Fitts law has been used in two different ways to estimate the motor system's capacity. The two methods of measuring capacity have produced conflicting developmental trends, which is not surprising because each measures a different aspect. Fitts and Peterson (1964) defined the capacity of the motor system as the *amount of information used per second*, which is expressed as the index of difficulty divided by movement time, or ID/MT. When movement time becomes faster (lower) for a particular information load, then capacity, as measured by this method, increases. For example, a group of children with a mean MT of 800 milliseconds on a task with an ID of 4 have a capacity of 5 bits per second (4 / .8 = 5). If an older group has a mean MT of 500 milliseconds on the same task, their capacity will be 8 bits per second (4 / .5 = 8). Notice that capacity is calculated separately for each test condition and then is compared among test conditions and different age groups. When comparing age groups for a single test condition, ID remains constant and is the same for each age group, with only MT varying, as shown in our example. Therefore, capacity in these terms increases as MT decreases. In all studies involving children and using this formula for capacity, there has been an increase in capacity with increasing age, because MT decreases with age up to the early adult years. Capacity values will be higher for discrete tasks and cannot be directly compared with capacity values for serial task.

Capacity also is viewed as the *rate of gain of information* that is measured by the reciprocal of the regression slope or $1/b$. Because the slope (b) is less than 1, the reciprocal $(1/b)$ is larger for a shallow slope and smaller for a steeper slope. A shallow slope indicates that MT increases slightly as the information load increases, indicating a higher rate of gain of information, compared with taking a larger amount of time to cope with the increase in information load. If the slopes of the regression lines for groups are the same, as seen for Groups B, C, and D in Figure 13-4, the rate of gain of information will be the same for each group. This means that MT increases as ID increases, but in a similar relationship among the three groups. Group A has a larger rate of increase for MT as ID increases, which is seen as a steeper slope (b) for the regression line and a smaller rate of gain of information $(1/b)$. This means that increases in processing load, as indicated by increases in ID, are relatively more difficult for Group A.

The findings from these two measures of capacity are discussed in the text. The formula of ID/MT must be calculated for each test condition (load), whereas $1/b$ is a single measure representing the general pattern of change across test conditions. Capacity as ID/MT is illustrated in Table 13-2, in which a set of scores shows the absolute level of capacity by age for each test condition. The pattern of change across test conditions is shown in Table 13-3 and is measured by the rate of change in the form of $1/b$.

as illustrated by Groups B, C, and D in Figure 13-4. Group values also are similar in the Salmoni-Pascoe study, except that 6-year-olds have a much lower $1/b$ value and thus a higher slope, as shown by Group A in Figure 13-4. Kerr (1975) reported no slope differences for children to support the Sugden findings, whereas Hay (1981) found slope differences to support the Salmoni-Pascoe findings.

There is no obvious and simple explanation for the discrepancy represented by Groups A and B in Figure 13-4. The tapping tasks and related procedures are similar and do not suggest any explanations. Salmoni and Pascoe tested only

FIGURE 13-4

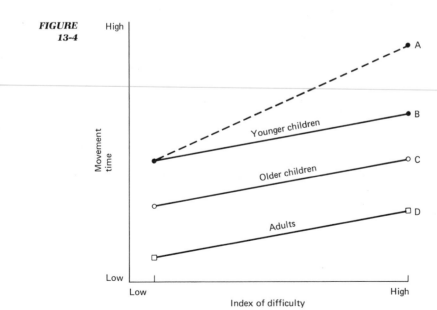

General relationship of movement time and index of difficulty for different age groups.

355

TABLE
13-2

Children's Capacity (ID/MT) on Serial and Discrete Tapping Tasks*

	INDEX OF DIFFICULTY (BITS OF INFORMATION)						
AGE	2	3	3.6	4	4.6	5	5.6
	Serial (Reciprocal) Tapping						
6	3.0	4.8	5.3	5.4	5.5	5.4	5.4
8	4.4	5.6	6.3	6.0	6.5	5.9	6.4
10	6.8	6.9	7.4	7.7	8.4	7.3	7.5
12	7.5	8.9	9.9	8.9	9.3	8.6	8.4
	Discrete (Single) Tap						
6		8.1	8.5	7.3	7.3	7.8	9.3
8		8.5	8.8	9.7	9.5	9.9	10.3
10		10.7	10.9	11.3	10.9	10.9	12.3
12		12.8	13.1	14.1	14.3	14.9	14.7

*Based on data from Sugden 1980b.

girls, but Hay studied both boys and girls. We suggest that the findings from these studies be interpreted in two ways. First, they both agree that older children and adults have similar slopes, which means that increases in processing load are not relatively more difficult for older children, even though their movement time is not as good. Older children have a smaller capacity in an absolute sense, but they adjust to increases in their processing load in a manner similar to the way adults do.

The second concern is the capacity of younger children who have a smaller absolute capacity and may or may not adjust as well to increases in their processing load. The latter may be that the capacity to adjust is marginal for younger children, and so we find a difference in one study and not in another. If there is a difference, we need to examine how younger children adjust. Sugden (1980b) suggests that as they grow older, children may program movements more effectively to function more efficiently with greater information loads. Some children also may need to use more visual correction, as discussed in Chapter 11, which will increase movement time. Adjustment to increases in processing load may be in transition, as seen in Chapter 7, which would identify an important time of change in an important aspect of change.

Another concern about capacity limitations is that changes in distance and accuracy might differentially affect movement time as load increases (Welford et

TABLE
13-3

Capacity on a Reciprocal Tapping Task As Measured by Rate of Gain of Information (1 / b)

	STUDY	
AGE	Salmoni and Pascoe (1978)	Sugden (1980b)
6	7.6	8.9
8		8.1
10	10.6	8.6
12		8.9
14	11.0	
Adults	9.8	

al. 1969). Salmoni and Pascoe (1978) tested this possibility with children by having nine load conditions arranged in two sets to keep either A or W constant.

A HELD CONSTANT			W HELD CONSTANT		
A	*W*	*Load*	*A*	*W*	*Load*
8	4	2	2	1	2
8	2	3	4	1	3
8	1	4	8	1	4
8	0.5	5	16	1	5
8	0.25	6	32	1	6

Notice that the middle condition (8, 1 = 4) of each set is the same, thus providing nine rather than ten load conditions. The middle condition is a common checkpoint in the two load sets, and the same five loads are represented in each. There were no significant differences in performance between the load sets, which means that distance and accuracy did not differentially affect the movement time as the load increased. This supports the robustness of Fitts law and also tells us that children perform in a manner similar to that of adults, although at a lower absolute level of performance. We still must determine whether younger children adjust to load increases as well as older children and adults do. If they do not, inefficient allocation of capacity, our next topic, may be an important factor.

Capacity Allocation. According to the view of attention presented in Chapter 12, there exists a limited amount of attentional capacity, in which processing takes place, and this capacity can be variably allocated to parts of the processing system as needed. If, for example, one part of the visual display is very complex and requires a great deal of attention, other parts of the system, such as those controlling movement, will suffer from a lack of attention unless the movements can be performed adequately and somewhat automatically to require very little attention. A corollary to this is that when young children first acquire a movement pattern, it takes most of their attentional capacity to control the movement, with little attention available for processing the complex visual display. All of this suggests that *time sharing* must exist in some form. Some individuals can do several tasks at once, such as walking, bouncing a ball, and seeing what is happening nearby. A mature adult's processing requirements for these tasks do not exceed the available attentional capacity. But young children trying to perform these tasks simultaneously may exceed the amount of attentional capacity available, which leads to a breakdown of one or more of the tasks. In Chapter 1 we explained how this could happen with other tasks, such as driving. Investigations of dual-task performance are one way to study time sharing in capacity allocation. However, what constitutes a dual task for babies and children is not clear. The general view is that if two actions or processes make separate demands on the pool of attentional capacity, then it is a dual task.

Several researchers have charted the development of performing two tasks simultaneously. Bruner (1970) outlined the action of sucking, which in young infants changes on a week-to-week basis. Sucking has been observed early in fetal development and is a well-established reflexive action at birth which eventually becomes a voluntary behavior. At first, young babies suck with their eyes shut.

If their eyes are open during sucking, object tracking begins and the sucking is disrupted. Around 9 weeks, babies suck in bursts and look up during the pauses. At 3 to 4 months, babies appear to be able to suck and to look up simultaneously, but this may be misleading because looking reduces suction amplitude. Bruner calls this "place holding" to mean maintaining the structure of a more inclusive act while executing the various parts separately. Later, babies can look up and not reduce their suction power, thus achieving a functional dual-task behavior.

As children develop, it is possible to examine their growing repertoire of dual-task behaviors, such as two-handed, or bimanual, action. Bruner (1970) did this by placing a toy in a box with a see-through lid that slid open. An efficient way to obtain the toy is to slide open the lid with one hand and hold it open while reaching for the toy with the other hand. The two hands need to be sequenced with all the constituent parts in order. Bruner observed babies who varied in age from 6 to 17 months and found overall success for 6 percent of the younger group, rising to 37 percent success for the older group. Another illustration of two-handed skill was described in Chapter 3 for the marble game used by Elliott and Connolly (1974, also see Box 3-3). A marble placed on the surface of a tray could be made to roll in directions parallel to the sides of the tray, by moving one knob at a time. To make the marble travel on the diagonal, it was necessary to use both knobs simultaneously. The overall results indicated that younger children could execute individual movements but had difficulty in performing simultaneous or sequential movements. But as they grew older, they became better able to turn the knobs together and with correct timing.

Sugden (1981) used a different dual-task paradigm, which was a modification of a TV game called "Variable Speed Brick Out." A paddle on the TV screen was controlled manually to hit a moving ball against a wall to remove bricks from it. The game objective was to knock down the wall. More than one brick could be knocked out if the ball hit closer to the center than to the edge of the wall. A brick score was continually shown in the bottom left corner of the screen. The dual task was manually controlling the paddle and verbally calling out the score. The score calling was to take place immediately after the ball hit the wall and before the next ball was hit. Children, ages 7 and 12, were tested in two different conditions. Group A in each age group had five practice trials (five balls per trial) of the single task of controlling the paddle to hit the balls before transferring to five trials of the dual task of controlling the paddle and calling out the brick score. Group B in each age group was a control group that did the dual task for each of the ten trials. In an attempt to control for the level of task difficulty, the ball was programmed to travel slower for the 7-year-olds than for the 12-year-olds. But as shown in Figure 13-5, the older children performed much better than the younger children did, even though the older children were hitting a faster moving ball.

The older children in Group A rapidly improved in the practice trials when controlling the paddle without having to call out the brick score. But their performance on the sixth trial dropped below the level of the older children in Group B when transferred to the dual task of controlling the paddle and calling out the score. Group A's older children also improved rapidly during the transfer trials, to perform as well on the ninth and tenth trials as the control group did, who performed the dual task on all the trials. The older children clearly did better when doing the single task, and they adjusted quickly when changing to the dual task. A somewhat similar pattern of change was reported for the younger children,

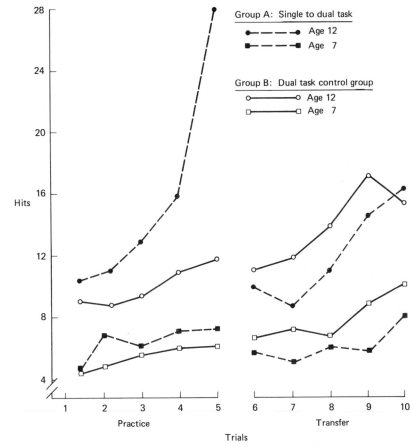

Number of hits per trial when practicing a single task and transfering to a dual task.
(Reproduced with the permission of Sugden, 1981.)

but the differences were quite small when comparing the practice trials of Groups A and B and the transfer of Group A from a single to a dual task. The overall results indicate the older children's capacity to handle greater processing loads in terms of responding to faster-moving objects and adjusting to simultaneously performing two tasks.

The impact upon the secondary task, which in this case was the verbal task of calling out the brick score, is shown in Figure 13-6. Again, the older children performed markedly better, with a calling accuracy of 90 percent or more on all trials for both conditions. The younger children in the control group quickly adjusted to doing the secondary task and had approximately 80 percent accuracy from the third trial to the tenth trial. But the younger children in Group A did not adjust well to the secondary task, in that they had only 60 percent accuracy when they transferred from the single to the dual task. The findings for the secondary task further demonstrate that younger children cannot allocate attention as well as older children can.

An interesting observation by Sugden was that the older children's strategic behavior in calling out scores changed more. The younger children, especially in Group A, had a quite random approach to calling out the score. Sometimes they called it just after the ball was hit and sometimes just before, with consid-

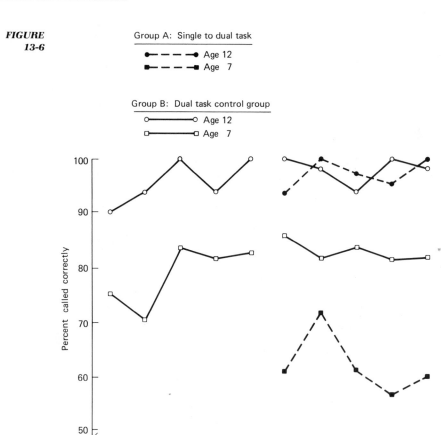

Percent of scores called correctly during practice and transfer trials.
(Reproduced with the permission of Sugden, 1981.)

erable variation from ball to ball. Older children, however, seemed to search actively for a strategy of when to call the brick score. They soon found it easier to call out the score just after the hit, and they stayed with that strategy. The older children seemed to have developed an active search strategy which Wright and Vlietstra (1975) propose as a major developmental shift in controlling attending behavior. A search strategy seemed to help improve performance in this dual task.

Another example of attention allocation is the study of Davids (1982) who used the general test arrangement shown in Figure 13-7 and described in Box 13-4. He examined time sharing in a dual task of catching a ball while detecting a light. The ball's speed was adjusted so that each group caught 75 percent of the balls when no light detection was required, which established a similar level of difficulty for the primary task of catching. As seen in Figure 13-8, the errors steadily decreased with age for both ball catching and light detecting. As expected, most of the light detection errors were at the wider angles.

An interesting finding was that children at ages 9 and 12 made most of their light detection errors when the light was switched on during the last third of the ball's flight time. The light detection errors of the older subjects, ages 15 and 18, were evenly distributed in relation to the light's being turned on during the first, second, or last third of the ball's flight time. It has been shown that information about a ball's being late in flight is not useful, because the information arrives too late to be used to make corrections (Sharp and Whiting 1974, Whiting et al. 1973, Whiting et al. 1970; Whiting and Sharp 1974). Therefore, the subjects in Davids's study presumably could allocate some of their attention to light detection in the last third of the ball's flight. This was not the case for the 9- and 12-year-olds, who seemed to allocate their attention to watching the ball late in flight and preparing for the catch, rather than to allocate some attention to light detection. The older subjects continued to perform both tasks, perhaps by ignoring information about the last part of the ball's flight, knowing that such information was not useful. Five- and 6-year-olds would probably have even more difficulty in allocating their attention to light detection during the final part of the flight path, and perhaps also to earlier parts of the flight path.

The preceding accounts of time-sharing performance are based on the idea of a limited amount of attentional space being variably allocated to tasks as needed, thus reducing the availability of attentional space for other duties. A neurological explanation is the notion of *functional cerebral space*, in which capacity limitations on dual-task performance, especially when done at speed, are due to intertask interference within a single, closely linked cerebral space (Kinsbourne and Cook 1971, Kinsbourne and Hicks 1978). The degree of interference is an inverse function of the distance between the cerebral control centers. In practical terms this means that a task involving the right hand, which is controlled by the left hemisphere, will be disrupted more by a secondary verbal task than will a task involving the left hand, which is controlled by the right hemisphere. This is because speech is controlled through the left hemisphere and is functionally closer to the cerebral control center for movement of the right hand. It is only when the left hemisphere has become dominant for language that this pattern is shown. This line of reasoning about functional cerebral space can be tested by comparing the decrements between right- and left-hand performance when verbalization is present, as shown in Figure 13-9.

If at some early age, language control is not completely located in the left hemisphere, then the pattern in Figure 13-9 will not be present. Because it would be useful to know if a developmental progression of this nature exists, Hiscock and Kinsbourne (1978) examined the tapping performance of children, ages 3 to 12, with and without the simultaneous performance of a verbal task. Changes noted with age were an increase in tapping speed and a decrease in the difference between single- and dual-task performances. They found that there was more disruption of tapping speed on the right hand than on the left hand at all ages when verbalization was present, which supports the presence of a functional cerebral space as early as age 3. But Archer (1980) did not find the right- and left-hand differences with verbalization until age 12, which places the development of functional cerebral space at an older age than Kinsbourne and his associates did. Finer-grained analyses are needed to determine whether this difference is present very early in life or whether it develops gradually with age.

Processing Error Information. Processing capacity is an important consideration in processing error information. After completing a movement, movers can evaluate its quality and their success in achieving the intended movement objective. This evaluation of error information in the form of feedback from many sources provides information to be used in preparing for subsequent movements. Knowledge of results (KR), as achievement information provided by the experimenter, is a source of feedback that has been studied with children in relation to *time needed to process* and *precision of performance information*, which the mover can translate into error information. These two concerns are interrelated because more precise error information should require more time to process. The level of precision of error information, however, may not be useful, regardless of the time available to process, if the information is too general or too precise.

The experimeter can control the processing time of KR in a number of ways.

ATTENTION ALLOCATION IN A DUAL TASK

The test arrangement shown in Figure 13-7 was used by Davids (1982) to examine attention allocation in a dual task requiring catching a ball while detecting a light. Subjects were twenty boys in four age groups (ages 9, 12, 15, and 18). A machine projected a ball at a constant speed and trajectory toward a subject seated 15 feet from the machine. The ball's speed was adjusted so that all the groups caught 75 percent or more of the "throws" when no light detection was required during a single-task condition. The ball's speed was 30.8 feet per second for 9-year-olds and 34.1 feet per second for the other three groups, so that the flight times, respectively, were 490 milliseconds and 440 milliseconds. Ten lights were arranged at the angles shown in Figure 13-7.

As the ball was released from the machine, a microswitch was triggered to activate a system that turned on one light for a period of 50 milliseconds during the first, second, or final third of the ball's flight time. The subjects had to catch the ball, name which side the light came on, and name the light. They had simultaneously to use visual information to read the ball's flight and detect the light, while also using some of their attentional capacity to control the catching movements.

Each subject did sixty trials, two trials for each light being lit during each of the three parts of the ball's flight, with order of trials randomized. There was a total of twelve hundred trials for each age group. The total number of ball-catching and light-detection errors is presented by age group in Figure 13-8. A light-detection error was naming the wrong light.

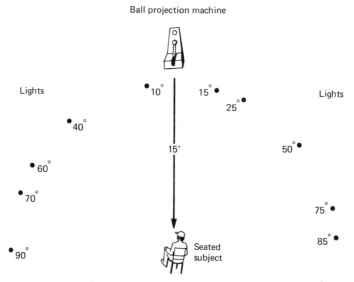

General test arrangement for a dual task of catching a ball while detecting a light (Davids, 1982).

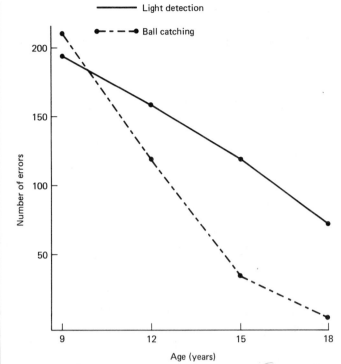

FIGURE
13-8

Total number of errors as a function of age on a dual task of ball catching and light detection. (Drawn from data reported by Davids, 1982.)

First, KR may be given immediately or may be delayed, so that there is a KR delay time. KR delay time becomes important when the delay is sufficient to produce a decay or loss in other feedback information that presumably needs to be processed for KR, but KR delay time in movement tasks has not been studied with children. Second, the time from receiving KR until the next trial begins is *post-KR delay time*, which is the time available to process KR. We are concerned here with post-KR delay time because this time period may be too short for children

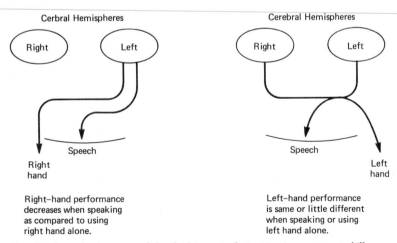

FIGURE
13-9

Functional cerebral space and the deployment of attention in movement skills.

to process KR adequately, which has been recognized as a difficulty for adults as well (Newell 1976).

The experimenter also can control the precision of error information when provided as KR. KR may be too general to be useful in one situation but be too precise or too complex in other situations. An optimal level of precision probably exists and may change with age in terms of what can be processed and used within the time available. Post-KR delay time and precision of error information are important and interactive conditions in studying the motor system's functional capacity.

Younger children often need more time to process information, as pointed out in Chapter 12. We should expect their movement performance to be affected when not given sufficient time to process. A clear demonstration is provided in the study of Gallagher and Thomas (1980), who varied post-KR delay time from 3 to 9 seconds on a curvilinear positioning task, with the results shown in Figure 13-10. The task was reasonably simple in terms of the error information to be processed, and so older children and adults needed very little processing time, whereas younger children were placed at a disadvantage when less processing time was available. Younger children (age 7) improved markedly as they were given more time, until they had a mean error score similar to that of older children (age 11) and adults. Notice that the performance of older children and adults did not change in relation to time available to process KR. This means that we must decide whether younger children are unable to process information or merely

FIGURE
13-10

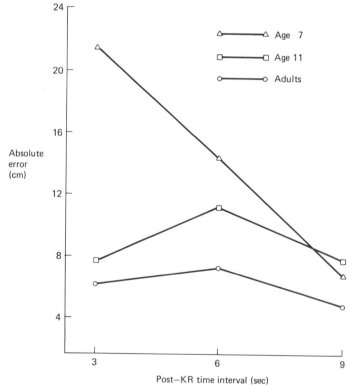

Performance as a function of processing time for younger children.
(Reproduced with permission from Gallagher and Thomas, 1980.)

do not have enough time to process it. For this simple movement, it was a lack of time and not an inability to process the necessary information. Barclay and Newell (1980) demonstrated this in another way: their subjects determined the length of the post-KR delay time on a linear positioning task by moving when they were ready. All of the subjects cut their post-KR time interval as they became more familiar with the task, but the adults continued to use less time to process.

An optimal precision level of KR for improving movement performance was demonstrated by Newell and Kennedy (1978) to be a direct function of age. Different levels of KR were given to four groups of children (ages 6, 8, 10, and 14) performing a positioning task. A curvilinear relationship between KR and age was found: performance was poorer with extreme levels of very imprecise and very precise KR, and the optimal level of KR became more precise with age. Thus, the younger children could not use more precise KR, and all of the children had difficulty using KR that was too general or too detailed. Newell and Carlton (1980) found that there were no differences among children at ages 9, 11, and 15 on a motor response recognition task, in contrast with a movement production task in which an intermediate level of KR precision was provided. However, 9-year-olds had larger means errors than 15-year-olds did when given extreme levels of very precise or very imprecise KR. Newell and Carlton suggest that developmental differences are more associated with planning and recall processes to produce movement than with processes related to recognition. The precision of KR also may be related to type of task (Salmoni 1980), level of task difficulty, and later performance when KR is removed. Thomas, Mitchell, and Solomon (1979) found that older children were better able to use more precise information on a difficult task and retain it for later use.

General Comment. Allocation and use of available processing resources seem to be major considerations in the development of movement control. We have offered several examples to illustrate the use of available processing capacity. Younger children not only need more time to process, but they also often cannot adjust as well to increases in processing load. They seem less able to allocate processing resources when the level of task difficulty increases and when another task must be done simultaneously, whereas older children and adults can adjust better to these changes in processing requirements. Feedback in the form of very precise or too general information may be less useful to younger children.

Motor Control

The production of movement in the most basic sense is the neuromotor system's control of the body parts' movements and positions. A movement's force, speed, and accuracy and related outcomes are external manifestations of neuromotor activity, as discussed in the framework presented in Chapter 1. *Motor control* is the general designation of a field of study that focuses on the production of movement by the neuromotor system. Motor control is expanding rapidly as a field of study, although it is mainly concerned with mature performance and often with high-level performance. This section is a brief and speculative look at some of the issues and concerns involved in development of motor control.

365

General Issues and Topics

Motor control research is concerned principally with how the neuromotor system produces movements. Some research deals directly with this issue by examining the structural and functional characteristics of certain aspects of the nervous system. Another approach to studying motor control is to infer motor control functioning from behavioral measurements. We shall limit our discussion here to the behavioral approach but recognize that work in both areas is progressing rapidly and that some efforts are being made to combine the direct study of neuromotor functioning with behavioral inferences. Schmidt (1982) provides a good review of the behavioral approach.

Motor control research from a behavioral perspective pertains to how movements are organized and regulated, and examples of research issues are the classical motor control problems of equivalence, variance, and complexity (Stelmach and Diggles 1982). Motor equivalence refers to the achievement of the same or a similar movement outcome when using different muscle combinations, and thus, movements may not correspond directly to the neural events causing them. Similarly, movements also may not be represented topologically in the nervous system. The variance or variability issue arises because apparently identical movements are not completely alike in biomechanical or other movement analyses, but they are enough alike to achieve an equivalent performance outcome. Complexity refers to Bernstein's (1967) notion of degrees of freedom when considering the difficulty in controlling the many degrees of freedom present in any movement.

The three motor control problems exemplify some of the general concerns in motor control research. We shall focus on two topics that characterize the current research and involve processing concerns. The first is the *mode of control* in which the motor system functions, and the second is the related topic of *response organization*.

The mode of control is how the motor system functions in relation to if and when feedback information is used. The two modes of control are *open loop* and *closed loop*, as shown in Figure 13-11. Mechanical and computer systems are constructed to be controlled in an open- or a closed-loop mode or in some combination of the two, and the human motor system is conceived as being controlled

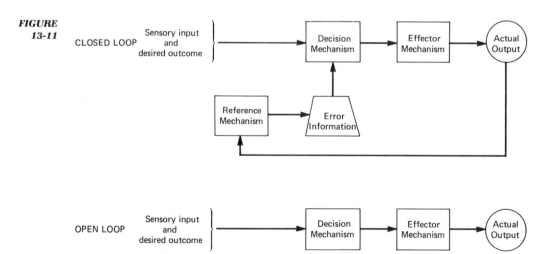

FIGURE 13-11

A general representation of open-loop and closed-loop modes of control.

in analogous ways. The idea of an open-loop mode is that a movement is pre-programmed and executed without ongoing correction. A closed-loop mode has a processing loop to bring information into the motor system while movement is occurring, rather than waiting until the movement is completed. The representations in Figure 13-11 are meant to show the open-end character of the open-loop mode and the information loop which creates the potential for ongoing correction in the closed-loop mode. Notice that a closed-loop mode uses feedback to generate error information which can be acted upon to reduce error during the movement. The motor control system functions in the same way during open-loop control, except that error information is not acted upon or is not useful until after the movement is finished.

Arguments for and against both modes of control have been presented and discussed extensively (see Schmidt 1980, Stelmach 1976, 1978). Supporters of the closed-loop mode of control point to the deterioration of performance when feedback is withdrawn and the lack of evidence for motor programming in humans. Those favoring an open-loop mode of control note that movements can take place without feedback and present evidence of motor programming in animals. The issue now is not that only one or the other mode exists but when each functions. The problem of how each functions still has not been solved.

Proponents of both open- and closed-loop modes of control now acknowledge that each may play a different role depending on the type of movement being performed. Schmidt (1980), using his concepts of "errors of selection" and "errors of execution," states that both modes of control operate. In a fast movement, for example, he believes that the selection of the response and most of the movement execution are controlled in an open-loop mode by generalized motor programs, which are abstract memory structures capable of being transformed into movement patterns. Any movement that is faster than one reaction time (for adults, about 180 to 200 milliseconds) is run off by a motor program, and *selection* of a new movement can occur only after the movement is completed. But there is evidence from neurophysiological studies that modifications, or corrections, in movement *execution* can be performed in less than this time (Smith 1978). Movements that take longer than 200 milliseconds clearly enable ongoing corrections to be made by a closed-loop mode of control. Time available is a principal determinant of the mode of control used. Other considerations are level of learning, task difficulty, and type of response required, but our concern is the extent to which the mode of control is related to the mover's development.

Our second topic is how a movement is organized for execution, which has been conceptualized as a movement program, much like a computer program. Motor programs initially were thought to decide what muscles will be contracted in what order and with what force and to determine the temporal relationships among the contractions. Another viewpoint is that muscle control is analogous to the functioning of a mass spring (Bizzi et al. 1978). The mass spring theory suggests that the muscles act together, like a vibratory system with the physical and behavioral characteristics of a mass spring. This means that a muscle unit, like a mass spring, will reach a final invariant position no matter how it is perturbed; that is, the motor program does not need to program all of these variables and does not need to deal with the associated problem of how the motor apparatus's degrees of freedom are regulated.

Another line of thinking is that there are generalized motor programs with as yet unknown but invariant features that determine a class of movements or actions.

Movements directed by a common generalized motor program may look quite different, though they have similar features and objectives. Schmidt and colleagues (1979) note that generalized motor programs with certain invariant features can explain how we can write our name on a piece of paper, on a blackboard, and in the snow with the same pattern but with different muscles around different joints.

Mode of Control

One general developmental concern is the shifts or changes in the motor system's mode of control. Movements initially are made in a more discontinuous or discrete manner before the mover can put the pieces together to make a more continuous and unified movement. The mode of control can change in several ways depending on the movement's need for ongoing regulation and the mover's capability to organize larger movement packages or programs that can be performed in an open-loop mode. The better-developed mover will be able to use both modes of control flexibly in order to adapt to environmental conditions and task requirements.

Beginning with a single and reasonably simple reaching movement, younger babies function in an open-loop mode to make corrections after a reach is completed, whereas older babies can correct during a reaching movement to indicate that they are using a closed-loop mode of control. This is evidence that babies soon have the capability of using both modes of control, but it does not mean that babies or young children can easily adjust to environmental conditions and task requirements by using the more effective mode of control. Hay (1979) reported that young children performed reaching movements in a ballistic or discrete manner, suggesting open-loop control, in contrast with older children who seemed to use selectively a combination of open- and closed-loop control. Hay also noted that children in the middle years seemed to overuse closed-loop control to overcorrect, as if not able to take in error information without immediately using it. Hay's three stages, which are discussed in Chapter 11 in regard to using visual information, demonstrate that children become more capable of using both modes of control selectively.

Reciprocal tapping tasks are a way to look at the mode of control in ongoing movements that are intended to be continuous. Younger children tend to make a series of discrete movements, for example, in which they lift up a pencil to "bomb" the target rather than to make a more direct and continuous movement to the target (Connolly et al. 1968). They also tend to look at each target, as if needing to check that they are on target with each tap (McCracken 1983). Older children seem to tap more continuously and also intermittently look at the target to check on their accuracy. Older children also adjust to make a more continuous movement after several trials on a small circle, in contrast with younger children who cannot adjust to making a more continuous movement, even when tapping with large circles. Again, older children are more capable of selectively using both modes of control. Another problem for younger children is that they may require more time to make what appears to be the same control adjustment (Salmoni 1983).

More continuous tapping indicates a larger packaging or programming of a movement, which is a good use of open-loop control but depends on the ability to combine movements units into a larger movement. This is discussed further in the next section on response organization, but we make the point now to illustrate that open-loop control can function in a simple, single movement or in a larger movement that may be part of an even larger movement. Intermittent monitoring is a more sophisticated use of closed-loop control than is limiting closed-loop control to continuous monitoring, which may be restrictive and even disruptive in some cases. Older children can use both modes of control in their more sophisticated forms and are better able to use them in combination.

Mounoud and Hauert (1982) studied the movements and related electromyographic (EMG) measurements of children, ages 6 months to 5 years, when picking up objects. They used EMG analyses to identify programmed (open-loop) movements and continuous control (closed-loop) movements, as well as movements with two other forms of control, which they called steps and ramps. Steps and ramps are a series of short feedback loops during a movement that makes a series of corrections rather than a continuous correction. Steps and ramps are not programmed, nor are they continuous corrections. Steps and ramps were not found when adults were tested on the same tasks, but they often were observed in children's EMG patterns during the initial trials of a new task, as if the children were trying to discover an appropriate control strategy. Mounoud and Hauert note that these different modes of control did not change or shift in a linear manner but, rather, appeared and disappeared at different ages. They suggest that the reappearance of a mode of control reflects a new structuring of the relationship between child and environment.

Both open-loop and closed-loop modes of control begin functioning at a very early age. As movements become organized in larger movement units and task requirements become more involved, it is difficult to tell whether the motor system is functioning in an open-loop or a closed-loop mode of control. Evidence from several experiments indicates that older children are better at combining the two modes of control, and more appropriately and more effectively. Mounoud and Hauert (1982) suggest ways to make finer-grained analyses, rather than to be limited to thinking of a mode of control as either open or closed. We now shall shift from the control of the motor system to the organization of a movement response in carrying out a movement plan.

Response Organization

We have come to a difficult and elusive question: How can a movement decision be translated into a movement? After a mover reads a movement situation and selects a solution to whatever is perceived to be the movement problem, how is the motor system commanded and guided in carrying out the action plan? It is at this point in the process of producing a movement that we know the least about the motor system's functioning. More microscopic analyses offer some knowledge of how motor units function, but we do not know how they are organized to produce movements, much less how they are organized in relation to situational requirements and mover intentions. We do know something about how a mover generally reads a movement situation and makes decisions, but we know very little about how preparation, knowledge, and intention are combined into a movement response.

General Organization. As noted earlier, one approach has been to think of *motor programs* as a way to conceptualize response organization. Motor programs are analogous to computer programs, and so generalized motor programs carry out general functions. Program instructions can be modified to provide response variations in relation to environmental conditions and task requirements, in much the same way that computer programs are varied by changing computer statements and parameters. A developmental concern is that motor programs somehow must be constructed and altered.

A quite different approach is to think of response organization in much broader terms and not be concerned with selecting and packaging a motor program. There may be *levels of organization* that interact in different ways. An executive level has only a few key elements that govern the working units, and the working units at various levels then carry out their functions with considerable freedom of execution. This means that the executive level controls only a few pieces of the puzzle and that the working units control the final execution leading to the movements we observe. An example of this view is the idea that coordinative structures, rather than a motor program, are the key to understanding movement organization. This is a new and rapidly emerging view detailed in a developmental context by Kugler, Kelso, and Turvey (1982) and, from a processing perspective, by Clark (1982).

These different proposals suggest the range of problems encountered in trying to understand how a movement is organized for execution, but very little has been done to test these ideas developmentally. We shall focus here on some ideas and data related to motor programs, because more has been done from this perspective, which also is more closely related to our review of processing.

Preprogramming. One line of research has concentrated on preprogramming to consider the extent to which a movement can be organized before it is executed. If the subjects know the movement to be performed, they presumably can prepare a motor program while waiting for the signal to move. Their reaction time will not be different for different movements, because they know what they must do and have a motor program selected and repackaged, if necessary. This seems to be true, because reaction time generally is not affected by the level of movement difficulty when the subjects know what the movement will be (Klapp et al. 1974). When the subjects do not know which movement among several will be required, their reaction time increases to indicate that programming is taking place. Thus preprogramming is characteristic of adults when they are given the opportunity for it.

Children also seem capable of preprogramming, as shown in several studies in which movement difficulty was manipulated and tested in relation to Fitts law (Sugden 1980b, Sugden and Gray 1981, Wallace et al. 1978). As illustrated in Figure 13-12 for the Sugden study (1980b, see also Box 13-3), the mean reaction time for each age group remained the same during increases in the index of difficulty (level of movement difficulty). The mean reaction times for the 6-year-olds were erratic, as was true somewhat for the 8-year-olds, but the differences within each age group were not significant. A problem may be that preprogramming is less efficient and thus leads to more attentional demands for corrections during the movement's execution (Forsstrom and von Hofsten, 1982; Schellekens et al. 1983).

Another important concern is the impact on preparation time when an unknown or uncertain (choice) situation is encountered, so that a movement must be selected and organized during the reaction time interval. Younger children presumably will need more time, but they may need proportionately more time for more difficult movements. It will not be easy to study this question because it is difficult to separate response selection from response organization. Another

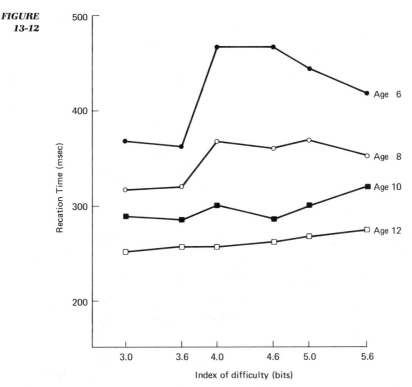

**FIGURE
13-12**

Mean reaction time preceding movements involving different levels of difficulty. (Reproduced with the permission of Sugden, 1980b.)

point to keep in mind is that these demonstrations of processing activity do not necessarily mean that a motor program is being selected and repackaged. Increased reaction time and similar evidence of processing activity might be used to control coordinative structures or whatever else might be proposed as an organizing and a controlling system. That is, individuals clearly are active in a general processing sense, but we do not know what they are doing.

Generalized Motor Programs: Schemas. Schmidt's (1975) schema theory of generalized motor programs is organized around rules called recognition schemas and recall schemas (see Shapiro and Schmidt 1982 for a current presentation of schema theory). The general sense of schemas is that a mover has rules defining the relationships among the information involved in the production and evaluation of a movement. For example, more force is needed to produce greater velocity or a longer distance when throwing an object. Schmidt names four pieces of information as stored or retained when an individual makes an intended movement: initial conditions that exist before movement, response specifications for the motor program, sensory consequences of the movement, and outcomes of the movement. When several similar movements have been attempted, the mover can abstract the relationships among these four sources of information in order to formulate the recognition schemas and recall schemas.

The idea of schemas and rules shifts our focus away from studying specific instructions in a motor program to studying its organization. This also takes our thinking in the direction of those who are more concerned with coordinative structures and similar, broader views of movement organization. (See Newell and Barclay 1982 for a discussion of this point.) However, schemas keep us tied to the concept of a motor program, and our general developmental concern is to understand the changes in the nature and function of schemas.

A fundamental proposition in schema theory is that the variability of experience (practice) will lead to the establishment of stronger schemas. The logic is that the variability of experience offers more information to the mover, who can extract from this information a more complete rule about means-ends relationships. It follows that a more complete schema allows the mover to organize movements better in unfamiliar or novel situations that involve the class of movements covered by a general motor program. In everyday events, this means that, for example, the force of a throw can be varied to propel an object toward targets at different distances and different spatial locations. In experiments, a group practicing at different distances and locations should do better when throwing to a new location and new distance than should a group practicing at only one distance and one location. Some studies of this kind have been done with children, because their schemas may be less well developed and easier to manipulate and test than are adults' schemas. As Moxley (1979) points out, that these studies merely use children as subjects but do not answer questions related to schema development. Recognizing this limitation, we shall briefly review some of these studies as our only source of evidence regarding children's movement schemas.

The general finding is that children seem to have schemas and can use them to organize movements in slightly different movement situations. This has been demonstrated for children at age 3 when pushing a toy car to different distances on a fixed trackway (Kelso and Norman 1978) and for somewhat older children (ages 6 to 8) when throwing at a target from different body orientations (Moxley 1979). The Moxley study is particularly interesting because she had children throw at the same target distance while *changing the initial conditions.* She did this by having the children sit on the floor and throw with their right hand from five different locations. She kept the force (distance) requirements constant but changed their body alignment in relation to the target. For example, the children in one location faced the target almost directly and in another location had to turn their bodies considerably to the right to make the throw. These test conditions show how one source of information (initial condition) can be manipulated. Most studies of schema hold initial conditions constant and vary force or other response specifications.

Some related concerns were examined by Carson and Wiegand (1979) in the study described in Box 13-5. Young children (ages 3 to 5) with more variable practice experiences had greater overall success when throwing a bean bag of a new weight at a target on the floor and at a relocated target attached to a wall. The variable practice group also maintained their performance level in all conditions after a period of 2 weeks, in contrast with a loss in performance by the other groups. Carson's and Wiegand's findings demonstrate that young children can establish a movement rule or relationship, can use it, and can retain it for later use.

This type of experiment has usually taken place in a movement situation with a stationary environment and usually with a stationary individual throwing objects at a target. Wrisberg and Mead (1981, 1983) investigated the same principles, but with a coincidence-timing task, thereby producing a moving environment. In the earlier study, there were no differences between the constant and variable practice regimes on transfer (learning) trials. In the later study, they increased the task's complexity by having two constant-speed groups, one slow and one fast, and two types of variable practice, one random and one blocked. The random group changed speeds on each trial, whereas the blocked group had six trials at one speed before moving to another. Each group improved during the acquisition trials, with no difference among them. But on the slow transfer condition, in which the differences were the most evident, slow constant-speed training and variable-blocked training were better than fast constant-speed training and variable-random speed training. The findings from the two studies show that not only is the type of practice important as being constant or variable but also that the organization of practice and the nature of the task can influence learning.

The findings in these studies are not surprising, although it is difficult sometimes to demonstrate experimentally the existence of what seem like sensible ideas. If children could not establish general rules of movement organization along the lines suggested by the schemas, it would be difficult for them to function in daily life. The studies of children and schema, however, do not offer anything to take us beyond the recognition that children have some means of organizing movement around their general knowledge about the relationship between means and ends, whether we call the relationship schemas or some other construct in a different perspective of movement response organization. We now need to determine the nature of these rules, how they develop, and how they are used in organizing movement.

Modularization. Another important consideration is the extent to which a movement unit is mastered to become a unit of action that can be combined with other units to form a larger movement. Bruner (1973) refers to this mastery and combining as *modularization,* to suggest that a module or unit is established (also see Hogan and Hogan 1975). Movement modules are quite reliable and are automated. Once modularized, a movement unit can be combined with other modules to form a larger movement that adapts to environmental conditions and task requirements. This includes using a particular module as part of many different, larger movements. Modules have been compared to language, that a module is the ability to say a word and to use it in many different sentences. This is like describing movement by means of movement vocabulary, with movement syntax used to produce movement sentences.

Bruner (1970) offers an example of modularization in his account of babies opening the lid of a box, holding it open, and reaching inside to retrieve an object. Bruner described improved performance in opening the lid until general mastery was established to have lid opening as a module or movement unit. Additional time then was needed to combine the lid-opening module with lid holding and reaching to retrieve (with the opposite hand) in order to form an appropriate movement sentence. Another way to describe this mastery of movement units and formation of larger movements is by comparing it to computer subroutines compiled into computer programs.

An obvious payoff in modularization is that less attentional capacity is needed to organize a movement. If modules or subroutines are available and can be combined to adapt to different environmental conditions and situational requirements, a mover can do more and can do it better with fewer attentional resources. A mover then can use the savings in attentional resources for dealing with other aspects of the movement situation which otherwise might not be possible. Time

373

BOX 13-5

VARIABILITY OF PRACTICE AND SCHEMA STRENGTH

Carson and Wiegand (1979) used several test conditions to examine children's ability to *establish* and *retain* a motor schema. The task was an underhand throw of a bean bag with the nondominant hand at a target placed on the floor. The children (ages 3, 4, and 5; total N = 92) practiced twenty throws per day for 5 days and were assigned to one of four practice conditions:

1. HI (High variability): Practiced with four different bag weights (5, 125, 227, 515 grams).
2. SP (Specificity): Practiced with one bag weight (211 grams), which was the weight used for the criterion test.
3. LO (Low variability): Practiced with one bag weight (61 grams), which was not the criterion weight.
4. CO (Control): Practiced a different movement task (kicking).

Three tests were administered after completing all of the practice throws. The test scores were used to indicate schema strength.

A. *Criterion weight:* Tossing a bean bag weighing 211 grams at the same target placed on the floor.
B. *Novel task:* Tossing a bean bag weighing 420 grams at the floor target.
C. *New task:* Tossing a small yarn ball (170 grams) at a target placed on a wall.

Group SP practiced at the criterion weight (Task A), whereas the other groups did not. Task B was novel (at least not practiced), because no group used a bean bag weighing 420 grams. Task C involved the same general movement (underhand toss) but used a different object and a different target location.

Each of the three tests was performed in the order A, B, C after completing the practice trials on the fifth day. The children were given the three tests in the same order 2 weeks after the initial test session. The postpractice tests provided three different measures of how well the children had established a schema for an underhand toss. The retention of the schema was measured by the performance level retained after an interval of 2 weeks.

The results are summarized in three graphs in Figure 13-13. According to the level

FIGURE 13-13

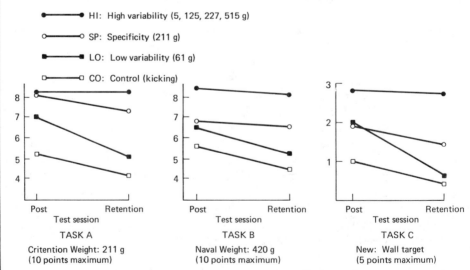

Mean target scores in relation to variability of practice in three tasks involving an underhand toss at a target. (See Box 13-5 for details.) (Graphs prepared from data reported by Carson and Wiegand, 1979.)

374

of performance for the postpractice session on each graph, Group HI matched Group SP for the criterion weight (Task A), maintained the same level of performance for the novel weight (Task B), and scored better than other groups did when changing to throw at a wall target (Task C). Group HI also seemed to have established a stronger schema, because its performance level was maintained after 2 weeks, in contrast with the loss in performance for all but Group SP on Tasks B and C.

These findings support the variability of practice as a means of establishing a strong schema. They also demonstrate that young children can formulate rules or relationships to be used in producing a general type of movement.

sharing in dual-task performance might well be explained in part by the extent to which modularization has been achieved in appropriate movement units and modular combinations.

In a test of modularization as a model of skill development, Moss and Hogg (1983) found an increase in movement variability rather than the increase in movement consistency predicted when modularization occurs. They propose that flexibility rather than consistency is characteristic of improvement in response organization. They offer a number of interesting ways to conceptualize and measure consistency and variability, including observing manipulation strategies related to grips, hand changing, and orientation when picking up rods to be placed in target locations. They also provide a comprehensive and critical analysis of modularization as a model for the development of movement organization.

General Comment. Our review of ideas about movement response organization has been primarily the metaphors of different scholars who are trying to capture the general sense of something we can observe as an outcome, but whose organization we cannot yet describe and understand. As another example, Connolly (1973) lists several sources of constraints on skill development that are pertinent to our discussion of the rules and modularization of organization. He suggests that the functional integrity of subroutines or modules will determine the extent to which modularization is possible. This appears to be the level of unity, that a movement module can stand on its own and be combined without losing its own unity. Connolly also states that the richness of motor syntax will govern the flexibility and complexity of an assembly of subroutines or modules. This is an interesting metaphor that points to rules of organization.

We now need to translate these metaphors and general statements into testable propositions, as shown in the work of Moss and Hogg (1983). An important decision is to select a level of analysis that will offer useful payoffs leading to broader understandings. Some researchers have chosen to look at motor programs, and others are concerned with levels of organization. Selecting a level of analysis becomes even more difficult when development is added to the search for understanding movement response organization. We cannot recommend where researchers should concentrate their efforts, but we believe that all should keep a broad perspective and be prepared for the coming flurry of ideas and studies.

Chapter Summary

The development of processing resources contributes to the development of movement control. This general statement captures what has been presented in

Chapters 10 through 13. Our focus in this chapter was, first, on the perspective of processing as an influence on movement control and, second, on the functioning of the motor control system in relation to processing. We can document that processing is important to movement control and that processing use and need change by situation in an interaction with age. These general points were well documented in Chapter 11 for vision as an information-gathering and processing system and in this chapter for processing as a general function.

Processing resources must be well developed when reading complex and abstract movement situations, when making continuous, simultaneous, and precise movement to coincide with external events, and when correcting accumulated movement errors. The level of development in general processing abilities can predict to some extent the movement performance in situations that require these abilities. A similar statement holds for more specific processing skills, such as rehearsal, if required. Younger children tend to have fewer and less-sophisticated processing skills, and they often do not use them as appropriately.

Younger children's attentional capacity is smaller than that of older children and young adults, and so their movement performance can be hampered, when not given enough time to process and when processing load increases, in making continuous and simultaneous movements, and in dealing with more precise error information. Older children and young adults often can adjust better to increased processing loads, perhaps because they have more ways to adjust and can better use the resources they have, such as how they allocate attention. It may be that in some situations, older children and young adults have better access to their central processing resources.

Improvements in the motor system's functioning sometimes reflect better processing. These improvements also help lessen the processing load which makes processing resources available for other uses. Young babies can function in an open-loop or closed-loop mode of control, but older children are better able to use both modes of control selectively and flexibly to adapt to environmental conditions and task requirements. Younger children can preprogram, that is, organize a movement unit, but we do not know how they function as the situations become more complex. Younger children can establish, use, and retain movement rules in organizing movement responses, but again we do not know how they develop movement rules and use them. An important achievement is movement modularization to master a movement unit and to combine movement units into larger movement packages, because a mover increases movement organization resources while freeing attentional resources for other uses.

A basic point in all aspects of producing a movement is that older children and young adults often are better able to adjust to environmental conditions and task requirements. They seem better able to use their resources flexibly and appropriately, thus they can handle greater processing loads. We must recognize that this is a somewhat circular argument because a better use of resources lowers individual demand, in the sense that we have been using demand as the relative load for an individual in a particular movement situation. An important point about younger children is that they have the basics in place at an early age. That is, they can track a slow-moving object and bring a hand to intercept the object; they have some basic processing strategies; they can execute movement in open-loop and closed-loop modes of control; and they have movement rules to use in response organization. But they seem to be quite limited in using their resources. Our point is that we must consider both the existence of a processing skill or a motor control operation and the use of each. An example is the need, first, to master a movement unit and, second, to use it in combination with other movement units to adjust better to movement situations and task requirements. The development of movement control must be understood as the development of basics and their use. We have described both in various ways, and so we now need to understand how the development of movement control progresses in relation to each type of resource and the interplay among aspects of each.

We can summarize this set of four chapters with a description of general achievements. Children with increasing age are more aware of their own bodies, are better at specifying the environment, possess better processing skills, have a larger general or semantic knowledge, make decisions more quickly, allocate attention more efficiently, and have a more accurate memory. All of these lead to a greater ability to prepare for movement. As they grow older, children also acquire more flexible means of organizing and controlling movements.

CHAPTER	
14	*General Contributions to Change*

The central theme in Part II is identifying and examining major influences on change in movement development. We shall conclude by discussing these many influences' contributions to change. Thus far we have examined biological systems and psychological functions. In this chapter, we shall include personal and social influences, necessarily in general terms. *Personal and social influences probably affect involvement in movement activity more than skill development*, a point we made in our introduction to Part II. Personal and social influences focus our attention on *participation experiences*, that is, what individuals do, an idea we have not included in our discussions, except in vague and undefined ways.

A recurring theme in each section of this chapter is the contribution of genes, as contrasted with the contribution of experience. This is the seemingly unresolvable issue of nature versus nurture: how much change is genetically predetermined and controlled and how much is a function of experience. Our position is that basic resources and abilities are prewired and in that sense are predetermined, but experience is necessary to stimulate and release these prewired changes and to shape predetermined behaviors. This means that we need both genes and experience to be what we are. Also, different resources and abilities are important at different times and for different types of movements.

Early Development

Early development is gaining control of self-movements in initial achievements and primary refinements and variations. General movements and reflexes give way to voluntary and adaptive movement control, and postural control is established as a basis on which other movements can be made. Body control becomes sufficient to enable babies to move in their immediate physical environment. Manual control progresses rapidly to give the arm linkage system and digits considerable spatial accuracy and dexterity. Movements become more continuous rather than discrete. Movement coordination is impressive in its sequencing and timing (phasing) of movement components, which comprise the general movement achievements we observe. Force can be monitored and regulated within

378

broad limits, but not to the level of precision achieved in later years. Babies can read some movements in the physical environment and can respond adequately in some limited but clearly open movement situations. They seem to be restricted more by their lack of proficiency in controlling their movements than by their difficulties in reading the environment. Our task now is to discover the major contributions to these changes in the early development of movement control.

Genetic Preadaptation

The early development of movement control is considered by some as genetic preadaptation. This means that babies' resources are prewired to adapt to many of the environmental conditions they encounter. If we observe babies' early movement development in different parts of the world, thus babies with different genetic backgrounds and living in different social-cultural environments, we will find the same general achievements and patterns of change. Werner's summary (1979) documents these similar patterns, although child-rearing practices do seem to alter the rate of development and the frequency of using some movements.

Kopp (1979) analyzes movement development findings to support genetic preadaptation as the principal influence on the early development of movement control. She recognizes individual variations in the rate and quality of achievement and presents a strong case for similarity in what she calls the *form* and *function* of initial achievements of locomotor and manual control movements. Form is the general repertoire of movements, and function is movements used in a similar way to achieve similar types of interactions. Kopp also reviewed studies of handicapped babies who had biological and medical limitations and/or environmental deprivations. She concludes that the form and function of the early movement development of handicapped babies is similar to that of intact babies with adequate care, except that handicapped babies often take longer to achieve these basic progressions of change. The early development of movement control seems to be genetically mapped to such an extent that all but the most severely impaired or deprived will achieve basic movement skills.

Kopp notes that the organism's integrity and the opportunities provided by the environment may enhance or impede the rate of development and the quality of response. She stresses genetic preadaptation as the primary contribution to the development of a general movement repertoire that is common to the species, but she reminds us of the importance of experience. The environment (experience) "activates change ... provides the 'materials and opportunities' for learning ... influences motivation to engage in activities, and promotes some early developmental precocities" (p. 16). With these statements about contributions to change as our background, we shall now consider the possible contributions of the various influences we discussed in Part II. *These are the changes in individual resources that are the agents of change we seek to identify and understand.*

Changes in Inner Surround Resources

Our focus in Part II was on changes in inner surround resources, that is, biological systems, sensory-perceptual functions, and a general processing system. The early development of movement control, as discussed in Chapter 9, seems to be a function of the level of development of the neuromuscular system. Until they can control self-movements, babies can do little to move in the outer surround of physical and social conditions. There does not appear to be any other reasonable alternative, even though we lack the evidence to verify such a sweeping generalization. The neuromuscular system must function to produce movement, with all other systems either enhancing or constraining it.

The sensory-perceptual and processing systems' level of functioning also contributes to the early development of movement control. However, the contributions of these systems become more apparent as multiple and simultaneous movements are made more continuously and in relation to surrounding conditions. The basic resources seem to be in place during the early years, but considerable time is needed to use them fully and in complex ways.

The difficulty in determining the contribution of different aspects of the inner surround to early movement development was demonstrated in an exchange between Zelazo (1983) and Thelen (1983). Zelazo argued that unaided walking may be made possible by a transition in cognitive development to provide the facility to integrate and coordinate the relevant reflexive components and postural adjustments. Thelen countered that it is not necessary to use cognitive explanations and offered a proposal based on changes in neural organization, body proportions, and muscle strength in concert with equilibrium development. She also discussed walking from an evolutionary point of view, by pointing out that the level of cortical development that Zelazo feels is necessary was not present 4 million years ago when bipedal locomotion evolved.

We next need to consider if early development of movement control is merely an accumulation of learning experiences. Bruner (1973) believes that learning in utero and during the first year of life after birth does not exist in the conventional sense of learning in later years. The appearance of many early movement achievements, such as reaching, grasping, standing upright, and walking, cannot be explained by a series of antecedent changes linked to repeated efforts (practice). Bruner views these achievements as quantum leaps, in which there is no observable sequence of changes that builds in a learning sense to create the emergence of new movement skills. It is possible that we are not yet clever enough to discover sequences of changes that lead to new movement skills, in all but the most severely impaired or deprived. Our position is that learning is a function of development, as discussed in Chapter 1.

The early development of movement control probably is genetically predetermined in form and function. The main determinant is the neuromotor control system's level of development. A secondary contribution is the level of development of sensory-perceptual and general processing systems to support the neuromuscular system. When movement control must be made in relation to the surrounding environments and in more continuous, multiple, and complex ways, the development of sensory-perceptual and processing resources becomes more important.

Outer Surround Influences: Child-rearing Practices

Babies' participation experiences are determined almost completely by the adults responsible for their early care and rearing. Parents and other primary caretakers establish and control their immediate environment and are the persons with whom the babies interact most directly. These adults determine their opportunities and provide either negative or positive personal-social reinforcements.

Adults' handling of babies is a natural part of early development because young babies cannot care for themselves. Babies are held and handled while adults transport, change, feed, talk, and play with them. Handling can be a stimulation to encourage movement and can place a baby in different positions and situations.

Additionally, handling is a social interaction between the baby and the handler. Dennis's early studies (1960), in which he observed caretaking practices in different types of institutions in Iran, offer some evidence that the lack of handling may delay early movement development. The attendants in two institutions did not handle the babies very much, that is, did not place them in prone and sitting positions, whereas the babies in a third institution were handled more frequently. The early development of sitting and locomotion was delayed in those institutions in which the babies were handled less frequently, presumably because their opportunities for movement experiences were fewer.

Handling in some cultural groups may be systematic in order to encourage movement development. Hopkins (1976) reviewed some of these systematic handling practices, which resemble the manipulation and massage techniques used by physical therapists and other medical personnel. He divides these handling practices into passive and active handling movements. Passive handling movements are initiated and effected by the caretaker in the form of stroking and massaging, and active handling movements consist of the caretaker's facilitating the baby's movements by encouraging voluntary movements, such as supporting the baby in an upright position to encourage walking. Hopkins also distinguishes formal and informal handling, with formal having long-term educational goals and informal having immediate, pleasing outcomes.

Hopkins studied the handling practices of West Indian parents living in Great Britain. The mothers' formal handling of their babies included passive stretching and massaging during the early months and active handling movements to encourage walking from the third month. The mothers reported that they did this because their mothers had done it as a way to help their bodies grow strong and healthy. Hopkins also found that at 6 months, the babies who had been handled more had more advanced manipulative skills. Hopkins's study points to the existence of systematic handling practices, presumably cultural, that can influence the early development of movement control. More definitive information and better analyses are needed to separate the many factors of such child-rearing practices.

A second example is that in some societies, parents focus on the early development of particular skills because the society values them. This really is just another example of active handling in which babies are propped up into certain positions or are encouraged in various ways to display valued behaviors. Kilbride (1980) studied the development of sitting and smiling in Kenyan tribal groups in which sitting and smiling are important behaviors in ceremonial events. Baganda parents formally train their babies to sit from about 2 to 3 months of age so that they can be in the presence of significant kinfolk. Kilbride compared the smiling and sitting development of the Baganda babies with another Kenyan group of Samia babies and with American babies. First social smiles appeared at the same mean age for each group of babies, but more advanced social smiling, such as smiling at a mirror image, was observed earlier in both Kenyan groups. The Baganda babies were earlier than the Samia babies in advanced social smiling, as expected with the Bagandas' emphasis on the social value of smiling. Both of the Kenyan groups were more advanced than the American babies. The Samia babies, who also received intensive training in sitting, were slightly ahead of the Baganda babies in sitting.

Another illustration is Super's work (1976) in studying the well-documented precocity of some groups of African babies in the early development of movement control, as compared with that of American and European babies. Super tested sixty-four Kenyan babies in a rural community during each month of their first year on selected test items of the Bayley Scales. Additionally, he made weekly observations of each Kenyan baby's home life. He confirmed an earlier finding that these African babies were able to sit, stand, and walk about 1 month earlier than were the American babies represented on the Bayley norms. However, the Kenyan babies were later in some movement skills, such as lifting their heads and crawling. Super found in his observations of home life that the mothers or other caretakers spent much time teaching and encouraging sitting and walking, as noted earlier for sitting for other Kenyan babies.

Super studied another sample of African babies who lived with their families in European houses in Nairobi. Many families had adopted European child care practices, although some mothers continued to teach and encourage their babies to sit and walk. The African rural babies could sit 3 weeks earlier than could the African urban babies, who were 3 weeks ahead of the American norms. Super's findings illustrate *the potential for child-rearing practices to influence the rate of early development.*

Our examples only touch on the many possibilities related to child-rearing practices. As suggested, societal or cultural values can direct caretakers to handle and interact with babies in specific ways. Sitting as a societal value leads some parents to hasten its achievement, even though their children will sit eventually, without intensive training and encouragement. More complex, pervasive, and subtle values are involved in what parents view as sex roles. Hopkins (1976) notes that mothers sometimes handle boys and girls differently, presumably because they are trying to achieve different outcomes for each. We know that parents interact differently with boy babies and girl babies, as shown in the style and color of clothing in which they are dressed and in the extent and kind of verbalizations. It is not difficult to imagine that some child-rearing practices are related to the baby's and the caretaker's genders. The impact probably is on the type of experiences that the caretaker arranges and encourages, as well as the caretaker's reinforcement when interacting with the baby.

The impact of child-rearing practices on the development of movement probably is not as intentional and directly visible as the handling practices described in our examples. Each caretaker likely affects the early development of movement control, but not in predictable ways that can be generalized across a group of caretakers. One mother may provide a wide range of opportunities for her girl baby, and another may be quite restrictive because she views sex roles differently from the way the first mother does. Our argument is that caretakers' child-rearing practices will influence babies' early movement development, but we cannot predict the nature or extent of that influence, except in circumstances in which major societal values are followed in a reasonably uniform manner.

Some other personal-social considerations should be recognized. The first is the baby's personality. Shirley's movement bibliographies (1931) in Chapter 2 illustrate differences in *movement personality*, such as the active movement behavior of "Winnie Walker," in contrast with the preference of her twin brother, "Freddie Talker," for verbal behavior. Differences in temperament likely contribute to general and specific preferences and satisfactions in movement. Some babies may like and, therefore, may seek certain movement activities, whereas others may avoid physical activity. Babies also are surrounded by things and people not included in our discussion of child-rearing practices; for example, the presence or absence of siblings may be important. Our general listing of considerations merely portrays the different sources of personal-social influences. Again, it does not seem likely that the form and function of early development of movement control are altered significantly by even the total impact of personal-social influences. Rather, it is more likely that personal-social influences are important in determining the rate and quality of early movement development.

Later Development: Biological Systems and Psychological Functions

The development of movement control beyond the first and second years is difficult to trace because movements become more complex combinations of basic movement units. The appearance of a "new" movement is not readily apparent, and the control of self-movements is more a matter of refining movements and creating variations and combinations, which progresses very rapidly, as seen in self-help skills and play-game skills. This aspect of movement development is a direct extension of the basic control established in the first and second years.

A striking change of another sort occurs in the early school years, when children become more capable of moving in a changing and an unstable movement situation. Older children become quite good in open movement situations that require reading and specifying changing conditions and using information about changing conditions to produce appropriate movements. The essence of these adjustments is to coincide self-movements with the positions and movements of objects and other people. Abstract conditions, which restrict movement situations by means of rules and strategies, also add another dimension to which adjustments must be made.

Movement development sometimes is measured as maximal performance that requires the perfection of movement control rather than the establishment of movement control. One consideration in maximal performance is the generation and control of force to move faster and more often, as well as to transmit force. Children improve steadily in maximal performance measures that control self-movements in closed movement situations. Very few data are available to describe change in maximal performance in complex, open movement situations, but children clearly improve in games and sports using movement in less stable and changing situations in which maximal performance is desired.

Our approach to analyzing the development of movement control has been to consider how movements are produced. We then identified what seem to be difficulties in three steps in producing movement. Step I is reading and specifying existing requirements and conditions; Step II is selecting a solution to the perceived movement problem and generating response specifications; and Step III is executing and regulating the movement. Babies and young children seem to have the basics for Step I to read and specify, although they may be limited in the amount of information they can process and have difficulty in processing certain types of information; that is, their knowledge base may be restricted in amount and quality. Younger children seem to need visual information, whereas older children and adults can use other information sources. Thus, babies and younger children seem to have the basics in place, but they do not seem able to use them as completely and flexibly as can older children and adults.

Step II is where babies and young children seem quite limited, particularly in translating their readings into response specifications. Many examples show that babies and young children can read a situation and make the requisite movement units but cannot make the overall movement. This is true for controlling the force of movements, as when moving slowly, and for more abstract conditions of drawing a figure. It is very difficult to study the translation of input into output, and little is known beyond that babies and younger children are markedly less effective than older children and adults are.

The mode of control in movement execution becomes more flexible as an important change in Step III. Babies clearly can function in either open-loop or closed-loop modes of control, but older children seem better able to change modes of control and to use them more appropriately. Closely related to the mode of control are the type and level of information needed and used in error corrections, whether in an open-loop mode after the movement is completed in preparation for a later movement or in a closed-loop mode during a movement's execution. Older children can use different sources of information and more levels of precision. As noted in our review of visual information, younger children seem to need certain information, even though alternate sources are available.

The continuous nature of many movements means that the three steps in movement production become part of one another, even though we have separated them for analysis and discussion. The unified process of producing movement is particularly apparent when considering the use of error information in correcting movements. Whatever the source of information, whether visual, kinesthetic, or verbal (experimenter or teacher saying "Too much" or "Too little"), error information becomes part of the preparation for the next movement or the next part of a continuing movement. This means that error information may need to go through the translation process included in Step II. Even more fundamental is that error information in some cases must be read (Step I) in the process of specifying the environment, and it may be internal as well as external information. In sum, the production of movement is a unified process, though it often is blurred by our need to focus on its parts.

Individual resources develop considerably during childhood, but it is not possible at this point to link directly the development in Resource A with the development in Movement Z. It is likely that such direct links do not exist in the simple and linear sense of changes in A being the major determinant of changes in Z. Developing systems and behaviors become so complex and interwoven that their relationships must be viewed in a larger context. We need to think of resource changes as producing *general functional capabilities* rather than specific capabilities. An illustration is our suggestion that younger children need to use vision, even though older children and adults are able to use more limited visual input in combination with other sources of information. This means that probably for younger children and in "new" situations for humans of all ages, the overall processing system is biased toward using visual information. Part of this bias may be that vision is a potent source of information for producing movement and seems to help regulate the internal sensory systems. A developmental consideration is that improvements in the general processing system make it possible to use alternate sources of information. These improvements are multiple and cumulative rather than a single change in a specific resource. The net effect is flexibility, which is an aggregate of the many changes we have noted, such as a variety of changes in control operations and a larger and more functional knowledge base. We see that a major contribution to change in moving in open movement situations is improvement throughout the processing system, including development in the visual-perceptual and other sensory-perceptual systems.

The development of the neuromotor system also helps change movement development beyond the early years, but in ways difficult to trace. The control of self-movements improves to regulate movements for more precise force control, as well as the control of force that is generated, and to summate force for maximal performance efforts. The overall control of movements improves in being able to do more things simultaneously and with more flexibility to adapt to different conditions.

The translation in Step II to use the environmental specifications to select and generate movement features seems to need the contributions of both a better processing system and a better functioning neuromotor system. This seems to be the area in which these two contributors are joined and are most dependent on each other.

The maximal performance of speeded and forceful movements requires summating force and biological resources in order to generate force in important segments of a movement sequence. Increased muscle mass is basic to the generation of force, and so young adults' physiological support systems are capable of higher-level functioning than are children's to support speeded and forceful movements. Skill in generating force is not well understood, but some individuals organize their movements more skillfully to generate force. Development within the neuromotor system would seem to be an important contribution to skill in maximal performance, although we do not know the nature of the changes that lead to better neuromotor functioning. Better processing also seems necessary, particularly as movement situations become more open.

Later Development: Personal-Social Influences

Personal-social influences can be viewed as affecting two aspects of participation experiences. First, *participation choice* refers to what a child chooses to do. What types of activities or experiences are selected, including the level of skill required, and how often does a child seek participation? This is the type and amount of involvement in movement experiences. Second, *participation effort* is what a child does when involved. Participation effort is a complex mixture of the effort that a child wants to make and the social conditions during the actual participation. If a child chooses to participate often and makes a strong effort, which is supported by others, the child's movement skill should improve. A child participating without positive support has a less favorable circumstance for improvement, and a child who does not participate is not likely to improve. Using the same reasoning, children will improve more in the types of movement skills that are part of the movement experiences in which they participate. The overall picture is that children become somewhat specialized in their movement skill development. They become better in those movement skills that they experience (practice) to a greater extent and in more favorable conditions. Lack of participation and unfavorable participation will limit skill development. Personal-social influences are important determinants of participation effort, which in turn will limit or enhance movement skill development.

Our general statements about personal-social influences on movement participation seem sensible to us, but very little evidence is available to evaluate them. Another problem is that personal-social influences probably are indirect, perhaps functioning as *mediators* to facilitate or interfere with the interplay of other factors.

Participation Arenas

One way to organize our thinking is to focus on participation arenas in which opportunities exist to experience movement. Young children participate in play, games, and organized sports, which we call general participation arenas. We include games to cover the wide range of individual and group movement activities that are not formally organized, as are youth sports. Participation arenas can be labeled more specifically as a particular type of play, game, or organized sport. The social conditions in a participation arena determine what children do in the movement activity. Participation arenas can be observed to discover differences in participation behavior and in conditions that affect individual behaviors.

Play is the basic arena in which children participate in movement activity, and differences in play behavior are readily apparent. An example is the many differences observed in the play behavior of boys and girls. Tauber (1979) lists some of these, which include boys and girls using different toys in different ways and boys' being more active and more aggressive. She examined family influences in regard to several hypotheses concerning sex roles and interactions with particular family members. Boys tended to be more active than girls when both were participating in the same activity. Tauber cites the example that girls sat more when boys at that time were standing. Boys also selected activities that called for more aggressive behavior, such as playing knights and castles, whereas girls selected activities with more opportunity to express nurturant behavior, such as playing in a dollhouse. Many significant correlations were reported for parental and sibling characteristics and play behaviors, but the correlations were seldom above .3, which means that many factors in many combinations must be considered when tracing family influences on play preferences and play behaviors.

Another important participation arena is youth sports, particularly when considering the current magnitude of participation in the United States. There has been much research during recent years on youth sports, in relation to interpersonal development, personal-social behaviors, and situational factors, including parents and coaches as agents of change. But there has been little study of movement performance and competence, other than children's feelings about their achievements. Nevertheless, the impact on movement skill development must be considerable, particularly in the encouragement to participate and positive support for efforts, as contrasted with what would be expected for discouragement and lack of support.

Group Membership

Social conditions related to movement activity can be analyzed in relation to group membership, because group membership is a basis for the social rules and social expectations that govern social conditions. Group membership in this context is a relationship sustained for a long period of time. There are many kinds of groups, with family and peers being among the most important. The influence of group membership can wax and wane, as well as change in kind. Group membership shapes and affects individual conduct on the basis of implicit or explicit rules and expectations. Perhaps the largest group to which each of us belongs is a national society. Another form of group membership is our biological identification as male or female, and sex roles are linked to societal, religious, and other group memberships.

Family membership during the early years is important to child-rearing practices and continues to be important in the early childhood years in defining participation opportunities. This is because a child lives in a particular location, and parents and other family members influence personal values that can determine participation choice and participation effort. Family membership is determined at birth, and changes in immediate family memberships can be caused by death, divorce, and other births.

Peer membership can be direct or indirect. Direct peer memberships are in the neighborhood, class in school, and special-interest groups (athletic teams, scout groups). Peer membership also can be extended to the generation or era in which an individual lives. This was mentioned earlier in Chapter 7 as a cohort, with the recognition that an individual can be a member of many cohorts, such as being a child during a depression followed by a war and later being a young adult woman in a time of social change for women. Peer groups can appear and disappear as an individual changes. Peer membership also may be defined in terms of age, with the obvious example being adolescence, when youths are striving for personal independence. Each of us will undergo such a period of change, although in different ways and at different times. The teenage years are a time when society members view youths as in transition from childhood to adulthood. Some of these societal perceptions are related to changes in physical appearance, in which boys and girls change into men and women. Societal expectations, which may vary markedly in different societal groups, change during the teen years to require more adult behavior.

Personal Values and Abilities

We need now to expand our discussion to include an individual's own self as influencing participation choice and participation effort. We are referring to the personality, temperament, feelings, motivations, attitudes, and values that comprise the personal self, as well as personal abilities for dealing with social involvements.

Participation motives and attitudes toward movement activity, as personal values, indicate some of the reasons for being involved in movement activity. Motives and attitudes clearly need to be considered as important influences on participation choice and participation effort. The findings from several studies are summarized in Table 14-1 as a comparison between adults and children in their personal values regarding movement activity.

Simon and Smoll (1974) measured children's attitudes toward physical activity, based on Kenyon's (1968) framework and related tests, as used with older youths and adults. Their findings are summarized in Table 14-1, along with a synthesis by Passer (1982) of several studies identifying children's general motives for participating in sports. Although different labels are used, the summary lists seem quite similar. The four participation motives that Passer offers—affiliation, fitness, excitement, and energy release—seem quite comparable to adults' and children's attitudes toward physical activity.

The overall match across studies and between children and adults suggests similar personal reasons for participating in movement activities. But the combinations are almost endless, which makes it difficult to determine precisely what an individual will choose and what his or her effort will be. Our task is further

TABLE 14-1 **Comparison of Participation Motives and Attitudes Toward Physical Activity**

ADULTS' ATTITUDES TOWARD PHYSICAL ACTIVITY (KENYON 1968)	CHILDREN'S ATTITUDES TOWARD PHYSICAL ACTIVITY (SIMON AND SMOLL 1974)	PARTICIPATION MOTIVES (PASSER 1982)
Social experience	Social experience	Affiliation
Health and fitness	Health and fitness	Fitness
Vertigo	Thrill involving some risk	Excitement
Catharsis	Release of tension	Energy release
		Skill development
		Success and status
Aesthetic	Beauty in human movement	
Ascetic	Long and hard training	

complicated by the need to consider the influence of social conditions. One conclusion is that social conditions and personal values can limit or enhance children's movement skill development, by influencing their participation choice and effort, even though we do not yet have the means of studying these influences.

A recent proposal by Griffin and Keogh (1982) about feelings of movement confidence illustrates the potential impact of several aspects of personal abilities and values on movement participation and movement performance. Their premise is that an individual's confidence or assurance when approaching a movement situation will help determine what an individual will choose to do and how adequate the movement performance will be. This is because the level of movement confidence will affect how information about a movement situation is processed and utilized.

Griffin and Keogh use the term *confidence* to mean more than a sense of competence, which generally is limited to meaning skill in achieving an outcome. Moving contains a wide range of sensory experiences thought to contribute to movement confidence, and sensory experiences are divided into those that may be enjoyed (or not enjoyed) and those that may cause physical harm. Sliding down a slide offers the sensation of moving fast and the potential of landing hard (both movement-related sensory experiences), as well as being able to control the body (skill or competence to achieve the intended movement).

The general model for movement confidence describes how movement confidence can be both a *consequence* (outcome) and a *mediator* (influence). Participation in a movement situation will influence an individual's movement confidence for that type of movement situation, because the individual now has some knowledge about personal ability to make the necessary movements and about the nature of the movement sensations involved. The level of movement confidence is an interplay of self-perceptions of competence, enjoyment of the movement sensations, and potential for physical harm. An individual's level of confidence will affect subsequent participation choices and effort. Thus, there is an involvement cycle in which the level of movement confidence affects the participation choice and effort, which in turn affect the changes in the level of movement confidence, and on and on.

Movement confidence in the early years is more likely to be a matter of personal reactions to movement sensations. Babies in their early months do not achieve much in the way of skilled movements, although they can generate movement sensations with their own movements and experience movement sensations when handled by others. Personal perceptions of ability or competence are complex aspects of development and apparently are not well developed in the early years. It seems likely in the early months that babies will evaluate movement sensations as enjoyed or not enjoyed and as involving or not involving physical harm. As examples, early efforts to roll over, sit, and stand may be influenced by preferences for movement sensations and perceptions of potential harm.

A general progression is proposed by Griffin and Keogh in which perceptions of movement sensation are developed early and affect the early development of movement control. Perceptions of competence develop later and are important when individuals strive for maximal performance in movement situations in which others contribute to competence expectations. Adults may shift back to being influenced more in their participation by perceptions of movement sensations and less by perceptions of movement competence. They may run in order to work hard and experience an emotional feeling rather than to finish ahead of others.

Chapter Summary

Contributions to change in movement development were discussed only in general terms. This was deliberate on our part to emphasize the importance of thinking about development as including many agents of change. Our position is that changes in individual resources provide the key to understanding changes in movement development, whether it be changes in the nervous system to alter directly the potential for the production of movement or changes in personal values to affect indirectly movement development by limiting or enhancing participation experiences. We also stressed the need to consider the nature of movement achievements, because different resources are important at different points in the early development of movement control, as contrasted with the later development of movement control when surrounding conditions are changing and unstable. We suggested further that contributions to change must be considered in several ways.

One distinction is that a contribution to change may be indirect rather than direct. This seems to be the case for personal abilities and values and social conditions. Personal-social considerations also are interwoven in ways that make them difficult to identify and study, but their contributions seem to be shaping participation opportunities and experiences. A more direct impact on movement development seems possible, with changes in what we call the inner surround. Form and function are determined principally by changes in inner surround resources, whereas the contributions of personal-social considerations are important early in the rate and quality of change and later in the kind and level of achievement.

Another way to look at the contributions to change is through the types of movement achievements. Early development is establishing and refining the basic control of self-movements. Later development has a wider range of achievements, including moving in relation to changing and unstable conditions and achieving maximal performance. Perceptual-cognitive development to process information

389

differently and more effectively seems to be particularly important in adapting to changing and unstable conditions, whereas the development of physiological support systems is more important in achieving maximal performance involving sustained movements. The general contributions of personal-social considerations in both examples will limit or enhance participation opportunities and experiences. We now need to formulate more precise hypotheses regarding the contributions to change.

AAHPER. 1965. *Youth fitness test manual.* Washington, D.C.: American Association for Health, Physical Education, and Recreation.

AAHPER. 1975. *Youth fitness test manual.* rev. ed. Washington, D.C.: American Alliance for Health, Physical Education, and Recreation.

Acheson, R. M. 1954. A method of assessing skeletal maturity from radiographs. *Journal of Anatomy* 88:498–508.

Adams, J. A., and S. Dijkstra. 1966. Short-term memory for motor responses. *Journal of Experimental Psychology* 71:314–318.

Adams, J. A., L. Gopher, and G. Lintern. 1977. Effects of visual and proprioceptive feedback on motor learning. *Journal of Motor Behavior* 9:11–22.

Ainsworth, M. D. S., and S. M. Bell. 1974. Mother-infant interaction and the development of competence. In *The growth of competence,* ed. K. Connolly and J. Bruner. New York: Academic Press.

Alderson, G. J. K. 1974. The development of motion prediction ability in the context of sports skills. Ph.D. diss., University of Leeds.

Ammons, R. B., S. I. Alprin, and C. H. Ammons. 1955. Rotary pursuit performance as related to sex and age of pre-adult subjects. *Journal of Experimental Psychology* 49:127–133.

Anderson, V. E. S., and P. M. McDonnell. 1979. The sinister infant: Unexpected laterality at three to eight weeks. Paper presented at meeting of Canadian Psychological Society, Quebec.

Annett, M. 1970. The growth of manual performance and speed. *British Journal of Psychology* 61:545–558.

———. 1976. A coordination of hand preference and skill replicated. *British Journal of Psychology* 67:587–592.

Anooshian, G. P. 1975. Component analysis of stabilometer performance for elementary school boys. Master's thesis, University of California, Los Angeles.

Apgar, V. 1953. A proposal for a new method of evaluation of the newborn infant. *Current Researches in Anesthesia and Analgesia* 32:260–267.

Archer, L. A. 1980. The effects of a concurrent verbal task on a unimanual motor task at two levels of difficulty in six-year-old children and adults. University of Leeds. Typescript.

Asmussen, E. 1973. Growth in muscular strength and power. In *Physical activity: Human growth and development,* ed. G. L. Rarick. New York: Academic Press.

Atkinson, J., and O. Braddick. 1982. Sensory and perceptual capacities of the neonate. In *Psychobiology of the human newborn,* ed. P. Stratton. New York: Wiley.

Atkinson, R. C., and R. M. Shiffrin. 1968. Human memory: A proposed system and its control processes. In *The psychology of learning and motivation,* vol. 2, ed. K. W. Spence and J. T. Spence. New York: Academic Press.

Auzias, M. 1975. *Enfants gauchers, enfants droiters.* Paris: Delachaux et Niestle.

Bachman, J. C. 1961. Motor learning and performance as related to age and sex in two measures of balance coordination. *Research Quarterly* 32:123–137.

Bailey, D. C. 1968. Longitudinal analyses of strength and motor development of boys ages twelve through seventeen years. Ph.D. diss., University of Oregon.

Bairstow, P. J., and J. I. Lazlo. 1981. Kinaesthetic sensitivity to passive movements and its relationship to motor development and motor control. *Developmental Medicine and Child Neurology* 23:606–616.

Ball, W., and E. Tronick. 1971. Infant responses to impending collision: Optical and real. *Science* (3973):818–820.

Barclay, C. R., and K. M. Newell. 1980. Children's processing of information in motor skill acquisition. *Journal of Experimental Child Psychology* 30:98–108.

Bard, C., M. Fleury, L. Carriere, and J. Bellec. 1981. Components of the coincidence-anticipation behavior of children aged from 6 to 16 years. *Perceptual and Motor Skills* 52:547–556.

Barry, A. J., and T. K. Cureton. 1961. Factor analysis of physique and performance in prepubescent boys. *Research Quarterly* 32:283–300.

Battig, W. F. 1979. The flexibility of human memory. In *Levels of processing in human memory*, ed. L. S. Cermak and F. I. M. Craik. Hillsdale, N.J.: Erlbaum.

Battig, W. F., and J. B. Shea. 1978–1980. Levels of processing of verbal materials: An overview. In *Motor learning and biomechnical factors in sport*, ed. P. Llouora and J. Flowers. Publications division, University of Toronto.

Baumeister, A. A., and G. Kellas. 1968. Distribution of reaction times of retardates and normals. *American Journal of Mental Deficiency* 72:715–718.

Bayer, L. M., and N. Bayley. 1976. *Growth diagnosis.* 2d ed. Chicago: University of Chicago Press.

Bayley, N. 1935. The development of motor abilities during the first three years. *Monographs of the Society for Research in Child Development* 1 (1, serial no. 1).

———. 1969. *The Bayley scales of infant development.* New York: Psychological Corp.

Bayley, N., and F. C. Davis. 1935. Growth changes in bodily size and proportions during the first three years: A developmental study of sixty-one children by repeated measurements. *Biometrika* 27:26–87.

Bechtoldt, H. P. 1970. Motor abilities in studies of motor learning. In *Psychology of motor learning*, ed. L. E. Smith. Chicago: Athletic Institute.

Belmont, L., and H. G. Birch. 1963. Lateral dominance and right-left awareness in normal children. *Child Development* 34:257–270.

Bernstein, N. 1967. *The co-ordination and regulation of movements.* New York: Pergamon Press.

Birch, H. G., and A. Lefford. 1963. Intersensory development in children. *Monographs of the Society for Research in Child Development* 28 (5, serial no. 89).

———. 1967. Visual differentiation, intersensory integration and voluntary motor control. *Monographs of the Society for Research in Child Development* 32 (2, serial no. 110).

Birren, J. E., and J. Botwinick. 1955. Age differences in finger, jaw, and foot reaction time to auditory stimuli. *Journal of Gerentology* 10:429–432.

Bisanz, J., and L. B. Resnick. 1978. Changes with age in two components of visual search speed. *Journal of Experimental Child Psychology* 25:129–142.

Bizzi, E., P. Dev, P. Morasso, and A. Polit. 1978. Effect of load disturbances during centrally initiated movements. *Journal of Neurophysiology* 41:542–556.

Bloom, B. S. 1964. *Stability and change in human characteristics.* New York: Wiley.

Bower, T. G. R. 1966. The visual world of infants. *Scientific American* 215(6):80–92.

———. 1977. *A primer of infant development.* San Francisco: Freeman.

———. 1979. *Human development.* San Francisco: Freeman.

———. 1982. *Development in infancy*, 2nd ed. San Francisco: Freeman.

Bower, T. G. R., J. M. Broughton, and M. K. Moore. 1970. Demonstration of intention in the reaching behaviour of neonates. *Nature* 228(5272):679–681.

———. 1971. Development of the object concept as manifested by changes in the tracking behavior of infants between 7 and 20 weeks of age. *Journal of Experimental Child Psychology* 11:182–192.

Bower, T. G. R., and J. G. Wishart. 1972. The effects of motor skill on object permanance. *Cognition* 1:165–172.

Bressan, E. S., and M. H. Woollacott. 1982. A prescriptive paradigm for sequencing instruction in physical education. *Human Movement Science* 1:155–175.

Bresson, F., L. Maury, G. Pierault-Le Bonniec, and S. de Schonen. 1977. Organization and lateralization of reaching in infants: An instance of asymmetric functions in hand collaboration. *Neuropsychologia* 15:311–320.

Broadbent, D. E. 1958. *Perception and communication.* London: Pergamon Press.

Bronson, G. W. 1982. Structure, status and characteristics of the nervous system at birth. In *Psychobiology of the human newborn*, ed. P. Stratton. New York: Wiley.

Brown, A. L. 1975. The development of memory: Knowing, knowing about knowing and knowing how to know. In *Advances in child development and behavior*, vol. 10, ed. H. W. Reese. New York: Academic Press.

————. 1978. Knowing when, where, and how to remember: A problem of metacognition. In *Advances in instructional psychology*, ed. R. Glaser. Hillsdale, N.J.: Erlbaum.

Bruininks, R. H. 1978. *The Bruininks-Oseretsky test of motor proficiency*. Circle Pines, Minn.: American Guidance Service.

Bruml, H. 1972. Age changes in preference and skill measures of handedness. *Perceptual and Motor Skills* 34:3–14.

Bruner, J. S. 1970. The growth and structure of skill. In *Mechanisms of motor skill development*, ed. K. Connolly. New York: Academic Press.

————. 1973. Organization of early skilled action. *Child Development* 44:1–11.

Bryant, P. E. 1968. Comments on the design of developmental studies of cross-modal matching and cross-modal transfer. *Cortex* 4:127–137.

Burnett, C. N., and E. W. Johnson. 1971a. Development of gait in childhood, part I: Method. *Developmental Medicine and Child Neurology* 13:196–206.

————. 1971b. Development of gait in childhood: Part II. *Developmental Medicine and Child Neurology* 13:207–215.

Burton, A. W. 1979. Age-related changes in error-detection and error-correction abilities in children. Master's thesis, University of California, Los Angeles.

Butterworth, G., and L. Hicks. 1977. Visual proprioception and postural stability in infants: A developmental study. *Perception* 6:255–262.

California. 1966. *The physical performance test for California*. Sacramento: State Department of Education.

————. 1971. *The physical performance test for California (revised)*. Sacramento: State Department of Education.

————. 1981. *The physical performance test for California (revised)*. Sacramento: State Department of Education.

Canada. 1966. *The CAHPER fitness-performance test manual*. Canadian Association for Health, Physical Education and Recreation.

Carmichael, L. 1970. Onset and early development of behavior. In *Carmichael's manual of child psychology*, vol. 1, 3rd ed., ed. P. H. Mussen. New York: Wiley.

Carron, A. V. 1971. Motor performance and response consistency as a function of age. *Journal of Motor Behavior* 3:105–109.

Carson, L. M., and R. L. Wiegand. 1979. Motor schema formation and retention in young children: A test of Schmidt's schema theory. *Journal of Motor Behavior* 11:247–251.

Carter, M. C. 1980. A preliminary analysis of children's ability to detect and correct movement errors. Master's thesis, University of California, Los Angeles.

Cavanaugh, J. C., and J. G. Borkowski. 1980. Searching for metamemory-memory connections: A developmental study. *Developmental Psychology* 16:441–453.

Cavanaugh, J. C., and M. Perlmutter. 1982. Metamemory: A critical examination. *Child Development* 53:11–28.

Chi, M. T. H. 1976. Short term memory limitations in children: Capacity or processing deficits? *Memory and Cognition* 4:559–572.

Chi, M. T. H., and E. T. Rees. 1983. A learning framework for development. In *Trends in memory development research*, ed. M. T. H. Chi. New York: Karger.

Clark, J. E. 1982. The role of response mechanisms in motor skill development. In *The development of movement control and co-ordination*, ed. J. A. S. Kelso and J. E. Clark. New York: Wiley.

Clarke, H. H. 1971. *Physical and motor tests in the Medford boys' growth study*. Englewood Cliffs, N.J.: Prentice-Hall.

Cohen, L. B., J. S. de Loache, and M. S. Strauss. 1979. Infant visual perception. In *Handbook of infant development*, ed. J. D. Osofsky. New York: Wiley.

Connell, R. A. 1980. Cognitive factors and the development of movement control. University of Leeds. Typescript.

Connolly, K. 1968. Some mechanisms involved in the development of motor skills. *Aspects of Education* 7:82–100.

393

————. 1970. Response speed, temporal sequencing and information processing in children. In *Mechanisms of motor skill development,* ed. K. Connolly. New York: Academic Press.

————. 1973. Factors influencing the learning of manual skills by young children. In *Constraints on learning,* ed. R. A. Hinde and J. S. Hinde. New York: Academic Press.

Connolly, K., K. Brown, and E. Bassett. 1968. Developmental changes in some components of a motor skill. *British Journal of Psychology* 59:305–314.

Connolly, K., and J. Bruner, eds. 1974. *The growth of competence.* New York: Academic Press.

Connolly, K., and J. Elliott. 1972. The evolution and ontogeny of hand function. In *Ethological studies of child behaviour,* ed. N. B. Jones. Cambridge, Engl.: Cambridge University Press.

Connolly, K., and B. Jones. 1970. A developmental study of afferent-reafferent integration. *British Journal of Psychology* 61:259–266.

Connolly, K., and P. Stratton. 1968. Developmental changes in associated movements. *Developmental Medicine and Child Neurology* 10:49–56.

Conroy, R. L., and P. Weener. 1976. The development of visual and auditory selective attention using the central-incidental paradigm. *Journal of Experimental Child Psychology* 22:400–407.

Constantini, A. F., D. A. Corsini, and J. E. Davis. 1973. Conceptual tempo, inhibition of movement and acceleration of movement in 4-, 7- and 9-year-old children. *Perceptual and Motor Skills* 37:779–784.

Constantini, A. F., and K. L. Hoving. 1973. The relationship of cognitive and motor response inhibition to age and IQ. *Journal of Genetic Psychology* 123:309–319.

Coren, S., C. Porac, and P. Duncan. 1981. Lateral preference behaviors in preschool children and young adults. *Child Development* 52:443–450.

Corlett, J. T., and J. Dickinson. 1983. Proactive and retroactive interference in children's motor short-term memory. *Journal of Human Movement Studies* 9:21–29.

Costa, L. D., L. M. Scarola, and I. Rapin. 1964. Purdue pegboard scores for normal grammar school children. *Perceptual and Motor Skills* 18:748.

Craik, F. I. M. 1979. Levels of processing: Overview and closing comments. In *Levels of processing in human memory,* ed. L. S. Cermak and F. I. M. Craik. Hillsdale, N.J.: Erlbaum.

Craik, F. I. M., and R. S. Lockhart. 1972. Levels of processing: A framework for memory research. *Journal of Verbal Learning and Verbal Behavior* 11:671–684.

Cratty, B. J., E. Apitzsch, and R. Bergel. 1973. Dynamic visual acuity: A developmental study. University of California, Los Angeles. Typescript.

Davids, K. 1982. An experimental paradigm for the examination of peripheral vision in children and adults during sport performance. University of Leeds. Typescript.

Davol, S. H., and S. L. Breakell. 1968. Sex differences in rotary pursuit performance of young children: A followup. *Perceptual and Motor Skills* 26:1199–1202.

Davol, S. H., M. L. Hastings, and D. A. Klein. 1965. Effect of age, sex, and speed of rotation on rotary pursuit performance by young children. *Perceptual and Motor Skills* 21:351–357.

Degelman, D., and R. Rosinski. 1979. Motion parallax and children's distance perception. *Developmental Psychology* 15:147–152.

de Jong, R. N. 1967. *The neurologic examination,* 3rd ed. New York: Hoeber.

Denckla, M. B. 1973. Development of speed in repetitive and successive finger-movements in normal children. *Developmental Medicine and Child Neurology* 15:635–645.

Denckla, M. B. 1974. Development of motor coordination in normal children. *Developmental Medicine and Child Neurology* 16:729–741.

Dennis, W. 1960. Causes of retardation among institutional children: Iran. *Journal of Genetic Psychology* 96:47–59.

de Oreo, K. L. 1976. Dynamic balance in preschool children: Quantifying qualitative data. *Research Quarterly* 47:526–531.

394

de Schonen, S. 1977. Functional asymmetries in the development of bimanual coordination in human infants. *Journal of Human Movement Studies* 3:144–156.

Deutsch, J. A., and D. Deutsch. 1963. Attention: Some theoretical considerations. *Psychological Review* 70:80–90.

di Franco, D., D. W. Muir, and P. C. Dodwell. 1978. Reaching in very young infants. *Perception* 7:385–392.

Dillman, C. J. 1975. Kinematic anlayses of running. In *Exercise and sport sciences reviews*, vol. 3, ed. J. H. Willmore and J. F. Keogh. New York: Academic Press.

Dodgson, M. C. H. 1962. *The growing brain*. Bristol, Engl.: Wright.

Doll, E. A., ed. 1946. *The Oseretsky tests of motor proficiency*. Trans. from Portugese adaptation. Circle Pines, Minn.: American Guidance Service.

Donders, A. F. 1969. On the speed of mental processes. *Acta Psychologica* 30:412–443.

Dorfman, P. W. 1977. Timing and anticipation: A developmental perspective. *Journal of Motor Behavior* 9:67–79.

Druker, J. F., and J. W. Hagen. 1969. Developmental trends in the processing of task-relevant and task-irrelevant information. *Child Development* 40:371–382.

Dunkeld, J., and T. G. R. Bower. 1978. The effect of wedge prisms on the reaching behaviour of infants. University of Edinburgh. Typescript.

Dusek, J. B. 1978. The effects of labeling and pointing in children's selective attention. *Developmental Psychology* 14:115–116.

Dyer, K. F. 1977. The trend of the male-female performance differential in athletics, swimming and cycling, 1948–1976. *Journal of Biosocial Science* 9:325–338.

Easton, T. A. 1978. Coordinative structures: The basis for a motor program. In *Psychology of motor behavior and sport: 1977*, ed. D. M. Landers and R. W. Christina. Champaign, Ill.: Human Kinetics.

Eckert, H. M., and G. L. Rarick. 1976. Stabilometer performance of educable mentally retarded and normal children. *Research Quarterly* 47:619–623.

Elkind, D., R. R. Koegler, and E. Go. 1964. Studies in perceptual development: II. Part-whole perception. *Child Development* 35:81–90.

Elliott, J. M., and K. J. Connolly. 1974. Hierarchical structure in skill development. In *The growth of competence*, ed. K. Connolly and J. S. Bruner. New York: Academic Press.

Elliott, R. 1972. Simple reaction time in children: Effects of incentive, incentive-shift and other training variables. *Journal of Experimental Child Psychology* 13:540–557.

Emmerich, W. 1964. Continuity and stability in early social development. *Child Development* 35:311–332.

Erickson, E. H. 1950. *Childhood and society*. New York: Norton.

Espenschade, A. 1960. Motor development. In *Science and medicine of exercise and sports*, ed. W. R. Johnson. New York: Harper.

Espenschade, A. S. 1940. Motor performance in adolescence. *Monographs of the Society for Research in Child Development* 5(1, serial no. 24).

Estes, W. K. 1978. The information processing approach to cognition. In *Handbook of learning and cognitive processes: Vol. 5, Human information processing*, ed. W. K. Estes. Hillsdale, N.J.: Erlbaum.

Eysenck, M. W. 1978. Levels of processing: A critique. *British Journal of Psychology* 69:157–169.

Fairweather, H., and S. J. Hutt. 1978. On the rate of gain of information in children. *Journal of Experimental Child Psychology* 26:216–229.

Fantz, R. L. 1958. Pattern vision in young infants. *Psychological Record* 8:43–47.

———. 1961. The origin of form perception. *Scientific American* 204(5):66–72.

———. 1965. Visual perception from birth as shown by pattern selectivity. *Annals of the New York Academy of Science* 118:793–814.

Faust, M. S. 1977. Somatic development of adolescent girls. *Monographs of the Society for Research in Child Development* 42(1, serial no. 169).

Faust, M. S., and W. L. Faust. 1980. Cognitive constructing: Levels of processing and developmental change. In *Advances in special education*, vol. 1, ed. B. K. Keogh. Greenwich, Conn.: JAI Press.

Ferris, B. G., and C. W. Smith. 1953. Maximum breathing capacity and vital capacity in female children and adolescents. *Pediatrics* 12:341–352.

Ferris, B. G., M. D. Whittenberger, and J. R. Gallagher. 1952. Maximum breathing capacity and vital capacity of male children and adolescents. *Pediatrics* 9:659–670.

Fiorentino, M. R. 1973. *Reflex testing methods for evaluating C.N.S. development*, 2d ed. Springfield, Ill.: Chas. C Thomas.

———. 1981. *A basis for sensorimotor development: Normal and abnormal*. Springfield, Ill.: Chas. C Thomas.

Fitts, P. M. 1954. The information capacity of the human motor system in controlling the amplitude of movement. *Journal of Experimental Psychology* 47:381–391.

———. 1962. Factors in complex skill learning. In *Training research and education*, ed. R. Glaser. Pittsburgh: University of Pittsburgh Press.

Fitts, P. M., and J. R. Peterson. 1964. Information capacity of discrete motor responses. *Journal of Experimental Psychology* 67:103–112.

Flavell, J. H. 1970. Developmental studies of mediated memory. In *Advances in child development and behavior*, vol. 5, ed. H. W. Reese and L. P. Lipsitt. New York: Academic Press.

———. 1972. An analysis of cognitive-developmental sequences. *Genetic Psychology Monographs* 86:279–350.

Fleishman, E. A. 1964. *The structure and measurement of physical fitness*. Englewood Cliffs, N. J.: Prentice-Hall.

———. 1966. Human abilities and the acquisition of skill. In *Acquisition of skill*, ed. E. A. Bilodeau. New York: Academic Press.

Fleishman, E. A., and J. F. Parker. 1962. Factors in the retention and relearning of perceptual-motor skill. *Journal of Experimental Psychology* 64:215–226.

Forman, G. E., ed. 1982. *Action and thought*. New York: Academic Press.

Forsstrom, A., and C. von Hofsten. 1982. Visually directed reaching of children with motor impairments. *Developmental Medicine and Child Neurology* 24:653–661.

Fortney, V. L. 1983. Kinematics and kinetics of the running pattern of two-, four-, and six-year-old children. *Research Quarterly for Exercise and Sport* 54:126–135.

Frankenburg, W. K., and J. B. Dodds. 1967. The Denver developmental screening test. *Journal of Pediatrics* 71:181–191.

Fulton, C. D., and A. W. Hubbard. 1975. Effect of puberty on reaction and movement times. *Research Quarterly* 46:335–344.

Gallagher, J. D., and J. R. Thomas. 1980. Effects of varying post-KR intervals upon children's motor performance. *Journal of Motor Behavior* 12:41–56.

Gardner, D. B. 1966. Intersensory aspects of children's judgments of short time intervals. Paper presented at meeting of American Psychological Association, New York.

Gardner, R. A. 1979. Throwing balls in a basket as a test of motor coordination: Normative data on 1350 school children. *Journal of Clinical Child Psychology* 8:152–155.

Gardner, R. A., and M. Broman. 1979. The Purdue pegboard: Normative data on 1334 school children. *Journal of Clinical Child Psychology* 8:156–162.

Gatev, V. 1972. Role of inhibition in the development of motor coordination in early childhood. *Developmental Medicine and Child Neurology* 14:336–341.

Gelfand, I. M., V. S. Gurfinkel, M. L. Tsetlin, and M. L. Shik. 1971. Some problems in the analysis of movements. In *Models of the structural-functional organization of certain biological systems*, ed. I. M. Gelfand, V. S. Gurfinkel, S. V. Fomin, and M. L. Tsetlin. Cambridge, Mass.: MIT Press.

Gentile, A. M., J. R. Higgins, E. A. Miller, and B. M. Rosen. 1975. The structure of motor tasks. *Mouvement* 7:11–28.

Gerson, R. F., and J. R. Thomas. 1977. Schema theory and practice variability within a neo-Piagetian framework. *Journal of Motor Behavior* 9:127–134.

————. 1978. A neo-Piagetian investigation of the serial position effect in children's motor learning. *Journal of Motor Behavior* 10:95–104.

Gesell, A., and C. S. Amatruda. 1941. *Developmental diagnosis.* New York: Harper.

————. 1947. *Developmental diagnosis*, 2d ed. New York: Harper.

Gibson, E. J., and R. D. Walk. 1960. The visual cliff. *Scientific American* 202(4):64–71.

Gibson, J. J. 1966. *The senses considered as perceptual systems.* Boston: Houghton-Mifflin.

————. 1977. The theory of affordances. In *Perceiving, acting and knowing*, ed. R. Shaw and J. Bransford. Hillsdale, N.J.: Erlbaum.

Ginsburg, H., and S. Opper. 1969. *Piaget's theory of intellectual development.* Englewood Cliffs, N.J.: Prentice-Hall.

Gipsman, S. C. 1973. Control of range of movement rate in primary school children. Master's thesis, University of California, Los Angeles.

Glassow, R. B., and P. Kruse. 1960. Motor performance of girls age 6 to 14 years. *Research Quarterly* 31:426–433.

Goetzinger, C. P. 1961. A re-evaluation of the Heath railwalking test. *Journal of Educational Research* 54:187–191.

Goodnow, J. 1971. The role of modalities in perceptual and cognitive development. In *Minnesota Symposia on Child Psychology*, vol. 5, ed. J. P. Hill. Minneapolis: University of Minnesota Press.

Goulet, L. R., and P. B. Baltes, eds. 1970. *Lifespan developmental psychology: Research and theory.* New York: Academic Press.

Grant, W. W., A. N. Boelsche, and D. Zin. 1973. Developmental pattern of two motor functions. *Developmental Medicine and Child Neurology* 15:171–177.

Griffin, N. S., and J. F. Keogh. 1982. A model for movement confidence. In *The development of movement control and co-ordination*, ed. J. A. S. Kelso and J. E. Clark. New York: Wiley.

Griffiths, R. 1954. *The abilities of babies.* New York: McGraw-Hill.

Guilford, J. P. 1958. A system of the psychomotor abilities. *American Journal of Psychology* 71:164–174.

Gutteridge, M. V. 1939. A study of motor achievements of young children. *Archives of Psychology* 34(serial no. 244).

Hagen, J. W. 1967. The effect of distraction on selective attention. *Child Development* 38:685–694.

Hagen, J. W., and S. R. Fisch. 1968. *The effects of incidental cues on selective attention.* Report no. 57, USPHS grant HD 03168. Ann Arbor, Mich.: Center for Human Growth and Development, University of Michigan.

Hale, G. A., and L. B. Alderman. 1978. Children's selective attention with variation in amount of stimulus exposure. *Journal of Experimental Child Psychology* 26:320–327.

Hall, R. J. 1980. An information-processing approach to the study of exceptional children. In *Advances in special education*, vol. 2, ed. B. K. Keogh. Greenwich, Conn.: JAI Press.

Halverson, H. M. 1931. An experimental study of prehension in infants by means of systematic cinema records. *Genetic Psychology Monographs* 10:107–286.

Halverson, L. E., M. A. Roberton, and S. Langendorfer. 1982. Development of the overarm throw: Movement and ball velocity changes by seventh grade. *Research Quarterly for Exercise and Sport* 53:198–205.

Harris, L. J. 1983. Laterality of function in the human infant: An historical review of theory and research. In *Manual specialization and the developing brain*, ed. G. Young, C. Corter, S. J. Segalowitz, and S. Trehub. New York: Academic Press.

Harway, N. I. 1963. Judgment of distance in children and adults. *Journal of Experimental Psychology* 65:385–390.

Hay, L. 1979. Spatial-temporal analysis of movements in children: Motor programs versus feedback in the development of reaching. *Journal of Motor Behavior* 11:189–200.

397

————. 1981. The effect of amplitude and accuracy requirements on movement time in children. *Journal of Motor Behavior* 13:177–186.

Heath, B. H., and J. E. L. Carter. 1966. A comparison of somatotype methods. *American Journal of Physical Anthropology* 24:87–99.

————. 1967. A modified somatotype method. *American Journal of Physical Anthropology* 27:57–74.

Heath, S. R. 1949. The railwalking test: Preliminary maturational norms for boys and girls. *Motor Skills Research Exchange* 1:34–36.

Hellebrandt, F. A., G. L. Rarick, R. Glassow, and M. L. Carns. 1961. Physiological analysis of basic motor skills: I. Growth and development of jumping. *American Journal of Physical Medicine* 40:14–25.

Henderson, L. 1982. *Orthography and word recognition in reading.* London: Academic Press.

Henry, F. M. 1956. Evaluation of motor learning when performance levels are heterogeneous. *Research Quarterly* 27:176–181.

————. 1961. Stimulus complexity, movement complexity, age, and sex in relation to reaction latency and speed in limb movements. *Research Quarterly* 32:353–366.

Hick, W. E. 1952. On the rate of gain of information. *Quarterly Journal of Experimental Psychology* 4:11–26.

Hicks, J. A. 1930. The acquisition of motor skill in young children. *Child Development* 1:90–105.

Hicks, R. E., and M. Kinsbourne. 1976. On the genesis of human handedness: A review. *Journal of Motor Behavior* 18:257–266.

Hiscock, M., and M. Kinsbourne. 1978. Ontogeny of cerebral dominance: Evidence from time-sharing asymmetry in children. *Developmental Psychology* 14:321–329.

Hodgkins, J. 1962. Influence of age on the speed of reaction and movement in females. *Journal of Gerentology* 17:385–389.

————. 1963. Reaction time and speed of movement in males and females of various ages. *Research Quarterly* 34:335–343.

Hoffman, E. R., A. Payne, and S. Prescott. 1980. Children's estimates of vehicle approach time. *Human Factors* 22:235–240.

Hoffman, S. J., C. H. Imwold, and J. A. Koller. 1983. Accuracy of prediction in throwing: A taxonomic analysis of children's performance. *Research Quarterly for Exercise and Sport* 54:33–40.

Hogan, J. C., and R. Hogan. 1975. Organization of early skilled action: Some comments. *Child Development* 46:233–236.

Hogan, J. C., and B. A. Yanowitz. 1978. The role of verbal estimates of movement error in ballistic skill acquisition. *Journal of Motor Behavior* 10:133–138.

Holbrook, S. F. 1953. A study of the development of motor abilities between the ages of four and twelve, using a modification of the Oseretsky scale. Ph. D. diss., University of Minnesota.

Hopkins, B. 1976. Culturally determined patterns of handling the human infant. *Journal of Human Movement Studies* 2:1–27.

Horn, P. W. 1975. Pursuit rotor speed, sex differences, and reminiscence in young children. *Journal of Psychology* 91:81–85.

Hyman, R. 1953. Stimulus information as a determinant of reaction time. *Journal of Experimental Psychology* 45:188–196.

Ilg, F. L., and L. B. Ames. 1964. *School readiness.* New York: Harper & Row.

Iliff, A., and V. A. Lee. 1952. Pulse rate, respiratory rate, and body temperature of children between two months and eighteen years of age. *Child Development* 23:237–245.

Jacklin, C. N., M. E. Snow, and E. E. Maccoby. 1981. Tactile sensitivity and muscle strength in new born boys and girls. *Infant Behavior and Development* 4:261–268.

Jahoda, G. 1976. Rapidity of bilateral arm movements: A cross-cultural study. *Psychologia Africana* 16:207–214.

398

Jenkins, L. M. 1930. A comparative study of motor achievements of children of five, six and seven years of age. *Contributions to Education* (no. 414). New York: Teachers College, Columbia University.

Jersild, A. T., and S. F. Bienstock. 1935. Development of rhythm in young children. *Child Development Monographs* (no. 22).

Jewett, A. E., and M. R. Mullan. 1977. *Curriculum design: Purposes and processes in physical education teaching-learning.* Washington, D.C.: AAHPER.

Jones, B. 1982. The development of intermodal co-ordination and motor control. In *The development of movement control and co-ordination,* ed. J. A. S. Kelso and J. E. Clark. New York: Wiley.

Jones, H. E. 1939. Principles and methods of the adolescent growth study. *Journal of Consulting Psychology* 3:157–159.

————. 1949. *Motor performance and growth.* Berkeley: University of California Press.

Jordan, D. B. 1966. Longitudinal analysis of strength and motor development of boys ages seven through twelve years. Ph.D. diss., University of Oregon.

Kahneman, D. 1973. *Attention and effort.* Englewood Cliffs, N.J.: Prentice-Hall.

Kaufman, A. S., R. Zalma, and N. L. Kaufman. 1978. The relationship of hand dominance to the motor coordination, mental ability, and right-left awareness of young normal children. *Child Development* 49:885–888.

Kay, H. 1970. Analyzing motor skill performance. In *Mechanisms of motor skill development,* ed. K. Connolly. New York: Academic Press.

Kelso, J. A. S., D. Goodman, C. L. Stamm, and C. Hayes. 1979. Movement coding and memory in retarded children. *American Journal of Mental Deficiency* 83:601–611.

Kelso, J. A. S., and P. E. Norman. 1978. Motor schema formation in children. *Developmental Psychology* 14:153–156.

Kenyon, G. S. 1968. A conceptual model for characterizing physical activity. *Research Quarterly* 39:96–105.

Keogh, B. K., and C. B. Kopp. 1978. From assessment to intervention: An elusive bridge. In *Communicative and cognitive abilities: Early behavioral assessment,* ed. F. D. Minifie and L. L. Lloyd. Baltimore: University Park Press.

Keogh, J. F. 1965. *Motor performance of elementary school children* (USPHS grants MH 08319-01 and HD 01059). Department of Physical Education, University of California, Los Angeles.

————. 1966. Physical performance test data for English boys, ages 6–9. *Physical Education* 58:65–69.

————. 1968a. *Analysis of individual tests in the Stott test of motor impairment.* Technical report 2-68 (USPHS grant HD 01059). Department of Physical Education, University of California, Los Angeles.

————. 1968b. *Developmental evaluation of limb movement tasks.* Technical report 1-68 (USPHS grant HD 01059). Department of Physical Education, University of California, Los Angeles.

————. 1969a. *Analysis of limb and body control tasks.* Technical report 1-69 (USPHS grant HD 01059). Department of Physical Education, University of California, Los Angeles.

————. 1969b. *Change in motor performance during early school years.* Technical report 2-69 (USPHS grant HD 01059). Department of Physical Education, University of California, Los Angeles.

————. 1970. A rhythmical hopping task as an assessment of motor deficiency. In *Contemporary psychology of sport,* ed. G. Kenyon. Chicago: Athletic Institute.

————. 1971a. Comments on Singer's study of differences between third- and sixth-grade children. *Research Quarterly* 42:96–97.

————. 1971b. Motor control as a unifying concept in the study of motor development. *Motor development symposium.* Berkeley: University of California.

————. 1975. Consistency and constancy in preschool motor development. In *Motor behavior of preschool children*, ed. H. J. Muller, R. Decker, and F. Schilling. Schorndorff, W. Ger.: Hofman.

————. 1977. The study of movement skill development. *Quest*, Monograph 28, pp. 76–88.

————. 1978. The use of visual information in control of movement force. University of California, Los Angeles. Typescript.

————. 1981. A movement development framework and a perceptual-cognitive perspective. In *Perspectives on the academic discipline of physical education*, ed. G. A. Brooks. Champaign, Ill.: Human Kinetics.

Keogh, J., G. Gardner, and G. Egstrom. 1965. Physical performance of peace corps volunteers. *Research Quarterly* 36:374–376.

Keogh, J. F. and J. N. Oliver. 1968. A clinical study of physically awkward educationally subnormal boys. *Research Quarterly* 39:301–307.

Kerr, B., C. Blanchard, and K. Miller. 1980. Children's use of sequence information in partially predictable reaction-time sequences. *Journal of Experimental Child Psychology* 29:529–549.

Kerr, R. 1975. Movement control and maturation in elementary-grade children. *Perceptual and Motor Skills* 41:151–154.

Kessen, W., M. M. Haith, and P. H. Salapatek. 1970. Human infancy: A bibliography and guide. In *Carmichael's manual of child psychology*, vol. 1, 3rd ed., ed. P. H. Mussen. New York: Wiley.

Kilbride, P. L. 1980. Sensorimotor behavior of Baganda and Samia infants: A controlled comparison. *Journal of Cross-Cultural Psychology* 11:131–152.

Kinsbourne, M., and J. Cook. 1971. Generalized and lateralized effects of concurrent verbalization on a unimanual skill. *Quarterly Journal of Experimental Psychology* 23:341–345.

Kinsbourne, M., and R. E. Hicks. 1978. Functional cerebral space: A model for overflow, transfer and interference effects in human performance: A tutorial review. In *Attention and performance VII*, ed. J. Requin. Hillside, N.J.: Erlbaum.

Klapp, S. T., E. P. Wyatt, and W. M. Lingo. 1974. Response programming in simple and choice reactions. *Journal of Motor Behavior* 6:263–271.

Knights, R. M., and A. D. Moule. 1967. Normative and reliability data on finger and foot tapping in children. *Perceptual and Motor Skills* 25:717–720.

Knobloch, H., and B. Pasamanick, eds. 1974. *Gesell and Amatruda's developmental diagnosis*, 3rd ed. New York: Harper & Row.

Kobasigawa, A. 1977. Retrieval strategies in the development of memory. In *Perspectives on the development of memory and cognition*, ed. R. V. Kail and J. W. Hagen. Hillsdale, N.J.: Erlbaum.

Kopp, C. B. 1979. Perspectives on infant motor system development. In *Psychological development from infancy*, ed. M. Bornstein and W. Kessen. Hillsdale, N.J.: Erlbaum.

Korner, A. E., E. B. Thoman, and J. H. Glick. 1974. A system for monitoring crying and noncrying, large, medium, and small neonatal movements. *Child Development* 45:946–952.

Kreutzer, M. A., C. Leonard, and J. H. Flavell. 1975. An interview study of children's knowledge about memory. *Monographs of the Society for Research in Child Development* 40(1, serial no. 159).

Krus, P. H., R. H. Bruininks, and G. Robertson. 1981. Structure of motor abilities in children. *Perceptual and Motor Skills* 52:119–129.

Kugler, P. N., J. A. S. Kelso, and M. T. Turvey. 1982. On the control and co-ordination of naturally developing systems. In *The development of movement control and co-ordination*, ed. J. A. S. Kelso and J. E. Clark. New York: Wiley.

Laabs, G. T. 1973. Retention characteristics of different reproduction cues in motor short-term memory. *Journal of Experimental Psychology* 100:168–177.

Laabs, G. T., and R. W. Simmons. 1981. Motor memory. In *Human skills*, ed. D. H. Holding. New York: Wiley.

Landmark, M. 1962. Visual perception and the capacity for form construction. *Developmental Medicine and Child Neurology* 4:387–392.

Lane, D. M. 1979. Developmental changes in attention-deployment skills. *Journal of Experimental Child Psychology* 28:16–29.

Langolf, G. D., D. B. Chaffin, and J. A. Foulke. 1976. An investigation of Fitts' law using a wide range of movement amplitudes. *Journal of Motor Behavior* 8:113–128.

Lasky, R. E. 1977. The effect of visual feedback of the hand on the reaching and retrieval behavior of young infants. *Child Development* 48:112–117.

Lazlo, J. I., and P. J. Bairstow. 1980. The measurement of kinaesthetic sensitivity in children and adults. *Developmental Medicine and Child Neurology* 22:454–464.

Leavitt, J. L. 1979. Cognitive demands of skating and stickhandling in ice hockey. *Canadian Journal of Applied Sports Sciences* 4:46–55.

Lee, D. N. 1978. The functions of vision. In *Modes of perceiving and processing information*, ed. H. L. Pick and E. Saltzman. Hillsdale, N.J.: Erlbaum.

Lee, D. N., and E. Aronson. 1974. Visual proprioceptive control of standing in human infants. *Perception and Psychophysics* 15:529–532.

Lee, D. N., and J. R. Lishman. 1975. Visual proprioceptive control of stance. *Journal of Human Movement Studies* 1:87–95.

Lewis, R. C., A. M. Duvall, and A. Iliff. 1943. Standards for the basal metabolism of children from 2 to 15 years of age, inclusive. *Journal of Pediatrics* 23:1–18.

Lindberg, M. A. 1980. Is knowledge base development a necessary and sufficient condition for memory development? *Journal of Experimental Child Psychology* 30:401–410.

Lockman, J. L., and D. H. Ashmead. 1983. Asynchronies in the development of manual behavior. In *Advances in Infancy Research*, vol. 2., ed. L. P. Lipsitt and C. K. Rovee-Collier. Norwood, N.J.: Ablex.

Lombard, O. M. 1950. Breadth of bone and muscle by age and sex in childhood. *Child Development* 21:229–239.

Long, A. B., and W. R. Looft. 1972. Development of directionality in children: Ages six through twelve. *Developmental Psychology* 6:375–380.

Lurcat, L., and I. Kostin. 1970. Study of graphical abilities in children. *Perceptual and Motor Skills* 30:615–630.

Maccoby, E. E., and H. L. Bee. 1965. Some speculations concerning the lag between-perceiving and performing. *Child Development* 36:367–377.

Maccoby, E. E., E. M. Dowley, J. W. Hagen, and R. Degerman. 1965. Activity level and intellectual functioning in normal preschool children. *Child Development* 36:761–770.

Malina, R. M. 1975. Anthropometric correlates of strength and motor performance. *Exercise and Sport Sciences Reviews* 3:249–274.

———. 1978. Adolescent growth and maturation: Selected aspects of current research. *Yearbook of Physical Anthropology* 21:63–94.

———. 1980. Biosocial correlates of motor development during infancy and early childhood. In *Social and biological predictors of nutritional status, physical growth, and neurological development*, ed. L. S. Greene and F. E. Johnstone. New York: Academic Press.

———. 1983. Unpublished data, 1968. Tabular summary reported in *Manual of physical status and performance in childhood. Vol. 2: Physical performance*, ed. A. F. Roche and R. M. Malina. New York: Plenum Press.

Malina, R. M., A. B. Harper, H. H. Avent, and D. E. Campbell. 1971. Physique of female track and field athletes. *Medicine and Science in Sports* 3:32–38.

Malina, R. M., and G. L. Rarick. 1973. Growth, physique, and motor performance. In *Physical activity: Human growth and development*, ed. G. L. Rarick. New York: Academic Press.

Manis, F. R., D. P. Keating, and F. J. Morrison. 1980. Developmental differences in the allocation of processing capacity. *Journal of Experimental Child Psychology* 29:156–169.

Mavrinskaya, L. F. 1960. On correlations of development of skeletal muscle nerve endings with appearance of motor activity in human embryos. *Arkhiv Anatomi* 38:61–68.

———. 1962. Histological changes of cholinesterase in developing somatic musculature of human embryos. *Arkhiv Anatomi* 42:30–43.

McCall, R. B. 1979. The development of intellectual functioning in infancy and the prediction of later IQ. In *Handbook of infant development*, ed. J. D. Osofsky. New York: Wiley.

McCaskill, C. L., and B. L. Wellman. 1938. A study of common motor achievements at the preschool ages. *Child Development* 9:141–150.

McCracken, H. D. 1983. Movement control in a reciprocal tapping task: A developmental study. *Journal of Motor Behavior* 15:262–279.

McDonnell, P. M. 1979. Patterns of eye-hand coordination in the first year of life. *Canadian Journal of Psychology* 33:253–267.

McDonnell, P. M., and W. C. Abraham. 1978. Application of signal detection theory in the analysis of oriented limb movements in the first two months. Paper presented at meeting of Canadian Psychological Association, Ottawa.

McGraw, M. B. 1963. *The neuromuscular maturation of the human infant* (reprint ed.). New York: Hafner.

Meeker, M. 1964. *Background for planning*. Los Angeles: Welfare Planning Council.

Meltzoff, A. N., and R. W. Borton. 1979. Intermodal matching by human neonates. *Nature* 282:403–404.

Meltzoff, A. N., and M. K. Moore. 1977. Imitation of facial and manual gestures by human neonates. *Science* 198:75–78.

———. 1983. The origins of imitation in infancy: Paradigm, phenomena, and theories. In *Advances in infancy research*, vol. 2, ed. L. P. Lipsitt and C. K. Rovee-Collier. Norwood, N.J.: Ablex.

Meyers, C. E., and H. F. Dingman. 1960. The structure of abilities at the preschool years: Hypothesized domains. *Psychological Bulletin* 57:514–532.

Michaels, C. F., and C. Carello. 1981. *Direct perception*. Englewood Cliffs, N.J.:Prentice-Hall.

Milani-Comparetti, A., and E. A. Gidoni. 1967. Routine developmental examination in normal and retarded children. *Developmental Medicine and Child Neurology* 9:631–638.

Millar, S. 1974. Tactile short-term memory by blind and sighted children. *British Journal of Psychology* 65:253–263.

———. 1975a. Effects of input conditions on intramodal and crossmodal visual and kinesthetic matches by children. *Journal of Experimental Child Psychology* 19:63–78.

———. 1975b. Spatial memory by blind and sighted children. *British Journal of Psychology* 66:449–459.

———. 1978. Short-term serial tactual recall: Effects of grouping on tactually probed recall of Braille letters and nonsense shapes by blind children. *British Journal of Psychology* 69:17–24.

Montoye, H. J., and D. E. Lamphier. 1977. Grip and arm strength in males and females, age 10 to 69. *Research Quarterly* 48:108–120.

Morris, A. M., J. M. Williams, A. E. Atwater, and J. H. Wilmore. 1982. Age and sex differences in motor performance of 3- through 6-year-old children. *Research Quarterly for Exercise and Sport* 53:214–221.

Moss, S. C., and J. Hogg. 1981. Observation and classification of prehension in preschool children: A reliability study. *Research Quarterly for Exercise and Sport* 52:273–277.

———. 1983. The development and integration of fine motor sequences in 12-month-old to 18-month-old children: A test of the modular theory of motor skill acquisition. *Genetic Psychology Monographs* 107:145–187.

Mounoud, P., and C. Hauert. 1982. Development of sensorimotor organization in young children: Grasping and lifting objects. In *Action and thought*, ed. G. E. Forman. New York: Academic Press.

402

Moxley, S. E. 1979. Schema: The variability of practice hypothesis. *Journal of Motor Behavior* 11:65–70.

Mugrage, E. R., and M. I. Andresen. 1936. Values for red blood cells of average infants and children. *American Journal of Diseases of Children* 51:775–791.

———. 1938. Red blood cell values in adolescence. *American Journal of Diseases of Children* 56:997–1003.

Mundy-Castle, A. C., and J. Anglin. 1969. The development of looking in infancy. Paper presented at meeting of Society for Research in Child Development, Santa Monica, Calif.

Napier, J. R. 1956. The prehensile movements of the human hand. *Journal of Bone and Joint Surgery* 38B:902–913.

Naus, M. J., P. A. Ornstein, and K. L. Hoving. 1978. Developmental implications of multistore and depth-of-processing models of memory. In *Memory development in children*, ed. P. A. Ornstein. Hillsdale, N.J.: Erlbaum.

Neumann, E., and R. B. Ammons. 1957. Acquisition and long-term retention of a simple serial perceptual-motor skill. *Journal of Experimental Psychology* 53:159–161.

Newell, K. M. 1976a. Knowledge of results and motor learning. In *Exercise and sport sciences reviews*, vol. 4, ed. J. F. Keogh and R. S. Hutton. Santa Barbara, Calif.: Journal Publishing Affiliates.

———. 1976b. More on absolute error, etc. *Journal of Motor Behavior* 8:139–142.

Newell, K. M., and C. R. Barclay. 1982. Developing knowledge about action. In *The development of movement control and co-ordination*, ed. J. A. S. Kelso and J. E. Clark. New York: Wiley.

Newell, K. M., and L. G. Carlton. 1980. Developmental trends in motor response recognition. *Developmental Psychology* 16:550–554.

Newell, K. M., and J. A. Kennedy. 1978. Knowledge of results and children's learning. *Developmental Psychology* 14:531–536.

Newell, K. M., D. C. Shapiro, and M. J. Carlton. 1979. Coordinating visual and kinaesthetic memory codes. *British Journal of Psychology* 70:87–96.

Newell, K. M., and M. G. Wade. 1974. Stabilometer trial length as a function of performance. *Research Quarterly* 45:16–20.

Nicolson, R. I. 1982. Cognitive factors in simple reactions: A developmental study. *Journal of Motor Behavior* 14:69–80.

Noble, C. E. 1978. Age, race, and sex in the learning and performance of psychomotor skills. In *Human variation: The biopsychology of age, race, and sex*, ed. R. T. Osborne, C. E. Noble, and N. Weyl. New York: Academic Press.

Noble, C. E., B. L. Baker, and T. A. Jones. 1964. Age and sex parameters in psychomotor learning. *Perceptual and Motor Skills* 19:935–945.

Oseretsky, N. I. 1948. A metric scale for studying motor capacity of children, 1923. Cited in *Annotated bibliography on the Oseretsky tests of motor proficiency*, by R. Lassner. *Journal of Consulting Psychology* 12:37–47.

Owings, R. A., and A. A. Baumeister. 1979. Levels of processing, encoding strategies and memory development. *Journal of Experimental Child Psychology* 28:100–111.

Ozer, M. N. 1968. The neurological evaluation of school-age children. *Journal of Learning Disabilities* 1:87–90.

Palmer, C. E. 1933. Seasonal variation of average growth in weight of elementary school children. *Public Health Reports* 48(1):211–233.

Parizkova, J. 1976. Growth and growth velocity of lean body mass and fat in adolescent boys. *Pediatric Research* 10:647–650.

Parmelee, A. H., and M. Sigman. 1983. Perinatal brain development and behavior. In *Biology and infancy*, ed. M. Haith and J. Campos. New York: Wiley.

Parnell, R. W. 1954. Somatotyping by physical anthropology. *American Journal of Physical Anthropology* 120:209–239.

———. 1958. *Behavior and physique: An introduction to practical and applied somatometry.* London: Arnold.

403

Pascual-Leone, J. 1970. A mathematical model for the transition rule in Piaget's developmental stages. *Acta Psychologica* 32:301–345.

Pascual-Leone, J., and J. Smith. 1969. The encoding and decoding of symbols by children: A new experimental paradigm and a neo-Piagetian model. *Journal of Experimental Child Psychology* 8:328–355.

Passer, M. W. 1982. Children in sport: Participation motives and psychological stress. *Quest* 33:231–244.

Peacock, W. H. 1960. *Achievement scales in physical education for boys and girls ages seven through fifteen.* Chapel Hill: University of North Carolina Press.

Perlmutter, M., and N. A. Myers. 1979. Development of recall in 2- to 4-year-old children. *Developmental Psychology* 15:73–83.

Peters, M., and B. M. Durding. 1978. Handedness measured by finger tapping: A continuous variable. *Canadian Journal of Psychology* 32:257–261.

Petterson, L., A. Yonas, and R. O. Fisch. 1980. The development of blinking in response to impending collision in preterm and full-term and postterm infants. *Infant Behavior and Development* 3:155–165.

Phillips, S., S. King, and L. Dubois. 1978. Spontaneous activities of female versus male newborns. *Child Development* 49:590–597.

Piaget, J. 1964. Development and learning. In *Piaget rediscovered,* ed. R. E. Ripple and V. N. Rockcastle. Ithaca, N.Y.: Cornell University Press.

Piaget, J., and B. Inhelder. 1956. *The child's conception of space.* London: Routledge and Kegan Paul.

———. 1973. *Memory and intelligence.* New York: Basic Books.

Poe, A. 1976. Description of the movement characteristics of two-year-old children performing the jump and reach. *Research Quarterly* 47:260–268.

Posner, M. I., and A. F. Konick. 1966. Short-term retention of visual and kinesthetic information. *Organizational Behavior and Human Performance* 1:71–86.

Poulton, E. C. 1957. On prediction in skilled movements. *Psychological Bulletin* 54:467–478.

Rarick, G. L., D. A. Dobbins, and G. D. Broadhead. 1976. *The motor domain and its correlates in educationally handicapped children.* Englewood Cliffs, N.J.: Prentice-Hall.

Rarick, G. L., and N. O. Oyster. 1964. Physical maturity, muscular strength, and motor performance of young school-age boys. *Research Quarterly* 35:523–530.

Rarick, G. L., and F. L. Smoll. 1967. Stability of growth in strength and motor performance from childhood to adolescence. *Human Biology* 39:295–306.

Reid, G. 1980a. The effects of memory strategy instruction in the short-term motor memory of the mentally retarded. *Journal of Motor Behavior* 12:221–227.

———. 1980b. Overt and covert rehearsal in short-term motor memory of mentally retarded and nonretarded persons. *American Journal of Mental Deficiency* 85:69–77.

Reynolds, E.L. 1949. The fat/bone index as a sex-differentiating character in man. *Human Biology* 21:199–204.

Richards, J.E., and N. Rader. 1981. Crawling-onset age predicts visual cliff avoidance in infants. *Journal of Experimental Psychology: Human Perception and Performance* 7:382–387.

Roberton, M.A. 1977. Stability of stage categorizations across trials: Implications for the "stage theory" of overarm throw development. *Journal of Human Movement Studies* 3:49–59.

Roberton, M. A., L. E. Halverson, S. Langendorfer, and K. Williams. 1979. Longitudinal changes in children's overarm throw ball velocities. *Research Quarterly* 50:256–264.

Robson, P. 1970. Shuffling, hitching, scooting or sliding: Some observations in 30 otherwise normal children. *Developmental Medicine and Child Neurology* 12:608–617.

Roche, A. F., ed. 1979. Secular trends in human growth, maturation, and development. *Monographs of the Society for Research in Child Development* 44(3–4, serial no. 179).

Rodier, P. M. 1980. Chronology of neuron development: Animal studies and their clinical implications. *Developmental Medicine and Child Neurology* 22:525–545.

Rosenbloom, L. and M. E. Horton. 1971. The maturation of fine prehension in young children. *Developmental Medicine and Child Neurology* 13:3–8.

————. 1975. Observing motor skill: A developmental approach. In Movement and child development, *Clinics in Developmental Medicine* no. 55.

Rosenbusch, M. H., and B. D. Gardner. 1968. Reproduction of visual and auditory rhythm patterns by children. *Perceptual and Motor Skills* 26:1271–1276.

Ryan, E. D. 1965. Retention of stabilometer performance over extended periods of time. *Research Quarterly* 36:46–51.

Saida, Y., and M. Miyashita. 1979. Development of fine motor skill in children: Manipulation of a pencil in young children aged 2 to 6 years. *Journal of Human Movement Studies* 5:104–113.

Salmoni, A. W. 1980. The effect of precision of knowledge of results on the performance of a simple line drawing task for children and adults. *Research Quarterly* 51:572–575.

————. 1983. A descriptive analysis of children performing Fitts' reciprocal tapping task. *Journal of Human Movement Studies* 9:81–95.

Salmoni, A. W., and C. Pascoe. 1978. Fitts' reciprocal tapping task: A developmental study. In *Psychology of motor behavior and sport*, ed. C. G. Roberts and K. M. Newell. Champaign, Ill.: Human Kinetics.

Sameroff, A. J., and M. J. Chandler. 1975. Reproductive risk and the continuum of caretaking causality. In *Review of child development research*, vol. 4, ed. F. D. Horowitz. Chicago: University of Chicago Press.

Sattler, J. M., and J. Englehardt. 1982. Sex differences on Purdue pegboard norms for children. *Journal of Clinical Child Psychology* 11:72–73.

Scammon, R. E. 1930. The measurement of the body in childhood. In *The measurement of man* by J. A. Harris, C. M. Jackson, D. G. Patterson, and R. E. Scammon. Minneapolis: University of Minnesota Press.

Schellekens, J. M. H., C. A. Scholten, and A. F. Kalverboer. 1983. Visually guided hand movements in children with minor neurological dysfunctions: Response time and movement time organization. *Journal of Child Psychology and Psychiatry* 24:89–102.

Schmidt, R. A. 1975. A schema theory of discrete motor skill learning. *Psychological Review* 82:225–260.

————. 1980. Past and future issues in motor programming. *Research Quarterly for Exercise and Sport* 51:122–140.

————. 1982. *Motor control and learning: A behavioral emphasis.* Champaign, Ill.: Human Kinetics.

Schmidt, R. A., H. Zelaznik, B. Hawkins, J. S. Frank, and J. T. Quinn. 1979. Motor-output variability: A theory for the accuracy of rapid motor acts. *Psychological Review* 86:415–451.

Scrutton, D. R. 1969. Footprint sequences of normal children under five years old. *Developmental Medicine and Child Neurology* 11:44–53.

Schulman, J. L., C. Buist, J. C. Kaspar, D. Child, and E . Fackler. 1969. An objective test of speed of fine motor function. *Perceptual and Motor Skills* 29:243–255.

Schutz, R. W., and E. A. Roy. 1973. Absolute error: The devil in disguise. *Journal of Motor Behavior* 5:141–153.

Second International Congress about the Physical Fitness of Youth. 1966. Prague.

Seefeldt, V., S. Reuschlein, and P. Vogel. 1972. Sequencing motor skills within the physical education curriculum. Paper presented at meeting of American Association of Health, Physical Education and Recreation, Houston.

Seth, G. 1973. Eye-hand coordination and "handedness": A developmental study of visuo-motor behavior in infancy. *British Journal of Educational Psychology* 43:35–49.

Shannon, C. E., and W. Weaver. 1949. *The mathematical theory of communication.* Urbana: University of Illinois Press.

Shapiro, D. C., and R. A. Schmidt. 1982. The schema theory: Recent evidence and developmental implications. In *The development of movement control and co-ordination,* ed. J. A. S. Kelso and J. E. Clark. New York: Wiley.

Sharp, R. H., and H. T. A. Whiting. 1974. Exposure and occluded duration effects in a ball-catching skill. *Journal of Motor Behavior* 6: 139–147.

Shea, C. H., J. B. Krampitz, C. C. Northam, and A. A. Ashby. 1982. Information processing in coincident timing tasks: A developmental perspective. *Journal of Human Movement Studies* 8:73–83.

Sheldon, W. H., C. W. Dupertuis, and E. McDermott. 1954. *Atlas of Men: A guide for somatotyping the adult male at all ages.* New York: Harper & Row.

Sheldon, W. H., and S. S. Stevens. 1942. *The varieties of human physique.* New York: Harper & Row.

Sheridan, M. R. 1979. A reappraisal of Fitts' law. *Journal of Motor Behavior* 11:179–188.

Shirley, M. M. 1931. *The first two years: A study of twenty-five babies. Vol. 1: Postural and locomotor development.* Minneapolis: University of Minnesota Press.

Shock, N. W. 1944. Basal blood pressure and pulse rate in adolescents. *American Journal of Diseases of Children* 68:16–22.

———. 1946. Some physiological aspects of adolescence. *Texas Reports on Biology and Medicine* 4:289–310.

Shuttleworth, F. K. 1939. The physical and mental growth of girls and boys age six to nineteen in relation to age at maximum growth. *Monographs of the Society for Research in Child Development* 4(3, serial no. 22).

Simard, T. 1969. Fine sensorimotor control in healthy children: An electromyographic study. *Pediatrics* 43:1035–1041.

Simon, H. A. 1972. What is visual imagery? An information processing interpretation. In *Cognition in learning and memory,* ed. L. W. Gregg. New York: Wiley.

Simon, J. A., and F. L. Smoll. 1974. An instrument for assessing children's attitudes toward physical activity. *Research Quarterly* 45:407–415.

Singer, R. N. 1965. Effects of spectators on athletes and non-athletes performing a gross motor task. *Research Quarterly* 36:473–482.

Singer, R. N., and R. F. Gerson. 1981. Task classification and strategy utilization in motor skills. *Research Quarterly for Exercise and Sport* 52:100–116.

Sloan, W. 1955. The Lincoln-Oseretsky motor development scale. *Genetic Psychology Monographs* 51:183–252.

Smith, J. L. 1978. Sensorimotor integration during motor programming. In *Information processing in motor control and learning,* ed. G. E. Stelmach. New York: Academic Press.

Smith, O. W., and P. C. Smith. 1966. Developmental studies of spatial judgments by children and adults. *Perceptual and Motor Skills Monograph Supplement* 22:3–73.

Smoll, F. L. 1973. A rhythmic ability analysis system. *Research Quarterly* 44:232–236.

———. 1974a. Development of rhythmic ability in response to selected tempos. *Perceptual and Motor Skills* 39:767–772.

———. 1974b. Development of spatial and temporal elements of rhythmic ability. *Journal of Motor Behavior* 6:53–58.

———. 1975. Variability in development of spatial and temporal elements of rhythmic ability. *Perceptual and Motor Skills* 40:140.

Smothergill, D. W. 1973. Accuracy and variability in the localization of spatial targets at three age levels. *Developmental Psychology* 8:62–66.

Spaeth-Arnold, R. K. 1981. Developing sport skills. *Motor Skills: Theory into Practice,* Monograph 2.

Statham, L., and M. P. Murray. 1971. Early walking patterns of normal children. *Clinical Orthopaedics and Related Reseach* 79:8–24.

Stelmach, G. E., ed. 1976. *Motor control: Issues and trends.* New York: Academic Press.

————. ed. 1978. *Information processing in motor control and learning*. New York: Academic press.

Stelmach, G. E., and V. A. Diggles. 1982. Control theories in motor behavior. *Acta Psychologica* 50:83–105.

Sternberg, S. 1969. The discovery of processing stages: Extensions of Donder's method. *Acta Psychologica* 30:276–315.

Sternberg, S. 1975. Memory scanning: New findings and current controversies. *Quarterly Journal of Experimental Psychology* 27:1–32.

Stott, D. H., F. A. Moyes, and S. E. Henderson. 1972. *Test of motor impairment*. Ontario, Can.: Brook.

Stratz, C. H. 1909. Wachstum und proportionen des menschen vor und nach der geburt. *Archiv fur Anthropologie* 8:287–297.

Stuart, H. C., and E. H. Sobel. 1946. The thickness of the skin and subcutaneous tissue by age and sex in childhood. *Journal of Pediatrics* 28:637–647.

Sugden, D. A. 1978. Visual motor short term memory in educationally subnormal boys. *British Journal of Educational Psychology* 48:330–339.

————. 1980a. Developmental strategies in motor and visual motor short-term memory. *Perceptual and Motor Skills* 51:146.

————. 1980b. Movement speed in children. *Journal of Motor Behavior* 12:125–132.

————. 1981. Dual task performance: A developmental perspective. *Information processing in motor skills*. Proceedings of British Society of Sports Psychology 13–32.

Sugden, D. A., and S. M. Gray. 1981. Capacity and strategies of educationally subnormal boys on serial and discrete tasks involving movement speed. *British Journal of Educational Psychology* 51:77–82.

Super, C. M. 1976. Environmental effects on motor development: The case of African infant precocity. *Developmental Medicine and Child Neurology* 18:561–567.

Surwillo, W. W. 1971. Human reaction time and period of EEG in relation to development. *Psychophysiology* 8:468–472.

————. 1977. Developmental changes in the speed of information processing. *Journal of Psychology* 97:102.

Taft, L. T., and H. J. Cohen. 1967. Neonatal and infant reflexology. In *Exceptional infant*, vol. 1, ed. J. Hellmuth. Seattle: Special Child Publications.

Tanner, J. M. 1962. *Growth at adolescence*, 2d ed. Oxford, Engl.: Blackwell.

————. 1964. *The physique of the olympic athlete*. London: Allen and Unwin.

————. 1970. Physical growth. In *Carmichael's manual of child psychology*, vol. 1, 3rd ed., ed. P. H. Mussen. New York: Wiley.

————. 1978. *Foetus into man*. London: Open Books.

————. 1981. *A history of the study of human growth*. Cambridge, Engl.: Cambridge University Press.

Tauber, M. A. 1979. Parental socialization techniques and sex differences in children's play. *Child Development* 50:225–234.

Temple, I. G., and H. G. Williams. 1977. Rate and level of learning as functions of information-processing characteristics of the learner and the task. *Journal of Motor Behavior* 9:179–192.

Thelen, E. 1979. Rhythmical stereotypies in normal human infants. *Animal Behaviour* 27:699–715.

Thelen, E. 1983. Learning to walk is still an "old" problem: A reply to Zelazo (1983). *Journal of Motor Behavior* 15:139–161.

Thelen, E., G. Bradshaw, and J. A. Ward. 1981. Spontaneous kicking in month-old infants: Manifestation of a human central locomotor program. *Behavioral and Neural Biology* 32:45–53.

Thomas, J. E., and E. H. Lambert. 1960. Ulnar nerve conduction velocity and H-reflex in infants and children. *Journal of Applied Physiology* 15:1–9.

Thomas, J. R., and P. R. Bender. 1977. A developmental explanation for children's motor behavior: A neo-Piagetian interpretation. *Journal of Motor Behavior* 9:81–93.

Thomas, J. R., D. J. Cotton, and F. Shelley. 1974. Effects of fulcrum heights on stabilometer performance. *Journal of Motor Behavior* 6:95–100.

Thomas, J. R., J. D. Gallagher, and G. J. Purvis. 1981. Reaction time and anticipation time: Effects of development. *Research Quarterly for Exercise and Sport* 52:359–367.

Thomas, J. R., B. Mitchell, and M. A. Solomon. 1979. Precision knowledge of results and motor performance: Relationship to age. *Research Quarterly* 50:687–698.

Thomas, J. R., and D. H. Moon. 1976. Measuring motor rhythmic ability in children. *Research Quarterly* 437:20–32.

Thomas, J. R., K. T. Thomas, A. M. Lee, E. Testerman, and M. Ashy. 1983. Age differences in use of strategy for recall of movement in a large scale environment. *Research Quarterly for Exercise and Sport* 54:264–272.

Tipps, S. T., M. P. Mira, and G. F. Cairns. 1981. Concurrent tracking of infant motor and speech development. *Genetic Psychology Monographs* 104:303–324.

Todor, J. I. 1978. A neo-Piagetian theory of constructive operators: Applications to perceptual-motor development and learning. In *Psychology of motor behavior and sport*, ed. D. M. Landers and R. W. Christina. Champaign, Ill.: Human Kinetics.

———. 1979. Developmental differences in motor task integration: A test of Pascual-Leone's theory of constructive operators. *Journal of Experimental Child Psychology* 28:314–322.

Turvey, M. T. 1977. Preliminaries to a theory of action with reference to vision. In *Perceiving, acting and knowing*, ed. R. Shaw and J. Bransford. Hillsdale, N.J.: Erlbaum.

Turvey, M. T., R. E. Shaw, and W. Mace. 1978. Issues in the theory of action: Degrees of freedom, coordinative structures and coalitions. In *Attention and performance VII*, ed. J. Requin. Hillsdale, N.J.: Erlbaum.

Uzgiris, I. C., and J. M. Hunt. 1975. *Assessment in infancy: Ordinal scales of psychological development.* Champaign-Urbana: University of Illinois Press.

von Hofsten, C. 1979. Development of visually directed reaching: The approach phase. *Journal of Human Movement Studies* 5:160–178.

———. 1980. Predictive reaching for moving objects by human infants. *Journal of Experimental Child Psychology* 30:369–382.

———. 1982. Eye-hand coordination in the newborn. *Developmental Psychology* 18:450–467.

———. 1983. Catching skills in infancy. *Journal of Experimental Psychology: Human Perception and Performance* 9:75–85.

von Hofsten, C., and K. Lindhagen. 1979. Observations on the development of reaching for moving objects. *Journal of Experimental Child Psychology* 28:158–173.

Wade, M. G. 1980. Coincidence anticipation of young normal and handicapped children. *Journal of Motor Behavior* 12:103–112.

Wade, M. G., and K. M. Newell. 1972. Performance criteria for stabilometer learning. *Journal of Motor Behavior* 4:231–239.

Walder, P. 1981. Contrasting theories of visuo-motor control with special reference to locomotion. University of Leeds. Typescript.

Wallace, S. A., K. M. Newell, and M. G. Wade. 1978. Decision and response times as a function of movement difficulty in preschool children. *Child Development* 49:509–512.

Walters, C. E. 1964. Reliability and comparison of four types of fetal activity and of total activity. *Child Development* 35:1249–1256.

———. 1965. Prediction of postnatal development from fetal activity. *Child Development* 36:801–808.

Washington. 1965. *Physical fitness test manual for elementary schools*, rev. ed. Olympia, Wash.: State Office of Public Instruction.

Wedell, K. 1964. Some aspects of perceptual-motor development in young children. In *Learning problems of the cerebral palsied*, ed. J. Loring. London: Spastics. Society.

Welch, M., and F. M. Henry. 1971. Individual differences in various parameters of motor learning. *Journal of Motor Behavior* 3:78–96.

Welford, A. T. 1968. *Fundamentals of skill.* London: Methuen.

Welford, A. T., A. H. Norris, and N. W. Shock. 1969. Speed and accuracy of movement and their changes with age. *Acta Psychologica* 30:3–15.

Wellman, B. L. 1937. Motor achievements of preschool children. *Childhood Education* 13:311–316.

Werner, E. E. 1979. *Cross-cultural child development.* Monterey, Calif.: Brooks/Cole.

Wetzel, N. C. 1941. Physical fitness in terms of physique, development and basal metabolism. *Journal of the American Medical Association* 116:1187–1195.

———. 1943. Assessing the physical condition of children. *Journal of Pediatrics* 22:82–110, 208–225, 329–361.

White, B. L. 1971. *Human infants: Experience and psychological development.* Englewood Cliffs, N.J.: Prentice-Hall.

White B. L., and J. C. Watts. 1973. *Experience and environment,* vol. 1. Englewood Cliffs, N.J.: Prentice-Hall.

Whiting, H. T. A., G. J. K. Alderson, and F. H. Sanderson. 1973. Critical time intervals for viewing and individual differences in performance of a ball-catching task. *International Journal of Sports Psychology* 4:155–164.

Whiting, H. T. A., and I. M. Cockerill. 1972. The development of a simple ballistic skill with and without visual control. *Journal of Motor Behavior* 4:155–162.

———. 1974. Eyes on hand—Eyes on Target? *Journal of Motor Behavior* 6:27–32.

Whiting, H. T. A., E. B. Gill, and J. M. Stephenson. 1970. Critical time intervals for taking in flight information in a ball-catching task. *Ergonomics* 13:265–272.

Whiting, H. T. A., and R. H. Sharp. 1974. Visual occlusion factors in a discrete ball-catching task. *Journal of Motor Behavior* 6:11–16.

Wickens, C. D. 1974. Temporal limits of human information processing: A developmental study. *Psychological Bulletin* 81:739–755.

Wickens, C. D., and D. C. R. Benel. 1982. The development of time-sharing skills. In *The development of movement control and co-ordination,* ed. J. A. S. Kelso and J. E. Clark. New York: Wiley.

Wickstrom, R. L. 1975. Developmental kinesiology: Maturation of basic motor patterns. In *Exercise and sport sciences reviews,* vol. 3, ed. J. H. Wilmore and J. F. Keogh. New York: Academic Press.

———. 1977. *Fundamental motor patterns,* 2d ed. Philadelphia: Lea and Febiger.

Wilcox, B. L., and M. Teghtsoonian. 1971. The control of relative size by pictorial depth cues in children and adults. *Journal of Experimental Child Psychology* 11:413–429.

Wild, M. R. 1938. The behavior pattern of throwing and some observations concerning its course of development in children. *Research Quarterly* 9:20–24.

Williams H. G. 1973. Perceptual-motor development in children. In *A textbook of motor development,* ed. C. B. Corbin. Dubuque, Ia.: Wm. C. Brown.

Wishart, J. G., T. G. R. Bower, and J. Dunkeld. 1978. Reaching in the dark. *Perception* 7:507–512.

Witkins, H. A., R. B. Dyk, H. F. Faterson, D. R. Goodenough, and S. A. Karp. 1962. *Psychological differentiation.* New York: Wiley.

Wolff, P. H. 1981. Theoretical issues in the development of motor skills. In *Developmental disabilities,* ed. M. Lewis and L. T. Taft. New York: Spectrum.

Wolff, P. H., and I. Hurwitz. 1976. Sex differences in finger tapping: A developmental study. *Neuropsychologia* 14:35–41.

Wright, J. C., and A. G. Vlietstra. 1975. The development of selecive attention: From perceptual exploration to logical research. In *Advances in child development and behavior,* vol. 10, ed. H. W. Reese. New York: Academic Press.

Wrisberg, C. A., and B. J. Mead. 1981. Anticipation of coincidence in children: A test of schema theory. *Perceptual and Motor Skills* 52:599–606.

————. 1983. Developing coincident timing skill in children: A comparison of training methods. *Research Quarterly for Exercise and Sport* 54:67–74.

Yonas, A., and M. Hagen. 1973. Effects of static and motion parallax depth information on perception of size in children and adults. *Journal of Experimental Child Psychology* 15:254—265.

Zdanska-Brincken, M., and N. Wolanski. 1969. A graphic model for the evaluation of motor development in infants. *Developmental Medicine and Child Neurology* 11:228–241.

Zelazo, P. R. 1983. The development of walking: New findings and old assumptions. *Journal of Motor Behavior* 15:99–137.

Zernicke, R. F., R. J. Gregor, and B. J. Cratty. 1982. Balance and visual proprioception in children. *Journal of Human Movement Studies* 8:1–13.

425